the JOY of MIXOLOGY

the JOY of MIXOLOGY

Including the History of Mixed Drinks; Compleat Instruction on the Methodology of the Cocktailian Bartender; A Thorough Explication of the Theory of Mixed Drinks; A Compleat Glossary Including All Categories of Spirits and Liqueurs; A Veritable Baedeker of the Bartender's Tools and Glassware; Prescriptions for Garnish Preparation; Recipes for the Preparation of, and Discussions on, the History and Makeup of All Manner of Popular Cocktails, Martinis, Highballs, Snappers, Sours, International Sours, New Orleans Sours, Sparkling Sours, Milanese Drinks, French-Italian Cocktails, Juleps, and Many Other Recently Created Cocktailian Masterpieces; Various Charts and Tables; and a Bit of Attitude.

GARY REGAN

CLARKSON POTTER / PUBLISHERS
NEW YORK

To Vi Regan. My mother and friend. 1924–2001.

Published by Clarkson Potter/Publishers, New York, New York.
Member of the Crown Publishing Group.

Random House, Inc. New York, Toronto, London, Sydney, Auckland
www.randomhouse.com

CLARKSON N. POTTER is a trademark and POTTER and colophon are registered trademarks of Random House, Inc.

Printed in the United States of America

Design by Maggie Hinders

Library of Congress Cataloging-in-Publication Data
is available upon request.

ISBN 0-609-60884-3

10 9 8 7 6 5 4 3 2

First Edition

ACKNOWLEDGMENTS

Give thanks to God. After all, it's his language you're cashing in on.

—Danielle Egnew

I KNOW THAT IF I TRY to mention everyone who helped get this book out, I'll forget some names and then I'll be slapping my forehead for years to come, so instead I'll attempt to list here the people to whom I'm most indebted. First and foremost must be Ted "Dr. Cocktail" Haigh. It should be noted that Doc's contribution of the beautiful line drawings in this book came at the last minute, and the fact that he did that has nothing whatsoever to do with the advice he contributed along the way. I could wax lyrical for a couple of dozen pages on all the things Doc has taught me, but I hope he'll understand if I leave it at this: Doc was my mentor. Thanks, Doc.

Robert Hess, from DrinkBoy.com, brought more than his share of bottles to this party; William Grimes from the *New York Times* turned up with a complete buffet in the form of his two editions of *Straight Up or On the Rocks,* and more than a few thoughts on many subjects by way of e-mail; the whole gang at DrinkBoy's MSN community has provided much stimulation, and led me down paths I might never have trodden; Dale DeGroff, a consummate bartender in every sense of the word, has always been just a phone call away when I needed guidance; Audrey Saunders, the Libation Goddess, has been integral in bringing the craft of mixology into the twenty-first century, and some of her creations have given me a better understanding of the creative mind of true cocktailians.

To everyone else who helped in various ways: those who eagerly submitted their cocktail recipes; all the people at various liquor and public relations companies who are always there to answer questions; students who have taken my bartender-training seminars and have taught me much; the crew at Painter's Tavern, who makes me feel like one of the gang; and others too numerous to mention but hopefully know who they are. Thanks, guys.

A big thanks to Sal Buttiglieri, the man behind the lens who made the photographs come to life.

Major debts of gratitude are due to Roy Finamore, my ardent and patient editor, who was 110 percent behind this project from the get-go. When other editors wanted this book in a short form, it was Roy who wanted more. Boy, did he get his wish.

Thanks, too, to Bonnie Thompson, the eagle-eyed copy editor on this project.

And finally, someone who doesn't deserve to be last on this list: Thanks to Mardee for making my life complete.

CONTENTS

Introduction . . . . *ix*

THE HISTORY OF COCKTAILS AND MIXED DRINKS 1

THE BARTENDER: DO YOU HAVE WHAT IT TAKES? 50

THE THEORY OF MIXOLOGY 69

THE CRAFT OF THE MIXOLOGIST 76

FOUNDATIONS OF THE BAR: GARNISHES, MIXERS, AND SUPPLEMENTAL INGREDIENTS 103

TOOLS AND VESSELS 123

GLASSWARE 131

BIRDS OF A FEATHER: COCKTAIL AND MIXED-DRINK FAMILIES 134

THE RECIPES 196

Tables and Charts *354*

Glossary *358*

Bibliography *370*

Index *377*

INTRODUCTION

We have a habit in writing . . . to cover up
all the tracks, to not worry about the blind alleys or describe
how you had the wrong idea first, and so on.
So there isn't any place to publish,
in a dignified manner, what you actually did
in order to get to do the work.

—RICHARD FEYNMAN

IF YOU WERE TO START WALKING from New York to Los Angeles, and were absolutely determined to get there, there is little doubt that you would eventually walk down Hollywood Boulevard. But you might lose your way a couple of times, and that's what happened when I wrote this book. I just had to get to Los Angeles, and I think I made it, but I took a few wrong turns along the way, visiting places I had no intention of going to. When the Pacific Ocean was in sight, though, I knew that my meanderings had been worthwhile.

While researching the history chapter of this book, consulting the thoughts and reasonings of the past masters of the craft and reading the words of people who had actually encountered such nineteenth-century superstar bartenders as Harry Johnson, holding forth from behind the bar at Little Jumbo, his joint on the Bowery, I found myself wishing that I could travel back to the Gay Nineties and watch a groundbreaking cocktailian at work. I could visit the old Waldorf-Astoria, order a Bronx Cocktail from Johnnie Solon himself, and sit back to take in the antics of Buffalo Bill Cody, a man who never refused a drink. Who knows, I might even find myself standing across the mahogany from Jerry Thomas, the man who wrote the world's first cocktail book, in 1862. What a treat that would be.

Later, though, when working on the recipes, and poring through formulas given to me by today's masters of the craft, I realized just how lucky I am to be living in the twenty-first century. I have watched Dale DeGroff making Blue Blazers at the Rainbow Room; I've been served marvelous creations by Tony Abou-Ganim when he was at Harry Denton's Starlight Room in San Francisco; and I have also had the honor of being served the best Manhattans in Manhattan by Norman Bukofzer at the Ritz-Carlton. I witnessed Audrey Saunders being mentored by Dale when they worked together at Blackbird, and before we knew it, she was a star. And I've bellied up to many a bar where the bartender wouldn't know how to make a Caipirinha if his or her life depended on it—but they were bartenders through and through.

THE COCKTAILIAN BARTENDER

A descriptor of sorts is needed to differentiate bartenders who merely know how to mix standard cocktails from the men and women behind the bar—or behind the stick, as I prefer—who thoroughly understand the theory behind mixing ingredients to achieve balance in their drinks and marry flavors successfully. I came up with the word *cocktailian* in 2001 when I was on a quest to find a word to replace *mixology,* and although it doesn't work in that instance, I think that *cocktailian bartender* fits the bill far better than *bar chef.*

WHAT YOU SHOULD KNOW ABOUT THIS BOOK

My aim in writing this book was twofold: I wanted to research the histories behind various cocktails and perhaps come up with some new theories, if not conclusions, along the way, and I also wanted to give the reader a feel for what it was like to be a bartender in various eras over the past two hundred years. I hope that the history chapter and the recipe chapter, where you'll find stories about individual drinks, accomplish that.

More important, though, I wanted to set some kind of standard for how people should learn the craft of the cocktailian bartender; but before you can be a cocktailian, you must first be a bartender, so I have tried to detail every aspect of the job to point out just how complex a task this is. Along the way I have tried to explain how drinks are born, and how relatively simple it is to take a proven formula and put your own twist on it. If you truly desire to know how to be a bartender, I hope that you don't make the mistake of jumping to the recipe chapter and fixing a drink—although there's no harm in doing that if you then sit down to read the rest.

If, on the other hand, you have no desire to work behind a bar but you're looking instead for advice on how to mix drinks at home, this book should serve you well. Using the methods described here, I have taught the cocktailian craft to many amateurs, as well as to people wanting to become professional bartenders. Once you thoroughly digest what I have to say, you will understand the theory of mixology to the point where you'll feel thoroughly at ease making cocktails and mixed drinks, as well as creating new potions of your own.

My Cocktails in the Country class takes only two days, and at the end of each course I've seen more than a few people with no prior knowledge of the craft mix drinks worthy of seasoned professionals. Read this book carefully, and you'll be able to *feel* your way through making a drink—it's really as simple as that.

Finally, I want you to know how privileged I feel to have spent much my life in barrooms. I don't know who first said this, but someone once pointed out to me that if you find a job you love, you'll never work another day in your life. I had a very early retirement.

the JOY of MIXOLOGY

THE HISTORY OF COCKTAILS AND MIXED DRINKS

Variety's the very spice of life,
That gives it all its flavour.

—WILLIAM COWPER, *The Task*, Book II, "The Time-Piece," 1785

THERE'S NOTHING quite like a good cup of tea. But do you prefer Earl Grey, Assam, Keemun, Lapsang souchong, jade oolong, Formosa oolong, or Ti Kuan Yin? Or perhaps English Breakfast is more your cuppa. And how do you take your tea? Plain and strong or with milk and sugar, a slice of lemon, a teaspoon of honey, a tot of whiskey, or a good measure of dark rum? One drink with myriad variations, all dependent on the taste of the consumer. And so it is, and always has been, with mixed drinks: The base ingredient can be consumed neat, but it can also be enhanced by the addition of one or more other ingredients. Why do people choose to adulterate fine wines, beers, and spirits? For variety's sake. It's the very spice of life.

It's more than possible that the world's first mixed drinks were created in order to mask the bad flavors of the base ingredient. Alcoholic potions of our dim and distant past were far inferior to the technologically clean products we enjoy today. Archaeological evidence shows that the ancient Egyptians used dates and other fruits to flavor their beer, and that Wassail, a spiced drink originally made with a base of hard cider, dates back to pagan England—it was served to celebrate a bountiful apple harvest. We also know that the Romans drank wine mixed with honey and/or herbs and spices. The practice could have arisen from the inferior quality of the wine, but it probably also had roots in the medicinal, restorative, or digestive qualities attributed to the various ingredients. Mulled wine and spiced beer date back thousands of years and are still enjoyed in the twenty-first century.

In order to see how the cocktails and mixed drinks of more modern times came into being, it's necessary to start in the 1600s, when taverns in New England were serving some creative concoctions. Sack Posset was a mixture of ale, sack (sherry), eggs, cream, sugar, and spices such as nutmeg and mace that was boiled over an open fire, sometimes for hours at a time. When the quaffers wanted their ale hot but didn't want to leave it on the fire, they would use a type of poker, known as a loggerhead, that was heated in the fire and then plunged into the tankard of ale. If a fight broke out in the tavern, these pokers could be used as weapons—the fighters were "at loggerheads" with each other.

It's possible that there were more than a few fights in seventeenth-century taverns, too—the colonists didn't drink in short measure. One description of the daily drinking habits of southern colonists states that they started their day with mint-flavored whiskey, stopped work at 11:00 A.M. in order to partake of Slings, Toddies, or Flips, drank whiskey or brandy with water before and during dinner, and finished their day with a whiskey or brandy without water. But overconsumption wasn't tolerated by all the colonists: In seventeenth-century Connecticut, for example, it was illegal to drink for more than thirty minutes at a time, or to down more than a half bottle of wine at one sitting. And if you dined at the Ship Inn in Boston circa 1634, you would have been allowed no more than one cup of wine with dinner.

Among the drinks consumed during the 1700s are Mulled Wines, sherry sweetened with fruit (such as raspberries), and Juleps. We're not sure whether these were the Mint Juleps familiar to us today since, according to Richard Barksdale Harwell, author of *The Mint Julep,* mention of such a drink wasn't recorded until 1803. All sorts of other mixed or flavored drinks were popular with the early colonists, and some of them, such as Toddies, Slings, and an assortment of Punches and Mulled Wines, are still made today, though probably not according to recipes that our forefathers would recognize.

Other drinks that cropped up in America around this time bear names that recall some of the cocktails we drink today. A potion called Mimbo was merely rum and sugar; Stonewall was a mixture of rum and cider; Black-Stripe was made of rum and molasses; a Stewed

Quaker was hard cider with a baked apple dropped into it; and one drink, made from simmered sour beer sweetened with molasses and thickened with crumbs from brown bread, had the wonderful moniker of Whistle-Belly-Vengeance. *Early American Beverages,* by John Hull Brown, details a New York City restaurant built in 1712 and known as Cato's Road House. Cato was a slave who had bought his freedom, opened his own joint, and sold New York Brandy Punch, South Carolina Milk Punch, and Virginia Eggnog to accompany dishes such as terrapin, curried oysters, fried chicken, and roast duck.

Our first president, George Washington, was known to be fond of a drink or two, and sometimes more. He indulged in thirteen toasts—one for each state—during a victory celebration at New York's Fraunces Tavern, and it's said that after he partook of Fish House Punch at Philadelphia's State in Schuylkill, essentially a fishing club, he couldn't bring himself to make an entry in his diary for the following three days. There's even a loose connection to Washington and Grog, the mixture of rum and water that Britain's Admiral Edward Vernon introduced to sailors in 1740. Lawrence Washington, George's half brother, served under Vernon and admired him so much that he named his estate for him. Later, of course, George became the chief resident at Mount Vernon.

By the end of the 1700s people in the newly formed United States were still tippling far more alcohol than we'd tolerate today; it's important to remember that at the time, alcohol was seen not only as a social drink but also as a medicine that would stave off, or maybe even cure, all manner of illnesses. John Brown, a medical professor at the University of Edinburgh in the mid-eighteenth century, prescribed liquor for many ailments. When one of his patients had the audacity to die, Brown simply opened up his body and declared the organs to be "fresh," which was proof that his "medicine" had been working. This, no doubt, was sufficient evidence to encourage a party of eighty people at Boston's Merchant's Club to down 136 bowls of Punch, 21 bottles of sherry, and a "large quantity" of cider and brandy during a dinner in 1792.

The eighteenth century also saw Americans become enamored of iced drinks, something that wouldn't gain favor in Europe for another two hundred years. European immigrants to these shores, unused to the hot summers in America, created a demand for ice from the frozen north to be brought down to the people in the sweltering south. Initially ice was fairly expensive and out of financial reach for many people, but prices gradually dropped, and by the mid-1800s iced drinks were the norm. While ice was becoming popular, though, something else happened behind a bar in America that would change the face of mixed drinks forever: At some point close to the year 1800, somebody created the world's first cocktail.

THE BIRTH OF THE COCKTAIL

On May 13, 1806, the *Balance and Columbian Repository* of Hudson, New York, answered a reader's query as to the nature of a cocktail: "Cocktail is a stimulating liquor, composed of spirits of any kind, sugar, water, and bitters—it is vulgarly called a bittered sling." The cocktail had been born, it had been defined, and yet it couldn't have been very well known by the general populace, or the newspaper wouldn't have considered it a fit topic for elucidation.

Where does the word *cocktail* come from? There are many answers to that question, and none is really satisfactory. One particular favorite story of mine, though, comes from *The Booze Reader: A Soggy Saga of a Man in His Cups,* by George Bishop: "The word itself stems from the English cock-tail which, in the middle 1800s, referred to a woman of easy virtue who was considered desirable but impure. The word was imported by expatriate Englishmen and applied derogatorily to the newly acquired American habit of bastardizing good British Gin with foreign matter, including ice. The disappearance of the hyphen coincided with the general acceptance of the word and its re-exportation back to England in its present meaning." Of course, this can't be true since the word was applied to a drink before the middle 1800s, but it's entertaining nonetheless, and the definition of "desirable but impure" fits cocktails to a tee.

Another theory has it that in England, horses of mixed blood had their tails docked to signify their lack of breeding, and were known as cocktailed horses. This is true, and since the cocktail comprises a mixture of ingredients, it makes sense that the term could have come from this source. But it's somewhat of a stretch.

A delightful story, published in 1936 in the *Bartender,* a British publication, details how English sailors of "many years ago" were served mixed drinks in a Mexican tavern. The drinks were stirred with "the fine, slender and smooth root of a plant which owing to its shape was called *Cola de Gallo* which in English means 'Cock's tail.'" The story goes on to say that the sailors made the name popular in England, and from there the word made its way to America.

Another Mexican tale about the etymology of *cocktail*—again, dated "many years ago"—concerns Xoc-tl (transliterated as Xochitl and Coctel in different accounts), the daughter of a Mexican king, who served drinks to visiting American officers. The Americans honored her by calling the drinks cocktails—the closest they could come to pronouncing her name. And one more south-of-the-border explanation for the word can be found in *Made in America,* by Bill Bryson, who explains that in the Krio language, spoken in Sierra Leone, a scorpion is called a *kaktel.* Could it be that the sting in the cocktail is related to the sting in the scorpion's tail? It's doubtful at best.

One of the most popular tales told about the first drinks known as cocktails concerns a tavernkeeper by the name of Betsy Flanagan, who in 1779 served French soldiers drinks garnished with feathers she had plucked from a neighbor's roosters. The soldiers toasted her by shouting, *"Vive le cocktail!"* William Grimes, however, points out in his book *Straight Up or On the Rocks: A Cultural History of American Drink* that Flanagan was a fictional character who appeared in *The Spy,* by James Fenimore Cooper. He also notes that the book "relied on oral testimony of Revolutionary War veterans," so although it's possible that the tale has some merit, it's a very unsatisfactory explanation.

A fairly plausible narrative on this subject can be found in *Famous New Orleans Drinks & how to mix 'em,* by Stanley Clisby Arthur, first published in 1937. Arthur tells the story of Antoine Amedie Peychaud, a French refugee from San Domingo who settled in New Orleans in 1793. Peychaud was an apothecary who opened his own business, where, among other things, he made his own bitters, Peychaud's, a concoction still available today. He created a stomach remedy by mixing his bitters with brandy in an eggcup—a vessel known to him in his native tongue as a *coquetier.* Presumably not all Peychaud's customers spoke French, and it's quite possible that the word, pronounced coh-KET-yay, could have been corrupted into *cocktail.* However, according to the Sazerac Company, the present-day producers of Peychaud's bitters, the apothecary didn't open until 1838, so there's yet another explanation that doesn't work.

If pushed to pick a story that rings truer than all others, I'll go for the one mentioned in Grimes's book that cites a paragraph from

H. L. Mencken's *The American Language. Cock,* it explains, refers to the tap on a barrel of spirits, and the *tailings* were the dregs from the bottom of the barrel. The last drops of all manner of spirits used to be mixed together and sold at a reduced rate, and thus the word *cocktail,* in a very unappealing manner, was born.

ADOLESCENCE

Although the cocktail had been created, not many people of the early 1800s were sipping well-constructed drinks. The name of the drinking game at that time was quantity, not quality. If you divided all the distilled spirits sold in the United States in the year 2000 among every man, woman, and child in the country, each person would be allotted just under half an ounce of liquor a day. Two hundred years earlier, though, when the cocktail was a mere babe in arms, enough spirits were sold to supply every man, woman, and child then in the States with almost two ounces of liquor a day. Thus, in 1800, Americans drank nearly four times the amount of distilled spirits as the good folk at the turn of the twenty-first century. The country was full of jitterbugs.

In the early 1800s liquor was often known as jitter sauce, and *jitterbug* was the moniker allocated to people who drank too much. One jitterbug in particular had his 1812 tavern bill detailed in *The Drunkard's Looking Glass,* a pamphlet issued by the Reverend Mason L. Weems. It seems that this hardy soul drank three Mint Slings before breakfast, nine tumblers of Grog before dinner, three glasses of wine and bitters with dinner, and two "ticklers" of brandy afterward. The total of the bill was six dollars, and it included breakfast, dinner, cigars, and supper (during which more wine was consumed).

Our nineteenth-century forefathers didn't just drink plentifully; they also gave weird and wonderful names to some of their newer creations. According to Richard Erdoes, author of *Saloons of the Old West,* house specialties became popular in the 1820s, and various inns and taverns offered such drinks as Moral Persuasion, Fiscal Agent, and Sweet Ruination. Drinks were also named for luminaries of the time: In 1824, when the Revolutionary War hero the Marquis de Lafayette returned to the United States from his native France, he not only was treated to Lafayette Punch but was also able to sip Lafayette brandy.

During the first half of the nineteenth century, although few people really cared, a new breed of bartenders started to emerge, and by the time Jerry Thomas wrote the world's first cocktail-recipe book, *How to Mix Drinks, or The Bon Vivant's Companion,* in 1862, he had collected formulas for Cobblers, Cocktails, Crustas, Fixes, Flips, Pousse-Cafés, Sangarees, Toddies, Sours, Slings, and Smashes, among others. Seven years later, when William Terrington published *Cooling Cups and Dainty Drinks* in London, he detailed drinks such as A Splitting Headache, a mixture of ale, rum, lime juice, cloves, cinnamon, ginger, and nutmeg, and Hour Before the Battle, a simple affair composed merely of sherry or madeira with bitters. The cocktail front was starting to pick up steam.

People down in Australia were also quaffing mixed drinks at this time, and during the mid-nineteenth-century gold rush there, at least one drink with a very strange name was being fashioned for the prospectors. *Spiers & Pond: A Memorable Australian Partnership,* a short nonfiction account by Phillip Andrew, details the circumstances:

> *In the early [18]50s there were no licensed inns on the fields. Consequently the sly grog trade had assumed enormous proportions. Weird were the drinks. One famous one, retailed at half a crown a wine glass, was known as "Blow-my-skull-off." It was made of* Cocculus indicus *[a poisonous berry found in Ceylon that was used to increase the potency of ale and porter], spirits of wine, Turkey opium, Cayenne pepper and rum, mixed with five parts of water. One good stir and it was ready for the table. A couple of good swigs and the mounted police turned out, hit everyone they could see, before the brawl reached the proportions of a riot.*

In the United States the demand for well-constructed mixed drinks grew steadily during the latter half of the nineteenth century until, in the 1890s, the Golden Age of Cocktails arrived. It would last right up to the enactment of Prohibition in 1920, but don't think for a moment that every bar in America was serving masterfully mixed drinks. Luc Sante, author of *Low Life: Lures and Snares of Old New York,* claims that in New York during the late 1800s, you could buy a concoction made from whiskey, rum, camphor, benzene, and cocaine sweepings. No name is given for this potent potable, but it cost only six cents per glass.

Bartenders who worked on the first riverboats enjoyed a decent reputation as cocktailians, but they used odd ingredients, such as a "brandy" made from burnt peach pits, nitric acid, cod-liver oil, and unaged whiskey. And according to *Hell's Best Friend,* by Jan Holden, if you were unfortunate enough to order a Manhattan at the Humboldt in Grays Harbor, Washington, the owner, Fred Hewett (who apparently didn't much care for anyone who drank cocktails), would pour a mixture of whiskey, gin, rum, brandy, aquavit, and bitters into a beer mug, top it up with beer, and stir it with his finger before handing it to you.

Bad liquor could be found in the barrelhouses of New Orleans, and for good measure you might also be treated to a blow or two to the head. *The French Quarter,* by Herbert Asbury, describes these dives as long rooms with a row of barrels on one side and drinking vessels on the other. For a nickel you could fill your glass from any barrel, but if you didn't buy another as soon as you emptied it you faced the chance of being turned out on your ear. And if you got drunk in these places after drinking too much "brandy" (here made from neutral spirits, sulfuric acid, tobacco, grape juice, and burnt sugar), you ran the risk of being rolled in a back room or in the back alley.

Certain dives on New York City's Bowery offered as much as you could drink from a rubber hose connected to a liquor barrel until you had to stop to take a breath; this would set you back a mere three cents. For two cents more, however, certain places would provide a shot of whiskey and a woman to go with it.

If you stopped by the Cosmopolitan Bar in Tucson, Arizona, in 1880, you could have a cocktail made with equal proportions of whiskey and mezcal that, the proprietor claimed, had had "the snakes strained out first." Various other saloons across the country served "Irish whiskey" made from neutral spirits mixed with creosote, hard cider that they called "champagne," and a medicinal drink, Dr. B. J. Kendall's Blackberry Balsam, which contained five grains of opium in every fluid ounce. Cocktails after work could be quite hazardous back then.

HELL'S HALF ACRE

While some cocktailian bartenders were hard at work creating formulas for drinks that have remained popular for over a century, and serving them to cigar-puffing sophisticates in elegant surroundings, many of the men holding forth from behind the mahogany during the latter half of the 1800s worked in shot-and-a-beer joints, served hard-working men, and contended with a far different kind of atmosphere. The drinks in these bars would hardly have qualified as "cocktailian," but the ways in which the customers were kept amused were innovative, to say the least.

In New Orleans, for instance, you could visit the Buffalo Bill House and watch two men butting their heads together for as long as forty-five minutes at a time. Nearby residents complained about the rough clientele that this type of activity enticed, but the owner rebutted that their objections were ridiculous, since he had purposefully opened his shop in an area of town where "no decent people lived." Far better, when visiting the Big Easy, to have a drink at the Conclave, a joint where the bartender dressed like an undertaker and the backbar was filled with gravestones, each one bearing the name of a different spirit. The bottles were kept in coffins beneath the gravestones.

In *Faces Along the Bar,* Madelon Powers points out that few bars of the late nineteenth century were owned by women, but those women who did get into the business must have been a little larger than life. Powers mentions Peckerhead Kate's in Chicago, Indian Sadie's in Green Bay, and Big Tit Irene's in Ashtabula, Ohio, as examples of such establishments. And some bars of the period catered to the man who didn't want to waste time when he had some serious drinking to do—for convenience's sake, urinals were installed at the foot of the bar.

A few bars in Ohio were so disreputable that they gained nicknames such as Shades of Death, Hell's Half Acre, Certain Death, and Devil's Den. And in the West certain bars fell into distinct categories: bug houses, whoop ups, snake ranches, bit houses (where every drink cost a bit, or twelve and a half cents), deadfalls, fandango houses (where dancing took place), and pretty-waiter saloons (the waiters were young girls in short skirts). Bars that were transported from one place to another on the railroad were known as Hell on Wheels.

Nineteenth-century bars also had standard attractions, such as billiards and ten-pin bowling, but gymnasium saloons, where men worked out before quaffing a few drinks, were available too. Dog fights, cock fights, and both bull- and bear-baiting were attractions guaranteed to draw crowds to a bar in the 1800s, and customers at one

West Coast saloon were once treated to the spectacle of a dog killing almost fifty rats in less than five minutes.

Gambling was another form of entertainment in the barrooms of the time, and many a man lost his newly mined gold in the saloons of San Francisco. One such joint had scales, sitting atop a small piece of carpet, on every card table. Nuggets were weighed and the appropriate number of gambling chips exchanged for them, but at the end of the night, when all the customers were gone, those pieces of carpet were carefully combed. The gold dust recovered could be enough to put an extra double sawbuck—twenty dollars—into the dealer's pocket.

Boxing matches were staged in some bars during the latter half of the nineteenth century. One of the most famous pugilists of the time, John L. Sullivan, world heavyweight champion from 1882 through 1892, made his New York debut at Harry Hill's, a halfway respectable bar. (Hill boasted that nobody was ever killed there.) But boxing wasn't the only form of entertainment offered at this bar on the corner of Houston and Crosby streets, and in an article he penned for the San Francisco *Alta California* in 1867, Mark Twain described some of the other spectacles that kept the crowds entertained:

> *Presently a man came out on a stage and sang "'Twas a Cold Winter's Night, and the Tempest was Snarling," and several parties accompanied him upon violins and a piano. After him came a remarkably black negro, whose clothes were ragged, and danced a boisterous dance and sang "I'm a happy contra band," though all his statements regarding himself would have warranted a different condition, I thought. After him came a man who mimicked fighting cats, and the buzzing of mosquitoes, and the squealing of a pig. Then a homely young man in a Highland costume entered upon the stage and danced—and he ought to have danced moderately, because he had nothing in the wide world on but a short coat and short stockings. This was apparent every time he whirled around. However, no one observed it but me. I knew that, because several handsomely dressed young ladies, from thirteen to sixteen and seventeen years of age, went and sat down under the foot-lights, and of course they would have moved away if they had noticed that he was only partly dressed.*

Theodore "The" Allen ran a similar joint on Bleecker Street, named Bal Mabille after the notorious Second Empire Parisian nightclub that had helped popularize the cancan. Nightlife at Allen's bar was described thus in the *Police Gazette,* a popular tabloid of the time: "The clinking of glasses keeps up a fitful accompaniment to the vocalization of the singers in the hall above, while down in the basement the dancers are rotating in the mazy. The lascivious waltz has become tame and the orchestra, catching the infection of the hour, strikes up the merry measures of Offenbach's cancan music. Lively feet keep time to the witching melody in all its lewd suggestiveness and dance themselves into an abandon till limbs of all shapes and sizes are elevated in dangerous proximity to male physiognomy."

Allen himself wasn't a man to be toyed with—he often started fights by putting his cigar out in his opponent's face—but he probably wasn't quite as feared as the western outlaw Johnnie Ringo, who once shot a man to death for refusing to drink champagne with him. Violence was not uncommon in nineteenth-century bars. Customers at the Tiger Saloon in Eureka, Nevada, bore witness to a knife fight between "Hog-Eyed" Mary Irwin and "Bulldog" Kate Miller, and the owner of a joint in lower Manhattan, Gallus Mag, not only bit the ears off customers who got out of control, she also kept the trophies in jars of alcohol on display behind the bar.

These joints are best described as dives, and indeed the majority of bars in the United States in the late 1800s are neatly summed up by Herbert Asbury in *The Great Illusion:* "[Saloons have] been rapturously eulogized as the workingmen's club, as a refuge of the harassed male, as the scene of wise and witty conversation, and as the home of sound liquor lovingly dispensed by a generous and understanding bartender. All this is mainly nonsense; it could apply only to the comparatively few barrooms, mostly in the large cities, which obeyed the laws and were operated as decently as any other business. . . . The stuff served in many saloons was frequently as vile as any of the concoctions guzzled by Americans during prohibition."

But in those comparatively few barrooms that Asbury mentions, there were men who took the job of mixing drinks very seriously. Even Harry Hill hung a sign outside his joint that read,

Punches and juleps, cobblers and smashes,
To make the tongue waggle with wit's merry flashes.

THE SMART SET

The people who went to watch men butting heads at New Orleans's Buffalo Bill House would likely have felt out of place at the Waldorf-Astoria Hotel, which opened in the 1890s on the site where the Empire State Building now stands. The bar at the old Waldorf-Astoria was the scene of the sort of decadence we often associate with the decade that became known as the Gay Nineties. In *The Old Waldorf-Astoria Bar Book,* Albert Stevens Crockett says that in the bar's heyday, "the air was rent with calls of 'Same here!' and 'Here's how!'" At 8:00 A.M., at least half a dozen customers attended the bar for "breakfast appetizers or something to take away what was left of the jag of the night before," and in the afternoons and evenings, twelve bartenders in white coats were kept busy "ministering to an endless array of thirsts."

Crockett's description of the original bar makes it sound very similar to the Bull and Bear bar in today's Waldorf-Astoria on Park Avenue: "The actual bar itself, a large, rectangular counter . . . had a brass rail running all around its foot. In its center was a long refrigerator topped by a snowy cloth and an orderly arrangement of drinking glasses. At one end of this cover stood a good-sized bronze bear, looking as if it meant business; at the other end, a rampant bull. Midway between them was placed a tiny lamb, flanked on either side by a tall vase of flowers." Regulars there joked that the flowers were all the public, represented by the lamb, ever saw after Wall Street's bulls and bears were through with them.

An interesting observation giving us a glimpse into the advanced cocktailian craft at the time is that Crockett lists ten brands of bitters commonly used "in small quantities" to construct cocktails at this bar, and the use of orange bitters exceeded that of Angostura. Even more intriguing is the fact that he mentions the use of Fernet Branca as a flavor enhancer, since this potable style of bitters is often sipped neat—nonpotable bitters such as Angostura and Peychaud's are used only as flavoring agents.

This was also the joint where Bat Masterson—buffalo hunter, railroad worker, army scout, gold prospector, newspaperman, and law enforcement officer—once emptied the bar by grabbing Colonel Dick Plunkett, a fellow U.S. marshall, by the throat and accusing him of "talking bad" about him. The situation came to nothing, though; Plunkett remained calm and offered Masterson a seat, a drink, and the chance to talk things over.

Colonel William F. Cody, otherwise known as "Buffalo Bill," was also a regular at the old Waldorf-Astoria, and he was well known for never refusing a drink on another man's tab—when asked, he would say, "Sir, you speak the language of my tribe." The tribes that frequented this bar were fairly well heeled, but not all of them had been that way for long. Henry Collins Brown, author of *In the Golden Nineties,* noted, "The Waldorf began to fill up with recently manicured iron workers from Pittsburgh, loggers from Duluth, copper miners from Michigan, brewers from Milwaukee and St. Louis, and other gentry who thought a cotillion was something to eat, but who could sign checks with numbers on them as long as a Santa Fe freight train."

Across the street from the old Waldorf-Astoria was the Manhattan Club: "In its window sat Tammany politicians hob-nobbing with broad-clothed bulwarks of the Solid South over Manhattan cocktails, and bowling the smoke of Henry Clay perfectos toward the frescoed ceiling in a futile effort to turn a stone refrigerator into a human habitation. There was Judge Truax telling Henry Watterson how many bottles of Medoc '69 reposed in the catacombs underneath; and Henry giving the Judge a recipe for mint julep that made the judicial bosom heave like a movie star's, and eye glisten like a bridegroom's," wrote Brown.

New York's Hoffman House Hotel, on Broadway between Twenty-fourth and Twenty-fifth streets, was home to another grand saloon of the late 1800s. George Ade, author of *The Old-Time Saloon,* refers to it as the home of the Manhattan but gives no other details. The Hoffman House regularly hosted luminaries of the day: Sarah Bernhardt kept suites there when she toured the States, and this was another haunt of Buffalo Bill's. Opposite the bar at the Hoffman House hung Bouguereau's *Nymphs and Satyr,* a work depicting naked women playfully teasing a half-human woodland creature of Greek mythology known for his lust and drunkenness. The painting was situated under a red velvet canopy and lit by a large chandelier, so that it could be easily seen in the mirror that hung behind the bar; customers could thus admire it without blatantly staring at the picture itself.

New York's Knickerbocker Hotel opened in the early years of the twentieth century, and the bar there, frequented, according to Ade, by "the convivial members of The Forty-Second Street Country Club," was initially home to another famous bar mural: Maxfield Parrish's *Old King Cole.* This rendering isn't offensive until you hear the story of its origin, but tradition has it that you must hear the tale from a bartender where the painting hangs. You can now find it behind the bar of the King Cole Room at New York's St. Regis Hotel on East Fifty-fifth Street.

In New Orleans during the nineteenth century you could find comfort at the Old Absinthe House, a Bourbon Street joint where you might spot such visiting celebrities as William Makepeace Thackeray, Oscar Wilde, or Walt Whitman availing themselves of a drop or two of the Green Fairy at the marble-topped bar. Even P. T. Barnum is said to have visited this joint, but since he was a teetotaler and temperance advocate he probably just sipped water from the dripper used by others to dilute their absinthe.

La Bourse de Maspero, or Maspero's Exchange, on St. Louis Street, was another hot spot in the Big Easy in the 1800s. It was here that Andrew Jackson is said to have planned to defend the city from the British after the War of 1812. This joint was taken over in 1838 by James Hewlett, a "well-known sporting man of the period," who completely renovated the place, renaming it Hewlett's Exchange and installing "the finest [bar] in the city," according to *The French Quarter,* by Herbert Asbury.

Other high-end bars of the time, mentioned in Ade's book, were "such gilt-edge and exceptional places as the . . . Ramos in New Orleans, . . . the splendiferous Righeimer's in Chicago, . . . the Planters' or Tony Faust's in St. Louis, . . . the Antlers in San Antonio, . . . the Palace in San Francisco, . . . the mint-julep headquarters in the Old White at White Sulphur Springs, [and] . . . the much frequented Touraine in Boston." But one posh joint deserves special mention: The Metropolitan, one of Manhattan's earliest grand hotels, opened in 1852, and an observer described it as standing "at the head of the hotels of the world in all points of elegance, comfort, and convenience." The bar at this hotel was graced by bartender Jerry Thomas—the man generally recognized as being the father of the craft of bartending.

THE COCKTAILIANS EMERGE

Jerry Thomas was born in 1832, and before he was thirty years old he had visited England and France, where he'd demonstrated his skills using a set of solid silver bar tools. Prior to this he had tended bar in

New Haven, Connecticut, and served as first assistant to the principal bartender at the El Dorado, the first gambling saloon in San Francisco, which housed a barroom complete with grand chandeliers and curtained booths, where certain ladies of the night plied their trade. One customer described the walls of the El Dorado's bar as being filled with "lascivious oil paintings of nudes in abandoned postures." There were huge mirrors on the backbar—the fixture behind the bar where bottles of liquor are displayed. An ornate backbar might not only be mirrored but also feature drawers, cupboards, and shelves; many barkeeps of the time referred to the backbar as the "altar."

Thomas also held forth for a time from behind the mahogany in South Carolina, where he studied the Mint Julep, and St. Louis, where he is said to have created the Tom and Jerry while serving as principal bartender at the Planter's House. New Orleans was also graced by Thomas's presence, and it was there that he encountered the Brandy Crusta (see page 161), the forerunner of some of today's best-loved cocktails, credited to a man known as Santina. Thomas describes this man as "a celebrated Spanish caterer," and Asbury claimed that in 1840 the same guy ran the City Exchange at Royal and St. Louis streets. From New Orleans, Thomas made his way to New York, and after a stint at the Metropolitan Hotel he traveled to Europe. Less than twelve months later, he was back; he worked in New York, San Francisco, and Virginia City, Nevada, before returning to the Big Apple, where he owned various bars, finally settling downtown at his own joint on Barclay Street.

Ten cocktails are contained in the recipe section of Thomas's 1862 book, and all of them contain bitters. Indeed, it would be decades before anyone dared give the name *cocktail* to a drink made without this ingredient. Various and sundry other drinks still popular today are also detailed in this tome: the Champagne Cocktail (which is erroneously shaken) and the Blue Blazer, a Thomas creation, which is actually more of a pyrotechnical display than a thoughtful mix. It has much in common with many drinks made by today's "flair" bartenders: looks good, tastes—well, okay. Thomas also wrote about the Mint Julep, various Milk Punches, and curiously enough, Punch Jelly. This "drink" must be considered to be a forerunner to today's Jelly Shots, although Thomas served it more as a dessert than a drink. It was rather potent, though—readers were warned, "This preparation is a very agreeable refreshment on a cold night, but should be used in moderation. . . . Many persons, particularly of the softer sex, have been tempted to partake so plentifully of it as to render them somewhat unfit for waltzing or quadrilling after supper."

Although Thomas didn't offer a great deal of advice to bartenders in his first tome, his second book, *The Bar-Tender's Guide, or How to Mix All Kinds of Plain and Fancy Drinks,* published in 1887, made up for his past sins of omission. In it, the great master counseled, "An efficient bartender's first aim should be to please his customers, paying particular attention to meet the individual wishes of those whose tastes and desires he has already watched and ascertained; and, with those whose peculiarities he has had no opportunity of learning, he should politely inquire how they wish their beverages served, and use his best judgment in endeavoring to fulfill their desires to their entire satisfaction. In this way he will not fail to acquire popularity and success." In a similar vein, Thomas's rival, Harry Johnson, wrote in his *New and Improved Illustrated Bartender's Manual,* a 1900 update of his own 1882 book,

> *The greatest accomplishment of a bartender lies in his ability to exactly suit his customer. This is done by inquiring what kind of drink the customer desires, and how he wishes it prepared. This is especially necessary with cocktails, juleps, "sours," and punches. The bartender must also inquire whether the drink is to be made stiff, strong, or medium, and then must use his best judgment in preparing it; but, at all times, he must make a special point to study the tastes of his customers and, strictly heeding their wishes, mix all drinks to their desires and tastes. In following this rule, the barkeep will soon gain the esteem and respect of his patrons.*

Johnson, like Thomas, had also spent time behind the bar in San Francisco, circa 1860; and in Chicago, some eight years later, he opened what he described as a place that was "generally recognized to be the largest and finest establishment of the kind in the country." It was destroyed by fire in 1871. Johnson also worked in Boston and New Orleans, but again like Thomas, he ended up in Manhattan, where he opened Little Jumbo, a cocktail bar on the Bowery, near Grand Street.

Henry Collins Brown recalled the joint well:

> *Harry Johnson's "Little Jumbo" saloon near Grand Street . . . had a sign before the door dating back to the time when a bartender had to serve an apprenticeship of several years. The bulk of the*

trade was then in mixed drinks, the drinks that carried the fame of American beverages around the world. Bartenders had black moustaches with waxed ends in those delectable days, and wore ornamental elastics on their sleeves to keep their cuffs from getting into the drinks. The sign, aforesaid, was a pyramid about four feet high. On the sides were the names of about one hundred mixed drinks. The pyramid tapered from the long-named mixed drink at the bottom to the short ones like "Gin Fizz" having fewer letters at the top. Oh, that this pyramid were as those of the Pharaohs, of aye enduring stone! And the legends thereon. Let me muse over them, as fond memory brings their glowing letters once more into view. Many of them are classics of concoctional nomenclature and as a faithful historian I must endeavor to reproduce one side of this pyramid to a generation that knows not the "Little Jumbo."

Harry Johnson's book sheds much light on the craft of the late-nineteenth-century cocktailian. Bartenders had to know how to reduce the proof of certain spirits properly, since at the time some liquors, especially imported products, were shipped at high proof to reduce the bulk, and therefore save on shipping charges. It was best to be cautious though, as Harry Rice, the owner of the Green Tree in New Orleans, found out in 1864; he was stoned almost to death by a group of sailors who weren't satisfied with the strength of his spirits.

The jigger, spelled *gigger* in Johnson's book, is mentioned as being "used by all first-class bartenders, except only a few experts in the art of mixing drinks who have had such experience and practice that they can measure accurately by eyesight alone, without even using a glass for measuring." He suggests that short-handled bar spoons be served with all drinks containing fruit garnishes so that customers can eat without using their fingers. Johnson also commands, "Bartenders should not . . . have a toothpick in their mouth, clean their fingernails while on duty, smoke, spit on the floor, or have other disgusting habits."

Thomas and Johnson were undoubtedly the two greatest masters of their craft in the 1800s, but they weren't the only ones to take their trade seriously. C. L. Sonnichsen, author of *Billy King's Tombstone,* describes two other professionals who plied their trade in the nineteenth-century Wild West: "Billy King, when he began operating his own saloon in the nineties, had [a white bar jacket] with five dollar gold pieces for buttons, which was considered in the best taste of the period." And Buckskin

GIN FIZZ

RAINBOW

EGG NOGG

ALABAZAM

GIN RICKEY

ROYAL FIZZ

MINT JULEP

SHANDY GAFF

TOM & JERRY

TOM COLLINS

POUSSE-CAFÉ

BRAIN DUSTER

CLARET PUNCH

WHISKEY SOUR

BRANDY TODDY

HAPPY MOMENT

WHISKEY SLING

PORT SANGAREE

CATAWBA PUNCH

SHERRY COBBLER

ABSINTHE FRAPPÉ

HANNIBAL HAMLIN

SITTING-BULL FIZZ

MANHATTAN COOLER

NEW ORLEANS PUNCH

MANHATTAN COCKTAIL

Frank Leslie, a bartender at the Oriental Saloon in Tombstone, was "a complete dandy. His slender body was erect and shapely, and he loved to adorn it with shiney boots, checked pants, Prince Albert coat, and a stiff shirt with black pearl studs. He had a stovepipe hat for special occasions, too." These were men who meant to be taken seriously—the bartender as an authoritarian figure was beginning to take shape.

> *For a time, the lawyer, the editor, the banker, the chief desperado, the chief gambler, and the saloon-keeper, occupied the same level in society, and it was the highest. The cheapest and easiest way to become an influential man and be looked up to by the community at large, was to stand behind a bar, wear a cluster-diamond pin, and sell whisky. I am not sure but that the saloon-keeper held a shade higher rank than any other member of society. His opinion had weight. It was his privilege to say how the elections should go. No great movement could succeed without the countenance and direction of the saloon-keepers. It was a high favor when the chief saloon-keeper consented to serve in the legislature or the board of aldermen. Youthful ambition hardly aspired so much to the honors of the law, or the army and navy as to the dignity of proprietorship in a saloon. To be a saloon-keeper and kill a man was to be illustrious.*

So wrote Mark Twain in *Roughing It,* a book detailing his adventures in the West.

Some of the western bartenders, often known as ganymedes (referring to the cupbearer to the gods in Greek mythology), could slide a glass of beer down the bar with the exact force that would cause it to come to a halt directly in front of whoever had ordered it, and it was common practice when serving whiskey for the bartender to grab the bottle with his right hand, a glass with his left, and cross hands before placing them both in front of the customer. The customer could pour as much whiskey as the glass would hold, but it wasn't considered seemly to fill the glass to the brim, lest a neighboring customer might inquire if you intended to bathe in it. (For simplicity's sake, I'm using the spelling "whiskey" generically—for American, Canadian, Irish, or Scotch. When referring only to Scotch or Canadian whiskies, however, the traditional spelling is "whisky.")

Although cities such as New York, San Francisco, and New Orleans sported most of the best cocktail bars, by the end of the nineteenth century mixed drinks were becoming popular throughout the country. *The Wild West Bartenders' Bible,* by Byron A. and Sharon Peregrine Johnson, mentions one Albuquerque, New Mexico, bar that in 1886 offered Whiskey, Gin, Vermouth, Chocolate, and Manhattan cocktails, and topped each one of them off with a splash of champagne. The bar menu also featured drinks such as the Charley Rose, Gold Band, Collins, Absinthe Frappé, Whiskey Daisy, Pousse-Café, Dide's Dream, Frozen Absinthe, Egg Nog, Egg Flip, Sherry Flip, Whiskey Flip, Gin Fizz, Silver Fizz, Gold Fizz, Blue Blazer, and Mint Julep.

In Chicago during the Gay Nineties you could order a variation on the Bell Ringer, a long-gone category of cocktails served in a glass rinsed with apricot brandy, from bartender James Maloney. And even in London, if you were fortunate enough to be served by Leo Engel, author of *American & Other Drinks* and bartender at the American Bar in the Criterion Hotel, you could request Alabama Fog Cutters, Connecticut Eye Openers, Thunderbolt Cocktails, Lightning Smashers, Boston Nose Warmers, Magnetic Crushers, Galvanic Lip Pouters, and Josey Ticklers. If you were feeling very brave, though, you might be tempted to try Leo's Knickebein: orange curaçao, crème de noyau, and maraschino liqueur mixed in the bottom of a port glass and topped with an egg yolk, which, in turn, was topped with the whisked white of an egg fashioned into the shape of a pyramid; the drink was finished off with a few drops of Angostura bitters dashed onto the pyramid. In order to drink the Knickebein you had to follow Engel's instructions:

1. Pass the glass under the Nostrils and Inhale the Flavor.—Pause.
2. Hold the glass perpendicularly, close under your mouth, open it wide, and suck the froth by drawing a Deep Breath.—Pause again.
3. Point the lips and take one-third of the liquid contents remaining in the glass without touching the yolk.—Pause once more.
4. Straighten the body, throw the head backward, swallow the contents remaining in the glass all at once, at the same time breaking the yolk in your mouth.

Leo's Knickebein, quite understandably, didn't catch on, but two drinks from the nineteenth century that did stand the test of time emanated from this side of the Atlantic. The Sazerac and the Ramos Gin Fizz are both New Orleans creations. Accounts vary as to who first created the Sazerac, originally a mixture of brandy, absinthe, sugar, and

Peychaud's bitters, but it's fairly safe to say that it originated at the Sazerac Coffee House sometime during the 1850s. (Bourbon is now the preferred base spirit, although straight rye whiskey has recently made a comeback in this drink.) The Ramos Gin Fizz, a sublime drink made with gin, cream, lemon and lime juices, egg white, simple syrup, orange flower water, and club soda, was the creation of Henry Ramos, a New Orleans saloon proprietor from 1888 right through until the enactment of Prohibition in 1920.

William "The Only William" Schmidt, author of 1892's *The Flowing Bowl* and a man who had been "active for a period of more than thirty years in the line of hotel and bar business," offered some early insights into the role of the man behind the stick when he wrote, "The situation of a bartender gives the holder the chance of studying human nature. A man fit for the position, and consequently a keen observer—for one thing cannot be separated from the other—will be able to tell a man's character very soon, as far as conduct, education, language, and general *savoir-vivre* are concerned." He also added a point of view that should be taken seriously by anyone who is tempted to use inferior products when making cocktails: "Mixed drinks might be compared to music; an orchestra will produce good music, provided all players are artists; but have only one or two inferior musicians in your band, and you may be convinced they will spoil the entire harmony."

The nineteenth-century harmony of which Schmidt speaks might strike a discord with cocktail fanciers of today. The majority of the drinks popular at the turn of the nineteenth century were, by and large, sweeter than they would become over the next twenty years. Something else happened, though, in the last decades of the 1800s. Something momentous. Something that left us with a range of drinks that must now be considered the capos of the cocktail family: Vermouth became popular among the cocktailian bartenders of America.

ITALY AND FRANCE LEND A HAND

There is no mention of vermouth whatsoever in Thomas's 1862 book, but in 1887 he detailed five recipes that called for vermouth: the Manhattan, the Martinez, the Vermouth and the Fancy Vermouth cocktails (the Vermouth made with bitters, the fancy version with bitters and maraschino) and the Saratoga, made with equal parts whiskey, brandy, and vermouth and a couple of dashes of bitters. The book doesn't, however, specify sweet or dry vermouth. Which did he use?

It's fairly obvious, when you look at recipes in other books of the period, that sweet vermouth, often referred to as Italian vermouth, for its country of origin, was far more common behind bars than was dry, or French, vermouth. Some cocktail books published in those years referred to both "vermouth," with no descriptor, and "dry vermouth"—which must signify that sweet vermouth was the norm, and dry vermouth a relative newcomer to the scene.

This isn't to say that dry vermouth wasn't available in the United States prior to the late 1800s—it was: Noilly Prat, the originator of dry vermouth in 1800, started shipping French vermouth to the States in 1853, some fourteen years before the first shipment of sweet vermouth, made by the Italian company that would eventually (in 1879) be named Martini & Rossi landed in America. But according to various sources, around the year 1900 Noilly Prat's sales of French vermouth were less than half of Martini & Rossi's of the Italian variety.

The first cocktail still popular today that called for vermouth was the Manhattan; and the Martinez—a precursor to the Martini made with a sweetened gin known as Old Tom, sweet vermouth, bitters, and maraschino liqueur—appeared shortly thereafter. Some of the early recipes for the Martini, which first appeared in the late 1800s, call for exactly the same ingredients used to make the Martinez, so it appears that the Martini started out as a drink made with sweet vermouth, and dry versions of the cocktail followed.

There can be no doubt that vermouth changed the face of mixed drinks in the twentieth century. The Manhattan, the Martini, and the Rob Roy might be considered to be the Triple Crown of cocktails, and you can't make one of them without vermouth. Indeed, Albert Stevens Crockett noted in *The Old Waldorf-Astoria Bar Book* that over half the cocktails known prior to World War I "had vermouth as an essential [ingredient]."

THE FIRST HUNDRED YEARS

The serious bartenders of the 1800s gave us the mixed-drink bases with which cocktailians still work today. The masters of the craft during the first century of cocktails formulated sours and the majority of other categorized drinks, and they learned to use liqueurs and other sweetening agents as substitutes for simple syrup. These men understood the importance of bitters, probably better than most present-day bartenders, and they knew that balance was the key to any well-constructed drink. What other drinks were commonplace at the dawn of the twentieth century?

Highballs—spirits and soda or water—were consumed before the turn of the nineteenth century, and drinks such as Brandy and Soda and Brandy and Ginger Ale are documented in recipe books of the time. The Tom Collins and John Collins both appeared in the nineteenth century, but few people seemed to agree on the base spirit of these drinks. The Shandy, then called the Shandy Gaff—originally ale and ginger ale—was also available, and by the very early 1900s the Dry Martini had been established as a cocktail. Indeed, in 1907 Heublein's Club Cocktails—Martinis and Manhattans among them—were being offered by the bottle by Park and Tilford, a wholesale wine and liquor company. The price was $10.50 for a dozen bottles (presumably quarts), or $14.40 for 144 individual bottles with presumably smaller capacities.

Modern American Drinks: How to Mix and Serve All Kinds of Cups and Drinks, by George J. Kappeler, detailed the oh-so-naughty Bosom Caresser way back in 1895, and although the formula has changed over the years, the drink is still found in most modern-day cocktail books. Kappeler's book was also one of the first—if not *the* first—to mention the Old-Fashioned Whiskey Cocktail, made with sugar, water, bitters, whiskey, and a twist of lemon.

Kappeler claimed that his recipes were "simple, practical and easy to follow, and . . . especially intended for use in first-class Hotels, Clubs, Buffets, and Barrooms, where, if adopted and concocted according to directions given, they will be entirely satisfactory to the caterer and pleasing to the consumer, the latter of whom will immediately notice a marked improvement in his favorite beverage." He included a couple of drinks in his book that bear somewhat modern sounding names: The Brain Duster was made with whiskey, sweet vermouth, absinthe, and simple syrup, and the Electric Current Fizz was constructed by shaking together gin, lemon juice, sugar, and the white of an egg, straining the mixture into a "fizz" glass, and topping it with seltzer; the drink was served with an egg yolk in the half shell, seasoned with salt, pepper, and vinegar, on the side.

George Du Maurier's *Trilby,* a novel that was first serialized in 1894 in *Harper's New Monthly Magazine* and later spawned the 1931 movie

Svengali, prompted a town in Florida, northeast of Tampa, to change its name to Trilby, complete with streets named after characters in the work and its very own Svengali Square. Of course, someone also had to create the Trilby Cocktail: whiskey, sweet vermouth, orange bitters, absinthe, and Parfait d'Amour, a violet-flavored liqueur.

Tonic water was first created in 1858, and in the 1870s Schweppes marketed the product, but it would take a while before Gin and Tonics were popular outside of India, where the quinine in the soda helped expatriate Brits ward off the effects of malaria. And although the Stinger wouldn't gain its moniker until the twentieth century, Schmidt's 1892 book details the Judge, a drink made with brandy, crème de menthe, and simple syrup. Someone had put the ingredients of the drink together, but it wouldn't get its sting until the simple syrup was omitted.

Before leaving the nineteenth century, a word or two from a guy who lived in the 1890s and reported on the bartenders who served him is in order: "The American bartender of the 'Gay Nineties' was an institution. His fame spread to the four corners of the globe, and visitors to our shores from the continent bowed before his skill in concocting tempting mixtures of 'liquid lightening.' He was and still is in a class by himself. We may go to Europe for our chefs, but Europe comes to us for its bartenders," wrote W. C. Whitfield in his 1939 book *Just Cocktails.*

TROUBLE AHEAD

As the sun rose on the twentieth century, temperance advocates were fast gaining a foothold in the States, and the movement that would lead to nationwide Prohibition had begun in earnest. When the word *temperance* was first used around the beginning of the nineteenth century by societies dedicated to the cause, it didn't mean abstinence, and many members of such clubs still indulged in an occasional glass of something or other, but they never drank to excess. Some people swore off liquor but still enjoyed beer and wine, and others might enjoy a glass of whiskey with friends, although always in moderation. People who shunned alcohol completely were classed as total abstainers and known as teetotalers. And some folks, of course, even prior to the Civil War, thought that all alcohol was evil incarnate.

Scare tactics were used by these latter-day enemies of John Barleycorn, and a good example of this method can be seen in an article published in *Cold Water Magazine* in 1842: "A wretched mother who had been imbibing strong ale in a dram shop, entered the door of her home with her child on one arm and a bag of flour on the other. By mistake she threw her child in the meal chest in a closet near at hand, and placed the bag of flour in the cradle; then threw herself on the bed to sleep. During the night the mother was occasionally aroused by the cries of the poor child and once or twice she actually got up and rocked the bag of flour. Morning came and with it the discovery of the darling babe dead in the meal chest. Since then that wretched mother has signed the Pledge."

Twenty-five years later, as the movement was gaining momentum, Mark Twain took a glimpse into the future when he wrote, "Prohibition only drives drunkenness behind doors and into dark places, and does not cure it or even diminish it." But it was the Anti-Saloon League, formed in 1893, that would prove to be the driving force behind the enactment of Prohibition. Just ten years after making its voice heard around the nation, the society had such an impact that H. L. Mencken wrote, "Americans reached their peak of their alcoholic puissance in the closing years of the last century. Along about 1903 there was a sudden and marked letting up."

By 1910 almost half the people in the United States were living in "dry" states or towns, and after America declared war on Germany in 1917, distillation of beverage alcohol was made illegal so that the grape and the grain would be eaten rather than sipped. Two years later, William Jennings Bryan, a politician and keen supporter of the Prohibition movement, said, "Ten years from now hundreds of thousands of men who voted against us and struggled to keep the saloon, will go down on their knees and thank God they were overwhelmed at the ballot-box and this temptation far removed from them."

William E. "Pussyfoot" Johnson, an agent for the Anti-Saloon League, wrote some of the organization's propaganda and lectured for the cause. He was so well known at the time that a nonalcoholic drink, the Pussyfoot, was named for him, but six years after Prohibition was enacted, Johnson admitted that during his campaign against American saloons he lied, bribed, and "drank gallons of [alcohol]."

During the nineteen years of the twentieth century that led up to Prohibition, although drinking was frowned upon by many, cocktails and mixed drinks continued to evolve in certain bars, and some bartenders of that period detailed the favorite drinks of the time, as well as the idiosyncrasies of the era.

Jere Sullivan, author of *The Drinks of Yesteryear: A Mixology,* tended bar prior to Prohibition, and he had some definite ideas of how things should be done. Among his admonitions, for example, he declared, "A Martini or a Manhattan cocktail should be stirred with a spoon instead of shaken unless the individual cares to have it shaken. (Results cloudy.)" Patrick Gavin Duffy, head bartender at New York's Ashland House for twelve years prior to Prohibition, and the man who claimed to have "first brought the highball to America, in 1895," wrote, "With very few exceptions, cocktails should be stirred and not shaken."

Sullivan described himself as a "wine clerk," a term that he defined as a gentleman who "mixed and served whatever little hearts desired." He worked at "the most epicurean hotel and restaurant east of the Hudson River," where he studied the "applied art of compounding and properly serving 'mixed and fancy drinks' for a clientele of most refined and exacting tastes," and he did us the favor of recording what he claimed were the "most popular and most used formulas when drinking was public and amateur mixers had not gone daft in trying by efforts of their own to approximate the enjoyed standards of the old regime." Included in his list were the Alexander, the Bacardi Cocktail, the Bronx, the Champagne Cocktail, the Clover Club, the Gibson, the Grasshopper, the Jacq [sic] Rose, the Manhattan, the Dry Martini, the Stinger, and the Yale Cocktail. It's important to note, though, that Sullivan's Bacardi Cocktail was made with rum, sweet vermouth, and Peychaud's bitters, although he does detail a second version that's nothing more than a Daiquiri. The Bacardi Cocktail that we know today, with grenadine as a sweetening agent, didn't appear until sometime during the years of Prohibition, when Americans first sampled the drink in Cuba.

These drinks would have set you back between fifteen and twenty-five cents at a high-class bar back then, whereas a mug of beer could be had for just a nickel; but many bars at the time offered a free lunch to boot, a tradition that dates back to at least the mid-1800s. Asbury maintains that the practice could have begun as early as 1838 at a New Orleans bar called the City Exchange. It was the brainchild, he claims, of an assistant bar manager named Alvarez, a man Asbury also credits with creating the world's first gumbo by cooking a bouillabaisse in a Creole style.

Free lunches were offered by many more bars when, in the 1880s, some of the bigger breweries acquired many saloons and subsidized the cost of the food. Quite naturally, the quality of the food on the table varied drastically, depending on the type of bar you frequented. Neighborhood saloons might offer stew, bread, ham, ribs, potato salad, and frankfurters, whereas at a high-class bar such as the Waldorf-Astoria it was possible to find delicacies such as "Russian caviar, . . . light and savory canapés, thirst-provoking anchovies in various tinted guises, . . . substantial slices of beef or ham, . . . a wonderful assortment of cheeses of robust odors, . . . crisp radishes and sprightly, delicate spring onions."

There were only two problems with the free lunch: Bartenders had to be on the lookout for people who sneaked in for food without buying a drink, and they could never be certain that every customer had good table manners. Bartender Harry Johnson reported having to make sure "that the patrons use a fork and not their fingers in digging out . . . the eatables." But customers didn't get the chance to do that at Righeimer's bar in Chicago just prior to World War I. As writer Charles W. Morton remembered in "When Money Was in Flower," an article that appeared in *The Atlantic Monthly* in 1962, "The free lunch was a ham or roast beef sandwich of extraordinary quality, prepared by an elderly Negro who used a slicing knife in each hand and turned out elegantly thin sandwiches without handling them, offering them to the customer on the extended blade of a knife; the style and dexterity in this operation were as attractive as the sandwich itself."

Attractive sandwiches needed to be accompanied by attractive drinks, and in 1906 Louis Muckensturm declared in his book *Louis' Mixed Drinks with Hints for the Care and Service of Wines* that a cherry was the appropriate garnish for "practically every cocktail, excepting when the cocktail is wanted extra dry. In that case olives can be used." But they had different ideas about garnishes at the old Waldorf-Astoria, where pickled rooster's combs were used to adorn their Chanticleer Cocktail, a mixture of orange-flavored gin, dry vermouth, and the white of an egg. Crockett wrote that Martinis were the most popular pre–World War I cocktail at the Waldorf, with the Manhattan running second, and customers at the time would gulp down five or six of either drink in succession.

The quantity of drinks that pre-Prohibition quaffers managed to down sounds quite startling considering that this was during a time when much of the country was behind the Prohibition movement, but

Crockett's statement is backed up by Charles Brown, author of *The Gun Club Drink Book,* who wrote, "A man would walk into his club or favorite bar perhaps on his way home from the office. He wants one drink and he needs it. . . . But by all the rules of the game he will find it impossible to get out of the club without taking six or more drinks." It should be noted, though, that drinks at that time were much smaller than today's often gigantic cocktails.

If the Martini was the most popular drink in New York at that time, the Manhattan reigned supreme in Baltimore, where, according to Mencken, it was always the cocktail of choice before a traditional Maryland dinner of oysters, terrapin, duck, and salad with ham. "No Baltimorean of condition ever drank gin," he wrote. And Mencken's fellow journalists were none too enamored of the temperance movement—Mencken claimed that there was only one reporter from the South who abstained from alcohol, and he was considered to be insane. Mencken could recall absolutely no newspapermen in New York City as being nondrinkers; he reminisced about one Christmas Eve when he could find only two people sober at the offices of the *New York Herald:* "All the rest were full of what they called hand-set whiskey. This powerful drug was sold in a saloon next door to the *Herald* office, and was reputed to be made in the cellar by the proprietor in person—of wood alcohol, snuff, tabasco sauce, and coffin varnish."

The coffin varnish could have come in handy on January 17, 1920, when the beverage alcohol industry was put to death and national Prohibition went into effect.

THE GREAT DROUGHT

Prohibition came in like a lion and left like a lamb, but the lion that roared in 1920 just got louder and louder as the dry years passed. And that lion was none too sober. Three years into the Noble Experiment, humorist Ring Lardner noted that the biggest difference in bars was that because, by law, there weren't any, they didn't have to close at any particular hour.

Speakeasies, illegal drinking establishments that patrons were encouraged to "speak easy" about, lest word spread to the wrong ears, flourished in every major city in the country and by all accounts were fun places to visit. Although it's often said that many modern cocktails were created during Prohibition because all sorts of extra ingredients were added to liquor to mask the flavor of the badly made spirits, there's little evidence to support such a claim.

Speakeasy bartenders used fruit juices, sometimes from canned fruit, as well as ginger ale, cream, honey, corn syrup, maple syrup, and even ice cream to make palatable the harsh flavors of spirits that Mencken described as "rye whiskey in which rats have drowned, Bourbon contaminated with arsenic and ptomaines, corn fresh from the still, gin that is three fourths turpentine, and rum rejected as too corrosive by the West Indian embalmers"; but they did little in the way of creating new drinks.

The fact of the matter is that although speakeasies existed in great number, lots of decent liquor was poured in regular restaurants and nightclubs around the country, and many of the owners encouraged customers to bring their own "atmosphere." These joints made most of their money from cover charges and from their exorbitant prices for setups—a glass full of ice with water or ginger ale on the side. Customers poured their whiskey from a flask or brought bottles to their favorite haunts. These bottles were kept out of view, labeled with the customer's name, and used for that one customer and anyone he or she chose to treat.

Although there is much evidence that some very bad liquor was sold by disreputable bootleggers, the biggest complaint heard during the era was that the whiskey had been watered down too much. Stanley Walker, author of *The Night Club Era* and city editor of the *New York Herald Tribune* at the time, claimed that less than half of one percent of methyl alcohol—a poison sometimes used by bootleggers—was ever found in bad bottles of booze, and since ethyl alcohol—the potable kind found in beer, wine, and spirits—is the antidote for methyl alcohol, this was not very dangerous, providing the drinker didn't make a habit of overconsuming.

Sidney E. Klein, a union organizer in Manhattan during the twenties, says that cocktails just weren't the point when bibbers of the time went out on the town, and that most people just wanted the "straight stuff." Although this doesn't mean that Martinis weren't made and Manhattans left the face of the earth, it certainly wasn't a period when bartenders could be very creative.

The new drinks that did appear during this era were mostly fashioned in Europe, where at least a few American bartenders fled to pursue their careers. Harry Craddock was one such man. He started work as a bartender at the Savoy Hotel, London, in 1925, and compiled *The Savoy Cocktail Book* (1930), in which he admonished bartenders, "Shake the shaker as hard as you can: don't just rock it: you are trying to wake it up, not send it to sleep!" Craddock is also credited with saying that the best way to drink a cocktail is "quickly, while it's laughing at you!"

The Brandy Alexander made its debut in Craddock's book, although it was named Alexander Cocktail (No. 2) at the time; the original Alexander Cocktail, which called for gin as a base liquor, was created before World War I. The Bacardi Cocktail, a variation of the Daiquiri, a late-nineteenth-century creation, also appears to have made its debut during the dry years in America, and is added as a "stick-in" in the only first-edition copy of *The Savoy Cocktail Book* I have seen. But Craddock didn't forget to detail the Bacardi Special—made like a Bacardi Cocktail but using Beefeater gin as well as Bacardi rum—before the book was typeset; the recipe hides behind the Bacardi Cocktail stick-in.

The first printed mention of the Aviation, Belmont, Income Tax, and Maurice cocktails that I can find are also in Craddock's book, but he doesn't lay claim to creating any of them, and since he did note that he was the man behind the Leap Year, Strike's Off, and Princess Mary's Pride cocktails, we must presume that the others were drinks with which he was familiar, but not the father of.

Of course, Americans did travel to Europe during Prohibition, and Craddock's bar at the Savoy was a popular destination for them. While it's more than likely that some new drinks created in Europe made their way back to the States during this time, one new creation stayed at home in Paris until the bars of America legally reopened their doors. That drink was a significant one.

The Bloody Mary was first made in the 1920s by French bartender Fernand "Pete" Petiot, who first married vodka and tomato juice behind the stick at Harry's New York Bar in Paris. Not until after Prohibition was repealed and John Astor installed him behind the bar at the King Cole Room in New York's St. Regis Hotel would the concoction be introduced to Stateside drinkers.

Although there *was* good liquor to be had, at least in the high-class speakeasies of America, and some good cocktails were served there, too, they came at a price. The fifteen-cent drinks of yesteryear would now set you back two bucks, and even in low-end clip joints, if you bought a "hostess" a drink, which was usually a Gin Highball made with water and ginger ale, you could count on spending more than a dollar for the privilege.

Speakeasy drinks varied in price, of course, depending on where you were; you could actually get a Sidecar for as little as sixty cents at one joint in South Carolina, where the owner had thought of a novel way to dispense liquor: He claimed to be giving it away. Printed on the bottom of the restaurant's wine and cocktail list were the following words: "As the sale of intoxicating beverages is prohibited by law, the above prices are for service only and do not include the price of the spirituous ingredients."

You could also buy pints of liquor in many speakeasies—whiskey would set you back about $10, and brandy, purportedly imported, went for $15. The speakeasy owners turned a good profit on this liquor: One bootlegger's price list offered brand-name bottles of bourbon and straight rye for $1.50 per pint, and Scotch—Johnnie Walker and Teacher's included—went for just fifty cents more. Gin was offered by the same guy, "Swift," at a paltry dollar a pint, and if you spent over ten bucks, you could choose between a quart of "Hiram Walker's Canadian Club Rye" or any "High Grade Scotch" as a bonus. Swift also noted, "All merchandise may be sampled before you pay."

Prohibition had been thrust upon America at a time when unemployment had been growing fast. After the conclusion of World War I, in 1918, strikes had hit almost all forms of industry; schools had been closed in some areas because of a lack of fuel (the result of almost half a million miners leaving the pits to protest wages and hours); and other schools had closed because teachers were unwilling to work for the pittance offered. Soldiers returning from the Great War were faced not only with a housing and job shortage but also with wives and sweethearts who were, well, not the same women they'd left at home.

The Lawless Decade, by Paul Sann, cites many symptoms of the new emancipated American women of the day, including a revolution in women's underwear that caused the popularity of the cotton variety to dwindle and silk to be the new fabric of choice. New short hairstyles, or "bobbed" hair, signaled a new freedom for women, and hemlines were rising rapidly. Flappers, "good-time girls" with their stockings rolled down below their knees and flashy makeup, danced and drank their way through the Roaring Twenties, arriving just in time for the speakeasies to open their doors.

In speakeasies, "the young women of the entertainment committee . . . are nearly as naked as can be managed with something ornamental still on. . . . The guests are from everywhere and are clothed . . . [in] every range from grave to gay and every origin from Paris to Podunk. . . . When a girl is doing her dance of contortion, a well-trained waiter at the back may let go a grating cry 'Throw her to the Li-ons!' That is just to make everybody feel at home," wrote H. I. Brock and J. W. Golinkin in *New York Is Like This.* Women had finally taken to the bars, and some of them had opened their own joints.

Mary Louise Cecilia "Texas" Guinan, Broadway chorus girl, musical actress, and star of movies such as *The Hellcat, The She Wolf, The Gun Woman,* and *Little Miss Deputy,* was, without doubt, the toast of the town in Manhattan nightclubs and speakeasies, though she also worked in Miami and Chicago during the dry years. "If [Police Commissioner] Grover Whalen is official host of [New York] . . . Texas is unofficial hostess," wrote one wag.

Although Guinan worked mostly as a hostess, greeting guests with her signature opening line, "Hello, sucker," she owned her own joints, too. Ruby Keeler, who went on to star in Busby Berkeley movies, making her film debut in his classic *42nd Street* in 1933, performed at the Texas Guinan Club, where Guinan could sometimes be spotted wearing a necklace of padlocks. The "Queen of the Night Clubs," who would sometimes encourage men to play leapfrog with her during the course of an evening, claimed that her headwaiter had a concession on all liquor sales in the club and that her money was made on cover and setup charges. In 1928, it cost twenty dollars just to gain access to Guinan's Club Intime, and the joint was very successful.

Guinan wasn't the only female speakeasy owner. Helen Morgan, the Torch Song chanteuse perhaps most famous for her performance as Julie in Florenz Ziegfield's Broadway production of *Show Boat,* entertained her guests from atop a piano in her "speak," and Belle Livingstone, known in the 1890s as the "chorus girl with the poetic legs," opened a Park Avenue "salon of culture, wit and bonhomie," which closed after being raided by the cops. Not to be deterred, Livingstone then opened a five-story "resort" on East Fifty-eighth Street, complete with miniature golf and Ping-Pong tables. That club, too, was raided, and her attempt to flee over the rooftops was thwarted when agents caught sight of her well-known red pajamas. After Livingstone spent her thirty days in prison, Texas Guinan sent an armored car to bring her back to Manhattan. Livingstone claimed afterward that her morals had not been impaired during her stay behind bars, saying, "On the contrary, . . . if anything, [they have] been improved."

Another woman who was famous during the dry years was Assistant Attorney General Mabel Walker Willebrandt, who said, "The ribaldry of the cocktail shaker . . . and the florid eagerness for false stimulation from what is almost always questionable liquor are rapidly fading from the social hours in Washington." Since the nation's capital was known as being one of the places where good liquor was, indeed, hard to come by, she might have been right. But elsewhere, the florid eagerness for false stimulation was not that easily quelled.

New York was home to speakeasies and nightclubs such as Peter's Blue Hour, the Peek Inn, the Metamora Club, the Crillon, Club Borgo, the Beaux Arts, the Silver Slipper, the Jungle Club, Club Richelieu, the Biarritz, Mouquin's, the Blue Ribbon, the Furnace, the Hyena Club, the Day Breakers, the Jail Club, and, funnily enough, the Ha! Ha! Most of these joints were in midtown or uptown, but down in Greenwich Village a certain Barney Gallant decided to open Club Gallant on Washington Square South. It was one of the swankiest joints in town.

According to Stanley Walker, Gallant had the distinction of being the first person in Manhattan to be jailed under Prohibition laws, an event that took place before national Prohibition went into effect. The war-time Prohibition Act of 1918, prohibiting the sale of alcohol until "the termination of demobilization," went into effect on June 30, 1919, and less than four months later Gallant's Greenwich Village Inn was raided. Gallant was arrested along with half a dozen of his waiters; he agreed to plead guilty providing the waiters were set free. Sentenced to thirty days in jail, he served far less, and about a month before national Prohibition began, his Club Gallant opened its doors.

The club, filled with "youngsters with strange stirrings in their breasts, who had come from remote villages on the prairie; women of social position and money who wanted to do things—all sorts of things—in a bohemian setting; businessmen who had made quick money and who wanted to breathe the faintly naughty atmosphere in safety, and ordinary people who got thirsty now and then and wanted to sit down and have a drink," thrived until 1924, when Gallant opened a new joint on West Third Street. If you wanted to drink at this place, you had to follow some rules:

1. Reserve a table in advance so as to be sure of admittance.
2. Do not offer any gratuities to the head waiter or the captain as soon as you enter the door. If the service was satisfactory tip one of them a moderate sum upon leaving.
3. Bring along your own "atmosphere" with you. It avoids controversy and is much safer all around.
4. Do not get too friendly with the waiter. His name is neither Charley nor George. Remember the old adage about familiarity breeding contempt.
5. Pinching the cigarette girl's cheek or asking her to dance with her is decidedly out of order. She is there for the sole purpose of dispensing cigars and cigarettes with a smile that will bring profits to the concessionaire.
6. Do not ask to play the drums. The drum heads are not as tough as many another head. Besides, it has a tendency to disturb the rhythm.
7. Make no requests of the leader of the orchestra for the songs of the vintage of 1890. Crooning "Sweet Adeline" was alright for your granddad, but times, alas, have changed.
8. Do not be overgenerous in tipping your waiter. Why be a chump? Fifteen percent of your bill is quite sufficient.
9. Examine your bill when the waiter presents it. Remember even they are human and are liable to err—intentionally or otherwise.
10. Please do not offer to escort the cloakroom girl home. Her husband, who is an ex-prizefighter, is there for that purpose.

Gallant claimed that his secret to success was exclusivity, and that this was the nightclub's "great and only stock in trade." Other places weren't quite as choosy about whom they let in. Walker noted that customers in various venues would "[complain] about the bill when they had expected to be robbed in the first place, . . . try to drink up the town's booze supply in one night, . . . drink too much and then try to lead the band, . . . lose their [money] and then blame the wrong people, . . . get reeling, blind drunk and try to steal their neighbor's girls, . . . [and] tip so much that they were ridiculous or so little that they would be snubbed. . . . In short, the lower stratum of customers were obstreperous, ill-mannered, unable to hold their liquor, and ripe for the plucking." There was quite a party going on.

In New York, the party stretched all the way uptown to Harlem, where, not long after the end of the First World War, white folk had discovered some marvelous clubs. Jimmie's, Small's, the Capitol, and the Palace Gardens were places where working-class African-Americans hung out, while the Cotton Club and the Exclusive Club catered more to Harlem's social leaders. At various nightspots you could catch acts by "Snake Hips" Earl Tucker, Cab Calloway, or Florence Mills, straight back from her success at Les Ambassadeurs in Paris, but one place that deserves special mention is Gilligan F. Holton's Broken Leg and Busted Bar and Grill, on West 138th Street. Holton described one incident in his speakeasy to journalist Joseph Mitchell:

> *One night the place was crowded, and a man and his wife came in. He looked like a big spender. I decided to use him for a psychological test. A test to determine just how much a human being would stand for.*
>
> *I sat him at a table right near the kitchen where it was so warm it would singe your hair. Then I had the waiters spill soup on him and step on his feet and scrape crumbs into his lap. His wife ordered some wine, and I said to myself, "I'll fix her." I got me some cold tea and I poured some kerosene in it and I dumped a little gin in it and I shook it up. Well, this couple stayed in the place until daybreak and spent $125—which was easy to do, of course—and then the man came up to me. I thought he was going to hit me.*
>
> *But no. He said, "Mr. Holton, I want to thank you for a wonderful night. I never had such an interesting time. I am going to tell all my friends about your place."*
>
> *And then his wife said, "And the wine, Mr. Holton! The most wonderful Amontillado sherry I ever tasted. How do you get such wonderful wine in this beastly prohibition country?"*

If Prohibition-era bars weren't filled with creative bartenders honing their collective craft, there were at least a few cocktailians around. A couple of cocktails that were served at speakeasies are detailed in Michael and Ariane Batterberry's *On the Town in New York:* The Goldfish Cocktail, sort of a Dry Martini with goldwasser (an herbal liqueur speckled with gold flakes), was the specialty of the Aquarium speakeasy that sported a huge fish tank as its bar; and at Zani's speakeasy, you could order a Zani Zaza, a drink made with gin, apricot brandy, egg white, lemon juice, and grenadine. No doubt other nightclubs of the time had bartenders who created cocktails during Prohibition, but the vast majority of drinks detailed in books published after repeal were either created prior to 1920, concocted during Prohibition but first made in Europe, or invented by those bartenders who took their place behind the mahogany on December 5, 1933, when the nation was, once again, allowed to drink in peace.

RESTORATION

On December 6, 1933, Sidney E. Klein looked out of his Times Square office window to see throngs of people standing in line to get schooners of beer from a wagon pulled by eight dray horses. Budweiser hadn't waited long to get back on the street. And neither did anyone else—Prohibition's repeal had been ratified at 5:32 P.M. the previous day, and the nation was ready to party in the open again. Too bad everyone was broke.

The Depression started by the stock market crash of 1929 had resulted in unemployment for over thirteen million Americans by the time Franklin Delano Roosevelt took office in March 1933. One of F.D.R.'s remedies for the situation, just one month after he became president, was to legalize near beer; he then made sure that the Twenty-first Amendment to the Constitution, which crushed the Prohibition amendment, was enacted before the year ended. On the following day, the *New York Times* carried such headlines as "City Toasts New Era," "Celebration in Streets," and "Machine Guns Guard Some Liquor Trucks—Supplies to Be Rushed Out Today."

No sooner did the bars of America reopen than the publishers started issuing new cocktail books to jog the memories of those who remembered the "Here's How" days prior to Prohibition, and to teach a new generation how to properly mix drinks. A few cocktail guides actually got published prior to the act's repeal, *Shake 'Em Up: A Practical Handbook of Polite Drinking,* by Virginia Elliot and Phil D. Stong, among them. The authors of this tongue-in-cheek party handbook admonished their readers to use nonalcoholic spirits when constructing their drinks, or to boil the alcohol off real spirits if that was all they could lay their hands on.

Sullivan's 1930 book *The Drinks of Yesteryear*—in which he claimed never to have served a flapper, saying that "her hiplash" was unknown to him—details, as the title suggests, pre-Prohibition drinks, not new cocktails. And even Patrick Gavin Duffy's 1934 *Official Mixer's Guide* isn't full of new American drinks, although the recipes suggest strongly that Duffy had read, and thoroughly digested, Craddock's book from the London Savoy.

Apart from the fact that Duffy categorized his recipes by the base liquor, whereas Craddock used the alphabetical approach, many instances point to Duffy referring to Craddock's work, at least as a guide; the one major difference lies in the use of absinthe, which was, and still is, legal in England but had been outlawed in the States. Duffy simply substituted Bénédictine in drinks such as the Monkey Gland Cocktail, and since that time various books have listed one or the other recipe, depending on which book was used for reference. In America, of course, absinthe substitutes such as Herbsaint, Absente, or Pernod are used when absinthe is called for.

Perhaps the most important aspect of drinking during the years that followed repeal, right up through the 1970s, is that overconsumption of beverage alcohol was rarely, if ever, mentioned. Drinking was fun. Being drunk was funny. Very few people took the role of the cocktailian too seriously, and some books of the era reflect the nation's attitude.

The Drunk's Blue Book, written by Norman Anthony and O. Soglow in 1933, for instance, details what the authors call the Drunk's Code:

1. Free lunch.
2. Free speech.
3. Free cheers.
4. Five-day week.
5. Every third drink on the house.
6. Lower curbstones.
7. Overstuffed gutters.
8. More lamp-posts.
9. Rubber nightsticks and rolling pins.
10. More keyholes for every door.
11. More farmers' daughters.
12. Colder ice.
13. Two cocktails for a quarter.
14. Bigger and better beers.

These wags also suggest that if you find yourself lying on the floor in front of a bar, it is improper to rest your elbows on the brass foot rail, and they recommend that if you discover you're driving the wrong way up a one-way street, you should keep to the right side of the road. A whole section of this book is devoted to "How to Get into Fights" and advises such activities as sitting on the curbstone shouting derogatory names at truck drivers, and approaching a couple at a table and, "chucking the lady in question under the chin, say[ing], 'Hello baby. Who's your funny-looking friend?'" Anthony and Soglow wouldn't have many twenty-first-century friends.

Some people, though, *were* interested in mixing a good drink, and Charles Brown noted that sweet drinks such as the Alexander had come into vogue in the thirties. There's no getting away from the fact that, in general, more women than men enjoy sweeter drinks. In contrast with pre-Prohibition nightlife, women were now every bit as important as men in bars across the country, and they were also throwing cocktail parties at home.

Charles Brown's 1939 *Gun Club Drink Book* noted: "Due to the speakeasy architecture of the Prohibition era, our own cocktail bars now look like . . . foreign imitations, and with their highly cushioned stools and female patrons they are quite different from the barrooms of preceding generations; but then too the women themselves have changed. . . . In the so called 'good old days' a woman's place was the home while the men frequented the bars; nowadays there is no sex discrimination in any sport and almost every home has its own bar."

In 1936 Harman Burney "Barney" Burke, an American bartender who had plied his trade in London, Paris, Berlin, and Copenhagen before returning to America after repeal, listed what he considered to be the fifteen "most popular conventional drinks in the Western world" in *Burke's Complete Cocktail & Drinking Recipes:*

1. Martini Cocktail (Dry or Sweet)
2. Manhattan Cocktail (Dry or Sweet)
3. Bronx Cocktail (Dry or Sweet)
4. Old Fashioned Whiskey Cocktail (Sweet)
5. Sidecar Cocktail (Sweet)
6. Clover Club Cocktail (Dry)
7. Gin Rickey (Dry)
8. Gin Fizz (Sweet or Dry)

9. Bacardi Cocktail (Dry)
10. Alexander Cocktail No. 1 (Sweet)
11. Rock and Rye (Sweet)
12. Whiskey Cocktail (Dry)
13. Sherry Cocktail (Sweet or Dry)
14. Dubonnet Cocktail (Sweet)
15. Champagne Cocktail

A little confusion arises here, since he lists the Bronx as being either dry or sweet but his recipe calls for both varieties of vermouth. Also, although he suggests that people enjoyed dry Bacardi Cocktails, his recipe calls for as much grenadine as citrus juice, so it couldn't have been very dry.

Burke's Dry Martini contained twice as much gin as vermouth, as well as a couple of dashes of orange bitters, a formula that would last in many cocktail books until well into the forties; and his Manhattan, which could be made with either rye or Irish whiskey, followed a similar path except that while he included bitters in the dry version, he used simple syrup in his Sweet Manhattan, and both Italian and French vermouths were called for.

The Old-Fashioned in Burke's book requires a slice of orange and a lemon twist to be "mulled" with bitters and sugar before the whiskey is added to the glass, and this method of preparing the drink caused many arguments among Old-Fashioned aficionados in the years to come. In the introduction to 1945's *Crosby Gaige's Cocktail Guide and Ladies' Companion,* writer and bon vivant Lucius Beebe wrote about his encounter with a bartender at the Drake Hotel in Chicago when he requested an Old-Fashioned without fruit. Apparently the bartender was so insulted at the thought of anybody imagining that he *might* put fruit in the drink that he admonished Gaige, "Young impudent sir . . . I've built Old-Fashioned cocktails these sixty years . . . and I have never yet had the perverted nastiness of mind to put fruit in an Old-Fashioned. Get out, scram, go over to the Palmer House and drink."

That the Sidecar is included in Burke's list is interesting, since this drink, reportedly created in France during the First World War, was still relatively new to the United States. While it did appear on at least one cocktail menu during Prohibition, "the 'Sidecar' and 'Presidente' cocktails are among the foreign importations that have a considerable following," wrote one mixed-drink fancier in 1934.

Drinks were named for people long before the 1930s. It's possible that the Bobby Burns, for example, was named not for the great Scottish poet but for a cigar salesman who frequented the old Waldorf-Astoria bar. But things got a little out of control when Sterling North and Carl Kroch decided to name drinks after popular books in their 1935 cocktail guide *So Red the Nose, or Breath in the Afternoon.*

The recipes in this lighthearted book were supplied by the author of each work referred to; Ernest Hemingway submitted the Death in the Afternoon cocktail—a simple mixture of absinthe and champagne. His instructions call for the imbiber to "Drink 3 to 5 of these slowly," and the editor's note at the bottom of the page advises, "After six of these cocktails *The Sun Also Rises.*"

Edgar Rice Burroughs submitted the Tarzan Cocktail, made with Bacardi, Cointreau, lime juice, and sugar. Hervey Allen contributed the Anthony Adverse Cocktail, which could help anyone through a little adversity: Barbados rum, lime juice, bitters, brown sugar, and "a strong dash of brandy."

One of the recipes that didn't make it into the main section of the book but was mentioned in the back (presumably because the authors couldn't resist it) came from H. L. Davis, author of *Honey in the Horn.* The drink contained two beer steins of high-proof rum; dark, strained honey; fresh huckleberries; mountain-ash berries; and "best black gunpowder." Davis instructed the bartender, "Mix (at room temperature) and stir savagely until it is no longer streaky in color. Each drink should be served with a toothpick impaling a dead bumblebee, a dead yellow jacket and a dead wasp. These are supposed to be eaten first to give the revelers a notion of what lies in store for them."

On the other side of the Atlantic, Booth's gin compiled a similar collection of cocktail recipes, but these were selected for people such as the Earl of Westmorland, who was assigned the London Buck—gin, lemon juice, and ginger ale—and made it into the book after he allowed them to print his quote: "A cocktail without Booth's is a cocktail under a handicap." The Countess of Oxford and Asquith declared, "It is popular to be liberal with Booth's gin, and then the party will be top of the poll," for which she was awarded the Empire Cocktail, a mixture of gin, calvados, and apricot brandy. And Dame Sybil Thorndike, whose theatrical break came when George Bernard Shaw took her under his wing, was honored with a Trilby cocktail when she said, "A cocktail in which Booth's plays a leading part receives an enthusiastic reception from the most captious critics."

Back in America, high society during the mid- to late thirties had marvelous nightclubs and bars to choose from, some of them being old speakeasies that had gone legit. The Stork Club in New York had been raided and closed on a couple of occasions during the early thirties, but now, in new premises, it was open to anyone with enough money to afford its food and drink. Similarly, El Morocco had been an illegal drinking club, but now people could drink there without fear of raids. On the West Coast, though, a new style of bar started to emerge when Donn "the Beachcomber" Beach started selling pseudotropical drinks at his new joint in Hollywood.

Jeff Berry and Annene Kaye detail Beachcomber originals such as the Missionary's Downfall and the Cobra's Fang in their book *Beachbum Berry's Grog Log,* but they note that the Zombie was his real claim to fame. The Beachcomber's first joint opened in 1934, but in 1937 he moved into bigger and better digs decorated with bamboo, tropical plants, waterfalls, burning torches, and even miniature volcanoes. The American tiki lounge had been born. Victor "Trader Vic" Bergeron copied the style in the late thirties, and he gave us the Mai Tai in 1944.

America didn't truly recover from the Depression until the end of the 1930s, just as the Second World War was beginning in Europe. But bon vivant Charles Henry Baker Jr. must not have been hit too hard by the stock market crash of 1929, since he had been spending his time drinking his way around the world, detailing his adventures in *The Gentleman's Companion.* "Each one of [our experiences that] fetches joyous memory of some friend, place, or adventure . . . is flanked with happy memory of a frosted glass, a smile, the sip of something perfect," he wrote, and went on to describe various and sundry cocktails, some of which he'd encountered at their place of origin.

Baker sipped Singapore Slings at the Raffles Hotel in Singapore, where the drink had been created in 1915 by bartender Ngiam Tong Boon, and declared it "a delicious, slow-acting, insidious thing." In New Orleans he drank Sazeracs and determined that the best way to enjoy them was to hold the glass under your nose, "inhale the fragrant blend of scents, sip and relax." And he was probably the first to instruct Americans on the ritual of drinking shots of tequila by sucking on a wedge of lemon (not lime), taking a pinch of salt, and shooting the spirit. Baker wasn't afraid to use top-shelf spirits in his cocktails, either; he wrote that it was as impossible to make a fine cocktail with "dollar gin" as it would have been for Whistler to depict his mother using "barn paint."

By the time the 1940s arrived, Americans had been introduced to the Bloody Mary. Vodka was being made in the States, though not many people knew much about it until around the middle of the decade, when Jack Morgan, the owner of the Cock and Bull Tavern in Los Angeles and an executive from the company that was making Smirnoff vodka, got together to create the Moscow Mule. Vodka would never look back.

Rum and Coca-Cola was another drink that became popular in the 1940s, popularized by the Andrews Sisters' version of the Trinidadian calypso by that name written by Lord Invader. The song was written about, and popular with, the servicemen at the American naval base in Trinidad.

Since the late 1800s, liquor companies have been aware that most of their products are poured into cocktail shakers, and they haven't been shy about bombarding us with "useful" pamphlets to guide us on our way. In 1941, Heublein issued *The Club Cocktail Party Book* to promote its range of bottled cocktails—Martinis, Manhattans, Old-Fashioneds, Sidecars, and Daiquiris—and to teach us how to make such party treats as heart-shaped canapés topped with a crab-flake spread and "your initials in capers."

Cocktail parties in those days were lots of fun, especially if you had Seagram's Magic Age Cards, each one advertising a different whiskey and filled with a "bingo card" of numbers: "Hand the six cards to a person telling him (or her) to return to you only those cards on which [their] age appears . . . simply add together the numbers appearing in the upper right-hand square." Oh, the fun they must have had.

Luckily for us all, some people started to take the subject of cocktails seriously again. In 1945, Lucius Beebe, once called "the outstanding dude among the journalists," wrote, "It is only fitting that the subject of cocktails should be approached with levity slightly tinctured with contempt because, for every good compound, arrangement, or synthesis of liquors, wines, and their adjacent or opposite fruits and flavors chilled and served in a variety of glasses, there are approximately a million foul, terrifying, and horrendous similar excitements to stupefaction, cuspidor hurling, and nausea." Beebe wasn't the only one putting a little thought into the subject—even James Beard, later to become the dean of American cookery, submitted a cocktail recipe for publication in 1945's *Crosby Gaige's Cocktail Guide and Ladies' Companion.*

But if Beebe, Beard, and others took the fine art of mixing drinks seriously, they were mere amateurs compared to David Embury, author of *The Fine Art of Mixing Drinks* (first published in 1948 and revised in 1952 and 1958) and the only true amateur among them. Embury was the first true cocktailian of the modern age, and he took time to analyze the components of a cocktail, breaking them down into a base (usually a spirit, it must be at least 50 percent of the drink); a modifying, smoothing, or aromatizing agent, such as vermouth, bitters, fruit juice, sugar, cream, or eggs; and "additional special flavoring and coloring ingredients," which he defined as liqueurs and nonalcoholic fruit syrups.

Embury taught us that the Ramos Gin Fizz must be shaken for at least five minutes in order to achieve the proper silky consistency, suggested that Peychaud's bitters be used in the Rob Roy, and noted that "for cocktails, such as the Side Car, a three-star cognac is entirely adequate, although a ten-year-old cognac will produce a better drink."

In the second edition of his book, Embury mentioned that he had been criticized for omitting two drinks from his original work: the Bloody Mary, which he described as "strictly vile," and the Moscow Mule—"merely mediocre." On the subject of Martinis, he explained that although most cocktail books call for the drink to be made with one-third to one-half vermouth, "quite recently, in violent protest of this wishy-washy type of cocktail, there has sprung up the vermouth-rinse method of making Martinis." He describes a drink made from chilled gin in a cocktail glass coated in vermouth. Embury didn't approve of either version, and went on to say that a ratio of seven parts gin to one part vermouth was his personal favorite.

While Embury was taking his drinking seriously, many Americans were quaffing Martinis by the pitcher, and *Playboy* magazine commissioned cocktail maven Thomas Mario and, later, Emanuel Greenberg to deliver cocktail news to a nation of people who drank for fun, and did it on a regular basis.

Esquire magazine issued its *Handbook for Hosts* as early as 1949, detailing drinks such as the Sloe Gin Fizz, the Pan American, the "I Died Game, Boys" Mixture, and the Ginsicle—gin with fruit juice or simple syrup poured over chipped ice in a champagne glass. A cartoon in the book depicts a frustrated bartender mopping his fevered brow and exclaiming, "She ordered it because it had a cute name." The world of cocktails was tilting slightly on its axis, and liquor companies lobbied long and hard to get into the act.

In the fifties, Southern Comfort got us to make Comfort Manhattans and Comfort Old-Fashioneds by issuing a booklet: *How to Make the 32 Most Popular Drinks.* By the seventies, when the Comfort Manhattan had become the Improved Manhattan, they were bringing us *Happy Hour Mixology Plus a Primer of Happy Hour Astrology,* presumably so we would have something to talk about at bars: "Oh, you're a Virgo—discriminating, keenly analytical, exacting, and often a perfectionist. Wanna drink?" Even roadside diners were using place mats filled with cocktail recipes to entice customers to have, perhaps, a Dubonnet Cocktail alongside their grilled-cheese sandwich, or a Crème de Menthe Frappé, which they could pour over their stack of silver-dollar pancakes.

Gordon's gin issued a recipe booklet in the late fifties detailing drinks such as the Major Bailey—a sort of gin-based Mint Julep—and the Spriuss Cocktail, "popular at the Hotel Excelsior, Rome," made with gin, apricot brandy, orange juice, and bitters. Monochrome photographs of foreign stamps appear on the pages of this pamphlet, and Gordon's deemed it necessary to warn readers, "All the stamps illustrated have been demonetized and are not valid for postage."

Bars in the last half of the twentieth century were also hit hard by convenience drinks. No need to squeeze lemons or limes anymore; "sweet and sour" is here—it's already sweetened, and you can use it in place of either juice. And the drinks you make with it will take you right back to your childhood—they taste like sherbet. Bloody Mary? Here's a bottle of tomato juice that's preseasoned with just enough sauces and spices to let you know they're there, but not enough to offend anyone on the face of the earth. How do you make a Daiquiri? It's easy—the instructions are on the packet. Not all of these drink mixes were terrible, but not one of them rendered potions worthy of the bartenders of yesteryear.

In the seventies, although there was a cornucopia of cocktails from which to choose, Martinis still reigned supreme, Manhattans took second place, just as they had at the old Waldorf-Astoria bar prior to World War I, and the sweeter drinks that had come into vogue right after the repeal of Prohibition were still popular in American bars. One cocktail was quickly gaining ground on the older classics, though, and it would become a shining star by the 1980s.

The Margarita (see page 290) had been around since the thirties, forties, or fifties, depending on whose story you believe, but tequila didn't really catch on in this country until the Swinging Sixties arrived, when hippies and would-be hippies alike heard a rumor that the spirit might act as a hallucinogen. By the seventies all bartenders knew how to fix a mean Margarita, and its popularity grew and grew, until nobody really cared about whether or not there were any mind-altering side effects—it had become a staple drink, and a classic in its own right.

THE NEW COCKTAILIANS

By the mid-1980s the health craze had swept the country, and the cocktail scene was all but dead. Or perhaps it simply lay in hibernation, since something came along that coaxed it out of its cave by screaming loudly, and out of tune: Punk Cocktails hit the scene. Young bartenders who had never been trained in the finer aspects of the cocktailian craft had grown bored of making wishy-washy White Wine Spritzers, tedious Tequila Sunrises, and lackluster Long Island Iced Teas, so they created obnoxious potions with vile-sounding names; you could order an Abortion or a Blow Job in any old bar and nobody would blink an eye. Bars selling dozens of flavors of frozen drinks seemed to spring up overnight, and few of them offered well-constructed Slurpies. And Jelly Shots, made from flavored gelatin and vodka, or sometimes tequila, were being sucked down by underage college kids on campuses everywhere.

Who created these drinks? Nobody seems to know. My friend Stuffy Shmitt learned how to make a drink called Windex at Barney's Beanery in Los Angeles, but he has no idea who first created it. And it was Stuffy who saw a sign outside a Lower East Side New York joint advertising a cocktail made with NyQuil as a base—but ask him which bar it was, and Stuffy shrugs. Nobody ever bothered to document Punk Cocktails—nobody really cared where they came from. Laughter at the bar, the chance to order a Sperm du Jour—a drink sipped through a straw inserted down the center of a fresh banana—and scantily clad women selling test-tube shooters of relatively harmless concoctions were welcomed, and very much needed, in the bars of America.

For me, this was a very exciting time in the world of mixed drinks; somebody was putting the fun back into drinking. We'd spent much of the 1980s hearing about the hazardous effects of overconsumption, and it seemed as though a whole generation of customers had entered adulthood being warned that they could have a drink providing they didn't have a good time. I dubbed the drinks of this period Punk Cocktails because they seemed to be liquid versions of bands like the Sex Pistols—they certainly didn't harmonize well, but they sure as hell made themselves heard. Bartenders revolted against the elevator-music drinks of their elders and created noisier potions of their own. This phenomenon was exactly what was needed to make potential cocktailians rethink their craft.

In no way am I suggesting that overconsumption of beverage alcohol should be encouraged, but neither am I one of those aficionados who claim to drink only for flavor. The effect of a couple of rounds on anyone unencumbered by ailments that prevent the use of alcohol is one of the rewards of a decent drink. So when Punk Cocktails gave bartenders and consumers a license to let loose a little at the bar, the path was opened for true cocktailians to once again take an interest in the subject of mixology and create new potions—some of which, no doubt, would bring a sparkle to the eyes to the likes of Harry Johnson and Jerry Thomas.

Dale DeGroff, probably the best-known cocktailian of our time, took over the bar at New York's legendary Rainbow Room in 1987, and a star was born. DeGroff brought us classics such as the Ritz of New York cocktail, and in turn, he mentored Audrey Saunders, the Libation Goddess, when he took over the bar at Blackbird. Audrey has given birth to such delicious potions as the Gin-Gin Mule and the Dreamy Dorini Smoking Martini.

Dr. Cocktail, a.k.a. Ted Haigh, a consummate cocktailian and a drink historian extraordinaire, has also sired some new drinks—the Delmarva Cocktail is one of my favorites—and has done much to bring back into vogue forgotten recipes such as the Twentieth-Century Cocktail, which dates to the 1930s. Robert Hess, known as DrinkBoy to most, goes bar-hopping armed with a palm-top full of cocktail recipes so he can teach worthy bartenders some drinks that might be new to them but are old favorites to him. He has also given us the Black

Feather Cocktail, a drink that displays his intimacy with classic methodology and an innate knowledge of ingredients.

In Las Vegas, Tony Abou-Ganim reigns supreme at the Bellagio, where his creations constantly marvel the in crowd of the gambling set, and regulars at Manhattan's Carnegie Club and Campbell Apartment are often treated to the best Mojitos in the city when they happen to catch beverage director Lou Cantres behind the stick.

Norman Bukofzer, my all-time favorite bartender, *feels* his way through the cocktailian craft at the newly opened Ritz-Carlton hotel on Central Park South, while Stuffy Shmitt mixes mean Manhattans just below Fourteenth Street, at the Tavern on Jane Street. Meanwhile, at the Town bar in Manhattan's Chambers hotel, a young Jonathan Pogash recently took his place behind the stick. Thirsty for knowledge, and striving for perfection, Jonathan took my Cocktails in the Country bartender course, and he, and others like him, hold the future of the craft in their hands. I think it will be safe there.

LAST CALL

Over 140 years have passed since Jerry Thomas published the world's first book of cocktail and mixed drink recipes—*How to Mix Drinks, or The Bon Vivant's Companion*—and most first-edition copies of this book are not in great condition. Even more scarce are copies of Harry Johnson's 1882 work, *New and Improved Illustrated Bartender's Manual,* a self-published book printed on inferior paper, much of which has started to disintegrate. Is it accurate to say, then, that if the current interest in mixology hadn't happened for, say, another fifty years, the basic theories of the cocktailian craft could have been entirely lost to history? It's certainly a possibility.

We are fortunate, indeed, that a few people realized that the fine art of mixing drinks is a serious matter, and have spent much time delving into the intricacies of the craft. And we are privileged to be living in an age when new cocktails are newsworthy, and when many bartenders take pride in their work not only as cocktailians but also as serious craftspeople who know every facet of the job, including when it's time to ring the bell and let everyone go home. If you have set your sights on being a professional bartender, you couldn't have wished for a better time in history to take your place behind the stick.

THOUGHTS FROM A COASTER

The first Kamikaze I ever saw was made with Stolichnaya vodka and two drops, no more, of sweetened lime juice. It was a shooter. "What's the difference between this and a very dry Vodka Gimlet?" my friend Dave Ridings asked of bartender Scott Lamb, who was holding forth at Hudson Bay on Manhattan's East Eighty-sixth Street at the time. "You don't feel like killing yourself after a Gimlet" was the answer.

I spent over two decades working in Manhattan bars, and I saw lots of changes along the way. Not all of my cocktail memories are worthy of short stories, but sometimes, as I sip my Manhattan at the end of the work day, the following images buzz around my head:

The first time I had Sex on the Beach in a bar . . . Pink Squirrels dying out . . . Dale DeGroff bringing our attention to the Pisco Sour . . . times when Presbyterians were regularly ordered drinks . . . discovering the joys of the Sazerac . . . an evening with friend Roy Finamore drinking absinthe, playing Parisian street music, using antique absinthe spoons, and making Tremblement de Terre cocktails . . . the couple who had business cards printed with their Sidecar recipe so bartenders wouldn't let them down . . . Southern Comfort Manhattans putting the finishing touch on a very long evening . . . huge Stingers at Martell's on Third Avenue . . . making a Ward Eight for old friend Trapper Al, who had been weaned on them . . . the Debonair cocktail (see page 246) making its way to the Rainbow Room cocktail list . . . almost bursting into tears when I realized that most bartenders had stopped adding bitters to Manhattans . . . predicting the Monkey Gland would make a comeback in 1991 and waiting years for it to happen . . . turning many people on to the joys of the Negroni . . . being taught how to make Mojitos by Lou Cantres, bar maestro at Manhattan's Carnegie Club . . . Godfathers hitting the scene shortly after the movie . . . an evening at Trader Vic's drinking Scorpions . . . being amazed that a ludicrous drink like the Long Island Iced Tea actually tasted okay . . . discovering, circa 1973, that someone who ordered an extra-dry Martini did not want me to put extra dry vermouth into his drink . . . making Ramos Gin Fizzes with Cornwall friends Chris and Leslie and shaking them until our hands were frozen to the shakers . . . being upset when I discovered that the vast majority of people thought that vodka was the base of the Bay Breeze—the fault of a certain vodka company . . . watching our friend Steve down Lemon Drop after Lemon Drop on Christmas Day, circa 1990; the same vodka company was responsible for that, now I think about it . . . discovering that the Hennessy Martini isn't just a good marketing ploy, it's a pretty good drink . . . countless arguments about what makes a cocktail a Martini . . . praying that the Blood Orange Cocktail would be a hit . . . the heavenly moment when I first sipped a Caipirinha . . . spending countless hours searching for the creator of the Cosmopolitan and coming up with nothing more than a sneaking suspicion that Cointreau was behind it . . . scoffing at the Green Apple Martini—until I actually tried one.

When my daily reward is almost drained, these memories and more sometimes spur me to pick up Bernard DeVoto's *The Hour* and read the passage describing cocktail hour: "This is the violet hour, the hour of hush and wonder, when the affectations glow and valor is reborn, when the shadows deepen along the edge of the forest and we believe that, if we watch carefully, at any moment we may see the unicorn." It makes my little heart glad.

THE BARTENDER: DO YOU HAVE WHAT IT TAKES?

The average bartender, despite the slanders of professional moralists, is a man of self-respect and self-possession; a man who excels at a difficult art and is well aware of it; a man who shrinks from ruffianism as he does from uncleanliness; in short, a gentleman. . . . The bartender is one of the most dignified, law abiding, and ascetic of men. He is girt about by a rigid code of professional ethics; his work demands a clear head and a steady hand; he must have sound and fluent conversation; he cannot be drunken or dirty; the slightest dubiousness is quick to exile him to the police force, journalism, the oyster boats or some other Siberia of the broken.

—H. L. MENCKEN, Baltimore *Evening Sun,* May 11, 1911

ALTHOUGH KNOWING HOW TO MIX a variety of good drinks is required of a professional bartender, if you really want to tend bar other qualities are absolutely necessary: how to deal with customers, how to deal with waitpeople, how to deal with the boss, and, perhaps most important, how to act professionally while keeping the customers happy, comfortable, and, if need be, entertained.

I have worked just about every job in bars and restaurants. I have managed some decent joints, unclogged toilets, cooked, washed dishes, heaved kegs, and in some very unfortunate circumstances, diners have had to put up with my gross inadequacies as a waiter. For some reason,

I just never got the hang of waiting tables. Most of all I tended bar. I love tending bar. I love the feeling of power supplied by the two feet of waist-high mahogany, I love being in control of the scene, and I love managing the moods of the customers.

Not everyone is cut out to be a bartender. I worked with a guy in the early 1970s who made money hand over fist as a waiter—he was the most popular guy on the floor. But what he really wanted was to tend bar, and when he was finally given a couple of shifts behind the mahogany, all hell broke loose. There was a subtle difference in his attitude that could be attributed only to his change of vocation. When disputes between customers arose and it was imperative that he intervene, I would watch him deliver the same lines he had heard spew forth from my lips in similar circumstances. But instead of taking notice of the all-powerful bartender, customers would become even more belligerent than they had been before he'd entered the fray. If you are new to this craft, you will quickly learn whether or not you are cut out for the job. If not, take heart; it doesn't make you a bad person—and maybe you'll be the best waiter in the world. But if you are a born bartender, take pride; it's a craft that deserves respect. And being paid to do a job you adore is a privilege—it's the dream of every sound-minded man and woman in the world.

It's also important to mention gender in this chapter, since some bars—though they are thankfully few—tend to hire only men or only women. In 1973, when I started tending bar in New York, there were very few female bartenders in the city. Bar owners justified their hiring practices by claiming they needed men to carry cases of beer, heave garbage pails full of ice, and deal with unruly customers. The times, however, have changed, and I would guess that there are now just as many women as men behind the stick in Manhattan. They carry cases, heave garbage pails full of ice, and deal with unruly customers just as successfully as any man—as long as they are cut out to be bartenders. And of course, the same applies to men—if bartending isn't in their hearts, they won't do a good job. The rule of thumb is this: A good bartender, male or female, can handle any given situation at any given time in any given bar.

Having said that, I must note that I have used the male gender throughout the rest of this book, just for readability's sake. If you read the words "he or she" every time it was necessary to employ them in order not to offend, it would surely drive you mad.

A WORD ABOUT THE BOSS

Depending on where you work, some of the guidelines detailed herein may be impossible for you to follow. Every bar has its own rules and regulations, and though I am a strong advocate of returning money to unsatisfied customers and a number of other actions that cost owners money in the short term (but save them a fortune in the long term), your boss may not agree with me. Don't risk losing your job for the sake of following my guidelines; you may, however, want to bring them to the attention of your employer by inviting him to read the pertinent sections of this book and mull over my reasons. In short, apply only the guidelines herein that the rules and regulations of your present employer allow. If he disagrees with my tips for dealing with customers and situations, remember: He's signing your paycheck, not me.

BASIC PHILOSOPHY AND GUIDELINES

My father, a landlord of distinction who ran three successful pubs in his lifetime, taught me that in order to be a good publican—which requires qualities very similar to those of a bartender—you must have "as many faces as the town hall clock." He didn't mean that you shouldn't be true to yourself and speak your mind when need be. What he was saying was that it's often necessary to react to situations in such a way as to guide the outcome to a pleasant conclusion. And that's something nobody can teach you.

It matters not whether you are a professional bartender or simply a person who makes drinks for guests at your home. Your role is the same. It is that of "Mine Host." Your job is to keep things running smoothly by not only mixing drinks but also guiding the ambience of your surroundings, and this is not always an easy task. Though the majority of this chapter is aimed at the professional bartender, amateur cocktailians, too, can gain by learning everything involved in the lot of a bartender.

It starts by being always well groomed and appropriately dressed, but appropriateness depends on the bar at which you work. Most managers or owners will either provide you with a uniform or tell you that you are expected to wear, say, black pants or a black skirt, a white shirt, and a black tie. In some joints, though, you might be expected to wear a T-shirt and jeans. Just follow the rules and regulations, arrive for work in clean clothes with clean hands, nails, and hair, and if you wear an apron behind the bar—which I happen to think looks just dandy—make sure that you change it as soon as anything spills on it.

Since the bartender is looked upon with reverence by most guests, it is up to him to prove that he is worthy of his position, and this is accomplished only with the utmost diplomacy. But diplomacy isn't achieved by words only; attitude also plays a major role.

The bartender must rule the roost from behind the mahogany; he must also be a benevolent dictator who truly cares about the well-being of his guests. If a situation arises that calls for him to, say, ask someone to leave the bar, he must be able to accomplish this task while causing as little upset as possible. It's of no use whatsoever to take on the attitude of "I'm your better," although there are times, when dealing with truly unruly people, when you must lay down the law. On most occasions, it's far better to take the guest in question to one side, explain why you have decided that it's time for him to leave, and assure him that he can return at a later date, providing he promises not to repeat whatever it is he has done to make you take action. You might also choose to talk to one of his friends—pick whoever seems to be either the leader of the group or the one with the most sense. Take that person to one side, explain the situation, and ask for advice on how to handle the fellow in question. Most people enjoy being put into the role of adviser, and often they will take care of the situation for you by departing with their friend.

Tricky situations aside, what do guests expect from bartenders? This really depends on what sort of bar you work in, but generalizations can be drawn. People usually come to bars to have a good time. Sometimes people meet at bars to discuss business or to have serious chats with friends, and if that's the case, they are usually best left alone, save for the times when you must converse with them in order to give good service.

Most of the time, though, it is the bartender's responsibility to "feel out" his customers, discover whether or not they want to meet other people, to chat to the bartender about almost any subject under the sun, to be left alone to muse, or maybe to read a book or newspaper. It's a good idea for a bartender to be well informed about current affairs and sports, but this isn't an essential quality if he has other attributes, such as being able to tell a good joke or perhaps perform acts of sleight of hand to keep his customers amused.

Politics and religion are two topics that, in the past, have been classically avoided by bartenders, but I don't believe that in this day and age they should be completely verboten, providing the bartender doesn't blatantly offend a guest. If you are completely ignorant about any particular topic—as I am when it comes to sports—you should play on that fact in one way or another. When I tended bar in the 1970s and my schedule called for me to be behind the stick when a football game was on television, I used to ask a fellow bartender for a comment or two that would be appropriate to use during the game. Then when I said something seemingly astute—about an injury a player had previously sustained, or a coach's style—my regular customers would look up in amazement, then burst out laughing. They knew I had no idea what I was talking about.

Similarly, I was always a speedy bartender, mainly because I was well organized, knew where everything was, and had trained my left hand to perform some jobs while my right hand was busy doing something else. But I was never any good at fancy movements behind the bar, and I'd never dare to try juggling bottles, or even catching ice cubes flicked into the air with a bar spoon—something that many other bartenders find easy. To compensate for this lack, I would flick ice cubes into the air knowing I would miss them by at least three or four feet. It was every bit as entertaining as catching the ice in a thimble behind my back.

Eavesdropping on guests' conversations is inevitable when you're behind the stick, and this is a good way to figure out how to entertain specific people. Of course, if they are talking about something personal, it's best to leave them alone. If, on the other hand, a couple happen to be talking about, say, a movie they've seen, you can usually jump in and add your comments about it if you've seen it, or about any of the actors in the film if you have something interesting to say. You just have to know when it's appropriate to volunteer your two cents' worth and when it's best to leave people alone.

When you are busy you will have to prioritize, putting specific duties in logical order: The waiter is asking for drinks, the telephone is ringing, new bar customers have just arrived, and a couple of regulars are asking for refills. What do you do first? The golden rule in this situation is: Make sure that everyone knows that you are aware that they need your attention. Verbally tell your customers and the waiter that you'll "be with them shortly," answer the phone (since it's not going to stop ringing) and make the call as short as possible, and then serve drinks to people in the order in which they were placed. If your regular customers are understanding, they'll sometimes wait patiently while you serve new customers who might otherwise leave in search of a drink elsewhere. And although it might not be the policy for the waitstaff to tip you, it's your job to serve them as quickly as possible—they've got to make a living, too, and you must always think about putting as much money in that register as possible in order to keep the boss happy.

Having prioritized that theoretical scenario, though, I should mention that situations vary from one day to another, and a good bartender must be able to assess the situation and act accordingly. For instance, perhaps the regulars at the bar have had enough to drink in your estimation; you might decide to pretend you haven't noticed that they need drinks in the hope that they might leave the bar without you having to confront them. A good bartender should be able to act appropriately in all situations.

In order for you to be able to serve drinks speedily, every bottle and every piece of equipment behind the bar must be in a predesignated spot. That way you know exactly where to go to prepare any drink. Usually the entire team of bartenders at a bar will agree on where to keep what, but some bartenders have specific idiosyncrasies and you might find, when taking over the bar, that a particular tool is not where you usually keep it. To avoid this sort of occurrence, make a thorough check of the bar before you allow your predecessor to leave the area.

If you are the first bartender of the day, make sure that you arrive at work in ample time to stock your bar, if necessary, ice down bottled beers, cut fresh garnishes, and check that everything is in its place before you open. Daytime bartenders often buy a selection of newspapers for their customers, and I have always found that to be a good practice.

You should never spend excessive time at the service end of the bar chatting to a member of the waitstaff. If you do, neither of you is doing your job properly. However, it's also important to have a good rapport with the servers. They need you to make drinks for them, and you need them to bring food for your customers and various and sundry other items, such as fruit from the kitchen if you suddenly find that you're running low.

Along with being amicable with the waitstaff, you should also be able to get along well with the manager, the owner, the chef, the line cooks, the dishwasher, the porter, and anyone else who works alongside you. This doesn't mean that you need to be best buddies with all these people, but it's imperative that you have a pleasant relationship with all of them. To tend bar properly, you must be a team player.

If you're a professional bartender, in all probability you're going to have to handle cash, and with this in mind, you should remember never to allow anyone other than the manager or owner behind your bar. You are in charge of the register, and you might be required to make up any shortages at the end of your shift. (This is illegal in some states, but if you're consistently short, you probably won't keep your job for long anyway.) Good bartenders, showing an orderly work ethic, tend to keep all the bills in the register facing the same way; they also take responsibility for cash belonging to customers left on the bar. I believe that when somebody's money is stolen, the bartender should replace it from his tip cup.

Keeping track of money on the bar, emptying and cleaning ashtrays regularly, and consistently wiping down the bar so that it's spotless are good ways to keep a bartender moving, and if he does all this regularly he will, in all likelihood, also be taking good care of his guests, since he will frequently be available to everyone at the bar. Bartenders must keep their eyes on glasses, asking guests if they would like a refill when their drinks are getting low. They must also keep their ears open to make sure that conversations are amicable, and that no guest is annoying another.

If you get into a conversation with one particular customer, you should frequently scan the bar as you talk in case somebody else requires your attention, but this isn't always sufficient for optimum service. It's also imperative to excuse yourself regularly and walk the length of the bar, since it's possible that a customer at the other end desires, say, to see a menu, and perhaps he doesn't want to interrupt your conversation. Unless you frequently give all of your customers an opportunity to speak to you, simply by strolling past each and every one of them, you aren't doing a thorough job.

Discretion is another quality that's needed in a good bartender. Guests tend to tell bartenders secrets they wouldn't share with their own mothers, and it's imperative that the bartender keep that information to himself. There really should be a law that protects bartenders, the same way that priests and doctors are covered when authorities demand information about their parishioners and patients. And if a telephone call comes through for someone at the bar or at a table, the bartender should always put the call on hold, first saying that he will check to see if that particular customer is in the establishment; then he must he ask whether or not the guest wishes to take the call. Also, if a customer tells you that he was never at the bar on a particular evening, he's right—he was never there (unless, of course, law enforcement agencies are involved).

In states where it is legal, most bars have a buy-back system wherein the bartender is allowed to give away, say, every fourth drink. It's important that the bartender not abuse this privilege by giving away too many drinks—especially to customers who tip well. This is a common mistake, since it can cause some guests to believe that they've "bought you," which can lead to trouble down the line. At the same time, you should always make sure that the customer is aware that "you" have bought the drink, since it often produces an extra dollar or two in your tip cup at the end of the night.

Unless you know both parties very well, if somebody wants to buy another customer at the bar or at a table a drink, you should always ask the intended recipient whether or not they want to accept the offer. Sometimes people don't want to feel obliged to the buyer. They might not want to enter into a situation wherein they then have to reciprocate, or the buyer could be making advances to someone of the opposite—or same—sex, and is using the drink as an invitation.

It's the bartender's job to make sure that no customer enters into an unwanted conversation with another, and you can do this only by watching body language and/or eavesdropping on conversations. If the seemingly unwanted guest goes to the bathroom, over to the jukebox, or anywhere else out of earshot, take the opportunity to ask whomever you believe he is bothering if they want you to intervene. Otherwise, you'll have to ask the offending party to step down the bar to a spot where you can talk to him privately and deal with the situation. There are few rules appropriate to every situation. The only advice I can offer here is that you shouldn't approach the offending guest in front of other customers, thereby embarrassing him; and it's usually a good idea to inform another member of staff of what you intend to do, just in case an argument breaks out and you find yourself in need of backup.

Remember, too, that you represent the management and owners of the bar, and therefore you should be prepared to enforce any rules that they have set down. If they don't want to serve guests wearing tank

THREE WISE BARTENDERS

MANY QUALITIES are needed in a bartender, and some are difficult, if not impossible, to define without simply telling stories about how certain people react to different situations when they are behind the stick. Here I detail three such stories in the hope that they will serve to point out some of the individual traits that go toward making a good bartender great.

CASE STUDY NO. 1

Let's first look at Dale DeGroff, an undisputed cocktailian master, whom I saw in action many times when he ruled the roost at New York's Rainbow Room and a couple of times since, most recently at Bemelmans Bar in the Carlyle Hotel on East Seventy-sixth Street.

Behind the Promenade Bar at the Rainbow Room, Dale was poetry in motion. His body was fluid, his methodology classic, his demeanor perfect for the environment. When he was behind the bar, usually with other bartenders to back him up, all eyes were always on Dale. His drinks, of course, were always perfect.

Now cut to Dale at work at Bemelman's Bar on February 22, 2002. The room was packed. This was one of the opening-night parties thrown after the joint was remodeled. Dale was consulting with the hotel and had brought Libation Goddess Audrey Saunders in as director of beverages. Audrey was working the floor, Dale was working the stick with a couple of old-timers who weren't used to the bar being so busy. I watched from a couple of yards back from the bar.

Dale kept his head down. He made no eye contact until he was ready to serve whoever was next. He was quick. Boy, was he quick. And he wasn't behind a bar that he'd worked for years, so his hands couldn't automatically reach out to whatever ingredient he needed next. The moment of truth came when he completed an order and served a drink. For a few short seconds that seemed like an unhurried eternity, Dale's eyes met the customer's eyes. The drink was perfect, and as he added the final touch—usually his signature flamed orange zest—he held the customer in the palm of his hand; then he moved to the next in line. I'd never seen Dale under so much pressure before. He's a consummate sophisticated cocktailian bartender, every bit as much at home when the bar's six deep as he is when he has time to exchange leisurely banter with his customers.

CASE STUDY NO. 2

Early in the year 2000 I found myself outside the Village Idiot, a bar on Manhattan's Fourteenth Street, with about forty-five minutes to kill before an appointment. I'd heard about this joint, so I thought I'd check it out.

Behind the bar was an attractive blond woman in her mid-twenties wearing low-cut jeans and a tiny tank top, and behind her, dozens of bras decorated the backbar. Country-and-western music blared from the jukebox as I yelled for a Manhattan "with bitters." I always order that way since so few bartenders in the twenty-first century know that the drink should always get bitters.

The bartender started pouring the bourbon, then stopped midway through the pour to tell me, "We ain't got no bitters." "Okay," I said, "I'll have it without bitters." She proved herself a little when she then told me that she was quite aware that the drink wasn't as good without bitters, but after pouring the rest of the bourbon into the mixing glass she then informed me that the bar "ain't got no vermouth" either. I told her I'd have a bourbon on the rocks, and she informed me that that was what I'd wanted all along.

Two minutes later, a couple of guys next to me ordered shooters, and the bartender started mixing something over ice, and placed three shot glasses on the bar—she'd decided to join them. Her moment of glory came when she strained the drinks, not through a strainer but through her fingers and into the shot glasses, then clinked her glass with the customers' glasses and shot it back in one.

That bartender was every bit as professional as anyone I've ever seen behind the stick. That's what the Village Idiot was all about. She was representing her bar to the nth degree.

CASE STUDY NO. 3

My wife, Mardee, and I first met Norman Bukofzer, bartender at New York's Ritz-Carlton hotel on Central Park South, in the early 1990s, and we were immediately impressed not only by his cocktailian skills but also by his warm hospitality and his ability to manage the bar and the customers as though he were conducting a symphony orchestra. Our only problem with Norman is that he insisted on calling us Mister and Missus Regan. Nobody gets away with that.

(Continues)

(Continued)

We pleaded with Norman to use our first names, and he always agreed to do so: "Okay, Mr. Regan, I'll remember in the future," he'd say with a wicked grin on his face. Eventually Norman explained that he had a reputation for remembering all of his customer's names, and that if he had to learn first names as well as surnames, his workload would be doubled, so we backed down and tried to get accustomed to our new mister-and-missus status.

All would have been well with this had we not introduced Roy Finamore, who happens to be the editor of this book, to Norman some six months later; Mr. Finamore joined the ranks of thousands addicted to Norman's wit and his cocktailian skills. A few months thereafter we were informed that Norman had taken to using Roy's first name at the bar, and we were livid. This called for action. We made the pilgrimage to Norman's bar.

We ordered our usual Manhattans: "Straight up. Your choice of bourbon." This is always the test we give Norman. He always selects a different brand of whiskey, and he always knows exactly how much vermouth to use to balance whichever whiskey he chooses. Ask Norman how he does it and he shrugs. "It's just a drink," he'll tell you. Our drinks arrived, and it was time for the confrontation.

"I hear that our friend Roy Finamore is a regular here now."

"That's right, Mister Regan, he's here three or four times a week."

"And what do you call him, Norman?"

"I call him Roy."

"And why is that, Norman?"

He leaned over the bar until our noses almost met.

"Just to piss you off."

It had taken Norman months to set up this one glorious moment. In my opinion, I was looking into the eyes of Manhattan's best bartender.

tops, then, obviously, you shouldn't serve people wearing tank tops. You need to get a feel for what kind of bar the management wants it to be and do your best to make it that way. If you're tending bar in a neighborhood joint, for instance, you will probably greet your guests in a casual manner and use their first names. At a tony restaurant, however, you might be required to say, "Good evening, sir"—or "madam"—when a guest approaches the bar.

Many people are attracted to the life of a bartender because it puts them in close proximity to alcohol. Don't fall into this trap. Although a nondrinking bartender is always desirable, I believe that it's useless to tell bartenders not to drink at all while on duty. A good rule of thumb is that you should never consume more than, say, one or two drinks during an eight-hour shift, and then only if this is allowed by the management. The reason I don't think that bartenders should be banned from drinking entirely while behind the bar is that if a bartender wants a drink, he will have one, and if he must wait until the manager's back is turned, he's likely to have, say, a quick shot of tequila. Bartenders who are allowed the odd drink at work are more likely to sip slowly on a beer.

In short, a good bartender should be the captain of his ship; the master of making moods; the dean of diplomacy; as honest as an Arctic summer day is long; as organized as a filing clerk; as punctual as the winter solstice; as neat and tidy as a seasoned librarian; congenial, amiable, and sociable on all occasions; as quick to make decisions as a broker on the stock-exchange floor; the very soul of discretion; a friend to those who need one (if only while on duty); and a dispenser of sound advice. Ideally he'll have a little psychic ability, too. And never forget: The demeanor of the bartender is every bit as important as his cocktailian skills.

A FEW EASY LESSONS

The one rule that all bartenders must learn is this: Nothing is written in stone. Every situation is different, different customers must be treated in different ways, and good bartenders should be able to assess all situations and deal with them appropriately. In the following scenarios, I offer some guidance about how to deal with some specific situations, but the guidelines won't work every time, simply because there's an infinite range of variation. I can only tell you some tricks of the trade that have worked for me in the past.

Being Early for Work Can Really Pay Off

I was always a "be prepared" kind of bartender. If I was working the day shift, my bar was always completely set up at least fifteen minutes before opening time, giving me a chance to sit down with a cup of coffee and relax before the onslaught. As a nighttime bartender, I always liked to get a *feel* for the crowd before I set foot behind the stick. It really pays to be prepared.

One bartender I knew in the late 1970s had a wonderful habit of showing up for his evening shift at least half an hour before it began. He would count his bank, make sure the "day guy" had set up his bar properly, and then he would join a couple of customers and buy them drinks before stepping behind the stick. This turned out to be a brilliant ploy. He usually bought drinks for the best tippers at the bar, and after he'd treated them to a drink, they felt obliged to stay for a while after he started his shift. They also felt special because their bartender wanted to socialize with them outside of work hours. His following grew and grew.

If you are going to be unavoidably late for your shift, you should let the management know as soon as possible. If you call, explain your situation, and give an estimated time of arrival, the manager will know what to do about the situation, whereas if you don't make contact, he might call another bartender to come in and you could lose your job. Communication is key in all aspects of tending bar.

If You Think a Customer *Might* Have Had Enough to Drink, You Are Probably Right

Oh, the number of times I got this wrong when I first started tending bar. Of course, that was back in the 1970s, when people weren't quite as uptight about "overconsumption," and I was in Manhattan, where most people didn't drive to and from bars. In these more enlightened days, however, it's imperative that you don't serve customers who are already three sheets to the wind. The fact is that you can't afford to serve people who are even slightly inebriated, and it's always best to err on the side of caution.

The Customer Is Always Right—The First Time

This is a guideline that sometimes involves swallowing your pride—but always getting the last laugh. Here's a scenario: A guy complains that his hamburger is overcooked; he ordered it medium-rare. You take a look at the burger and see a nice bright pink interior, no sign of overcooked meat at all. This guy is wrong, but do you really want to start an argument? It's only a burger, after all. Here's what to do: Tell the customer that you will order another burger, and inform him that you are going to ask for a rare burger. Explain that the chef always cooks medium-rare burgers to that exact stage of doneness, so if he ever again orders a medium-rare burger in your joint, he should try to remember what to expect. On the first offense, don't ever tell the customer he is wrong; instead, blame the chef, blame the owner, blame the cat if you must, but never argue with the customer.

If, a week later, this guy pulls the same stunt again, it's time to act. You have two choices, and your decision should be based on exactly how much damage this customer is doing to your bar scene. If he is complaining loudly and telling everyone around him about the terrible chef or the lousy bartender, you may just want to get rid of him immediately. Be a good scout: Be prepared. Take money from the register or your tip cup to pay him back for his burger and the last drink he ordered and have it at the ready. Now try to get him off his bar stool and down to the service area, or come out from behind the bar and ask if you can talk to him alone. The important aspect of this act is to make sure that this guy isn't losing face in front of others—that will make him feel compelled to save face by creating a scene. Explain that this bar clearly isn't right for him (not that *he* isn't right for the bar), push the money into his hand while telling him that his burger and last drink were on the house, and ask him to leave. Keep in mind that you're probably not the first person to oust him from a bar, so there's a good possibility that he'll be out of your hair quite quickly.

The second option is waiting until this grouse is about to leave of his own accord. Then try to get him out of hearing range of the other customers and explain that, in your opinion, since he isn't happy with your bar, he shouldn't return. If he argues that he wants to come back, you must pull the plug and tell him that you will refuse to serve him again. Whichever tack you take, always make sure that other members of staff are around in case the customer makes a scene or turns violent.

How to Treat a Bad Tipper

Bad tippers can be really infuriating. You call them sir, you call them madam, you make sure they get a buy-back at the appropriate time, you give them a horse that wins the Belmont Stakes, but still, when it comes time to pay the piper, they leave you next to nothing. How to cure them of this habit? Well, I wouldn't suggest spilling drinks over their best suits, although I've known bartenders who have tried it. You should always keep in mind that even though these ne'er-do-wells don't put any money in your pocket, they are spending some hard-earned bucks at your bar. And those dollars are keeping your boss happy. In turn, your boss lets you keep your job and the bar stays open. It's long-term thinking, but it's better than pounding the pavement looking for a new gig every six months.

This is how you should treat bad tippers: Exactly the same way that you treat everyone else. Maybe they'll come around and maybe they won't, but your tip cup is, after all, a result of swings and roundabouts. One guy stiffs you, the next guy leaves you five dollars for pouring him a beer. It all evens out at the end of the shift.

How to Deal with Unwanted Invitations

I have met some of my favorite people while tending bar, and a few of them have gone on to become true friends. But such occurrences are few and far between. Unfortunately, many bar customers want to be the bartender's best friend, and this can lead to some embarrassing situations. On top of this, the people who want you to come over for dinner or spend the weekend at their country house are very often people with few other friends, and there's usually a good reason for that. You could, of course, invent a house policy that prevents you from socializing with customers, but be sure to inform the boss and the rest of the staff if you do this—the customer is bound to ask about it. It's probably best just to have an automatic excuse for every day of the week: Saturday? Sorry, I have people coming over for dinner myself. Next Wednesday? No, it's my kung fu night. Two weeks from Thursday? Let me look in my diary at home and I'll get back to you.

The truth is, there's no really good method of getting these people off your back. Remember, the most persistent ones, those who never take the hint, are probably lonely souls who desperately need some company. Treat them kindly. Let them down gently. They need a little T.L.C.

How to Deal with Unwanted Advances

Wear a wedding band at all times—whether you're married or single.

Things to Do During Slow Periods

Polish bottles and glassware; write memos to the boss with suggestions about how to improve service, or noting brands of liquor, beer, or wine that have been requested but your bar doesn't stock; clean the bar and backbar; check your backup inventory; cut garnishes; make Bloody Mary mix; wash the pourers from the liquor bottles. In short, make sure that you've done everything possible to ready the bar for the next shift. (If you don't, it will come back to haunt you.)

Things Not to Do During Slow Periods

Read a newspaper or book; sit on the backbar or on a bar stool (I've seen it done); make phone calls; drink.

How to Arrange Liquor Bottles

All liquor bottles should be positioned so that the label points toward the customers, and all pourers should face the left side of the label from the customer's viewpoint. If you are exacting in this, your bar will have a symmetry that people will notice, at least subliminally. They may never comment, but there's something about a symmetrical backbar that's very pleasing to the eye.

How to Make Sure That New Customers Come Back

You should always win new customers one at a time, so go the extra yard whenever the opportunity arises. If someone's new to your bar, ask him about himself, get him talking, find out his interests, and, if possible, introduce him to a regular customer whom you think he might get along with.

If a customer asks where the nearest fabric store is, don't say that you don't know; instead, ask other members of staff or other customers at the bar. If you have time, get out the Yellow Pages and look it up. Or offer up the phone book.

If you work in, say, a trendy lounge bar and the customers are new to your neighborhood, tell them about other bars and restaurants nearby: the nearest sports bar, the best Chinese restaurant, the best pizza place. They aren't going to come to your joint every night of the week, but if you help them get to know their new surroundings they're bound to remember you and what you did for them. And if you know bartenders at any of the other restaurants you recommend, tell these new guys those bartenders' names, adding, "Tell them I sent you." The other bartenders are bound to reciprocate.

You can also advise them about the best dry cleaner, liquor store, locksmith, and myriad other services available in your neck of the woods. Rest assured that you'll see a lot of these new customers in the future.

How to Seat People

Bar customers usually sit wherever they wish, but if you see the opportunity to introduce two people who have similar interests or similar demeanors, there's nothing wrong with saying, "Come sit down here, there's someone I want you to meet." (One bartender did that for me once, but it turned out that he didn't want to introduce me to anyone—he was just making sure that I didn't sit next to the bore at the other end of the bar. I've never forgotten him for that.)

How to Deal with Angry Customers

If it's at all possible, never allow a customer to leave your bar angry. If somebody complains that there's not enough liquor in his drink, pour a little extra into his glass while explaining that, in the future, you'll only be able to give him your standard pour. He might not return, but he probably won't give you any bad press, either. Whatever the situation, even if it means losing face, you should always try to pacify, not further anger an upset customer.

How to Deal with Problems in the Bathroom

From time to time you'll probably hear that someone is ill in the bathroom, and you might have to investigate. *Always* take another member of the staff with you. If the bathroom is reserved for the opposite sex, bring a member of the opposite sex with you. There could be someone waiting to accost you in there, or it could be a scam in which you'll be accused of some impropriety, and if there are no witnesses you'll find yourself in a sticky situation.

How to Deal with Money

Nobody wants to be accused of being wrong when it comes to making change or totaling a bill, but mistakes do happen. They must be dealt with in the most delicate manner. If somebody at the bar is paying cash, be it a customer or a waitperson, take the money from their hands and announce exactly how much they owe and how much they are handing to you: "That's fifteen fifty out of a twenty, sir." This way you have both agreed upon how much money is changing hands, and you are giving the customer an opportunity to disagree before you proceed to the register. When you hand back their change, clearly state how much you are giving them: "Four fifty change out of a twenty, sir."

There's an old trick played by grifters (you can see it in the movie *The Grifters,* but I've also had it played on me on more than one occasion) in which a customer will get your attention by waving a twenty-dollar bill in the air, but after you make his drink he'll hand you a ten. You might make change for a twenty, remembering seeing it previously. If you make change for a ten, the grifter will say, "I gave you a twenty—don't you remember?" And nine times out of ten, you will lose ten bucks. But if you follow the instructions above, the grifter will always lose.

In another moneymaking scheme, a con man at a busy bar will ask to see a menu as soon as he sidles up to the bar. Then, using the menu as a shield, he will steal money from the bar while the customer it belongs to is locked in conversation and you are occupied serving other customers. Be wary of anyone who asks to see a menu without first purchasing a drink. Most times they will turn out to be innocent prospective customers who merely want to peruse the bar's bill of fare, but sometimes they'll turn out to be thieves.

When people run a tab (ask to pay at the end of the evening rather than paying for each drink when it's served), these days it's best to ask for a credit card, which you will keep behind the bar until they are ready to leave. The bar in which you work should have rules about this procedure—ask the management about them. A problem sometimes occurs with these people, though, when it comes time to pay and they disagree with their bill. Perhaps they forgot that they sent drinks to a couple of friends down the bar, or maybe they just don't realize that they had four Margaritas, not three. Whatever the case, the situation must be handled with discretion.

You can start by going back over the evening and trying to pinpoint events that will jog their memory: "Remember, Bill and Jane came in about an hour ago and you sent them drinks" or "You ordered one drink when you came in, another when you got your burger, a third when you were talking to Alice, and I've just served you a fourth." If they still disagree, first check with a manager or refer to the house rules. In my opinion, though, it's best to go along with the customer—but only once. When this happened to me and the situation involved a particularly angry customer, I offered to disregard the bill entirely, but informed the person in question that in the future I would expect him to pay for drinks as he went along. He paid the bill. I don't suggest that you use that tactic every time, but there are occasions when it might come in handy. If you back down and allow the customer to "beat you" for a couple of drinks, when you serve him in the future, inform him how many drinks he's had every time you serve him: "That's your third," and so forth.

THE THEORY OF MIXOLOGY

An Indian likes a cocktail swizzled; a North American, within the last few years, will not take one unless it is stirred with a spoon; a South American will have it shaken; an Englishman, who has traveled in America, is more particular than any one of the others until you find out his taste, and is most difficult to please.

—LEO ENGEL, *American & Other Drinks*

WHAT'S IN A NAME?

In spring of 2000 a contestant appeared on *Jeopardy!* who claimed to have invented chili. Thankfully, he wasn't serious. This man was an amateur chef who dabbled in the kitchen, and one day he had thrown together a few ingredients, thoughtfully marrying spices, meat, beans, and a few other edibles he had lying around until he thought that he'd concocted a flavorful "stew." His wife was called into the kitchen to taste his new creation. Her reaction: "It's good. But it's chili." Such is the way with cocktails and mixed drinks.

The recent past has brought a plethora of new creations to the world of the bartender. It's possible to find the same drink masquerading under different names in different areas of the country, and it's also quite common to discover that a given cocktail is made with different ingredients depending on which bartender you happen to order from on any particular night. Sex on the Beach is a great example. I once went through my files to see how many recipes for this drink

I'd collected over the years and found no less than twenty-two different versions.

As far as I was concerned, Sex on the Beach was a highball comprising vodka, peach schnapps, orange juice, and cranberry juice. It's a fairly simple affair, and in its heyday—probably around 1977—it's possible that it was ordered more for its name than for the quality of the mixture. But I found recipes from bartenders nationwide who were using melon liqueur, raspberry liqueur, and even scotch in their rendition of this drink. Which is the correct recipe? It's impossible to track down.

Only when someone properly documents a new creation can we be certain of the original recipe, and even then there's bound to be a bartender, probably about two thousand miles away, who came up with the same drink at the same time. It might have a different name, but it's the same drink. A good example of this phenomenon is the Blood Orange Cocktail, which was created when a new orange-flavored vodka was introduced to the market. A Manhattan bartender, John Simmons, decided that it would mix well with Campari. Simmons presented his creation to Bob Camillone, who worked at the company that imported Campari at the time, and Camillone in turn took it to Molly Lynch, brand manager for the Italian aperitif. But Lynch had already thought of this drink. It made sense; Campari marries very well to orange juice, so of course it would be a natural match to orange-flavored vodka.

What can be done to properly record new drinks? Absolutely nothing, as far as I'm concerned. Is this a problem? Well, no. We will have to live with the fact that we might never know who created many cocktails, or the correct ingredients in the original versions.

WHEN IS A MARTINI NOT A MARTINI?

In the 1990s young people started calling all drinks served in a cocktail, or Martini, glass Martinis, but you shouldn't think for a second that this is a new phenomenon. So-called purists will hold that any drink containing ingredients other than gin and dry vermouth doesn't deserve to be called a Martini. They are wrong. True purists would make Martinis with sweetened gin, sweet vermouth, orange bitters, and perhaps a dash of curaçao or maraschino liqueur, since this is how the drink was first made (see page 294). If the so-called purists argue that they are referring to a *Dry* Martini, true purists could still argue that orange bitters must be added to the drink, as well as liberal amounts of dry vermouth, since that's the way the first Dry Martinis were made.

It's useless to argue this point, and a whole generation, if not two, now uses the term *Martini* when referring to drinks that, in the past, would have been dubbed *cocktails*. Can anybody change this habit? I think not. Furthermore, using the word *Martini* has helped cocktails come back into vogue, and if this happenstance has helped, in any way, spur young bartenders to create new drinks, then I'm willing to stand by and watch it happen without uttering a word. English is an ever evolving language.

ACHIEVING BALANCE

Mixed drinks of all kinds should glide down the throat easily, and since most cocktails have a spirit base, the addition of ingredients containing less or no alcohol is needed to cut the strength of the drink and make it more palatable. In most cases, the base spirit, be it gin, vodka, whiskey, or any other relatively high-proof distillate, makes up over fifty percent of the cocktail, and its soul must be soothed if the bartender wants to achieve balance. The other ingredients come in all guises: wines, liqueurs, fruit juices, dairy products, soft drinks, and even water.

Although mixing drinks is akin to cookery in many respects, it is not an exact science. For instance, when you're baking a cake, it's imperative that the ingredients be precisely measured according to whichever recipe is being followed; otherwise the cake might not rise, or it could be too crumbly, too moist, too dry, or simply a disaster. Other aspects of cookery, such as the ratio of flour to butter or oil to make a roux, must also be fairly strictly adhered to. But there are times when liberties can be taken in the kitchen. For instance, you can add extra spices to a jambalaya if you know that the people who will be eating it enjoy extra-hot or more fully flavored dishes.

Cocktailian bartenders are akin to chefs who specialize in sauces, soups, and stews—they should be able to experiment with recipes. Some people enjoy Martinis with just a drop of vermouth; others like Martinis on the "wet" side, with at least one part vermouth to every two parts gin or vodka. And who's to say how much Drambuie belongs in a Rusty Nail? At one time this drink was made with a fifty-fifty mix of scotch and Drambuie, but it's a far more sophisticated potion when made with less liqueur—eighty to twenty is a good ratio to use. You disagree? Good. We're off to a promising start.

In the cocktail and mixed-drinks recipes in this book, the amounts given for ingredients are guidelines. Prepare a drink exactly according to my instructions and you'll end up with a well-balanced potion; but if you decide that you enjoy the drink more with, say, a tad extra gin, you should feel free to follow your heart. To a point.

The most important aspect of any cocktail or mixed drink is balance, and although guidelines can be set to make, say, a Rob Roy, this drink can vary considerably depending on:

1. Which bottling of scotch is used. Scotches vary vastly from one brand to another, and you'll need less sweet vermouth to soothe the soul of a mild-mannered blended bottling than you would to properly balance the drink when made with a bold single malt from Islay, bearing heavy smoke notes and a good dose of iodine.

2. Which bottling of sweet vermouth is used. Some vermouths have far lighter bodies than others, and the degree of spiciness can differ enormously from one bottling to another.

3. Will you add bitters to the Rob Roy? If so, will you use Angostura, Peychaud's, or orange bitters? Each will bring its own nuances to the drink, but some scotches can be so complex that bitters might not be desirable at all.

Similar options apply to almost any drink you can name, and although it's necessary to follow guidelines such as the recipes in this book, a good bartender will consider all these aspects when preparing any given drink.

So where does this leave you when you're looking for someone to tell you exactly how to make a specific cocktail? As with culinary endeavors, you should initially make the drink according to a standard recipe. Taste it, and if you deem it well balanced you can continue to use that recipe, providing you employ the same bottlings of ingredients each time. It's up to you to familiarize yourself with many different bottlings of spirits, and after years of experience you should be able to alter the proportions in the drink when need be in order to create a well-balanced drink every time.

A chef leaves culinary school armed with a good basic knowledge of how to prepare many different dishes, but it could take years before he is able to instinctively add, say, a touch more paprika to a dish because he has bought a new brand that isn't quite as strong as the one he's used to.

The best method of preparing yourself to make any drink is to taste each ingredient before you start. Whenever possible, pour a small amount of the base spirit into a glass; then do the same with all the other liquid components of the drink. Now dip a straw or sipstick into the first glass and, by putting your finger over the top of the straw, capture a tiny amount of the liquid; drizzle this over your tongue by releasing your finger. Repeat the process with each ingredient until you have a clear picture of what all the individual elements are bringing to the party, and you'll be amazed at how easily you're able to make a well-balanced potion.

More than a few bartenders these days also taste the finished drink, using the straw method, before serving it to a customer. This gives you a chance to make sure you've made the cocktail correctly, and adjust it if need be. Would a chef pour sauce over a dish without tasting it first, and maybe adding a little extra salt if he deemed it necessary?

INDIVIDUAL TASTE

It's the job of the cocktailian bartender to take into account the taste of the individual customer. Some folk like sweeter drinks, while others prefer a mouth-puckering sour cocktail. Bartenders must make a habit of finding out about their customer's preferences before making drinks for them. If someone orders, say, a Manhattan, the bartender can politely ask how they like that drink made. If the customer isn't sure what's meant by that, the bartender should be able to guide them through the individual components of the drink, making suggestions along the way.

Start by asking which whiskey the customer wants you to use in the drink; then describe that bottling to them, making suggestions as to the ratio of vermouth that you would recommend in order to balance the cocktail. Tell them that you recommend bitters in the drink to add depth and complexity, and suggest they try the Manhattan with bitters. If the customer seems to like sweeter drinks, you can even suggest adding a teaspoon or more of juice from the maraschino cherries, even though this strays from the classic formula. If that's what the customer wants, that's what the customer should get. A friend of mine did this recently and was rewarded by the customer declaring that her Manhattan was the best one she'd ever had in a bar—only her husband had been able to make the drink exactly the way she liked it until then.

Don't think for a moment that you'll automatically be a world-class bartender after reading this book; you'll just be very well armed to handle a job behind the bar. The rest takes time.

INGREDIENTS

The best cocktails and mixed drinks are made with the best ingredients, but that doesn't necessarily mean that you must use only the most expensive items. Many bargain bottlings, especially those that aren't advertised extensively, can be of very high quality.

Much to the dismay of many people in the beverage industry, in the early 1990s I started making cocktails with single-malt scotch. Single malts can be rather expensive, but the bold flavors of this type of whisky can transform a great drink like the Rob Roy into a world-class masterpiece. However, a line must be drawn somewhere. In 1998 a forty-year-old bottling of Bowmore single malt was offered to the public at $7,000 per bottle. Would I dare use this scotch in a Rob Roy? Truth be told, as long as someone else was footing the bill, I'd love to try such a drink. But as a rule, although I recommend using only top-quality ingredients in cocktails, I'm more likely to use a $30 to $50 bottling than anything that costs more than, say, $100.

Opting for high quality applies to all the ingredients in any given drink, not just the spirituous items, so it's important to use fresh fruit juices whenever possible. Also make sure that your spices are fresh, that your garnishes are newly cut, and that any other ingredient called for in a drink is of the finest caliber.

IN CONCLUSION

Perhaps you're beginning to realize that in order to become an accomplished cocktailian bartender you're going to have a long journey ahead of you. Don't despair. The truth of the matter is that if you follow the guidelines in this book, practice, practice, practice, and learn the formulas for the most-requested drinks, you can become a bartender in either a professional or a home setting in a relatively short time.

You'll quickly discover that the vast majority of drinks called for in any bar are simple Highballs such as Scotch and Soda, as well as Martinis, Manhattans, Cosmopolitans, and other perennial favorites that are quite easy to master. Every bar also has its idiosyncratic cocktails, such as house specialties or weird potions peculiar to that one particular joint. Most bartenders will tell you that it's seldom necessary to know how to make more than a couple dozen drinks in any one bar. And when someone requests a drink a bartender has never heard of, the true professional will either ask the customer how to make it or refer to a good recipe book. Even the most accomplished chefs consult cookbooks before making a dish for the very first time, and sometimes they'll refer back to a printed recipe if they haven't made a particular sauce for a while and want to be sure that they are using the correct ingredients.

One good way to get a handle on what to expect when you get a job at a particular bar is to go there and notice which drinks are being called for on a regular basis. Situate yourself near the service area, where you can observe not only the drinks being prepared for bar customers but also the cocktails being requested by the waitstaff. Watch how the present bartenders make these drinks so you can absorb the house style. Ask questions when you're not sure about specific formulas—you'll probably find that the bartender on duty is more than willing to share his knowledge with you.

You should also be prepared to make mistakes and, as in any other job, to learn from them. In 1973, I arrived in New York from England not knowing how to make anything more complicated than a Gin and Tonic, so I observed bartenders for a full month before even applying for a job. Even then, when I eventually got a position behind the stick, I made more than a few errors. In England, for example, if you order "whisky," you will be served scotch, so I was making Scotch Sours for a while when Whiskey Sours were ordered. It wasn't until a waitress caught me that I learned what I was doing wrong. That's right—not even the customers noticed. Or if they did, they certainly didn't tell me.

A basic knowledge of how to handle bar equipment, a good grasp of a few dozen classic drinks, and a good attitude are really all you need before you set foot behind the stick. Those things, and a true desire to be a bartender, will get you off to a good start.

THE CRAFT OF THE MIXOLOGIST

A bartender in those days was a combination of artist and scientist, who was looked upon with some awe by mere statesmen, bankers and leaders in other professions. To know just how many dashes of lemon juice to introduce into a Manhattan Cooler was no small accomplishment. Great friendships have sprung up there from between white jackets and their steady patrons. A bartender who knew the exact proportions of a Supreme Court Judge's tipple might expect any favor from His Honor, short of causing the latter's impeachment.

—HENRY COLLINS BROWN, *In the Golden Nineties,* 1928

ANYONE CAN MAKE a good drink if he puts his mind to it. It's just a case of using the best ingredients in the correct proportions and mixing them according to the prescribed method. No method of mixing a drink takes too long to learn or perform. What does take time, however, is becoming a speedy bartender, and anyone new at the job should know from the beginning that speed will come only with practice, and by memorizing the exact location of every bottle and tool behind the bar.

Some bartenders are graceful souls when they mix drinks. They move with extreme fluidity, sometimes flipping an ice cube into the air with a barspoon and catching it in a mixing glass held behind their back. And I saw one bartender in London who did just the opposite:

When making a drink his body became robotic, moving in short jolts that reminded me of a character in a silent movie. Personally, I am not a graceful bartender, nor do I turn into a windup toy when mixing drinks. But I quickly learned how to be both precise and speedy when behind the bar.

However you move when you are mixing drinks, try to develop your own personal style and to be consistent. Make customers remember you because of something you do differently from anyone else. I saw that London bartender only once, and that was in the mid-1990s, but since then I've told countless people traveling to London that they must go to Quaglino's to see him if he's still there—he was a joy to behold.

The examples given below—how to hold a shaker and the other meticulous details of how to mix drinks—should be taken as mere guidelines, since personal style is far more important for a good bartender. Take note of specific instructions on such things as how long to stir or shake a cocktail, but feel free to develop your own personal way of actually holding, say, a Boston shaker—just as long as it works well for you and the drink doesn't end up on the floor.

GARNISHES

You will learn how to prepare garnishes in the next chapter, but before you start to actually mix drinks, you should know that certain garnishes are also ingredients. Lime and lemon wedges and any citrus twist (a strip of peel from limes, lemons, oranges, and the like) are the "ingredient garnishes." All too often I see bartenders affix lime or lemon wedges on the rim of a glass, effectively handing the job of squeezing it into a drink over to the customer, who, in turn, gets sticky fingers. Worse still is the bartender who simply tosses a lemon twist into a drink without twisting it, thereby making the customer fish it out of his cocktail if he wants to enjoy its aromatic essences.

When you add a wedge of lime to, say, a Gin and Tonic, its juices must first be squeezed into the drink. To squeeze the wedge of fruit, take it between your thumb and forefinger and hold it directly above the drink. Use your other hand as a shield, cupping it around the far side of the glass so as to prevent any stray squirts of juice from flying into your customer's face. Now simply squeeze the juice from the fruit, drop it into the drink, add a sipstick, and stir the drink briefly to incorporate the juice.

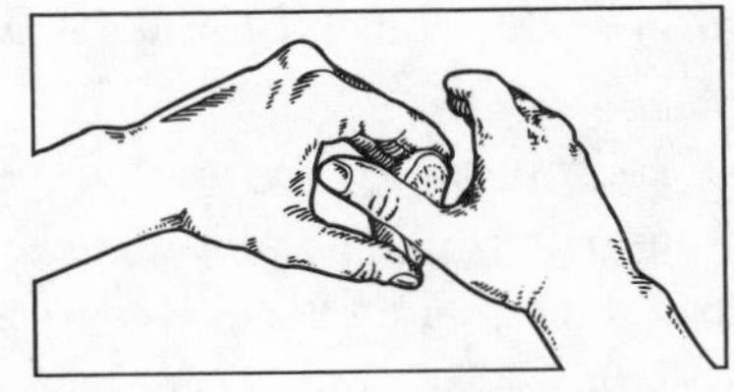

Citrus twists—strips of citrus zest that incorporate a little of the white inner pith for sturdiness—offer their essential oils to any drink that calls for them, and they can also add a flare of showmanship if the oils are ignited. To properly introduce a twist to a drink, hold it over the glass with the colored side pointing downward. Holding each end of the twist between your thumb and forefinger, turn one end clockwise and the other counterclockwise, releasing the oils from the zest onto the top of the drink. Next, rub the colored side of the twist around the rim of the glass so that any remaining oils are left there, and drop the garnish into the drink.

Many bartenders, for some reason, hate rubbing a twist around the rim of the glass, and some refuse to put the twist into the drink after it has released its secret ingredient. I'm very much in favor of the method described above, which results in a fresh citrus flavor on the rim of the glass and a far prettier drink with the garnish floating on top.

If you wish to flame the oils from a twist, which adds an extra dimension to a drink by caramelizing the oils before they land, a little practice will be necessary. First of all, when you cut the twist from the fruit you should make it as wide as possible; larger fruits, such as oranges, are best suited to this maneuver since it's fairly easy to cut a twist from them that's almost one inch wide. Have the twist close at hand as you light a match, and hold the match close to the top of the drink. Take the twist in your other hand and grasp it by the sides, using your thumb and first two or three fingers, depending on the length of the twist. (The colored side of the twist should, of course, be pointing toward the drink.) Now position the twist over the match and squeeze it to release its oils. You will see them sparkle as they leap through the flame onto the top of the drink.

TO RIM A GLASS

Very few bartenders know how to properly coat the rim of a glass with sugar (for a Sidecar, for instance), salt (for a Margarita), or other dry ingredients, such as cocoa powder (for a Chocolate Martini). Poor rimming techniques drive me crazy. When a glass is rimmed with one of these items, it's imperative that the dry ingredient stick to the exterior of the glass only. If the salt, for instance, is applied to the interior of the glass, when you add the cocktail it will fall into the drink, thus adding an extra ingredient that doesn't belong in the recipe.

To rim a glass properly, you must first moisten the rim, and this can be accomplished in two ways; you'll need a shallow saucer full of the dry ingredient for both methods. The first technique—my favorite—is to take a wedge of an appropriate citrus fruit (lime for a Margarita, lemon for a Sidecar, for instance) and slot the inner fruit side over the rim of the glass. Now, squeezing the fruit gently to release a little juice, slide the wedge around the rim of the glass until the whole perimeter is moist. Take the base of the glass in one hand, holding the other hand vertically to form a bridge. Rest the glass on the index finger of your free hand so that the rim faces downward at a forty-five-degree angle. Allowing the rim of the glass to rest on the surface of the dry ingredient, rotate it until the whole rim is coated. If you have time, you can use a napkin to remove any of the dry ingredient that might have stuck to the glass below the rim—you're trying to achieve a straight line, about a quarter inch deep, around the perimeter of the glass.

The second method is different only in that to moisten the rim, you dip the glass into a saucer full of one of the ingredients in the drink. Triple sec, for instance, works well for both the Sidecar or the Margarita. If the drink contains any liqueur, use that instead of a straight liquor, since the dry ingredient will adhere to it more readily. Admittedly, with both methods a little liquid will make its way into the interior of the glass, but the amount is negligible and the alternative is simply too fastidious to be viable.

If you expect to make large quantities of any drink that calls for a glass with a coated rim, it's best to prepare glasses before your customers or guests arrive. This is also preferable because, given time to air thoroughly, the dry ingredient will adhere better to the glass. Whatever you do, though, don't ever upturn a moistened glass into a saucer of the dry ingredient, coating the inside of the rim as well as the outside. I might just be watching you.

OTHER FANCIFUL GLASSWARE DECORATIONS

It isn't my style to go overboard with garnishes and decorations—quite honestly, I'm just not very good at that sort of thing, and I'd rather spend the time ensuring that my drinks are thoughtfully made and well balanced. However, I've been very impressed by some bartenders who excel at this skill. For instance, I saw one bartender use a zester—more of a kitchen tool than a piece of bar equipment—to cut a very long, very thin spiral of lemon peel. He put one end of the spiral into the drink and draped the rest around the glass a few times until the other end rested on the base of the glass. Very pretty. (His drinks were great, too.)

Another glass garnish that you might see in some antique cocktail books involves cutting a wider spiral of lemon zest with a paring knife, inserting it into a glass, and arranging it so that it coats the interior. In my experience this is viable only when using very slim glasses, such as a champagne tulip—otherwise the spiral simply keeps falling into the bottom of the glass.

One recipe in this book—for the Banana-Split Martini—calls for the glass to be drizzled with chocolate and strawberry syrups. If you attempt this—it's visually wonderful—I advise you to be sparing with the syrups and prepare the glass well before making the drink, leaving time to refrigerate it so that the syrups harden somewhat.

WHAT'S ON FIRST?

The old rule of thumb about which ingredient should be poured first when making a cocktail or mixed drink was "Least expensive leads." The reasoning behind this was that if you made the mistake of pouring too much of any one ingredient, less money would have been wasted. However, this isn't a hard-and-fast rule by any stretch of the imagination. You would never, for example, pour tonic into a highball glass before adding gin or vodka. I'm a great believer in always pouring the base ingredient of any drink first. This way you get a "feel" for how much of the other ingredients to pour. Hence, when making, say, a Sidecar, I will always pour brandy first, followed by triple sec, then lemon juice—precisely the opposite of the rule dictated by price.

Be careful about ingredients that present a freshness issue. Tomato juice, fruit juices, milk, half-and-half, cream, and eggs have a definite shelf life, so these ingredients should be tested before being added to drinks. Fruit juice that has passed its prime can be hard to detect by the nose alone, so it's advisable to shake the container before pouring and observe—effervescence is a sure sign that the juice should be discarded.

Raw eggs, if you choose to use them (see page 112), should be cracked into a receptacle other than the mixing glass and checked for freshness before being added to the drink.

PRECISE POURING

Some bartenders pour by eye. That is, they watch the glass into which they are pouring and judge the depth of the liquid to deem the pour complete. This is a very inadequate way of measuring a shot, since it is dependent on the size of the glass and, more important, the ice cubes. If the cubes are small or if the ice is crushed, you will use less liquid to achieve a predetermined depth than you will if the ice cubes are large. If the ice cubes are large, much depends on how they fall into the glass: If one cube wedges against another in such a way as to prevent other cubes from falling alongside them, there will be a large space to fill with liquid before the desired depth is achieved.

I have seen Audrey Saunders pour by eye, but she did this in an empty mixing glass, and she knows how far up the glass to pour for specific measurements. There's nothing wrong at all with this practice, but it wasn't the way I was taught, so I'm going to recommend that you use the method detailed below.

Jiggers and other measuring devices are, of course, very precise and can be used satisfactorily for most drinks. Personally, I prefer the very American free-pour system, wherein the bartender judges, without the use of measuring devises, how much of any ingredient he pours. This gives the bartender a chance to show a little flair in his pouring style and allows him to "feel" his way through a drink—which, in my opinion, is the only way to be a good cocktailian bartender. Also, with drinks that will be served straight up, there's nothing better than seeing a full

Martini glass after the bartender drains every last drop from a shaker or mixing glass, thus showing that precision is part of his craft.

Before learning how to free-pour, you should first know about the hidden ingredient in mixed drinks: water. When drinks are properly prepared over ice in a shaker or a mixing glass, one-quarter of the resultant cocktail will be water melted from the ice. This water is a very necessary ingredient, since it lowers the alcohol level of the cocktail and thus makes the drink more palatable.

In order to learn how to free-pour you should first practice with a bottle of water fitted with a pourer. When you hold the bottle, be sure to wrap your index finger or your thumb over the base of the pourer. This is a safety precaution. If the pourer is a little loose, you run the risk of it falling from the bottle. Even if you know that a particular pourer has a tight fit, it's imperative that you make a habit of holding bottles in this fashion so that you never make a mistake.

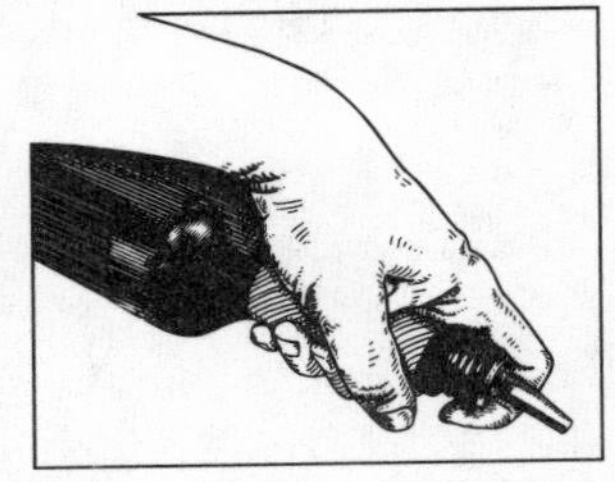

Pour water from the bottle into a measuring device such as a 1½-ounce jigger, and as you pour, count silently in your head. When the jigger is full, stop pouring and remember how far you got in your counting. That's your "shot count." Since people count at different rates, there's no use telling anyone to count to, say, four in order to achieve a perfect shot—every bartender should have his own number. You must practice this with a jigger and/or other devices of different measures until you are confident that you can pour any given measurement simply by counting to the appropriate number in your head.

If you are a professional bartender, the management of your bar should give you guidelines about the size of the shot you are expected to serve; this is usually about 1½ ounces. In practice, though, most bartenders pour about two ounces of liquor into a highball glass, and however much is needed into a drink that will be served in a cocktail glass. Since cocktail glasses come in many sizes, it's up to you to familiarize yourself with the ones used at your bar or in your home, and to develop a "count" that will result in a drink that fits your glass.

The most difficult aspect of making perfectly sized cocktails is that you're usually dealing with three or more ingredients that must be poured with balance in mind; at the same time, it's imperative that the sum of those ingredients be sufficient to fill your cocktail glass after they have been shaken or stirred together. How can I possibly teach you to achieve this without being there with you as you work? I can't. It will have to be sufficient for me to tell you that if you have what it takes to be a cocktailian bartender, you will be amazed at how quickly you develop this skill.

Don't, however, fill cocktail glasses to the rim. Why challenge the customer to see if he can get it to his mouth without spilling? And if the drink is being made for a customer at a table, the waitperson must deliver it without the drink sloshing over the side of the glass, which results in a sloppy mess on the serving tray, as well as some pretty sticky fingers for both the server and the customer.

The amount of liquor poured into a drink also varies when it comes to drinks served on the rocks. Unless you are pouring into oversized glasses, these drinks should be filled to within about half an inch of the rim.

TO SERVE A DRINK

All drinks should be served in sparkling clean glasses on a coaster or a napkin that will absorb condensation from the glass. Coasters should also be provided for beer bottles if the whole bottle doesn't fit into the glass or if the customer wishes to pour it himself. Drinks are normally prepared in the small trough on the bartender's side of the bar and then placed in front of the customer, but sometimes a drink such as a Martini straight up is strained into a glass that has already been placed in front of the customer.

It's very important that the customer is able to see you prepare his drink, so don't assemble it out of his view. Ideally you should stand directly in front of the customer whose drink you are mixing, and make sure that he is able to see the label on any bottles you use, either before you start to pour or as you are pouring. This way the customer knows that he is getting what he asked for, and he will also enjoy the show as you mix the drink.

If a drink contains a sipstick or other inedible garnishes—plastic mermaids and the like—watch to see when the customer removes these from his drink and sets them down on the bar, and then remove them immediately. You should also keep an eye on coasters and napkins. When one becomes wet because of condensation from the glass or because a customer spilled his drink when picking it up, remove the offending coaster and replace it immediately.

The home bartender should also follow the guidelines above, although it can sometimes be difficult to make the drink directly in front of your guests without a real bar. All of the other rules, though, are just as important when making drinks for friends.

TEMPERATURE

The temperature of the drink is another important factor to consider when shaking or stirring. Shaking requires approximately one-half of the time in order to reach the correct temperature as does stirring. As a rule of thumb, you should shake a drink for between ten and fifteen seconds, or stir it for twenty to thirty seconds.

Some people think that if you use a metal receptacle such as a cocktail shaker or the metal half of a Boston shaker, the resultant drink will be far colder than if you use glass. This is true, but not significantly so. Experimentation has shown me that a drink stirred in an ice-filled metal receptacle for twenty-five seconds will have a temperature of thirty-eight degrees; the same drink stirred in a mixing glass will take about five seconds longer to attain the same temperature.

You might hear some people say that Gin Martinis should be stirred rather than shaken in order to avoid "bruising" the gin, but this is a misconception—gin can't be bruised. It's more than likely that the "bruising" referred to here is, in fact, a chill haze—the cloudiness that can occur when certain items get too cold. Martinis used to be made with as much dry vermouth as gin, and vermouth, when well chilled, will develop this haze. There is nothing wrong with a cloudy Martini save for its appearance.

Showmanship is very important when tending bar, and drinkers love to see those ice cubes move up and down and round and round when you prepare their drink in a mixing glass, so this is the receptacle that I recommend above all others for preparing a stirred drink.

TO CHILL GLASSWARE

Any chilled cocktail that is served without ice should be poured into a prechilled glass, and the easiest and best way of achieving this is to keep glasses in the fridge or the freezer. But if you don't have room there, a couple of other methods can be used. One way to chill a glass is to keep it upturned or buried in a mound of crushed ice, but this is possible only at bars that have space for a suitable receptacle. Ideally the crushed ice will be held in a bowl or sink that is fitted with a drain so that melted ice will not become a problem; if this is not viable you can use a punch bowl or similar receptacle. Be aware, though, that you'll have to drain the bowl periodically, so be sparing with the ice or it will become unmanageable.

The most commonly used method of prechilling glasses is to fill them with ice and water and let them sit while you mix the drink. I recommend that whenever possible you stand the ice-filled glass in a sink and run water into it until it overflows—the water that clings to the outside of the glass will help chill it more quickly. Before pouring the drink you must, of course, empty the glass of the ice and water. Holding it by the base or the stem, shake the glass vigorously for a few seconds, allowing the cold water to spill over the outside of the glass; then empty it and once again shake it vigorously to rid it of any last drops of water. When properly chilled, the glass should be frosted on the outside.

TO BUILD A DRINK

Drinks such as the Screwdriver, a Scotch and Soda, and a Gin and Tonic are served in a highball glass and are known as "built" drinks. To build a highball, simply fill the glass with ice; add the ingredients, liquor first; stir the drink with a sipstick a few times; add any garnish that's called for; and serve it complete with the sipstick. If the garnish is a citrus wedge or twist, it should be added before the drink is stirred, but if it's an ornamental garnish such as an orange wheel, stir the drink and then add the garnish.

Most people drinking highballs will stir the drink a few extra times with the sipstick before discarding it and proceeding to drink. Now you have a wet sipstick on your sparkling clean bar—don't let it languish there. Discard it immediately. Some customers, however, insist on keeping their used sipsticks so they know how many drinks they've had. If this is the case there's not much you can do about it, but you might want to put them on an extra coaster so they don't look quite so untidy. Home bartenders should also be on the lookout for discarded sipsticks—they can end up all over the house—and discard them as quickly as possible.

Drinks such as the Black Russian (vodka and Kahlúa) and the Godfather (scotch and amaretto) are often built in the glass in which they will be served, but they are far better when stirred over ice, then strained into an ice-filled old-fashioned glass. This method ensures that the drink is cold before it's poured into the glass, and the ice in the glass will not melt as readily.

TO STRAIN A DRINK

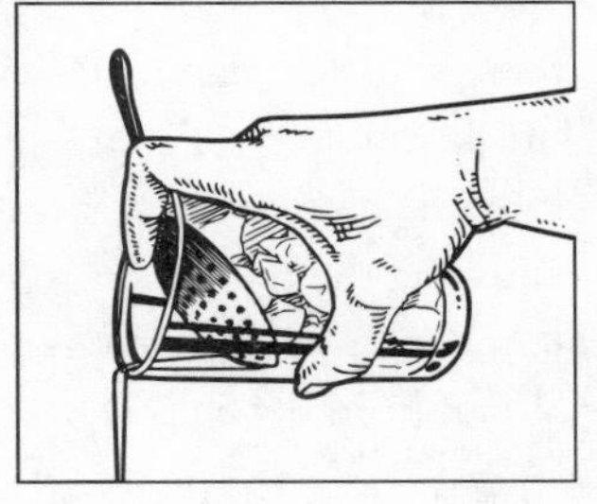

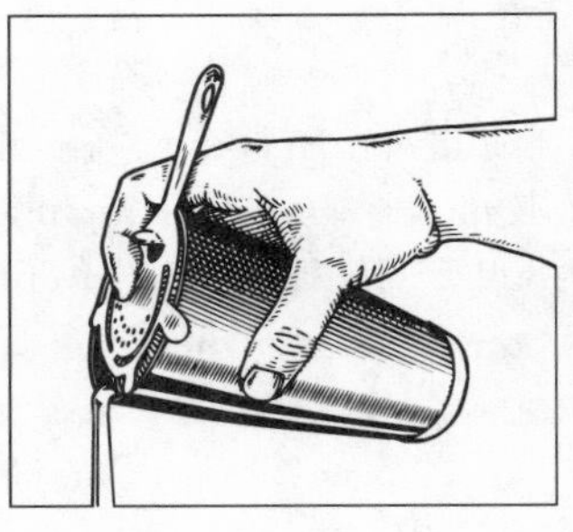

Although cocktail shakers are fitted with their own strainers, I'm far more enamored of using a spring-loaded Hawthorne strainer or a standard julep strainer in tandem with a Boston shaker when straining drinks. It simply looks more professional. The Hawthorne strainer should be used when pouring from the metal half of the shaker, and the julep strainer is used to strain drinks from the mixing glass. After preparing a cocktail as detailed below, simply fit the strainer firmly onto the mouth of the metal or glass, put your index finger over the top of the strainer to hold it in place, and strain the drink into the serving glass. Once you've emptied the liquid, give the glass a sharp twist in any direction as you return it to an upright position, so that any remaining drops don't fall to the bartop as you remove the mixing glass.

Some bartenders strain shaken drinks by holding a complete Boston shaker horizontally over the glass after "breaking" the two parts, a method similar to one used by bartender William Schmidt in the 1890s. Instead of using a shaker, he put one goblet on top of another and "turned them upside down five or six times," held them up together as high as he could with both hands, and let the liquid drip down into a "tall, fancy glass." When using a Boston shaker for this maneuver, the shaker halves are pulled apart slightly so that the liquid pours from the broken seal. I like the showmanship involved in this procedure but recommend that if you want to adopt this style, you practice with water until you have mastered the maneuver.

WHETHER TO STIR OR SHAKE

Most bartenders will agree that, as a generalization, drinks containing eggs; fruit juices; cream liqueurs, such as Baileys; or dairy products (cream, half-and-half, or milk) should be shaken, while clear drinks, such as the classic Martini or Manhattan, are usually stirred. It's fairly easy to determine why some drinks should be shaken: It's far easier, for instance, to thoroughly combine a spirit with heavy cream or a fruit juice by shaking rather than stirring, whereas the Martini and the Manhattan, made with a spirit and vermouth, are easily mixed together when stirred. Bear in mind, however, that there are exceptions to the rule, and that some bartenders choose to stray from classical methods as a matter of personal style.

I prefer to stick to the classical procedures for making drinks as described above when it comes to shaken drinks, but in the case of cocktails that should be stirred I allow certain exceptions. The Stinger, for instance, is a clear drink (brandy and white crème de menthe) that is normally shaken, not stirred. I like the fact that this has become the norm for one particular cocktail, so I, too, use the shaker when making a Stinger. A classic Gin Martini, however, should be stirred, even though some old recipe books prescribe shaking the drink. Some customers, however, will specifically ask for a shaken Martini. Their wish is your command.

TO STIR A DRINK

Before you prepare a drink that calls for stirring as the prescribed methodology, be sure to have at the ready a chilled glass, or a glass containing ice cubes if the drink is to be served on the rocks. You can stir drinks in the base of a cocktail shaker if you wish, but I prefer, by far, to use the mixing-glass half of a Boston shaker. If you choose to use a Martini pitcher to stir your drinks, you'll find that it comes with a long glass rod—which, in my opinion, is a comely but functionally poor substitute for a good barspoon.

The standard barspoon has a twisted shaft, and this isn't merely stylistic; it's a functional part of the design. To stir a drink properly, hold the twisted part of the shaft between your thumb and first two fingers. Plunge the spoon into the mixing glass, twirl the spoon back and forth by twisting your fingers away from, then toward yourself, and simultaneously move the spoon up and down in the glass. This sounds hard but it isn't. Stir the drink for between twenty and thirty seconds in order to bring the temperature down to approximately thirty-eight degrees and to incorporate enough water to make the cocktail palatable. One-fourth of the chilled drink will be water melted from the ice, and this is a highly desirable amount.

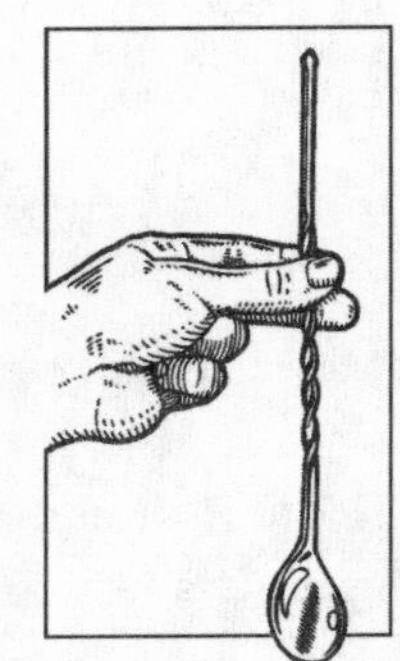

TO SHAKE A DRINK

Once again, although I love to look at a beautiful all-metal cocktail shaker, I prefer to use a Boston shaker, with its simple components: two cones, one metal, one glass. There's something about a Boston shaker that makes me think that a bartender means business. It's a serious tool. First you must prepare the glassware needed for the cocktail, then fill the mixing-glass half of the shaker about two-thirds full of ice. Pour in the ingredients for the drink and place the metal half of the shaker on top of the glass, giving it a sharp tap on the base to ensure that you have formed a watertight seal.

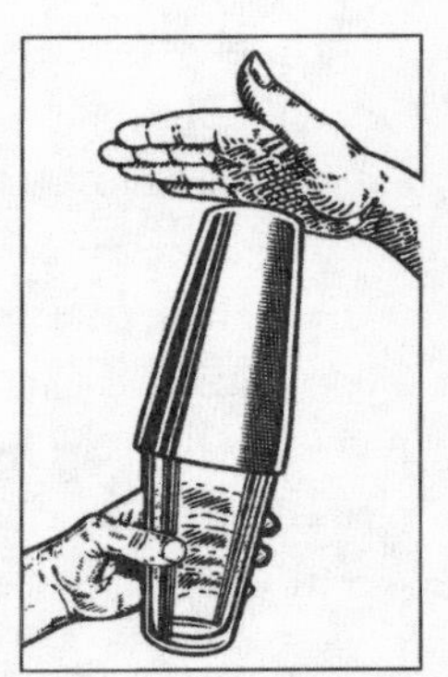

The classic method of holding a shaker involves placing your thumbs on the base of both halves of the Boston shaker with your pinkies intertwined in the middle—which, for me at least, is very uncomfortable. I believe that you should hold the shaker however it feels most comfortable to you, just as long as you keep the two parts together during the shaking. It is important, though, that the glass half of the shaker faces the backbar as you shake, with the metal half pointing towards your customer. In the unlikely event that the shaker breaks apart as you work, the glass will thus fall behind you, and won't fly out into the customer's face.

To chill a drink down to the correct temperature—about thirty-eight degrees—it's necessary to shake it for only about ten to fifteen seconds. Then, holding the shaker so that the metal part is on the bottom, tap the metal sharply with the heel of your hand at the point where the two receptacles are joined. This will break the seal and you will be able to lift the glass off the metal container. It's very important to keep the metal on the bottom when breaking the seal—if the glass is on the bottom, sometimes the action of hitting the shaker will cause liquid to spill over the lip of the glass, wetting your hand and the glass, and thus causing the glass to slip to the floor. If the metal is on the bottom, this can't happen. If you have a problem breaking the seal with the heel of your hand—and this happens occasionally to even the most seasoned professionals—tap the metal sharply at the same place on the edge of the bar or another solid surface. Some people worry that this action could break the glass, but I have yet to see that happen. I prefer to transfer the drink from the metal to the glass before pouring—this makes the performance more visually exciting for the customer.

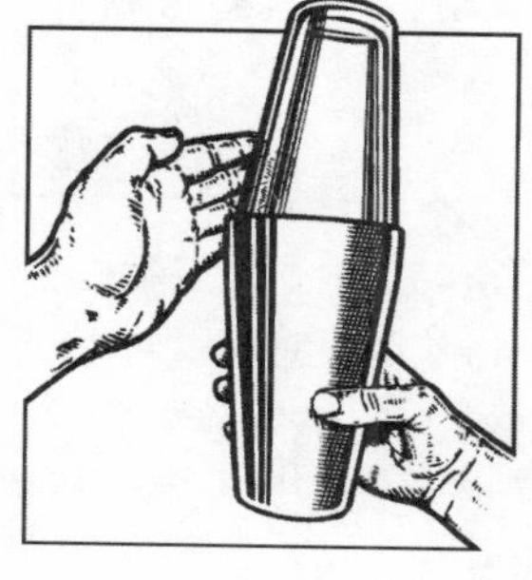

TO ROCK OR ROLL A DRINK

I have heard this method referred to as both rocking and rolling, and it's a way of mixing ingredients without incorporating too much air. Dale DeGroff, a.k.a. King Cocktail, refers to the method as rolling and suggests that the technique is a good one to use when making a Bloody Mary because it won't aerate the tomato juice too much. To rock or roll a drink, simply pour the ingredients into the glass half of a Boston shaker that is two-thirds full of ice. Then repeatedly pour it back and forth between the glass and the metal half of the shaker. To thoroughly incorporate the ingredients in a Bloody Mary, this action should be repeated about half a dozen times, ending up with the drink in the mixing glass; it should then be strained into an ice-filled serving glass.

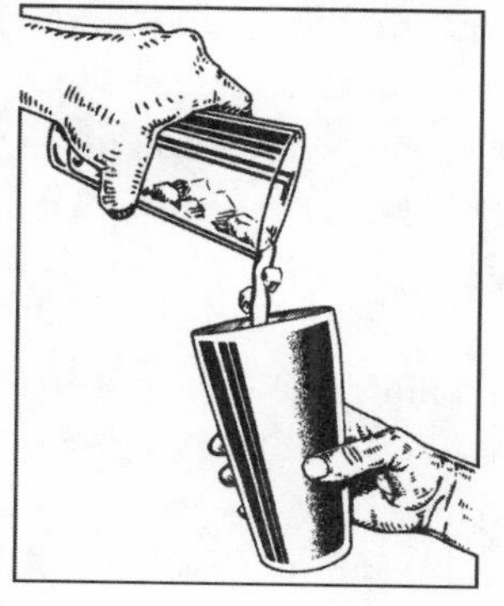

TO MUDDLE A DRINK

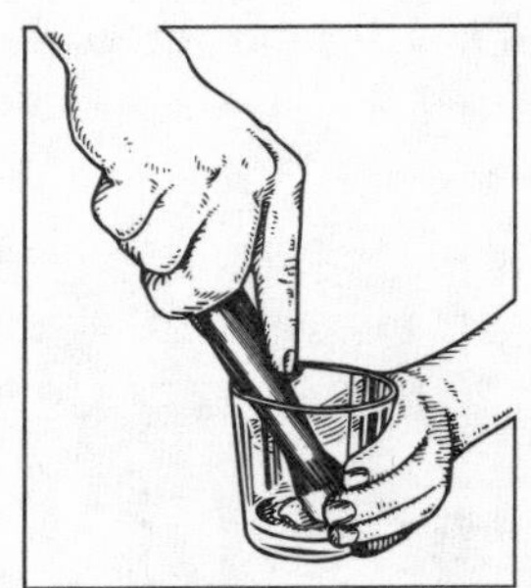

The term *muddling* refers to the action of combining ingredients, usually in the bottom of a glass, by pressing down on them with a muddler—a short wooden pestle, similar in shape to a baseball bat, with one rounded end and one flattened end. The flattened end is used to mix the ingredients together.

The Old-Fashioned is probably the most popular drink that requires muddling, but other drinks can also benefit greatly from this. For instance, you can muddle lemon wedges with granulated sugar to make a Tom Collins or a Whiskey Sour. The sugar abrades the zest of the lemons and produces a far fresher-tasting drink. This phenomenon also occurs in a Caipirinha when granulated sugar is muddled along with lime wedges.

Although muddling can be achieved by using the back of the bowl of a sturdy spoon, I highly recommend that you use a muddler. As with the Hawthorne or julep strainer and the Boston shaker, I think that the use of a wooden muddler shows that a bartender takes his craft seriously.

When muddling ingredients together, be sure to choose a glass that's sturdy enough to hold up to the force of muddling. A double old-fashioned glass without a stem works well if you're preparing a drink suitable for that glass. If you're making, say, a Whiskey Sour or a Tom Collins, muddle the appropriate ingredients in the bottom of a mixing glass, prepare the drink in that glass, and then strain it into the serving glass.

When sugar is called for as an ingredient to be muddled, some liquid will be needed in order to dissolve it. Sometimes the liquid will be produced by the juice of whatever fruit is being muddled; it might also come from a few dashes of bitters. Don't hold back when muddling—squeeze every last drop of juice from fruit wedges by pressing on them firmly and repeatedly with the pestle, and grind the sugar into the liquid until it completely dissolves.

I have witnessed one other form of muddling drinks in just one city, Seattle, and hence have dubbed it the Seattle Muddle, though I'm sure that bartenders in other cities must sometimes use this method of mixing. In order to perform the Seattle Muddle you must first pour all

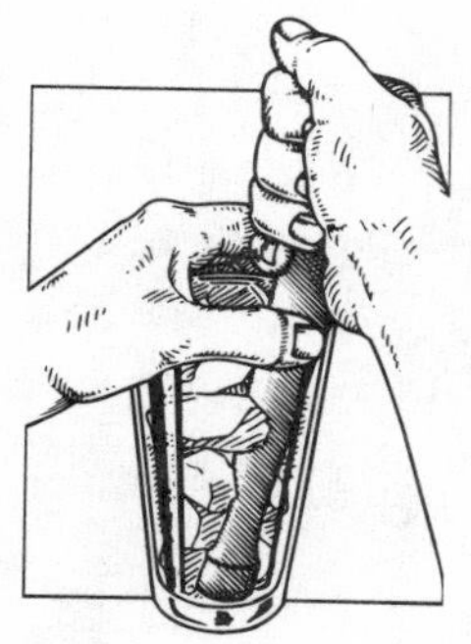

the ingredients of any given cocktail or mixed drink into a mixing glass two-thirds full of ice. Next wrap your hand over the top of the glass, and with the other hand insert the pestle into the glass between your thumb and forefinger. Now plunge the pestle up and down, mixing the drink thoroughly before straining it into the serving glass.

The Seattle Muddle is a somewhat messy affair, and it's slightly unhygienic, since the drink splashes against your palm as you mix it, sometimes actually spilling out of the glass if you don't form a watertight seal with your hand. However, this method has the advantage of breaking tiny shards off the ice, and these morsels will remain in the drink after it has been strained. In the case of a cocktail that's being served straight up, these shards will form sparkling little "stars" that float on top of the drink—the visual effect is quite appealing.

TO LAYER A DRINK

Layered drinks are generically known as Pousse-Cafés, and the preparation of these drinks displays the height of showmanship of the bartender. Layering is usually achieved by slowly pouring liqueurs, spirits, and sometimes even cream or fruit juice over the back of a small spoon, or a barspoon, so that the liquid falls very gently onto the previously poured liquid and rests atop it in a new layer. Other objects can be used instead of a spoon; and I first witnessed this in 1993, when New Orleans bartender Lane Zellman poured the ingredients for his creation—the AWOL—over a maraschino cherry. He held the cherry by the stem, and the effect was very entertaining.

In order to ascertain which ingredients will float on top of others you should know the density of each component of the drink. This can be somewhat difficult, however, since liqueurs such as, say, white crème de menthe are made by many different producers, and depending on the formulas used, the density of one bottling is not necessarily the same as another.

Having said that, though, I will also add that it can be fairly simple to guess correctly what will float on what, just by knowing the texture of a spirit or liqueur. Cassis, crème de banane, crème de menthe, and crème de cacao, for instance, are all fairly heavy, syrupy liqueurs, so it stands to reason that lighter products such as triple sec, kirsch, and sloe gin will float on any of the above products. Spirits such as brandy, whiskey, rum, tequila, vodka, and gin will usually float on top of almost any liqueur, since they contain no sugar and are, therefore, lighter. And heavy syrups such as grenadine will usually withstand the weight of most liqueurs and so should be considered as one of the first ingredients added to the glass.

Here's a list of specific liquors, liqueurs, and their densities. These densities apply only to bottlings for sale in the United States; products bearing the same names might vary in other countries. Start with a high-density product from the bottom of the list, and float fluids from higher up the list, with lower densities, on them:

PRODUCT	DENSITY
Plymouth Gin (114 proof)	0.9156
Maker's Mark Bourbon	0.941
Hiram Walker Kirschwasser	0.941
Buffalo Trace Bourbon	0.9414
Sauza Silver Tequila	0.945
Old Smuggler Blended Scotch	0.945
Plymouth Gin (82.4 proof)	0.9461
Jameson's Irish Whiskey (80 proof)	0.948
Türi Vodka	0.94916
Rain Vodka	0.9498
Sauza Gold Tequila	0.95
SKYY Citrus	0.9555
SKYY Vodka	0.9841

PRODUCT	DENSITY
Pernod	0.985
Mathilde XO Cognac à l'Orange	0.9881
Southern Comfort	0.99337
Hiram Walker Ginger-Flavored Brandy	0.995
Tuaca	1.0157
Celtic Crossing Liqueur	1.0221
B&B	1.0245
Marie Brizard Grand Orange	1.0245
Mathilde Triple Sec	1.025
Hiram Walker Peppermint Schnapps (90 proof)	1.027
Grand Marnier	1.03
Mathilde Anisette	1.03
Mathilde Café	1.03
Artic Flavored Vodkas	1.032
Hiram Walker Amaretto and Cognac	1.033
Hiram Walker Root Beer Schnapps (90 proof)	1.037
Cointreau	1.0385
Marie Brizard Triple Sec	1.0398
DuBouchett Sloe Gin	1.04432
Harlequin Liqueur	1.04583
Hiram Walker Peach Schnapps (90 proof)	1.046
DuBouchett Apricot Brandy	1.04725
Hiram Walker Blackberry-Flavored Brandy	1.048
Amarula Liqueur	1.0484
Hiram Walker Apricot-Flavored Brandy	1.049
Hiram Walker Cherry-Flavored Brandy	1.049
Marie Brizard Poire William	1.0496
Hiram Walker Peach-Flavored Brandy	1.05

(Continues)

(Continued)

PRODUCT	DENSITY
Hiram Walker Sloe Gin	1.051
Marie Brizard Watermelon Liqueur	1.0516
Marie Brizard Mango Passion	1.054
Baileys Irish Cream	1.0548
Hiram Walker Snowstorm	1.055
Hiram Walker Cocorhum	1.056
Hiram Walker Peppermint Schnapps (60 proof)	1.056
Hiram Walker Raspberry-Flavored Brandy	1.057
Villa Massa Limoncello	1.06
DuBouchett Peach Brandy	1.06396
DuBouchett Anisette	1.06401
Vandermint Mint Chocolate Liqueur	1.06452
Hiram Walker Peach Schnapps (30 proof)	1.065
Galliano	1.065
Hiram Walker Raspberry Schnapps	1.068
DuBouchett Peppermint Schnapps	1.06851
DuBouchett Cherry Brandy	1.07005
Lazzaroni Sambuca	1.07099
Bénédictine	1.0725
Hiram Walker Coffee-Flavored Brandy	1.073
Hiram Walker Spearmint Schnapps	1.073
Marie Brizard Peach Liqueur	1.0732
Hiram Walker Sambuca	1.075
DuBouchett Triple Sec	1.07547
Hiram Walker Hazelnut Schnapps	1.076
Hiram Walker Amaretto Liqueur	1.078
Hiram Walker Peppermint Schnapps (30 proof)	1.078
Hiram Walker Cinnamon Schnapps	1.079
Marie Brizard Blackberry Liqueur	1.0801

PRODUCT	DENSITY
DuBouchett Orange Curaçao	1.08026
Marie Brizard Amaretto	1.08152
DuBouchett Blue Curaçao	1.08319
Dr. McGillicuddy's Mentholmint Schnapps	1.0841
Disaronno Liqueur	1.085
Hiram Walker Triple Sec	1.085
Dr. McGillicuddy's Vanilla Schnapps	1.0863
DuBouchett Blackberry Brandy	1.08674
DuBouchett Peach Schnapps	1.08692
DuBouchett White Crème de Menthe	1.08718
Hiram Walker Root Beer Schnapps (30 proof)	1.088
Oro di Mazzetti (Grappa Liqueur)	1.088
Hiram Walker Anisette	1.09
Hiram Walker Blue Raspberry Sourball	1.09
Hiram Walker Rock & Rye	1.09
Hiram Walker Apple Sourball	1.091
Marie Brizard Orange Curaçao	1.0916
Tia Maria	1.094
DuBouchett Amaretto	1.09437
Hiram Walker Red Hot Schnapps	1.095
DuBouchett Green Crème de Menthe	1.09515
Hiram Walker Strawberry Cordial	1.097
Marie Brizard Apricot Liqueur	1.0976
Marie Brizard Blue Curaçao	1.0999
DuBouchett Crème de Banana	1.1009
Marie Brizard Raspberry Liqueur	1.10468
Marie Brizard Strawberry Liqueur	1.1068
Mathilde Pêche	1.116
Marie Brizard Parfait Amour	1.1163

(Continues)

(Continued)

PRODUCT	DENSITY
Mathilde Poire	1.117
Hiram Walker Blue Curaçao	1.118
Mathilde Framboise	1.12
Marie Brizard Green Crème de Menthe	1.1204
Marie Brizard White Crème de Menthe	1.1204
Hiram Walker Green Crème de Menthe	1.124
Hiram Walker White Crème de Menthe	1.125
Lazzaroni Amaretto	1.12503
Hiram Walker Butterscotch Schnapps	1.126
Hiram Walker Café Aztec Liqueur	1.132
Hiram Walker Orange Curaçao	1.132
Hiram Walker Dark Crème de Cacao	1.136
Marie Brizard Anisette	1.1371
Hiram Walker Crème de Banana	1.14
Hiram Walker Black Raspberry Liqueur	1.141
Praline, Pecan Liqueur	1.1418
Marie Brizard Coffee Liqueur	1.142
DuBouchett Crème de Cassis	1.14224
DuBouchett White Crème de Cacao	1.14529
Hiram Walker Crème de Noyaux	1.148
Hiram Walker White Crème de Cacao	1.149
DuBouchett Coffee Liqueur	1.14909
DuBouchett Dark Crème de Cacao	1.15143
Kahlúa	1.152
Copa de Oro Coffee Liqueur	1.1545
Marie Brizard White Crème de Cacao	1.1592
Marie Brizard Dark Crème de Cacao	1.1602
Hiram Walker Crème de Cassis	1.179
Mathilde Cassis	1.192

TO FLAME A DRINK

Be careful. Be very careful. Flaming drinks can be a hazardous affair at best. Once ignited, if that drink spills you have a fire on your hands, and if it spills onto a person you might have a human torch in the bar. You should always have a working fire extinguisher on hand when making flaming drinks; make sure that you know how to use it before you show off your pyrotechnical skills.

But a raging fire isn't all you have to worry about when you make these drinks. If a drink is allowed to flame for too long, the rim of the glass will become very hot, and it will stay that way for quite some time. You must warn anybody who insists on a flaming drink of this danger and advise him not to bring the drink to his lips until he can touch the rim of the glass with his finger, and keep his finger there without it being burned.

A few different kinds of drinks can be flamed before service. Straight liqueurs such as sambuca, for instance, are often flamed, and sometimes the top layer of a Pousse-Café is set alight. Other drinks—the Zombie is a good example—have a high-proof spirit, such as 151-proof rum, floated on top, and this can also be ignited to impress customers. To flame drinks such as these, simply touch a lighted match to the surface of the drink until it catches fire, and allow it to burn for approximately ten seconds before extinguishing it by placing a small saucer on top of the glass. It's okay to allow the customer to blow the flame out, although a saucer is the more effective method. The bartender should never blow out the flame on a customer's drink—it's unsanitary behavior.

TO BLEND A DRINK

Making a frozen drink in a blender looks like a comparatively easy affair, but it's a little more troublesome than you might imagine if you want the resultant drink to be as smooth as silk and easy to sip through a straw. If you don't have a frozen-drink machine at hand you'll have to use a blender to make frozen drinks. It's best to buy a sturdy commercial blender with a strong motor to make blended drinks, since crushing ice places a lot of stress on the machine's motor.

After adding ice and the drink ingredients to the blender, set the top in place and run the blender on high speed (many commercial blenders have only one speed: fast) for twenty to thirty seconds. Turn the blender off, wait until you are sure that the blades are stationary, then remove the lid and thoroughly stir the ingredients with a barspoon. Return the lid to the bowl, start the motor again, and repeat the procedure. You might have to stir the drink more than once in order to achieve a perfect frozen drink, but the results are very worthwhile.

You should also use your ears when making frozen drinks in a blender. You'll notice that the sound of the motor changes as the ice is crushed and incorporated into the drink, and that's when it's time to turn off the blender and check the drink's consistency.

The amount of ice needed to make any specific frozen drink is in direct relationship to the size of the serving glass, so if you're in doubt, simply build the drink in the glass and then pour the whole thing into the blender. You'll find that this results in a full glass with a slightly convex dome, which is visually appealing.

If you use fruit such as pineapple, peaches, or strawberries in a frozen drink, cut it into manageable pieces before adding it to the blender. Hull strawberries and cut them in half; pineapples, peaches, and other fruits should be cut into one-inch cubes. Of course, the pit must be removed from stone fruits, and you shouldn't use the core of a fresh pineapple.

TO INFUSE SPIRITS

The infusion of distilled spirits has gained much popularity in the past decade or so, yet infusion is an ancient practice. According to renowned food scientist Shirley Corriher, ethyl, or beverage, alcohol has the power to boost the flavors of any ingredient with which it is married. "Why do we put vodka into Penne alla Vodka?" she offered as a good example. After all, vodka, for all intents and purposes, is without flavor, so how could it possibly enhance a food dish?

Dairy products and water can also "grab" flavors, distribute them throughout a dish, and enhance them somewhat, but according to

Corriher, alcohol does more than those two products combined. With that in mind, it's good to remember that a high-proof spirit will yield better results than one of low proof when it comes to infusion, and you can always bring the resultant flavored spirit down to a suitable drinking proof after it has been infused, using bottled water, simple syrup, or even fruit juices.

I prefer to use neutral grain spirits instead of vodka when infusing. At 95 percent alcohol by volume, it seems to literally suck the flavors out of whatever ingredient you add to it. However, that product isn't available in every state (I have to travel to Connecticut or New Jersey to procure mine), so if you can't find it locally, use 150-proof vodka—which is legal throughout the country.

In order to infuse a spirit with any ingredient, you must first find a jar with a tight-fitting lid that's large enough to hold the liquor and the fruit (or whatever ingredient you choose) and still have air space at the top so that you can shake the jar periodically. Prepare your ingredients (see list on the next page), add them to the jar along with the liquor, tightly screw the lid onto the jar, and give it a good shake. Now place it somewhere away from direct sunlight but where you'll see it at least once a day, preferably twice or three times. Whenever you walk past it, give it another good shake.

You should taste your infusion regularly—at least once a day after the first twenty-four hours, and twice a day if you are infusing hot peppers or similar strong-flavored ingredients, since they tend to take over the drink.

The average amount of time required to infuse spirits ranges from two to five days, depending on the ingredients used and the proof of the liquor. After seven days it's highly unlikely that any more flavor will be extracted from any ingredient.

When the infusion is ready, strain it through a double layer of dampened cheesecloth, preferably into another large jar. The main problem with infused spirits is that it's sometimes difficult to remove from the spirit tiny particles of the ingredient used for the infusion, so it's a good idea to allow it to rest for a day or so after you've strained it, allowing these particles to drop to the bottom of the jar. Then you should carefully decant it into a bottle, leaving the residue in the bottom of the jar just as you would if you were decanting a bottle of vintage port.

If you use a high-proof spirit for infusion, you'll need to dilute it to a drinkable strength when it is decanted. Use bottled still water to do

Preparing Various Ingredients for Infusions

INGREDIENT	AMOUNT PER 750 ML. DISTILLED SPIRIT	PREPARATION METHOD
APRICOTS	4–5	Wash well. Remove the stone and cut into 1-inch cubes. Peel can be left in place or removed.
BELL PEPPERS	1–2	Wash well.Remove the top and tail, cut into 6 to 8 pieces, and discard the seeds.
BING OR QUEEN ANNE CHERRIES	1 pound	Wash well. Crush with a pestle, breaking the pits. Don't discard the pits.
COFFEE BEANS	6–8 ounces	Crack the beans using the back of the blade of a large sturdy knife.
FRESH HERBS	1–2 bunches	Wash well and dry. Roughly chop.
GRAPEFRUIT ZEST	4–6 grapefruits	Wash well. Remove the zest carefully, making sure not to cut into the bitter white pith.
HOT PEPPERS	1	Wash well. Remove the top and tail, cut into quarters, and discard the seeds.
LEMON ZEST	12 lemons	Wash well. Remove the zest carefully, making sure not to cut into the bitter white pith.
LIME ZEST	12 limes	Wash well. Remove the zest carefully, making sure not to cut into the bitter white pith.
ORANGE ZEST	6–8 oranges	Wash well. Remove the zest carefully, making sure not to cut into the bitter white pith.

INGREDIENT	AMOUNT PER 750 ML. DISTILLED SPIRIT	PREPARATION METHOD
PEACHES	3–4	Wash well. Remove the stone and cut into 1-inch cubes. Peel can be left in place or removed.
PINEAPPLE	1	Remove top and tail. Peel and core, then cut the flesh into 1-inch cubes.
PLUMS	6	Blanch briefly in hot water. Remove the skin and stone and cut into quarters.
STRAWBERRIES	1 pound	Wash well. Hull and slice in half.
TOMATOES	1 pound	Blanch in hot water. Remove the skins, cut into quarters, and discard the seeds.

this—I recommend Poland Spring as a brand with very little, if any, flavor of its own. And you'll have to do some math if you want to bring your infusion down to a specific proof. One liter of spirit at 151 proof contains 75.5 centiliters of pure alcohol. Since 200 proof is equivalent too 100 percent alcohol, for 100 proof, the amount of alcohol in the diluted infusion must be equal to 50 percent of the whole; thus here you'll need to end up with 1.51 liters of infused liquor. Therefore, you must add just over half a liter of bottled water to your infusion to bring it down to the right proof.

I recommend that you don't bring infusions down to less than 100 proof. At that level infusions tend to keep a clear appearance, but when they are diluted beyond that, they can become murky when chilled.

Many infusions require the addition of sugar before serving, a good example being Limoncello, the Italian infusion of lemon zest, which needs to be sweetened to become more palatable. Add sugar in the form of simple syrup, which is made by mixing one cup of granulated sugar into one cup of hot water over medium heat, stirring frequently until the sugar dissolves and the liquid is transparent. Allow the syrup to cool to room temperature before adding it to your infusion.

You can also add honey to your infusions, but be careful to add it in small amounts lest it overcome the other ingredients. Another way of sweetening an infused spirit is by adding a liqueur to it, but again, you should take care not to add too much at once.

FOUNDATIONS OF THE BAR: GARNISHES, MIXERS, AND SUPPLEMENTAL INGREDIENTS

Fill a mixing glass half full of fine ice; add three dashes of gum syrup, 2 dashes maraschino, the juice of a quarter of a lemon, two dashes Peychaud or Angostura bitters, and one jigger brandy; mix. Take a lemon the size of a fancy sauterne or claret glass; peel the rind from three-fourths of it all in one piece; fit it into the glass; moisten the edge of the glass with a piece of lemon, and dip it into fine sugar, which gives it a frosted appearance. Strain your mixture into this glass, trim with fruit, and serve.

—GEORGE J. KAPPELER, *Modern American Drinks: How to Mix and Serve All Kinds of Cups and Drinks,* 1895

THE ITEMS LISTED and discussed on the next page are integral to the cocktailian craft. They can turn a mediocre drink into a masterpiece, whether by adding depth, character, and individual nuances to the drink itself or merely as an eye-pleasing garnish. It is of utmost importance that the bartender be intimate with these items, and that he understand what each one looks like, how it tastes, what other ingredients are suitable to mix with it, and the drinks in which it plays an integral part.

BITTERS
- Angostura Bitters
- Peychaud's Bitters
- Orange Bitters
- Various Other Bitters

SAVORY PRODUCTS
- Clam Juice and Beef Bouillon
- Tomato Juice
- Tomato Water
- Horseradish
- Hot Sauces
- Worcestershire Sauce

SWEETENING AGENTS
- Simple Syrup and Various Other Sweeteners
- Grenadine
- Lime Cordial
- Elderflower Syrup
- Orgeat Syrup
- Various Fruit Syrups
- Coconut Cream

DAIRY PRODUCTS AND EGGS
- Eggs
- Milk, Cream, and Butter

FRUIT JUICES
- Lime Juice and Lemon Juice
- Orange, Tangerine, and Grapefruit Juices
- Cranberry Juice
- Pineapple Juice
- Tamarind Juice
- Other Fruit Juices and Nectars

VARIOUS AND SUNDRY SUPPLEMENTAL INGREDIENTS
- Dry Ingredients
- Orange Flower Water
- Gelatin
- Food Coloring

TEA

SODAS

GARNISHES
- Lemon and Lime Wedges
- Lemon, Lime, and Orange Twists
- Fruit Wheels
- Pineapple Garnishes
- Maraschino Cherries
- Celery
- Fresh Herbs
- Olives and Other Savory Garnishes
- Chocolate Syrups, Shells, Sprinkles, and Shavings
- Various Other Garnishes

BITTERS

Of all the items listed in this chapter, bitters are the most important. Bartenders of yesteryear had far more varieties of bitters from which to choose, and they used them fairly liberally and very frequently. Two drops of bitters added to a Lemon Drop cocktail will drastically alter the drink, giving it an added dimension. Many customers won't even know there are bitters in the drink, but most will be able to discern that this cocktail stands head and shoulders above the vast majority of Lemon Drops.

Potable bitters, such as Fernet-Branca, are commonly used as postprandial drinks in Italy because they are believed to aid digestion, but most of the bitters dealt with below are nonpotable, meaning that they are not meant to be consumed neat or on the rocks. Most nonpotable bitters are commonly employed as a flavor enhancer in cocktails and mixed drinks. Usually high in alcohol—between 70 and 90 proof—they therefore have a long shelf life, lasting for twelve months without refrigeration.

Angostura Bitters

In 1820, after serving in the Prussian army and tending to the wounded at the 1815 Battle of Waterloo, Dr. Johann Gottlieb Benjamin Siegert traveled to the Venezuelan port of Angostura to help General Simón Bolívar liberate the country from the Spanish. Bolívar succeeded in his mission in 1821 and moved on to liberate Ecuador, Peru, and Colombia. Dr. Siegert stayed on in Angostura (renamed Ciudad Bolívar in 1846) to study native botanicals and determine if they could be used medicinally. By 1824, he had developed a tonic known as *amargos aromáticos,* which he marketed commercially. Now called Angostura bitters, the product is made in Trinidad, and is the best-known cocktail ingredient of its kind in the world.

The Angostura company claims that the product gained worldwide renown when, shortly after its creation, it became a staple of ships' provisions; it was used to treat seasickness, fever, and scurvy. The recipe for this potion, though, remains a well-guarded secret.

Without Angostura bitters, many cocktails are somewhat one-dimensional, but when just a dash or three of Angostura are added, they are transformed into complex, multidimensional potions. This ingredient should be constantly on the mind of the creative cocktailian as a possible item to add to new drinks, especially those made with a base of brown spirits, such as whiskey, or brandy, but these bitters are amazingly adaptable to other spirits too. If you dash a little Angostura onto vanilla ice cream, you'll understand how versatile this product can be.

Bartenders should also know that Angostura bitters can help cure hiccups. Coat a lemon wedge with granulated sugar and douse it with Angostura bitters. The person suffering from the malady should then bite down on the lemon wedge. You should be aware, however, in case a customer is a strict teetotaler, that this product contains 45 percent alcohol by volume.

Angostura bitters are available in most supermarkets, as well as specialty food and beverage stores, but if you have any difficulty finding them, or need to find out more about the company, you can call (800) 355-6221 or go to www.angostura.com.

Peychaud's Bitters

The second most important cocktail bitters, Peychaud's is an integral ingredient in the Sazerac cocktail and can be used as a substitute for Angostura in many drinks, especially such cocktails as the Manhattan. The resultant cocktail will not duplicate the same drink made with Angostura, but Peychaud's will add its own nuances and complexities.

In 1795, Antoine Amedie Peychaud arrived in New Orleans after fleeing San Domingo (now Haiti) following the slave revolt there in 1791. His son, Antoine Amedie Peychaud Jr., was born in 1813. Twenty-five years later, Junior opened an apothecary at 123 Royal Street in the French Quarter.

Using a secret family recipe brought to New Orleans by his father, Peychaud Jr. dispensed brandy mixed with bitters as a tonic; the same drink was served, circa 1850, at the Sazerac Coffee House in New Orleans. By the late 1860s, Peychaud had been hired by the coffeehouse, where the owner, Thomas H. Handy, marketed the product, which won a gold medal at the 1869 Grand Exhibition in Germany.

Peychaud's bitters can be hard to find in certain areas of the country, but they can be obtained from the Sazerac Company, Inc., 803 Jefferson Highway, P.O. Box 52821, New Orleans, LA 70121. You can call (504) 831-9450 or go to www.sazerac.com for more details and a downloadable order form. If you wish to pay by credit card, go to www.buffalotrace.com.

Orange Bitters

Orange bitters used to be an integral ingredient in Dry Martinis but started to fall from favor after Prohibition, and now they have almost disappeared. These bitters work very well in Manhattans, and are called for in a number of different cocktail recipes.

If you wish, you can make your own orange bitters by following this recipe for Regans' Orange Bitters No. 5, but Regans' Orange Bitters No. 6, a product I developed with help from the Sazerac Company, should be released in 2003, and should be available by the time you are reading this book. Write to the Sazerac Company, Inc., 803 Jefferson Highway, P.O. Box 52821, New Orleans, LA 70121. You can call (504) 831-9450 or go to www.sazerac.com for more details and a downloadable order form. If you wish to pay by credit card, go to www.buffalotrace.com.

REGAN'S ORANGE BITTERS NO. 5

Allow four weeks to prepare.

Adapted from guidelines set down in *The Gentleman's Companion,* volume 2: *Exotic Drink Book,* by Charles H. Baker Jr.

Warning: These bitters have a very high alcohol content and should not be consumed undiluted. Their purpose is for use in small quantities in cocktails and mixed drinks.

8 ounces dried orange peel, chopped very fine
1 teaspoon cardamom seeds (taken out of their pods)
½ teaspoon caraway seeds
1 teaspoon coriander seeds
1 teaspoon quassia chips
½ teaspoon powdered cinchona bark
¼ teaspoon gentian
2 cups grain alcohol
4½ cups water, divided into ½ cup, 3½ cups, and ½ cup
1 cup granulated sugar

NOTE: Cinchona bark, dried orange peel, gentian, and quassia are available from the Isis Magick Web site: www.isismagick.com/herbs.htm.

Place the peel, cardamom seeds, caraway seeds, coriander seeds, quassia, cinchona bark, gentian, grain alcohol, and ½ cup water into a half-gallon mason jar and push the ingredients down so that they are covered by the alcohol and water. Seal the jar.

Shake the jar vigorously once a day for fourteen days.

Strain the alcohol from the dry ingredients through a cheesecloth. Gather the ends of the cheesecloth to form a pouch and squeeze tightly to extract as much alcohol as possible. Place the dry ingredients in a strong bowl or mortar; reserve the alcohol in a clean mason jar and seal tightly.

Muddle the dry ingredients with a pestle or strong spoon until the seeds are broken.

Place the dry ingredients in a nonreactive saucepan and cover with 3½ cups of water. Bring to a boil over a medium-high heat, cover, turn the heat down, and simmer for 10 minutes. Allow to cool, still covered (about 1 hour).

Return the dry ingredients and water to the original mason jar that contained the alcohol, seal, and leave for seven days, shaking vigorously once a day.

Strain the water from the dry ingredients through a cheesecloth. Discard the dry ingredients and add the water to the alcohol.

Put sugar in a small nonstick saucepan and place over a medium-high heat. Stir constantly until the sugar becomes liquid and turns dark brown. Remove from heat and allow to cool for two minutes.

Pour the sugar into the alcohol-and-water mixture. At this point the sugar may solidify, but it will quickly dissolve.

Allow the mixture to stand for seven days. Skim off any bits that float to the surface and carefully decant the clear liquid to separate it from any sediment resting on the bottom.

Measure the bitters; there should be about 12 fluid ounces. Add 6 ounces (or half the amount of bitters produced) of water, and shake thoroughly.

Pour the bitters into a bitters bottle. Store for up to twelve months.

Various Other Bitters

Peach bitters are seldom called for, and I have not tasted a commercial brand of this product that I can recommend. Potable bitters such as Underberg from Germany (www.underberg.com) are mainly used as digestive remedies; this can also be said about many Italian bitters, such as Fratelli Averna and Cynar.

Campari, another potable form of bitters from Italy, is regularly used as a cocktail ingredient in superb drinks such as the Negroni and the Americano. Campari can be very useful to the cocktailian bartender, and it, along with other potable bitters, should be considered as a viable ingredient, even when used in very small amounts. Like the nonpotable bitters described above, they can add much depth and complexity to mixed drinks.

SAVORY PRODUCTS

Clam Juice and Beef Bouillon

These potables are used in a few savory drinks, such as the Bloody Caesar and the Bull Shot, and should be purchased in small bottles or cans to eliminate waste. Both of these products should be refrigerated after being opened.

Tomato Juice

Tomato juice is one of my big downfalls—I just hate the texture. Therefore, my Bloody Mary skills are somewhat lacking. However, people whose opinions I respect assure me that most reputable commercial brands of tomato juice are perfectly viable in drink preparation.

Tomato Water

Although I'm not enamored of tomato juice, I do like tomato water—it makes for a wonderful ingredient in cocktail preparation. To make tomato water, simply roughly cut flavorful tomatoes, place them in a double layer of dampened cheesecloth, and squeeze the liquid from the fruit. This ingredient can be successfully employed in the Bloody Mary Martini (see page 222), and it also has many other possibilities in mixed-drink preparation.

Horseradish

Prepared horseradish, used in savory drinks such as the Bloody Mary, should be purchased in small jars and refrigerated after being opened.

Hot Sauces

Although the regular bottling of Tabasco sauce is the norm behind the bar, that brand is now available in different flavors, such as garlic and chipotle, and there are many other brands of hot sauce from which to choose. Think about using these flavorings to differentiate your own Bloody Marys or to create a drink that's tied to a specific cuisine, such as Mexican food.

Worcestershire Sauce

Bottles of Worcestershire sauce, which is used in savory drinks such as the Bloody Mary, should always be at hand behind the bar.

SWEETENING AGENTS

Simple Syrup and Various Other Sweeteners

There has been much debate among cocktailians about the correct ratio of sugar to water when making simple syrup; the truth is that it doesn't really matter. I make my syrup using a fifty-fifty ratio, and because I'm aware of the sweetness it delivers, I usually know how much to add to a drink to achieve a good balance between it and any sour components, such as lemon juice. You may choose to use more sugar, so that you're adding less water to a drink when using this ingredient. Then you will get used to using simple syrup made to your formula, and as long as you always make it the same way, you'll end up with nicely balanced drinks.

I recommend that you store simple syrup refrigerated, in a clean bottle that can be fitted with a speed pourer for easy service.

SIMPLE SYRUP

One quarter ounce of this syrup is equal in sweetness to one teaspoon of granulated sugar.

MAKES 1½ CUPS SIMPLE SYRUP

1 cup granulated sugar
1 cup water

Combine both ingredients in a saucepan and cook over medium heat, stirring frequently, until the sugar is dissolved. Allow the syrup to rest until it cools to room temperature, then transfer it to a clean bottle.

Although superfine sugar dissolves easily in cold liquids, I far prefer to use simple syrup, which distributes itself quickly in cocktails and mixed drinks. Since confectioners' sugar contains traces of cornstarch to prevent clumping, it's not a viable alternative, either. I do, however, recommend the use of granulated sugar in the preparation of certain drinks.

When making drinks such as the Caipirinha, lime wedges should be muddled with granulated sugar until the sugar is completely dissolved. During this process, the coarse sugar abrades the zest of the lime and introduces the lime's essential oils to the drink. This method can be employed when making all sorts of cocktails that contain lime or lemon juice, and it adds an extra dimension to drinks like the Tom Collins.

Confectioners' sugar, though not suitable for making simple syrup, can be successfully used as a garnish when sprinkled onto items such as mint sprigs in a Julep. Brown sugar, bearing somewhat richer molasses notes, can be a good choice for Irish Coffee and many other hot drinks.

Two other sweetening agents—honey and maple syrup—are sometimes called for as ingredients in mixed drinks, but I find them overly sweet, and their flavors can easily mask other nuances in a cocktail if extreme care isn't taken to introduce them in very small quantities.

Grenadine

True grenadine is a syrup made from pomegranate juice, so check the labels on commercial brands to make sure that the word *pomegranate* appears as an ingredient. The Angostura company produces a pomegranate-based nonalcoholic grenadine, and both Jacquin's and Boulaine sirop de grenadine liqueurs are very low in alcohol (2.5 percent and 2 percent alcohol by volume, respectively); they are also made from pomegranates.

To make your own grenadine you must first juice some pomegranates—each one should yield two to three ounces of juice—and I find that this is easily accomplished by using a levered citrus fruit juicer. Add one ounce of simple syrup (see page 110) to every three ounces of pomegranate juice, and you'll have a flavorful sweetening agent that will add extra depth to cocktails such as the Monkey Gland.

Lime Cordial

In 1867, sweetened lime juice was first produced commercially in Edinburgh, Scotland, by Lauchlin Rose, who patented his method of preserving the juice without the addition of alcohol. That same year it was made mandatory for all ships in both the Royal Navy and British merchant fleet to include lime juice in the sailors' daily rations, and Rose's lime juice soon became known throughout the world.

Sweetened lime juice should never be used in cocktails calling for fresh lime juice, but it is an integral part of such drinks as the Gimlet and Lager and Lime. The cocktailian might experiment with lime cordial as a sweetening agent, using it instead of, say, grenadine or simple syrup when creating new drinks.

You might notice that some bottlings of lime juice change color, becoming golden brown after a time as a result of oxidization. This isn't of great concern to most bars, since sweetened lime juice is used too quickly for it to oxidize. For home use, though, the Angostura company once again comes to the rescue here—Angostura Reconstituted Lime Juice is a sweetened product that always retains its original color.

Elderflower Syrup

Used in only one recipe in this book—the Lola Martini—this product can usually be found at specialty German food stores or can be ordered online from www.germandeli.com.

Orgeat Syrup

Flavored with almonds and orange flower water, this sweet, nutty, citrusy syrup is used primarily in tropical drinks; it can usually be found in specialty food stores.

Various Fruit Syrups

Various recipes call for a variety of fruit syrups, such as strawberry, raspberry, and black currant. These syrups are often available at specialty food stores and can be ordered online from Monin (www.monin.com), a fine company, in my experience.

Coconut Cream

Canned coconut cream, used in drinks such as the Piña Colada, is very thick and syrupy. The can should be shaken well before it is opened, and even then, it's often necessary to stir the cream until all the oils, which float to the top, are incorporated into the cream.

DAIRY PRODUCTS AND EGGS

Eggs

Very few drinks call for the use of raw eggs, but you can't make a Pisco Sour or a Ramos Gin Fizz without raw egg white. Although salmonella contamination in raw eggs is rare, it is certainly a consideration; in some states, it is illegal to serve raw eggs, so you should check your local laws. Eggs that have been pasteurized in their shells are now available (see www.safeeggs.com, or call (800) 410-7619, ext. 205, for more details). These are recommended by the F.D.A. for making drinks such as Eggnog that call for raw eggs.

Milk, Cream, and Butter

Recipes calling for milk, cream, or half-and-half can be made with any one of these products, but the resultant drink, of course, will be thicker and have a more pleasing consistency if cream is used. You should always check dairy products for freshness before using them.

If you want whipped cream, heavy cream is the easiest to whisk to the right consistency. Although some people like to whip it until it forms stiff peaks, I prefer to stop when the cream thickens somewhat but is still pourable. This way the cream will float easily on top of the drink and become part of it, as opposed to a food item that's better eaten with a spoon.

Butter, called for in a Hot Buttered Rum, should be kept refrigerated at all times, and for drink service you must use unsalted butter unless the recipe specifies otherwise.

FRUIT JUICES

Lime Juice and Lemon Juice

Whenever possible, fruit juices used in drink preparation should be fresh, especially in the case of lime and lemon juice. Many bars use commercial products known as "sweet and sour" instead of either of these juices, but I've yet to find one that isn't overly sweet—not to mention that no one product could possibly take the place of two different juices. Doubtless it won't be long before some company issues viable products that save the bartender time. Meanwhile, if you use so much juice that squeezing your own fruit simply isn't viable, it's worth seeking out companies that offer frozen fresh juices.

If you work in a busy bar, you might want to presweeten your fresh lemon and lime juices; I recommend using 1½ ounces of simple syrup to each cup of lime juice, and 2 ounces simple syrup to each cup of lemon juice. You can experiment with these ratios until you find a recipe that works for you, but I strongly suggest that you don't add too much syrup, since this results in unbalanced drinks. It's easy to add a little more sweetener to individual cocktails in order to satisfy the tastes of individual customers.

Orange, Tangerine, and Grapefruit Juices

With orange, tangerine, and grapefruit juices, once again, fresh is best and frozen fresh juice comes in second. Some commercial brands of juice in cartons have gotten far better recently than they were a mere five years ago, so if that's all you have at hand, I can't say that I object to their use in drink preparation.

Cranberry Juice

If you look at the label on a bottle or can of cranberry juice, you'll note that it's usually sold as "cranberry juice cocktail." This is because straight cranberry juice is far too bitter to drink, so it must be sweetened for use at home or behind the bar. Most commercial brands of cranberry juice cocktail are perfectly acceptable for drink preparation.

Pineapple Juice

As with cranberry juice, I find that most commercial brands of canned pineapple juice are perfectly acceptable behind the bar.

Tamarind Juice

This sweet-tart tropical fruit juice can be found in many specialty food stores, especially those with an Asian focus. It can easily overpower other flavors in a cocktail, so be sure to add it to a drink gradually.

Other Fruit Juices and Nectars

Various other juices and nectars—made from papayas, mangoes, guavas, apples, peaches, and all manner of exotic fruits—are on the market, and their number seems to grow daily. Although fresh is always best, most of these commercial products are quite acceptable for drink preparation. Make sure to shake the container of nectars well before opening, since some of these products tend to settle and separate even before they hit the shelves.

VARIOUS AND SUNDRY SUPPLEMENTAL INGREDIENTS

Dry Ingredients

Granulated sugar, coarse salt, cocoa powder, Old Bay seasoning, and other dry ingredients are often used to coat the rims of glasses for drinks such as Sidecars, Margaritas, Chocolate Martinis, and Bloody Marys. These ingredients should be stored in airtight containers overnight, but during service it's advisable to have them in saucers behind the bar, ready for use.

Orange-Flower Water

Used in few drinks—the Ramos Gin Fizz is the only one that easily springs to mind—this delicately perfumed ingredient, made from orange blossoms, is readily available at specialty food stores.

Gelatin

Used in the Jelly Shots on pages 211, 292, and 350, unflavored gelatin, in my opinion, is the only way to go when making this type of "drink."

Food Coloring

Usually found in the baking department of most food stores, food colorings are seldom used behind the bar, but you'll need some if you intend to make any of the Jelly Shots on pages 211, 292, and 350. It's also possible to substitute triple sec and blue food coloring for blue curaçao, but be sure to add the coloring sparingly until you arrive at the correct hue.

TEA

Tea is seldom used as a cocktail ingredient, but when it's called for there is simply no substitute. Since there are so many flavored teas on the market, the cocktailian bartender might look in this direction when composing new drinks. I have experimented a little with this ingredient, and advise you to make a somewhat stronger brew than you would if you were going to drink it from a cup. You should also prepare it well in advance of use so that it has time to cool to room temperature.

SODAS

Like commercial brands of fruit juices, soda from "guns" has improved over the years, but I've yet to taste one that's acceptable to the cocktailian bartender, no matter which flavor you choose. Good bars stock the smallest bottles available of the best brands of lemon-lime soda, cola, ginger ale, ginger beer, club soda, and tonic water, as well as a selection of the various new and wonderful fanciful flavors that, as with fruit juices, appear on a regular basis. If you use these small bottles of soda, pour just a little soda into the glass, place the bottle on a cocktail napkin or coaster next to the drink, and allow the customer to use his judgment in adding more soda to the drink.

It's important to understand the difference between ginger ale and ginger beer—the latter is usually far spicier and bears fuller flavors than the former. This isn't to say that ginger beer is better than ginger ale; they have different uses. And it's also true that some brands of ginger ale outrank others in terms of flavor and spiciness. Blenheim ginger ale is a good case in point—it's available in diet, hot, and mild and is very flavorful. You can order it at www.beveragesdirect.com.

Root beer, sarsaparilla, birch beer, and various other spicy sodas are readily available, and these are wonderful additions to the basic line of sodas. Since the better brands are not overly sweet, they provide a viable alternative for adult customers who don't drink alcohol or are driving. Most other sodas are too sweet for many adults to drink more than one.

An ingredient that can be very successfully used as a nonalcoholic cocktail ingredient and is also very refreshing when served over ice is San Pellegrino San Bitter, a soda that tastes very much like Campari. The company also makes sophisticated lemon and orange sodas, known respectively as limonata and aranciata, and all three of these bottlings can be found in many Italian specialty food stores. For professional use, wholesalers that stock San Pellegrino bottled water should be able to supply bars and restaurants with these products. Alternatively, try the Soda Shop Web site: store.yahoo.com/soda-pop/index.html.

One more soda should be mentioned here. It's seldom seen in the United States, but it's a very good mixer when used with gin or vodka. Bitter lemon soda is merely tonic water with lemon flavoring, and it's easily made by adding fresh lemon juice to regular tonic, then adjusting the sweetness with a little simple syrup to suit individual tastes.

GARNISHES

Fruit garnishes are very important to the bartender, and it's imperative that they be as fresh as possible. There's nothing I enjoy better than seeing a bartender cut a lemon twist from the fruit immediately before using it, but this isn't always possible in busy bars. The vast majority of bartenders must prepare garnishes prior to service, endeavoring to cut only as much as he thinks he will need that day or evening.

Some garnishes, such as lemon twists, will keep overnight provided they are covered with a dampened paper napkin. It's up to the bartender to check these for freshness the following day and decide whether or not they are fit for use.

As the name suggests, garnishes are additional ingredients meant to make drinks more pleasing to the eye; some of them are also drink ingredients, so again, freshness comes into play. Citrus wedges, for example, will start to lose juice the moment they are cut, so it's essential that they be discarded as soon as it becomes apparent that they are no longer viable. This is easily accomplished by squeezing one wedge out of a batch and observing how much juice is left in it (one quarter of a lime, for example, should contain about a quarter ounce of juice).

Lemon and Lime Wedges

I like to use large wedges of both of these fruits. Although it depends on the size of the lemon or lime you are cutting, most limes won't yield much more than four wedges, or six at the very most; lemons will normally yield six to eight wedges.

To prepare lemon and lime wedges, first remove both ends with a sharp paring knife; then slice the fruit in half either vertically or horizontally, depending on the style of wedge you prefer. Because of size variances, I usually cut limes horizontally and lemons vertically. Now cut each half into equal-sized wedges, remembering that size matters; you need to end up with a wedge large enough to yield about a quarter ounce of juice. A rule of thumb is that one quarter of one lime or one sixth of one lemon should contain this amount.

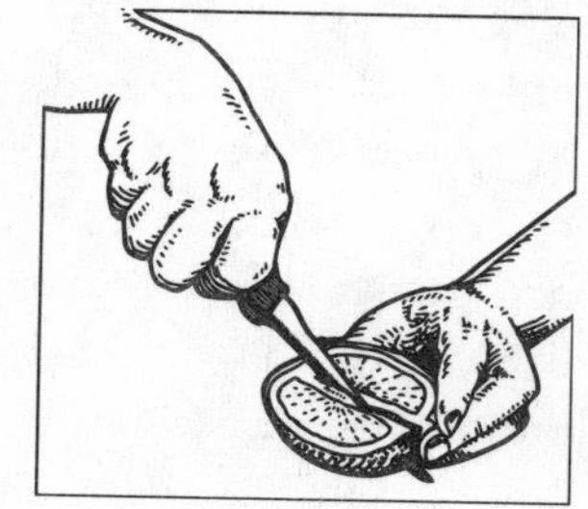

One half of a lemon that has been cut vertically will yield long slender wedges that are easy to squeeze. One half of a lime, cut horizontally, will give you shorter, squat wedges, but they, too, will be easy to handle during service.

Lemon, Lime, and Orange Twists

Citrus twists can be cut in many different ways, but in my opinion, bigger is better. The twists give up their essential oils to the cocktail being garnished with them (see page 78), so the larger the twist, the more oils will be added to the drink.

To prepare citrus twists, remove the stem end of the fruit in order to give it a base, stand it on that base, and carefully cut strips of the zest away from the fruit. The width of the twist will depend on the size and shape of the fruit you are using, but try for as wide as possible in each case. Some of the white inner pith must remain on the twist so that it will be sturdy enough to use properly, but you should make sure that you never cut into the inner pulp of the fruit. The length of each twist, once again, will depend on the size of the fruit, but long is preferable, short is not.

You can also produce twists in the form of spirals by cutting around the fruit in one continuous motion, but these twists can prove difficult to handle. If, however, you'd like to line the inside of a glass with a citrus spiral, you should prepare the glass prior to service and use a slim glass—champagne flutes are ideal for this type of garnish.

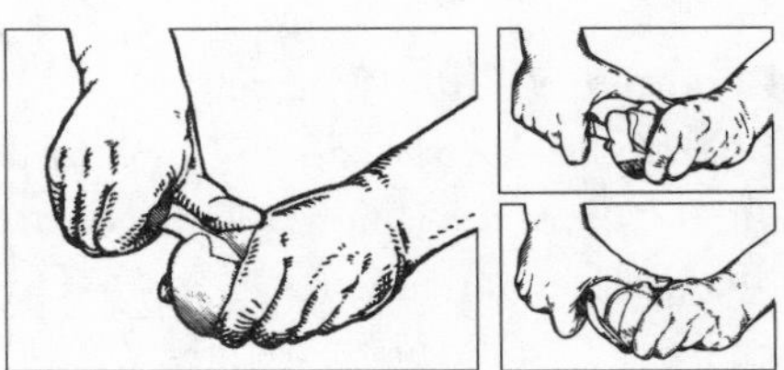

Fruit Wheels

Oranges are the garnishes most commonly cut into the shape of a wheel, but limes and lemons are sometimes cut in this fashion, too. Orange wheels, however, can be eaten by the customer, while this is seldom the case with limes and lemons. Lime and lemon wheels are not good substitutes for wedges since they are almost impossible to squeeze successfully, and hence don't do the same job as wedges, but they can be visually pleasing.

Orange wheels are often cut in half, depending on the size of the fruit. It's the job of the bartender to assess the size of both the fruit and the glass before deciding whether a whole wheel or a half wheel would be more suitable for any specific drink.

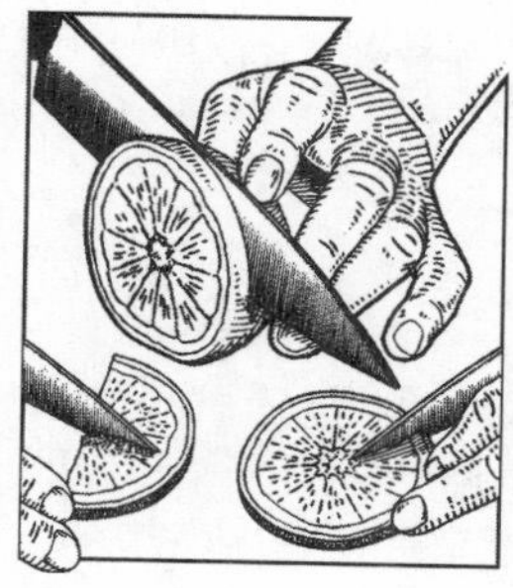

To cut fruit wheels, first remove both ends of the fruit, cutting deep enough to expose the inner pulp. Then, holding the fruit steady, slice off quarter-inch wheels. If a whole wheel is called for, cut through the peel up to the center of the fruit, creating a slit that will fit over the rim of a glass. When using half wheels, you should cut a slit from the center of the fruit up to the white pith, so that the garnish can be hung over the side of the glass.

Pineapple Garnishes

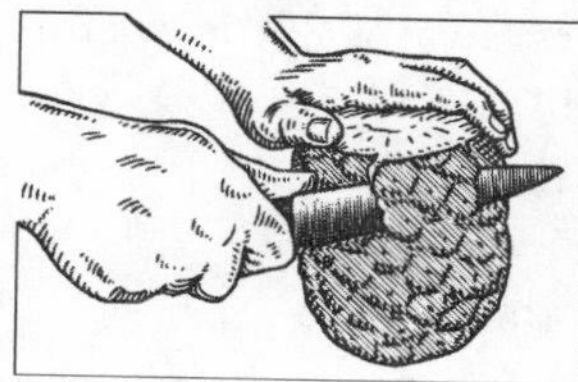

Pineapples are delicious edible garnishes, but this fruit can be hard to handle, and the shape into which you cut it will largely depend on the ripeness of the fruit, which governs the sturdiness of the resultant garnishes. Sturdier pineapples can be cut into spears, whereas riper ones are usually best cut into chunks or cubes. You can also use small cookie cutters to make all manner of shapes; if this is your desire, there's no need to remove the outer skin first. Simply cut the fruit into half-inch wheels and use the cookie cutter to create the garnish, making sure to avoid the hard center core.

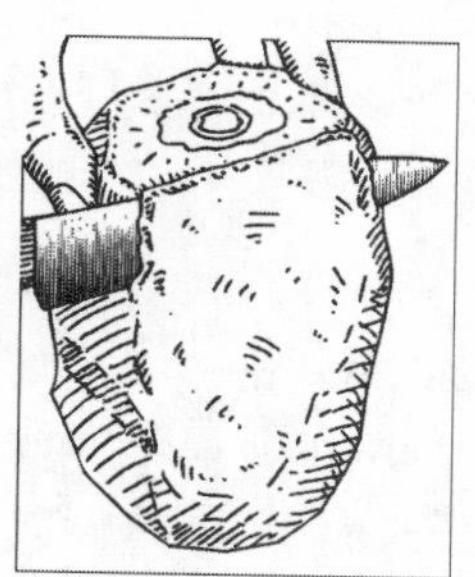

To make spears or cubes, slice off the top and bottom of the pineapple, then remove the outer skin by cutting downward, following the shape of the fruit. Any black spots remaining on the outside of the fruit should be cut out with a paring knife. Next, cut slices from the side of the fruit, about a half inch wide, until you reach the hard center. You can now cut spears from these slices; pare them down,

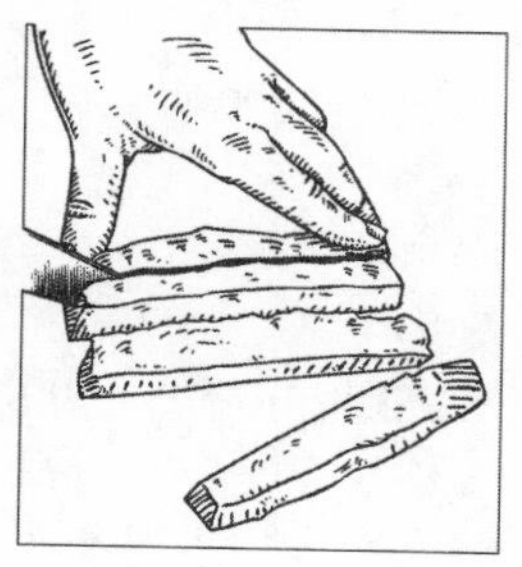

if need be, to fit the glass you intend to garnish. Otherwise, cut the fruit into half-inch cubes and impale them with toothpicks or cocktail picks for easy handling.

Maraschino Cherries

Just what are maraschino cherries? The Cherry Marketing Institute sent me information on how these garnishes are made; the process doesn't make them sound appealing, but they *are* real cherries. They go through a few steps involving calcium chloride, sugar, food coloring, pasteurization, and flavorings before being bottled and sold to Manhattan lovers everywhere. I don't find these garnishes abhorrent, and I frequently use them, but I have also taken fresh cherries, pierced each one a few times with a wooden skewer, and marinated them in a mixture of bourbon and vermouth. These make fine garnishes, although the color leaves a little to be desired. Commercial maraschino cherries are available in the traditional red color, and also in a bright emerald green—perfect around the holidays, or perhaps on St. Patrick's Day.

Celery

Stalks of celery, thoroughly washed, trimmed, and usually shortened to fit the glass, are a great way to garnish a Bloody Mary. You must make sure, though, that the celery is crisp and fresh; if you keep some on display, it's best to place them in a container with some iced water at the bottom.

Fresh Herbs

Herbs such as rosemary, thyme, cilantro, sage, basil, and mint can be used as very successful garnishes, but the bartender must be careful to match the scent of the herb with the appropriate cocktail. Rosemary and thyme, for instance, both go well with gin-based mixed drinks, cilantro works in Bloody Marys, and mint is commonly called for in the Mojito—a rum-based tall drink—and, of course, the Mint Julep. Fresh herbs are best stored in a container with iced water at the bottom.

Olives and Other Savory Garnishes

Olives can be found in a variety of sizes, and stuffed with any number of other ingredients, such as almonds, blue cheese, pimientos, and anchovies. Since these fruits are usually used as a Dry Gin Martini garnish and Martini drinkers tend to be very specific about their drinks, many customers are very choosy when it comes to which type of olive they want. Using plain pitted olives in some sort of brine is the safest way to go, but you might want to keep some stuffed olives on hand in order to offer a selection.

If you would like to personalize your olives, you can make your own "brine" by adding fresh herbs such as basil, thyme, and/or rosemary to dry vermouth, simmering the liquid for about five minutes on the stovetop, covering the mixture, and allowing it to return to room temperature. Discard the brine from the bottle of olives, and replace it with the herbed vermouth.

Caper berries also make good Martini garnishes, and I've even seen regular capers added to the drink, but the most common "other" Martini garnish is the pearl onion, again packed in brine, which turns the Martini into a Gibson. The only real rule of thumb when using any of these berry-type garnishes is that an odd number of them must always be used: One olive is standard, three are acceptable, but two are verboten. This, I believe, comes from an old superstition, but I can't find a good reference to it. The same rule, incidentally, applies to coffee beans when added to a glass of sambuca.

I have also seen Martini recipes that call for dilly beans (pickled green beans), pickled okra, tiny pickled tomatoes, and even pickled mirliton (also known as chayote), a squash that should be cut into small cubes for use as a garnish. There are no rules here—simply pick something edible that suits your fancy.

Chocolate Syrups, Shells, Sprinkles, and Shavings

Most commercial brands of chocolate syrups and sprinkles are fine to use in drink preparation, and one recipe in this book calls for Chocolate Magic Shell, a product made by Smuckers that hardens when chilled. Chocolate shavings, sometimes used as a garnish, are easily made by simply grating cold chocolate, but if you do this prior to service, keep the shavings refrigerated.

Various Other Garnishes

Almost anything edible that looks good in or on a drink can be employed by the cocktailian bartender. Hershey's Hugs or Kisses dress up a clear Chocolate Martini, multicolored sprinkles can be used to adorn the lip of a glass with a chocolate-syrup-coated rim, and miniature candy canes look splendid in holiday-time cocktails.

Whole cloves are often used in hot drinks such as the Hot Toddy, and although they serve as a garnish, their primary purpose is to add flavor to the drink. Cinnamon sticks, candied ginger, and vanilla beans can also be used as garnishes, and kiwis, strawberries, bananas, and countless other fruits are perfectly acceptable, providing they are matched to the appropriate drink. Kiwis and bananas should be peeled and sliced, and strawberries hulled; "notches" should then be cut into these fruits to enable them to be placed on the lip of the glass.

One practice that faded from fashion about a hundred years ago is the custom of topping drinks, especially those made with crushed ice, with mounds of berries and small slices of other fruits, such as strawberries and bananas. In the days when these drinks were served at first-class bars, the customers were provided with short spoons with which to eat the fruit—it's a practice I'd love to see return to the barrooms of America.

TOOLS AND VESSELS

Liquor Pump, Mallet, Filtering Bag or Paper, Brace and Bit, Liquor Gauge, Gimlet, Bung Starter, Rubber Hose for drawing Liquor, Liquor Thieves, Thermometer, Hot Water Kettle, Lemon Squeezers, Liquor Gigger, Cork Press, Champagne Faucets, Molasses Jugs, Postal Cards, Demijohns, Spittoons, Shot for Cleaning Bottles, Railroad Guide.

—HARRY JOHNSON,
excerpted from "Complete List of Utensils, Etc., Used in a Bar Room," *New and Improved Bartender's Manual of How to Mix Drinks,* 1900

IT'S ESSENTIAL FOR THE BARTENDER to have the right tools on hand to mix every sort of drink, and it's also necessary to know how to use bar equipment properly. That said, there's nothing wrong with adding your own style when it comes to drink preparation. I once saw a bartender using two metal cones instead of one glass and one metal piece, the usual set that makes up the Boston shaker. Since the cones came from different manufacturers, one had a slightly larger mouth than the other, so the combination worked well, and the all-metal shaker looked very smart when in use. It turned out that the bar hadn't ordered the correct glassware for a Boston shaker, so this guy had just improvised. Even when the right glasses arrived, he decided to keep using the two metal pieces. Nothing wrong with that—it displays showmanship and imagination. Here's a list of equipment you'll need to properly set up a bar.

COCKTAIL AND MIXED-DRINK PREPARATION

Boston Shaker: This consists of two pieces: a mixing glass, usually sixteen-ounce capacity, and a slightly larger, flat-bottomed metal cone. The glass can be used on its own when drinks are stirred over ice; the two are used in tandem, with the metal part fitting over the glass, for shaking drinks.

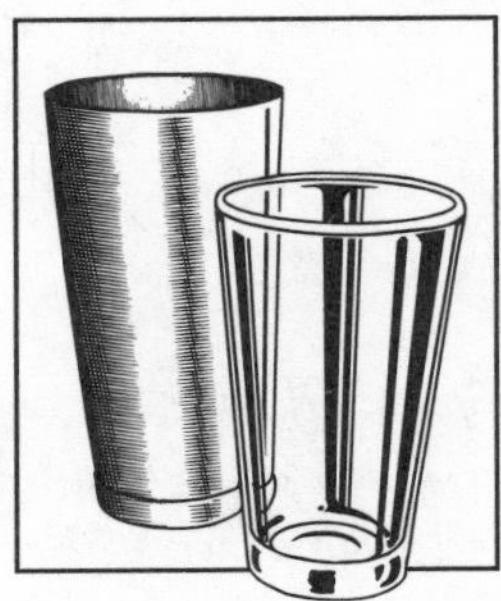

Barspoon: This long-handled spoon with a twisted shaft and shallow bowl is used for stirring drinks in order to chill and dilute them.

Hawthorne Strainer: This flat-topped, perforated metal device with a continuous coil of wire around its perimeter, which helps keep the strainer snugly in place, has a short handle and either two or four "thumbs" that extend from the top and sides to keep it in place on the Boston shaker. The Hawthorne strainer is used when drinks are strained from the metal half of the Boston shaker.

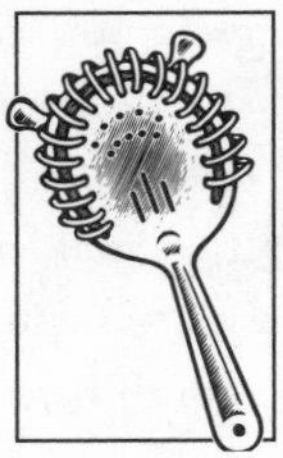

Julep Strainer: A perforated metal soupspoon-shaped strainer used when drinks are strained from a mixing glass.

Martini Pitcher: Seldom used these days, glass Martini pitchers are usually tall and elegant, have a tightly pinched spout to prevent ice from falling into the drinks, and generally come with a glass rod for stirring cocktails.
Cocktail Shaker: A metal cocktail shaker has a tight-fitting top, which covers a strainer, and the strainer fits into a metal cone. Cocktail shakers come in many elegant designs and are considered completely acceptable for use in the home or behind a professional bar.

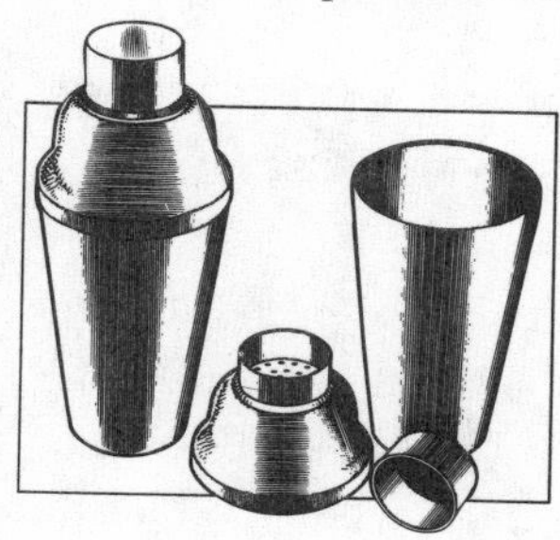

Short Shaker: This is a miniature version of the metal half of the Boston shaker. It is placed on top of a glass—usually an old-fashioned glass (see the following chapter)—in order to shake a drink that has already been poured into the glass. I find these devices more or less useless.
Electric Blender: Used to prepare frozen drinks, crush ice, and puree fruit, commercial blenders with strong motors are essential for bar use, since crushing ice demands a great deal of force. You'll need to use a barspoon (see page 124) in conjunction with the blender to make smooth frozen drinks (see page 97).

GARNISH PREPARATION

Cutting Board: Small wooden or plastic cutting boards are necessary for preparing fruit garnishes and are easily stored behind the bar.
Paring Knives: Small, sharp paring knives are needed to prepare fruit garnishes.
Muddler: A wooden pestle, used to crush and blend ingredients in the serving glass or a mixing glass. The flattened end is used for this procedure.

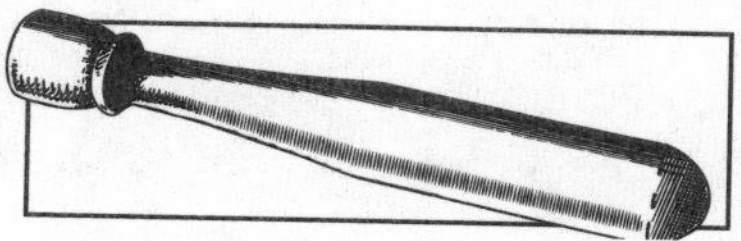

Grater: A small metal grater is useful for grating items such as nutmeg onto the top of cocktails.

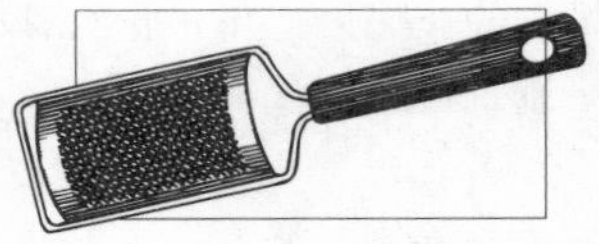

BOTTLE AND CAN OPENERS AND STORAGE

Bottle Opener: Most bars have professional bottle openers, complete with a receptacle to catch the tops, installed behind the bar. Otherwise, bartenders should keep a pocket-sized bottle opener at hand.

Church Key: Metal church keys serve a dual purpose: one end punches holes in cans so the liquid contents can be poured out, and the other end opens bottles.

Corkscrew: There are many different kinds of corkscrews from which to choose. The **Winged Corkscrew** fits easily onto the neck of the bottle; two arms extend when the cork is impaled, and pushing the arms downward removes the cork. The **Screw-Pull Corkscrew** removes the cork by first impaling it; as the user keeps turning the wingnut-shaped handle clockwise, the device pulls the cork from the bottle. The **Rabbit Corkscrew** is simple to use and highly recommendable—it has easy-to-handle grips, and the cork can be swiftly ejected from the worm after being pulled from the bottle. The **Ah-So Cork Puller** works when the two thin blades are inserted between the cork and bottle—they grip the cork, and the user can pull it from the bottle; I find this style of cork remover unsatisfactory. **Waiter's Corkscrews** are penknife-like tools that fit easily into the pocket. They have a blade for cutting the foil from the top of a bottle, a worm that screws into the cork, and a fitting that rests on the lip of the bottle so that when the user pulls the handle upward, the cork is removed. I highly recommend this style of corkscrew for professional bartenders.

Champagne Keepers: These spring-loaded devices clamp onto the top of an opened bottle of champagne or sparkling wine and seal the bottle to prevent carbonation from escaping. A necessary tool for the bartender.

JUICE EXTRACTORS AND SERVICE

Citrus Reamers: Reamers come in two basic styles. One is the typical glass or plastic reamer with a pointed cone, onto which the fruit is pressed to extract the juice. The cone is surrounded by a well that collects the juice; nubbles in the well are meant to prevent seeds from falling into the juice, but they seldom do the job satisfactorily. Wooden reamers, consisting of a handle topped with a pointed cone, look very professional when wielded behind the bar. This tool should be used in conjunction with a strainer to catch the seeds.

Lever-Pull Juice Extractors: These professional-quality contraptions look wonderful on the bar and do a great job of extracting all the juice from the fruit. The fruit is placed on top of a perforated metal cone; when the lever is pulled downward, a metal cap pushes the fruit onto the cone, and the juice drips down into a glass or other container. If you want to prepare large quantities of juice for use during the day, this type of juicer is highly recommendable; I use it in tandem with a strainer to catch both seeds and the majority of the pulp from the fruit.

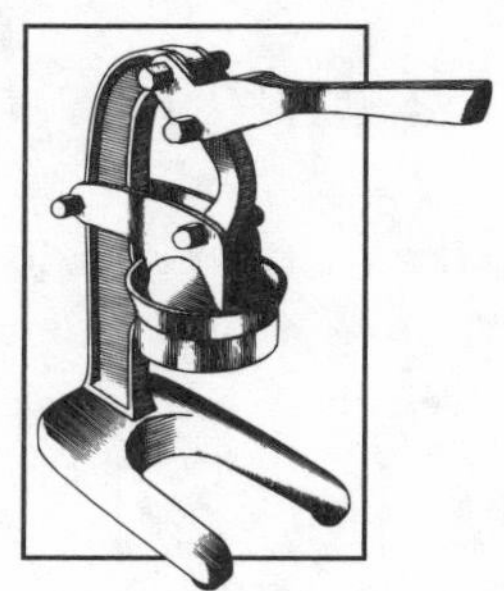

Electric Juicers: Similar in design to glass reamers, the cone on these machines spin around to supposedly make juice extraction easier, but you still have to apply lots of pressure to release the juice. I find these machines unsatisfactory.

Pitchers and Carafes: Glass pitchers and carafes can be used for fruit-juice storage and service.

Juice Bottles: These liter-sized plastic juice bottles have detachable necks fitted with pourers for easy service. The pourer, as well as the lid that screws onto the bottle when the neck is removed, is available in many colors, thus making it possible to color-code your juices.

ICE STORAGE, PREPARATION, AND SERVICE

Ice Buckets: Metal ice buckets are needed for the service of chilled wine. For keeping ice cubes handy, look for a smaller plastic ice bucket fitted with a perforated interior, through which water can drip into the bottom of the container, keeping it separate from the ice. These are useful in a home-bar setting but seldom needed in a professional bar, where ice is usually stored in sinks.

Ice Crushers: Ice can be crushed in a lint-free tea towel using a rubber mallet, or even a rolling pin, but electric and hand-cranked machines are available. The hand-cranked machines can be hard to use, and many electric models are very noisy, so professional bartenders should crush ice prior to service.

Ice Scoop and Tongs: Metal ice scoops make it easy to fill glasses quickly, whereas only one ice cube at a time can be moved with tongs. Nevertheless, in small, tony bars and in home bars, the use of ice tongs is a tasteful touch.

MEASURING DEVICES

Jiggers: Most metal jiggers have two cones, joined at the pointed end; one cone holds 1 ounce, and the other 1½ ounces. The use of jiggers is visually pleasing when precise measurements are needed.

Measuring Spoons: A set of metal or plastic measuring spoons is sometimes necessary for dry ingredients—for example, when a quarter teaspoon of salt is called for in a savory drink.

Measured Pourer: Some pourers are fitted with measuring devices that make sure that the bartender cannot pour more than a certain amount—usually 1½ ounces—without returning the bottle to an upright position and pouring another shot. I hate these devices. They are an insult to the cocktailian.

Bitters Bottles: Commercial brands of bitters are fitted with a device that ensures that only small amounts can be released from the bottle. Antique bitters bottles are available from various sources and are very pleasing to the eye. Empty commercial bitters bottles, once they are thoroughly washed and their labels removed, can be used to dispense absinthe substitutes, Bénédictine, and other strongly flavored ingredients called for in small quantities. Antique bitters bottles, of course, can be used in this fashion, too.

Speed Pourers: Metal (preferred) or plastic (despised) pourers should fit snugly into the neck of bottles for fast, efficient service. Since bottles have varying neck sizes, pourers can be hard to work into some bottles, and can be a little loose in others. Pourers' spouts also vary in width—the larger ones, which pour liquor more quickly, are usually referred to as **California Pourers.** Individual bars should select one specific size and brand of pourer so that bartenders know how quickly the liquor will pour. It will also be pleasing to the eye if every bottle is fitted with the same style of pourer. Pourers should also be affixed to bottles used for lime juice, lemon juice, and simple syrup—ingredients that are normally used in small quantities.

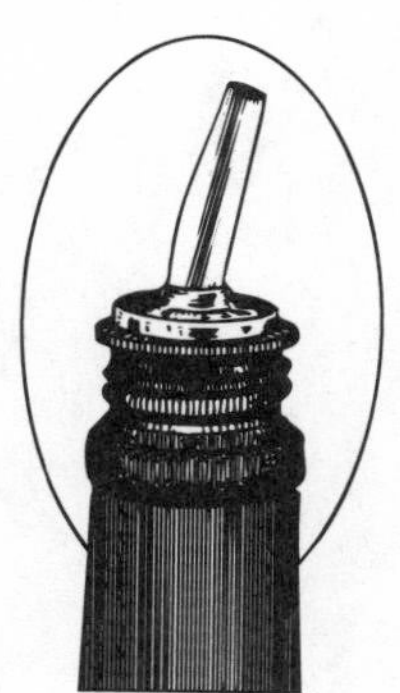

DRINK SERVICE

Sipsticks or Stirrers: These short, thin straws and stirrers (those with no hole through the center) are usually used in Highballs and drinks served on the rocks. They should be stored on or behind the bar, within easy reach of the bartender.

Straws: Various sizes and lengths of drinking straws should be readily available for frozen drinks, Juleps, and many other drinks.

Cocktail Napkins and Coasters: Paper cocktail napkins or sturdier cardboard coasters are placed underneath glasses to absorb condensation and spillage.

Cocktail Picks: Short, pointed, sticks, usually plastic, are used to impale garnishes and are then usually rested on top of the serving glass.

GLASSWARE

The bartender's particular attention must be given to keeping the glassware in a clean, bright condition. The glasses he hands out to the customers for the purpose of allowing them to help themselves, as well as the glasses he uses for mixing drinks, should be without a speck on them.

—HARRY JOHNSON,
New and Improved Bartender's Manual of How to Mix Drinks, 1900

EVERY BAR, whether commercial or in the home, needs a good stock of many styles and sizes of glasses if lots of different drinks are to be served. It's important to think about what drinks will be offered at any bar before investing in glassware. For simplicity and economy, consider using one style of glass for a variety of drinks. Hurricane glasses, for instance, won't be necessary unless you intend to offer Hurricanes, but if you do wish to serve that particular drink, consider using the glasses for all frozen drinks, and perhaps for other tropical-style drinks, such as the Planter's Punch.

It's also advisable to check the space available behind the bar for glass storage—some glasses can be quite tall and might not fit onto your shelves. Also check the space between the beer spigots and the drainage tray so you won't buy beer glasses that don't fit between the two. I can tell you from personal experience that this situation can prove very frustrating. Here's a list of various styles of glassware, along with approximate capacities; be aware, however, that glasses are available in so many shapes and sizes that if you look hard enough, you'll probably be able to find almost any glass in any size.

LIQUOR AND FORTIFIED WINE SERVICE

BRANDY SNIFTER
5–8 ounces

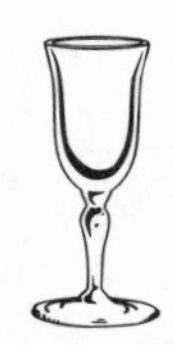

CORDIAL GLASS
2–3 ounces

SHERRY COPITA
3–4 ounces

SHOT GLASS
1–2 ounces

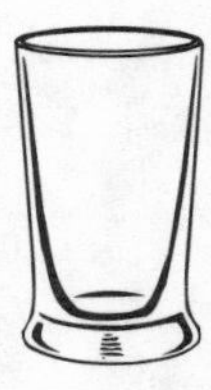

VODKA GLASS
1–3 ounces

WINE SERVICE

CHAMPAGNE FLUTE
6–8 ounces

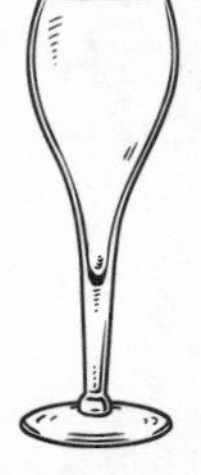

CHAMPAGNE TULIP
6–8 ounces

CHAMPAGNE SAUCER
6–8 ounces

RED-WINE GLASS
8–12 ounces

WHITE-WINE GLASS
8–12 ounces

BEER SERVICE

BEER MUG
10–14 ounces

BRITISH BEER MUG
20 ounces

MIXING GLASS
(also used for beer service) 16 ounces

PILSNER GLASS
10–14 ounces

COCKTAIL AND MIXED-DRINK SERVICE

COCKTAIL OR MARTINI GLASS

4–8 ounces

COLLINS GLASS

8–12 ounces

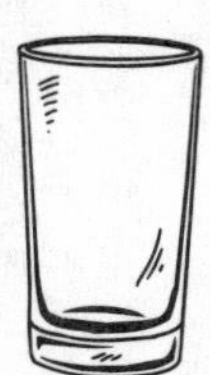

HIGHBALL GLASS

8–10 ounces

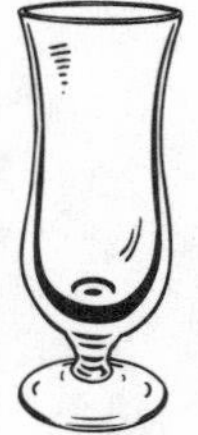

HURRICANE GLASS

14–20 ounces

IRISH COFFEE GLASS

8–10 ounces

OLD-FASHIONED OR ROCKS GLASS

6–8 ounces

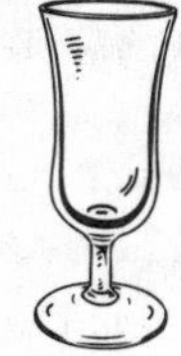

POUSSE-CAFÉ GLASS

2–4 ounces

SOUR GLASS

3–6 ounces

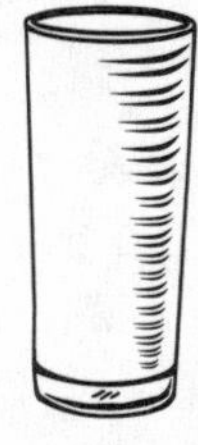

ZOMBIE GLASS

10–12 ounces

BIRDS OF A FEATHER: COCKTAIL AND MIXED-DRINK FAMILIES

A family is a place where minds come in contact with one another. If these minds love one another, the home will be as beautiful as a flower garden. But if these minds get out of harmony with one another, it is like a storm that plays havoc with the garden. If discord arises within one's family, one should not blame others but should examine one's own mind and follow a right path.

—BUDDHA

BY THE END OF THE 1800s many "families" of drinks had been established, but some of the old-master cocktailians disagreed about the correct ingredients needed to make Sours, Daisies, Fixes, Fizzes, and other categories of drinks. After consulting many old cocktail books, I have taken a consensus and have redefined some of the existing families, discarded families that I consider to be arcane, and created new families when I've spotted similarities among a number of cocktails or mixed drinks. Now, why would I want to do that?

My journey to define drink families began when I started to compile notes on how various other writers have described drinks in the past. Paying much attention to the works of Thomas, Johnson, Embury, and Grimes, and consulting with other cocktailians—Ted Haigh being my most frequently used source and mentor—I looked at definitions, then came to arbitrary decisions about which ingredients must be used in order for a drink to belong in a specific group.

It was Ted Haigh, again, who steered me toward creating new families, when he pointed out that the Margarita was nothing more, and certainly nothing less, than a variation on the Sidecar: Both call for a base spirit, a citrus juice, and an orange-flavored liqueur—tequila, lime juice, and triple sec in the first instance, and brandy, lemon juice, and triple sec in the second. There must be more drinks that follow this rule, I thought. And I was right.

The purpose of grouping these drinks together, though, is not merely for the sake of giving them somewhere to hang their hats. In many cases, listing these drinks and their ingredients one under the other—as you will see in the various charts that follow—makes whole strings of drinks far easier to memorize. Once you know the formula for, say, New Orleans Sours, the family in which you'll find the Margarita and the Sidecar, you will understand that the Kamikaze is just a vodka-based Margarita, and that the Cosmopolitan, using citrus vodka as a base, follows the same formula, with just a little cranberry juice thrown in for color. Hopefully, you will be able to use this, and other formulas, when creating drinks of your own.

Not all of the families listed below lend themselves to being arranged in a chart format, but many of the world's most important drinks do, and I hope that these lists will become a valuable learning tool for amateurs and professional alike. If you are seriously interested in becoming a cocktailian bartender who understands the theory of mixed drinks, I urge you to read these definitions carefully. Then, when you make any of the drinks listed in the recipe chapter, check which family it belongs to, and refer back to these definitions so that you'll have a better understanding of exactly why the drink calls for its various components.

My definitions for the following families are sometimes based on historical texts and are sometimes of my own making. Arguments both pro and con can be made in many cases. And remember the first rule of the bartender:

Nothing Is Written in Stone.

BEER- AND CIDER-BASED MIXED DRINKS

This category of mixed drinks doesn't present a great challenge to the cocktailian bartender, but it is important, as always, to achieve balance in these drinks, and much of this depends on the beer being used. I tend to shy away from light-bodied American lagers and opt for microbrewed products, which tend to be sturdier. Sometimes I'll even substitute a pale ale for a lager—the Sierra Nevada bottling is a good choice here.

On the stout front, I'm likely to stick to Guinness for the most part, though Brooklyn Brewery's Black Chocolate Stout is another great choice, and Sam Smith's Imperial Stout is incredibly dry and works well in mixed drinks. For other styles of beer mentioned here, look again to the Sam Smith's line, Brooklyn Brewery, Sierra Nevada, or other smallish breweries with long-standing good reputations.

Definition: Beer- and cider-based mixed drinks contain beer or cider; it doesn't matter what ratio the beer or cider has to any other ingredient or groups of ingredients.

Beer- and cider-based mixed drinks listed in the recipe chapter:

- Black and Tan
- Black Velvet
- Black Velveteen
- Boilermaker
- Dog's Nose
- Lager and Lime
- Pernod and Cider
- Shandy

BOTTLED COCKTAILS

My wife, Mardee, and I experimented with this concept for an article published in *Wine Enthusiast* magazine, December 2000, but it's not our own original idea—Jerry Thomas wrote this about bottled cocktails in 1862: "The 'Cocktail' is a modern invention, and is generally used on fishing and other sporting parties, although some *patients* insist that it is good in the morning as a tonic."

Thomas's "Bottle Cocktail" contained water as an ingredient, presumably to make up for the meltage from ice that would get into the drink if it was stirred or shaken over ice. We, too, added water to our bottled cocktails, and found them to be very successful. The Bottled Cocktails included in the recipe chapter are formulated to fit into 750-milliliter bottles, so I had to tinker a little with ratios. If you experiment with this kind of drink, a good rule of thumb is that the amount of water in the recipe should be approximately equal to one-third of the sum of the other ingredients.

Bottled Cocktails are ideal to make for large parties since, like punch, they leave the host free to mingle, while the guests just help themselves. These drinks can be prepared days prior to the event at which they will be served, and you can keep the drinks at room temperature providing you don't add the water until, say, twelve hours before the party; once the water is added, they must be refrigerated. Without the water, there's enough alcohol in all of the recipes that follow to keep the fruit juices stable for at least three days.

If you are throwing a party, it's best to prepare more than one variety of bottled cocktail so that your guests will have a choice of beverage. For service, it's a good idea to take a large container, big enough to hold at least one bottle of each cocktail, fill it with ice, and arrange the bottles, each fitted with a speed pourer, decoratively—perhaps surrounded by sliced fruits, or even flowers. You can take another ice-filled container and arrange upturned cocktail glasses on top of the ice so that they'll be well chilled when the party begins.

Definition: Bottled cocktails are mixed drinks made for gatherings and parties, usually in advance of the event. Water should be added to the recipe to compensate for the lack of ice meltage present in cocktails mixed in a shaker or mixing glass.

Bottled Cocktails included in the recipe chapter:

Cosmopolitan
Jack Rose Royale
Manhattan
Margarita
Martini, Circa 1900
Sidecar DeLuxe

CHAMPAGNE COCKTAILS

The original Champagne Cocktail, classically made by placing a cube of sugar in the bottom of a champagne flute, soaking it with bitters, and filling the glass with chilled champagne, invites myriad variations. It should be seriously considered as a base for new creations, especially as new spirits and liqueurs are released.

It's quite easy to employ a small amount—say, one-half ounce—of brandy, bourbon, Chartreuse, Bénédictine, or any other liquor or liqueur to make this drink distinctive, but there are other paths you might want to wander, too. If you use bourbon in a Champagne Cocktail, try adding Peychaud's bitters rather than Angostura; if you decide to add cognac, experiment with orange bitters. Another creative twist is to add a spirit *and* a liqueur—for instance, brandy and Grand Marnier—to chilled champagne.

As mentioned in the history chapter, *The Wild West Bartenders' Bible,* by Byron A. and Sharon Peregrine Johnson, noted that in 1886 one Albuquerque bar topped off all of their cocktails with a splash of champagne. This style of champagne cocktail has been making a comeback of late, as you will see in modern-day recipes such as the Old Cuban Cocktail, the Pierce Brosnan, and the Ritz of New York. You can also use classic cocktails, adding, say, one ounce of a Rob Roy, a Manhattan, or a Blood Orange Cocktail to a flute before filling it with champagne. Or you might want to reverse the ratios and top off a cocktail glass almost filled with the primary drink with a splash of champagne. I highly recommend this for both the Manhattan and the Margarita.

It's true that you can use inexpensive bubbly when creating these drinks, since the other ingredients will mask the finer points of better bottlings somewhat, but you can use good champagne, even the very best, and the resultant cocktail will benefit greatly from it. Most important here is which style of champagne you use; since most champagne cocktails contain either a cube of sugar or a sweet liqueur, choose one of the drier bottlings: extra dry, brut, or extra brut (the driest of the three). I have included drinks made with prosecco, an Italian sparkling wine, in the Champagne Cocktail family, but if you don't have any on hand, champagne will suffice.

Definition: Champagne Cocktails are drinks that contain champagne or any other sparkling wine, no matter what ratio the champagne has to any other ingredient or groups of ingredients.

Champagne Cocktails listed in the recipe chapter:

Alfonso
Bellini
B9 Martini
Champagne Cocktail
Esquivel Cocktail
Eve's Seduction Apple Martini
Fallen Angel Cocktail
French 75
Kir Royale
Mimosa
Moon Walk
Nelson's Blood
Old Cuban Cocktail
Pierce Brosnan
Punt e Mes Fizz
Ritz of New York
Seelbach Cocktail
Tbilisi Royale
Tiepolo
Tsar's Champagne Cocktail
Tulio Oro

COBBLERS

This family of drinks was around by the mid-1800s, and although I'm tempted to say that cobblers are now arcane, they do provide a base for creativity and should probably be reconsidered by professional and amateur bartenders alike. The first Cobblers were made by simply adding sugar and either wine or spirits to a glass filled with crushed ice, then decorating the drink with an abundance of fruit.

In the 1950s, David Embury suggested that other sweetening agents, such as pineapple juice or fruit-flavored liqueurs, could be added to Cobblers, and in the late 1990s, famed bartender Dale DeGroff offered Cobblers made by reversing the order of the ingredients and muddling the fruit garnish in the bottom of the glass before building the drink. DeGroff's Bourbon Cobbler was delightful.

I'm not much in favor of using wines, such as sherry, madeira, or champagne, to make Cobblers; I think it best these days to restrict the base to distilled spirits. Try DeGroff's method if you wish—he used lemon, orange, and pineapple as his base fruits. Experiment with different combinations of base spirits and liqueurs or fruit syrups, and remember to garnish these drinks heavily in order to stay true to the concept. Also make sure that the glass is fully filled with crushed ice to form a base for the elaborate garnishes. If you stir Cobblers for a couple of minutes before serving them, a thin sheet of ice should form on the exterior of the glass.

You'll find one true Cobbler recipe in this chapter—the Brandy Cobbler—and you can substitute whiskey or even dark rum to make variations on this drink. I will throw my hat into the ring with Embury on this one, though, and include recipes for Cobblers that call for sweetening agents other than simple syrup in order to illustrate what can be done with these drinks. I've also allowed the Crème de Menthe Frappé to join this family before it drops from sight completely.

Definition: Cobblers call for a base liquor and a sweetening agent, such as simple syrup, grenadine, or a liqueur; they are built in glasses filled to the brim with crushed ice and are garnished with an abundance of fruits.

Cobblers listed in the recipe chapter:

- Bourbon Peach Cobbler
- Brandy Cobbler
- Crème de Menthe Frappé
- French Connection Cobbler
- Jamaican Cobbler

DUOS AND TRIOS

Duos call for two ingredients, usually a spirit and a liqueur; Trios call for cream or a cream liqueur to be added to a Duo to make a whole new drink. Although two-ingredient drinks look simplistic, and some of them are, when one of the ingredients is a complex liqueur, such as Chartreuse, or perhaps a multilayered single-malt scotch, they can be quite intricate.

The drinks in this category, perhaps more than any other, are ideal for experimentation. If a recipe calls for two parts spirit and one part liqueur, for instance, you can easily make a drier, more sophisticated drink by altering the ratios and using far more liquor in relationship to the liqueur. With Trios, it's often possible to substitute a cream liqueur, such as Baileys, for the cream called for in drinks such as the Brandy Alexander, to make an interesting variation. The reason I chose to group these drinks together is far more obvious when you look at the chart on page 166.

Definition: Duos are composed of two ingredients, usually a base spirit and a liqueur, and are normally served in an old-fashioned glass. Trios are Duos to which cream or a cream liqueur has been added. Not all Duos can be made into Trios. Not all Trios start out as Duos.

Duos and Trios listed in the recipe chapter:

- Alaska
- Alexander
- Amaretto Alexander
- Apple Martini
- Black Russian
- Brandy Alexander
- Brave Bull
- Burnet
- Burnished Gold Martini
- Chocolate Martini

Copper Swan Cocktail
Debonair
Dubonnet Cocktail
French Connection
Goddaughter
Godfather
Godmother
Godson
Golden Cadillac
Grasshopper
Irish Peach Cream
Mudslide
Pacific Rim Martini
Pink Squirrel
Planter's Cocktail
Raspberry Martini
Rusty Nail
Starry Night Cocktail
Stinger
Toasted Almond
Tremblement de Terre
White Russian
White Spider

FRENCH-ITALIAN DRINKS

Drinks included in the French-Italian family all contain vermouths, either sweet, dry, or both, or sometimes brand-named products, such as Lillet, an aperitif wine that's closely related to vermouth. The name of this family of drinks is derived from the fact that people used to call sweet vermouth "Italian" and dry vermouth "French," referring to their countries of origin (regardless of where specific bottlings were actually produced).

The French-Italian family is headed by the Manhattan and the Martini; you'll notice that many other classic cocktails—the Rob Roy and the Bronx Cocktail among them—belong here, too. As you look at the recipes, note the similarities as well as the differences between each one; also observe that when these drinks call for gin or vodka as a base, they *usually* employ dry vermouth as the secondary ingredient, whereas the cocktails with a base of whiskey or brandy *normally* call for sweet vermouth as a modifier.

You will find two sets of charts detailing French-Italian drinks on pages 170–175. One set features drinks based on gin and vodka, while the other details whiskey- and brandy-based cocktails; if you compare them, you will discover how similar many of these recipes can be. By soothing the soul of a distilled spirit, vermouth creates a great cornerstone for a cocktail, and can often be successfully used as a base for creative new drinks.

Bitters often come into play in French-Italian drinks, especially when whiskey or brandy is called for as a base, and the creative bartender should always bear that in mind when composing new formulas. By experimenting with Angostura, Peychaud's, or orange bitters, you can change the character of the resultant cocktail quite dramatically.

Definition: French-Italian drinks contain a distilled spirit and sweet or dry vermouth, or sometimes both. They can be modified by other ingredients.

French-Italian drinks with a gin or vodka base listed in the recipe chapter:

Abbey Cocktail
Allies Cocktail
Bermuda Rose Cocktail
Bronx Cocktail
Caricature Cocktail
Chanticleer Cocktail
Claridge Cocktail
Dirty Martini
Gibson
Goldfish Cocktail
Income Tax Cocktail
Martinez
Martini
Maurice Cocktail
Pompier Cocktail

Riveredge Cocktail
The Third Degree, or Martini with a Spot
Vesper Martini

French-Italian drinks with a whiskey or brandy base listed in the recipe chapter:

Algonquin Cocktail
Arawak Cocktail
Black Feather Cocktail
Blackthorne
Blood-and-Sand Cocktail
Bobby Burns Cocktail
CEO Cocktail
Corpse Reviver No. 1
Deadly Sin
Dubliner Cocktail
Manhattan
Manhattan (Dry)
Manhattan (Perfect)
Manhattan (Kentucky's Best)
Millennium Manhattan
Paddy Cocktail
Phoebe Snow Cocktail
Preakness Cocktail
Remember the Maine
Rob Roy
Rob Roy (Dry)
Rob Roy (Perfect)

FROZEN DRINKS

For a frozen drink to be palatable, it's imperative that it have a smooth consistency and be easy to sip through a straw. Unless you have a frozen-drink machine, you'll have to follow the instructions on page 97 to learn how to use a blender properly if you want to make consistently great frozen drinks.

Although most cocktails could be frozen, sweeter drinks are usually the ones that find their way to the blender—I pale at the idea of, say, a frozen Rob Roy. With respect to ice, if you use enough cubes to fill the glass intended for service, you'll find that you end up with the semisolid consistency expected in a frozen drink; but you can vary this with some very interesting results, as can be seen in the Riveredge Cocktail (see page 324), a member of the French-Italian family that is made in a blender but because of its liquid consistency isn't, strictly speaking, a frozen drink. For instance, if you intend to serve the drink in a twelve-ounce glass, you would normally use a total of six ounces of ingredients and a glassful of ice, but if, instead, you use eight ounces of ingredients and enough ice to fill the glass to the halfway mark, you'll find that the drink still fits the glass. Although it will be ice-cold, the consistency will be more liquid than usual, and this makes for very pleasant quaffing.

The recipe section lists some standard frozen drinks, as well as a couple of unusual formulas, but you can modify other recipes, such as the Baileys Chocolate Martini or the the Boston Cream Martini. Formulate the drink by using a glass that holds twice the amount of ingredients called for, and freeze them with one glassful of ice.

Definition: Frozen drinks, made in an electric blender, call for enough ice to achieve a semisolid consistency after being thoroughly blended.

Frozen drinks listed in the recipe chapter:

- Cognac Coulis
- Frozen Banana Colada
- Frozen Banana Daiquiri
- Frozen Chi-Chi
- Frozen Daiquiri
- Frozen Margarita
- Frozen Piña Colada
- Hemingway Daiquiri
- Rum Runner

HIGHBALLS

Patrick Gavin Duffy, author of *The Official Mixer's Guide* (1934), claimed that he had "first brought the Highball to America, in 1895." He went on to say that the Parker House in Boston had previously claimed that distinction, but the *New York Times* of "not many years ago" had given Duffy credit. I must confess, though, that if I had been the first person to think of marrying whiskey and ginger ale, or gin and tonic—both drinks that fit the category—I'm not sure how much fuss I'd make about it.

Highball is a railroad term formerly used to indicate to the conductor on a steam train that there was enough water in the tank, and thus the train could go full speed ahead. The water level was indicated by a ball connected to a float inside the tank, so when the ball was high, the tank was full. In a television documentary that aired in 1999, a guy who'd ridden the rails during the Depression said that when a train was about to leave, "they gave you the highball—that's two shorts [whistle blows] and a long. Man, you better be ready then 'cause he's pulling out." This appeals to me, since the whistle signal could be perverted to mean two shots of liquor and a long drink, such as ginger ale; but why Duffy chose the name, we'll probably never know.

I have listed recipes for Highballs with names that don't easily indicate the ingredients, such as the Dark and Stormy and the Moscow Mule. I've also included popular drinks, such as the Scotch and Soda and Gin and Tonic, but I haven't listed every single combination of spirit and soda, since you can fairly easily figure out these drinks without my help.

There are two subcategories of Highballs: Florida Highballs and New England Highballs. All three Highball families are also detailed in the charts on pages 176–181.

Definition: Highballs are built in highball glasses; they call for a base spirit and a mixer, such as soda or water.

Highballs listed in the recipe chapter:

Bourbon and Branch
Bourbon and Coke
Brandy and Soda
Cuba Libre
Dark and Stormy
Gin and Tonic
Gin Buck
Jack and Coke
Mamie Taylor
Moscow Mule
Pimm's Cup
Presbyterian
Rye and Ginger
Scotch and Soda
Scotch and Water
Seven and Seven
Vodka and Tonic

HIGHBALLS: FLORIDA HIGHBALLS

Florida Highballs are mixed drinks built in a highball glass that contain orange or grapefruit juice but not cranberry juice, since that's the defining ingredient in New England Highballs. You'll understand why I chose to group these drinks together when you see the chart on pages 178–181. Pay close attention to the relationship between Sex on the Beach, a New England highball, and the Fuzzy Navel, its Floridian sister.

Florida highballs included in the recipe chapter:

Alabama Slammer
Black-Eyed Susan
Bocce Ball
Freddie Fudpucker
Fuzzy Navel
Greyhound

- Harvey Wallbanger
- The Salty Chihuahua
- Salty Dog
- Screwdriver
- Sloe Comfortable Screw
- Tequila Sunrise

HIGHBALLS: NEW ENGLAND HIGHBALLS

All New England Highballs contain cranberry juice and are built in a highball glass. These are close relatives of the Florida Highballs, as you'll see when you look at the chart on pages 178–181. Although there are only six drinks in the New England Highball family, it's interesting to note the relationship between the Cape Codder, the Madras, Sex on the Beach, and the Woo Woo.

New England Highballs included in the recipe chapter:

- Bay Breeze
- Cape Codder
- Madras
- Sea Breeze
- Sex on the Beach
- Woo Woo

HOT DRINKS

Most hot drinks are fairly simple to prepare, but some, such as Café Brûlot, require a little skill. Remember, though, when making hot drinks in which spices are called for, to use the freshest ingredients possible in order to extract more flavor. For hot drinks served with cream floating on top, please avoid the use of artificial products.

Hot drinks included in the recipe chapter:

- Café Brûlot
- Hot Buttered Rum
- Hot Toddy
- Irish Coffee
- International Coffees:
  - American Coffee No. 1
  - American Coffee No. 2
  - American Coffee No. 3
  - American Coffee No. 4
  - Caribbean Coffee
  - French Coffee
  - Gaelic Coffee
  - German Coffee
  - Greek Coffee No. 1
  - Greek Coffee No. 2
  - Italian Coffee No. 1
  - Italian Coffee No. 2
  - Italian Coffee No. 3
  - Jamaican Coffee No. 1
  - Jamaican Coffee No. 2
  - Keoke Coffee
  - Mexican Coffee
  - New Orleans Coffee
  - Spanish Coffee

INFUSIONS

You'll find guidance on infusing distilled spirits on pages 98–102, but in the recipe chapter you'll see just five such formulas, and one of those, Minted Simple Syrup, is nonalcoholic. The Lark Creek Inn Tequila Infusion is well worth making, and shows that chefs—Bradley Ogden in this case—can be extremely talented behind the bar.

Infusions included in the recipe chapter:

- Lark Creek Inn Tequila Infusion
- Limecello
- Limoncello
- Raspberry Vodka

JELLY SHOTS

Looked upon by most people as an abomination created by young bartenders in the 1980s, these "drinks" actually date back to at least the mid-1800s. A recipe detailed in Thomas's 1862 book calls for gelatin to be added to a punch made with cognac, rum, and lemon juice. The mixture was then poured into molds and allowed to set. Thomas wrote, "This preparation is a very agreeable refreshment on a cold night, but should be used in moderation. . . . Many persons . . . have been tempted to partake so plentifully of it as to render them somewhat unfit for waltzing or quadrilling after supper."

In more modern times, but still far before the 1980s, Jelly Shots were used by men in the armed forces. *Classic Home Desserts,* a wonderful book by the late, great Richard Sax, details a letter reprinted from the *New York Times* that told a tale about songwriter Tom Lehrer. Apparently, during his army days, from 1954 until 1956, Lehrer made orange-flavored jelly shots spiked with vodka for noncommissioned officers, who weren't allowed alcohol, even at the annual Christmas party.

Of course it's easy to substitute spirits for part of the water when making commercial fruit-flavored jellies, but this is akin to using commercial sweet-and-sour mix in a Margarita. And equally awful. Far better to use unflavored gelatin mixed with spirits, fresh fruit juices, and water. Experiment with classic cocktail recipes and you can make Manhattan Jelly Shots, Mint Julep Jelly Shots, or almost any other drink you care to mention. The secret is to get the proportions of gelatin to spirits and juices correct; the sugar content must also be taken into consideration.

If you make a Jelly Shot by simply adding gelatin to a prepared cocktail and allowing it to set, you'll often find that the resultant shot is too tart. In those cases, it's necessary to add more sugar, in the form of simple syrup, than you would when preparing a mixed drink. Sometimes the simple syrup can take the place of a portion of the water in the recipe.

Water is necessary in Jelly Shots since you won't be shaking or stirring the ingredients over ice; you therefore need to compensate for the water from the ice that would normally have melted into the drink. A general rule of thumb is to add one-third as much water, sometimes in the form of simple syrup, as the sum of the rest of the ingredients.

Unflavored gelatin usually comes in small quarter-ounce packets. This amount is ideal to use with approximately eight ounces of liquid, so for the best results when formulating recipes, try to arrive at amounts that add up to between seven and nine ounces.

Most mixed drinks, when turned into Jelly Shots, are unappealing to the eye. I recommend that you add a couple of drops of food coloring to the recipe, but be careful not to add too much—stir the mixture after every drop and test for color. Coloring also makes the shots easy to distinguish from one another if you make a variety of shots: Green Margarita Shots, Yellow Whiskey Sour Shots, Red Planter's Punch Shots, and so on.

Generally speaking, Jelly Shots will set in a fridge after about two hours, but the results will be better if you leave them overnight. Although it's easier to use ice-cube trays to form your Jelly Shots, I highly recommend the use of a small baking tray—one measuring eight inches by four inches will yield a sheet of shots about a half inch thick if you use eight ounces of ingredients. The sheet of jelly can be cut into cubes with a knife, but I prefer to use small cookie cutters of various shapes, which produces shots that are fun to look at.

Definition: Jelly Shots are drinks gelatinized by the addition of unflavored gelatin.

Jelly Shots included in the recipe chapter:

Banana Daiquiri Jelly Shot
Margarita Jelly Shot
Whiskey Sour Jelly Shot

JULEPS

Although the word *julep* has no true connection to mint, we have come to instantly think of that fragrant herb whenever the word is spoken. The drinks in this family, therefore, all depend on fresh mint as a flavoring agent, or simply as an aromatic garnish.

Juleps included in the recipe chapter:

- Massa Mojito
- Mint Julep No. 1
- Mint Julep No. 2
- Mojito
- Southside Cocktail
- Southside Fizz

MILANESE DRINKS

This is a small but very important family of drinks, all of which call for Campari. Campari is a form of bitters first produced in Milan, circa 1867, by Gaspare Campari, owner of the Café-Patisserie Campari; it's said that you must try this drink three times before you'll enjoy it.

I love Campari, and I've written advertorials for the company on a few occasions—something that's quite easy to do when you truly appreciate the product. This is an underutilized ingredient in modern-day cocktail bars and should be considered for use when you're in a creative mode.

Milanese drinks included in the recipe chapter:

- Americano
- Astor Martini
- Blood Orange
- Negroni
- Teresa
- Valentino
- Valentino (Vodka)

MUDDLED DRINKS

When granulated sugar is muddled with wedges of citrus fruit (see page 90), it can add an extra dimension to some otherwise ordinary potions. The recipe for the Tom Collins, for instance, calls for lemon juice—it's basically no more than gin, lemonade, and club soda, and it's a very refreshing drink. But if, instead of making the Tom Collins with lemon juice squeezed from the fruit, you muddle lemon wedges with granulated sugar, you'll find that the sugar extracts the essential oils from the lemon zest and adds an extra sparkle to the drink. This doesn't happen in every muddled drink; nevertheless, the act of muddling is part of the show for the customer, and it should be performed where you, the bartender, can easily be seen.

Definition: Muddled drinks are made by crushing some of the ingredients with a wooden muddler, or pestle, before adding ice and spirits.

Muddled drinks included in the recipe chapter:

- Caipirinha
- Caipiroska
- Whiskey Old-Fashioned
- Whiskey Old-Fashioned, Fruit-Style
- Whiskey Old-Fashioned (Peach)

Other drinks that call for muddling included in the recipe chapter:

- Massa Mojito: Julep family
- Mojito: Julep family
- Old Cuban Cocktail: Champagne Cocktail family
- Southside Cocktail: Julep family
- Southside Fizz: Julep family

ORPHANS

The thirty-three drinks included here don't fit into any family at all, as far as I can ascertain, so I've labeled them Orphans. Many of the Orphans, such as the Boston Cream Martini, the Glenkinchie Clincher, and the Russian Walnut Martini, are modern-day creations and are quite sweet. Some new cocktails that also fall into the Orphan category—the Dreamy Dorini Smoking Martini, being, perhaps, the prime example—aren't sweet at all, however, and show off the craft of the twenty-first-century cocktailian bartender.

Surprisingly enough, some of the old classics refused to be members of any family that I could figure out, the Sazerac and the Monkey Gland Cocktail among them. These are recipes important to every bartender who wants to have a complete repertoire. Don't ignore the Orphans.

Orphans included in the recipe chapter:

Baileys Chocolate Martini
Banana-Split Martini
Betsy Ross
Blow My Skull Off
Bobbo's Bride Straight Up
Boston Cream Martini
Dreamy Dorini Smoking Martini
Elegant Without Number
Flame of Love
Flirtini Martini
Gimlet
Glenkinchie Clincher
Hawaiian Cocktail
Haymaker Special
Jamaican Ten-Speed
Kentucky Long Shot
Kir
Lewis & Martin Cocktail
Libation Goddess
Mandrintini

Mary Pickford Cocktail
Millennium Cocktail
Monkey Gland Cocktail No. 1
Monkey Gland Cocktail No. 2
Mousques Cocktail
Oatmeal Cookie Cocktail
Royale
Russian Walnut Martini
Satan's Whiskers
Sazerac
Tart Gin Cooler
Tiramisu Martini
White Wine Spritzer

POUSSE-CAFÉS

Pousse-café literally translates as "push the coffee," although the intent is unclear. Did this category of drinks originate as something to "push" the coffee down your throat? Or perhaps, as some people have suggested, the phrase might have originally meant "Push the coffee away, I'll have myself a drink."

Pousse-Cafés are layered drinks (see page 91), and can be quite beautiful, but although some people love making them, others don't think it's worth the time and effort. I normally stand alongside the latter, but drinks like the AWOL have at times persuaded me to join the former group.

Just when people started making these drinks is difficult to determine, but we do know that they were around prior to 1862, since Jerry Thomas included four such drinks in his book from that year. He didn't seem to have a firm grasp on the category, though—below the ingredients for the first recipe, he instructed the bartender to "mix well." However, the book includes an illustration of the Pousse l'Amour, and here we see a conical glass with separate layers of maraschino, vanilla cordial, and brandy. Not visible, though, is the "pure yolk of an egg," which is dropped into the maraschino before the cordial is added.

Definition: Pousse-Cafés are drinks made by floating one ingredient on top of another, or several others, to create a multilayered effect.

Pousse-Cafés included in the recipe chapter:

Angel's Tit
AWOL
B-52
Black-and-White Cocktail
Blue-Eyed Blonde
Fifth Avenue
French-Kiss Shooter

PUNCHES

In *Early American Beverages,* John Hull Brown suggests that the first printed mention of Punches, in New England at least, was in 1682. He goes on to say that the word *punch* comes from the Hindustani *panch,* meaning five, and referring to the number of ingredients used to make it. That, of course, doesn't hold true today, and many Punches have far more than a dozen ingredients.

Punches make life easy for the host at large parties and even small gatherings. The drink is made beforehand, and guests enjoy the ritual of helping themselves whenever they are ready for a second or third drink. It's best to keep punches cold by using large blocks of ice in the bottom of the bowl; these are easily achieved by using thoroughly washed juice or milk cartons, which can be peeled away from the ice without a great deal of effort.

Although water is a necessary ingredient in the vast majority of cocktails, Punches usually contain enough water in the form of fruit juices, or low-alcohol beverages such as wine, to be at their best when first made. Therefore, I recommend that Punches be chilled in the fridge prior to service, helping them stay true to their flavors for a longer period of time, without taking on too much water from the ice.

I have included a couple of Sangrias in the Punch category, and just two classic Punches. The chief reason I have not included more Punch recipes involves space restrictions; I prefer to devote most of that precious space to cocktails and mixed drinks more pertinent to the twenty-first-century bartender. You will find more prepared-in-advance drinks under the heading of Bottled Cocktails (see page 136), and these, I believe, are far more important than Punches.

Definition: Punches are mixed drinks made in large quantities for parties and other social gatherings.

Punches included in the recipe chapter:

- Artillery Punch
- Bolo's Pomegranate Sangria
- Bolo's White Peach Sangria
- Fish House Punch

SNAPPERS

I have grouped all the savory drinks together in the Snapper family because they are all, more or less, based on the Bloody Mary, which was once called the Red Snapper (see page 220). The variations on these drinks are countless, since all sorts of different spices can be married to tomato juice, clam juice, or beef bouillon, and it can be interesting to create cuisine-specific snappers by using, say, cumin and turmeric to make an Indian Bloody Mary, or caraway seeds in conjunction with aquavit for a Swedish-style drink. When making a Snapper, many people like to coat the rim of the glass with Old Bay Seasoning, paprika, salt and pepper, or just about any spice combination you can imagine. Play with all these aspects of drinks in the Snapper family, and you can end up with myriad variations.

Definition: Snappers are mixed drinks made with savory ingredients such as tomato juice, beef bouillon, and clam juice and seasoned with a variety of condiments.

Snappers included in the recipe chapter:

- Bloody Bull
- Bloody Caesar
- Bloody Mary
- Bloody Mary Martini
- Bullshot
- Red Snapper

SOURS

When Jerry Thomas detailed Sours in 1862, he was making them with a base spirit, sugar, water, a quarter of a lemon (the use of which he neglected to mention, but we'll presume he squeezed it), and another "small piece of lemon, the juice of which must be pressed in the glass." By 1887, he had revised his formula and was calling for sugar dissolved in carbonated water, lemon juice, and a spirit. Thomas's rival, Harry Johnson, also used carbonated water to make his sours, but in 1895 George J. Kappeler made an Apple Brandy Sour using gum (simple) syrup, lemon juice, and apple brandy, and that formula fits the one used today by cocktailian bartenders.

The Sour family can be broken down into many different categories. For instance, Sours that are sweetened by grenadine, rather than simple syrup, were once known as Daisies, and Fixes were Sours sweetened by pineapple juice. I have incorporated Daisies and Fixes into the Sour family, and I have devised three more families of Sours: International Sours, New Orleans Sours, and Sparkling Sours, all of which are described below. In the charts on pages 182–195, you can see at a glance the similarities between drinks in these groups.

Definition: Sours contain a base liquor, lime or lemon juice, and a nonalcoholic sweetening agent, such as simple syrup, grenadine, or pineapple juice. If the base of a sour is a liqueur, no additional sweetening agent is required.

Sours included in the recipe chapter:

- Amaretto Sour
- Apple Sidecar
- Apricot Sour
- Bacardi Cocktail
- Bennett Cocktail
- Bolero Cocktail
- Clover Club Cocktail
- Daiquiri
- Delicious Cocktail
- El Presidente
- Fish House Cocktail
- Jack Rose
- Lemon Drop
- Old San Juan Sour
- Pisco Sour
- Scofflaw Cocktail
- Tea Tini
- Tropical Cocktail
- Ward Eight
- Whiskey Sour

SOURS: INTERNATIONAL SOURS

These Sours, sweetened by liqueurs, offer the cocktailian bartender a wonderful opportunity for experimentation. It's possible to take almost any of these recipes and make it your own simply by substituting different liqueurs for the one called for in the formula. I have attempted to display this with the Delmarva Cocktail on page 247; you'll find two variations on the Delmarva, both of which work very well. You can also learn more about this family from the chart on pages 185–188.

Definition: International Sours call for a base liquor and either lime or lemon juice, and are sweetened by a liqueur, another fruit juice, or both.

International Sours included in the recipe chapter:

An Apple a Day
Aviation Cocktail
Bistro Sidecar
Canteen Martini
Charlie Chaplin Cocktail
Chatham Cocktail
Chaya Candy Apple Cosmo
Delmarva Cocktail
Delmarva Cocktail No. 2
Delmarva Cocktail No. 3
Disaronno Margarita
El Floridita No. 1
El Floridita No. 2
English Rose Cocktail
Fernandito Cocktail
Gotham Cocktail
Hop Toad Cocktail
Jockey Club Cocktail No. 2
Kretchma Cocktail
Leap-Year Cocktail
Millionaire Cocktail No. 4
Millionaire's Margarita
Modernista
Paradise Cocktail
A Quick Little Pick-Me-Up
RBS Special Cocktail
Stiletto Cocktail
Twentieth-Century Cocktail

SOURS: NEW ORLEANS SOURS

Discovering this category of drinks was the most exciting thing that happened to me while writing this book. I owe a debt of gratitude to Dr. Cocktail, a.k.a. Ted Haigh, for pointing out that the Sidecar is a variation on the Brandy Crusta, and that the Margarita is also built on the same formula.

The Brandy Crusta first appeared in New Orleans, probably in the first half of the nineteenth century. It was the creation of Joseph Santini (or Santina—reports vary), a restaurateur who once managed the City Exchange, a bar and restaurant where, reportedly, gumbo was first created. The first recorded recipe for the Brandy Crusta appears in Jerry Thomas's 1862 book on mixology; it calls for brandy, curaçao (more or less a sweeter version of triple sec), bitters, simple syrup, and lemon juice. The drink was served in a glass with a sugared rim and a spiral of lemon peel that covered the interior of the glass. Some later recipes for the Brandy Crusta substituted maraschino liqueur for the curaçao. The drink is now arcane, but the formula has spawned many classics, and New Orleans Sours are highly important to the cocktailian bartender.

You will notice that some of the world's greatest cocktails are members of this family, the Sidecar, the Margarita, and the Cosmopolitan among them. Study these drinks carefully, referring to the charts on pages 189–192. Having a grasp of the formula that New Orleans Sours follow is imperative to the cocktailian bartender.

Definition: New Orleans Sours call for a base spirit, lemon or lime juice, and triple sec or another orange-flavored liqueur, such as curaçao.

New Orleans Sours included in the recipe chapter:

Beachcomber Cocktail
Between the Sheets
Big Pine Key Cocktail
Blue Train Cocktail
Cacharita
Calvados Cocktail
Caribbean Cosmopolitan
Cherry Blossom Cocktail
Classic Cocktail
Corpse Reviver No. 2

Cosmopolitan
Crux Cocktail
Deauville Cocktail
Footloose Cocktail
James Joyce Cocktail
Lola Martini
Maiden's Blush Cocktail
Maiden's Prayer Cocktail
Margarita
Marin-i-tini
Metropolitan
Millionaire's Margarita
Oriental Cocktail
Pegu Club Cocktail
Pink Lemonade Cocktail
Rosebud Cocktail
Sage Margarita
Sidecar

SOURS: SPARKLING SOURS

Since relatively few Collinses, Slings, and Fizzes are relevant to the twenty-first-century bartender, I have chosen to group them all together in this family; you'll see how they relate to each other in the chart on pages 193–194. Although Sparkling Sours call for lemon or lime juice, these drinks can instead be made by muddling citrus wedges with granulated sugar, skipping the simple syrup called for in the formula; when the sugar abrades the zest of the fruit, it will release the oils from the zest. Since these drinks are usually served in collins glasses, the muddling can be done in the glass, but I prefer to muddle the fruit and sugar in a mixing glass, add all the ingredients except for the carbonated beverage, and then strain the mixture into an ice-filled collins glass before adding the soda.

Definition: Sparkling Sours contain a base spirit, lemon or lime juice, a sweetening agent, and a carbonated beverage.

Sparkling Sours included in the recipe chapter:

- Apricot Fizz
- Carbonated Piston Slinger
- John Collins
- Long Island Iced Tea
- Maravel Sling
- Pretty in Pink
- Ramos Gin Fizz
- Singapore Sling No. 1
- Singapore Sling No. 2
- Tom Collins

SQUIRREL SOURS

This, I believe, is a whole new genre of cocktails, and it's a result of Mardee insisting that we buy some crème de noyau, a pink almond-flavored liqueur that's readily available in liquor stores but is seldom seen behind bars of the twenty-first century. In March 2002, a friend requested that I make her a drink that was "on the sweet side," so I shook up some Van Gogh Wild Appel vodka with crème de noyau and lemon juice, strained it into an ice-filled collins glass, and topped it with a little club soda. The result was a sparkling sour, quickly dubbed Pretty in Pink, and the process started me thinking: Suppose I substitute crème de noyau for the triple sec in some of the New Orleans Sours? A new category was born. (See the chart on page 195.)

Crème de noyau works best in these drinks, since it delivers such a wonderful pinkish hue, but this is a good category for experimentation with other nut-flavored liqueurs, such as amaretto (also almond-flavored), Frangelico hazelnut liqueur, and Nocello, a walnut-based liqueur.

Definition: Squirrel Sours call for a base spirit, lemon or lime juice, and crème de noyau or another nut-flavored liqueur.

Squirrel Sours included in the recipe chapter:

British Squirrel
Caribbean Squirrel
Dutch Squirrel
French Squirrel
Irish Squirrel
Kentucky Squirrel
Maryland Squirrel
Mexican Squirrel
New Jersey Squirrel
Russian Squirrel
Scottish Squirrel

TROPICAL DRINKS

The tropical-drink craze was started in America by Donn the Beachcomber (real name: Ernest Raymond Beaumont-Gantt), who opened a tiki-themed joint in Hollywood in 1934. "Trader" Vic Bergeron took the concept and ran with it, evidently granting bartenders nationwide permission to throw together lots of fruit juices and three or four different rums, give the resultant drink an exotic name, and consider it a masterpiece. I wonder if he knew what kind of devil he was unleashing onto civilized society.

That said, *some* tropical drinks can be wonderfully refreshing—the Piña Colada, for instance, is a personal favorite—and *some* of these potions are made from well-thought-out formulas. It's important that the cocktailian bartender know how to make the most popular of these drinks, so I have included recipes for those drinks that should be preserved.

Tropical drinks included in the recipe chapter:

Bahama Mama
Fog Cutter
Hurricane
Mai Tai (Original)

Mai Tai No. 2
Piña Colada
Planter's Punch
Scorpion
Zombie No. 1
Zombie No. 2

DUOS AND TRIOS: CHART 1

Of particular note in this family is the bond that ties the Black and White Russians to the Mudslide. Could Baileys be substituted for the cream in any of these Trios? It certainly looks that way.

Godfather	scotch	amaretto	
Godson	scotch	amaretto	cream
Godmother	vodka	amaretto	
Goddaughter	vodka	amaretto	cream
Chocolate Martini	vodka	white crème de cacao	
Alexander	gin	white crème de cacao	cream
Brandy Alexander	cognac	dark crème de cacao	cream
Planter's Cocktail	rum	Godiva Chocolate Liqueur	
Amaretto Alexander	amaretto	white crème de cacao	cream
Pink Squirrel	crème de noyau	white crème de cacao	cream
Golden Cadillac	Galliano	white crème de cacao	cream

Black Russian	vodka	Kahlúa	
White Russian	vodka	Kahlúa	cream
Mudslide	vodka	Kahlúa	Baileys
Brave Bull	tequila	Kahlúa	
Toasted Almond	amaretto	Kahlúa	cream
Stinger	brandy	white crème de menthe	
White Spider	vodka	white crème de menthe	
Grasshopper	white crème de cacao	green crème de menthe	cream
French Connection	cognac	Grand Marnier	
Raspberry Martini	raspberry vodka	Grand Marnier	
Pacific Rim	gin or vodka	ginger liqueur	
Debonaire	scotch	ginger liqueur	

DUOS AND TRIOS: CHART 2

The second chart in this family is composed entirely of Duos, tied together by their base ingredient. The room for expansion in this family is massive.

Tremblement de Terre	cognac	absinthe
Burnished Gold	cognac	Frangelico
Dubonnet Cocktail	gin	Dubonnet
Starry Night	gin	Goldschläger cinnamon schnapps
Alaska	gin	yellow Chartreuse
Apple Martini	gin or vodka	green-apple schnapps
Irish Peach Cream	peach vodka	Baileys
Copper Swan Cocktail	scotch	apricot brandy
Burnet	scotch	cherry brandy
Rusty Nail	scotch	Drambuie

DUOS AND TRIOS: CHART 3

The most important Duos and Trios are in this chart; all are also listed in the previous charts.

Godfather	scotch	amaretto	
Godmother	vodka	amaretto	
Rusty Nail	scotch	Drambuie	
Dubonnet Cocktail	gin	Dubonnet	
Apple Martini	gin or vodka	green-apple schnapps	
Black Russian	vodka	Kahlúa	
White Russian	vodka	Kahlúa	cream
Mudslide	vodka	Kahlúa	Baileys
Toasted Almond	amaretto	Kahlúa	cream
Chocolate Martini	vodka	white crème de cacao	
Alexander	gin	white crème de cacao	cream
Brandy Alexander	cognac	dark crème de cacao	cream
Stinger	brandy	white crème de menthe	
White Spider	vodka	white crème de menthe	
Grasshopper	white crème de cacao	green crème de menthe	cream

FRENCH-ITALIAN FAMILY: GIN AND VODKA: CHART 1

The similarities between the first five drinks here are obvious, but you should also pay attention to the following two, and to the band of three that follow them. The Caricature Cocktail makes a bridge for liqueurs to be introduced to this family, and the remaining drinks omit any fruit juices but remain fairly closely bound.

Dry Martini	gin or vodka	dry vermouth			
Gibson	gin or vodka	dry vermouth			(onion garnish)
Dirty Martini	gin or vodka	dry vermouth			olive brine
Third Degree	gin	dry vermouth			absinthe
Vesper Martini	gin and vodka	Lillet			
Riveredge Cocktail	gin	dry vermouth	orange juice		orange zest and orange bitters
Abbey Cocktail	gin	Lillet	orange juice		Angostura

Bronx Cocktail	gin	dry and sweet vermouth	orange juice		orange bitters
Income Tax Cocktail	gin	dry and sweet vermouth	orange juice		Angostura
Maurice Cocktail	gin	dry and sweet vermouth	orange juice		absinthe
Caricature Cocktail	gin	sweet vermouth	grapefruit juice	triple sec	Campari
Chanticleer	gin	dry vermouth		triple sec	
Claridge Cocktail	gin	dry vermouth		triple sec	apricot brandy
Pompier Cocktail	gin	dry vermouth		crème de cassis	
Goldfish Cocktail	gin	dry vermouth		Danziger goldwasser	
Allies Cocktail	gin	dry vermouth		kümmel	
Martinez	gin	sweet vermouth		maraschino	Angostura
Bermuda Rose	gin	sweet vermouth		apricot brandy	grenadine

FRENCH-ITALIAN FAMILY: GIN AND VODKA: CHART 2

The cocktails in the chart below, which are also listed in the previous chart, are the most important drinks in this family.

Dry Martini	gin or vodka	dry vermouth		
Gibson	gin or vodka	dry vermouth		(onion garnish)
Dirty Martini	gin or vodka	dry vermouth		olive brine
Vesper Martini	gin and vodka	Lillet		
Bronx Cocktail	gin	dry and sweet vermouth	orange juice	orange bitters
Martinez	gin	sweet vermouth	maraschino	Angostura

FRENCH-ITALIAN FAMILY: WHISKEY AND BRANDY: CHART 1

You should pay attention to a number of aspects in these formulas. Note the relationship between the Paddy Cocktail and the Blackthorne; the Bobby Burns and the Preakness; and Remember the Maine and Blood and Sand. Also of note here are the similarities between Deadly Sin, created by a Spanish cocktailian, and the Millennium Manhattan, a creation of Mardee's and mine. Both drinks were conceived independently, but we all went in the same direction. The same thing happened with the Black Feather and the CEO Cocktails, the first created by Robert Hess, the second by Dr. Cocktail.

Paddy Cocktail	Irish whiskey	sweet vermouth		Angostura
Blackthorne	Irish whiskey	sweet vermouth		Angostura and absinthe
Manhattan	bourbon	sweet vermouth		Angostura
Rob Roy	scotch	sweet vermouth		Peychaud's
Phoebe Snow Cocktail	brandy	Dubonnet	absinthe	
Corpse Reviver No. 1	applejack	sweet vermouth	brandy	
Bobby Burns	scotch	sweet vermouth	Bénédictine	
Preakness Cocktail	bourbon	sweet vermouth	Bénédictine	Angostura
Remember the Maine	bourbon	sweet vermouth	cherry brandy	Angostura and absinthe

FRENCH-ITALIAN FAMILY: WHISKEY AND BRANDY: CHART 1 *(CONTINUED)*

Blood and Sand	scotch	sweet vermouth	cherry brandy	orange juice
Dubliner	Irish whiskey	sweet vermouth	Grand Marnier	orange bitters
Deadly Sin	bourbon	sweet vermouth	maraschino	orange bitters
Millennium Manhattan	bourbon	sweet vermouth	peach schnapps	Angostura
Algonquin Cocktail	rye whiskey	dry vermouth	pineapple juice	
Arawak Cocktail	bourbon	dry vermouth	pineapple juice	tamarind juice and Angostura
Princess Mary's Pride	applejack	dry vermouth	Dubonnet	
Black Feather Cocktail	brandy	dry vermouth	triple sec	Angostura
CEO Cocktail	brandy	Lillet Blonde	crème de cassis	orange bitters

FRENCH-ITALIAN FAMILY: WHISKEY AND BRANDY: CHART 2

This quartet of cocktails includes the most important drinks in this family.

Manhattan	bourbon	sweet vermouth		Angostura
Rob Roy	scotch	sweet vermouth		Peychaud's
Bobby Burns	scotch	sweet vermouth	Bénédictine	
Blood and Sand	scotch	sweet vermouth	cherry brandy	orange juice

HIGHBALLS

This is, by definition, a simple family of drinks, and most of these formulas are obvious from the name of the drink. Note the lime juice in both the Gin Rickey and the Cuba Libre; it can be incorporated by squeezing extra wedges into the glass or by the addition of fresh juice, but it's an integral part of both drinks.

Bourbon and Branch	bourbon	bottled water	
Bourbon and Coke	bourbon	Coca-Cola	
Brandy and Soda	brandy	club soda	
Gin Rickey	gin	club soda	lime juice
Gin Buck	gin	ginger ale	
Gin and Tonic	gin	tonic water	
Jack and Coke	Jack Daniel's	Coca-Cola	
Pimm's Cup	Pimm's No. 1	ginger ale, lemon-lime soda, or club soda	
Cuba Libre	rum	cola	lime juice

Dark and Stormy	rum	ginger beer	
Presbyterian	rye whiskey	ginger ale, club soda	
Rye and Ginger	rye whiskey	ginger ale	
Scotch and Water	scotch	bottled water	
Scotch and Soda	scotch	club soda	
Mamie Taylor	scotch	ginger ale	
Seven and Seven	Seagram's Seven-Crown whiskey	7UP	
Moscow Mule	vodka	ginger beer	
Vodka and Tonic	vodka	tonic water	

FLORIDA HIGHBALLS

It's easy to see how these drinks come together as a family. It's also quite obvious that if one were to start substituting different liqueurs in some of these drinks, the family could explode.

Screwdriver	vodka		orange juice		
Fuzzy Navel	vodka	peach schnapps	orange juice		
Harvey Wallbanger	vodka	Galliano	orange juice		
Freddie Fudpucker	tequila	Galliano	orange juice		
Tequila Sunrise	tequila	grenadine	orange juice		

Bocce Ball			amaretto	orange juice	
Sloe Comfortable Screw	vodka	sloe gin	amaretto	orange juice	
Alabama Slammer	Southern Comfort	sloe gin	amaretto	orange juice	
Black-Eyed Susan	vodka	rum	triple sec	orange juice, pineapple juice	
Greyhound	vodka			grapefruit juice	
Salty Dog	vodka			grapefruit juice	salt-rimmed glass
Salty Chihuahua	tequila			grapefruit juice	salt-rimmed glass
Muddy Waters	rum			grapefruit juice	lime wedges

NEW ENGLAND HIGHBALLS

The New Englanders are a small family, but it's fun to look at how secondary juices are introduced; then comes peach schnapps, and finally the Woo Woo holds on to the schnapps but decides against a second juice.

Cape Codder	vodka		cranberry juice	
Sea Breeze	vodka		cranberry juice	grapefruit juice
Bay Breeze	rum		cranberry juice	pineapple juice
Madras	vodka		cranberry juice	orange juice
Sex on the Beach	vodka	peach schnapps	cranberry juice	orange juice
Woo Woo	vodka	peach schnapps	cranberry juice	

FLORIDA MEETS NEW ENGLAND

This small chart points out what can happen to Floridian Highballs when they visit New England.

Greyhound	Florida	vodka			grapefruit juice
Sea Breeze	New England	vodka		cranberry juice	grapefruit juice
Fuzzy Navel	Florida	vodka	peach schnapps		orange juice
Sex on the Beach	New England	vodka	peach schnapps	cranberry juice	orange juice

SOURS: CHART 1

In this, the first of the Sour families, it's best to separate the drinks by base liquor—you can see at a glance how similar many of these drinks are. The curveball here is the Jack Rose, which I placed among the rums just to illustrate that it's a Bacardi Cocktail made with applejack as a base.

Amaretto Sour	amaretto		lemon juice	
Apricot Sour	apricot brandy		lemon juice	
Delicious Cocktail	gin		lime juice	simple syrup
Bennett Cocktail	gin		lime juice	simple syrup, Angostura
Clover Club	gin	egg white	lemon juice	raspberry syrup
Daiquiri	rum		lime juice	simple syrup
Bacardi Cocktail	rum (Bacardi)		lime juice	grenadine
Jack Rose	applejack		lemon juice	grenadine
El Presidente	rum		lime juice, pineapple juice	grenadine

Tropical Cocktail	rum		lime juice, pineapple juice	grenadine, Angostura
Old San Juan Sour	rum	cranberry juice	lime juice	simple syrup
Fish House Cocktail	rum and brandy	peach brandy	lime juice, lemon juice	simple syrup
Bolero Cocktail	rum and brandy	orange juice	lime juice	simple syrup
Apple Sidecar	vodka	apple brandy	lemon juice	tangerine juice
Lemon Drop	citrus vodka		lemon juice	simple syrup
Tea Tini	orange vodka		lemon juice	sweet iced tea
OP Lemonade	OP vodka	peach puree	lemon juice	simple syrup
Whiskey Sour	bourbon		lemon juice	simple syrup
Scofflaw Cocktail	bourbon	dry vermouth	lemon juice	grenadine, orange bitters
Ward Eight	rye whiskey	orange juice	lemon juice	grenadine
Pisco Sour	pisco brandy	egg white	lemon juice	simple syrup, Angostura

SOURS: CHART 2

The Sours in this chart, which also appear on the previous chart, are the most important drinks in this family.

Amaretto Sour	amaretto		lemon juice	
Apricot Sour	apricot brandy		lemon juice	
Daiquiri	rum		lime juice	simple syrup
Bacardi Cocktail	rum (Bacardi)		lime juice	grenadine
Jack Rose	applejack		lemon juice	grenadine
Lemon Drop	citrus vodka		lemon juice	simple syrup
Whiskey Sour	bourbon		lemon juice	simple syrup
Pisco Sour	pisco brandy	egg white	lemon juice	simple syrup, Angostura

INTERNATIONAL SOURS: CHART 1

When these drinks are arranged by the secondary ingredient, their similarities immediately become apparent.

Stiletto	bourbon	amaretto		lime juice	
Disaronno Margarita	tequila	amaretto		lime juice	
Jockey Club Cocktail	gin	amaretto		lemon juice	Angostura
Delmarva No. 3	rye whiskey	amaretto	dry vermouth	lemon juice	
Canteen Martini	rum	amaretto	Southern Comfort	lime juice	
Charlie Chaplin		apricot brandy	sloe gin	lime juice	
Millionaire Cocktail No. 4	rum	apricot brandy	sloe gin	lime juice	
Hop Toad	rum	apricot brandy		lime juice	Angostura
English Rose	gin	apricot brandy	dry vermouth	lemon juice	grenadine
Paradise Cocktail	gin	apricot brandy	orange juice	lemon juice	

INTERNATIONAL SOURS: CHART 1 ***(CONTINUED)***

Twentieth-Century Cocktail	gin	white crème de cacao	dry vermouth	lemon juice	
Delmarva No. 2	rye whiskey	white crème de cacao	dry vermouth	lemon juice	
El Floridita No. 2	rum	white crème de cacao	sweet vermouth	lime juice	grenadine
Kretchma Cocktail	vodka	white crème de cacao		lemon juice	grenadine
Aviation Cocktail	gin	maraschino liqueur		lemon juice	
El Floridita No. 1	rum	maraschino liqueur		lime juice	simple syrup
An Apple a Day	gin	maraschino liqueur	apple liqueur	lime juice, grapefruit juice	simple syrup
Millionaire's Margarita	tequila	Grand Marnier		lime juice	
Leap-Year Cocktail	gin	Grand Marnier	sweet vermouth	lemon juice	

INTERNATIONAL SOURS: CHART 2

The remaining International Sours.

Chatham Cocktail	gin	ginger liqueur		lemon juice	
Delmarva Cocktail	rye whiskey	white crème de menthe	dry vermouth	lemon juice	
Gotham Cocktail	brandy	crème de cassis	dry vermouth	lemon juice	
Modernista	scotch and rum	absinthe		lemon juice	orange bitters
RBS Special	rye whiskey	kümmel		lemon juice	grenadine
A Quick Little Pick-Me-Up	bourbon	Branca Menta		lemon juice	simple syrup
Fernandito	spiced rum	Chambord		lime juice, orange juice	
Bistro Sidecar	brandy	Tuaca	Frangelico	lemon juice, tangerine juice	
Chaya Candy Apple Cosmo	apple vodka	Cuarenta y Tres		lime juice, cranberry juice	

INTERNATIONAL SOURS: CHART 3

All these formulas are listed on the previous two charts, but these are the most important International Sours to the cocktailian bartender.

Stiletto	bourbon	amaretto		lime juice	
Aviation Cocktail	gin	maraschino liqueur		lemon juice	
Twentieth-Century Cocktail	gin	white crème de cacao	dry vermouth	lemon juice	
Millionaire Cocktail No. 4	rum	apricot brandy	sloe gin	lime juice	
El Floridita No. 1	rum	maraschino		lime juice	simple syrup
El Floridita No. 2	rum	white crème de cacao	sweet vermouth	lime juice	grenadine

NEW ORLEANS SOURS: CHART 1

It's obvious that this is a very important family—look who's here: the Margarita, the Sidecar, the Cosmopolitan, the Metropolitan, and the Kamikaze. This chart displays how relatively simple it is to take a proven formula and run with it.

Margarita	tequila	triple sec		lime juice	
Sidecar	brandy	triple sec		lemon juice	
Cacharita	pisco brandy	triple sec		lime juice	
Deauville Cocktail	brandy and applejack	triple sec		lemon juice	
Crux Cocktail	brandy	triple sec	Dubonnet Rouge	lemon juice	
Classic Cocktail	brandy	triple sec	maraschino liqueur	lemon juice	
Cherry Blossom	brandy	triple sec	cherry brandy	lemon juice	
East India Cocktail	brandy	triple sec	pineapple juice	lemon juice	Angostura
Calvados Cocktail	calvados	triple sec	orange juice	lemon juice	orange bitters
Kamikaze	vodka	triple sec		lime juice	
Footloose Cocktail	raspberry vodka	triple sec		lime juice	Peychaud's
Cosmopolitan	citrus vodka	triple sec	cranberry juice	lime juice	
Metropolitan	currant vodka	triple sec	cranberry juice	lime juice	
Rosebud Cocktail	citrus vodka	triple sec	grapefruit juice	lime juice	
Marin-i-tini	vodka	triple sec	peach schnapps	lime juice	blue curaçao
Lola Martini	OP vodka	triple sec	cranberry juice	lime juice	elderflower syrup

NEW ORLEANS SOURS: CHART 2

The rest of the New Orleans Sours. It's no coincidence that both whiskey-based drinks in this family call for sweet vermouth; the James Joyce was based on the Oriental.

Mount Gay Rumrita	rum	triple sec		lime juice	
Missing Link	rum	triple sec		lemon juice	
Between the Sheets	rum and brandy	triple sec		lemon juice	
Caribbean Cosmopolitan	citrus rum	triple sec	cranberry juice, pineapple juice	lime juice	Angostura
Beachcomber Cocktail	rum	triple sec	maraschino liqueur	lime juice	

Big Pine Key Cocktail	gin	triple sec		lime juice	
Pegu Club Cocktail	gin	triple sec		lime juice	Angostura and orange bitters
Maiden's Blush Cocktail	gin	triple sec	grenadine	lemon juice	
Corpse Reviver No. 2	gin	triple sec	Lillet	lemon juice	absinthe
Maiden's Prayer	gin	triple sec	orange juice	lemon juice	Angostura
James Joyce Cocktail	Irish whiskey	triple sec	sweet vermouth	lime juice	
Oriental Cocktail	rye whiskey	triple sec	sweet vermouth	lime juice	

NEW ORLEANS SOURS: CHART 3

All these formulas are in Chart 1, but these are the most important drinks in the New Orleans Sour family—a six-pack that every cocktailian bartender should know.

Margarita	tequila	triple sec		lime juice
Sidecar	brandy	triple sec		lemon juice
Kamikaze	vodka	triple sec		lime juice
Cosmopolitan	citrus vodka	triple sec	cranberry juice	lime juice
Metropolitan	currant vodka	triple sec	cranberry juice	lime juice
Pink Lemonade	citrus rum	triple sec	cranberry juice	lemon juice

SPARKLING SOURS

As you can see from this chart, Tom and John Collins have a third brother in the Sloe Gin Fizz. Those three drinks, along with the Singapore Sling No. 2 and the Long Island Iced Tea, are the most important drinks in this family. The Ramos Gin Fizz is also a handy formula to have memorized.

Apricot Fizz	apricot brandy			lemon juice	club soda	
John Collins	bourbon	simple syrup		lemon juice	club soda	
Tom Collins	gin	simple syrup		lemon juice	club soda	
Sloe Gin Fizz	sloe gin	simple syrup		lemon juice	club soda	
Carbonated Piston Slinger	rum	sloe gin		lime juice	club soda	
Pretty in Pink	Van Gogh Wild Appel Vodka	crème de noyau		lemon juice	club soda	

SPARKLING SOURS ***(CONTINUED)***						
Long Island Iced Tea	vodka, gin, rum, and tequila	triple sec		lemon juice	cola	
Singapore Sling No. 1	gin	Bénédictine	kirsch	lemon juice	club soda	Angostura and orange bitters
Singapore Sling No. 2	gin	Bénédictine and triple sec	cherry brandy	lime juice, pineapple juice	club soda	Angostura
Ramos Gin Fizz	gin	simple syrup		lime juice, lemon juice	club soda	cream, egg white, orange-flower water
Maravel Sling	gin	Bénédictine		lemon juice, mango nectar	club soda	Angostura, tamarind juice

SQUIRREL SOURS

This simple category is easy to remember. I named the drinks for the country or state most representative of the base spirit; the "squirrel," of course, is derived from the nutty flavor of crème de noyau.

British Squirrel	gin	crème de noyau	lime juice
Caribbean Squirrel	rum	crème de noyau	lemon juice
Dutch Squirrel	Van Gogh Wild Appel Vodka	crème de noyau	lemon juice
French Squirrel	brandy	crème de noyau	lemon juice
Irish Squirrel	Irish whiskey	crème de noyau	lemon juice
Kentucky Squirrel	bourbon	crème de noyau	lemon juice
Maryland Squirrel	rye whiskey	crème de noyau	lemon juice
Mexican Squirrel	tequila	crème de noyau	lime juice
New Jersey Squirrel	applejack	crème de noyau	lemon juice
Russian Squirrel	vodka	crème de noyau	lime juice
Scottish Squirrel	scotch	crème de noyau	lemon juice

THE RECIPES

It is only fitting that the subject of cocktails should be approached with levity slightly tinctured with contempt because, for every good compound, arrangement, or synthesis of liquors, wines, and their adjacent or opposite fruits and flavors chilled and served in a variety of glasses, there are approximately a million foul, terrifying, and horrendous similar excitements to stupefaction, cuspidor hurling, and nausea.

—LUCIUS BEEBE, 1945

WHEN COMPILING COCKTAIL and mixed-drink recipes, the writer is always faced with having to decide the order in which to list them. When I first wrote the recipe chapter, I put the drinks into categories, or families of drinks, and listed them under each family's heading. After a while, however, this method got too confusing, and I decided that listing the drinks alphabetically made more sense. The only curveball you're likely to find here involves variations on a drink. For instance, the Dry Rob Roy is listed right after the Rob Roy and is headed "Rob Roy (Dry)." In the previous chapter you'll find charts detailing most, but not all, of the drink families into which I have divided the drinks. In each recipe, I have included the family to which the drink belongs, and I strongly urge you to read about each family before constructing any drink included here.

THE CHOSEN MANY

There are over 350 recipes in this chapter. How did I decide which drinks to include and which to leave by the wayside? I started with a list of well over a thousand drinks, and initially I chose the obvious—the Martini, the Manhattan, and all the drinks that are regularly ordered in twenty-first-century bars. The next step was to research old books looking for drinks that are seldom ordered but had formulas that *looked* as though they would work for today's consumers.

Next I took advice from my cocktailian friends at DrinkBoy.com, who constantly experiment with old recipes and often write lists of their all-time favorites. And finally I pleaded with bartenders, both amateur and professional; restaurateurs; and friends to submit recipes for their own creations.

Then came the testing phase, and that was the point at which many drinks bit the dust. Others, some of which looked as though they didn't deserve a clean glass, grabbed my attention, and appear in these pages.

BRAND NAMES

For the most part I have called for generic ingredients in these recipes, but there are exceptions. If I have personally formulated a drink to be made with a specific brand-name product and if I believe that it's important to use that product in that particular drink, then I've used the brand name. This happens far more often with whiskeys than any other spirit.

If a recipe has been formulated at the request of a specific company, whether by the company itself (although it's a rare spirits company that creates well-balanced drinks), by me, or by other bartenders or consultants, I have included the brand name and discussed the origin of the drink in the headnote.

Have I worked for any company in the spirits industry? Yes—many times. Have I ever represented a brand that I don't believe to be of high quality? No—I have turned down work when I haven't believed in the product concerned. Most spirits companies have many products, and it's a rare firm that issues only the best of the best, so even though I might have taken on projects involving one specific brand, there's a good possibility that I have also said negative things about other brands issued by that company. Why do these companies put up with this sort of behavior? Because if I told you I liked everything they had to offer, you would never know when to believe me. Do I have a favorite spirits company? No, but I do have favorite friends within many of these firms.

Triple Sec

Triple sec is such an important ingredient in many recipes that for years I have taken a stand, saying that Cointreau is the best bottling of triple sec on the market, bar none. At the time of this writing, Van Gogh O'Magnifique triple sec has just been introduced. It is issued at 80 proof (the same proof as Cointreau), and it equals Cointreau in quality, as far as I'm concerned. I highly recommend that you use either of these bottlings wherever triple sec is called for in a recipe. (The owner of Van Gogh and the brand manager for Cointreau are both acquaintances of mine, but I have no financial stake in either product.)

Absinthe Substitute

Since absinthe is illegal in the United States, we must use substitutes for this anise-flavored spirit. The main choices of brand names are Absente, Herbsaint, Pernod, and Ricard. Absente is by far the driest of these bottlings, but dryness isn't always what to look for when constructing cocktails. Any one of these products can be used when an absinthe substitute is called for in a recipe, and you should learn to adjust quantities depending on which bottling you use.

DATES

Wherever possible, I have included the birthdates of individual cocktails, but although some of these dates are absolutely verifiable, in other cases, as I have noted, they refer only to the first printed mention I have been able to find. My library of vintage cocktail books is extensive but by no means complete; I welcome any information that challenges the dates used here.

INGREDIENTS AND RATIOS

It's important to note that even though I might refer to a certain book as having detailed specific drinks, the recipe that follows is not necessarily the exact formula in the original drink. For the most part, ratios have been altered to suit today's tastes, and at times I have substituted certain ingredients—usually because the original spirit or liqueur is no longer available or is very hard to find.

NAMES AND CREATORS

As discussed on page 69, ingredients for almost every cocktail can vary from bar to bar, and drinks calling for the exact same formulas can masquerade under different names in different places. The recipes in this chapter detail the ingredients that I believe to be correct, or at least each recipe is the best of the various versions I have tested; and wherever possible, I have credited the person who I believe created the drink.

MEASUREMENTS

All the measurements given in these recipes are based on specific sizes of glasses; in the case of drinks served on ice, I have arbitrarily chosen to assume that ice will take up one-half of the space in the glass. This is not an absolute fact, of course, since the space taken up by ice will vary depending on whether you're using crushed ice, the size of the ice cubes, and how the ice cubes fall into the glass. Remember, too, that a cocktail made with three ounces of ingredients, after being stirred or shaken over ice, will result in a four-ounce drink. You should also note that the cocktail glasses specified here will not be filled to the brim if you use the amounts given in the recipe. This makes the glass much easier to handle.

Here are the sizes of the glasses I used when formulating these recipes:

collins glass: 12 ounces
highball glass: 10 ounces
champagne flute: 6 ounces
cocktail glass: 5 ounces
old-fashioned glass: 8 ounces
sour glass: 3 ounces
beer glass: 16 ounces
Irish coffee glass: 8 ounces
pousse-café glass: 4 ounces
wine glass: 8 ounces

THE MOST IMPORTANT LESSON FOR THE COCKTAILIAN BARTENDER

I strongly believe that bartenders should not follow recipes precisely. They should learn to be able to feel their way around a drink by developing a keen taste memory for ingredients, or should actually taste all the ingredients in a drink before putting them together. I have worked with students who had no prior cocktailian experience, and I have observed them successfully utilizing this method of making drinks after as little as two days' instruction.

That said, the fact is that recipes must have measurements; but in the vast majority of cases, I hope that you will regard them as mere guidelines. You must learn to alter proportions when making drinks such as the Rob Roy, since the ratios depend on which particular bottling of scotch you use, and you should learn to vary proportions in order to satisfy individual tastes. Again, never forget:

Nothing Is Written in Stone.

APPROPRIATE GLASSWARE

All of the recipes here call for specific glasses to be used. These are the glasses that most bartenders will automatically reach for when the drink is ordered, but don't think for a moment that you *must* use that type of glass. Most drinks served in cocktail glasses can also be presented in an ice-filled old-fashioned glass, and some cocktails can be transformed into Highballs by increasing the amount of the fruit juice called for. The Blood and Sand Cocktail is a good example of this: I often increase the orange juice component in this drink and serve it as a Highball with lunch or brunch—it's far more interesting than, say, a Screwdriver. And as for cocktail glasses, I personally detest them, and far prefer to serve cocktails in champagne flutes.

METHODOLOGY

Instead of repeating specific instructions over and over again on how to make each drink included in this chapter, I have elected to provide one set of instructions here. The key words in each recipe will indicate which instructions to follow. For instance, if you see **STIR AND STRAIN** into a chilled cocktail glass," simply follow the directions given below under the heading *stir and strain.* For discussions of all methods of mixing drinks, refer to the chapter entitled "The Craft of the Mixologist."

Build

Fill the glass with ice, if called for, and add the ingredients in the order given. Add any garnish called for, stir briefly, and serve.

Float

After making the drink, float the last ingredient on top by pouring it slowly over the back of a barspoon.

Layer

Pour the first ingredient into the glass. Then slowly pour each of the other ingredients, in the order given, over the back of a barspoon, so that each successive ingredient floats on top of the previous ingredient.

Mix and Chill

Combine the ingredients in a large container, stir thoroughly, and store the container in a refrigerator until well chilled.

Muddle

Put the ingredients into an empty glass and grind them with a muddler until all the juices have been extracted from the fruit and any sugar in the recipe is completely dissolved.

Rinse

Pour the ingredient called for into the glass and, by tilting the glass and rotating it at the same time, coat the entire interior of the glass. Discard any excess.

Shake and Strain

Fill a shaker two-thirds full of ice and add the ingredients in the order given. Shake for approximately fifteen seconds and strain the drink into the appropriate glass.

Stir and Strain

Fill a mixing glass two-thirds full of ice and add the ingredients in the order given. Stir for approximately thirty seconds, then strain the drink into the appropriate glass.

Yield

Unless otherwise noted, each recipe makes one drink.

ABBEY COCKTAIL

FAMILY: **FRENCH-ITALIAN: GIN AND VODKA** ~ Originally developed in the 1930s, this drink works well with Peychaud's bitters instead of Angostura; also, orange bitters may be either substituted for or used in conjunction with the Angostura bitters. The ratios can easily be tinkered with here, but the gin should remain predominant.

1½ ounces gin
¾ ounce Lillet
¾ ounce fresh orange juice
2 dashes Angostura bitters

SHAKE AND STRAIN into a chilled cocktail glass.

ALABAMA SLAMMER

FAMILY: **FLORIDA HIGHBALLS** ~ There are many different recipes for this drink, which is normally served as a shooter, but the main base ingredients are usually equal measures of amaretto, sloe gin, and Southern Comfort. The Highball version works well as a brunch drink.

MAKES FIVE SHOOTERS OR ONE HIGHBALL

1 ounce sloe gin
1 ounce amaretto
1 ounce Southern Comfort
2 ounces fresh orange juice

SHAKE AND STRAIN into an ice-filled highball glass, or five shot glasses.

ALASKA

FAMILY: **DUOS AND TRIOS** ~ Experiment with ratios when preparing this drink. Chartreuse can easily overpower other ingredients, and it's vital to consider which brand of gin you are using. Tanqueray, for example, will stand up to more Chartreuse than, say, Bombay will.

1½ ounces gin
½ ounce yellow Chartreuse

STIR AND STRAIN into a chilled cocktail glass.

ALEXANDER

FAMILY: **DUOS AND TRIOS** This mixture of gin, crème de cacao, and cream was devised prior to 1917. Mixing gin and chocolate might sound strange, but the combination is delicious; the best result of this mixture can be seen in the Twentieth-Century Cocktail (see page 346).

2 ounces dry gin
1 ounce white crème de cacao
1 ounce cream

SHAKE AND STRAIN into a chilled cocktail glass.

A rehearsal of "Red, Hot and Blue!" was in progress. The star of the show, Jimmy Durante, sat on a shaky chair tilted against the bare bricks in the back wall of the stage. He looked as if he were trying to get as far away from other humans as possible. His face was haggard. When he took his cigar out of his big, ragged mouth his hands shook.

"I can't drink," he said, shivering. "Only my great sense of responsibility forced me to show up at the pickle works today. I can't drink. It's alright if I take a glass of vermoot, or some red wine. Yeh, that's all right. But last night I'm feeling thirsty, so I go to this joint across the street and I say to the bartender, 'recommend me something.' So he give me what he called an Alexander. I had about six of these Alexanders, and I get dizzy. When I go home I hit the bed and it whirls around like an electric fan. I am seasick. I'm in an awful fix. I want to die."

—JOSEPH MITCHELL, *MY EARS ARE BENT*

ALFONSO

FAMILY: **CHAMPAGNE COCKTAILS** This drink dates back to at least 1930, when it was detailed in Harry Craddock's *The Savoy Cocktail Book*. The recipe there, though, calls for a now-defunct brand of bitters known as Secrestat. Use less Dubonnet for a sweeter drink.

1 sugar cube soaked in Angostura bitters
1 ounce Dubonnet Rouge
4½ ounces chilled champagne
1 lemon twist, for garnish

BUILD in the order given in a champagne flute. Add the garnish.

ALGONQUIN COCKTAIL

FAMILY: **FRENCH-ITALIAN: WHISKEY AND BRANDY** ~ I always thought that this drink had been created in the 1930s, when the renowned literati of the time frequented what was know as the Round Table for fun, frivolity, and many, many cocktails. However, I can't find reference to it in its present form until the 1980s. There's a recipe for an Algonquin Special in a 1945 book, but it's made with sherry and port, and the Algonquin Cocktail detailed in *Ted Saucier's Bottoms Up* (1951), which the author says came from the hotel, is composed of light rum, blackberry brandy, Bénédictine, and lime juice.

This is one of those recipes that calls for precision pouring lest the drink get out of balance. The recipe I chose to use was devised by Ted Haigh—Dr. Cocktail himself.

1½ ounces straight rye whiskey
¾ ounce dry vermouth
¾ ounce pineapple juice

STIR AND STRAIN into a chilled cocktail glass.

ALLIES COCKTAIL

FAMILY: **FRENCH-ITALIAN: GIN AND VODKA** ~ Adapted from a recipe in Harry Craddock's *The Savoy Cocktail Book* (1930). The caraway flavors of kümmel can overpower this drink if too much is used, so be careful with it unless you love caraway.

2 ounces gin
1 ounce dry vermouth
¼ ounce kümmel

STIR AND STRAIN into a chilled cocktail glass.

AMARETTO ALEXANDER

FAMILY: **DUOS AND TRIOS** ~ I have no idea when this drink was created or who first put the ingredients together, but it was a good idea. This drink is made up of two liqueurs, thus not quite fitting the category, but it belongs here with its sibling Alexanders. Experiment with ratios until you find your favorite formula.

2 ounces amaretto
1½ ounces white crème de cacao
1 ounce cream
slivered almonds, for garnish

SHAKE AND STRAIN into a chilled cocktail glass. Add the garnish.

AMARETTO SOUR

FAMILY: **SOURS** ⸻ For a tarter drink, add more lemon juice or less amaretto.

2 ounces amaretto
1 ounce lemon juice
1 maraschino cherry, for garnish
1 half wheel orange, for garnish

SHAKE AND STRAIN into a chilled sour glass or an ice-filled rocks glass. Add the garnishes.

AMERICANO

FAMILY: **MILANESE DRINKS** ⸻ Legend has it that this drink was created in late-nineteenth-century Italy by an unknown bartender who was trying his hand at making an American-style drink. The recipe was not recorded, however, as far as I can ascertain, until 1937, when W. J. Tarling included it in his *Café Royal Cocktail Book*, a British publication.

I think this drink fares well when made with equal parts Campari and vermouth, but this is purely a matter of personal preference—experiment with ratios until you find your own perfect Americano. The drink also works well with lemon-lime soda instead of club soda, and is sometimes served in a large old-fashioned glass with just a splash of soda.

1½ ounces Campari
1½ ounces sweet vermouth
2 ounces club soda
1 orange twist, for garnish

BUILD in the order given in an ice-filled highball glass. Add the garnish.

AN APPLE A DAY

FAMILY: **INTERNATIONAL SOURS** — Adapted from a recipe by Audrey Saunders, New York City's Libation Goddess, this is a complex potion that you should initially make with the exact quantities listed here, so that all the ingredients play their part in the balance.

1 ounce Gordon's gin
1 ounce Sour Apple Pucker liqueur
¾ ounce fresh lime juice
½ ounce simple syrup
¼ ounce maraschino liqueur
½ ounce fresh grapefruit juice
1 maraschino cherry, for garnish

SHAKE AND STRAIN into a chilled cocktail glass. Add the garnish.

ANGEL'S TIT

FAMILY: **POUSSE-CAFÉS** — Known in the 1930s as the Angel's Tip, this drink is sometimes called the Witch's Tit, and without the cherry garnish it becomes the King Alphonse.

2 ounces dark crème de cacao
1 tablespoon whipped cream
1 maraschino cherry, for garnish

Pour the crème de cacao into a pousse-café glass and **FLOAT** the whipped cream on top. Skewer the cherry with a toothpick and rest it over the glass.

APPLE MARTINI

FAMILY: **DUOS AND TRIOS** — Rick Marin detailed many recipes for Apple Martinis in the *New York Times* in October 2000. Some contained apple puree, some used calvados, and some called for green-apple schnapps. The latter ingredient, or at least something similar, was featured previous to these drinks in the Maker's Mark Big Apple Manhattan, a drink unveiled at the Bourbon Festival in Bardstown, Kentucky, circa 1998. It was made by simply stirring together two parts bourbon and one part apple liqueur, and this is the way I prefer to make Apple Martinis, using vodka or, preferably, gin and green-apple schnapps.

2 ounces gin or vodka
1 ounce green-apple schnapps

STIR AND STRAIN into a chilled cocktail glass.

APPLE SIDECAR

FAMILY: **SOURS** Adapted from a recipe by Ryan Magarian of Restaurant Zoe, in Seattle. There is no real substitute for the Clear Creek apple brandy, but you can experiment with applejack here to make a variation on the theme.

1½ ounces vodka
½ ounce Clear Creek apple brandy
1 ounce fresh lemon juice
1 ounce simple syrup
½ ounce fresh tangerine juice
shredded tangerine zest, for garnish

SHAKE AND STRAIN into a chilled, sugar-rimmed cocktail glass. Add the garnish.

APRICOT FIZZ

FAMILY: **SPARKLING SOURS**

2½ ounces apricot brandy
¾ ounce fresh lemon juice
club soda

SHAKE AND STRAIN the brandy and lemon juice into an ice-filled collins glass. Pour in soda to fill the glass.

APRICOT SOUR

FAMILY: **SOURS**

2 ounces apricot brandy
1 ounce fresh lemon juice
1 maraschino cherry, for garnish
1 half wheel orange, for garnish

SHAKE AND STRAIN into a chilled sour glass or an ice-filled old-fashioned glass. Add the garnishes.

ARAWAK COCKTAIL

FAMILY: **FRENCH-ITALIAN: WHISKEY AND BRANDY** ~ I created this drink for Trotter's bar, in Trinidad; it's a tropical variation on the Algonquin. Be very careful when you add the tamarind juice—it can overpower the drink.

2 ounces bourbon
½ ounce dry vermouth
¼ ounce pineapple juice
1 dash tamarind juice
Angostura bitters to taste
1 pineapple cube, for garnish

SHAKE AND STRAIN into a chilled cocktail glass. Add the garnish.

ARTILLERY PUNCH

FAMILY: **PUNCHES** ~ A very similar recipe for this punch was detailed in 1958 by David Embury, and following his instructions I use simple syrup—without it, it's far too dry.

MAKES 24 SIX-OUNCE SERVINGS

1 bottle (750 milliliters) rye whiskey
1 bottle (750 milliliters) red wine
25 ounces chilled strong tea
12 ounces dark rum
6 ounces gin
6 ounces brandy
1 ounce Bénédictine
12 ounces fresh orange juice
6 ounces fresh lemon juice
6 ounces simple syrup
1 large block of ice
lemon wheels, for garnish

Pour all of the liquid ingredients into a large nonreactive pan or bowl. Stir well, cover, and refrigerate for four hours or longer. Place the block of ice in the center of a large punch bowl, then add the punch and the garnish.

ASTOR MARTINI

FAMILY: **MILANESE DRINKS** ~ Adapted from a recipe from Astor Place, in South Beach, Miami, this is a great drink to play with. Try building it in a highball glass and adding extra grapefruit juice, and if you're fond of Campari, increase the amount to one ounce or even more.

2 ounces Ketel One vodka
½ ounce Campari
1 ounce fresh grapefruit juice

SHAKE AND STRAIN into a chilled cocktail glass.

AVIATION COCKTAIL

FAMILY: **SOURS** ~ Dating back to at least 1930, this is a great drink, but the ratios depend entirely on how dry the maraschino liqueur is. Taste your bottling first, then add the lemon juice accordingly.

2 ounces gin
½ ounce maraschino liqueur
½ ounce fresh lemon juice

SHAKE AND STRAIN into a chilled cocktail glass.

AWOL

FAMILY: **POUSSE-CAFÉS** ~ Adapted from a recipe by New Orleans bartender Lane Zellman. This must be shot back in one go if you want to get the full effect.

¾ ounce melon liqueur
¾ ounce chilled pineapple juice
¾ ounce vodka
¾ ounce 151-proof rum

LAYER in the order given in a pousse-café glass. Flame the rum for a few seconds, then extinguish the flame. Caution the customer to make sure that the rim of the glass is cool enough before drinking.

BACARDI COCKTAIL

FAMILY: **SOURS** ~ In 1936 this drink had become so popular that the Bacardi family took a bar owner to court for using a rum other than Bacardi in his Bacardi Cocktails, and an injunction was granted. Let that be a lesson to you. The Bacardi Cocktail is basically a Daiquiri made with grenadine.

2 ounces Bacardi light rum
1 ounce fresh lime juice
½ ounce grenadine

SHAKE AND STRAIN into a chilled cocktail glass.

BAHAMA MAMA

FAMILY: **TROPICAL DRINKS** ~ This is a decent tropical drink, but you might want to try adding less pineapple juice to cut the sweetness a little.

¼ ounce Kahlúa
½ ounce dark rum
½ ounce coconut liqueur
½ ounce 151-proof rum
1 ounce fresh lemon juice
4 ounces pineapple juice

SHAKE AND STRAIN into an ice-filled collins glass.

BAILEYS CHOCOLATE MARTINI

FAMILY: **ORPHANS** ~ Taught to me by my Trinidadian friends in Port of Spain, 2001.

2 ounces vodka
¾ ounce Baileys Irish Cream
¾ ounce dark crème de cacao
1 Hershey's Kiss, for garnish

SHAKE AND STRAIN into a chilled cocktail glass. Add the garnish.

BANANA DAIQUIRI JELLY SHOT

FAMILY: **JELLY SHOTS** ~ See page 150 for advice about what molds to use for jelly shots.

1 ounce fresh lime juice
1 ounce simple syrup
1 ounce water
1 package unflavored gelatin (¼ ounce)
3 ounces rum
3 ounces crème de banane
food coloring, if desired

Place the lime juice, simple syrup, and water in a small glass measuring cup, and add the gelatin. Allow this to sit for one minute, then microwave the mixture on high for thirty seconds. Stir thoroughly to make sure that all the gelatin has dissolved, then add the rum, banana liqueur, and food coloring (if desired). Stir thoroughly again and pour the mixture into a mold. Refrigerate for at least one hour or, preferably, overnight.

BANANA-SPLIT MARTINI

FAMILY: **ORPHANS** ~ Adapted from a recipe by Christie Hartmann and Gage Tschyevkosky, Wolfgang Puck's Grand Cafe, Denver.

1½ ounces Grey Goose vodka
1½ ounces Godiva White Chocolate liqueur
¾ ounce crème de banane
1 slice of banana, for garnish

SHAKE AND STRAIN into a chilled cocktail glass drizzled with strawberry and chocolate syrup. Add the garnish.

BAY BREEZE

FAMILY: **NEW ENGLAND HIGHBALLS** ~ This drink is now often made with vodka instead of rum, but the rum version is by far the better drink.

2 ounces light rum
1½ ounces cranberry juice
1½ ounces pineapple juice
1 lime wedge, for garnish

BUILD in the order given in an ice-filled highball glass. Add the garnish.

BEACHCOMBER COCKTAIL

FAMILY: **NEW ORLEANS SOURS** ~ I've reformulated this drink from Trader Vic's 1948 recipe; you can reformulate it again by using more maraschino liqueur and less triple sec.

2 ounces light rum
1 ounce triple sec
¼ ounce maraschino liqueur
½ ounce fresh lime juice

SHAKE AND STRAIN into a chilled cocktail glass.

BELLINI

FAMILY: **CHAMPAGNE COCKTAILS** ~ According to *Harry's Bar,* by Arrigio Cipriani, the Bellini—perhaps the most sophisticated Italian drink—was created in 1948 by Harry Cipriani at Harry's Bar in Venice. It was named for the fifteenth-century Italian artist Jacopo Bellini, most of whose works apparently included a "pink glow," which is reproduced in the resultant drink. In 1990, Arrigio licensed the drink to an entrepreneur, who promptly added raspberry juice to the recipe. This angered Arrigio so much that in 1995 he took the entrepreneur to arbitration and regained ownership of the name.

Classically made with white peaches, this is a beautiful drink, but it can be somewhat hard to pour since the fruit puree makes the wine effervesce more than usual. The drink should be made with prosecco, an Italian sparkling wine that's sweeter than most champagnes used in this type of cocktail; if you use champagne instead, go with a sec or demi-sec bottling. And if white peaches aren't available, use any fresh peach.

You can also experiment with this drink by substituting purees of fruits other than peaches, such as raspberries, strawberries, or apricots, but you should remember to take into consideration the relative sweetness of the fruit, and alter the amount of lemon juice accordingly.

I was given a recipe for this drink by Giovanni Venturini, a bartender at the private palace of the Ciprianis in Venice. It contained a little too much peach puree for my liking, so although I've used Venturini's recipe for the puree itself, I've altered his proportions for what I think it a better-balanced drink.

2 ounces white peach puree (see below)
3½ ounces chilled prosecco

Add the peach puree to a champagne flute, then slowly add the chilled prosecco, stirring constantly to incorporate the ingredients.

WHITE PEACH PUREE

In a blender, puree the flesh, including the skin, of one white peach together with two or three ice cubes and a half teaspoon of fresh lemon juice.

BENNETT COCKTAIL

FAMILY: **SOURS** — The original version of the Bennett Cocktail, circa 1930, had no sweetening agent and was mouth-puckering, to say the least. With a little simple syrup added for balance, though, the combination of gin, lime juice, and bitters comes alive.

2 ounces gin
1 ounce fresh lime juice
½ ounce simple syrup
Angostura bitters to taste

SHAKE AND STRAIN into a chilled cocktail glass.

BERMUDA ROSE COCKTAIL

FAMILY: **FRENCH-ITALIAN: GIN AND VODKA** — Adapted from a somewhat confusing 1950s recipe detailed by David Embury. The apricot brandy plays well with the vermouth in this drink, and I find that just a drop or two of grenadine suffices—any more and it's a little too sweet for my liking.

2 ounces gin
½ ounce sweet vermouth
½ ounce apricot brandy
grenadine to taste

STIR AND STRAIN into a chilled cocktail glass.

BETSY ROSS

FAMILY: **ORPHANS** ➸ I enjoy the combination of brandy and port, so this recipe from the 1950s caught my eye. It's a little too sweet without the bitters—I recommend at least three dashes. Orange bitters can also be successfully used in the drink.

1½ ounces brandy
1½ ounces ruby port
½ ounce curaçao
Angostura bitters to taste

STIR AND STRAIN into a chilled cocktail glass.

BETWEEN THE SHEETS

FAMILY: **NEW ORLEANS SOURS** ➸ Adapted from a recipe in *Jones' Complete Barguide,* this is one the few recipes that successfully marries two different spirits. You can experiment with dark rum in this cocktail, too.

1 ounce brandy
1 ounce light rum
1 ounce triple sec
¾ ounce fresh lemon juice

SHAKE AND STRAIN into a chilled cocktail glass.

B-52

FAMILY: **POUSSE-CAFÉS** ➸ A Pousse-Café created in the late twentieth century.

¾ ounce Kahlúa
¾ ounce Baileys Irish Cream
¾ ounce Grand Marnier

LAYER in the order given in a pousse-café glass.

BIG PINE KEY COCKTAIL

FAMILY: **NEW ORLEANS SOURS** ➸ Adapted from a recipe by Robert Semmes, a cocktailian I met on the DrinkBoy community board.

1½ ounces gin
1 ounce triple sec
¾ ounce fresh lime juice
1 orange twist

SHAKE AND STRAIN into a chilled cocktail glass. Add the garnish.

BISTRO SIDECAR

FAMILY: **INTERNATIONAL SOURS** — Adapted from a recipe by chef Kathy Casey, founder of Kathy Casey Food Studios in Seattle, a creative chef who uses her skills behind the bar. The Tuaca and Frangelico work well together here, but it's actually the tangerine juice that makes this drink so special.

1½ ounces brandy
½ ounce Tuaca
½ ounce Frangelico
¼ ounce fresh lemon juice
½ ounce fresh tangerine juice
1 roasted hazelnut, for garnish

SHAKE AND STRAIN into a chilled, sugar-rimmed cocktail glass. Add the garnish.

BLACK AND TAN

FAMILY: **BEER- AND CIDER-BASED DRINKS** — The name for this drink probably came from the soldiers recruited by the British to quell the Irish Rebellion of 1920—they wore khaki uniforms and black caps.

Before the late 1980s the Black and Tan was a divine mixture of ale and stout, but since that time the drink has been promoted as a layered drink—sort of a beer pousse-café. Personally, I prefer the mixed version, but many drinkers who have come of age in the past decade would look askance at the original concoction.

8 ounces amber ale
8 ounces stout

Pour the ale into a beer glass and top with the stout. (If you want a layered drink, pour the stout over the back of a spoon.)

BLACK-AND-WHITE COCKTAIL

FAMILY: **POUSSE-CAFÉS** ~ A chilled coffee drink that Mardee and I came up with for a formal function. It's only a Pousse-Café inasmuch as the cream floats on a mixture of the other ingredients.

1½ ounces brandy
½ ounce dark crème de cacao
3 ounces chilled strong coffee
1 teaspoon whipped cream
chocolate sprinkles, for garnish

Pour the brandy, crème de cacao, and coffee into a chilled champagne flute. FLOAT the whipped cream on top of the drink, and garnish with a few chocolate sprinkles.

BLACK-EYED SUSAN

FAMILY: **FLORIDA HIGHBALLS** ~ The Black-Eyed Susan was created as Pimlico Race Course's answer to Churchill Downs' Mint Julep, as the drink to be seen with when the Preakness is running. It was originally a prepackaged cocktail issued by the Heublein company in 1973, but when Heublein refused to divulge the recipe, Pimlico came up with its own formula. This recipe has been adapted from the official drink, and it was given to Ted Haigh, the ardent researcher, by the good folks at Pimlico.

1 ounce vodka
1 ounce Mount Gay Eclipse rum
¾ ounce triple sec
1½ ounces fresh orange juice
1½ ounces pineapple juice
1 maraschino cherry, for garnish
1 orange wheel, for garnish
1 pineapple cube, for garnish
1 lime wedge, for garnish

BUILD in a collins glass filled with crushed ice. Add the garnishes.

NOTE: It's imperative to squeeze the juice from the lime wedge into the drink.

BLACK FEATHER COCKTAIL

FAMILY: **FRENCH-ITALIAN: WHISKEY AND BRANDY** ~ Adapted from a recipe created in 2000 by Robert Hess (a.k.a. DrinkBoy) in Seattle, this is a clear case of a classically styled cocktail formulated in a modern era.

2 ounces brandy
1 ounce dry vermouth
½ ounce triple sec
Angostura bitters to taste
1 orange twist, for garnish

STIR AND STRAIN into a chilled cocktail glass. Add the garnish.

BLACK RUSSIAN

FAMILY: **DUOS AND TRIOS** ~ Here's a perfect drink for experimentation: Try using far less Kahlúa for a drier drink, then make it again using light rum instead of vodka. My favorite version, though, is the Brave Bull (see page 230), which calls for tequila.

2 ounces vodka
1 ounce Kahlúa

STIR AND STRAIN into an ice-filled old-fashioned glass.

BLACKTHORNE

FAMILY: **FRENCH-ITALIAN: WHISKEY AND BRANDY** ~ Adapted from a recipe in Harry Craddock's *The Savoy Cocktail Book* (1930), this variation on the Manhattan is delightful—when made with caution. The trick is to be very careful not to overpower the drink with too much absinthe substitute.

2 ounces Irish whiskey
1 ounce sweet vermouth
Angostura bitters to taste
absinthe substitute to taste (go easy)
1 lemon twist, for garnish

STIR AND STRAIN into a chilled cocktail glass. Add the garnish.

BLACK VELVET

FAMILY: **BEER- AND CIDER-BASED DRINKS** ➸ This drink is said to have been created in 1861 when the steward of the Brooks Club in London deemed that champagne should be drunk in mourning for Albert, Queen Victoria's husband, then added stout to every glass so that the drink would be black. That story, though entertaining, is hard to verify. Since I've yet to see the drink mentioned in print before 1946, when Charles H. Baker Jr. described it in *The Gentleman's Companion,* dubbing it Champagne Velvet, I'm pretty sure it's not true. The earliest reference I've found under the name Black Velvet is in the 1945 book *Crosby Gaige's Cocktail Guide and Ladies' Companion.* Later David Embury wrote that he had been introduced to the drink in Canada, but he neglects to put a date on the experience.

The first recipes for the Black Velvet called for a fifty-fifty mix of stout and champagne, and many recipes suggest that you make it in a pint glass. I'm in favor of using far less stout in the mix and serving it in a champagne flute.

4½ ounces chilled champagne
1 ounce chilled stout

BUILD in the order given in a champagne flute.

BLACK VELVETEEN

FAMILY: **BEER- AND CIDER-BASED DRINKS** ➸ A refreshing drink based, of course, on the Black Velvet.

8 ounces hard cider
8 ounces stout

BUILD in the order given in a beer glass.

BLOOD-AND-SAND COCKTAIL

FAMILY: **FRENCH-ITALIAN: WHISKEY AND BRANDY** ➸ This is an unusual bunch of ingredients, but the drink works very well indeed. Introduced to Mardee and me by Dale DeGroff, the recipe here is from *The Savoy Cocktail Book* (1930); the drink was probably named for Rudolph Valentino's 1922 silent movie about bullfighting and, of course, love, which was based on the 1908 book by Vicente Blasco Ibáñez. I'm fond of making this drink in a highball glass, using considerably more orange juice, and serving it at lunch or brunch.

¾ ounce scotch
¾ ounce sweet vermouth
¾ ounce cherry brandy
¾ ounce fresh orange juice

SHAKE AND STRAIN into a chilled cocktail glass.

BLOOD ORANGE

FAMILY: **MILANESE DRINKS** Adapted from a recipe devised by John Simmons of Petaluna, New York, in 1995. Simmons created this drink shortly after Stolichnaya released its orange-flavored vodka, and although the recipe here is designed for a cocktail glass, he also serves the drink on the rocks or in a highball glass with club soda.

2 ounces Stolichnaya Ohranj
1 ounce Campari
1 half wheel blood orange, for garnish

STIR AND STRAIN into a chilled cocktail glass. Add the garnish.

BLOODY BULL

FAMILY: **SNAPPERS** The bouillon in this drink makes it more palatable for me than a Bloody Mary, but I'm still not a fan. Use different spices for variations.

2 ounces vodka
2 ounces tomato juice
2 ounces beef bouillon
fresh lemon juice to taste
salt or celery salt to taste
black pepper to taste
prepared horseradish to taste
Worcestershire sauce to taste
hot sauce to taste
1 lemon wedge, for garnish
1 celery stalk, for garnish

SHAKE AND STRAIN into an ice-filled collins glass. Add the garnishes.

BLOODY CAESAR

FAMILY: **SNAPPERS** ⁓ Use different spices for variations.

2 ounces vodka
2 ounces tomato juice
2 ounces clam juice
fresh lemon juice to taste
black pepper to taste
salt or celery salt to taste
prepared horseradish to taste
Worcestershire sauce to taste
hot sauce to taste
1 lemon wedge, for garnish
1 celery stalk, for garnish

SHAKE AND STRAIN into an ice-filled collins glass. Add the garnishes.

BLOODY MARY

FAMILY: **SNAPPERS** ⁓ One story about the birth of the Bloody Mary has it that the owner of a New York speakeasy created it, as the Bloody Meyer, during Prohibition. But the more popular, and almost certainly true, tale is that it was first concocted at Harry's New York Bar in Paris, circa 1924, by bartender Fernand "Pete" Petiot.

In 1934, Petiot was hired by John Astor, then owner of New York's St. Regis Hotel, and there he presided over the King Cole Room, introducing New Yorkers to his creation. At some point the Bloody Mary was known as the Red Snapper; one story has it that Astor objected to the Bloody Mary name and insisted it be changed. A recipe for the Red Snapper is detailed in the 1945 book *Crosby Gaige's Cocktail Guide and Ladies' Companion.* It was donated to the author by Gaston Lauryssen, manager of the St. Regis at the time, and it's a far cry from the drink we know today as the Bloody Mary. The main differences between today's and yesteryear's versions is that the latter contained as much vodka as tomato juice and was served straight up as a cocktail, as opposed to being presented on the rocks in a highball glass.

When did the Red Snapper regain its original name? Probably sometime during the late 1940s. The first printed recipe for a Bloody Mary I can find is in *The Bartender's Book* (1951), and the authors, Jack Townsend and Tom Moore McBride, didn't much care for the drink, calling it "a savage combination of tomato juice and vodka." The following year, David Embury, in the second edition of *The Fine Art of Mixing Drinks,* described the Bloody Mary as being "strictly vile."

Bloody Mary Tips for the Professional Bartender

1. If you prepare a batch of Bloody Mary mix in quantity rather than mixing drinks individually, base your recipe on the amount of tomato juice in a standard No. 5 can (46 fluid ounces).
2. Never add the vodka to the mix until the drink is ordered. Many customers want Virgin Marys.
3. To make enough mix to last a week—and still be able to serve freshly made drinks: Combine all the spices, seasonings, and sauces (without the lemon juice) in a small jar and shake well. Prepare as many of these jars as you will need in the course of a week, and refrigerate them. When you need a batch of Bloody Marys, mix one jar of spices with one can of tomato juice and the lemon juice.

In the mid-1950s comedian George Jessel was featured in a Smirnoff vodka advertising campaign for the Bloody Mary, in which he claimed to have invented the drink at "five in the morning" when the bartender was asleep. The tale, of course, isn't true, but the campaign served to popularize the drink throughout the United States.

Personally, I'm not a fan of Bloody Marys—I'd even go so far as to put myself in Embury's camp and call it strictly vile—but my dislike for this potion doesn't have anything to do with the flavor; it's the texture of tomato juice that I can't stand. I love tomatoes, and I enjoy the Bloody Mary Martini recipe detailed on the next page, but in general, savory drinks are not to my liking. One tip I can offer, though, is that lemon juice marries with tomato juice far better than does lime juice.

This is a generic recipe—use different spices and/or spirits, for variations.

2 ounces vodka
4 ounces tomato juice
fresh lemon juice to taste
black pepper to taste
salt or celery salt to taste
prepared horseradish to taste
Worcestershire sauce to taste
hot sauce to taste
1 lemon wedge, for garnish
1 celery stalk, for garnish

SHAKE AND STRAIN into an ice-filled collins glass. Add the garnishes.

BLOODY MARY MARTINI

FAMILY: **SNAPPERS** ~ An August 30, 2000, article in the *New York Times* detailed a drink created by chef-owner Kurt Gutenbrunner of Wallse, an Austrian restaurant in Greenwich Village. It was called the Peppar Tomato. Based on the description given by writer Amanda Hesser (there was no actual recipe), my wife, Mardee, developed this drink.

1½ ounces pepper-flavored vodka
1 ounce vodka
2 ounces tomato water (see below)
1 pinch of celery seed
1 lemon twist, for garnish

SHAKE AND STRAIN into a chilled cocktail glass. Add the garnish.

TOMATO WATER

Simply puree some ripe tomatoes and place them in a fine sieve lined with a double layer of dampened cheesecloth. Place the sieve on top of a bowl or large measuring jug, and allow the tomato water to drain into the bowl. (If you're in a hurry, make the cheesecloth containing the tomato puree into a pouch and squeeze out the water.)

BLOW MY SKULL OFF

FAMILY: **ORPHANS** ~ The story behind the original drink of this name can be found in the history chapter (see page 7), but I loved the name so much that, since the ingredients used in the original formula are hard to come by, I was compelled to create a modern-day drink of the same name.

2 ounces cognac
½ ounce peach schnapps
½ ounce Jägermeister

STIR AND STRAIN into a chilled cocktail glass.

The Blue Blazer

HERBERT ASBURY, in the introduction to the 1928 edition of Jerry Thomas's book *How to Mix Drinks, or The Bon Vivant's Companion,* states that this drink was created by Thomas in San Francisco, circa 1850. The recipe is detailed in Thomas's 1862 edition. According to Asbury, the drink was a result of a gold prospector who demanded, "Fix me up some hell-fire that'll shake me right down to my gizzard!"

This is a somewhat simple drink, and its main attribute is pyrotechnical, since when it's properly prepared, a stream of flaming whisky is poured back and forth between two mugs (Thomas recommended silver-plated receptacles). The problem with this recipe is that if you follow Thomas's formula, combining equal amounts of Scotch and boiling water, the mixture will be hard to ignite.

It's highly probable that Thomas used a high-proof whisky to make this drink, since to save on shipping charges, spirits were often shipped at high proof, then diluted by saloon keepers upon arrival. This practice was fairly common right up to the early years of the twentieth century. I have seen Dale DeGroff make this drink when he was at the Rainbow Room, and he tells me that he heats the whisky, ignites it, then pours it into the second mug, which contains the hot water. He assures me that the mixture stays lit if you use this method. With the addition of a little sugar and lemon, as Thomas prescribed, the Blue Blazer is a heart-warming drink. This is a legitimate opportunity for accomplished bartenders to display their dexterity, but when you get right down to brass tacks, this is a showman's drink, not a cocktailian masterpiece. Here's Thomas's original formula:

(Use two silver-plated mugs, with handles.)
1 wine-glass Scotch whiskey
1 wine-glass boiling water
Put the whiskey and the boiling water in one mug, ignite the liquid with fire, and while blazing mix both ingredients by pouring them four or five times from one mug to the other. . . . If well done this will have the appearance of a continued stream of liquid fire.

Sweeten with one teaspoonful of pulverized white sugar, and serve in a small bar tumbler, with a piece of lemon peel.

> *The "blue blazer" does not have a euphonious or classic name, but it tastes better to the palate than it sounds to the ear. A beholder gazing for the first time upon an experienced artist, compounding this beverage, would naturally come to the conclusion that it was a nectar for Pluto rather than Bacchus. The novice in mixing this beverage should be careful not to scald himself. To become proficient in throwing the liquid from one mug to the other, it will be necessary to practise [sic] for some time with cold water.*

BLUE-EYED BLONDE

FAMILY: **POUSSE-CAFÉS** ❧ Taught to me by my friends at Trotter's, in Trinidad.

½ ounce Frangelico
½ ounce crème de banane
½ ounce blue curaçao

LAYER in the order given in a pousse-café glass.

BLUE TRAIN COCKTAIL

FAMILY: **NEW ORLEANS SOURS** ❧ In 1930 Harry Craddock used Cointreau and "blue vegetable extract" to make this drink.

1½ ounces gin
1 ounce blue curaçao
½ ounce fresh lemon juice

SHAKE AND STRAIN into a chilled cocktail glass.

B9 MARTINI

FAMILY: **CHAMPAGNE COCKTAILS** ❧ Adapted from a recipe from Butterfield 9, in Washington, D.C.

1½ ounces Grey Goose orange-flavored vodka
½ ounce peach schnapps
chilled champagne

STIR AND STRAIN the vodka and peach schnapps into a chilled cocktail glass. Top with a splash of chilled champagne.

BOBBO'S BRIDE STRAIGHT UP

FAMILY: **ORPHANS** — Adapted from a recipe by Laurel Semmes, wife of Robert Semmes, who created the Big Pine Key Cocktail on page 214.

1 ounce gin
1 ounce vodka
½ ounce peach schnapps
½ ounce Campari
1 slice peach, for garnish

STIR AND STRAIN into a chilled cocktail glass. Add the garnish.

BOBBY BURNS

FAMILY: **FRENCH-ITALIAN: WHISKEY AND BRANDY** — Albert Stevens Crockett, author of *The Old Waldorf-Astoria Bar Book,* noted that this drink, then called the Robert Burns, was created prior to Prohibition. He intimated that it was born at the Waldorf-Astoria: "It may have been named after the celebrated Scotsman. Chances are, however, that it was christened in honor of a cigar salesman, who 'bought' in the Old Bar."

The Waldorf recipe includes a dash of absinthe, whereas the Savoy recipe (1930) calls for three dashes of Bénédictine instead. In the 1950s, David Embury suggested that Drambuie could be used in this drink instead of either absinthe or Bénédictine. My personal preference for a Bobby Burns is to use Bénédictine, but it is interesting to try these variations.

2 ounces scotch
1 ounce sweet vermouth
Bénédictine to taste (try 2 dashes, then adjust)
1 lemon twist, for garnish

STIR AND STRAIN into a chilled cocktail glass. Add the garnish.

BOCCE BALL

FAMILY: **FLORIDA HIGHBALLS**

2 ounces amaretto
3 ounces fresh orange juice

BUILD in an ice-filled highball glass.

BOILERMAKER

FAMILY: **BEER- AND CIDER-BASED DRINKS** ~ The Perdue Boiler Makers achieved their nickname in 1891 when an Indiana reporter wrote about their 44–0 victory over the Wabash football team. But this drink, which is actually a drinking ritual, most likely gets its name from the steelworkers in western Pennsylvania, one of whom—a certain Vince Orend (now retired)—wrote me a very passionate letter about Boilermakers:

> *The steel mills are all gone but Boilermakers are still served at every local in the area. Not the Yuppie bars with their White Wine Spritzers, but the bars that have been, and will always be neighborhood bars. Three and four generations have been thrown out of them. The Boilermaker is a drink that cuts right through the heat, dirt, and dust of the steel mills. It was a drink that a MAN would belt down after eight hours in the heat and dirt of the mills. It was a way to get your energy fast and replace the fluids that you lost in the heat of the day. It was a way to forget how hard you worked, and how hard you will work the next day, and the day after, and the day after that. . . . The whiskey was cheap & the beer was cold. The glasses were dirty just like the rest rooms, but you stopped every day with the guys you worked with and had a Boilermaker with the boys. The idea was you were a team. We picnicked with each other's families and knew all the kids' names. We ate, drank, worked, cried, and loved together. The Boilermaker was the cement that held us together.*

I must admit that Orend's letter gave me a new respect for the Boilermaker.

Generally speaking, the Boilermaker is merely a glass of beer with a shot of whiskey served on the side. The shot goes down in one, and the beer follows, being sipped rather than quickly downed. You can have fun with this drink, though, if you try matching whiskeys and beers: wheat beer with a wheated bourbon such as Maker's Mark or Old Fitzgerald; or perhaps a stout alongside a fruity whiskey such as the Wild Turkey twelve-year-old or the Elijah Craig eighteen-year-old.

1 glass beer
2 ounces whiskey of choice

BOLERO COCKTAIL

FAMILY: **SOURS** — Adapted from a 1950s recipe.

1 ounce dark rum
1 ounce brandy
½ ounce fresh orange juice
1 ounce fresh lime juice
½ ounce simple syrup

SHAKE AND STRAIN into a chilled cocktail glass.

BOLO'S POMEGRANATE SANGRIA

FAMILY: **PUNCHES**

MAKES TEN 6-OUNCE DRINKS

This recipe and the one following were both created by Bobby Flay, chef-owner of Bolo restaurant in New York. Mardee and I have many friends who swear that these drinks have been the center of attraction at their parties.

1 bottle (750 milliliters) dry red wine
1 cup American brandy
1 cup simple syrup
2 cups fresh orange juice
¾ cup pomegranate molasses or pomegranate juice
2 oranges, sliced into thin rounds
3 green apples, cored and cut into thin slices
2 lemons, sliced into thin rounds

Combine all the ingredients, except the fruit, and let sit, refrigerated, for at least two hours and up to two days. Add the fruit before serving.

BOLO'S WHITE PEACH SANGRIA

FAMILY: **PUNCHES**

MAKES TEN 6-OUNCE DRINKS

Created by Bobby Flay, Bolo, New York.

1 bottle (750 milliliters) pinot grigio
1 cup American brandy
1 cup simple syrup
2 cups fresh orange juice
¾ cup white peach puree (see page 213)
4 white peaches, pitted and sliced
3 green apples, cored and cut into thin slices
2 lemons, sliced into thin rounds

Combine all the ingredients and let sit, refrigerated, for at least two hours and up to two days.

BOSTON CREAM MARTINI

FAMILY: **ORPHANS** ❧ Adapted from a recipe by Russ Hovermale, Buzz restaurant, Boston, MA

2½ ounces Grey Goose vodka
½ ounce Baileys Irish Cream
1 dash vanilla extract

SHAKE AND STRAIN into a frozen martini glass rimmed with Chocolate Magic Shell (an ice-cream topping).

BOURBON AND BRANCH

FAMILY: **HIGHBALLS** ❧ Branch water is water from the branch of a river or a stream. It's a southern term, and I'm assured that any still water will suffice in this drink.

2 ounces bourbon
3 ounces bottled still water

BUILD in an ice-filled highball glass.

BOURBON AND COKE

FAMILY: **HIGHBALLS** ~ If you use any soda other than Coca-Cola, make sure that the customer is aware of this and that the brand you use is acceptable.

2 ounces bourbon
3 ounces Coca-Cola

BUILD in an ice-filled highball glass.

BOURBON PEACH COBBLER

FAMILY: **COBBLERS**

3 ounces bourbon
1 ounce peach schnapps
fruits in season, for garnish

BUILD in the order given in a wine glass filled with crushed ice. Add the garnish.

BRANDY ALEXANDER

FAMILY: **DUOS AND TRIOS** ~ Created before 1930, this drink was once known as Alexander No. 2, then as the Panama. It had gotten the name Brandy Alexander by 1936, but it was often still referred to as the Panama until well into the 1940s.

2 ounces brandy
1 ounce dark crème de cacao
1 ounce cream
freshly grated nutmeg, for garnish

SHAKE AND STRAIN into a chilled cocktail glass. Add the garnish.

BRANDY AND SODA

FAMILY: **HIGHBALLS** ~ Ask the customer what type of brandy he would like, and then ask if any one particular brand would be preferable.

2 ounces brandy
3 ounces club soda

BUILD in an ice-filled highball glass.

BRANDY COBBLER

FAMILY: **COBBLERS** You can make this drink with bourbon, blended whiskey, or even dark rum, but white spirits such as gin or tequila don't work very well. Adjust the ratio of spirit to simple syrup to make a drink with the sweetness desired by your customer.

3 ounces brandy
1 ounce simple syrup
fruits in season, for garnish

BUILD in the order given in a wine glass filled with crushed ice. Add the garnish.

BRAVE BULL

FAMILY: **DUOS AND TRIOS**

2 ounces white tequila
1 ounce Kahlúa

STIR AND STRAIN into an ice-filled old-fashioned glass.

BRITISH SQUIRREL

FAMILY: **SQUIRREL SOURS** This drink works well with lemon juice instead of lime juice. If you go the lemon route, add a lemon-twist garnish, too.

1½ ounces gin
¾ ounce crème de noyau
¾ ounce fresh lime juice

SHAKE AND STRAIN into a chilled cocktail glass.

BRONX COCKTAIL

FAMILY: **FRENCH-ITALIAN: GIN AND VODKA** The story of the creation of this drink is detailed in Albert Stevens Crockett's *The Old Waldorf-Astoria Bar Book,* and although the book claims that it was created prior to 1917, no clue is given as to the precise year of its birth. According to the book, the bartender who first made the Bronx was a certain Johnnie

Solon (or Solan), and he made the drink as a response to a challenge from a waiter by the name of Traverson. The Bronx was a variation of a popular drink of the time known as the Duplex (sweet and dry vermouth with orange bitters), and it became so popular that the bar was soon using more than a case of oranges per day. The book quotes Solon as saying, "I had been at the Bronx Zoo a day or two before, and I saw, of course, a lot of beasts I had never known. Customers used to tell me of the strange animals they saw after a lot of mixed drinks. So when Traverson said to me, as he started to take the drink in to the customer, 'What'll I tell him is the name of this drink?' I thought of those animals, and said, 'Oh, you can tell him it is a Bronx.'"

I have added orange bitters to the original recipe and have increased the amount of both vermouths to give the drink better balance.

2 ounces gin
¼ ounce sweet vermouth
¼ ounce dry vermouth
1 ounce fresh orange juice
orange bitters to taste
1 orange twist, for garnish

SHAKE AND STRAIN into a chilled cocktail glass. Add the garnish.

BULLSHOT

FAMILY: **SNAPPERS** — This isn't a favorite of mine, but if you have homemade beef bouillon and serve this drink hot, it's a good cold-weather drink. Use different spices for variations.

2 ounces vodka
4 ounces beef bouillon
fresh lemon juice to taste
black pepper to taste
salt or celery salt to taste
Worcestershire sauce to taste
hot sauce to taste
1 lemon wedge, for garnish
1 celery stalk, for garnish

SHAKE AND STRAIN into an ice-filled collins glass. Add the garnishes.

BURNET

FAMILY: **DUOS AND TRIOS** ⁓ I created this drink in 2001 for my friends at Glenmorangie. Their whisky is delicate compared to many other single malts, so it's imperative that you go easy on the Cherry Heering. A good way to develop your cocktailian skills is to take this simple formula and experiment with other scotches, tasting them neat before making the drink and attempting to balance the cocktail properly. Another good experiment with this formula is to substitute other liqueurs—amaretto, for instance—for the Cherry Heering.

2½ ounces Glenmorangie single-malt scotch
½ ounce Cherry Heering
1 lemon twist, for garnish

STIR AND STRAIN into a chilled cocktail glass. Add the garnish.

BURNISHED GOLD

FAMILY: **DUOS AND TRIOS** ⁓ Just a variation on the Rusty Nail theme. Add more Frangelico for extra sweetness.

2 ounces brandy
½ ounce Frangelico

STIR AND STRAIN into a chilled cocktail glass or an ice-filled old-fashioned glass.

CACHARITA

FAMILY: **NEW ORLEANS SOURS** ⁓ Marty Friedland, the president of Efco Importers, the company that brings Pitú cachaça into the United States, called me in 2001 and asked if I thought it would be possible to make a Margarita-style drink with his spirit. I tinkered with it a little and came up with this new New Orleans Sour. Notice that I needed more triple sec to balance the drink than I use in my Margarita recipe, which calls for just one ounce; the cachaça simply needed more sweetness to soothe its soul.

1½ ounces Pitú cachaça
1½ ounces triple sec
½ ounce fresh lime juice

SHAKE AND STRAIN into a chilled cocktail glass.

CAFÉ BRÛLOT

FAMILY: **HOT DRINKS** Adapted from a recipe from Commander's Palace, New Orleans.

MAKES 2 DRINKS

1 lemon
1 orange
1 ounce triple sec
1 ounce brandy
1 cinnamon stick
4 whole cloves
1½ cups hot, strong coffee

Remove the lemon and orange peel in one continuous strip so that it forms a spiral. As you peel the fruit, hold it over a brûlot bowl (or fondue pot) so that any juices drop into the bowl. Place the lemon peel in the brûlot bowl and set it over a Sterno heater. Add the triple sec, brandy, and cinnamon stick. Stud the orange peel with the cloves and hold it over the brûlot bowl on a fork. Carefully ignite the brandy mixture and ladle the flaming liquid over the orange peel. Slowly pour the coffee into the bowl to extinguish the flames. Ladle the coffee into demitasse cups and sweeten to taste with fresh-squeezed juice from the peeled orange.

CAIPIRINHA

FAMILY: **MUDDLED DRINKS** ◆ A Brazilian drink that's been in vogue for the past half dozen years or so, and justifiably so. The name (pronounced k-EYE-pir-een-YA) translates roughly to "country bumpkin," and the drink calls for cachaça, a somewhat rough Brazilian style of rum that bears what I can describe only as a musty fruitiness. When married to the limes and sugar, though, cachaça becomes an elixir. There are a few different brands of this spirits, but Pitú is the one most easily found, and it makes for a great Caipirinha. It's difficult to tell you how many wedges of lime to use when making this drink because limes can differ quite drastically in size; my rule of thumb is to add wedges until they fill the glass to the halfway mark.

The possibilities for variations on the Caipirinha are endless. Dale DeGroff makes a drink with lemon wedges and Bacardi O, an orange-flavored rum, and I have used lemons and pisco brandy quite successfully, too. This is a good drink to play around with.

4 to 6 lime wedges
1 tablespoon granulated sugar
3 ounces cachaça

MUDDLE the limes and sugar in an old-fashioned glass. Add crushed ice and cachaça, and stir thoroughly.

CAIPIROSKA

FAMILY: **MUDDLED DRINKS** ◆ The vodka-based cousin to the Caipirinha, for those who aren't enamored of cachaça.

4 to 6 lime wedges
1 tablespoon granulated sugar
3 ounces vodka

MUDDLE the limes and sugar in an old-fashioned glass. Add crushed ice and vodka, and stir thoroughly.

CALVADOS COCKTAIL

FAMILY: **NEW ORLEANS SOURS** ◆ Adapted from a recipe in *Jones' Complete Barguide*. I played with ratios here and added lemon juice to the original formula to give it a little more bite.

2 ounces calvados
½ ounce triple sec
½ ounce fresh orange juice
½ ounce fresh lemon juice
orange bitters to taste

SHAKE AND STRAIN into a chilled cocktail glass.

CANTEEN MARTINI

FAMILY: **INTERNATIONAL SOURS** ~ Adapted from a recipe by Joey Guerra, at the Canteen, New York City, this is a sweet drink that you can adjust by using less Southern Comfort or increasing the amount of lime juice.

1½ ounces white rum
1½ ounces Southern Comfort
½ ounce amaretto
½ ounce fresh lime juice

SHAKE AND STRAIN into a chilled cocktail glass.

CAPE CODDER

FAMILY: **NEW ENGLAND HIGHBALLS**

2 ounces vodka
3 ounces cranberry juice
1 lime wedge, for garnish

BUILD in the order given in an ice-filled highball glass. Add the garnish.

CARBONATED PISTON SLINGER

FAMILY: **SPARKLING SOURS** ~ Adapted from a recipe by Dr. Cocktail.

2 ounces 151-proof Demerara rum
¾ ounce sloe gin
¾ ounce fresh lime juice
club soda
1 maraschino cherry, for garnish
1 lime wedge, for garnish

SHAKE everything except for the club soda and STRAIN into an ice-filled collins glass. Top with club soda. Add the garnishes.

CARIBBEAN COSMOPOLITAN

FAMILY: **NEW ORLEANS SOURS** ~ This is a simple twist on the Cosmopolitan that I created for Trotter's bar, Port of Spain, Trinidad. Experiment with different base spirits, such as citrus vodkas or Bacardi O, the orange-flavored rum.

2 ounces Bacardi Limón
½ ounce triple sec
½ ounce fresh lime juice
¼ ounce pineapple juice
¼ ounce cranberry juice
Angostura bitters to taste
1 maraschino cherry, for garnish

SHAKE AND STRAIN into a chilled cocktail glass. Add the garnish.

CARIBBEAN SQUIRREL

FAMILY: **SQUIRREL SOURS** ~ If you use dark instead of light rum in this drink, experiment with Frangelico to replace the crème de noyau.

1½ ounces light rum
¾ ounce crème de noyau
¾ ounce fresh lime juice

SHAKE AND STRAIN into a chilled cocktail glass.

CARICATURE COCKTAIL

FAMILY: **FRENCH-ITALIAN: GIN AND VODKA** ~ I created this in 2001 for graphic artist Jill DeGroff, Dale's wife, but it's nothing more than a variation on Dale DeGroff's Old Flame cocktail.

1½ ounces gin
½ ounce sweet vermouth
¾ ounce triple sec
½ ounce Campari
½ ounce fresh grapefruit juice
1 orange twist, for garnish

SHAKE AND STRAIN into chilled cocktail glass. Add the garnish.

CEO COCKTAIL

FAMILY: **FRENCH-ITALIAN: WHISKEY AND BRANDY** Adapted from a recipe by Dr. Cocktail (Ted Haigh), who shakes all his drinks, regardless of the ingredients. For a variation you could use dry vermouth instead of the Lillet, or it might be interesting to try bourbon as a base liquor instead of the brandy.

2 ounces brandy
½ ounce Chambord or crème de cassis
1 ounce Lillet Blonde
2 dashes orange bitters
1 lemon twist, for garnish

SHAKE AND STRAIN into a chilled cocktail glass. Add the garnish.

CHAMPAGNE COCKTAIL

FAMILY: **CHAMPAGNE COCKTAILS** The original Champagne Cocktail is detailed in Jerry Thomas's 1862 book *How to Mix Drinks, or The Bon Vivant's Companion,* but his methodology is a little strange: "Fill tumbler one-third full of broken ice, and fill balance with wine. Shake well and serve." The ingredients are listed as champagne, a half teaspoon of sugar, one or two dashes of bitters, and one piece of lemon peel, and that's pretty much what we use to make a Champagne Cocktail today; but the idea of shaking the drink is somewhat mystifying—the shaker would explode when opened.

We know that our forefathers were sipping Champagne Cocktails in the mid–nineteenth century, but what else do we know about the history of this drink? In 1906, bartender Louis Muckensturm recommended rubbing the sugar cube onto lemon peel before adding it to the glass—not a bad idea at all—and in 1927 a book titled *Here's How,* by Judge Jr., proclaimed that the drink had been created at the Ritz Hotel in Paris and was considered "very high hat." By the 1930s, the Champagne Sour, using lemon juice instead of bitters, had been introduced into the mix, and W. J. Tarling's *Café Royal Cocktail Book* prescribed "a dash of brandy as required" in 1937. Variations were springing up.

A couple of years later, Charles H. Baker Jr. detailed quite a few deviations from the norm in his book *The Gentleman's Companion.* They included the Maharajah's Burra-Peg: "And we would sip various things, including—on Washington's birthday, of course—a quartet of champagne Burra Pegs, and he [their host] would recount to us certain toothsome bits of 'under the punkah' tales about maharajahs and people; and how, actually, the young new one we'd just met preferred one wife to the regiment of 400 or so that his dad had thoughtfully left to him." Baker suggested that the Burra Peg was best made in a sixteen-ounce glass, into which he poured three ounces of brandy, which was topped off with champagne. He also dropped a bitters-soaked sugar cube into the glass, along with a spiral of lime peel.

In 1945, recipes for eight Champagne Cocktails with names such as She Couldn't Say No, Her Sarong Slipped, and Widow's Might appeared in *Crosby Gaige's Cocktail Guide and Ladies' Companion.* Crosby also noted, "Maidens wed without champagne . . . are bound to become husband beaters."

More variations on this drink have appeared every decade—perhaps even every month or every week—since the forties. We now have such a wide array of ingredients suitable to add to champagne that I dare say there are thousands of recipes out there, and thousands more are on their way.

1 sugar cube soaked in Angostura bitters
5½ ounces chilled champagne
1 lemon twist, for garnish

BUILD in the order given in a champagne flute. Add the garnish.

CHANTICLEER COCKTAIL

FAMILY: **FRENCH-ITALIAN: GIN AND VODKA** Adapted from a pre–Prohibition era drink of the same name, the original recipe called for orange-flavored gin and the white of an egg. I reformulated the Chanticleer using triple sec for the orange flavor and dropping the egg white altogether. The word *chanticleer* is French for rooster, and at the old Waldorf-Astoria bar, the drink was served with "a Cock's Comb, if desired."

1 ounce gin
1½ ounces dry vermouth
½ ounce triple sec
1 orange twist, for garnish

STIR AND STRAIN into a chilled cocktail glass. Add the garnish.

CHARLIE CHAPLIN COCKTAIL

FAMILY: **INTERNATIONAL SOURS** This is the exact formula used at the old Waldorf-Astoria prior to 1920, in honor of the silent movie star.

1 ounce apricot brandy
1 ounce sloe gin
1 ounce fresh lime juice

SHAKE AND STRAIN into a chilled cocktail glass.

CHATHAM COCKTAIL

FAMILY: **INTERNATIONAL SOURS** I had never heard of this drink until Dr. Cocktail pointed it out to me, but it's a very pleasing formula. Try using liqueurs other than the ginger brandy called for here—cherry brandy would be a good place to start. Adapted from a recipe in *Jones' Complete Barguide.*

2 ounces gin
½ ounce ginger brandy or ginger liqueur
½ ounce fresh lemon juice

SHAKE AND STRAIN into a chilled cocktail glass.

CHAYA CANDY APPLE COSMO

FAMILY: **INTERNATIONAL SOURS** Adapted from a recipe by Eric Schreiber at Chaya Brasserie, San Francisco.

1½ ounces Van Gogh Wild Appel vodka
½ ounce Cuarenta y Tres liqueur
½ ounce fresh lime juice
½ ounce cranberry juice

SHAKE AND STRAIN into a chilled cocktail glass.

CHERRY BLOSSOM COCKTAIL

FAMILY: **NEW ORLEANS SOURS** Reformulated from Harry Craddock's 1930 recipe, this is a simple variation on the Sidecar, employing cherry brandy as an extra ingredient.

1 ounce brandy
1 ounce cherry brandy
½ ounce triple sec
½ ounce fresh lemon juice

SHAKE AND STRAIN into a chilled cocktail glass.

CHOCOLATE MARTINI

FAMILY: **DUOS AND TRIOS** ❧ Adapted from a recipe from Max's South Beach, Miami, 1993.

2 ounces vodka
1½ ounces white crème de cacao
1 Hershey's Hug, for garnish

STIR AND STRAIN into a chilled, cocoa-rimmed cocktail glass. Add the garnish.

CLARIDGE COCKTAIL

FAMILY: **FRENCH-ITALIAN: GIN AND VODKA** ❧ Adapted from Harry Craddock's 1930 recipe.

1 ounce gin
1 ounce dry vermouth
½ ounce triple sec
½ ounce apricot brandy

STIR AND STRAIN into a chilled cocktail glass.

CLASSIC COCKTAIL

FAMILY: **NEW ORLEANS SOURS** ❧ Note that this is essentially a Sidecar with maraschino liqueur added. Craddock's original 1930 recipe called for curaçao, for which I have substituted triple sec.

1½ ounces brandy
½ ounce triple sec
½ ounce maraschino liqueur
½ ounce fresh lemon juice

SHAKE AND STRAIN into a chilled, sugar-rimmed cocktail glass.

CLOVER CLUB COCKTAIL

FAMILY: **SOURS** ❧ According to Albert Stevens Crockett, author of *The Old Waldorf-Astoria Bar Book,* this drink originated at the "old Belleview-Stratford, where the Clover Club, composed of literary, legal, financial and business lights of the Quaker City, often dined and wined, and wined again." And therein lies a tale, since George Charles Boldt, the first manager of the old Waldorf-Astoria, hailed from Philadelphia.

Born on the Isle of Rügen, in the Baltic Sea, Boldt came to the United States in 1864, at age thirteen. By 1888, he owned two hotels in Philadelphia—the Bellevue and the Stratford. It was a dark and stormy night, circa 1890, when a couple entered the lobby of one of these hotels looking for a room; but since there were three conventions being held in the city, all of the rooms were booked. Boldt, though, let the couple sleep in his own room. Before they left the following morning, the man told Boldt that he ought to be operating a better hotel, and that one day he might build one for him. The stranger turned out to be William Waldorf Astor, and that's how Boldt ended up at the Waldorf-Astoria.

Boldt eventually returned to Philadelphia, where in 1904 he opened the Bellevue-Stratford, the hotel to which Crockett refers as being host to the Clover Club, but it's possible that the drink could actually predate this grand hotel: In 1881, Boldt's Bellevue Hotel had been host to Philadelphia's Clover Club, and the society obviously had quite an impact on his life. He married in 1877, and he and his wife, Louise, had two children, George Jr., and Louise Clover.

The first recipes for the Clover Club Cocktail called for raspberry syrup, which has been replaced by grenadine over time. Use raspberry syrup if you have it at hand—without it this drink isn't much to talk about.

2 ounces gin
1 ounce fresh lemon juice
1 egg white
raspberry syrup or grenadine to taste

SHAKE AND STRAIN into a chilled cocktail glass.

COGNAC COULIS

FAMILY: **FROZEN DRINKS** Adapted from a recipe by Mardee and me for *Food & Wine* magazine in 1996.

2 ripe kiwi fruits, peeled and sliced
5 large ripe strawberries, hulled
3 ounces cognac
1 ounce Grand Marnier

Reserve two slices of the kiwi for garnish. Blend with enough ice to almost fill a 12-ounce collins glass. Add the garnish.

COPPER SWAN COCKTAIL

FAMILY: **DUOS AND TRIOS** ❧ I came up with this one a couple of years ago for an article in *Whisky* magazine. Highland Park is a great malt to pair with apricot brandy, and other brands, especially those with a goodly amount of smoke in their character, will fare well in this drink if you alter the proportions according to their intensity. For example, if you use Laphroaig or Ardbeg malts, both of which are extremely peaty, you'll need more apricot brandy for balance.

2½ ounces Highland Park single-malt scotch
¾ ounce apricot brandy
1 lemon twist, for garnish

STIR AND STRAIN into an ice-filled rocks glass or a chilled cocktail glass. Add the garnish.

CORPSE REVIVER NO. 1

FAMILY: **FRENCH-ITALIAN: WHISKEY AND BRANDY** ❧ Corpse Revivers were a category of drinks that we might call eye-openers, or a hair of the dog. Craddock detailed two of these in *The Savoy Cocktail Book,* and underneath this one he instructed the reader that the drink should be "taken before 11 a.m., or whenever steam and energy are needed."

In 2001, Steve Gilberg, publisher of happyhours.com, made this drink using applejack as the base spirit, whereas Craddock put the emphasis on the brandy. Gilberg's version, in my opinion, was the better of the two, so this recipe is adapted from his formula.

2 ounces applejack
¾ ounce sweet vermouth
¾ ounce brandy

STIR AND STRAIN into a chilled cocktail glass.

CORPSE REVIVER NO. 2

FAMILY: **NEW ORLEANS SOURS** ❧ Based on Craddock's 1930 recipe, about which he noted, "Four of these taken in swift succession will unrevive the corpse again."

¾ ounce gin
¾ ounce triple sec
¾ ounce Lillet Blonde
¾ ounce fresh lemon juice
absinthe substitute to taste (go easy)

SHAKE AND STRAIN into a chilled cocktail glass.

COSMOPOLITAN

FAMILY: **NEW ORLEANS SOURS** We may never know the truth about where this drink originated—it's a mystery as deep as the Martini's. Although I suspect that it could have been the product of a marketing genius who was charged with promoting Cointreau, the people at the company today truly don't seem to know. This runaway hit of the 1990s continues to be successful today. And deservedly so.

1½ ounces citrus vodka
1 ounce triple sec
½ ounce fresh lime juice
1 or 2 dashes cranberry juice, for color
1 lime wedge, for garnish

SHAKE AND STRAIN into a chilled cocktail glass. Add the garnish.

COSMOPOLITAN (BOTTLED)

FAMILY: **BOTTLED COCKTAILS**

MAKES 22 OUNCES

10 ounces citrus vodka
4 ounces triple sec
2 ounces fresh lime juice
1 ounce cranberry juice
5 ounces bottled water

MIX AND CHILL for a minimum of six hours.

CRÈME DE MENTHE FRAPPÉ

FAMILY: **COBBLERS** — In American barspeak, the acute accent on the *e* in *frappé* is traditionally ignored.

2½ ounces green crème de menthe

Simply pour the crème de menthe into a champagne saucer glass filled with crushed ice and serve with short straws.

CRUX COCKTAIL

FAMILY: **NEW ORLEANS SOURS** — Adapted from a recipe in *Jones' Complete Barguide.*

¾ ounce brandy
¾ ounce Dubonnet Rouge
¾ ounce triple sec
¾ ounce fresh lemon juice

SHAKE AND STRAIN into a chilled cocktail glass.

CUBA LIBRE

FAMILY: **HIGHBALLS** — In the late 1930s, when Charles H. Baker Jr. wrote *The Gentleman's Companion,* this drink was just coming into vogue. According to his book, the best way to make it is to squeeze the juice from a whole small lime into a collins glass, drop the lime into the glass, and muddle it so that the oils coat the interior of the glass; then add the rum and lots of ice and cola. These days it seems that most bartenders merely make a rum and cola with a wedge of lime—a very unsatisfactory drink.

Although it isn't necessary to muddle the lime—with no sugar to abrade the zest, few of the essential oils are released, and with sugar the drink becomes unbearably sweet—it is necessary to add at least one ounce of lime juice to balance out the sweetness of the cola. This drink is seldom held in high regard, but when made properly it can be a heavenly potion.

2 ounces light rum
1 ounce fresh lime juice
3 ounces cola
1 lime wedge, for garnish

BUILD in the order given in an ice-filled highball glass. Add the garnish.

DAIQUIRI

FAMILY: **SOURS** Most sources claim that the Daiquiri was created in 1898, by a couple of Americans working in Cuba just after the Spanish-American War. It's said that the drink was made as a cure for or a medicine to ward off malaria. Whatever the truth, this Sour calls for lime juice instead of lemon juice; and of course the base spirit is rum.

The first printed mention of the Daiquiri I can find appears in Frank Shay's 1929 book *Drawn from the Wood,* and the authors insist that Bacardi rum be used if the drink is to be properly constructed. Of course, any white rum will suffice in the making of this drink, but the same is not true of the Bacardi Cocktail (see page 210).

2 ounces light rum
1 ounce fresh lime juice
½ ounce simple syrup
1 lime wedge, for garnish

SHAKE AND STRAIN into an ice-filled wine glass. Add the garnish.

DARK AND STORMY

FAMILY: **HIGHBALLS** A Bermudan drink made with dark Bermudan rum and cloudy, if not quite stormy, ginger beer.

2 ounces Gosling's Black Seal rum
3 ounces ginger beer
1 lime wedge, for garnish

BUILD in an ice-filled highball glass. Add the garnish.

DEADLY SIN

FAMILY: **FRENCH-ITALIAN: WHISKEY AND BRANDY** Adapted from a recipe by Rafael Ballesteros of Spain, a member of the DrinkBoy community board of cocktailians.

2 ounces bourbon
⅓ ounce sweet vermouth
¼ ounce maraschino liqueur
1 dash orange bitters
1 orange twist, for garnish

STIR AND STRAIN into a chilled cocktail glass. Add the garnish.

DEAUVILLE COCKTAIL

FAMILY: **NEW ORLEANS SOURS** — The original recipe, from the 1930s, called for calvados, but I find that applejack works very well here.

¾ ounce brandy
¾ ounce applejack or calvados
¾ ounce triple sec
¾ ounce fresh lemon juice

SHAKE AND STRAIN into a chilled cocktail glass.

DEBONAIR

FAMILY: **DUOS AND TRIOS** — My wife and I came up with this one in the early nineties. It's based on the Whisky Mac, a somewhat popular drink in the United Kingdom that calls for scotch and green ginger wine. If you can't get ginger liqueur in your neck of the woods, experiment with green ginger wine instead. I suggest two bottlings of single malt here, chosen for their briny characteristics, which play well off the ginger liqueur. Remember that if you use any bottling other than the ones suggested here, you'll have to fool around with ratios to get the right balance.

2½ ounces Oban or Springbank single-malt scotch
1 ounce Original Canton Delicate Ginger liqueur
1 lemon twist, for garnish

STIR AND STRAIN into a chilled cocktail glass. Add the garnish.

DELICIOUS COCKTAIL

FAMILY: **SOURS** — Adapted from a recipe by Ryan Magarian of Restaurant Zoe in Seattle, this drink is similar in concept to the Southside Cocktail (see page 339). Aside from the fact that this recipe calls for lime juice, rather than the lemons in the Southside, note that the mint in this drink is used as an aromatic garnish only—the other cocktail calls for incorporating the mint into the drink. When you use mint in a cocktailian manner, you should weigh these options.

2 ounces Tanqueray No. 10 gin
1 ounce fresh lime juice
1 ounce simple syrup
5 fresh mint sprigs, dusted with confectioners' sugar, for garnish

SHAKE AND STRAIN into a chilled, sugar-rimmed cocktail glass. Add the garnish.

DELMARVA COCKTAIL

FAMILY: **INTERNATIONAL SOURS** Adapted from a recipe by Ted Haigh, Dr. Cocktail, Los Angeles. Below, you'll find two variations on this drink—it turned out to be the perfect vehicle for a little cocktailian experimentation.

2 ounces straight rye whiskey
½ ounce dry vermouth
½ ounce white crème de menthe
½ ounce fresh lemon juice
1 fresh mint leaf, for garnish

SHAKE AND STRAIN into a chilled cocktail glass. Add the garnish.

DELMARVA COCKTAIL NO. 2

FAMILY: **INTERNATIONAL SOURS** When I tried Doc's Delmarva Cocktail, above, I thought that it would be an ideal drink to play with by changing just one ingredient. Instead of crème de menthe, I went for the chocolate flavors in crème de cacao. The two drinks are entirely different from each other and offer a good example, I believe, of how relatively simple it can be to create a new drink, providing that the original recipe works well.

2 ounces straight rye whiskey
½ ounce dry vermouth
½ ounce white crème de cacao
½ ounce fresh lemon juice
1 fresh mint leaf, for garnish

SHAKE AND STRAIN into a chilled cocktail glass. Add the garnish.

DELMARVA COCKTAIL NO. 3

FAMILY: **INTERNATIONAL SOURS** — Experimenting further on Doc's original recipe, this time I substituted amaretto for the crème de menthe, but I had to add a little more lemon juice before the drink was properly balanced. I took away the mint leaf garnish, too.

2 ounces straight rye whiskey
½ ounce dry vermouth
½ ounce amaretto
¾ ounce fresh lemon juice

SHAKE AND STRAIN into a chilled cocktail glass.

DIRTY MARTINI

FAMILY: **FRENCH-ITALIAN: GIN AND VODKA** — This is probably one of the world's worst drinks when made incorrectly, but when properly prepared, with not too much olive brine added, it can be a sterling potion.

2½ ounces gin or vodka
½ ounce dry vermouth
olive brine to taste (go easy)
1 olive, for garnish

STIR AND STRAIN into a chilled cocktail glass. Add the garnish.

DISARONNO MARGARITA

FAMILY: **INTERNATIONAL SOURS** — I developed this for Disaronno in 2001, and it's a good example of needing to adjust proportions when making changes to a standard drink. The Disaronno liqueur is far sweeter than the triple sec in the original Margarita formula, so I had to experiment with ratios until the drink was balanced. I ended up with only half as much Disaronno as triple sec, and although its almond flavor still shines through, the tart lime juice is also evident.

1½ ounces white tequila
½ ounce Disaronno liqueur
½ ounce fresh lime juice

SHAKE AND STRAIN into a chilled cocktail glass.

DOG'S NOSE

FAMILY: **BEER- AND CIDER-BASED DRINKS** — The Dog's Nose is mentioned in Dickens's *Pickwick Papers,* and his great-grandson, Cedric Dickens, claimed in his book *Drinking with Dickens* that a certain Mr. Walker thought that tasting a Dog's Nose twice a week for twenty years had lost him the use of his right hand. Mr. Walker had since joined a temperance society. This is a strange mixture, indeed, but it works very well.

12 ounces porter or stout
2 teaspoons brown sugar
2 ounces gin
freshly grated nutmeg, for garnish

Pour the porter or stout into a large sturdy glass and heat it in a microwave for about one minute. Add the brown sugar and gin and stir lightly. Add the garnish.

DREAMY DORINI SMOKING MARTINI

FAMILY: **ORPHANS** — Adapted from a recipe by Audrey Saunders, New York City's Libation Goddess, this drink displays the height of the cocktailian craft. If you know the Laphroaig single-malt scotch at all, you'll be aware that the ten-year-old bottling is unforgiving in terms of peat and smoke, and Pernod can easily take over a drink if it's not used with caution. Here Audrey thought it all out: One thing that Pernod can't easily quell is Laphroaig, and adding the vodka brings both the scotch and the Pernod to their knees. The whole drink comes together in harmony, and a masterpiece is born. I've also used Ardbeg ten-year-old single-malt scotch to make this one, and I've been delighted with the results.

2 ounces Grey Goose vodka
½ ounce Laphroaig ten-year-old single-malt scotch
2 to 3 drops Pernod
1 lemon twist, for garnish

STIR AND STRAIN into a chilled cocktail glass. Add the garnish.

DUBLINER

FAMILY: **FRENCH-ITALIAN: WHISKEY AND BRANDY** — Created by Mardee and me for St. Patrick's Day 1999, this is an easy recipe to break down and analyze. Without the Grand Marnier, the formula is a Manhattan-style drink that calls for Irish whiskey instead of bourbon. Add the Grand Marnier—a cognac-based orange liqueur—and supplement the orange flavors with some orange bitters, and voilà, it's a new drink.

2 ounces Irish whiskey
½ ounce sweet vermouth
½ ounce Grand Marnier
orange bitters to taste
1 maraschino cherry (green, if possible), for garnish

STIR AND STRAIN into a chilled cocktail glass. Add the garnish.

DUBONNET COCKTAIL

FAMILY: **DUOS AND TRIOS** — The original Dubonnet Cocktail, from the 1930s, had no garnish, but I find that a lemon twist works well here. If you alter the ratios, using twice as much gin as Dubonnet, and add a couple of dashes each of curaçao and Angostura bitters, plus one dash of Absente, you have yourself a Dubonnet Royal, as detailed in W. J. Tarling's *Café Royal Cocktail Book* (1937).

1½ ounces Dubonnet Rouge
1½ ounces gin
1 lemon twist, for garnish

STIR AND STRAIN into a chilled cocktail glass. Add the garnish.

DUTCH SQUIRREL

FAMILY: **SQUIRREL SOURS**

2 ounces Van Gogh Wild Appel vodka
¾ ounce crème de noyau
¾ ounce fresh lemon juice

SHAKE AND STRAIN into a chilled cocktail glass.

ELEGANT WITHOUT NUMBER

FAMILY: **ORPHANS** ~ Adapted from a recipe by Rafael Ballesteros of Spain.

2 ounces vodka
¾ ounce calvados
½ ounce Grand Marnier
1 maraschino cherry, for garnish

STIR AND STRAIN into a chilled cocktail glass. Add the garnish.

EL FLORIDITA NO. 1

FAMILY: **INTERNATIONAL SOURS** ~ There are two versions of El Floridita, the first found by Ted Haigh in a 1930 recipe book from El Floridita bar in Havana, where Hemingway sipped these delicious drinks. The second is a more widely known version that calls for crème de cacao rather than maraschino liqueur. Both are delightful. This version is adapted from the first recipe.

2 ounces light rum
¾ ounce fresh lime juice
½ ounce simple syrup
maraschino liqueur to taste

SHAKE AND STRAIN into a chilled cocktail glass.

EL FLORIDITA NO. 2

FAMILY: **INTERNATIONAL SOURS** ~ This is a complicated drink to construct, but when properly made, it's a classic. The chocolate notes from the crème de cacao should appear only in the finish—if you taste it straight off you've added too much.

1½ ounces light rum
½ ounce sweet vermouth
½ ounce fresh lime juice
white crème de cacao to taste (go very easy)
grenadine to taste

SHAKE AND STRAIN into a chilled cocktail glass.

EL PRESIDENTE

FAMILY: **SOURS** ~ I found a few different recipes for drinks under this name, but this one, adapted from the 1949 edition of *Old Mr. Boston,* works best for today's tastes. This is an obvious variation on the Daiquiri—just a little pineapple juice and a dash of grenadine have been added instead of simple syrup.

2 ounces light rum
½ ounce fresh lime juice
½ ounce pineapple juice
dash of grenadine

SHAKE AND STRAIN into a chilled cocktail glass.

ENGLISH ROSE COCKTAIL

FAMILY: **INTERNATIONAL SOURS** ~ This cocktail is adapted from a recipe in the first edition (1935) of *Old Mr. Boston.*

1½ ounces gin
¾ ounce dry vermouth
¾ ounce apricot brandy
¼ ounce fresh lemon juice
grenadine to taste

SHAKE AND STRAIN into a chilled, sugar-rimmed cocktail glass.

ESQUIVEL COCKTAIL

FAMILY: **CHAMPAGNE COCKTAILS** ~ Adapted from a recipe by Dr. Cocktail (Ted Haigh), who wrote, in 2002, "Esquivel was the name of the bandleader who just died; he wrote *Space Age Bachelor Pad Music.* The drink was created for Byron Werner, who rediscovered Esquivel after years of obscurity and allowed him several years of revitalized fame before his demise. The drink was a characterization of Esquivel himself: sweet, spicy, tropical, tangy."

2 ounces light rum
½ ounce Kahlúa
1 ounce pineapple juice
Angostura bitters to taste
orange bitters to taste
chilled champagne
1 orange twist, for garnish
ground cinnamon, for garnish

SHAKE AND STRAIN the rum, Kahlúa, pineapple juice, and bitters into a chilled cocktail glass. Top with a little champagne. Add the garnishes.

EVE'S SEDUCTION APPLE MARTINI

FAMILY: **CHAMPAGNE COCKTAILS** — Adapted from a recipe by Matt Knepper of the Fifth Floor Bar, Hotel Palomar, San Francisco.

1½ ounces Van Gogh Wild Appel vodka
¼ ounce amaretto
¼ ounce fresh lemon juice
¼ ounce fresh lime juice
¼ ounce simple syrup
chilled champagne

SHAKE AND STRAIN the vodka, amaretto, lemon juice, lime juice, and simple syrup into a chilled champagne flute. Top with a little champagne.

FALLEN ANGEL COCKTAIL

FAMILY: **CHAMPAGNE COCKTAILS** — Adapted from a recipe from Drovers Tap Room, New York City.

1 ounce Bacardi Limón
¼ ounce triple sec
¼ ounce cranberry juice
chilled champagne

SHAKE AND STRAIN the Bacardi Limón, triple sec, and cranberry juice into a chilled cocktail glass. Top with a little champagne.

FERNANDITO COCKTAIL

FAMILY: **INTERNATIONAL SOURS** Adapted from a recipe created in 1997 by Mardee and me for *Food & Wine* magazine. We named it for Fernando Martinez, then with Rums of Puerto Rico.

2 ounces Bacardi Spice rum
½ ounce Chambord
½ ounce fresh orange juice
½ ounce fresh lime juice
1 lime wedge, for garnish

SHAKE AND STRAIN into a chilled cocktail glass. Add the garnish.

FIFTH AVENUE

FAMILY: **POUSSE-CAFÉS** Adapted from Craddock's 1930 recipe.

¾ ounce white crème de cacao
¾ ounce apricot brandy
¾ ounce cream

LAYER in the order given in a pousse-café glass.

FISH HOUSE COCKTAIL

FAMILY: **SOURS** Based on the Punch recipe below but with a little extra sweetness, gained by increasing the amounts of the peach brandy and the simple syrup.

1½ ounces dark rum
½ ounce brandy
½ ounce peach brandy
½ ounce simple syrup
¼ ounce fresh lime juice
¼ ounce fresh lemon juice

SHAKE AND STRAIN into a chilled cocktail glass.

FISH HOUSE PUNCH

FAMILY: **PUNCHES** — The Fish House Club in Philadelphia was founded in 1732 when a group of fishermen formed a society dedicated to gastronomy as well as angling. Although the club is officially known as the State in Schuylkill, it's often referred to as the Schuylkill Fishing Company or the Fish House Club. George Washington dined at this club, and some historians say that three blank pages in his diary reflect the effects of the Fish House Punch that he indulged in during his visit.

MAKES 10 TO 12 FIVE-OUNCE SERVINGS

1 bottle (750 milliliters) dark rum
9 ounces brandy
4 ounces peach brandy
4 ounces simple syrup
5 ounces fresh lime juice
5 ounces fresh lemon juice
1 large block of ice, for serving

Pour all of the ingredients into a large nonreactive pan or bowl; stir well. Cover and refrigerate until chilled, at least 4 hours. Place the large block of ice in the center of a large punch bowl. Add the punch.

FLAME OF LOVE

FAMILY: **ORPHANS** — Adapted from a recipe created for Dean Martin by Pepe, the longtime bartender at Chasen's in West Hollywood. The drink has been served to Frank Sinatra, Gregory Peck, Tommy Lasorda, and (then presidential hopeful) George Bush.

½ ounce dry sherry
2 orange twists
3 ounces gin or vodka

RINSE a chilled cocktail glass with the sherry and discard the excess. Flame one of the orange twists into the glass. STIR AND STRAIN the gin or vodka into the glass, then flame the remaining orange twist over the drink.

FLIRTINI MARTINI

FAMILY: **ORPHANS** — As seen on *Sex and the City.*

2 ounces vodka
1 ounce pineapple juice
¼ ounce Chambord

SHAKE AND STRAIN into a chilled cocktail glass.

FOG CUTTER

FAMILY: **TROPICAL DRINKS** — Adapted from a recipe in *Jones' Complete Barguide.*

1½ ounces light rum
½ ounce brandy
½ ounce gin
2 ounces fresh orange juice
½ ounce fresh lemon juice
½ ounce orgeat syrup
¼ ounce cream sherry

SHAKE AND STRAIN everything except the sherry into an ice-filled collins glass. FLOAT the sherry.

FOOTLOOSE COCKTAIL

FAMILY: **NEW ORLEANS SOURS** — Adapted from a recipe by Wesly Moore, from Pasadena, California.

2 ounces Stolichnaya Razberi
1 ounce triple sec
½ ounce fresh lime juice
Peychaud's bitters to taste
1 lime twist, for garnish

SHAKE AND STRAIN into a chilled cocktail glass. Add the garnish.

FREDDIE FUDPUCKER

FAMILY: **FLORIDA HIGHBALLS** — A variation on the Harvey Wallbanger.

2 ounces tequila
3 ounces fresh orange juice
¼ to ½ ounce Galliano

BUILD the tequila and the orange juice in an ice-filled highball glass. Stir briefly, then **FLOAT** the Galliano on top of the drink.

FRENCH CONNECTION

FAMILY: **DUOS AND TRIOS** Here's a simple little drink that I thought I had created in 2001. The good people at Grand Marnier, however, informed me that it had been around for quite a while before I came up with it. The cocktailian bartender might want to experiment with this formula by adding some fresh lemon juice, shaking the ingredients over ice, and straining it into a chilled cocktail glass.

3 ounces cognac
1 ounce Grand Marnier

STIR AND STRAIN into an ice-filled old-fashioned glass.

FRENCH CONNECTION COBBLER

FAMILY: **COBBLERS**

3 ounces brandy
1 ounce Grand Marnier
fruits in season, for garnish

BUILD in the order given in a wine glass filled with crushed ice. Add the garnish.

FRENCH-KISS SHOOTER

FAMILY: **POUSSE-CAFÉS**

½ ounce Frangelico
½ ounce Baileys Irish Cream
½ ounce amaretto

LAYER in the order given in a pousse-café glass.

FRENCH 75

FAMILY: **CHAMPAGNE COCKTAILS** ❧ The French 75 is one of those wonderful cocktails that is bound to stir up controversy: Should it be prepared with gin or cognac, lemon juice or lime juice? The oldest recipe that I've seen is in *The Savoy Cocktail Book* (1930); Harry Craddock prescribes gin and lemon juice and remarks, "Hits with remarkable precision." To my knowledge, it wasn't until David Embury stated that the drink should be made with cognac that the brandy version reared its head. I'm going to stick with the original gin-based recipe.

½ teaspoon simple syrup
½ ounce fresh lemon juice
1 ounce gin
4 ounces chilled champagne

BUILD in the order given in a collins glass filled with crushed ice. Stir briefly.

FRENCH SQUIRREL

FAMILY: **SQUIRREL SOURS** ❧ This is my favorite in the Squirrel-Sour family, and it truly lends itself to experimentation with other nut-flavored liqueurs, such as Frangelico or Nocello, instead of the crème de noyau.

2 ounces cognac
½ ounce crème de noyau
½ ounce fresh lemon juice
1 lemon twist, for garnish

SHAKE AND STRAIN into a chilled cocktail glass. Add the garnish.

FROZEN BANANA COLADA

FAMILY: **FROZEN DRINKS**

2 ounces dark rum
1 ripe banana, peeled and roughly chopped
2 ounces pineapple juice
1 ounce coconut cream
1 maraschino cherry, for garnish
1 pineapple cube, for garnish

Blend with enough ice to almost fill a 12-ounce collins glass. Add the garnishes.

FROZEN BANANA DAIQUIRI

FAMILY: **FROZEN DRINKS**

2 ounces light rum
1 overripe banana, peeled and sliced
1 ounce fresh lime juice

Blend with enough ice to almost fill a 12-ounce collins glass.

FROZEN CHI-CHI

FAMILY: **FROZEN DRINKS**

2 ounces vodka
½ cup pineapple cubes or 2 ounces pineapple juice
1½ ounces coconut cream
1 maraschino cherry, for garnish
1 pineapple cube, for garnish

Blend with enough ice to almost fill a 12-ounce collins glass. Add the garnishes.

FROZEN DAIQUIRI

FAMILY: **FROZEN DRINKS**

2 ounces light rum
1½ ounces fresh lime juice
¾ ounce simple syrup
1 lime wedge, for garnish

Blend with enough ice to almost fill a 12-ounce collins glass. Add the garnish.

FROZEN MARGARITA

FAMILY: **FROZEN DRINKS**

3 ounces white tequila
2 ounces triple sec
1 ounce fresh lime juice
1 lime wedge, for garnish

Blend with enough ice to almost fill a 12-ounce collins glass. Add the garnish.

FROZEN PIÑA COLADA

FAMILY: **FROZEN DRINKS** ⁓ There are a couple of stories about the birth of this drink, but the most plausible is that it was created in 1954 by bartender Ramón (Monchito) Marrero at the Caribe Hilton Hotel, in Puerto Rico. It is one of the very few sweet drinks that I love. I like to use fresh pineapple to make Piña Coladas, but canned pineapple chunks will suffice, and the sweetness of the canned variety is more dependable.

2 ounces dark rum
½ cup pineapple cubes or 2 ounces pineapple juice
1½ ounces coconut cream
1 maraschino cherry, for garnish
1 pineapple cube, for garnish

Blend with enough ice to almost fill a 12-ounce collins glass. Add the garnishes.

FUZZY NAVEL

FAMILY: **FLORIDA HIGHBALLS**

1 ounce vodka
1 ounce peach schnapps
3 ounces fresh orange juice

BUILD in an ice-filled highball glass.

GIBSON

FAMILY: **FRENCH-ITALIAN: GIN AND VODKA** ⁓ Reportedly created in the 1930s at New York's Players Club by bartender Charlie Connolly. It was named for famed magazine illustrator Charles Dana Gibson, who requested "something different" from Connolly. This is merely a Martini with a different garnish, but the cocktail onions work very well as a foil to either gin or vodka, so perhaps it does deserve a name all its own.

2½ ounces gin or vodka
½ ounce dry vermouth
1 or 3 cocktail onions, for garnish

STIR AND STRAIN into a chilled cocktail glass. Add the garnish.

GIMLET

FAMILY: **ORPHANS** — This is from www.royal-navy.mod.uk: "Gimlette: Common name for gin laced with lime-juice cordial. The name comes from the name of the naval surgeon—Gimlette—who introduced this drink as a means of inducing his messmates to take lime juice as an anti-scorbutic. Sir Thomas D. Gimlette, KCB, joined the Navy in October, 1879, as a Surgeon; he retired in June, 1913, as a Surgeon General."

Although gin was the primary liquor in this drink, many people now drink Vodka Gimlets, and as you see, common usage has resulted in a change of spelling over the past century or so.

2½ ounces gin or vodka
¾ ounce lime-juice cordial, such as Rose's
1 lime wedge, for garnish

STIR AND STRAIN into an ice-filled old-fashioned glass. Add the garnish.

GIN AND TONIC

FAMILY: **HIGHBALLS**

2 ounces gin
3 ounces tonic water
1 lime wedge, for garnish

BUILD in an ice-filled highball glass. Add the garnish.

GIN BUCK

FAMILY: **HIGHBALLS**

1 lemon wedge
2 ounces gin
3 to 4 ounces ginger ale

Squeeze the juice from the lemon wedge into a highball glass, then add the wedge to the glass. Fill the glass with ice, add the gin and ginger ale, and stir briefly.

GIN RICKEY

FAMILY: **HIGHBALLS** ❧ "The Rickey owes its name to Colonel 'Joe' Rickey . . . [who] had been a lobbyist in Washington, and as such used to buy drinks for members of Congress in the glamorous days before they had come to depend upon the discreet activities of gentlemen in green hats to keep them wet while they voted dry. The drink was invented and named for him at Shoemaker's, famous in Washington as a Congressional hangout," reported Albert Stevens Crockett in *The Old Waldorf-Astoria Bar Book* (1935).

I'm not a fan of this drink, which can be made with any white liquor as a base, but I have known people who love it. The secret is in the amount of lime juice used, and many bartenders are guilty of serving merely a Gin and Club Soda Highball with a squeeze of juice from just one wedge of lime.

¾ ounce fresh lime juice
2 ounces gin
3 to 4 ounces club soda
1 lime wedge, for garnish

BUILD in an ice-filled collins glass. Add the garnish.

GLENKINCHIE CLINCHER

FAMILY: **ORPHANS** ❧ I was hired by Glenkinchie to create this one. It was served at a reception for Tony Bennett in London in 2000.

2 ounces Glenkinchie single-malt scotch
½ ounce amaretto
½ ounce triple sec
1 maraschino cherry, for garnish

STIR AND STRAIN into an ice-filled rocks glass or a chilled cocktail glass. Add the garnish.

GODDAUGHTER

FAMILY: **DUOS AND TRIOS**

2 ounces vodka
1 ounce amaretto
1 ounce cream

SHAKE AND STRAIN into an ice-filled old-fashioned glass.

GODFATHER

FAMILY: **DUOS AND TRIOS**

2 ounces scotch
1 ounce amaretto

STIR AND STRAIN into an ice-filled old-fashioned glass.

GODMOTHER

FAMILY: **DUOS AND TRIOS**

2 ounces vodka
1 ounce amaretto

STIR AND STRAIN into an ice-filled old-fashioned glass.

GODSON

FAMILY: **DUOS AND TRIOS**

2 ounces scotch
1 ounce amaretto
1 ounce light cream

SHAKE AND STRAIN into an ice-filled old-fashioned glass.

GOLDEN CADILLAC

FAMILY: **DUOS AND TRIOS** — This drink, which appeared in the sixties or seventies, was reputedly created at Poor Red's, a barbecue joint in El Dorado, California. This place is now the nation's leading "consumer" of Galliano, reportedly going through as many as 1,700 bottles in 2000, and a whopping 87 bottles during "one remarkable evening." At three-quarters of an ounce of Galliano per drink, that works out to some 2,940 Golden Cadillacs; if the "remarkable evening" lasted for as long as eight hours, the poor guys behind the stick at Poor Red's had to make, serve, take money, and give change for a Golden Cadillac every ten seconds.

2 ounces white crème de cacao
¾ ounce Galliano
1 ounce cream

SHAKE AND STRAIN into a chilled cocktail glass.

GOLDFISH COCKTAIL

FAMILY: **FRENCH-ITALIAN: GIN AND VODKA** ~ Served at the Aquarium Speakeasy in Manhattan during Prohibition, the original recipe, detailed in *On the Town in New York* by Michael and Ariane Batterberry, called for equal amounts of each ingredient. The proportions in my recipe below result in the gin not being so overpowered by the goldwasser, and the vermouth forms a subtle backdrop.

2 ounces gin
1 ounce dry vermouth
½ ounce Danziger goldwasser

STIR AND STRAIN into a chilled cocktail glass.

GOTHAM COCKTAIL

FAMILY: **INTERNATIONAL SOURS** ~ Adapted from a recipe created by David Wondrich in 2001 for the debut issue of New York's *Gotham* magazine.

2 ounces cognac
1 ounce Noilly Prat dry vermouth
½ ounce crème de cassis
2 dashes fresh lemon juice
1 lemon twist, for garnish

STIR vigorously with cracked ice. **STRAIN** into a chilled cocktail glass and garnish with the lemon twist.

GRASSHOPPER

FAMILY: **DUOS AND TRIOS** ~ I have been guilty of scoffing this drink. If you enjoy chocolate-covered mints, don't make the same mistake. The formula below is fairly generic and results in a well-balanced drink, but you can experiment by using more or less of either of the two liqueurs.

1½ ounces green crème de menthe
1½ ounces white crème de cacao
1 ounce cream

SHAKE AND STRAIN into a chilled cocktail glass.

GREYHOUND

FAMILY: **FLORIDA HIGHBALLS**

2 ounces vodka
3 ounces fresh grapefruit juice

BUILD in an ice-filled highball glass.

HARVEY WALLBANGER

FAMILY: **FLORIDA HIGHBALLS** ~ According to an article by Brooks Clark in *Bartender* magazine, the Harvey Wallbanger was created at a party in the mid-1960s in Newport Beach, California. The host of the party was a certain Bill Doner, then a sports editor for a small newspaper, who, finding that the only potables he had on hand were vodka, frozen orange juice, and a bottle of Galliano, simply mixed them all together. In the early hours of the morning a guest by the name of Harvey was found banging his head against the wall and blaming Doner's concoction for his misery. A drink was born.

2 ounces vodka
3 ounces fresh orange juice
¼ to ½ ounce Galliano

BUILD the vodka and the orange juice in an ice-filled highball glass. Stir briefly, then **FLOAT** the Galliano on top of the drink.

HAWAIIAN COCKTAIL

FAMILY: **ORPHANS** ~ Adapted from the recipe in the 1935 edition of *Old Mr. Boston*. I added bitters to this drink to give it some complexity.

2 ounces gin
½ ounce triple sec
½ ounce pineapple juice
2 dashes of Angostura bitters

SHAKE AND STRAIN into a chilled cocktail glass.

HAYMAKER SPECIAL

FAMILY: **ORPHANS** ~ Adapted from a recipe by Dr. Cocktail (Ted Haigh).

2 ounces calvados
½ ounce Dubonnet Rouge
½ ounce triple sec
½ ounce fresh grapefruit juice
1 lime spiral, for garnish

SHAKE AND STRAIN into a chilled cocktail glass. Add the garnish.

HEMINGWAY DAIQUIRI

FAMILY: **FROZEN DRINKS** ~ Not to be confused with El Floridita, this frozen drink is very tart and very refreshing. The following recipe is a result of experimentation—the ingredients are true to the original, but the ratios aren't.

3 ounces light rum
1½ ounces fresh lime juice
1½ ounces fresh grapefruit juice
1 ounce maraschino liqueur

BLEND with enough ice to almost fill a 12-ounce collins glass.

HOP TOAD COCKTAIL

FAMILY: **INTERNATIONAL SOURS** ~ Adapted from a recipe in Crockett's *The Old Waldorf-Astoria Bar Book*. I played around with ratios on this one and added bitters for complexity.

1½ ounces dark rum
1 ounce apricot brandy
½ ounce fresh lime juice
Angostura bitters to taste

SHAKE AND STRAIN into a chilled cocktail glass.

HOT BUTTERED RUM

FAMILY: **HOT DRINKS** A recipe titled Buttered Toddy, calling for rum, water, honey, nutmeg, lemon juice, and "a piece of fresh butter about the size of a walnut," appeared in the 1860 book *Practical Housewife.* The best Hot Buttered Rum I ever tasted was a fairly simple affair made with spiced rum, and hot apple cider instead of hot water. It was created by bartender Nick Hydos at Painter's Tavern, in Cornwall on Hudson, New York.

1 teaspoon honey
1 whole clove
4 ounces hot water or hot apple cider
2 ounces dark rum or spiced rum
½ teaspoon unsalted butter
ground cinnamon to taste
1 cinnamon stick, about 4 inches long

Place the honey, clove, and hot water or apple cider into an Irish coffee glass, and stir well to dissolve the honey completely. Add the rum, butter, and ground cinnamon. Stir briefly with the cinnamon stick, and serve with the cinnamon stick in the glass.

HOT TODDY

FAMILY: **HOT DRINKS** The name may derive from the Hindu *tári tádi,* which refers to fermented coconut milk or the fermented sap from various trees. When the drink arrived in Europe, Toddies were made with a base spirit, various spices, sometimes a twist of lemon or orange, and water. *The American Herbal,* published in 1801, called the toddy a "salutary liquor," and Dickens mentions a Whisky Toddy in *The Pickwick Papers:* "I don't quite recollect how many tumblers of whisky toddy each man drank after supper."

Although Toddies were, at least in the 1700s, made with either cold or hot water, today all Toddies are hot. You can prepare Toddies with hot tea instead of plain hot water, and the abundance of flavored teas currently on the market makes this drink ideal for experimentation.

You can also experiment with different herbs and spices with which to flavor your Toddies, although most recipes call for the usual bunch of what I refer to as "Christmas spices"—cinnamon, cloves, nutmeg, allspice, and the like. A Hot Toddy is one of the very few drinks I can think of in which I recommend the use of honey as a sweetening agent, and this works very well indeed when using scotch as your base liquor. Other sweetening agents can be introduced in the form of liqueurs, of course, but many aren't suited to this drink, since they can detract from the subtle spiciness of the Toddy and overwhelm the drink completely. Nutty liqueurs such as amaretto or hazelnut liqueur work well here.

On the liquor front, I recommend that you stick with brown goods—whiskey, brandy, and dark rum all work well as a base for a Toddy, but white goods such as gin, vodka, tequila, and light rum aren't the best vehicles here.

3 whole cloves
1 cinnamon stick, about 4 inches long
1 teaspoon honey
4 to 5 ounces boiling water
2 ounces bourbon, scotch, rye, brandy, or dark rum
freshly grated nutmeg or allspice
1 lemon twist, for garnish

Place the cloves, cinnamon stick, and honey into a preheated Irish coffee glass and add the boiling water. Stir briefly to dissolve the honey, and allow the mixture to stand for 3 to 4 minutes. Add the liquor, stir briefly, then dust the top of the drink with the nutmeg or allspice. Add the garnish.

HURRICANE

FAMILY: **TROPICAL DRINKS** This drink was created at Pat O'Brien's in New Orleans sometime during the 1940s, but the original recipe seems to be lost. The good folk at www.patobriens.com, who sell Hurricane mix, told me that they believe "passion fruit juice, lemon, sugar, and probably a few other flavors" were used, but they had no other information, so I turned to Chuck Taggart, from www.gumbopages.com, for a little guidance. The following recipe is based on Chuck's version of the Hurricane, but I used lemon juice, whereas he uses lime juice.

1½ ounces light rum
1½ ounces dark rum
1 ounce fresh orange juice
1 ounce fresh lemon juice
2 ounces passion fruit juice
½ ounce simple syrup
grenadine to taste
1 maraschino cherry, for garnish
1 orange wheel, for garnish

SHAKE AND STRAIN into an ice-filled hurricane glass. Add the garnishes.

INCOME TAX COCKTAIL

FAMILY: **FRENCH-ITALIAN: GIN AND VODKA** ~ Note that this is merely a Bronx with Angostura bitters—it's an ideal drink to offer when April 15 rolls around.

2 ounces gin
¼ ounce sweet vermouth
¼ ounce dry vermouth
1 ounce fresh orange juice
Angostura bitters to taste
1 orange twist, for garnish

SHAKE AND STRAIN into a chilled cocktail glass. Add the garnish.

IRISH AND INTERNATIONAL COFFEES

FAMILY: **HOT DRINKS** ~ Irish Coffee was originally created in the 1940s by Joe Sheridan, a bartender at Shannon Airport, Ireland, who wanted to fix a drink that would appeal to American tourists.

Stanton Delaplane, a reporter for the *San Francisco Chronicle,* sampled one of Sheridan's coffees and took the recipe to his local hangout, the Buena Vista in San Francisco, which now claims to sell over fifteen hundred Irish Coffees per day. The plaque on the wall outside the Buena Vista claims that it sold its first one in 1952.

Irish Coffee is a fairly simple affair, but it can be a very appealing drink providing that fresh cream is used. The drink should be sweetened according to the customer's liking—always ask before you make the drink, as once the cream is floated on top there's no turning back.

It's far easier to use whipped cream when making an Irish Coffee, since it can be spooned on top of the drink, where it will float with no problem whatsoever. It's better, though, to whip fresh light cream until it thickens, but not enough to achieve stiff peaks. Depending on the consistency of the cream at this point, you might be able to pour it slowly onto the top of the drink, where, if it's thick enough, it will float; or pour it over the back of a teaspoon as though you were making a Pousse-Café.

I prefer to use simple syrup rather than sugar to sweeten this drink, since it's already dissolved and it distributes itself quickly in the coffee. You might want to try making simple syrup with brown sugar for this one, too. It works very well. You can also think about using a liqueur to sweeten your Irish Coffee; of course, Irish Mist would be the natural choice, but other liqueurs, such as Bénédictine, can work quite well here, too—just be sure to let the customer know of your intentions.

2 ounces Irish whiskey
4 to 5 ounces hot coffee
simple syrup to taste
whipped cream

BUILD in an Irish coffee glass. Float the whipped cream on top.

INTERNATIONAL COFFEES

These coffees are made exactly like an Irish Coffee, but various spirits and sweetening agents are used to symbolize whichever country the drink represents. French Coffee, therefore, would call for cognac, and although simple syrup can be used as a sweetening agent, you might think about trying a French liqueur, such as Grand Marnier, instead.

There are no strict rules about the names and ingredients in these coffees, but it is important to make sure that the customer is aware of which ingredients you are using, and that those ingredients represent the name of the drink. Some International Coffees call for a liqueur as a base, and then, of course, no additional sweetening agent is needed. Here are some suggestions for various styles. In all cases the drink is **BUILT** with 4 to 5 ounces of hot coffee in an Irish coffee glass.

NAME	LIQUOR OR LIQUEUR 1	LIQUOR OR LIQUEUR 2
American No. 1	Bourbon	Peach Schnapps
American No. 2	Bourbon	Southern Comfort
American No. 3	Rye Whiskey	Cinnamon Schnapps
American No. 4	Bourbon	Wild Turkey Liqueur
Caribbean	Spiced Rum	Tia Maria
French	Cognac	Grand Marnier
Gaelic	Scotch	Drambuie or Glayva
German	Jägermeister	
Greek No. 1	Metaxa	Simple Syrup
Greek No. 2	Ouzo	
Italian No. 1	Frangelico	
Italian No. 2	Amaretto	
Italian No. 3	Limoncello	
Jamaican No. 1	Dark Rum	Tia Maria
Jamaican No. 2	Tia Maria	
Keoke	Brandy	Kahlúa and dark crème de cacao (optional)
Mexican	Kahlúa	
New Orleans	Rye Whiskey	Herbsaint
Spanish	Brandy de Jerez	Cuarenta y Tres

IRISH PEACH CREAM

FAMILY: **DUOS AND TRIOS** My wife, Mardee, and I developed this simple recipe for Baileys Irish Cream in the late 1990s. It's a sweet drink but highly adaptable—you can substitute any flavor of vodka in this recipe and change the name appropriately.

2 ounces Baileys Irish Cream
2 ounces peach-flavored vodka

SHAKE AND STRAIN into in ice-filled rocks glass.

IRISH SQUIRREL

FAMILY: **SQUIRREL SOURS**

1½ ounces Irish whiskey
¾ ounce crème de noyau
½ ounce fresh lemon juice
1 lemon twist, for garnish

SHAKE AND STRAIN into a chilled cocktail glass. Add the garnish.

JACK AND COKE

FAMILY: **HIGHBALLS** Be aware that the customer is requesting Jack Daniel's Tennessee whiskey—not bourbon—and Coca-Cola. If you don't stock these brands, be sure that the customer knows, and that he agrees to the brand names you suggest. At the time of this writing, the only other brand name of Tennessee whiskey on the market is George Dickel. If you use bourbon in this drink, once again, make sure that the customer knows. Suggest a lemon wedge for garnish.

2 ounces Jack Daniel's Tennessee whiskey
3 ounces Coca-Cola

BUILD in an ice-filled highball glass.

JACK ROSE

FAMILY: **SOURS** The Jack Rose is nothing more than an applejack sour that's sweetened with grenadine, but the dryness of Laird's applejack works wonders for this drink. Who was Jack Rose? As far as I can ascertain, there was no such person: *Jack* probably referred to the applejack in the recipe, and *rose* could easily have been used to describe the pinkish hue of the drink. In fact, in *The Old Waldorf-Astoria Bar Book,* Albert Stevens Crockett states that when properly concocted, the drink should be the exact shade of a Jacqueminot rose; he suggests that the true name could have been Jacque Rose.

As you'll see in the recipe for the Jack Rose Royale below, you can easily tweak this recipe by substituting a red liqueur for the grenadine—experiment with cherry brandy, crème de noyau, Chambord, and the like.

2½ ounces applejack
¾ ounce fresh lemon juice
grenadine to taste
1 lemon twist, for garnish

SHAKE AND STRAIN into a chilled cocktail glass. Add the garnish.

> *"In the morning all the ashtrays would be full of butts and the wastebaskets would hold piles of crumpled copy paper and empty applejack bottles. Whenever I see a bottle of applejack I think of the Hauptmann trial."*
>
> —JOSEPH MITCHELL, *MY EARS ARE BENT*

JACK ROSE ROYALE (BOTTLED)

FAMILY: **BOTTLED COCKTAILS**

MAKES 22 OUNCES

12 ounces applejack
2½ ounces Chambord black raspberry liqueur
2½ ounces fresh lemon juice
5 ounces bottled water
maraschino cherries, for garnish

MIX AND CHILL for a minimum of six hours.

JAMAICAN COBBLER

FAMILY: **COBBLERS**

3 ounces dark rum
1 ounce Tia Maria
fruits in season (raspberries and blueberries work well here), for garnish

BUILD in the order given in a wine glass filled with crushed ice. Add the garnish.

JAMAICAN TEN-SPEED

FAMILY: **ORPHANS** ❧ Created by Roger Gobler of Café Terra Cotta in Scottsdale, Arizona. This is one of those drinks that makes you think the bartender simply threw some ingredients together and it happened to work, but nothing could be further from the truth; Roger explained to me, in detail, his methodology for creating the Jamaican Ten Speed, and it involved much experimentation. This is also the type of drink that I would shy away from after perusing the list of ingredients—it looks too sweet for my palate—but this formula has perfect balance and is well worth re-creating.

1 ounce vodka
¾ ounce Midori melon liqueur
¼ ounce crème de banane
¼ ounce Malibu rum
½ ounce half-and-half

SHAKE AND STRAIN into a chilled cocktail glass.

JAMES JOYCE COCKTAIL

FAMILY: **NEW ORLEANS SOURS** ❧ I created this one in 2001 while conducting bartender-training seminars. It's a simple variation on the Oriental Cocktail.

1½ ounces Irish whiskey
¾ ounce sweet vermouth
¾ ounce triple sec
½ ounce fresh lime juice

SHAKE AND STRAIN into a chilled cocktail glass.

JOCKEY CLUB COCKTAIL NO. 2

FAMILY: **INTERNATIONAL SOURS** — The original 1930 recipe for the Jockey Club Cocktail called for crème de noyau, for which I have substituted amaretto. I also dropped the orange bitters from this drink and played around with ratios, so although I started out with an old formula, this is a new drink.

2 ounces gin
¾ ounce amaretto
¾ ounce fresh lemon juice
Angostura bitters to taste (go easy)

SHAKE AND STRAIN into a chilled cocktail glass.

JOHN COLLINS

FAMILY: **SPARKLING SOURS** — Most of the old cocktail books agree that this drink was originally made with geneva gin as a base, but these days bourbon is usually the spirit of choice.

2½ ounces bourbon
1 ounce fresh lemon juice
¾ ounce simple syrup
club soda
1 maraschino cherry, for garnish
½ orange wheel, for garnish

SHAKE everything except for the club soda, and STRAIN into an ice-filled collins glass. Top with club soda. Add the garnishes.

KAMIKAZE

FAMILY: **NEW ORLEANS SOURS** — When I first met this drink on the Upper East Side of Manhattan in the early seventies, it was a shooter, made with only Stolichnaya vodka and just two or three drops of Rose's lime juice. It did much damage. Today's formula is far more sophisticated.

1½ ounces vodka
1 ounce triple sec
½ ounce fresh lime juice

SHAKE AND STRAIN into a chilled cocktail glass.

KENTUCKY LONGSHOT

FAMILY: **ORPHANS** ~ Adapted from a recipe by the late Max Allen Jr. of the Seelbach Hilton Hotel in Louisville, Kentucky, who created the drink as a signature cocktail for the 1998 Breeders' Cup. The three garnishes represent win, place, and show.

2 ounces bourbon
½ ounce ginger liqueur
½ ounce peach brandy
1 dash Angostura bitters
1 dash Peychaud's bitters
3 pieces candied ginger, for garnish

STIR AND STRAIN into a chilled cocktail glass. Add the garnishes—if you are using long strips of candied ginger, hang them over the lip of the glass; smaller pieces can be dropped into the drink.

KENTUCKY SQUIRREL

FAMILY: **SQUIRREL SOURS** ~ This is another member of the Squirrel Sour family that lends itself to experimentation with nut-flavored liqueurs other than crème de noyau. Frangelico works particularly well here.

1½ ounces bourbon
¾ ounce crème de noyau
½ ounce fresh lemon juice
1 lemon twist, for garnish

SHAKE AND STRAIN into a chilled cocktail glass. Add the garnish.

KIR

FAMILY: **ORPHANS** ~ This drink was originally called Vin Blanc Cassis in France, and it was a favorite of the mayor of Dijon, Canon Felix Kir, who was revered for his work in the French resistance during World War II. He served what came to be known as Kirs at official functions during his twenty-year service to Dijon, from 1945 until 1965. The drinks comprised two products made in the Burgundy region, a white wine known as aligoté, and crème de cassis, a black-currant liqueur. The crème de cassis sweetens the wine; usually a quarter to a half ounce works well with five ounces of wine, but you should experiment until you achieve the ratios right for your taste.

5 ounces chilled dry white wine
crème de cassis to taste
1 lemon twist, for garnish

BUILD in the order given in a wine glass. Add the garnish.

KIR ROYALE

FAMILY: **CHAMPAGNE COCKTAILS**

5 ounces chilled champagne
½ ounce crème de cassis
1 lemon twist, for garnish

BUILD in a champagne flute in the order given. Add the garnish.

KRETCHMA COCKTAIL

FAMILY: **INTERNATIONAL SOURS** ➸ Adapted from a recipe in the 1958 edition of David Embury's *The Fine Art of Mixing Drinks.*

2 ounces vodka
1 ounce white crème de cacao
¾ ounce fresh lemon juice
grenadine to taste

SHAKE AND STRAIN into a chilled cocktail glass.

LAGER AND LIME

FAMILY: **BEER- AND CIDER-BASED DRINKS** ➸ Made with sweetened lime juice, such as Rose's, the Lager and Lime is one of my favorite thirst quenchers. In Britain there's a variation on this drink known as a Lager and Black, which is made with nonalcoholic black-currant juice. This product can be hard to find in America, but the best-known brand name is Ribena, and Monin (www.monin.com/us/en/index.html) makes a terrific range of fruit syrups, black currant among them.

12 ounces chilled lager
1½ ounces sweetened lime juice such as Rose's

Pour into a beer glass in the order given.

LARK CREEK INN TEQUILA INFUSION

FAMILY: **INFUSIONS** ❧ Created by Bradley Ogden of the Lark Creek Inn in Larkspur, California, in 1995. This is one of my all-time favorite infusions, but beware: It's important to taste this as soon as the first forty-eight hours are over, and to strain the ingredients from the tequila as soon as you get a hint that the chili pepper might be taking charge of the drink—it can soon overpower the rest of the ingredients. I usually serve this drink in small portions—about two ounces—straight from the freezer. It makes a great shooter or sipper, but don't let it get too warm.

MAKES 24 TO 30 OUNCES

1 serrano chili
1 pineapple, peeled and cut into 1-inch chunks
1 sprig tarragon
1 bottle (750 milliliters) reposado tequila

Cut the top and tail from the chili and discard them. Slice the chili lengthways down the center, remove the seeds, and place the chili halves in a large glass container with the pineapple chunks and the tarragon.

Pour in the tequila and allow it to rest for forty-eight to sixty hours in a cool, dark place, tasting the infusion frequently to make sure that the chili doesn't overpower it.

Strain the tequila from the pineapple, chili, and tarragon through a double layer of dampened cheesecloth. Return the tequila to the bottle and chill it in the refrigerator or freezer for at least twelve hours.

LEAP-YEAR COCKTAIL

FAMILY: **INTERNATIONAL SOURS** ❧ "This Cocktail was created by Harry Craddock, for the Leap Year celebrations at the Savoy Hotel, London, on February 29th, 1928. It is said to have been responsible for more proposals than any other cocktail that has ever been mixed," reports *The Savoy Cocktail Book* (1930).

This recipe is adapted from Craddock's original, but the drink is one that bartenders should keep in mind to serve as a specialty when February 29 rolls around.

2 ounces gin
½ ounce Grand Marnier
½ ounce sweet vermouth
¼ ounce fresh lemon juice
1 lemon twist, for garnish

SHAKE AND STRAIN into a chilled cocktail glass. Add the garnish.

LEMON DROP

FAMILY: **SOURS** ⸺ In memory of Steve Wilmot, who introduced us to this drink, and who drank far too many of them one Christmas Day. I believe the Lemon Drop was created shortly after citrus vodkas gained popularity in the early 1990s. If you use triple sec instead of simple syrup, you'll find that the cocktail has more depth and character than this early formula. When you make the drink with triple sec, though, it automatically gets adopted by the New Orleans Sour family.

2 ounces citrus-flavored vodka
1 ounce fresh lemon juice
½ ounce simple syrup
1 lemon wedge, for garnish

SHAKE AND STRAIN into a chilled, sugar-rimmed cocktail glass. Add the garnish.

LEWIS & MARTIN COCKTAIL

FAMILY: **ORPHANS** ⸺ Adapted from a recipe by Ted Haigh, Dr. Cocktail, of Los Angeles. This is a very complex potion, and you'll note that Doc shakes this, whereas I think it should be stirred. When asked about this incorrect methodology, Doc said, "You know me. I'm a savage. I shake everything." It just goes to prove that in the world of the cocktailian bartender, there are no rules.

2 ounces bourbon
1 ounce Lillet Blonde
¾ ounce crème de banane
2 dashes Peychaud's bitters
1 lemon twist, for garnish

SHAKE AND STRAIN into a chilled cocktail glass. Add the garnish.

LIBATION GODDESS

FAMILY: **ORPHANS** Created by Mardee and me in 2002, when we were experimenting with crème de cacao. We named it for New York cocktailian bartender extraordinaire Audrey Saunders (who uses Libation Goddess as a nickname), simply because we thought it was time she had an eponymous cocktail.

2 ounces gin
¾ ounce white crème de cacao
½ ounce cranberry juice
1 lime wedge, for garnish

STIR AND STRAIN into a chilled cocktail glass. Add the garnish.

LIMECELLO

FAMILY: **INFUSIONS** Based on the recipe for Limoncello (on the next page), this drink should be served neat, straight from the freezer.

MAKES APPROXIMATELY 60 OUNCES

9 medium limes
1 liter grain alcohol
2 cups granulated sugar
2 cups water

Carefully pare the zest from the limes, taking care not to take any of the white pith along with the zest. Place the zest in a large glass container with a close-fitting lid, reserving the pulp and juice for another use. Pour in the grain alcohol and close the container. Leave the mixture in a dark place for one week, to mellow.

Combine the sugar and the water in a small saucepan. Bring to a boil over medium heat, stirring frequently, until the sugar has dissolved. Allow the syrup to cool to room temperature, then add it to the lime-zest mixture. Close the container again and allow the limecello to mellow for one more week.

Strain the mixture through a double layer of dampened cheesecloth into bottles, and place the bottles in the freezer.

LIMONCELLO

FAMILY: **INFUSIONS** ➸ Adapted from a recipe by George Germon and Johanne Kileen of Al Forno in Providence, Rhode Island, where Mardee and I were introduced to the drink in the 1990s. Limoncello is a traditional Sicilian after-dinner drink and should be served neat, straight from the freezer.

MAKES APPROXIMATELY 60 OUNCES

12 medium lemons
1 liter grain alcohol
2 cups granulated sugar
2 cups water

Carefully pare the zest from the lemons, taking care not to take any of the white pith along with the zest. Place the zest in a large glass container with a close-fitting lid, reserving the pulp and juice for another use. Pour in the grain alcohol and close the container. Leave the mixture in a dark place for one week, to mellow.

Combine the sugar and the water in a small saucepan. Bring to a boil over medium heat, stirring frequently, until the sugar has dissolved. Allow the syrup to cool to room temperature, then add it to the lemon-zest mixture. Close the container again and allow the limoncello to mellow for one more week.

Strain the mixture through a double layer of dampened cheesecloth into bottles, and place the bottles in the freezer.

LOLA MARTINI

FAMILY: **NEW ORLEANS SOURS** ➸ Adapted from a recipe by Alex Freuman and Kurt Eckert of Jean Georges restaurant in New York.

2 ounces OP flavored vodka
½ ounce triple sec
½ ounce fresh lime juice
½ ounce elderflower syrup (available from www.german-deli.com and specialty German food stores)
1 splash cranberry juice
1 thin slice strawberry, for garnish

SHAKE AND STRAIN into a chilled cocktail glass. Add the garnish.

LONG ISLAND ICED TEA

FAMILY: **SPARKLING SOURS** ~ Robert Bott, a bartender at the Oak Beach Inn in Babylon, Long Island, lays claim to this drink's creation, but many years ago an executive at the T.G.I. Friday's chain told me that it was a Friday's bartender who came up with it. In 2002, I called T.G.I. Friday's to confirm this information, but they could find no record of it being true. Whoever it was gets my vote as best monkey at a typewriter. This is not a well-thought-out drink, and the notion of mixing all these spirits together is horrifying. Nevertheless, it's undeniable that the Long Island Iced Tea works. It's pleasant, refreshing, and somewhat lethal.

1 ounce vodka
1 ounce gin
1 ounce light rum
1 ounce white tequila
1 ounce triple sec
1 ounce fresh lemon juice
¾ ounce simple syrup
cola
1 lemon wedge, for garnish

SHAKE everything except for the cola and STRAIN into an ice-filled collins glass. Top with cola. Add the garnish.

MADRAS

FAMILY: **NEW ENGLAND HIGHBALLS**

2 ounces vodka
1½ ounces cranberry juice
1½ ounces fresh orange juice

BUILD in the order given in an ice-filled highball glass.

MAIDEN'S BLUSH COCKTAIL

FAMILY: **NEW ORLEANS SOURS** ~ Adapted from Craddock's 1930 recipe in *The Savoy Cocktail Book,* this gin-based New Orleans Sour employs grenadine for color; the syrup also serves to slightly soften the spirit. This is a good lesson for the cocktailian bartender seeking to create gin-based cocktails.

2 ounces gin
¾ ounce triple sec
½ ounce fresh lemon juice
grenadine to taste

SHAKE AND STRAIN into a chilled cocktail glass.

MAIDEN'S PRAYER COCKTAIL

FAMILY: **NEW ORLEANS SOURS** — Adapted from Craddock's 1930 recipe. I find that the addition of bitters works well here, but they weren't in the original drink—consider them optional. The cocktailian bartender should take time to compare this recipe with the Maiden's Blush Cocktail, above. Here we see orange juice being used to soften the gin slightly, whereas grenadine is employed for the same purpose in the recipe above.

1 ounce gin
1 ounce triple sec
½ ounce fresh lemon juice
½ ounce fresh orange juice
Angostura bitters to taste

SHAKE AND STRAIN into a chilled cocktail glass.

MAI TAI (ORIGINAL)

FAMILY: **TROPICAL DRINKS** — It's generally agreed that the Mai Tai was created by "Trader" Vic Bergeron, so I went to www.tradervics.com for the scoop. According to that site, in 1970 Victor J. "Trader Vic" Bergeron wrote the following:

> *I originated the Mai Tai and have put together a bit of the background on the evolution of this drink. . . . In 1944, after success with several exotic rum drinks, I felt a new drink was needed. I thought about all the really successful drinks: martinis, manhattans, daiquiris. . . . All basically simple drinks. . . . I took down a bottle of 17-year-old rum. It was J. Wray Nephew from Jamaica; surprisingly golden in color, medium bodied, but with the rich pungent flavor particular to the Jamaican blends. . . . I took a fresh lime, added some orange curaçao from Holland, a dash of Rock Candy Syrup, and a dollop of French Orgeat, for its subtle almond flavor. A generous amount of shaved ice*

and vigorous shaking by hand produced the marriage I was after. Half the lime shell went in for color. . . . I stuck in a branch of fresh mint and gave two of them to Ham and Carrie Guild, friends from Tahiti, who were there that night. Carrie took one sip and said, "Mai Tai—Roa Ae." In Tahitian this means "Out of This World—The Best." Well, that was that. I named the drink "Mai Tai." . . . In fairness to myself and to a truly great drink, I hope you will agree when I say, "Let's get the record straight on the Mai Tai."

This recipe is adapted from the original formula; below I've included a variation that calls for ingredients a little easier to find.

2 ounces seventeen-year-old J. Wray Nephew Jamaican rum
½ ounce French Garnier orgeat
½ ounce Holland DeKuyper orange curaçao
¼ ounce Rock Candy syrup
1 ounce fresh lime juice
1 sprig fresh mint, for garnish

SHAKE AND STRAIN into an old-fashioned glass filled with crushed ice. Add the garnish.

MAI TAI NO. 2

FAMILY: **TROPICAL DRINKS** — If you don't have all of the exact ingredients for Trader Vic's original recipe on hand, here's a good variation.

1 ounce dark rum
1 ounce light rum
½ ounce triple sec
¾ ounce orgeat syrup
1 ounce fresh lime juice
1 mint sprig, for garnish

SHAKE AND STRAIN into an old-fashioned glass filled with crushed ice. Add the garnish.

MAMIE TAYLOR

FAMILY: **HIGHBALLS** — This is a drink with a little history. It used to belong in a category of drinks known as Bucks, but aside from the Gin Buck, the Mamie Taylor is more or less the last surviving member of the family. I have therefore taken the liberty of having the Highball family adopt Miss Mamie.

To make a Buck, one always squeezed the citrus wedge into an empty highball glass before the ice was added, and the drink was then built in the glass. I'd like to hold on to this tradition and keep the Mamie Taylor intact, so that this distinct methodology will hopefully live on in at least one drink. The recipe for this drink that appears in Craddock's 1930 edition of *The Savoy Cocktail Book* calls for it to be made with a wedge of lime, but I prefer a lemon wedge.

1 lemon wedge
2 ounces scotch
3 ounces ginger ale

Squeeze the juice from the lemon wedge into a highball glass, and add the wedge to the glass. Add ice, the scotch, and the ginger ale, and stir briefly.

MANDRINTINI

FAMILY: **ORPHANS** ~ Adapted from a recipe by Peter George of Trotter's in Port of Spain, Trinidad.

2½ ounces Absolut Mandrin
¾ ounce fresh orange juice
¾ ounce cranberry juice

SHAKE AND STRAIN into a chilled cocktail glass.

MANHATTAN

FAMILY: **FRENCH-ITALIAN: WHISKEY AND BRANDY** ~ The drink that changed the face of cocktails. The Manhattan, as far as I can ascertain, is the first drink that called for vermouth as a modifier, and it is still going very strong today. It is the father of the Martinez, the grandpop of the Martini, and the founder of all French-Italian cocktails. Quite simply, when properly constructed, it is the finest cocktail on the face of the earth.

2 ounces bourbon or straight rye whiskey
1 ounce sweet vermouth
Angostura, Peychaud's, or orange bitters to taste (start with 2 dashes and adjust)
1 maraschino cherry, for garnish

STIR AND STRAIN into a chilled cocktail glass. Add the garnish.

THE HISTORY of the Manhattan is lost to us, but we do have some clues as to its origin, mostly uncovered by the ardent efforts of cocktail historian William Grimes, who detailed a few theories in his 2001 edition of *Straight Up or On the Rocks: The Story of the American Cocktail.* Dismissing as unsubstantiated the theory that the drink was created for a banquet thrown at the Manhattan Club in 1874 to celebrate an electoral success for Governor Samuel Tilden, Grimes says that the club's records indicate that the drink was, in fact, invented there, but no dates were noted. He also says that a certain William Mullhall, who tended bar in New York in the 1880s, claimed that the drink was created by a Broadway saloonkeeper named Black. We'll never know for sure, but without doubt this cocktail, with its simple formula and complex delivery, was a direct result of vermouth's increasing popularity with bartenders in the late 1800s. It could—as were many other cocktails and mixed drinks—have been created by more than one person, at around the same time: Bottles of Italian vermouth were new at the bar; cocktailians experimented with them.

The recipe that appears in Jerry Thomas's *The Bar-Tender's Guide, or How to Mix All Kinds of Plain and Fancy Drinks* (1887) calls for one pony of rye whiskey, a wine glass of vermouth, two dashes of curaçao or maraschino, and three dashes of Boker's bitters (now unavailable); the Manhattan Club's recipe indicates that its bartenders used equal amounts of whiskey and vermouth, with some orange bitters. By 1906, though, Louis Muckensturm, author of *Louis' Mixed Drinks with Hints for the Care and Service of Wines,* was calling for twice as much whiskey as vermouth, as well as dashes of curaçao, Angostura, and orange bitters—a drink that's not too far removed from the Manhattan we serve today.

The "drying" of the Martini that occurred in the 1940s almost happened to the Manhattan in the 1990s, and some untrained bartenders out there still think that the drink should be made with just a dash or two of vermouth. But to a large extent, cocktail drinkers know that the vermouth should make up at least one-quarter of the drink, and it usually takes Muckensturm's base proportion to properly balance this cocktail. However, as with all drinks made with a whiskey base, it's imperative to alter the ratios according to the whiskey you use to construct the Manhattan.

Although straight rye whiskey was the original spirit to grace the glass of Manhattan quaffers, I far prefer to use bourbon; but when it comes to which bottling to choose, I fluctuate according to my mood. For the sake of thrift, the Evan Williams seven-year-old is an excellent choice if you use about twice as much whiskey as vermouth. My other two favorite brands, selected when I'm feeling a little more flush, are Maker's Mark and Wild Turkey 101 proof, but with these it's important to watch how you pour. Maker's, a gentle soul, needs only just under one-third its volume of vermouth to achieve good balance, whereas the far spicier palate of the Wild Turkey requires just a little less than 1½ parts vermouth to two parts whiskey. Other bourbons recommendable when using a two-to-one ratio include the seven-year-old Jim Beam Black Label; eight-year-old Old Charter; Knob Creek nine-year-old; Old Rip Van Winkle Bourbon, ten summers old; Buffalo Trace; and Woodford Reserve Distiller's Select. Spicier drams that will take more vermouth include Old Forester Bonded, Old Grand-Dad 114 Barrel Proof, seventeen-year-old Eagle Rare, and Booker's barrel-proof bourbon (which needs almost as much vermouth as bourbon to soothe its soul).

As for bitters, Angostura is the standard way to go here, but Peychaud's and orange bitters both work well in this drink. If you go the Peychaud route, you will notice a marked difference in your Manhattan—it works for some people, though not everybody. I make my Manhattans this way occasionally; more often than not, though, I enjoy the fruity-spicy notes of orange bitters in this drink. Most important, however, is that there *must* be bitters of some kind in a Manhattan. Unless, of course, a customer requests that you leave them out.

I stick with two brands of vermouth: Martini & Rossi and Noilly Prat. You'll need a tad more vermouth if using the former; the latter is the more robust bottling.

I hope, after digesting all the variables discussed here, you have some idea of why I think that the Manhattan is the best cocktail on earth. It's so simple, but it's so darned complicated. You should take the construction of this drink as a challenge. For the record, the best Manhattans in Manhattan, according to an unscientific survey conducted by Mardee and me some years ago, are made by Norman Bukofzer at the Ritz-Carlton hotel, on Central Park South.

MANHATTAN (DRY)

FAMILY: **FRENCH-ITALIAN: WHISKEY AND BRANDY**

2 ounces bourbon or straight rye whiskey
1 ounce dry vermouth
Angostura, Peychaud's, or orange bitters to taste (start with 2 dashes and adjust)
1 lemon twist, for garnish

STIR AND STRAIN into a chilled cocktail glass. Add the garnish.

MANHATTAN (PERFECT)

FAMILY: **FRENCH-ITALIAN: WHISKEY AND BRANDY**

2 ounces bourbon or straight rye whiskey
½ ounce sweet vermouth
½ ounce dry vermouth
Angostura, Peychaud's, or orange bitters to taste (start with 2 dashes and adjust)
1 maraschino cherry, and/or 1 lemon twist, for garnish

STIR AND STRAIN into a chilled cocktail glass. Add the garnish.

In 1998, on *Homicide*, the NBC police drama, Detective Munch was seen ordering a Manhattan from Billie Lou, a forty-something bartender in a very seductive mood:

BILLIE LOU: Cherry?

DETECTIVE MUNCH: Always. Why do you think they call it a Manhattan?

BILLIE LOU: It's beautiful, seductive, intoxicating, and really bad for you.

DETECTIVE MUNCH: Thoughts on a maraschino cherry.

BILLIE LOU: Forbidden fruit?

DETECTIVE MUNCH: An allegory in a glass.

MANHATTAN (BOTTLED)

FAMILY: **BOTTLED COCKTAILS**

MAKES 22 OUNCES

12 ounces bourbon
4 ounces sweet vermouth
5 ounces bottled water
1 teaspoon Angostura bitters
maraschino cherries, for garnish

MIX AND CHILL for a minimum of six hours.

MANHATTAN (KENTUCKY'S BEST)

FAMILY: **FRENCH-ITALIAN: WHISKEY AND BRANDY** Loosely adapted from a recipe from the Bull's Head Inn in Campbell Hall, New York, developed by Jeff Traphagen, Charles Bennedetti, and Fred Whittle. The winner of Knob Creek's Manhattan competition, New York City, 1998.

2 ounces Knob Creek bourbon
¼ ounce maraschino cherry juice
3 dashes ruby port
3 dashes Martini & Rossi sweet vermouth
2 dashes crème de cassis
1 dash Angostura bitters
1 maraschino cherry, for garnish

STIR AND STRAIN into a chilled cocktail glass. Add the garnish.

MARAVEL SLING

FAMILY: **SPARKLING SOURS** ❧ I created this drink for Trotter's, in Port of Spain, Trinidad.

2 ounces gin
¼ ounce Bénédictine
¼ ounce mango nectar
½ ounce fresh lemon juice
tamarind juice to taste
Angostura bitters to taste
club soda
1 pineapple cube, for garnish
1 maraschino cherry, for garnish

SHAKE AND STRAIN the gin, Bénédictine, mango nectar, lemon juice, tamarind juice, and bitters into an ice-filled collins glass. Top with club soda. Add the garnishes.

MARGARITA

FAMILY: **NEW ORLEANS SOURS** ❧ One of America's most popular cocktails, the Margarita has almost as many histories as rabbits have bunnies. Which is true? Let's take a look at these oft-told tales:

1. Daniel (Danny) Negrete created the drink for his girlfriend, Margarita, when he was the manager of the Garci Crespo Hotel in Puebla, Mexico, in 1936. Apparently Margarita liked to eat salt with whatever she drank, so the salted rim on the glass made it unnecessary for her to keep reaching into salt bowl.

2. Vern Underwood, a tequila distributor for Jose Cuervo, named Johnnie Durlesser, a bartender at the Los Angeles restaurant the Tail of the Cock in the 1950s, as being the man who re-created a drink he'd had in Mexico, dubbing it the Margarita. Underwood took out full-page advertisements in various magazines that depicted himself wearing white tie and tails and red shoes, of all things, saluting a goddess, and declaring, "Margarita, more than a girl's name."

3. Jazz musician Teddy Stauffer, among others, attributed the drink to Margarita Sames of San Antonio, Texas. This claim was backed up by Helen Thompson, who wrote, in *Texas Monthly* magazine in 1991, that socialite Sames, noting that she didn't like weak drinks or weak men, claimed to have created the drink for Nicky Hilton—one of the Hotel

Hiltons, of course, and coincidentally, the owner of the Tail of the Cock at the time.

4. Sara Morales, an expert on Mexican folklore, claimed that it was created, circa 1930, by Doña Bertha, the owner of Bertha's Bar in Taxco, Mexico. Morales added that the first drink created by this woman was called the Bertha; the Margarita was her second creation. This is partially substantiated by Charles H. Baker Jr. in *The Gentleman's Companion* (1946): "Tequila Special *à la* Bertita, Garnered, among other Things, in Lovely Taxco, in February of 1937. This is a shocker from the place of Bertita, across from the cathedral steps in Taxco. . . . It is a cooler as well and Americans find it very unusual. Take 2 ponies of good tequila, the juice of 1 lime, 1 tsp sugar, and 2 dashes of orange bitters. Stir in a collins glass with lots of small ice, then fill with club soda. No garnish except crushed halves of the lime." If Baker's account is true, then it's not much of a stretch to imagine Bertha, or Bertita, substituting triple sec for the orange bitters, and coming up with a Margarita.

5. Carlos "Danny" Herrera is also said to have invented this drink in 1948, when he was running Rancho La Gloria, a hotel and restaurant close to Tijuana. Herrera supposedly named the drink for starlet Marjorie King, who, when in Mexico, took the name Margarita.

Margarita Sames has toured the United States for Cointreau, publicly laying claim to this creation, but of course this could also be a case of the same drink being created by more than one person, at approximately the same time. I'm at a loss to pick any of these stories as being the "one and only" true one, but no matter how you look at it—and whether or not the real creator was aware of this—the Margarita formula follows the same path as other classics such as the Sidecar: It's a base spirit made sour by the addition of lime juice and balanced for sweetness with triple sec.

As for what ratios of ingredients to use when making this superb drink, I follow the instructions of Anne and Larry Walker, mavens of all things Spanish and Mexican, who instructed me to use three parts tequila to two parts triple sec and one part fresh lime juice. This version of the Margarita is not sweet enough for some customers, but for me, it's perfect—this is one of the few drinks for which I will actually measure the ingredients before shaking. If you desire a sweeter version, I suggest that you add simple syrup.

For the tequila, I like to use 100 percent agave white bottlings, also known as silver, or *blanco,* and I find Don Julio, El Tesoro, Chinaco, and Herradura all to be of top quality for Margaritas. For the triple sec, I use either Cointreau or the less expensive Van Gogh O'Magnifique, the finest bottlings on the market. When it come to the garnish, I don't use one.

Normally this drink would take a wedge of lime, but if you squeeze it into the drink you can throw off the balance, so I stay clear of any garnish at all.

1½ ounces white tequila
1 ounce triple sec
½ ounce fresh lime juice

SHAKE AND STRAIN into a salt-rimmed (optional), chilled cocktail glass.

MARGARITA (BOTTLED)

FAMILY: **BOTTLED COCKTAILS**

MAKES 22 OUNCES

8 ounces white tequila
6 ounces triple sec
3 ounces fresh lime juice
5 ounces bottled water
lime wedges, for garnish

MIX AND CHILL for a minimum of six hours.

MARGARITA JELLY SHOT

FAMILY: **JELLY SHOTS** See page 150 for advice about what molds to use for Jelly Shots.

1 ounce fresh lime juice
1 ounce simple syrup
1 ounce water
1 package unflavored gelatin (¼ ounce)
3 ounces white tequila
2 ounces triple sec
food coloring, if desired

Place the lime juice, simple syrup, and water in a small glass measuring cup, and add the gelatin. Allow this to sit for one minute, then microwave the mixture on high for thirty seconds. Stir thoroughly to make sure that all the gelatin has dissolved, then add the tequila, triple sec, and food coloring (if desired). Stir thoroughly again and pour the mixture into a mold. Refrigerate for at least one hour or, preferably, overnight.

THE MARIN-I-TINI

FAMILY: **NEW ORLEANS SOURS** ~ Adapted from a recipe by Manne Hinojosa of the Walnut Creek Yacht Club in California.

1½ ounces Pearl vodka
½ ounce triple sec
½ ounce peach schnapps
½ ounce fresh lime juice
¼ ounce blue curaçao
1 lime twist, for garnish

SHAKE the vodka, schnapps, and lime juice, and STRAIN into a chilled cocktail glass. Pour the blue curaçao down the side of the glass so that it rests on the bottom. Add the garnish.

MARTINEZ

FAMILY: **FRENCH-ITALIAN: GIN AND VODKA** ~ Adapted from the recipe in Jerry Thomas's 1887 book *The Bar-Tender's Guide, or How to Mix All Kinds of Plain and Fancy Drinks*. Thomas used more vermouth than gin is his Martinez, and his choice of bitters was Boker's, which is no longer made. This drink, I believe, was born of the Manhattan (see the Martini, below) and is the father, or perhaps grandfather, of the Dry Gin Martini. It tastes nothing like a Dry Gin Martini, of course, mainly because it calls for sweet vermouth, but this is a glorious drink that's well worth trying.

2 ounces gin
1 ounce sweet vermouth
¼ ounce maraschino liqueur
Angostura bitters to taste
1 lemon twist, for garnish

STIR AND STRAIN into a chilled cocktail glass. Add the garnish.

MARTINI

FAMILY: **FRENCH-ITALIAN: GIN AND VODKA** ~ We'll never know with absolute certainty when the Martini was born, or who was its creator, but my research points toward the drink being a direct descendant of the Manhattan. Recipes for the Martini started to appear in cocktail books in the late 1800s, and many of them were very similar, and sometimes identical, to recipes for the Martinez, a cocktail that appeared in print in the

1880s and was often described as "a Manhattan, substituting gin for the whiskey." Thus, theoretically at least, the Martinez was a variation on the Manhattan, and the Martini is, for all intents and purposes, a Martinez.

The first Martinis were made with Old Tom (sweetened) gin, sweet vermouth, bitters, and maraschino liqueur, and even when the Dry Martini came into being, circa 1906, it contained bitters as well as dry gin and dry vermouth. Orange bitters remained an ingredient in Dry Martinis right through to the 1930s, but by the late 1940s the drink was being made with just dry gin and dry vermouth, and the amount of vermouth used was getting smaller and smaller.

Many of the first Dry Martinis were made with equal amounts of gin and vermouth, but by the early 1950s some bartenders had already started to use atomizers to dispense the vermouth into the drink, and bitters had been dropped from the recipe. So the Dry Gin Martini, as we know it today, has been around for over half a century.

These days, many cocktails are known as Martinis even though they contain no gin (or even vodka) and vermouth, dry or sweet, is nowhere to be found in the recipe. These drinks are merely cocktails, but for one reason or another, during the cocktail craze of the 1990s, they were dubbed Martinis. *Martini,* therefore, has become another word for a cocktail of any kind, just as long as it can be served in a Martini glass. Many purists abhor this phenomenon. Personally, I think that it helped spur bartenders to create new drinks, many of which are wonderful, so it doesn't bother me in the least. Recipes for cocktails known as Martinis, though, are not listed in this category unless they fit the criteria detailed above.

Martinis should be stirred and not shaken, simply because the sight of a bartender lovingly stirring this drink for at least twenty to thirty seconds is something that people enjoy. Stirring for approximately thirty seconds will yield a drink that's just as cold as one that has been shaken for about ten seconds—it's worth the time. Shake it if you must, and if a customer requests that the drink be shaken, then that's how it should be made. Never use gin or vodka from the fridge or the freezer, since the spirit will be too cold to melt enough ice—a very necessary ingredient in a well-made Martini.

You can make Martinis with white rum or tequila, but they aren't very good drinks. Gin marries perfectly with vermouth, and vodka, too, is a good base spirit to use. The ratio of gin or vodka to vermouth is entirely up to your discretion, but although many people prefer a mere hint of vermouth in their Martinis, I suggest that you start by using one part vermouth to each four or five parts base spirit. Taste the drink, and on future occasions you can alter the proportions to suit your preferences. If you're a professional bartender, of course, you must cater to the whims of your customers in this regard.

Choosing specific bottlings of gin, vodka, and vermouth is of tantamount importance when making a Martini, and the ratio of vermouth to base spirit can vary with your choice of gin or vodka. Some gins—Bombay, Leyden, and Gordon's, for instance—aren't as intensely perfumed and dry as such bottlings as Tanqueray, Beefeater, Boodles, Van Gogh, Junipero, or Plymouth. The "softer" bottlings, therefore, will need less vermouth than the latter category of gins. The same applies, though to a far lesser extent, to vodkas. These spirits, however, don't vary enough in character for the ratios to be differentiated from one bottling to another, so it's pretty futile to attempt to give guidance in this respect. Experiment until you find your favorite ratio.

Vermouths, too, vary from one label to another, though most of the recognizable brands, such as Noilly Prat, Cinzano, and Martini & Rossi, are fine products. A new vermouth from California called Vya is also a great choice for Martinis. You might also want to experiment with other

Shaken, Not Stirred

In 1999, shortly after the James Bond flick *The World Is Not Enough* was released, I received the following missive from Kathleen Talbert, a New York public relations maven who represents Coate's Plymouth gin:

> *In the latest Bond flick . . . Bond orders his martini by uttering those famous words, "shaken not stirred." A recent Canadian study, just published in that unimpeachable source, the* British Medical Journal, *concludes that a martini shaken, not stirred, may have contributed to the good health of James Bond. The Scripps Howard News Service reported on the study. "Testing the drinks against chemical yardsticks, the scientists found that the more vigorous mixing of gin and vermouth gives them greater antioxidant properties than when the two ingredients are merely stirred. . . . 'The science is serious,' said John Trevithick, a professor of biochemistry at the University of Western Ontario and senior author of the report. 'Of the two active ingredients, vermouth had more powerful anti-oxidant properties, but it was a well-mixed combination of the two that proved to be the most effective in deactivating hydrogen peroxide. The peroxide was used in the lab as a surrogate for the free radicals that are thought to cause arterial damage.'"*

aperitif wines, such as Lillet Blonde and Dubonnet Blanc, when making Martinis. These are perfectly good products, though they tend to be a little fruitier than most vermouths. Take this into consideration and add less aperitif wine than you would vermouth when making your Martinis.

As for garnishes, I prefer a pimiento-stuffed olive in a Gin Martini and a lemon twist in a Vodka Martini, but many new garnishes, such as olives stuffed with almonds or anchovies, are now available, and you should experiment with whatever takes your fancy. Always remember that the Martini is a purely American drink, and therefore people should be able to exercise freedom of speech when requesting one: If somebody wants a Gin Martini made with equal parts gin and vermouth, a splash or two of bitters, and a pickled tomato for a garnish, then that's the way the Martini should be made.

2½ ounces gin or vodka
½ ounce dry vermouth
1 olive or lemon twist, for garnish

STIR AND STRAIN into a chilled cocktail glass. Add the garnish.

MARTINI CIRCA 1900 (BOTTLED)

FAMILY: **BOTTLED COCKTAILS**

MAKES 22 OUNCES

8 ounces gin
8 ounces dry vermouth
5½ ounces bottled water
½ teaspoon orange bitters
lemon twists, for garnish

MIX AND CHILL for a minimum of six hours.

MARYLAND SQUIRREL

FAMILY: **SQUIRREL SOURS**

1½ ounces straight rye whiskey
¾ ounce crème de noyau
½ ounce fresh lemon juice
1 lemon twist for garnish

SHAKE AND STRAIN into a chilled cocktail glass. Add the garnish.

MARY PICKFORD COCKTAIL

FAMILY: **ORPHANS** Loosely adapted from Craddock's 1930 recipe. The ingredients remain true to the original, but I have been pretty drastic in altering the ratios. Craddock called for as much pineapple juice as rum in his recipe, but that version is far too sweet, as far as I'm concerned, so that was the first thing I modified. Next came the maraschino liqueur—only six drops were used in Craddock's recipe, and the liqueur can hardly be detected in that quantity. I increased the amount to ¼ ounce and find that a pleasant nuttiness comes through in the backdrop.

2 ounces light rum
1 ounce pineapple juice
¼ ounce maraschino liqueur
1 dash grenadine

SHAKE AND STRAIN into a chilled cocktail glass.

MASSA MOJITO

FAMILY: **JULEPS** Adapted from a recipe from Pizzicato Restaurant, in Philadelphia, this interesting variation on the classic Mojito calls for Villa Massa Limoncello. This particular bottling of limoncello isn't as sweet as most of the other commercial brands, so if you experiment with other bottlings you must take their relative sweetness into account.

This drink helps point out the limitless possibilities for variations on the Mojito: Experiment with different flavors of spirits and liqueurs married to lemon or lime juice and mint.

4 wedges lemon
1 to 2 teaspoons granulated sugar
15 to 20 fresh mint leaves
2½ ounces Villa Massa Limoncello
club soda
2 to 3 mint sprigs, for garnish

MUDDLE the lemon wedges, sugar, and mint leaves in a mixing glass until the sugar is completely dissolved, all the juice is extracted from the lemons, and the mint is thoroughly integrated into the juice. Add ice and the limoncello to the mixing glass, shake briefly, and strain into a collins glass filled with crushed ice. Top with club soda, and add the garnish.

MAURICE COCKTAIL

FAMILY: **FRENCH-ITALIAN: GIN AND VODKA** Note that this is a Bronx Cocktail with absinthe substitute, which should be added in a very small quantity—I suggest no more than one or two dashes—lest it take over the drink.

2 ounces gin
¼ ounce sweet vermouth
¼ ounce dry vermouth
1 ounce fresh orange juice
absinthe substitute to taste
1 orange twist, for garnish

SHAKE AND STRAIN into a chilled cocktail glass. Add the garnish.

METROPOLITAN

FAMILY: **NEW ORLEANS SOURS** Adapted from a recipe created by Chuck Coggins, bartender at Marion's Continental Restaurant and Lounge, New York, in 1993. The recipe here calls for triple sec as a sweetening agent, rather than the sweetened lime juice used in Coggins's original formula.

1½ ounces Absolut Kurant vodka
1 ounce triple sec
½ ounce fresh lime juice
cranberry juice to taste
1 lime wedge, for garnish

SHAKE AND STRAIN into a chilled cocktail glass. Add the garnish.

MEXICAN SQUIRREL

FAMILY: **SQUIRREL SOURS** This member of the Squirrel-Sour family was very hard to balance, but the vegetal notes in the tequila work very well with the almond flavors in the crème de noyau.

2 ounces white tequila
¾ ounce crème de noyau
¾ ounce fresh lime juice

SHAKE AND STRAIN into a chilled cocktail glass.

MILLENNIUM COCKTAIL

FAMILY: **ORPHANS** Created for New Year's Eve 1999 by Mardee and me. This is a simple recipe, but the drink can be quite complex if enough bitters are added—that one ingredient makes the cocktail come alive. It's obviously easy to tinker with ratios here, making the drink drier or sweeter by altering the amount of peach schnapps (the sweet ingredient), but how else could the cocktailian bartender play with this formula? You might think about adding lemon juice to the recipe and creating a Millennium Sour; then take that formula, strain the drink into an ice-filled collins glass, add club soda, and call it the Millennium Collins. There are many possibilities here.

2½ ounces straight bourbon
½ ounce peach schnapps
3 dashes Angostura bitters
1 lemon twist, for garnish

STIR AND STRAIN into a chilled cocktail glass. Add the garnish.

MILLENNIUM MANHATTAN

FAMILY: **FRENCH-ITALIAN: WHISKEY AND BRANDY** After we created our Millennium Cocktail (see above)—and there must have been hundreds of cocktailians inventing their own drink with the same name that year—Mardee pointed out that the mixture would be far more complex if we added some sweet vermouth, and thus another drink was born. A simple observation such as this serves to point out that the best new drinks aren't normally created from scratch—it's far more likely that a new recipe will be successful if it's based on a tried-and-true formula.

2 ounces bourbon
1 ounce sweet vermouth
½ ounce peach schnapps
Angostura bitters to taste
1 maraschino cherry, for garnish

STIR AND STRAIN into a chilled cocktail glass. Add the garnish.

MILLIONAIRE COCKTAIL NO. 4

FAMILY: **INTERNATIONAL SOURS** Adapted from a recipe by Dr. Cocktail (Ted Haigh). Doc altered the ratios of Craddock's Millionaire No. 1 from *The Savoy Cocktail Book* (1930) to come up with this perfectly balanced drink—he made them for Mardee and me on one glorious weekend in 2000. Since tinkering with Doc's ratios would throw the drink off balance, and I would then incur his wrath, I've left the ingredients and the amounts exactly as he gave them to me, but note that you'll need a large cocktail glass for this one—after shaking, the drink is over six ounces.

2 ounces Myers's rum
1 ounce sloe gin
1 ounce apricot brandy
1 ounce fresh lime juice

SHAKE AND STRAIN into a chilled cocktail glass.

MILLIONAIRE'S MARGARITA

FAMILY: **INTERNATIONAL SOURS** Adapted from a recipe by fellow cocktailian and spiritsmeister Steve Olson, this drink changed my mind about the use of Grand Marnier in a Margarita. Note, though, that in a regular Margarita I use two parts triple sec to one part lime juice, but the added sweetness brought to this party by the Grand Marnier requires that the ratios be pretty drastically altered. At 1999 prices, if you bought these ingredients from a liquor store, this drink would set you back around thirty dollars.

2 ounces El Tesoro de Don Felipe Paradiso añejo tequila
¾ ounce Grand Marnier Cuvée du Centenaire
¾ ounce fresh lime juice
1 half orange wheel, for garnish

SHAKE AND STRAIN into a chilled cocktail glass. Add the garnish.

MIMOSA

FAMILY: **CHAMPAGNE COCKTAILS** This drink can be varied by the addition of a splash of grenadine, in which case it's sometimes known as a Buck's Fizz. Or try adding a little cognac or substituting Grand Marnier for the triple sec. Many people omit the triple sec altogether in the Mimosa. It's a big mistake.

½ ounce triple sec
1½ ounces fresh orange juice
3½ ounces chilled champagne
1 orange slice for garnish

BUILD in the order given in a champagne flute. Add the garnish.

MINT JULEP

FAMILY: **JULEPS** Here's a drink worthy of much debate. It dates back, in its present form of spirit, mint, and sugar, to around the late 1700s, although according to *The Mint Julep,* by Richard Barksdale Harwell, the first printed mention of mint as an ingredient in a Julep didn't appear until 1803. The English used the term *julep* to describe simple syrup as far back as 1400, and the word, according to various sources, appears to have been derived from the Persian *gul-ab* or the Arabic *julab,* meaning rose water.

Many people drink Mint Juleps only on Kentucky Derby day (when, at Churchill Downs, they serve premixed Juleps hardly worthy of the name), but hidden in Harwell's book you can find other dates suitable for serving this wonderful drink: May 28 marks the opening of Julep season as celebrated by members of the General P.G.T. Beauregard Marching and Burial Society. No mention is given of the closing date of the season, so we must presume that it lasts, well, as long as you would like. In 1837, English captain Frederick Marryat wrote that during New York's Independence Day celebrations, Mint Juleps were served (along with porter, ale, cider, mead, brandy, wine, ginger beer, pop, soda water, whiskey, rum, punch, cocktails and "many other compounds to name which nothing but the luxuriance of American-English could invent a word"), so July Fourth seems as though it, too, is an appropriate date on which to drink Juleps.

My all-time favorite story about the Mint Julep, though, involves a South Carolinian by the name of William Heyward Trapier, who is said to have taken several casks of bourbon with him when visiting England in 1845. Harwell states that the casks of bourbon were "pure assumption" on the part of the original reporter of this event, but he does agree that the following took place:

While visiting England, Trapier went to New College, Oxford (formally named the College of the Blessed Virgin Mary of Winchester), and was there entertained by the "warden and fellows." He was surprised to find out that nobody at New College knew how to make a Mint Julep and took it on himself to demonstrate. The drinks were so well received that ever since, on June 1, Mint Juleps are served at New College, and a seat there remains empty in case Trapier returns to join in the festivities. So now you can add June 1 to your Julep calendar. (I e-mailed New College in 2000 to confirm this story and was told that, yes, they still celebrate Mint Julep Day on June 1, but they no longer keep a chair open for Trapier. Shame on them.)

May 15 marks the anniversary of the founding of the Old Dominion Society of New York City, which, in 1860, was given a poem about the Mint Julep to be read at its annual banquet by John Reuben Thompson, a poet from Richmond. The end of the first verse states, "A whiskey julep is the drink that typifies the nation!" So now you can pick any of these dates on which to serve a Mint Julep. Or, as long as the weather is warm, serve it whenever you like.

The major issue concerning the Mint Julep is whether or not the mint leaves should be crushed to release their essential oils, and I've previously taken a stand on this, maintaining that the mint should serve only as an aromatic garnish. I must admit, however, that a Julep that tastes of mint is also a thing of beauty; but rather than crushing mint leaves with sugar and water in the bottom of a julep cup, I prefer to infuse the mint into simple syrup, and use that as the sweetener for the drink. And I still believe that an abundance of mint should be placed atop the drink in order that the drinker's nose be buried in the garnish whilst he sips it through short straws.

Of primary importance when preparing a Mint Julep is making sure that a thin layer of ice forms on the outside of the julep cup (preferably made of silver) or the glass in which it is served. In order to achieve this, the bartender must use the finest crushed ice available to him and stir the drink until the ice forms. Then the drink must be topped with mint, and straws should be inserted into the drink, short enough to ensure that the customer gets the full benefit of the mint aromas. Always serve a Mint Julep with a coaster of some sort, since the condensation from the ice on the glass can be a problem.

Silver julep cups can be prohibitively expensive, and although they are the proper vessel for this drink, I don't think that regular glasses—collins glasses are preferable—should be considered improper.

The first Mint Juleps were probably not made with bourbon. Rum, peach brandy, and regular brandy have all been cited in recipes dating back to 1787, and at that time bourbon was only just coming to be known by that name. The recipes here call for straight bourbon, but you should feel free to experiment with other spirits, though brown goods (whiskey, brandy, and the like), are far preferable in this drink to their lighter cousins.

A good way to make variations on the Mint Julep is to substitute liqueurs for the simple syrup; you can also use a different base liquor and match that with other liqueurs. For instance, try using peach schnapps in a bourbon-based Julep; then switch over to brandy as a base and sweeten the drink with triple sec or Grand Marnier. The possibilities are endless.

finely crushed ice
3 ounces bourbon
1 to 2 ounces simple syrup or minted simple syrup (see below)
5 or 6 stems of fresh mint, for garnish

Cut straws so that they are approximately 2 inches taller than the serving glass. Add crushed ice to a julep cup or collins glass until it is two-thirds full. Add the bourbon and syrup and stir for ten to twenty seconds. Add more crushed ice and stir again until a thin layer of ice forms on the outside of the glass; then add more crushed ice so that it domes slightly over the rim of the glass. Garnish with the fresh mint stems and insert the straws. Serve with a cocktail napkin to catch the condensation.

MINTED SIMPLE SYRUP

FAMILY: **INFUSIONS**

1 cup water
1 cup granulated sugar
1 bunch fresh mint

Combine the ingredients in a small saucepan over medium heat. Stir frequently until the mixture reaches a simmer; then cover the pan, turn the heat down to low, and allow it to simmer for 5 minutes. Remove the pan from the heat and let the mixture come down to room temperature (approximately one hour). Remove the mint before storing the syrup.

MINT JULEP NO. 2

FAMILY: **JULEPS** ➛ This recipe is loosely based on a formula detailed in Jerry Thomas's 1862 book *How to Mix Drinks, or The Bon Vivant's Companion.* Thomas states that it was a recipe taken to England by Captain Frederick Marryat (1792–1848), a British naval officer who wrote books about his seafaring adventures after he retired from the navy. Marryat related that he had overheard an American woman saying, "Well, if I have a weakness for any one thing, it is for a mint julep!" He remarked that the drink was, "like the American ladies, irresistible."

1½ ounces brandy
1½ ounces peach brandy
1 to 2 ounces simple syrup or minted simple syrup
5 or 6 stems of fresh mint, for garnish
1 pineapple spear, for garnish

Cut straws so that they are approximately 2 inches taller than the serving glass. Add crushed ice to a julep cup or collins glass until it is two-thirds full. Add the brandy, peach brandy, and syrup and stir for ten to twenty seconds. Add more crushed ice and stir again until a thin layer of ice forms on the outside of the glass; then add more crushed ice so that it domes slightly over the rim of the glass. Garnish with the fresh mint stems and the pineapple spear, and insert the straws. Serve with a cocktail napkin to catch the condensation.

MISSING LINK

FAMILY: **NEW ORLEANS SOURS** ➛ Created in 2002 when I discovered that, as far as I could ascertain, nobody had come up with a simple New Orleans Sour with a rum base.

1½ ounces dark rum
1 ounce triple sec
½ ounce fresh lemon juice

SHAKE AND STRAIN into a chilled cocktail glass.

MODERNISTA

FAMILY: **INTERNATIONAL SOURS** ➛ Adapted from a recipe by Ted Haigh (Dr. Cocktail), who in turn adapted it from the formula for the Modern Cocktail in Craddock's *The Savoy Cocktail Book.* Doc uses a teaspoon of absinthe substitute in his recipe, but I prefer just two or three dashes. Experiment with this, but remember how easy it is for absinthe to take over a drink.

2 ounces scotch
½ ounce dark Jamaican rum
½ ounce fresh lemon juice
orange bitters to taste
absinthe substitute to taste
1 maraschino cherry, for garnish
1 lemon twist, for garnish

SHAKE AND STRAIN into a chilled cocktail glass. Add the garnishes.

MOJITO

FAMILY: **JULEPS** Lou Cantres—who used to bill himself as "General Manager of Bar and Books and the Carnegie Club, Beverage Director for Hospitality Holdings, Inc., and Social Chemist to the Civilized and Uncivilized World"—taught me how to make this drink properly. Lou, a bartender's bartender if there ever was one, knows what he's doing.

Although you can use simple syrup in the Mojito, granulated sugar makes a far better cocktail, since, as with the Caipirinha, the sugar abrades the zest of the limes and releases their essential oils to the drink.

4 lime wedges
2 to 3 teaspoons granulated sugar
8 to 10 fresh mint leaves
2 ounces light rum
club soda
2 or 3 mint sprigs, for garnish

MUDDLE the lime wedges, sugar, and mint leaves in a mixing glass until the sugar is completely dissolved, all the juice is extracted from the limes, and the mint is thoroughly integrated into the juice. Add ice and the rum to the mixing glass, SHAKE briefly, and STRAIN into a collins glass filled with crushed ice. Top with club soda, and add the garnish.

MONKEY GLAND COCKTAIL NO. 1

FAMILY: **ORPHANS** There are two legitimate Monkey Gland Cocktails, one of which takes absinthe substitute as an accent; the other calls for Bénédictine. I discovered this in 1997 when Dale DeGroff made this drink for me at the Rainbow Room and I saw him reaching for an absinthe substitute, whereas I had always used Bénédictine. It turned out that Dale followed Harry Craddock's recipe from the 1930 *Savoy Cocktail Book,* whereas I had learned the drink from Patrick Gavin Duffy's *The Official Mixer's Guide* (1934). Craddock, based in London, had access to absinthe, but Duffy changed the recipe to make it easier on American bartenders. Both versions are well worth trying.

2 ounces gin
1 ounce fresh orange juice
Bénédictine to taste
grenadine to taste

SHAKE AND STRAIN into a chilled cocktail glass.

MONKEY GLAND COCKTAIL NO. 2

FAMILY: **ORPHANS**

2½ ounces gin
¾ ounce fresh orange juice
absinthe substitute to taste
grenadine to taste

SHAKE AND STRAIN into a chilled cocktail glass.

MOON WALK

FAMILY: **CHAMPAGNE COCKTAILS** Adapted from a recipe by Joe Gilmore, bartender at the Savoy Hotel, London, to commemorate Neil Armstrong's 1969 walk on the moon.

1 ounce fresh grapefruit juice
1 ounce Grand Marnier
1 dash rose water
3½ ounces chilled champagne

BUILD in the order given in a champagne flute.

MOSCOW MULE

FAMILY: **HIGHBALLS** ~ Created in 1941 by Jack Morgan, owner of the Cock 'n' Bull Tavern in Los Angeles, and John G. Martin of the Heublein company. Morgan had a surplus of ginger beer, and Heublein's executives were trying to get Americans to drink their newly acquired Smirnoff vodka. This drink is traditionally served in a small copper tankard.

2 ounces vodka
3 ounces ginger beer
2 lime wedges, for garnish

BUILD in an ice-filled highball glass. Add the garnish.

MOUNT GAY RUMRITA

FAMILY: **NEW ORLEANS SOURS** ~ After thinking that there was no such thing as a rum-based New Orleans sour, and therefore formulating the Missing Link (see page 304), I learned that Jane Scott, brand manager for Cointreau in New York, had been drinking this Mount Gay rum version of the cocktail for quite a while. There's nothing new on the face of the earth.

1½ ounces Mount Gay rum
1 ounce Cointreau
½ ounce fresh lime juice

SHAKE AND STRAIN into a chilled cocktail glass.

MOURESQUE COCKTAIL

FAMILY: **ORPHANS** ~ The French usually drink this on the rocks, with a little more orgeat than is called for here and a splash of water. Orgeat can be syrupy, so I shake this drink.

2 ounces absinthe substitute
1 ounce orgeat syrup

Pour the absinthe substitute and the orgeat syrup into a highball glass full of ice cubes. Top with water, stir, and serve. Alternatively, SHAKE AND STRAIN into a chilled cocktail glass.

MUDDY WATERS

FAMILY: **FLORIDA HIGHBALLS** ❧ Created by Jimmy Daukas of Maryland, this drink was introduced to me by Doug Land, a good friend, in 2002. It's imperative to use Myers's dark rum to get the exact flavor that Daukas intended for this Highball.

3 to 4 lime wedges
2 ounces Myers's dark rum
3 ounces fresh grapefruit juice

Squeeze the lime wedges into a highball glass and drop them into the glass. Add ice and BUILD in the order given.

MUDSLIDE

FAMILY: **DUOS AND TRIOS**

2 ounces vodka
1 ounce Kahlúa
1 ounce Baileys Irish Cream

SHAKE AND STRAIN into an ice-filled old-fashioned glass.

NEGRONI

FAMILY: **MILANESE DRINKS** ❧ It's said that a certain Count Negroni created this drink by asking an Italian bartender to substitute gin for the club soda in his Americano (see page 205); this event supposedly occurred circa 1919. The first printed recipes I can find for the Negroni, however, are in two books, both printed in 1955: *The U.K.B.G. Guide to Drinks,* a British book compiled by the United Kingdom Bartenders' Guild, and Oscar Haimo's *Cocktail and Wine Digest,* published in New York.

Whether or not Count Negroni ever existed is of no consequence: This is one of the world's finest drinks. Some people have started to automatically make Negronis with vodka instead of gin, and these days the wise bartender will ask his customer which version is desired. Don't experiment with the proportions here—the balance is of primary importance in a Negroni, and using equal parts of each ingredient is absolutely necessary to achieve perfection.

1½ ounces Campari
1½ ounces sweet vermouth
1½ ounces gin
1 orange twist, for garnish

BUILD in any order in an ice-filled rocks glass. Add the garnish.

NEGRONI (VODKA)

FAMILY: **MILANESE DRINKS**

1½ ounces Campari
1½ ounces sweet vermouth
1½ ounces vodka
1 orange twist, for garnish

BUILD in any order in an ice-filled rocks glass. Add the garnish.

NELSON'S BLOOD

FAMILY: **CHAMPAGNE COCKTAILS** ~ I was first made aware of this drink by Richard Ward, a good friend who used to serve it aboard cruise ships in the 1970s.

1½ ounces ruby port
4 ounces chilled champagne

BUILD in the order given in a champagne flute.

NEW JERSEY SQUIRREL

FAMILY: **SQUIRREL SOURS**

1½ ounces applejack
¾ ounce crème de noyau
¾ ounce fresh lemon juice
1 lemon twist, for garnish

SHAKE AND STRAIN into a chilled cocktail glass. Add the garnish.

OATMEAL COOKIE COCKTAIL

FAMILY: **ORPHANS** — You must be careful about ratios in this drink, or it won't taste like an oatmeal cookie.

1 ounce Baileys Irish Cream
1 ounce butterscotch schnapps
1 ounce Jägermeister
½ ounce cinnamon schnapps
3 skewered raisins, for garnish

SHAKE AND STRAIN into a chilled cocktail glass. Add the garnish.

OLD CUBAN COCKTAIL

FAMILY: **CHAMPAGNE COCKTAILS** — Adapted from a recipe by Audrey Saunders, New York City's Libation Goddess. Audrey makes her own sugared-vanilla-bean garnishes (see below). But if you don't have one, better to omit the garnish than miss out on this fabulous drink.

½ ounce fresh lime juice
¾ to 1 ounce simple syrup
6 fresh mint leaves
1½ ounces Bacardi 8 añejo rum
2 dashes Angostura bitters
Moët & Chandon champagne
1 sugared vanilla bean, for garnish

MUDDLE the lime juice, simple syrup, and mint leaves in the bottom of a mixing glass. Add the rum, bitters, and ice. SHAKE AND STRAIN into a chilled cocktail glass, and top with a little champagne. Add the garnish, if you have one.

SUGARED VANILLA BEANS

Slice a vanilla bean lengthwise, remove the seeds, and reserve them for other uses. Sprinkle granulated sugar over the bean, and press lightly so the sugar adheres to the bean. If you want to make these garnishes in quantity, simply prepare like this, then store the beans in a container full of granulated sugar—you'll end up with sugared-vanilla-bean garnishes, and vanilla-scented sugar to boot.

OLD SAN JUAN SOUR

FAMILY: **SOURS** A fairly tart drink I created after a trip to Puerto Rico, circa 1997.

1½ ounces amber rum
½ ounce cranberry juice
1 ounce fresh lime juice
¼ ounce simple syrup
1 lime wedge, for garnish

SHAKE AND STRAIN into a chilled cocktail glass. Add the garnish.

THE OP LEMONADE COCKTAIL

FAMILY: **SOURS** Adapted from a recipe by Audrey Saunders, New York City's Libation Goddess. OP, for all intents and purposes, is a flavored vodka, and a darned good one, too. The sweetening agent here is peach puree, which makes for an interesting dimension. Of OP, Audrey wrote, "It's light, delicate, and has a wonderfully fragrant nose. I created this drink because I wanted to highlight its nuances, instead of masking them with overpowering flavors. The lemon and the peach seem to enhance the flavors nicely in this one."

1½ ounces OP vodka
½ ounce white (or yellow) peach puree (see page 213)
½ ounce fresh lemon juice
½ ounce simple syrup
1 lemon wedge, for garnish

SHAKE AND STRAIN into a small ice-filled wine glass. Add the garnish.

ORIENTAL COCKTAIL

FAMILY: **NEW ORLEANS SOURS** ~ Adapted from a recipe in *The Savoy Cocktail Book* (1930), which also notes that an American man desperately ill with fever in the Philippines in 1924 gave the doctor who saved his life the recipe for this drink by way of thanks. I've tinkered with ratios here and have offered a choice of whiskey styles (the original was made with rye); instead of curaçao, I went with triple sec to cut down somewhat on the sweetness of the drink.

1½ ounces straight rye whiskey or bourbon
¾ ounce sweet vermouth
¾ ounce triple sec
½ ounce fresh lime juice

SHAKE AND STRAIN into a chilled cocktail glass.

PACIFIC RIM MARTINI

FAMILY: **DUOS AND TRIOS** ~ Adapted from a recipe created in 1993 by Ginger DiLello, head bartender at Philadelphia Fish and Company, in Philadelphia. The gin version is by far the better way to go with this drink.

2½ ounces gin or vodka
½ ounce Original Canton Delicate Ginger liqueur
1 small piece crystallized ginger, for garnish

STIR AND STRAIN into a chilled cocktail glass. Add the garnish.

PADDY COCKTAIL

FAMILY: **FRENCH-ITALIAN: WHISKEY AND BRANDY** ~ This is an Irish Manhattan—I hate its name, but that's how it was first detailed in 1930. Play with the ratios to suit the Irish whiskey you use, although the following formula works well with most bottlings. The 1930 recipe called for no garnish, but I find that a twist of lemon works well here—it brings a wonderful aromatic dimension not present in the original.

2 ounces Irish whiskey
1 ounce sweet vermouth
Angostura bitters to taste
1 lemon twist, for garnish

STIR AND STRAIN into a chilled cocktail glass. Add the garnish.

PARADISE COCKTAIL

FAMILY: **INTERNATIONAL SOURS** — Loosely based on Craddock's 1930 recipe. I've added much more lemon juice here for a less sweet drink. Like the Blood-and-Sand Cocktail, this drink can be served as a Highball by increasing the amount of orange juice and building it in a highball glass; but I suggest that you also add a half ounce more gin to the formula if you make it that way.

1½ ounces gin
¾ ounce apricot brandy
½ ounce fresh orange juice
½ ounce fresh lemon juice

SHAKE AND STRAIN into a chilled cocktail glass.

PEGU CLUB COCKTAIL

FAMILY: **NEW ORLEANS SOURS** — Adapted from the recipe in Harry Craddock's *The Savoy Cocktail Book* (1930). Craddock noted, "The favourite cocktail of the Pegu Club, Burma, and one that has traveled, and is asked for, round the world."

2 ounces gin
1 ounce triple sec
½ ounce fresh lime juice
Angostura bitters to taste
orange bitters to taste

SHAKE AND STRAIN into a chilled cocktail glass.

PERNOD AND CIDER

FAMILY: **BEER- AND CIDER-BASED DRINKS** — This one is dedicated to the memory of Ken Tittle, a dear friend who turned me on to Pernod and Cider in the early seventies. It's an incredibly good mixture.

2 ounces Pernod
1 chilled bottle (12 ounces) hard cider

Pour in the order given into a 16-ounce beer glass.

PHOEBE SNOW COCKTAIL

FAMILY: **FRENCH-ITALIAN: WHISKEY AND BRANDY** ❧ A curveball in the French-Italian family, since it calls for Dubonnet rather than sweet vermouth, but a great drink nevertheless. You'll be tempted to think that this one was named for the singer, probably best known for her 1974 hit "Poetry Man," but actually both the drink and the singer borrowed their names from a fictitious character, first seen circa 1900, who always dressed in a spotless white dress and gloves to promote the Lackawanna railroad trains' use of anthracite, a clean-burning form of coal. Here's one of the jingles used in the campaign:

I won my fame and wide acclaim
For Lackawanna's splendid name
By keeping white and snowy bright
Upon the Road of Anthracite.

I have altered the ratios here, but the ingredients come from a 1930s recipe. I suggest that you use just one or two dashes of absinthe substitute when you first make this drink.

2 ounces brandy
1 ounce Dubonnet Rouge
absinthe substitute to taste

STIR AND STRAIN into a chilled cocktail glass.

PIERCE BROSNAN

FAMILY: **CHAMPAGNE COCKTAILS** ❧ Adapted from a recipe created for Pierce Brosnan by Salvatore Calabrese at the Lanesborough Hotel in London. Look at the methodology employed in the making of this drink—it's a wonderful display for the customer, and it points out that part of the bartender's job is to keep his customers entertained.

1½ ounces vodka, straight from the freezer
½ ounce chilled champagne
1 sugar cube
¼ ounce absinthe substitute

Pour the vodka into a well-chilled cocktail glass, add the champagne, and stir briefly. Place the sugar cube on a barspoon or teaspoon, soak it with the absinthe substitute, and ignite it with a match. Drop the flaming sugar cube into the drink.

PIMM'S CUP

FAMILY: **HIGHBALLS** This drink isn't too well known in the States, but it's a marvelously refreshing summertime quaff that's not too high in alcohol. James Pimm opened his first London restaurant in 1823, and by 1840 he had a chain of five establishments. Pimm himself is said to have created this gin-based aperitif, flavored with fruit liqueurs and herbs; it was traditionally served in tankards. Pimm's Cup became so successful that it was exported throughout the British Empire, and eventually five more bottlings were released, each with a different base: Pimm's No. 2 Cup was made with scotch, No. 3 with brandy, No. 4 with rum, No. 5 with rye, and No. 6 with vodka. Today only Pimm's No. 1 Cup is still available.

In the north of England, Pimm's is usually served in a highball glass, topped off with club soda or ginger ale and an abundance of fruit—a wedge of apple, a slice of orange, a maraschino cherry, and maybe a small slice of lemon. On the Thames, however, drinkers look down their noses at this fruit salad, preferring to take their Pimm's in the more traditional fashion with just a sliver of cucumber rind. Another great way to garnish the drink is with a huge bunch of basil on top. Serve, like a Julep, with straws cut short enough so that the drinker must bury his nose in the basil while sipping through the straw.

2 ounces Pimm's No. 1 Cup
5 to 7 ounces ginger ale, lemon-lime soda, or club soda
1 sliver cucumber rind, for garnish

BUILD in a 16-ounce mixing glass. Add the garnish.

PIÑA COLADA

FAMILY: **TROPICAL DRINKS** ~ You'll note that I use fresh pineapple, or canned pineapple chunks, in the frozen version of this drink, but pineapple juice in this one. This is easy to explain: The frozen drink is made in a blender where the chunks will be liquidized, and here the drink is merely shaken, so juice is needed. You could, of course, puree pineapple chunks in the blender, but you'll have to dilute the puree with a certain amount of juice to make it mixable. The dark rum is merely personal preference—light rum will work in this drink.

2 ounces dark rum
2 ounces pineapple juice
1½ ounces coconut cream
1 maraschino cherry, for garnish
1 pineapple cube, for garnish

SHAKE AND STRAIN into an ice-filled collins glass. Add the garnishes.

PINK LEMONADE COCKTAIL

FAMILY: **NEW ORLEANS SOURS** ~ Adapted from a recipe by Bryna O'Shea, San Francisco.

2 ounces Bacardi Limón
¾ ounce triple sec
½ ounce fresh lemon juice
¼ ounce cranberry juice
1 lemon wheel, for garnish

SHAKE AND STRAIN into a chilled, sugar-rimmed cocktail glass. Add the garnish.

PINK SQUIRREL

FAMILY: **DUOS AND TRIOS** ~ The first printed mention of this drink I can find is in a 1966 edition of *Old Mr. Boston*. It was still going fairly strong in the mid-seventies when I tended bar at New York's Drake's Drum, and the formula works well for those with a sweet tooth. This is best made with crème de noyau; amaretto doesn't yield as pink a drink.

1 ounce crème de noyau
1 ounce white crème de cacao
1 ounce cream

SHAKE AND STRAIN into a chilled cocktail glass.

PISCO SOUR

FAMILY: **SOURS** ➸ Modern-day drinkers owe a debt of gratitude to Dale DeGroff for bringing this incredible drink to our attention. Dale, in turn, credits the late Joe Baum for featuring the Pisco Sour on his cocktail menu at La Fonda Del Sol, New York, in the late 1960s, and says that the drink can be found on other drinks lists from the 1930s.

The Pisco Sour is detailed by Charles H. Baker Jr. in *The South American Gentleman's Companion,* where he wrote that the Angostura bitters, which are dashed on top of the drink rather than being shaken with the other ingredients, were "the finishing touch put-on by the talented bar-maestro at the wonderful and luxurious Lima Country Club, before they served them to your pastor and Limenian good friends on our suite balcony overlooking the polo fields and possibly the handsomest swimming pool you'll find in the world."

2 ounces Pisco brandy
1 ounce fresh lemon juice
½ ounce simple syrup
1 raw egg white, from a small egg (see page 112)
Angostura bitters, as an aromatic garnish

SHAKE AND STRAIN into a chilled champagne flute. Dash some bitters on top.

PLANTER'S COCKTAIL

FAMILY: **DUOS AND TRIOS** ➸ I created this simple drink for an advertorial for Captain Morgan's Private Stock Rum in the late 1990s.

2 ounces Captain Morgan's Private Stock rum
½ ounce Godiva chocolate liqueur
1 maraschino cherry

STIR AND STRAIN into a chilled cocktail glass. Add the garnish.

PLANTER'S PUNCH

FAMILY: **TROPICAL DRINKS** ❧ If there was ever a drink with no definitive recipe, this is it. In *The Gentleman's Companion,* Charles H. Baker Jr. detailed ten different recipes for Planter's Punch, noting, "Any set rules for these tropical institutions would last about as long as a set rule for a mint julep to please Louisville and Baltimore."

My personal favorite recipe for Planter's Punch relies heavily on grapefruit juice and both Angostura and Peychaud's bitters. Mardee and I came up with this one for a 1998 issue of *Wine Enthusiast,* but I've tweaked it a little since then.

2 ounces dark rum
½ ounce fresh lime juice
½ ounce fresh lemon juice
1 ounce fresh orange juice
2 ounces fresh grapefruit juice
Angostura bitters to taste
Peychaud's bitters to taste
freshly grated nutmeg, for garnish

SHAKE AND STRAIN into an ice-filled collins glass. Add the garnish.

POMPIER COCKTAIL

FAMILY: **FRENCH-ITALIAN: GIN AND VODKA** ❧ Based on the Pompier Highball found in Charles Baker Jr.'s *The Gentleman's Companion.* I came up with this variation for a cocktail dinner at Painter's Tavern, in Cornwall on Hudson, New York, in 2001.

The gin in this recipe isn't present in the Pompier Highball, but in order to turn the drink into a cocktail of sorts, a spirit had to be added. I opted to use only a very small amount of gin here, simply because the drink was created to accompany food and I wanted to keep the alcohol level down. Nevertheless, the spirit did its job and added a dry quality to the drink, which balanced the fruitiness of the cassis and made this cocktail perfect to sip alongside our salad course.

2½ ounces dry vermouth
¼ ounce crème de cassis
¼ ounce gin
1 lemon twist, for garnish

STIR AND STRAIN into a chilled cocktail glass. Add the garnish.

PREAKNESS COCKTAIL

FAMILY: **FRENCH-ITALIAN: WHISKEY AND BRANDY** I believe that this drink was formulated in the 1940s; later recipes call for blended whiskey as a base. Bourbon or straight rye works best in this one.

2 ounces bourbon or straight rye whiskey
1 ounce sweet vermouth
Bénédictine to taste (go easy)
Angostura bitters to taste
1 lemon twist, for garnish

STIR AND STRAIN into a chilled cocktail glass. Add the garnish.

PRESBYTERIAN

FAMILY: **HIGHBALLS** I haven't heard of this drink being ordered for years, but most people who are familiar with it would expect it to be made with blended whiskey. Ask the customer before you make it.

2 ounces straight rye whiskey
1½ ounces club soda
1½ ounces ginger ale
1 lemon twist, for garnish

BUILD in an ice-filled highball glass. Add the garnish.

PRETTY IN PINK

FAMILY: **SPARKLING SOURS** I created this for a good friend, Brook Wilkinson, on March 30, 2002, when she wanted "something on the sweet side." It was the inspiration for a new family of drinks—Squirrel Sours.

2 ounces Van Gogh Wild Appel vodka
¾ ounce crème de noyau
¾ ounce fresh lemon juice
club soda

SHAKE AND STRAIN into an ice-filled collins glass. Top with club soda.

PRINCESS MARY'S PRIDE COCKTAIL

FAMILY: **FRENCH-ITALIAN: WHISKEY AND BRANDY** ❧ Adapted from a recipe created by Harry Craddock in 1922 to mark the wedding of H.R.H. Princess Mary.

1½ ounces applejack
¾ ounce Dubonnet Rouge
¾ ounce dry vermouth

STIR AND STRAIN into a chilled cocktail glass.

PUNT E MES FIZZ

FAMILY: **CHAMPAGNE COCKTAILS** ❧ Adapted from a recipe by Audrey Saunders, New York City's Libation Goddess.

¾ ounce Punt e Mes
1½ ounces sweet vermouth
1½ to 2 ounces prosecco
1 lemon twist, for garnish

STIR AND STRAIN the Punt e Mes and vermouth into a chilled cocktail glass. Top with the prosecco. Add the garnish.

A QUICK LITTLE PICK-ME-UP

FAMILY: **INTERNATIONAL SOURS** ❧ Adapted from a recipe by Audrey Saunders, New York City's Libation Goddess—this one's a shooter.

¾ ounce Maker's Mark bourbon
¼ ounce Branca Menta
½ ounce fresh lemon juice
¾ ounce simple syrup
1 maraschino cherry, for garnish

SHAKE AND STRAIN into a sour glass. Add the garnish.

RAMOS GIN FIZZ

FAMILY: **SPARKLING SOURS** ❧ Henry Ramos, creator of this Fizz, had his own methods of making sure that the drink was prepared correctly: He hired a bevy of bartenders, who passed the shaker from one to the next until the drink reached the desired consistency. In *Famous New Orleans Drinks & how to mix 'em,* author Stanley Clisby Arthur states that at Mardi Gras in 1915 "35 shaker boys nearly shook their arms off, but still were unable to keep up with the demand."

Ramos himself, a native of Baton Rouge, owned the Imperial Cabinet Saloon in New Orleans from 1888 until 1907. At that point he took over the Stag Saloon, which served his special gin fizzes until 1920, when Prohibition was enacted. Here, it is said, customers would wait as long as an hour to get their hands on an authentic Ramos Fizz.

Following the directions of various old masters, a couple of friends and I once shook three shakers of this drink for a full five minutes, at which point it was hard to pry our hands from the shakers—we were as one with them. The point of the long shake is to achieve a "ropy" consistency. This is somewhat hard to describe, but "silky" also fits the bill, and once you experience this texture, you'll swear you're in heaven.

In *The Gentleman's Companion,* Charles H. Baker Jr. prescribes making the Ramos Gin Fizz in a blender, but with less ice than you would use to make a frozen drink. I've found this to deliver a perfect fizz, with the correct consistency and without the pain of frozen hands.

An optional ingredient in this drink is vanilla extract, and if you decide to use it (which I don't recommend), you should be very sparing; add only a couple of drops to the recipe below, which will make enough for two champagne flutes. Since at one ounce of gin per drink the alcohol content is very low, this is a great brunch drink, or something to consider if you're planning on having more than one.

MAKES 2 COCKTAILS

2 ounces gin
1 ounce cream
1 raw egg white (see page 112)
½ ounce simple syrup
½ ounce fresh lime juice
½ ounce fresh lemon juice
¼ ounce orange-flower water
club soda
2 half wheels orange, for garnish

Blend everything except for the club soda with enough ice to fill one champagne flute. Divide the mixture between two champagne flutes, and top each drink with a splash of club soda. Add the garnishes.

RASPBERRY MARTINI

FAMILY: **DUOS AND TRIOS** ~ Adapted from a recipe by Roy Finamore, New York City.

2½ ounces homemade raspberry vodka (see below)
½ ounce Grand Marnier
1 lemon twist, or 1 fresh raspberry, for garnish

SHAKE AND STRAIN into a chilled cocktail glass. Add the garnish.

RASPBERRY VODKA

FAMILY: **INFUSIONS** ~ Adapted from a recipe by Roy Finamore.

Place two pints of fresh raspberries in a large jar and add 1.75 liters vodka. Allow to infuse for three to four weeks, agitating the jar every few days. Strain through a double layer of dampened cheesecloth.

NOTE: Roy developed this infusion to use in his Raspberry Martinis, which contain Grand Marnier as a sweetening agent. If you wish to serve straight raspberry-infused vodka, I suggest you add simple syrup, to taste, to this recipe for balance.

RBS SPECIAL COCKTAIL

FAMILY: **INTERNATIONAL SOURS** ~ Adapted from a recipe created by David Wondrich in 2001 for New York's *RBS Gazette,* a "paper put out by the Rubber Band Society, a New York–based coalition of writers and artists, many of whom are Russian." Wondrich also notes, "The rye combines with the caraway notes of the kümmel (a liqueur formerly quite popular in Russia) to give the drink a faint and (I hope) [not unpleasant] flavor of rye bread, which New Yorkers and Russians are known to be particularly fond of. The grenadine gives the drink a faint red cast, to commemorate the former Soviet Union, from which many of the artists in the Rubber Band Society escaped."

2 ounces Wild Turkey straight rye whiskey
¼ ounce Gilka kümmel
½ ounce fresh lemon juice
¼ ounce grenadine

SHAKE AND STRAIN into a chilled cocktail glass.

RED SNAPPER

FAMILY: **SNAPPERS** ~ Adapted from the recipe donated by Gaston Lauryssen, then manager of the St. Regis Hotel, to the 1945 book *Crosby Gaige's Cocktail Guide and Ladies' Companion.*

1½ ounces tomato juice
1½ ounces vodka
2 dashes Worcestershire sauce
2 dashes fresh lemon juice
salt and cayenne pepper to taste

SHAKE AND STRAIN into a chilled cocktail glass.

REMEMBER THE MAINE

FAMILY: **FRENCH-ITALIAN: WHISKEY AND BRANDY** ~ Adapted from a recipe detailed by Charles H. Baker Jr., who insisted that the drink be stirred in a clockwise direction.

2 ounces bourbon
¾ ounce sweet vermouth
¼ ounce cherry brandy
absinthe substitute to taste
Angostura bitters to taste

STIR, in a clockwise direction, and STRAIN into a chilled cocktail glass.

RITZ OF NEW YORK

FAMILY: **CHAMPAGNE COCKTAILS** ~ Adapted from a recipe by Dale DeGroff, King Cocktail, of New York City.

1 ounce cognac
½ ounce triple sec
2 dashes maraschino liqueur
¼ ounce fresh lemon juice
chilled dry champagne or sparkling wine
1 orange twist, for garnish

SHAKE AND STRAIN the cognac, triple sec, maraschino liqueur, and lemon juice into a large, chilled cocktail glass. Top with champagne. Flame the garnish.

RIVEREDGE COCKTAIL

FAMILY: **FRENCH-ITALIAN: GIN AND VODKA** I came across this drink in *Crosby Gaige's Cocktail Guide and Ladies' Companion* (1945) and was immediately intrigued when I found that the recipe had been donated to Gaige by none other than James Beard, the dean of American cookery. The recipe in Gaige's book called for "four or five inch-wide strips of rind from a fine ripe orange" to be added to a blender "that is well filled with ice," along with 4½ jiggers of gin, 1 jigger of dry vermouth, and ½ jigger of water. It is interesting to note that this drink harks back to the Martinis of the 1940s and '50s, which almost always included a few dashes of orange bitters.

The Riveredge Cocktail

And now, ladies and gentlemen, I present to you one of man's best friends. No, it's not the dog—it's Jimmy Beard, father and mother of cooking in the open, harbinger of hors d'oeuvre, *and creator by royal decree of the* canapé. *If you do not possess his magnum opus,* Cook It Outdoors *or his encyclopedia,* Hors d'Oeuvre and Canapés, *you are not properly equipped to deal with present-day existence.*

Mr. Beard leads a life of splendor in a casserole near Washington Square. He dips a vanilla bean into homogenized ink and writes me as follows:

Dear Mr. Gaige:
May I call you Mr. Gaige?

Here is the drink . . . you requested of me. The cocktail is one that was a favorite of a great lady of long acquaintance. You may rest assured that I will never give you her telephone number. Years of tasting with a keen palate had given her, if possible, definite ideas of what, among other things, constituted a true "aperitif" or introduction to the waltz and I believe she had twins when she started this one. . . . Somehow or other after six or eight of these I find that the world is a fascinating place after all and the lady's phone number if you must know it is Eldorado something.

—FROM *CROSBY GAIGE'S COCKTAIL GUIDE AND LADIES' COMPANION*

Unfortunately, the recipe in Gaige's book just doesn't work. The bitterness from the orange rind masks all the other flavors; I'm sure that Mr. Beard meant for orange zest to be used, without any of the inner white pith. In the interest of keeping this drink alive, though, I experimented and came up with a new version of the Riveredge Cocktail.

MAKES 16 OUNCES; SERVES 4

6 ounces gin
2 ounces dry vermouth
2 ounces fresh orange juice
grated zest of 1 orange
2 dashes orange bitters
4 orange twists, for garnish

Blend with one cup of ice cubes. Pour immediately into four chilled cocktail glasses. Add the garnishes.

ROB ROY

FAMILY: **FRENCH-ITALIAN: WHISKEY AND BRANDY** ~ Crockett's *The Old Waldorf-Astoria Bar Book* states that this drink was named after a Broadway show of the same name, so it's possible that it dates back to 1894, when *Rob Roy,* an operetta by Reginald De Koven, opened on the Great White Way. Given that bartenders of that period were using more and more vermouth in their drinks than had their predecessors, there's a fair chance that the date is close to being correct. Rob Roy, of course, is a fictional character detailed in Sir Walter Scott's book of the same name, and is best described as a sort of Scottish Robin Hood who stole from the rich to give to the poor in the late seventeenth and early eighteenth centuries.

The Rob Roy is always made with sweet vermouth, unless otherwise requested. A Dry Rob Roy (sometimes referred to as the Beadlestone Cocktail) is made by substituting dry vermouth for the sweet, and a Perfect Rob Roy calls for half sweet and half dry vermouths. Classically, the basic Rob Roy calls for a cherry garnish, whereas the other two variations are usually served with twists of lemon. Personally I prefer to use lemon twists in all three versions.

Few people these days add bitters to the Rob Roy, and Angostura bitters don't work well in this drink. However, as David Embury suggested in the 1950s, Peychaud's bitters marry very well to the scotch in the Rob Roy, and I highly recommend that you try using them as an ingredient.

2 ounces scotch
1 ounce sweet vermouth
Peychaud's bitters to taste (optional)
1 maraschino cherry, for garnish

STIR AND STRAIN into a chilled cocktail glass. Add the garnish.

ROB ROY (DRY)

FAMILY: **FRENCH-ITALIAN: WHISKEY AND BRANDY**

2 ounces scotch
1 ounce dry vermouth
Peychaud's bitters to taste (optional)
1 lemon twist, for garnish

STIR AND STRAIN into a chilled cocktail glass. Add the garnish.

ROB ROY (PERFECT)

FAMILY: **FRENCH-ITALIAN: WHISKEY AND BRANDY** ➸ This was Mardee's favorite drink in 1978, when we first met.

2 ounces scotch
½ ounce sweet vermouth
½ ounce dry vermouth
Peychaud's bitters to taste (optional)
1 maraschino cherry, and/or 1 lemon twist, for garnish

STIR AND STRAIN into a chilled cocktail glass. Add the garnish.

ROSEBUD COCKTAIL

FAMILY: **NEW ORLEANS SOURS** ➸ Adapted from a recipe contributed to webtender.com by Michael Henderson in 1997. I played around with this drink because the ingredients looked as though they would work well together. The original was quite different.

1½ ounces citrus vodka
1 ounce triple sec
½ ounce fresh pink grapefruit juice
¼ ounce fresh lime juice

SHAKE AND STRAIN into a chilled cocktail glass.

ROYALE

FAMILY: **ORPHANS** — Adapted from a recipe by Peter Brown of the Craigellachie Hotel, Scotland, who wasn't too keen on making it with a single malt.

2 ounces Macallan twelve-year-old single-malt scotch
1 ounce apple schnapps
3 to 4 ounces ginger ale

BUILD in a wine glass filled with crushed ice.

RUM RUNNER

FAMILY: **FROZEN DRINKS** — Adapted from several recipes found on the Web. I never had made this drink prior to 2000, thinking that it was just another tropical frozen drink with no merit. I was wrong.

2 ounces 151-proof rum
1½ ounces blackberry brandy
1 ounce crème de banane
½ ounce fresh lime juice
grenadine to taste
1 lime wedge, for garnish

Blend with enough ice to almost fill a 12-ounce collins glass. Add the garnish.

RUSSIAN SQUIRREL

FAMILY: **SQUIRREL SOURS**

2 ounces vodka
½ ounce crème de noyau
½ ounce fresh lime juice

SHAKE AND STRAIN into a chilled cocktail glass.

RUSSIAN WALNUT MARTINI

FAMILY: **ORPHANS** — Adapted from a recipe from 2087: An American Bistro, in Thousand Oaks, California.

2 ounces Stolichnaya vodka
1 ounce Nocello walnut liqueur
½ ounce dark crème de cacao

STIR AND STRAIN into a chilled cocktail glass.

RUSTY NAIL

FAMILY: **DUOS AND TRIOS** — This is a good recipe for experimentation, since by using different bottlings of scotch and altering the ratios of base spirit to liqueur, the cocktailian bartender can learn much about ingredients. Blended scotch is normally used in this drink, but to display the cocktailian craft, try using different bottlings of single malt, tasting each one before adding the Drambuie (which should also be tasted prior to experimentation). You'll find that you need far less Drambuie if you use a lightly peated malt, such as Glenmorangie, than with a pungent malt from Islay, such as Ardbeg. The Macallan and Aberlour have much character of their own, without being heavily peated, but it's imperative that you add only enough Drambuie to either of these bottlings to flavor the scotch without completely destroying its personality.

2½ ounces scotch
½ ounce Drambuie

STIR AND STRAIN into an ice-filled old-fashioned glass.

RYE AND GINGER

FAMILY: **HIGHBALLS** — Most people expect this drink to be made with a blended whiskey, such as Canadian Club, which is not a straight rye whiskey. Ask the customer.

2 ounces straight rye whiskey
3 ounces ginger ale

BUILD in an ice-filled highball glass.

SAGE MARGARITA

FAMILY: **NEW ORLEANS SOURS** ~ Adapted from a recipe by Ryan Magarian of Restaurant Zoe, Seattle.

2 ounces Sauza Hornitos tequila
½ ounce triple sec
¾ ounce fresh lime juice
¼ ounce simple syrup
3 large fresh sage sprigs (preferably pineapple sage)
1 sage leaf, for garnish

SHAKE, with the sage sprigs, and STRAIN into a chilled cocktail glass. Add the garnish.

THE SALTY CHIHUAHUA

FAMILY: **FLORIDA HIGHBALLS**

2 ounces tequila
3 ounces fresh grapefruit juice

BUILD in an ice-filled, salt-rimmed highball glass.

SALTY DOG

FAMILY: **FLORIDA HIGHBALLS**

2 ounces vodka
3 ounces fresh grapefruit juice

BUILD in an ice-filled, salt-rimmed highball glass.

SATAN'S WHISKERS

FAMILY: **ORPHANS** ➤ There are two formulas for Satan's Whiskers. This one, known as "straight," calls for Grand Marnier, whereas the "curled" potion takes orange curaçao. This formula is adapted from *Jones' Complete Barguide.*

½ ounce gin
½ ounce dry vermouth
½ ounce sweet vermouth
½ ounce fresh orange juice
¼ ounce Grand Marnier
orange bitters to taste

SHAKE AND STRAIN into a chilled cocktail glass.

SAZERAC

FAMILY: **ORPHANS** ➤ The Sazerac Company of New Orleans pins down 1850 for the creation of this drink and says it was served at the Sazerac Coffee House in the French Quarter. Stanley Clisby Arthur, author of *Famous New Orleans Drinks & how to mix 'em,* wrote that Leon Lamothe was the bartender who first made the drink. He suggests that Lamothe merely added the absinthe component to the cocktail of brandy, sugar, and Peychaud's bitters that Peychaud himself is credited with serving as early as 1838. That brandy was the original base liquor is agreed upon by the Sazerac Company, which has a photograph of an early bottling of premixed Sazerac Cocktails. On the label, these words can be found: "Sazerac Cocktail, Prepared and bottled by Thomas H. Handy, Limited, Sole Proprietors. Guaranteed . . . under the food and drugs act, June 30, 1906. Martini." We don't know exactly when this bottle was issued, but we can be sure that it was prior to the onset of Prohibition in 1920; and already, cocktails other than a mixture of gin and vermouth were being referred to as Martinis, a phenomenon that's usually attributed to the 1990s.

We aren't quite sure when straight rye whiskey replaced the brandy in this drink, but it's possible that the phylloxera epidemic that devastated European vineyards during the latter years of the nineteenth century had something to do with it. The Sazerac Company's records indicate that the change occurred during the 1870s.

Peychaud's bitters are an integral ingredient in the Sazerac, as is absinthe substitute, and for this drink I recommend the use of Herbsaint, a New Orleans bottling made by the Sazerac Company. Herbsaint is drier than Pernod or Ricard, sweeter than Absente, and provides a perfect foil to the Peychaud's bitters. And since there's now a superb straight rye whiskey being issued by Sazerac, I'll go the whole hog and suggest that, if it's available, why not use this bottling and make a Sazerac Sazerac.

The ritual of making this drink involves chilling an old-fashioned glass with crushed ice, muddling sugar into the bitters in another glass, adding ice and whiskey to the bitters, and stirring the mixture to chill and dilute it. The ice is then discarded from the first glass, the glass is rinsed with Herbsaint and filled with fresh crushed ice, and the chilled whiskey is strained into the Herbsaint-rinsed glass. Finally, a twist of lemon is added, though some old recipes dictate that the twist not be dropped into the drink—just its oils should be released onto the drink's surface.

Sazerac aficionados have come up with various changes in the methodology of making this classic drink, and not wanting to be left out, I'm going to prescribe that the Sazerac be served straight up in a champagne flute—or a cocktail glass, if you must—simply because newcomers to the drink might be more tempted to try it if the glassware is a little more elegant. If you'd like to sample the original drink made with cognac, select a dryish bottling such as Hennessy or Hine, rather than fruitier brandies like Courvoisier.

3 ounces straight rye whiskey
¾ ounce simple syrup
Peychaud's bitters to taste (be fairly liberal)
Herbsaint to rinse the glass
1 lemon twist, for garnish

STIR AND STRAIN into a chilled, Herbsaint-rinsed champagne flute or cocktail glass. Add the garnish.

SCOFFLAW COCKTAIL

FAMILY: **SOURS** ▸ According to Michael B. Quinion, publisher of www.worldwidewords.org, the word *scofflaw* came about after the sum of two hundred dollars was offered, in 1923, to whoever came up with the best word to describe "a lawless drinker of illegally made or illegally obtained liquor." The prize money was donated by a rich Prohibitionist who wanted to "stab awake the conscience" of those who drank alcohol during Prohibition.

The following year, it was reported in the *Chicago Tribune* that "Jock," a bartender at Harry's New York Bar in Paris, had created the Scofflaw Cocktail. This recipe is adapted from the one found in Patrick Gavin Duffy's 1934 book *The Official Mixers Manual.*

2 ounces bourbon or straight rye whiskey
1 ounce dry vermouth
½ ounce fresh lemon juice
¼ ounce grenadine
orange bitters to taste

SHAKE AND STRAIN into a chilled cocktail glass.

SCORPION

FAMILY: **TROPICAL DRINKS** ▸ Adapted from a recipe in Jeff Berry and Annene Kaye's *Beachbum Berry's Grog Log,* this drink is commonly made with regular brandy, but it once called for pisco brandy from Peru—try both versions. The Scorpion is also traditionally served in a bowl, for two or more people. This recipe is for a single serving.

2 ounces light rum
½ ounce brandy
2 ounces fresh orange juice
¾ ounce fresh lemon juice
½ ounce orgeat syrup
½ ounce 151-proof rum

SHAKE AND STRAIN everything except the 151-proof rum into an ice-filled collins glass. FLOAT the 151-proof rum.

SCOTCH AND SODA

FAMILY: **HIGHBALLS** ~ Ask if the customer would like a lemon twist.

2 ounces scotch
3 ounces soda water

BUILD in an ice-filled highball glass.

SCOTCH AND WATER

FAMILY: **HIGHBALLS** ~ Ask if the customer would like bottled water.

2 ounces scotch
3 ounces water

BUILD in an ice-filled highball glass.

SCOTTISH SQUIRREL

FAMILY: **SQUIRREL SOURS** ~ Scotch and almonds work incredibly well together, and this drink is also well suited to Frangelico, Nocello, and other nut-flavored liqueurs.

1½ ounces scotch
¾ ounce crème de noyau
¾ ounce fresh lemon juice
1 lemon twist, for garnish

SHAKE AND STRAIN into a chilled cocktail glass. Add the garnish.

SCREWDRIVER

FAMILY: **FLORIDA HIGHBALLS**

2 ounces vodka
3 ounces fresh orange juice

BUILD in an ice-filled highball glass.

SEA BREEZE

FAMILY: **NEW ENGLAND HIGHBALLS**

2 ounces vodka
1½ ounces cranberry juice
1½ ounces fresh grapefruit juice
1 lime wedge, for garnish

BUILD in the order given in an ice-filled highball glass. Add the garnish.

SEELBACH COCKTAIL

FAMILY: **CHAMPAGNE COCKTAILS** — Adapted from a recipe created in 1917 at the Seelbach Hotel, in Louisville, Kentucky.

¾ ounce bourbon
½ ounce triple sec
7 dashes Angostura bitters
7 dashes Peychaud's bitters
4 ounces chilled brut champagne
1 orange twist, for garnish

BUILD in the order given in a champagne flute. Add the garnish.

SEVEN AND SEVEN

FAMILY: **HIGHBALLS** — At the time of this writing, another company had just bought the brand of whiskey called for in this drink from Seagram's, so there's no guaranteeing its future. If you use any other whiskey, or any other lemon-lime soda, the drink will not be a Seven and Seven. You must discuss this with the customer so that he knows exactly what he's getting, and agrees to the brands you have on hand.

2 ounces Seagram's Seven-Crown whiskey
3 ounces 7UP

BUILD in an ice-filled highball glass.

SEX ON THE BEACH

FAMILY: **NEW ENGLAND HIGHBALLS**

1½ ounces vodka
½ ounce peach schnapps
1½ ounces cranberry juice
1½ ounces fresh orange juice

BUILD in the order given in an ice-filled highball glass.

SHANDY

FAMILY: **BEER- AND CIDER-BASED DRINKS** ~ Originally known as a Shandy Gaff, this drink has been around since at least the 1880s, when it was usually made with ginger ale rather than lemon-lime soda. The old ginger ale version is superior to today's lemon-lime drink. But to make it better than that, build a Shandy with Jamaican ginger beer—it's a crisp, mouth-puckering treat. However you make this drink, though, be sure to pour the soda into the glass first; otherwise it will foam over the top before you can finish pouring.

8 ounces lemon-lime soda, ginger ale, or ginger beer
8 ounces amber ale

BUILD in the order given in a beer glass.

SIDECAR

FAMILY: **NEW ORLEANS SOURS** ~ In *The Fine Art of Mixing Drinks,* David Embury claims that the Sidecar was created during the First World War by a friend of his who traveled to his favorite "little bistro" in Paris in the sidecar of a motorbike. Popular legend has it that the bistro was Harry's New York Bar, but Embury doesn't mention this fact. Other accounts claim that it was first created by Frank Meier at the Paris Ritz, but that account was challenged by Meier's successor, a man by the name of Bertin.

Whoever made the world's first Sidecar had probably never heard of the Brandy Crusta, and he can't have been aware of what would become of the formula he used—that this combination of a spirit, an orange-flavored liqueur, and a citrus juice eventually spawned the Margarita, the Kamikaze, and the Cosmopolitan, to name just a few. The original drink, claims Embury, "contained six or seven ingredients," but his recipe calls for just cognac or armagnac, triple sec, and lemon juice—the ingredients we still use today. Embury used eight parts brandy to one of triple sec and two of lemon juice, but that formula doesn't work well for me—it's far too sour. After much enjoyable experimentation with this drink, I present the ratios I now use below. But the cocktailian bartender should experiment for himself. And with good reason.

Cognacs vary drastically in style, so it's impossible to make a Sidecar with Courvoisier, a plump, fruity brandy, the same way you'd fix the drink using a drier bottling such as Hennessy. The Hennessy Sidecar needs more triple sec for sweetness, and just a tad more lemon juice to balance it out. The Sidecar is a French cocktail, so cognac and armagnac are the obvious choices when it comes to the base brandy, but customers with a sweeter tooth might enjoy brandy de Jerez, a Spanish brandy that's usually on the sweet side (though bottlings vary), and true, blue Americans could request that their Sidecar be made with a great Californian brandy, such as those coming from the Germain-Robin distillery in Ukiah, or the Mendocino County Jepson distillery. But don't think for a second that their brandies are similar—Jepson bottlings are usually far drier than the Germain-Robin brandies.

Where does this leave the cocktailian? On his own, I'm afraid. Start with the formula below, tasting each ingredient before making the drink. Then make it again, altering the proportions after reconsidering the attributes of the brandy you are using.

1½ ounces cognac
1 ounce triple sec
½ ounce fresh lemon juice
1 lemon twist, for garnish

SHAKE AND STRAIN into a chilled, sugar-rimmed cocktail glass. Add the garnish.

SIDECAR DELUXE (BOTTLED)

FAMILY: **BOTTLED COCKTAILS**

MAKES 24 OUNCES

12 ounces cognac
3 ounces Grand Marnier
3 ounces fresh lemon juice
6 ounces bottled water
lemon twists, for garnish

MIX AND CHILL for a minimum of six hours.

SINGAPORE SLING NO. 1

FAMILY: **SPARKLING SOURS** The discussions about the original recipe for this drink are endless, and many members of the DrinkBoy.com community have debated the subject in depth. Although the truth may never be known, the Raffles Hotel in Singapore, where the drink is said to have been created by bartender Ngiam Tong Boon, in 1915, puts forth a recipe, and there are also a couple of other formulas worthy of note. Dr. Cocktail discovered the first recipe here in a 1922 book. It was called Straights Sling but was referred to as a "well-known Singapore drink." Since it calls for dry cherry brandy, Doc surmises that a cherry eau-de-vie, such as kirsch, was used in this version. The recipe below is adapted from the one in Doc's book and is included chiefly for historical interest, although it's not a bad drink at all. The second recipe, though, produces a Singapore Sling that most people will recognize.

2 ounces gin
½ ounce Bénédictine
½ ounce kirsch
¾ ounce fresh lemon juice
orange bitters to taste
Angostura bitters to taste
club soda

SHAKE everything except the club soda, and **STRAIN** into an ice-filled collins glass. Top with club soda.

> *Just looking around the terrace porch we've seen Frank Buck, the Sultan of Johore, Aimee Semple McPherson, Somerset Maugham, Dick Halliburton, Doug Fairbanks, Bob Ripley, Ruth Elder and Walter Camp. . . . When our soft footed Malay boy brings the 4th Sling and finds us peering over the window sill at the cobra-handling snake charmers tootling their confounding flutes below he murmurs "jaga baik-baik Tuan"—"jaga bye-bye too-wan," as it is in English—or "take care master" as it means in English. The Singapore Sling is a delicious, slow-acting, insidious thing.*
>
> —CHARLES H. BAKER JR., *THE GENTLEMAN'S COMPANION*, 1946

SINGAPORE SLING NO. 2

FAMILY: **SPARKLING SOURS** ~ The ingredients in this version are listed on a coaster from the Raffles Hotel, but no measurements were given, and club soda wasn't mentioned.

2 ounces Beefeater gin
½ ounce Cherry Heering
¼ ounce Bénédictine
½ ounce triple sec
2 ounces pineapple juice
¾ ounce fresh lime juice
Angostura bitters to taste
club soda

SHAKE everything except the club soda, and **STRAIN** into an ice-filled collins glass. Top with club soda.

SLOE COMFORTABLE SCREW

FAMILY: **FLORIDA HIGHBALLS**

¾ ounce vodka
¾ ounce sloe gin
¾ ounce Southern Comfort
3 ounces fresh orange juice

BUILD in an ice-filled highball glass.

SLOE GIN FIZZ

FAMILY: **SPARKLING SOURS**

2½ ounces sloe gin
1 ounce fresh lemon juice
½ ounce simple syrup
club soda

SHAKE everything except the club soda, and **STRAIN** into an ice-filled collins glass. Top with club soda.

SOUTHSIDE COCKTAIL

FAMILY: **JULEPS** I confess to not having known this drink very well until recently, but research pointed to it usually being not much more than a Gin Sour with a mint-sprig garnish. I have therefore taken the liberty of playing with it a little, employing the same technique used to make a Mojito and incorporating the mint into the drink, as well as using mint as a garnish.

4 lemon wedges
2 to 3 teaspoons granulated sugar
4 or 5 fresh mint leaves
2½ ounces gin
1 mint sprig, for garnish

MUDDLE the lemon wedges, sugar, and mint leaves in a mixing glass until the sugar is completely dissolved, all the juice is extracted from the lemons, and the mint is thoroughly integrated into the juice. Add ice and the gin to the mixing glass, and **SHAKE AND STRAIN** into a chilled cocktail glass. Add the garnish.

SOUTHSIDE FIZZ

FAMILY: **JULEPS** This is, more or less, a Mojito made with gin, but you can vary this drink by using tonic water instead of the club soda. Adding just one dash of Peychaud's or Angostura bitters to this drink can also make for interesting variations on the theme.

4 lemon wedges
2 to 3 teaspoons granulated sugar
6 to 8 fresh mint leaves
2½ ounces gin
club soda
3 mint sprigs, for garnish

MUDDLE the lemon wedges, sugar, and mint leaves in a mixing glass until the sugar is completely dissolved, all the juice is extracted from the lemons, and the mint is thoroughly integrated into the juice. Add ice and the gin to the mixing glass, and **SHAKE AND STRAIN** into an ice-filled collins glass. Add the soda and the garnish.

STARRY NIGHT COCKTAIL

FAMILY: **DUOS AND TRIOS** ⁓ I created this one for Van Gogh gin.

2½ ounces Van Gogh gin
1 ounce Goldschläger cinnamon schnapps

Pour all of the ingredients into a mixing glass two-thirds full of ice cubes. **STIR AND STRAIN** into a chilled cocktail glass.

STILETTO COCKTAIL

FAMILY: **INTERNATIONAL SOURS** ⁓ Adapted from a recipe by Al Romeo of Anthony's, in Houston, Texas. This formula is interesting since it directs that lime juice be used in conjunction with bourbon, whereas lemon juice is usually called for in most whiskey-based drinks. I admit that I raised my eyebrows when I first saw this recipe, but it works well despite itself.

2 ounces bourbon
½ ounce amaretto
½ ounce fresh lime juice

SHAKE AND STRAIN into a chilled cocktail glass.

STINGER

FAMILY: **DUOS AND TRIOS** ⁓ The combination of brandy and crème de menthe dates back to at least 1892, when William Schmidt detailed a drink called the Judge in his book *The Flowing Bowl.* "Shake to the freezing-point," he instructed, and his words have stayed with us, for the Stinger is the only drink I can name that will be shaken by the most professional bartenders, even though it contains no fruit juices, eggs, or dairy products.

The Stinger can be served straight up or over ice, but it's more often served over crushed ice. Be wary of the ratios here, since the crème de menthe can easily overpower the brandy, especially if you choose a dryish brandy such as Hennessy or Hine rather than a fruitier bottling like Courvoisier. And dry brandy *is* the best way to go with this drink.

3 ounces cognac
¼ to ½ ounce white crème de menthe

SHAKE AND STRAIN into a large brandy glass filled with crushed ice.

TART GIN COOLER

FAMILY: **ORPHANS** ⁓ This drink came into being as a result of experimentation with tonic water, which, when mixed with a little lemon juice, tastes like bitter lemon, a soda that's popular in the United Kingdom. Mardee and I tried it with grapefruit juice, and the rest of the drink just evolved.

2 ounces gin
2 ounces fresh pink grapefruit juice
2 ounces tonic water
Peychaud's bitters to taste

BUILD in an ice-filled collins glass.

TBILISI ROYALE

FAMILY: **CHAMPAGNE COCKTAILS** ⁓ Adapted from a recipe from the FireBird Russian Restaurant in New York City.

¼ ounce Stolichnaya Limonnaya vodka
½ ounce peach schnapps
chilled champagne
1 orange twist, for garnish
1 maraschino cherry, skewered onto a stirrer, for garnish

BUILD in the order given in a champagne flute. Add the garnishes.

TEA TINI

FAMILY: **SOURS** ⁓ Adapted from a recipe from the Peninsula Grill in Charleston, South Carolina.

1¾ ounces Stolichnaya Ohranj vodka
1 ounce sweet iced tea
¼ ounce fresh lemon juice
1 lemon wedge, for garnish

SHAKE AND STRAIN into a chilled, sugar-rimmed cocktail glass. Add the garnish.

TEQUILA SUNRISE

FAMILY: **FLORIDA HIGHBALLS** ~ A curveball in the Highball family, since this drink is normally served in a collins glass.

2½ ounces tequila
3 ounces fresh orange juice
splash grenadine

BUILD the tequila and orange juice in an ice-filled collins glass. Drop the grenadine into the center of the drink.

TERESA

FAMILY: **MILANESE DRINKS** ~ Adapted from a recipe by Rafael Ballesteros of Spain. This drink shows a cocktailian mind at work. Campari, a bitter aperitif from Italy, is often married to fruit juices such as grapefruit juice or orange juice, but Raphael took it a step further and used crème de cassis, a liqueur made from black currants; then he added lime juice to the mix. I'm at a loss to fathom how this dedicated cocktailian put these flavors together in his head, but the resultant drink is a complex marvel.

2 ounces Campari
¾ ounce crème de cassis
1 ounce fresh lime juice

SHAKE AND STRAIN into a chilled cocktail glass.

THE THIRD DEGREE, OR MARTINI WITH A SPOT

FAMILY: **FRENCH-ITALIAN: GIN AND VODKA** ~ When absinthe was still a legal substance, some people would add just a drop, or a spot, of it to their Martinis. This practice can have interesting results: If the absinthe substitute is added in drops, rather than even dashes, its anise notes are barely detectable, but the juniper flavors in the gin seem to be enhanced. Alchemy is at work here.

2½ ounces gin or vodka
½ ounce dry vermouth
absinthe substitute to taste (go easy)
1 olive or lemon twist, for garnish

STIR AND STRAIN into a chilled cocktail glass. Add the garnish.

TIEPOLO

FAMILY: **CHAMPAGNE COCKTAILS** ⁓ This is simply a strawberry version of the Bellini, brought to my attention by Roy Finamore, my editor. It was probably named for the eighteenth-century Italian artist Giovanni Battista Tiepolo.

2 ounces strawberry puree (see below)
3½ ounces chilled prosecco

Add the strawberry puree to a champagne flute, then slowly add the chilled prosecco, stirring constantly to incorporate the ingredients.

STRAWBERRY PUREE

In a blender, puree six hulled strawberries together with two or three ice cubes and a half teaspoon of fresh lemon juice.

TIRAMISU MARTINI

FAMILY: **ORPHANS** ⁓ Adapted from a recipe by Alan Kearney and Salvatore Como of the Pen-Top Bar, in New York City.

1 ounce Godiva white chocolate liqueur
1 ounce Stolichnaya Vanil
1 ounce Kahlúa
½ ounce Disaronno liqueur
½ ounce cream
chocolate shavings, for garnish

SHAKE AND STRAIN into a chilled cocktail glass. Add the garnish.

TOASTED ALMOND

FAMILY: **DUOS AND TRIOS**

1½ ounces amaretto
1½ ounces Kahlúa
1 ounce cream

SHAKE AND STRAIN into an ice-filled old-fashioned glass.

TOM COLLINS

FAMILY: **SPARKLING SOURS** "This is a long drink, to be consumed slowly with reverence and meditation," wrote cocktailian David Embury in the 1950s, and the Tom Collins is certainly a drink worthy of more respect than it gets. It isn't a complex drink, and neither is it made from a formula that required genius to figure it out—it's no more than a carbonated gin Sour—but this refreshing quaff can be delightful in hot weather.

The debate over the base of the Tom Collins will rage forever, but it's fairly safe to say that Old Tom, a sweetened gin no longer available, was first used in this drink; dry gin is now commonly used. The recipe here calls for fresh lemon juice and simple syrup, but if you would like to experiment with the Tom Collins, try muddling fresh lemon wedges with granulated sugar instead. The sugar will abrade the zest of the fruit and add a sparkle to the drink.

2½ ounces gin
1 ounce fresh lemon juice
¾ ounce simple syrup
club soda
1 maraschino cherry, for garnish
1 half orange wheel, for garnish

SHAKE everything except the club soda, and STRAIN into an ice-filled collins glass. Top with club soda. Add the garnish.

TREMBLEMENT DE TERRE (EARTHQUAKE)

FAMILY: **DUOS AND TRIOS** A drink mentioned in *Absinthe: History in a Bottle,* by Barnaby Conrad III, but without measurements. This was apparently a cocktail favored by Henri de Toulouse-Lautrec, a French artist who died in 1901, at the age of thirty-six. Considered yourself forewarned.

2½ ounces cognac
¼ ounce absinthe substitute
1 lemon twist, for garnish

STIR AND STRAIN into a chilled cocktail glass. Add the garnish.

TROPICAL COCKTAIL

FAMILY: **SOURS** — David Embury detailed this drink in the 1950s, but he muddled fresh pineapple with sugar and didn't include bitters. I have reformulated the recipe; you'll note that, depending on which style of bitters you use, the drink can change tremendously.

2 ounces dark rum
½ ounce pineapple juice
½ ounce fresh lime juice
grenadine to taste
Angostura, Peychaud's, or orange bitters to taste

SHAKE AND STRAIN into a chilled cocktail glass.

TSAR'S CHAMPAGNE COCKTAIL

FAMILY: **CHAMPAGNE COCKTAILS** — This recipe was submitted by pioneer spirits writer Herb Silverman, who says that he heard of it from a Russian in 1945. It was supposedly a favored drink of the tsars of Russia.

2 ounces chilled vodka
3½ ounces chilled champagne

BUILD in the order given in a champagne flute.

TULIO ORO

FAMILY: **CHAMPAGNE COCKTAILS** — Adapted from a recipe from Turo restaurant, in Seattle, Washington.

1 lemon twist
¾ ounce Limoncello
½ ounce Punt e Mes champagne
6 ounces prosecco

In a shaker half-filled with ice, combine the lemon twist, Limoncello, and Punt e Mes. SHAKE AND STRAIN into a champagne flute. Add the prosecco.

TWENTIETH-CENTURY COCKTAIL

FAMILY: **INTERNATIONAL SOURS** ~ Detailed in Tarling's *Café Royal Cocktail Book* (1937), this drink was created by a certain C. A. Tuck. Dr. Cocktail brought it to my attention a few years ago, and I've been mixing and drinking it ever since. The citrus juice acts as a foil to the sweet liqueur in this delightful drink, but it's the mixture of gin and chocolate that intrigues me. Did C. A. Tuck envisage these flavors before he put the drink together? We'll never know, but however he came up with the formula, nobody can argue with the fact that this drink is a masterpiece.

1½ ounces gin
½ ounce Lillet Blonde
½ ounce white crème de cacao
½ ounce fresh lemon juice

SHAKE AND STRAIN into a chilled cocktail glass.

VALENTINO

FAMILY: **MILANESE DRINKS** ~ After saying that you shouldn't adjust the ratios when making a Negroni, Mardee and I did just that when we created this drink in February 1999, for the Valentine's Day issue of *Ardent Spirits e-letter.* This was a no-brainer, but the resultant cocktail is far different from the Negroni, and I believe that it's a good example of what can be done with a tried-and-true recipe.

2 ounces gin
½ ounce Campari
½ ounce sweet vermouth
1 orange twist, for garnish

STIR over ice and STRAIN into a chilled cocktail glass. Add the garnish.

VALENTINO (VODKA)

FAMILY: **MILANESE DRINKS** ~ Merely the vodka-based version of the Valentino.

2 ounces vodka
½ ounce Campari
½ ounce sweet vermouth
1 orange twist, for garnish

STIR AND STRAIN into a chilled cocktail glass. Add the garnish.

VESPER MARTINI

FAMILY: **FRENCH-ITALIAN: GIN AND VODKA** Named for Vesper Lynd, a character in Ian Fleming's *Casino Royale.* James Bond insisted that this Martini be shaken, he preferred Lillet to vermouth, and he suggested that a grain-based vodka worked better than a potato vodka. The cocktailian bartender might pause to wonder why somebody would add vodka to this gin-based drink, and in this instance the vodka acts as a diluting agent, taking the edge off the gin. If you use a softer gin, such as Bombay, you'll find that this drink has little character. Far better to employ a sturdier bottling, like Tanqueray, lest the gin get completely lost in the mix.

2 ounces gin
½ ounce vodka
¼ ounce Lillet Blonde
1 lemon twist, for garnish

SHAKE AND STRAIN into a chilled cocktail glass. Add the garnish.

VODKA AND TONIC

FAMILY: **HIGHBALLS**

2 ounces vodka
3 ounces tonic water
1 lime wedge, for garnish

BUILD in an ice-filled highball glass. Add the garnish.

WARD EIGHT

FAMILY: **SOURS** Although politician Martin M. Lomasney was known to many as "the Boston Mahatma," others called him "the Czar of Ward Eight." It's generally accepted that this drink was created at the Locke-Ober Café in Boston, circa 1898, to celebrate his victory in a race for the state legislature. The twist to the story, though, is that the drink was made before the election results were in. Lomasney has been quoted as saying, "Just before the election we send out suggestions to the voters. We don't tell 'em how to vote. We just suggest." In her 1993 essay "The Business of Elections," Rebecca Mercuri wrote, "The old-timers used to tell stories of how Martin Lomasney . . . would greet them at the polls on election day. 'Here's your ballot,' he'd say, 'I've already marked it for you. When you get in there, pick up the ballot they give you and give them back this one.' When you came out you'd give Martin the clean ballot, and he'd mark it off and give it to the next guy in line."

2 ounces straight rye whiskey
1 ounce fresh orange juice
1 ounce fresh lemon juice
grenadine to taste

SHAKE AND STRAIN into a chilled cocktail glass.

WHISKEY OLD-FASHIONED

FAMILY: **MUDDLED DRINKS** This drink was old-fashioned way back in 1895, when Kappeler called it the Old-Fashioned Whiskey Cocktail in his book *Modern American Drinks: How to Mix and Serve All Kinds of Cups and Drinks.* He made the drink by dissolving a lump of sugar with a little water, then adding two dashes of Angostura bitters, a small piece of ice, lemon peel, and a jigger of whiskey. Seven years prior to that, Harry Johnson had made a similar drink with the addition of a couple of dashes of curaçao. His recipe was titled the Whiskey Cocktail, so presumably those seven years seemed like a generation to Kappeler.

The Old-Fashioned can be a controversial drink on more than one front. Some bartenders add a splash of club soda, either before muddling or after mixing the drink, and others will add a little water. Neither of these ingredients should be in there as far as I'm concerned. But the thing that really raises the hackles of many cocktailians is the question of fruit. Is it correct to muddle, say, a slice of orange and a maraschino cherry with the bitters and sugar before adding the ice and whiskey?

Historically, this is not the prescribed method—most vintage recipes call only for a twist of lemon to be added to the drink, the way in which President Eisenhower sipped the drink at New York's '21' Club,

The Old-Fashioned

This was brought to the Old Waldorf in the days of its "sit-down" Bar, and was introduced by, or in honor of, Col. James E. Pepper, of Kentucky, proprietor of a celebrated whiskey of the period. It was said to have been the invention of a bartender at the famous Pendennis Club in Louisville, of which Col. Pepper was a member.

—ALBERT STEVENS CROCKETT,
THE OLD WALDORF-ASTORIA BAR BOOK, 1935

according to a 1973 *Playboy* article by Emanuel Greenberg. And in 1945, Crosby Gaige, a playboy himself, wrote, "Serious-minded persons omit fruit salad from 'Old-Fashioneds,' while the frivolous window-dress the brew with slices of orange, sticks of pineapple, and a couple of turnips."

So when did the fruit find its way into this drink? It could have been during Prohibition if you listen to Ted Saucier, who said as much in his 1951 book *Bottoms Up*. Be that as it may, the fruit question is a serious one, and although many people in the twenty-first century expect a small fruit salad to be muddled into the drink, a good bartender will always ask before proceeding.

Personally, I like the fruit-salad Old-Fashioned over the historically correct version, but both have their merits. Here I detail an old-fashioned Old-Fashioned, a fruity Old-Fashioned, and a variation on the latter. You should also experiment with very small quantities—a couple of dashes at most—of liqueurs such as curaçao and maraschino, both of which have been previously recorded as ingredients, to fashion your own Old-Fashioned.

Although whiskey was the base liquor in the world's first Old-Fashioned, you can also experiment with other dark spirits, such as brandy or dark rum, to make this style of drink.

1 sugar cube
3 dashes Angostura bitters
3 ounces bourbon or straight rye whiskey
1 lemon twist, for garnish

MUDDLE the sugar and bitters in an old-fashioned glass. Add ice and the whiskey. Add the garnish. STIR briefly.

WHISKEY OLD-FASHIONED (FRUIT-STYLE)

FAMILY: **MUDDLED DRINKS** The way in which I was taught to make the drink at Drakes Drum, New York City, circa 1973.

1 sugar cube
3 dashes Angostura bitters
1 maraschino cherry
1 half wheel orange
3 ounces bourbon or straight rye whiskey

MUDDLE the sugar, bitters, cherry, and orange in an old-fashioned glass. Add ice and the whiskey. STIR briefly.

WHISKEY OLD-FASHIONED (PEACH)

FAMILY: **MUDDLED DRINKS** ~ I made this drink for Peter Buttiglieri, a partner at Painter's, our local joint, when he popped over one afternoon to "get away from it all" and demanded an Old-Fashioned. With no other fruit in the house, I used ripe peach slices; Peter was happy with the results. Note that there is no sugar in this formula—the sweetness of the peaches made it unnecessary. Experiment with other ripe fruits, such as pineapple or apricots, for variations on this theme, and take into account the relative sweetness of the fruit before deciding on whether or not sugar will be necessary.

3 dashes Angostura bitters
2 ripe peach wedges
3 ounces bourbon or straight rye whiskey

MUDDLE the bitters and peach wedges in an old-fashioned glass. Add ice and the whiskey. STIR briefly.

WHISKEY SOUR

FAMILY: **SOURS**

2 ounces bourbon, rye, or blended whiskey
1 ounce fresh lemon juice
½ ounce simple syrup
1 maraschino cherry, for garnish
1 half wheel orange, for garnish

SHAKE AND STRAIN into a chilled sour glass or an ice-filled rocks glass. Add the garnishes.

WHISKEY SOUR JELLY SHOT

FAMILY: **JELLY SHOTS** ~ See page 150 for advice about what molds to use for Jelly Shots.

2 ounces fresh lemon juice
1 ounce simple syrup
1 ounce water
1 package unflavored gelatin (¼ ounce)
4 ounces whiskey
food coloring, if desired

Place the lemon juice, simple syrup, and water in a small glass measuring cup, and add the gelatin. Allow this to sit for one minute, then microwave the mixture on high for thirty seconds. Stir thoroughly to make sure that all the gelatin has dissolved, then add the whiskey and food coloring (if desired). Stir thoroughly again and pour the mixture into a mold. Refrigerate for at least one hour or, preferably, overnight.

WHITE RUSSIAN

FAMILY: **DUOS AND TRIOS**

2 ounces vodka
1 ounce Kahlúa
1 ounce cream

SHAKE AND STRAIN into an ice-filled old-fashioned glass.

WHITE SPIDER

FAMILY: **DUOS AND TRIOS** ~ Often known as a Vodka Stinger, which is exactly what this drink is.

3 ounces vodka
¼ to ½ ounce white crème de menthe

SHAKE AND STRAIN into a chilled cocktail glass or a wine glass filled with crushed ice.

The White Spider

Its body consists of ice and eternal snow. Its legs and its predatory arms, all hundreds of feet long, are white, too. From that perpetual, fearfully steep field of frozen snow nothing but ice emerges to fill gullies, cracks, and crevices. . . .

And there the "Spider" waits.

—HEINRICH HARRER, *THE WHITE SPIDER*

WHITE WINE SPRITZER

FAMILY: **ORPHANS** ~ I honestly can't imagine a drink more boring than this.

6 ounces dry white wine
1 to 2 ounces club soda
1 lemon twist, for garnish

BUILD in an ice-filled collins glass. Add the garnish.

WOO WOO

FAMILY: **NEW ENGLAND HIGHBALLS** ~ Sometimes called a Pierced Navel.

2 ounces vodka
½ ounce peach schnapps
2½ ounces cranberry juice

BUILD in the order given in an ice-filled highball glass.

ZOMBIE NO. 1

FAMILY: **TROPICAL DRINKS** ~ Created by Donn the Beachcomber, the Zombie was reportedly first served at the Hurricane Bar during the 1939 World's Fair. Donn's original recipe has never, to my knowledge, been published, so here are two other versions. The first is adapted from a recipe that Mardee and I formulated in 1998 for an article in *Wine Enthusiast,* and the second is adapted from a recipe in Jeff Berry and Annene Kaye's *Beachbum Berry's Grog Log.*

2 ounces añejo rum
1 ounce light rum
1 ounce dark rum
½ ounce fresh lime juice
¾ ounce pineapple juice
¼ ounce apricot brandy
¼ ounce 151-proof rum
Angostura bitters to taste
1 maraschino cherry, for garnish
1 fresh pineapple spear, for garnish
1 mint sprig, for garnish

SHAKE all the liquid ingredients except for the 151-proof rum, and **STRAIN** into an ice-filled zombie glass. **FLOAT** the 151-proof rum, and add the garnishes.

ZOMBIE NO. 2

FAMILY: **TROPICAL DRINKS**

1 ounce dark rum
1½ ounces añejo rum
1½ ounces light rum
¾ ounce applejack
¾ ounce papaya nectar
¾ ounce pineapple juice
1 ounce fresh lime juice
½ ounce simple syrup
½ ounce 151-proof rum
1 maraschino cherry, for garnish
1 fresh pineapple spear, for garnish
1 mint sprig, for garnish

SHAKE all the liquid ingredients except for the 151-proof rum, and **STRAIN** into an ice-filled zombie glass. **FLOAT** the 151-proof rum, and add the garnishes.

TABLES AND CHARTS

Minim.—There are 60 minims in a dram or teaspoon; 120 in a dessertspoon; 240 in a tablespoon; 480 in an ounce; 960 in a wineglass; 1,920 in a teacup or gill; 3,840 in a breakfast-cup or tumbler; 7,680 in a pint; 15,360 in a quart; 61,440 in a gallon; 2,935,360 in a barrel; 3,970,720 in a hogshead. Its equivalent weight is .9493 grams. A Minim is equal to a drop."

—CUYLER REYNOLDS, *The Banquet Book,* 1902

BOTTLE SIZES

375 milliliters: half a standard spirit or wine bottle
750 milliliters: standard spirit or wine bottle
Magnum: 1.5 liters
Double magnum: 3 liters
Jeroboam: 3 liters
Rehoboam: 4.5 liters
Imperial: 6 liters
Methuselah: 6 liters
Salmanazar: 8 to 9 liters
Balthazar: 12.3 liters
Nebuchadnezzar: 15.4 liters

FRESH FRUIT JUICE YIELDS

The following approximate yields are a result of some five years of noting how much juice I squeezed from each fruit, then arriving at an average.

1 grapefruit yields 6 ounces juice
1 lemon yields 1½ ounces juice
1 lime yields 1 ounce juice
1 orange yields 2½ to 3 ounces juice

FLUID MEASUREMENT CONVERSIONS

There is much confusion about the term *gill,* and I believe this arises because of the confusion between British and American pints. Although British and American fluid ounces are slightly different, the British measurement containing four-hundredths of an ounce more than the American ounce, it's generally accepted that a British pint contains 20 ounces and a pint in the States contains 16 ounces—the difference in ounce size being disregarded.

A gill, which is a more or less arcane measurement, *usually* referred to one-quarter of a pint; so in Britain, a gill would be five ounces, and in the States, it would contain four ounces.

BARSPEAK	**U.S.A.**	**U.K.**	**METRIC**
1 pony	1 ounce	1.04 ounces	2.96 centiliters
1 jigger	1.5 ounces	1.56 ounces	4.44 centiliters
1 gill	4 ounces	5 ounces	14.19 centiliters

U.S.A.	**U.K.**	**METRIC**
1 ounce	1.04 ounces	2.96 centiliters
1.5 ounces	1.56 ounces	4.44 centiliters
1 pint	0.83 pint	47.32 centiliters
1 gallon	0.83 gallon	3.79 liters

U.K.	**U.S.A.**	**METRIC**
1 ounce	0.961 ounce	2.841 centiliters
1 pint	1.201 pints	56.825 centiliters
1 gallon	1.201 gallons	4.546 liters

METRIC	U.S.A.	U.K.
1 liter	33.82 ounces	35.195 ounces
750 millileters	25.36 ounces	26.396 ounces
1 milliliter	0.034 ounce	0.035 ounce
1 centiliter	0.338 ounce	0.352 ounce

HOW MANY SHOTS ARE IN THAT BOTTLE?

BOTTLE SIZE	SHOT SIZE	NUMBER OF SHOTS
750 milliliters	1 ounce	25.36
750 milliliters	1¼ ounces	20.29
750 milliliters	1½ ounces	16.91
750 milliliters	2 ounces	12.68
750 milliliters	2½ ounces	10.14
1 liter	1 ounce	33.82
1 liter	1¼ ounces	27.01
1 liter	1½ ounces	22.55
1 liter	2 ounces	16.91
1 liter	2½ ounces	13.53

HOW MUCH ALCOHOL IS IN THAT BOTTLE?

Thankfully, most producers of alcoholic beverages have started to steer away from using *proof* as an indicator of the amount of alcohol in any one product and now use *abv,* "alcohol by volume," to show strength. Therefore, a bottle of liquor at 40 percent abv contains 40 percent pure alcohol by volume (as opposed to by weight, which would get very confusing).

Britain, which used to use the Sikes scale to display proof, now uses the European scale set down by the International Organization of Legal Metrology (IOLM). This scale, for all intents and purposes the same as the Gay-Lussac scale, previously used by much of mainland Europe, was adopted by all the countries in the European Community in 1980. Using the IOLM scale or the Gay-Lussac scale is essentially the same as measuring alcohol by volume, except that their figures are expressed as degrees, not percentages.

ALCOHOL BY VOLUME	U.S.A. PROOF	IOLM
40%	80°	40°
43%	86°	43°
50%	100°	50°

GLOSSARY

ABSENTE A dry French absinthe substitute.

ABSINTHE A high-proof spirit with a predominant anise flavor. Absinthe was declared illegal in the United States in 1912, because the wormwood used in its production was deemed to be harmful.

ABSINTHE SUBSTITUTE Spirits or liqueurs with a predominant anise flavor meant to be used in place of the now illegal absinthe. Absente, Herbsaint, La Muse Verte, Pernod, and Ricard are all examples of absinthe substitutes.

ABRICOTINE An apricot-flavored liqueur from France.

ADVOCAAT A brandy-based liqueur made with eggs, vanilla, and various other flavorings.

AGED SPIRITS Spirits labeled with a specific age statement have spent the indicated number of years aging in wooden barrels. The contents of the bottle can contain spirits older than the given age, but not younger.

AGING DISTILLED SPIRITS Some spirits, such as whiskey, aged brandy, and aged rum, require time in oak barrels before being bottled. During that time, the congeners, which are basically impurities in the liquor, oxidize, forming acids that react with other congeners to produce pleasant-tasting esters. The alcohol also reacts with the wood, extracting vanillins, wood sugars, tannins, and color.

ALE A style of beer made with a top-fermenting yeast. Subcategories of ales include amber ales, barley wines, India pale ales, lambics, porters, stouts, and wheat beers.

ALIZÉ A proprietary passion-fruit-flavored liqueur from France.

ALIZÉ RED PASSION A proprietary passion-fruit- and cranberry-flavored liqueur from France.

AMARETTO An almond-flavored liqueur, usually made in Italy. Disaronno is a great example of this liqueur, but at the time of this writing, the company is considering taking the word *amaretto* off its label. This will leave it in the same boat as Cointreau, and future generations might not realize that Disaronno *is* an amaretto, just as there are people today who don't realize that Cointreau is a triple sec.

AMER PICON A hard-to-find French aperitif with orange notes and a bitter herbal backdrop.

AMERICAN BRANDY Primarily produced on the West Coast and usually distilled from a fermented mash of grapes. The less expensive bottlings can be overly sweet, but some of the newer artisanal American brandies rank among the finest in the world. American brandy makers are not restricted as to which variety of grape may be used, so a few distilleries, using traditional French-style *alembique* stills and employing varietals such as chardonnay, chenin blanc, meunière, muscat, and pinot noir grapes, produce great aged brandies.

Anisette An anise-flavored liqueur.

Aperitif A beverage designed to whet the appetite.

Applejack An American product, currently available only from Laird's in New Jersey, made from a blend of distilled cider, neutral spirits, and "apple wine," which is produced from hard cider and apple brandy. I'd like to see applejack back behind every bar in America, just as it was just a few decades ago—it's a very versatile spirit and can be of great use to the cocktailian bartender.

Apricot brandy An apricot-flavored liqueur.

Apry A proprietary apricot-flavored liqueur from France.

Ardent spirits
1. From the Latin *adere,* meaning "to burn," this term was used to describe the first distilled spirits, simply because they could be ignited. The word *spirit,* in all probability, referred to the vapors that rose from the liquid being distilled. 2. An e-mail newsletter free to anyone sending their e-mail address to gary@ardentspirits.com.

Armagnac A brandy distilled from a fermented mash of grapes, made in the Gascony region of France. Armagnac is made from ugni blanc (Saint-Émilion), colombard, and/or folle blanche grapes, and although this practice is starting to wane, it is traditionally aged in Monlezun oak. Like cognac, much Armagnac is aged for longer than the law requires, but the following guidelines were set in 1994: 3 stars: 3 years; V.O.: 5 years; V.S.O.P.: 5 years; Réserve: 5 years; Extra: 6 years; Napoléon: 6 years; X.O.: 6 years; Vielle Reserve: 6 years, and Hors d'Age: 10 years.

Aromatized wines Wines flavored with botanicals such as herbs and spices and slightly fortified by the addition of brandy.

Aurum A proprietary orange-flavored liqueur from Italy.

B & B A proprietary bottling of Bénédictine and cognac.

Baileys Irish Cream A cream-based liqueur flavored with Irish whiskey.

Beer A beverage made by fermenting grains. There are two groups: ales and lagers.

Bénédictine A French herbal liqueur developed in 1510 by the Bénédictine monk Dom Bernardo Vincelli.

Bitters 1. A nonpotable high-proof infusion of various botanicals used as an accent in many cocktails. 2. A potable spirit, emanating mainly from Italy, where it is known as *amaro* and is flavored with bitter botanicals, as well as, sometimes, fruits and other flavorings. Campari and Averna are two good examples, and if you compare these two bottlings, you'll get a grasp of how diverse this category can be. Since the Bureau of Alcohol, Tobacco, and Firearms doesn't have a category for potable bitters, they are often labeled as liqueurs.

Blackberry brandy A blackberry-flavored liqueur.

Blue curaçao An blue-colored, orange-flavored liqueur; it is similar to triple sec, but usually sweeter.

Botanicals A collection of flavoring agents that can be made up of a variety of barks, fruits, herbs, spices, and various other ingredients. Juniper, for example, is one botanical used to flavor gin, and orange peel is a botanical employed in the flavoring of Cointreau.

Bourbon A whiskey made in the United States from a fermented mash of grains; corn must make up at least 51 percent, but no more than 79 percent, of the mash. Bourbon must be aged in new, charred oak barrels for at least two years, but if it is bottled at less than four years of age, its age must be noted on the label.

Brandy A spirit distilled from a fermented mash of fruit. Usually when we think of brandy we think of a grape-based spirit that has been aged in wood, but that isn't always the case. *See also* American brandy, armagnac, brandy de Jerez, cognac, eau-de-vie, grappa, marc.

Brandy de Jerez An aged grape-based brandy made in the Jerez region of Spain. The liquor is aged using the solera system of adding young spirits to older spirits in a pyramid fashion: The top row of a solera holds new distillates, and the bottom row holds the oldest brandies, with barrels full of ascending ages in between. Airén or palomino grapes are the usually used varietals, and the brandy can be sweeter than most other grape brandies. Bottlings of brandy de Jerez that use the word *Solera* on the label have been aged for about one year; *Solera Reserva* brandies spend around twenty-four months in the wood, and *Solera Gran Reserva* bottlings can be over seven years old.

Calvados A spirit distilled from a fermented mash of apples, usually with a small percentage of pears. Made in the Calvados region of Normandy, France, it is aged in oak.

Campari An Italian form of potable bitters.

Canadian blended whisky Many people erroneously think of Canadian whisky as being rye whisky, but that's just not true unless you see the words *rye whisky* on the label. The vast majority of Canadian blended whisky is made in continuous stills from a base of corn and is mixed with neutral grain whisky after aging. Flavorings are commonly added to the end product. Bourbon, cognac, rum, and sherry are all employed by one distillery or another to flavor Canadian whiskies, and even a product known as prune wine can be an additive. By law, the distillers are allowed to add 9.09 percent flavoring to their products, but in practice a far smaller percentage is actually used.

Chambord A black-raspberry-flavored liqueur from France.

Champagne A French sparkling wine from the Champagne district of northeastern France. Although sparkling wines from the United States are sometimes labeled "champagne," they are not recognized as such by the knowledgeable.

Charcoal filtration In most cases, these words refer to filtration with activated carbon, a process used on many spirits, after they have been aged, to eliminate impurities that can cause them to develop a chill haze when cold. (This is not to be confused with the charcoal filtration used in the production of Tennessee whiskey.) The problem with filtration is that the impurities that are removed during the process are flavorful, and if the spirit is chilled before filtration, even more impurities are lost. The alternative is to bottle spirits at high proof—around 50 percent alcohol by volume—since these spirits won't easily develop a chill haze.

Chartreuse An herbal liqueur from France said to have been created by Carthusian monks in 1737, though the recipe supposedly dates back to 1605. Available in green and yellow bottlings. Yellow Chartreuse, introduced in 1838, is the sweeter variety.

Cheri Suisse A proprietary chocolate- and cherry-flavored liqueur from Switzerland.

Cherry brandy A cherry-flavored liqueur.

Cherry Heering A proprietary cherry-flavored liqueur from Denmark.

Cherry Marnier A cherry-flavored, cognac-based liqueur from France.

Cognac An aged grape-based spirit from the Cognac region of France. Cognac must be made from at least 90 percent ugni blanc (also known as Saint-Émilion), folle blanche, and/or colombard grapes, and is usually aged in Limousin oak barrels. Much cognac is aged for longer than the law requires; however, in order to put the following codes on the bottle, it must spend the time noted in wood: V.S. (Very Special): 2.5 years; V.S.O.P. (Very Special Old Pale): 4.5 years; V.O. (Very Old): 4.5 years; Réserve: 4.5 years; X.O. (Extra Old): 6 years; and Napoléon: 6 years.

Cointreau A highly recommendable proprietary brand of triple sec from France.

Continuous still A type of still patented by Aeneas Coffey, circa 1860, that's sometimes referred to as a Coffey still, a column still, or a patent still. The still contains a series of perforated metal plates; the fermented mash is entered at the top of the still, and steam is piped into the bottom. The steam strips the mash of its alcohol, and the alcohol-laden vapors are collected at the top. It's possible to attain a spirit with around 96 percent alcohol in a single distillation in this type of still. Similar stills were in use in France in the late 1700s.

Cordial A sweetened and flavored low-alcohol beverage usually referred to as a liqueur.

CORN WHISKEY A spirit distilled from a grain mash, a minimum of 80 percent of which must be corn. If aged, it must rest in previously used barrels.
CRÈME DE ANANAS A pineapple-flavored liqueur.
CRÈME DE BANANE A banana-flavored liqueur.
CRÈME DE CACAO A chocolate-flavored liqueur available in both white and dark bottlings.
CRÈME DE CASSIS A black-currant-flavored liqueur.
CRÈME DE MENTHE A mint-flavored liqueur available in both green and white bottlings.
CRÈME DE NOYAU An almond-flavored liqueur.
CRÈME YVETTE A now-unavailable proprietary violet-flavored liqueur. At the time of this writing, you can order a violet liqueur at www.sallyclarke.com.
CUARENTA Y TRES A Spanish herbal liqueur with a predominance of vanilla.
CURAÇAO An orange-flavored liqueur similar to triple sec but usually sweeter.
DANZIGER GOLDWASSER A proprietary aniseed- and caraway-flavored liqueur flecked with gold flakes, from Germany.
DIGESTIF A beverage, such as Underberg bitters, designed to aid digestion.
DISTILLATION The distillation of beverage alcohol, as far as we know, dates back to the century between 1050 and 1150 and most probably occurred at the University of Salerno, in Italy. The word *distillation* is derived from the Latin *dis* or *des,* which implies separation, and *stilla,* which translates to "drop." In a literal sense, therefore, it means separation drop by drop. In the case of distilled spirits, the object is to separate alcohol from water using heat. Since beverage alcohol evaporates at a little under 173° F, whereas water turns to steam at 212° F, if a liquid containing both water and alcohol is heated to a point above the boiling point of alcohol but below that of water, the resultant vapors can be condensed into a liquid that contains more alcohol that the original liquid.
DISTILLED SPIRITS Beverages distilled from fermented food products, such as grains, fruits, or vegetables, that are bottled at a minimum of 40 percent alcohol by volume.
DRAMBUIE A scotch-based herbal liqueur flavored with honey. The word *Drambuie* is derived from the Gaelic *an dram buidheach,* meaning "the drink that satisfies."
DUBONNET An aromatized wine, similar to vermouth, available in rouge and blanc.
EAU-DE-VIE A generic French term meaning "water of life" that can be applied to all unaged fruit brandies.
FERMENTATION This term refers to the process that occurs when yeast feeds on sugar, producing carbon dioxide, heat, and alcohol. In the case of fruit-based spirits, such as brandy, this is easy: The sugar is ready, willing,

and able. But grain-based spirits like whiskey are a little trickier. Grains contain starches, though, and starches are merely complex forms of sugar, so they can be broken down to yield fermentable sugars.

Forbidden Fruit A proprietary American brandy-based, fruit-flavored liqueur. Very hard to find.

Fortified wine A wine such as madeira, port, or sherry that has been fortified by the addition of brandy.

Framboise 1. An eau-de-vie made from a fermented mash of raspberries. 2. A raspberry-flavored liqueur.

Frangelico A proprietary hazelnut-flavored Italian liqueur.

Galliano A proprietary Italian vanilla-herbal liqueur with orange notes.

Gin A spirit distilled from a fermented mash of grains and flavored with a number of botanicals, of which juniper must be predominant. Having written that, I must now say that some gins on the market these days do not show a predominance of juniper. These bottlings seem to be very popular, and some vodka drinkers have been converted to gin as a result of experimentation with these products.

London dry gin need not be produced in London—the phrase is used to describe a dry style of gin. *Plymouth gin,* on the other hand, although it displays characteristics similar to London dry bottlings, must be made in Plymouth, England. *Old Tom gin* is a defunct product; it was a slightly sweetened gin that was very popular during the latter decades of the 1800s, right through to the onset of Prohibition in 1920. *Hollands* or *geneva gin,* made in Holland, can be fairly sweet, although some bottlings are similar in style to the lightly junipered gins favored by vodka drinkers.

Glayva A proprietary scotch-based herbal-honey liqueur.

Grand Marnier A proprietary orange-flavored, aged cognac-based liqueur from France. Available in three bottlings: Grand Marnier Cordon Rouge; Grand Marnier Cuvée du Centenaire, made with ten-year-old cognac; and Grand Marnier Cuvée du Cent-Cinquantenaire, made with X.O. cognac.

Grappa An Italian eau-de-vie distilled from a fermented mash of grape pomace, the leftovers from the winemaking process.

Herbsaint A proprietary absinthe substitute from New Orleans.

Irish Mist A proprietary Irish-whiskey-based liqueur flavored with herbs and honey.

Irish whiskey A spirit distilled in Ireland from a fermented mash of grains and aged in wooden barrels for a minimum of three years. There are some fine single-malt Irish whiskeys distilled in pot stills, and their number is growing. Most Irish whiskeys, though, are blended products. The Irish Distillers company, which owns many of the major brands, has a policy to not bottle any of its whiskeys, blended or single malt, until all the whiskey used has been aged for a minimum of five years. I'd wager that the same could be said of the independent Irish whiskeymakers.

One of the major differences between Irish whiskey and scotch is that the Irish rarely use peat fires to dry their malt. Another is that Irish whiskeymakers usually distill their whiskey three times, whereas scotch is normally distilled only twice. The benefits of triple distillation have been described to me time and again, but they never quite seem to make sense. If you can attain the desired proof by double distillation, which is fairly easy, why bother distilling again?

Izarra A proprietary brandy-based herbal liqueur from the Basque region of France. Like Chartreuse, Izarra is available in both yellow and green bottlings.

Jägermeister A proprietary herbal liqueur from Germany that tastes somewhat medicinal.

Kahlúa A proprietary coffee-flavored liqueur from Mexico.

Kirsch Sometimes called kirschwasser; an eau-de-vie made from a fermented mash of cherries.

Kümmel A predominantly caraway-flavored herbal liqueur, usually from Holland or Germany.

La Muse Verte A proprietary French absinthe substitute.

Lager A style of beer made with a bottom-fermenting yeast. Subcategories of lager include pilsners, Vienna lagers, and bocks.

Limoncello An Italian liqueur flavored with lemon zest. There's an excellent recipe for homemade Limoncello on page 281. The best proprietary bottlings I've tasted are Massa and Giori—many others are far too sweet.

Liqueur A sweetened and flavored low-alcohol beverage sometimes referred to as a cordial.

Madeira A fortified wine from the island of Madeira.

Malibu A proprietary rum-based, coconut-flavored liqueur.

Mandarine Napoléon A proprietary cognac-based, tangerine-flavored French liqueur.

Maraschino A European liqueur flavored with whole Dalmatian marasca cherries.

Marc A French eau-de-vie distilled from a fermented mash of grape pomace, the leftovers from the winemaking process.

Mash A "soup" that can be made up of fruits, fruit juices, grains, vegetables, sugars, or any other edible material and can be fermented by the addition of yeast to produce alcohol.

Metaxa Commonly thought of as a brandy, Metaxa is actually Greek brandy mixed with aged muscat wine, blended with a secret mix of botanicals, and aged in oak casks.

Mezcal A spirit distilled in Mexico from a fermented mash of agave, mezcal is to tequila what brandy is to cognac: All tequilas are forms of mezcal, but not all mezcals can be called tequila.

Midori A proprietary melon-flavored liqueur.

Neutral grain alcohol Distilled at high proof from a fermented mash of any grains, this is basically high-proof vodka that is never aged. Neutral grain alcohol can be used in gin production, and it's sometimes diluted to make vodka. It also has many other uses in the liquor business, especially when flavors need to be extracted from raw materials, such as for liqueurs.

Neutral grain whiskey A spirit distilled from grains that leaves the still containing few impurities and much alcohol, and therefore it doesn't develop much flavor, even if it is aged. Neutral grain whiskey is used in blended whiskeys, along with other, more flavorful spirits. The age statement on any bottle of blended whiskey refers to the number of years of aging of the neutral whiskey, or the other components, whichever is smaller.

Ouzo A Greek anise-flavored liqueur.

Peach brandy A peach-flavored liqueur.

Peach schnapps A peach-flavored liqueur, usually drier than peach brandy.

Peat reek The smoky odor found in scotch whisky, a result of the barley being dried over peat fires.

Peppermint schnapps A peppermint-flavored liqueur, usually drier than crème de menthe.

Pernod A proprietary French absinthe substitute.

Pisco brandy A Peruvian grape brandy also made in other South American countries. Aged for a few months in clay containers, pisco is more of an eau-de-vie than an aged brandy.

Port A fortified Portuguese wine produced in the Douro region of Portugal. Other countries also produce fortified wines that are labeled as ports; although this practice has been scoffed at in the past, there are now some good bottlings on the market, and the practice is gaining legitimacy.

Pot still Pot stills come in many styles; most people automatically think of the Scottish or Irish pot still, a beautiful, bulbous, onion-shaped copper vessel with a graceful tall swan's neck sprouting from it. The French, too, have very elegant pot stills, known as *alembiques;* these are somewhat more elaborate affairs, with a tank that holds wine waiting to be distilled that is warmed by the vapors from the wines *being* distilled, thus making use of the heat. Quite simply, though, pot stills are more labor-intensive than continuous stills. They require at least two distillations to attain a high enough proof in the spirit, but they tend to produce spirits with a character that's specific to the individual still.

Pot-stilled A term found on some liquor bottles, most notably Irish whiskey, that describes the method of distillation but not the grains used to make the product. Pot-stilled does not imply single malt.

Ricard A proprietary French absinthe substitute.
Rock and Rye A whiskey-based liqueur flavored with fruit juices and horehound.
Rum A spirit distilled from a fermented mash of molasses or sugarcane juice. Rum is almost impossible to define, since it emanates from so many countries, each of which has its own regulatory laws. Styles include dark, amber, añejo (aged), and white, or light, rum. Various bottlings are made in pot stills, though most come from continuous stills. There are some fabulous rums on the market, and these are well-suited to be sipping rums. Almost any rum can be successfully employed as a cocktail ingredient, as long as you remember, of course, that better-quality products will yield superior cocktails and mixed drinks.
Rye whiskey Although legally this product can be made anywhere, at the time of this writing the term refers to a whiskey produced in the United States from a fermented mash of grains including at least 51 percent rye. Straight rye whiskey made in America must be aged in new, charred oak barrels for at least two years, and if it is bottled at less than four years of age, its age must be noted on the label. Many people refer to Canadian blended whiskies as ryes; this practice began during and right after Prohibition, when American whiskey stocks were depleted and much of the bootleg trade came from our northern neighbors, who, at that time, used a great deal of rye in their whisky.
Sambuca An Italian anise-based liqueur. Available in white and black bottlings; black Sambuca has notes of lemon zest.
Scotch (blended) A whisky made in Scotland from a blend of single-malt scotches and neutral grain whisky and aged for a minimum of three years. More expensive bottlings usually contain a higher percentage of single malts than those sold at bargain prices.
Scotch (single malt) A whisky made in Scotland, distilled from a fermented mash of malted barley that, traditionally, is dried over peat fires. Single-malt scotches are aged for a minimum of three years and are always the product of a single distillery.

Single-malt scotches emanate from different areas of Scotland. They bear regional characteristics due, in part, to the climate where they are aged, and also to various other idiosyncrasies, such as the height of the still and the amount of time the barley spends over peat fires in the malting process. Traditionally, descriptions of single-malt Scotches from different areas divide Scotland into five regions—the following characteristics attributed to malts from those regions are gross generalizations:

Islay (EYE-luh): Single-malt scotches from this small island just off the western coast of Scotland are usually characterized by their peaty-seaweed-iodine-medicinal tones.

Lowland: This southern part of Scotland usually produces single-malt scotches that are lighter and somewhat "cleaner" than all others.

Campbeltown: This small town on Scotland's western coast is primarily known for single-malt scotches bearing a briny character, along with some peaty-iodine notes.

Highlands: The northern areas of Scotland tend to produce fresh, heathery, medium-bodied malts. But since this is where most single-malt scotches are made, bottlings can differ tremendously, and not all of them fit this description accurately.

Speyside The Speyside region is actually a subregion of the Highlands that is home to over fifty distilleries, each with its own style. Although Speyside produces light-, medium-, and heavy-bodied malts, all of these single-malt scotches can be loosely characterized as complex and mellow, with hints of peat.

SCOTCH (VATTED) Usually labeled "Pure Malt Scotch" in the United States, vatted malts contain a blend of single-malt scotches from different distilleries.

SHERRY A fortified wine from the region of Spain around the city of Jerez.

SINGLE-BARREL WHISKEY These whiskeys come from one specific barrel of whiskey that the blender or distiller has deemed good enough to bottle without the addition of whiskeys from any other barrels.

SINGLE-MALT AMERICAN WHISKEY A few single-malt American whiskeys are now on the market, and I have no doubt that at some point in the future we'll see some great bottlings. The distillers producing them—most notably Jorg Rupf at the St. George Distillery in California and Steve McCarthy at the Clear Creek distillery in Oregon—are very skilled at their craft, so watch out for new releases.

SLOE GIN A liqueur flavored with the fruit of the blackthorn and sometimes, though seldom, made with a gin base.

SMALL BATCH A term used by many spirits companies to describe superior bottlings of their products. Each company has its own definition of the term; although you might be tempted to think that the spirit was produced in small batches, this isn't always the case. Sometimes it refers to, say, whiskey taken from a small batch of casks, for instance. I don't know of a company that uses the term *small batch* on inferior products, but personally, I put greater stock in age statements.

SOUTHERN COMFORT A proprietary fruit-flavored liqueur.

SPARKLING WINE Wine, such as champagne or prosecco, that is carbonated by a secondary fermentation.

STRAWBERRY BRANDY A strawberry-flavored liqueur.

STREGA A proprietary Italian herbal liqueur. *Strega* translates from the Italian to "witch."

TENNESSEE WHISKEY A spirit distilled in Tennessee from a fermented mash of grains that is filtered through large vats of sugar-maple charcoal before being aged in new, charred oak barrels. The charcoal filtration adds a sooty sweetness to the whiskey not found in bourbons or straight ryes.

TEQUILA A spirit distilled in demarcated regions of Mexico from a fermented mash of cooked *Agave tequilana Weber,* otherwise known as blue agave. Most tequila falls under the category of *mixto* (MEES-toh); that word denotes that the spirit can be made with as little as 51 percent blue agave—the rest of the distillate is usually made from sugar in one form or another.

Tequilas made entirely from blue agaves is known as "100 percent blue agave," and those words appear on the label of such bottlings. These are the finest tequilas, and some are suitable as an after-dinner drink, being taken neat at room temperature. *Blanco* ("silver" or "white") tequilas are unaged and bear the vegetal, sharp, and peppery notes that I love in tequila. *Gold* tequilas must, by law, contain a small percentage of *reposado* tequila (see below), but the amount is not specified. *Reposado,* or "rested," tequilas are, by law, aged in oak barrels—usually used bourbon casks—for a minimum of two months. They can be more complex than *blanco* bottlings, and many, especially 100 percent agave bottlings, can be successfully used in mixed drinks. *Añejo,* or "aged," tequilas are, again by law, aged in oak for a minimum of one year. These are the sipping tequilas, especially the 100 percent agave bottlings, but although they can be delightful, like aged gin, most have lost their delightful vegetal bite. Among the exceptions to this rule are the Don Julio and Herradura tequilas, which retain their character even after being aged. *Muy añejo,* or "extra-aged," tequilas, are aged for longer than one year, and the amount of time they have spent in wood is usually noted on the label.

TIA MARIA A proprietary rum-based, coffee-flavored Jamaican liqueur.

TRIPLE SEC A generic orange-flavored liqueur. Many bottlings are fairly sweet and low in alcohol. The best bottlings on the market are Cointreau and Van Gogh O'Magnifique, both of which, at 80 proof, are dry, sophisticated, and perfect for cocktailian bartenders.

TUACA A proprietary herbal liqueur from Italy with predominant orange and vanilla notes.

USQUEBAUGH or **UISGA BEATHA** Both are Gaelic terms meaning "water of life"; they were later anglicized to "whiskey."

VERMOUTH An aromatized wine that's slightly fortified by the addition of a little brandy. Available in sweet (red), also known as Italian vermouth, and dry (white), also known as French vermouth.

VINTAGE-DATED SPIRITS Aged spirits that were distilled in the specific year noted as the vintage. These are different from other aged spirits, which bear an age statement but no vintage year since they might contain a percentage of spirits distilled earlier than the age statement indicates.

VODKA A spirit distilled from almost any vegetal matter, although most are grain based and there are quite a few potato vodkas available. The rest—some made from beets or molasses—are less expensive, and producers of these vodkas rarely boast about the base of their products. Although by American legal definition, vodka should have no distinctive flavor, if you taste different bottlings, side by side and at room temperature, it's easy to find nuances from one label to the next. In the vast majority of mixed drinks, however, it's virtually impossible to distinguish which brand is in the glass.

VODKA (FLAVORED) Many flavored vodkas are now available, and new ones are released regularly. These products can be wonderful bases on which new cocktails can be built.

WHISKEY, WHISKY A spirit distilled from a mash of fermented grains. The *e* is usually, but not always, included when the word refers to Irish or American whiskeys, whereas scotch and Canadian products leave the *e* out.

WOOD FINISHES Some whiskeys are aged in one barrel for, say, twelve years, then are transferred to another cask for "finishing," which usually takes between six and eighteen months. The time the whiskey spends in the secondary barrel is usually left to the distiller's discretion. He will sample the whiskey regularly until he thinks it is perfect. The finishing process usually takes place in barrels that previously held products such as sherry, madeira, or port, each of which adds its own nuance to the final product.

BIBLIOGRAPHY

The ABC of Cocktails. New York: Peter Pauper Press, 1953.

Ade, George. *The Old-Time Saloon.* New York: Old Town Books, 1993.

Amis, Kingsley. *Kingsley Amis on Drink.* New York: Harcourt Brace Jovanovich, 1973.

Angostura Bitters Complete Mixing Guide. New York: J. W. Wupperman, 1913.

An Anthology of Cocktails Together with Selected Observations by a Distinguished Gathering and Diverse Thoughts for Great Occasions. London: Booth's Distilleries, n.d.

Anthony, Norman, and O. Soglow. *The Drunk's Blue Book.* New York: Frederick A. Stokes Company, 1933.

Armstrong, John: *VIP's All New Bar Guide.* Greenwich, CT: Fawcett Publications, 1960.

Arthur, Stanley Clisby. *Famous New Orleans Drinks & how to mix 'em.* 1937. Reprint, Gretna: Pelican Publishing Company, 1989.

Asbury, Herbert. *The Barbary Coast: An Informal History of the San Francisco Underworld.* New York: Garden City Publishing Company, 1933.

———. *The French Quarter: An Informal History of the New Orleans Underworld.* New York: Garden City Publishing Company, 1938.

———. *The Gangs of New York.* New York: Thunder's Mouth Press, 2001.

———. *The Great Illusion: An Informal History of Prohibition.* New York: Doubleday & Co., 1950; New York: Greenwood Press, 1968.

Baker, Charles H., Jr. *The Gentleman's Companion: An Exotic Drinking Book.* New York: Crown Publishers, 1946.

———. *The South American Gentleman's Companion.* New York: Crown Publishers, 1951.

Barr, Andrew. *Drink.* London: Bantam Press, 1995.

———. *Drink: A Social History of America.* New York: Carroll & Graf Publishers, 1999.

Barrett, E. R. *The Truth About Intoxicating Drinks.* London: Ideal Publishing Company, Limited, 1899.

Batterberry, Michael, and Ariane Batterberry. *On the Town in New York.* New York: Routledge, 1999.

Bayley, Stephen. *Gin.* England: Balding & Mansell, 1994.

Beebe, Lucius. *The Stork Club Bar Book.* New York: Rinehart & Company, 1946.

Behr, Edward. *Prohibition: Thirteen Years That Changed America.* New York: Arcade Publishing, 1996.

Behrendt, Axel, and Bibiana Behrendt. *Cognac.* New York: Abbeville Press, 1997.

Bernard [pseud.]. *100 Cocktails: How to Mix Them.* London: W. Foulsham & Co., n.d.

Berry, Jeff, and Annene Kaye. *Beachbum Berry's Grog Log.* San Jose, CA: SLG Publishing, 1998.

Bishop, George. *The Booze Reader: A Soggy Saga of a Man in His Cups.* Los Angeles: Sherbourne Press, Inc., 1965.

Blochman, Lawrence. *Here's How.* New York: New American Library, 1957.

Brinnin, John Malcolm. *Dylan Thomas in America.* London: Harborough Publishing Company, 1957.

Brock, H. I., and J. W. Golinkin. *New York Is Like This.* New York: Dodd, Mead & Company, 1929.

Broom, Dave. *Spirits and Cocktails.* London: Carlton, 1998.

Brown, Charles. *The Gun Club Drink Book*. New York: Charles Scribner's Sons, 1939.

Brown, Gordon. *Classic Spirits of the World*. New York: Abbeville Press, 1996.

Brown, Henry Collins. *In the Golden Nineties*. Hastings-on-Hudson, NY: Valentines's Manual, 1928.

Brown, John Hull. *Early American Beverages*. New York: Bonanza Books, 1966.

Bryson, Bill. *Made in America*. London: Martin Secker & Warburg, 1994.

Bullock, Tom. *The Ideal Bartender*. St. Louis, MO: Buxton & Skinner, 1917.

Bullock, Tom, and D. J. Frienz. *173 Pre-Prohibition Cocktails*. Oklahoma: Howling at the Moon Press, 2001.

Burke, Harman Burney. *Burke's Complete Cocktail and Drinking Recipes*. New York: Books, 1936.

Carling, T. E. *The Complete Book of Drink*. London: Practical Press Limited, 1951.

Carson, Johnny. *Happiness Is a Dry Martini*. New York: Doubleday and Company, 1965.

Charles and Carlos [pseuds.]. *The Cocktail Bar*. London: W. Foulsham & Co., Ltd., 1977.

Charles of Delmonicos. *Punches and Cocktails*. New York: Arden Book Company, 1930.

Cipriani, Arrigo. *Harry's Bar: The Life and Times of the Legendary Venice Landmark*. New York: Arcade Publishing, 1996.

The Cocktail Book: A Sideboard Manual for Gentlemen. 1900. Reprint, Boston: Colonial Press, C. H. Simonds Company, 1926.

Conrad, Barnaby, III. *Absinthe: History in a Bottle*. San Francisco: Chronicle Books, 1988.

Cotton, Leo, comp. and ed. *Old Mr. Boston De Luxe Official Bartender's Guide*. Boston: Ben Burke, Inc., 1935.

———. *Old Mr. Boston De Luxe Official Bartender's Guide*. Boston: Berke Brothers Distilleries, 1949.

———. *Old Mr. Boston De Luxe Official Bartender's Guide*. Boston: Berke Brothers Distilleries, 1953.

———. *Old Mr. Boston De Luxe Official Bartender's Guide*. Boston: Mr. Boston Distiller, 1966.

———. *Old Mr. Boston De Luxe Official Bartender's Guide*. Boston: Mr. Boston Distiller Corporation, 1970.

Craddock, Harry. *The Savoy Cocktail Book*. New York: Richard R. Smith, 1930.

Craig, Charles H. *The Scotch Whisky Industry Record*. Scotland: Index Publishing, 1994.

Crewe, Quentin. *Quentin Crewe's International Pocket Food Book*. London: Mitchell Beazley International, 1980.

Crockett, Albert Stevens. *The Old Waldorf-Astoria Bar Book*. New York: A. S. Crockett, 1935.

Culver, John Breckenridge. *The Gentle Art of Drinking*. New York: Ready Reference Publishing Co., [1934].

Daiches, David. *Scotch Whisky: Its Past and Present*. London: Macmillan Company, 1969.

Davies, Frederick, and Seymour Davies. *Drinks of All Kinds*. London: John Hogg, n.d.

DeVoto, Bernard. *The Hour*. Cambridge, MA: Riverside Press, 1948.

Dickens, Cedric. *Drinking with Dickens*. Goring-on-Thames, Eng.: Elvendon Press, 1980.

Dickson, Paul. *Toasts*. New York: Crown Publishers, 1991.

Downard, William L. *Dictionary of the History of the American Brewing and Distilling Industries*. Westport, CT: Greenwood Press, 1980.

Doxat, John. *The Book of Drinking*. London, Eng.: Triune Books, 1973.

———. *Stirred—Not Shaken: The Dry Martini.* London: Hutchinson Benham, 1976.

Duffy, Patrick Gavin. *The Official Mixer's Manual.* New York: Alta Publications, Inc., 1934.

———. *The Official Mixer's Manual.* New York: Blue Ribbon Books, 1948.

———. *The Official Mixer's Manual.* Revised and enlarged by James A. Beard, New York: Garden City Books, 1956.

———. *The Standard Bartender's Guide.* New York: Permabooks, 1948.

———. *The Standard Bartender's Guide.* Revised and enlarged by James A. Beard, New York: Permabooks, 1958.

———. *The Standard Bartender's Guide.* Revised and enlarged by James A. Beard, New York: Permabooks, 1959.

Earle, Alice Morse. *Customs and Fashions in Old New England.* New York: Charles Scribner's Sons, 1913.

Edmunds, Lowell. *Martini, Straight Up: The Classic American Cocktail.* Baltimore: Johns Hopkins University Press, 1998.

Edwards, Bill. *How to Mix Drinks.* Philadelphia: David McKay Company, 1936.

Elliot, Virginia, and Phil D. Stong. *Shake 'Em Up: A Practical Handbook of Polite Drinking.* N.P.: Brewer and Warren, 1932.

Embury, David A. *The Fine Art of Mixing Drinks.* 2nd ed. New York: Garden City Books, 1952.

———. *The Fine Art of Mixing Drinks.* New revised ed. New York: Doubleday & Company, 1958.

Emmons, Bob. *The Book of Tequila: A Complete Guide.* Chicago: Open Court Publishing Company, 1997.

Engel, Leo. *American and Other Drinks.* London: Tinsley Brothers, [1883].

Erdoes, Richard. *Saloons of the Old West.* New York: Gramercy Books, 1997.

Erenberg, Lewis A. *Steppin' Out: New York Nightlife and the Transformation of American Culture, 1890–1930.* Chicago: University of Chicago Press, 1981.

Faith, Nicholas, and Ian Wisniewski. *Classic Vodka.* London: Prion Books, 1997.

Feery, William C. *Wet Drinks for Dry People.* Chicago: Bazner Press, 1932.

Fields, W. C. *W. C. Fields by Himself: His Intended Biography.* Commentary by Ronald J. Fields. New Jersey: Prentice-Hall, 1973.

Gaige, Crosby. *Crosby Gaige's Cocktail Guide and Ladies' Companion.* New York: M. Barrows & Company, 1945.

———. *The Standard Cocktail Guide.* New York: M. Barrows & Company, 1944.

Gale, Hyman, and Gerald F. Marco. *The How and When.* Chicago: Marco's, 1940.

Gordon, Harry Jerrold. *Gordon's Cocktail and Food Recipes.* Boston: C. H. Simonds Company, 1934.

Gorman, Marion, and Felipe de Alba. *The Tequila Book.* Chicago: Contemporary Books, 1978.

Gregory, Conal R. *The Cognac Companion: A Connoisseur's Guide.* Philadelphia: Running Press, 1997.

Grimes, William. *Straight Up or On the Rocks: A Cultural History of American Drink.* New York: Simon & Schuster, 1993.

———. *Straight Up or On the Rocks: The Story of the American Cocktail.* New York: North Point Press, 2001.

Grossman, Harold J. *Grossman's Guide to Wines, Beers, and Spirits.* 6th ed. Revised by Harriet Lembeck. New York: Charle's Scribner's Sons, 1977.

Haimo, Oscar. *Cocktail and Wine Digest.* New York: International Cocktail, Wine, and Spirits Digest, 1955.

Hamilton, Edward. *The Complete Guide to Rum.* Chicago: Triumph Books, 1997.

Harrington, Paul, and Laura Moorhead. *Cocktail: The Drinks Bible for the Twenty-first Century.* New York: Viking, 1998.

Harwell, Richard Barksdale. *The Mint Julep.* Charlottesville, VA: University Press of Virginia, 1985.

Haskin, Frederic J. *Recipes for Mixed Drinks, Wines: How to Serve Them.* Hartford, CT: N.P., 1934; circulated by the *Hartford Courant.*

Hastings, Derek. *Spirits and Liqueurs of the World.* Consulting editor: Constance Gordon Wiener. London, Eng.: Footnote Productions, 1984.

Hewett, Edward, and Axton, W. F. *Convivial Dickens: The Drinks of Dickens and His Times.* Athens: Ohio University Press, 1983.

Holden, Jan. *Hell's Best Friend: The True Story of the Old-Time Saloon.* Stillwater, OK: New Forums Press, 1998.

Holmes, Jack D. L. *New Orleans Drinks and How to Mix Them.* New Orleans: Hope Publications, 1973.

Hunt, Ridgely, and George S. Chappell, comp. *The Saloon in the Home, or A Garland of Rumblossoms.* New York: Coward-McCann, 1930.

Hutson, Lucinda. *Tequila! Cooking with the Spirit of Mexico.* Berkeley: Ten Speed Press, 1995.

Jackson, Michael. *Michael Jackson's Complete Guide to Single Malt Scotch.* Philadelphia: Running Press, 1999.

Jeffs, Julian. *Sherry.* London: Faber and Faber, 1992.

Johnson, Byron A., and Sharon Peregrine Johnson. *The Wild West Bartenders' Bible.* Austin, TX: Texas Monthly Press, 1986.

Johnson, Harry. *New and Improved Illustrated Bartender's Manual.* New York: Harry Johnson, 1900.

Jones, Andrew. *The Apéritif Companion.* London: Quintet Publishing, 1998.

Jones, Stanley M. *Jones' Complete Barguide.* Los Angeles: Barguide Enterprises, 1977.

Judge Jr. *Here's How.* New York: Leslie-Judge Company, 1927.

———. *Here's How Again!* New York: John Day Company, 1929.

Kappeler, George J. *Modern American Drinks: How to Mix and Serve All Kinds of Cups and Drinks.* New York: Merriam Company, 1895.

Kinross, Lord. *The Kindred Spirit: A History of Gin and the House of Booth.* London: Newman Neame, 1959.

Lawlor, C. F. *The Mixicologist, or How to Mix All Kinds of Fancy Drinks.* Cleveland: Burrow Brothers, 1897.

Lass, William, ed. *I. W. Harper Hospitality Tour of the United States.* New York: Popular Library, 1970.

Lewis, V. B. *The Complete Buffet Guide, or How to Mix Drinks of All Kinds.* Chicago: M. A. Donahue & Company, 1903.

London, Robert, and Anne London. *Cocktails and Snacks.* Cleveland: World Publishing Company, 1953.

Lord, Tony. *The World Guide to Spirits, Aperitifs and Cocktails.* New York: Sovereign Books, 1979.

Lowe, Paul E. *Drinks: How to Mix and How to Serve.* Toronto: Gordon & Gotch, 1927.

Mahoney, Charles S. *Hoffman House Bartender's Guide: How to Open a Saloon and Make It Pay.* New York: Richard K. Fox Publishing Company, 1912.

Mamma's Recipes for Keeping Papa Home. Texas: Martin Casey & Co., 1901.

Mario, Thomas. *Playboy's Bar Guide.* Chicago: Playboy Press, 1971.

———. *Playboy's Host and Bar Book.* Chicago: Playboy Press, 1971.

Marquis, Don. *The Old Soak's History of the World.* New York: Doubleday, Page & Company, 1925.

Marrison, L. W. *Wines and Spirits.* Baltimore: Penguin Books, 1957.

Martin, Paul. *World Encyclopedia of Cocktails.* London: Constable and Company, 1997.

Mason, Dexter. *The Art of Drinking.* New York: Farrar & Rinehart, 1930.

McNulty, Henry. *The Vogue Cocktail Book.* New York: Harmony Books, 1982.

Mencken, H. L. *Heathen Days.* New York: Alfred A. Knopf, 1943.

———. *Newspaper Days.* New York: Alfred A. Knopf, 1963.

———. *The Young Mencken: The Best of His Work.* Collected by Carl Bode. New York: Dial Press, 1973.

Mendelsohn, Oscar A. *The Dictionary of Drink and Drinking.* New York: Hawthorne Books, 1965.

———. *Drinking with Pepys.* London: Macmillan & Co., 1963.

Mew, James, and John Ashton. *Drinks of the World.* London: Leadenhall Press, 1892.

Miller, Anistasia, Jared Brown, and Don Gatterdam. *Champagne Cocktails.* New York: Regan Books, 1999.

Mitchell, Joseph. *McSorley's Wonderful Saloon.* New York: Grosset & Dunlap, 1943.

———. *My Ears Are Bent.* New York: Pantheon Books, 2001.

Montague, Harry. *New Bartender's Guide.* Baltimore: I. & M. Ottenheimer, 1914.

Mr. Boston Official Bartender's Guide: Fiftieth Anniversary Edition. New York: Warner Books, 1984.

Muckensturm, Louis. *Louis' Mixed Drinks with Hints for the Care and Service of Wines.* New York: Dodge Publishing Company, 1906.

Murray, Jim. *Classic Bourbon, Tennessee, and Rye Whiskey.* London: Prion Books, 1998.

———. *Classic Irish Whiskey.* London: Prion Books, 1997.

———. *The Complete Guide to Whiskey.* Chicago: Triumph Books, 1997.

North, Sterling, and Carl Kroch. *So Red the Nose, or Breath in the Afternoon.* New York: Farrar & Rinehart, 1935.

Pace, Marcel. *Selected Drinks.* Paris: Hotel Industry Mutualist Association, 1970.

Phillips, Louis. *Ask Me Anything About the Presidents.* New York: Avon Books, 1992.

Plotkin, Robert. *The Original Guide to American Cocktails and Mixed Drinks.* Tucson: BarMedia, 2001.

Pokhlebkin, William. *A History of Vodka.* Translated by Renfrey Clarke. London: Verso, 1992.

Powers, Madelon. *Faces Along the Bar: Lore and Order in the Workingman's Saloon, 1870–1920.* Chicago: University of Chicago Press, 1998.

Proskauer, Julien J. *What'll You Have.* New York: A. L. Burt Company, 1933.

Rae, Simon, ed. *The Farber Book of Drink, Drinkers and Drinking.* London: Farber and Farber, 1991.

Ray, Cyril. *Cognac.* London: Peter Davis, 1973.

Ray, Cyril, ed. *The Compleat Imbiber.* New York: Rinehart & Company, 1957.

———. *The Compleat Imbiber Six: An Entertainment.* New York: Paul S. Eriksson, 1963.

———. *The Compleat Imbiber Twelve.* London: Hutchinson and Company, 1971.

———. *The Gourmet's Companion.* London: Eyre & Spottiswood, 1963.

Red Jay Bartender's Guide. Philadelphia: Dr. D. Jayne and Son, 1934.

The Reminder. Worcester, MA: N.P., 1899; compliments of M. J. Finnegan High Grade Beverages.

Reynolds, Cuyler. *The Banquet Book.* New York: Knickerbocker Press, 1902.

Sante, Luc. *Low Life: Lures and Snares of Old New York.* New York: Farrar, Straus and Giroux, 1991.
Sardi, Vincent, with George Shea. *Sardi's Bar Guide.* New York: Ballantine Books, 1988.
Saucier, Ted. *Ted Saucier's Bottoms Up.* New York: Greystone Press, 1951.
The Savoy Cocktail Book. London: Pavilion Book Limited, 1999.
Sax, Richard. *Classic Home Desserts.* Vermont: Chapters Publishing, 1994.
Schmidt, William (the Only William). *The Flowing Bowl: When and What to Drink.* New York: Charles L. Webster & Co., 1892.
Schoenstein, Ralph, ed. *The Booze Book.* Chicago: Playboy Press, 1974.
Shane, Ted. *Authentic and Hilarious Bar Guide.* New York: Fawcett Publications, 1950.
Shay, Frank. *Drawn from the Wood: Consolations in Words and Music for Pious Friends and Drunken Companions.* New York: Macaulay Company, 1929.
Sonnichsen, C. L. *Billy King's Tombstone.* Caldwell, ID: Caxton Printers, 1942.
Southworth, May E., comp. *One Hundred and One Beverages.* San Francisco: Paul Elder and Company, 1906.
Spence, Godfrey. *The Port Companion: A Connoisseur's Guide.* New York: Macmillan, 1997.
Spenser, Edward. *The Flowing Bowl.* New York: Duffield and Company, [1925].
Steedman, M. E., and Cherman Senn, M.B.E. *Summer and Winter Drinks.* London: Ward, Lock & Co., 1924.
Stephen, John, M.D. *A Treatise on the Manufacture, Imitation, Adulteration, and Reduction of Foreign Wines, Brandies, Gins, Rums, Etc.* Philadelphia: Published for the Author, 1860.
Straub, Jacques. *Drinks.* Chicago: Marie L. Straub–Hotel Monthly Press, 1914.
Sullivan, Jere. *The Drinks of Yesteryear: A Mixology.* N.P.: N.P., 1930.
Tarling, W. J., comp. *Café Royal Cocktail Book.* London: Publications from Pall Mall, 1937.
Terrington, William. *Cooling Cups and Dainty Drinks.* London: Routledge and Sons, 1869.
Thomas, Jerry. *The Bar-Tender's Guide, or How to Mix All Kinds of Plain and Fancy Drinks.* New York: Fitzgerald Publishing Corporation, 1887.
———. *How to Mix Drinks, or The Bon Vivant's Companion.* New York: Dick & Fitzgerald, 1862.
———. *How to Mix Drinks, or The Bon Vivant's Companion.* New York: Grosset & Dunlap, 1928.
Tirado, Eddie. *Cocktails and Mixed Drinks Handbook.* Australia: Tradewinds Group, 1976.
Townsend, Jack, and Tom Moore McBride. *The Bartender's Book.* New York: Viking Press, 1951.
Trader Vic [Victor Bergeron]. *Bartender's Guide.* New York: Garden City Books, 1948.
United Kingdom Bartender's Guild, comp. *The U.K.B.G. Guide to Drinks.* London: United Kingdom Bartender's Guild, 1955.
Van Every, Edward. *Sins of New York, as "Exposed" by the Police Gazette.* New York: Frederick A. Stokes Company, 1930.
Vermeire, Robert. *Cocktails: How to Mix Them.* London: Herbert Jenkins, [1930s?].
Wainwright, David. *Stone's Original Green Ginger Wine: Fortunes of a Family Firm, 1740–1990.* London: Quiller Press, 1990.
Walker, Stanley. *The Night Club Era.* New York: Frederick A. Stokes Company, 1933.
Whitfield, W. C., comp. and ed. *Just Cocktails.* N.P.: Three Mountaineers, 1939.
Williams, H. I. *Three Bottle Bar.* New York: M. S. Mill Co., 1945.

Wilson, Ross. *Scotch: The Formative Years.* London: Constable & Company, 1970.

MAGAZINES

National Review, December 31, 1996.
Playboy, August 1973.

PAPERS

Liebmann, A. J. "The History of Distillation." New York: Reprinted from *Journal of Chemical Education,* vol. 33 (April 1956): p. 166.

Underwood, A. J. V., D.Sc., F.I.C. (Member). "The Historical Development of Distilling Plant." London: Reprinted from the *Transactions of the Institute of Chemical Engineers,* vol. 13 (1935): pp. 34–61.

WEB SITES

Architectural Record: www.archrecord.com.
The Atlantic: www.theatlantic.com.
Babe Ruth: www.baberuth.com.
Cocktail database: cocktaildb.com.
Cocktail Times: www.cocktailtimes.com.
Cyber Boxing Zone: cyberboxingzone.com.
DrinkBoy: drinkboy.com.
DrinkBoy MSN community: groups.msn.com/drinkboy.
Paul Sann, Journalism, Letters, Writings: www.paulsann.org.
State University of New York at Potsdam: www2.potsdam.edu.
Texas State Historical Association: www.tsha.utexas.edu.
Twain quotes: www.twainquotes.com.
Webtender: www.webtender.com.

INDEX

Note: Page numbers in **boldface** refer to recipes.

Abbey Cocktail, **202**
Abou-Ganim, Tony, xii, 47
absinthe, substitutes for, 37, 198
Alabama Slammer, **202**
Alaska, **202**
alcohol. *See* liquor
Alexander, **203**
Alfonso, **203**
Algonquin Cocktail, **204**
Allies Cocktail, **204**
Amaretto Alexander, **204–5**
Amaretto Sour, **205**
Americano, **205**
Angel's Tit, **206**
Angostura bitters, 105–6
Apple a Day, An, **206**
Apple Martini, **206–7**
Apple Sidecar, **207**
Apricot Fizz, **207**
Apricot Sour, **207**
Arawak Cocktail, **208**
Artillery Punch, **208**
Astor Martini, **209**
Aviation Cocktail, **209**
AWOL, 91, **209**

Bacardi Cocktail, 26, 30, **210**
Bahama Mama, **210**
Baileys Chocolate Martini, **210**
Banana Daiquiri Jelly Shot, **211**
Banana-Split Martini, 80, **211**
barspoons, 88, 124
bartenders. *See also* mixology
  arranging liquor bottles, 65
  being early for work, 61–62
  characteristics of, 52–53
  cocktailian, defined, xii
  famous 19th century, 9, 14–19
  handling angry customers, 66
  handling bad tippers, 63–64
  handling difficult customers, 62–63
  handling inebriated customers, 62
  handling money, 66–68
  handling problems in bathroom, 66
  handling unwanted invitations, 64
  learning most-requested drinks, 75
  seating people, 66
  skills and responsibilities, 16, 17, 52–61, 74–75
  tasks for slow periods, 64–65
  winning new customers, 65–66
Bay Breeze, **211**
Beachcomber Cocktail, **212**
beef bouillon, 109
Beer- and cider-based mixed drinks, 135–36
  in ancient times, 1
  Black and Tan, **215**
  Black Velvet, **218**
  Black Velveteen, **218**
  Boilermaker, **226**
  Dog's Nose, **249**
  Lager and Lime, 111, **277**
  Pernod and Cider, **313**
  Shandy, 23, **335**
beer mug, 132
beer service glassware, 132
Bellini, **212–13**
Bennett Cocktail, **213**
Bergeron, "Trader" Vic, 41, 164
Bermuda Rose Cocktail, **213**
Betsy Ross, **214**
Between the Sheets, **214**
B-52, **214**
Big Pine Key Cocktail, **214–15**
Bistro Sidecar, **215**
bitter lemon soda, 116
bitters, 5, 43, 70, 104–8, 152
bitters bottles, 129
Black and Tan, **215**
Black-and-White Cocktail, **216**
Black-Eyed Susan, **216**
Black Feather Cocktail, **217**
Black Russian, **217**
Blackthorne, **217**
Black Velvet, **218**
Black Velveteen, **218**
blenders, electric, 97–98, 125
Blood-and-Sand Cocktail, **218–19**
Blood Orange, 70, **219**
Bloody Bull, **219**
Bloody Caesar, 109, **220**
Bloody Mary, **220–21**
  garnishes for, 120
  history of, 30, 42, 43
  ingredients for, 109
  mixing ingredients in, 89
  premade mixers for, 44
Bloody Mary Martini, 109, **222**
Blow My Skull Off, **222**
Blue Blazer, 15, **223–24**
Blue-Eyed Blonde, **224**

Blue Train Cocktail, **224**
B9 Martini, **224**
Bobbo's Bride Straight Up, **225**
Bobby Burns, **225**
Bocce Ball, **225**
Boilermaker, **226**
Bolero Cocktail, **227**
Bolo's Pomegranate Sangria, **227**
Bolo's White Peach Sangria, **228**
Boston Cream Martini, **228**
Boston shakers, 84, 86–89, 124
Bottled Cocktails, 136–37
  Cosmopolitan, **243**
  Jack Rose Royale, **273**
  Manhattan, **289**
  Margarita, **292**
  Martini Circa 1900, **296**
  Sidecar Deluxe, **336**
bottle openers, 126
bottles, number of shots in, 356
bottles, sizes of, 354
Bourbon and Branch, **228**
Bourbon and Coke, **229**
Bourbon Peach Cobbler, **229**
Brandy Alexander, 30, **229**
Brandy and Soda, 23, **229**
brandy-based French-Italian drinks. *See* French-Italian drinks
Brandy Cobbler, **230**
Brandy Crusta, history of, 15, 161
brandy snifter, 132
Brave Bull, **230**
British beer mug, 132
British Squirrel, **230**
Bronx Cocktail, **230–31**
building drinks, 85–86, 201
Bukofzer, Norman, xii, 47, 59–60
Bullshot, 109, **231**
Burnet, **232**
Burnished Gold, **232**
butter, 113

Cacharita, **232–33**
Café Brûlot, **233**
Caipirinha, 90, 110–11, **234**
Caipiroska, **234**
Calvados Cocktail, **234–35**
Campari bitters, 70, 108, 152
Canteen Martini, **235**
Cape Codder, **235**
carafes, 127
Carbonated Piston Slinger, **235**
Caribbean Cosmopolitan, **236**
Caribbean Squirrel, **236**
Caricature Cocktail, **236**
celery, 120
CEO Cocktail, **237**
Champagne Cocktails, 138–39
  Alfonso, **203**
  Bellini, **212–13**
  B9 Martini, **224**
  Champagne Cocktail, 15, **237–38**
  Esquivel Cocktail, **252–53**
  Eve's Seduction Apple Martini, **253**
  Fallen Angel Cocktail, **253**
  French 75, **258**
  Kir Royale, **277**
  Mimosa, **300–301**
  Moon Walk, **306**
  Nelson's Blood, **309**
  Old Cuban Cocktail, **310**
  Pierce Brosnan, **314–15**
  Punt e Mes Fizz, **320**
  Ritz of New York, **323**
  Seelbach Cocktail, **324**
  Tbilisi Royale, **341**
  Tiepolo, **343**
  Tsar's Champagne Cocktail, **345**
  Tulio Oro, **345**
champagne flute, 132
champagne keepers, 126
champagne saucer, 132
champagne tulip, 132
Chanticleer Cocktail, **238**
Charlie Chaplin Cocktail, **238–39**
Chatham Cocktail, **239**
Chaya Candy Apple Cosmo, **239**
cherries, maraschino, 120
Cherry Blossom Cocktail, **239**
chocolate garnishes, 121
Chocolate Martini, 79, 121, **240**
church key, 126
cider-based mixed drinks. *See* Beer- and cider-based mixed drinks
citrus reamers, 127
clam juice, 109
Claridge Cocktail, **240**
Classic Cocktail, **240**
Clover Club Cocktail, **240–41**
coasters, 83–84, 130
Cobblers, 139–40
  Bourbon Peach Cobbler, **229**
  Brandy Cobbler, **230**
  Crème de Menthe Frappé, **244**
  French Connection Cobbler, **257**
  Jamaican Cobbler, **274**
cocktail glass, 133
cocktailian bartender, defined, xii
cocktail napkins, 83–84, 130
cocktail picks, 130
cocktails
  definition of, 4
  during Prohibition, 28–36
  during the 1600s, 2

during the 1700s, 2–4
during the 1800s, 6–24
during the 1900s, 24–47
etymology of, 4–6
glassware for, 133
"Golden Age of," 7
"Punk," 45–47
serving, 129–30
cocktail shakers, 84, 86, 125
coconut cream, 112
Coffee, Irish, 111, **269–70**
Coffees, International, **270–71**
Cognac Coulis, **241**
Collins glass, 133
Copper Swan Cocktail, **242**
cordial glass, 132
corkscrews, 126
Corpse Reviver No. 1, **242**
Corpse Reviver No. 2, **242–43**
Corriher, Shirley, 98–99
Cosmopolitan, **243**
Cosmopolitan (Bottled), **243**
Craddock, Harry, 30, 37
cranberry juice, 114
cream, 81, 113
Crème de Menthe Frappé, **244**
Crux Cocktail, **244**
Cuba Libra, **244**
cutting boards, 125

Daiquiri, 44, **245**
dairy products, 112–13
Dark and Stormy, **245**
Deadly Sin, **245**
Deauville Cocktail, **246**
Debonair, **246**
DeGroff, Dale, xii, 46, 58, 89, 140
Delicious Cocktail, **246–47**
Delmarva Cocktail, **247**
Delmarva Cocktail No. 2, **247**
Delmarva Cocktail No. 3, **248**
Dirty Martini, **248**
Disaronno Margarita, **248**
Dog's Nose, **249**
Dreamy Dorini Smoking Martini, **249**
drinks. *See* cocktails; mixed drinks
Drunk's Code, 37–38
Dubliner, **250**
Dubonnet Cocktail, **250**
Duffy, Patrick Gavin, 26, 37, 146
Duos and Trios, 141–42
Alaska, **202**
Alexander, **203**
Amaretto Alexander, **204–5**
Apple Martini, **206–7**
Black Russian, **217**
Brandy Alexander, 30, **229**
Brave Bull, **230**
Burnet, **232**
Burnished Gold, **232**
Chocolate Martini, 79, 121, **240**
comparative charts for, 166–69
Copper Swan Cocktail, **242**
Debonair, **246**
Dubonnet Cocktail, **250**
French Connection, **257**
Goddaughter, **262**
Godfather, **262**
Godmother, **263**
Godson, **263**
Golden Cadillac, **263**
Grasshopper, **264**
Irish Peach Cream, **272**
Mudslide, **308**
Pacific Rim Martini, **312**
Pink Squirrel, **316–17**
Planter's Cocktail, **317**
Raspberry Martini, **322**
Rusty Nail, **328**
Starry Night Cocktail, **340**
Stinger, 24, 87, **340**
Toasted Almond, **344**
Tremblement de Terre (Earthquake), **344–45**
White Russian, **351**
White Spider, **351**
Dutch Squirrel, **250**

eggs, 81, 112–13
elderflower syrup, 112
electric blender, 97–98, 125
electric juicers, 127
Elegant without Number, **251**
El Floridita No. 1, **251**
El Floridita No. 2, **251**
El Presidente, **252**
Embury, David, 43, 140
English Rose Cocktail, **252**
Esquivel Cocktail, **252–53**
Eve's Seduction Apple Martini, **253**

Fallen Angel Cocktail, **253**
Fernandito Cocktail, **254**
Fifth Avenue, **254**
Fish House Cocktail, **254**
Fish House Punch, 3, **255**
Flame of Love, **255**
flaming drinks, 97
Flirtini Martini, **256**
floating ingredients, 201
Florida Highballs, 147–48
Alabama Slammer, **202**
Black-Eyed Susan, **216**
Bocce Ball, **225**

Florida Highballs (*cont.*)
  comparative charts for, 178–79, 181
  Freddie Fudpucker, **256–57**
  Fuzzy Navel, **260**
  Greyhound, **265**
  Harvey Wallbanger, **265**
  Salty Chihuahua, **329**
  Salty Dog, **329**
  Screwdriver, **333**
  Sloe Comfortable Screw, **338**
  Tequila Sunrise, **342**
fluid measurement conversions, 355–56
Fog Cutter, **256**
food coloring, 115
Footloose Cocktail, **256**
fortified wine glassware, 132
Freddie Fudpucker, **256–57**
French Connection, **257**
French Connection Cobbler, **257**
French-Italian drinks, 142–44
  gin- or vodka-based
    Abbey Cocktail, **202**
    Allies Cocktail, **204**
    Bermuda Rose Cocktail, **213**
    Bronx Cocktail, **230–31**
    Caricature Cocktail, **237**
    Chanticleer Cocktail, **238**
    Claridge Cocktail, **240**
    comparative charts for, 170–72
    Dirty Martini, **248**
    Gibson, **260**
    Goldfish Cocktail, 35, **264**
    Income Tax Cocktail, **269**
    Martinez, **293**
    Martini, 22, 27, 39, 43, 44, 70–71, 87, 120–21, **293–96**
    Maurice Cocktail, **298**
    Pompier Cocktail, **318**
    Riveredge Cocktail, **324–25**
    Third Degree, or Martini with a Spot, **342–43**
    Vesper Martini, **347**
  whiskey- or brandy-based
    Algonquin Cocktail, **204**
    Arawak Cocktail, **208**
    Black Feather Cocktail, **217**
    Blackthorne, **217**
    Blood-and-Sand Cocktail, **218–19**
    Bobby Burns, **225**
    CEO Cocktail, **237**
    comparative charts for, 173–75
    Corpse Reviver No. 1, **242**
    Deadly Sin, **245**
    Dubliner, **250**
    Manhattan, 27, 28, 39, 44, 87, **285–87**
    Manhattan (Dry), **288**
    Manhattan (Kentucky's Best), **289**
    Manhattan (Perfect), **288**
    Millennium Manhattan, **299**
    Paddy Cocktail, **312**
    Phoebe Snow Cocktail, **314**
    Preakness Cocktail, **319**
    Remember the Maine, **323**
    Rob Roy, 43, **325–26**
    Rob Roy (Dry), **326**
    Rob Roy (Perfect), **326**
French-Kiss Shooter, **257**
French 75, **258**
French Squirrel, **258**
Frozen drinks, 144–45
  Cognac Coulis, **241**
  Frozen Banana Colada, **258**
  Frozen Banana Daiquiri, **259**
  Frozen Chi-Chi, **259**
  Frozen Daiquiri, **259**
  Frozen Margarita, **259**
  Frozen Piña Colada, **260**
  Hemingway Daiquiri, **266**
  preparing, 97–98
  Rum Runner, **327**
fruit
  for frozen drinks, 98
  for garnishes, 118–19, 122
  syrups, 112
fruit juices
  bottles for, 128
  extractors and service, 127–28
  testing freshness of, 81
  types of, 113–14
  yields of, 354
Fuzzy Navel, **260**

garnishes
  adding, tips for, 80
  early 20th century, 27
  preparing, tools for, 125–26
  types of, 117–22
  used as ingredients, 77–78
gelatin, 115
Gibson, **260**
Gimlet, 111, **261**
gin, Booth's, 40
gin, "bruising," 84
gin, Gordon's, 44
Gin and Tonic, 24, **261**
gin-based French-Italian drinks. *See* French-Italian drinks
Gin Buck, **261**
ginger ale, 116
ginger beer, 116
Gin Rickey, **262**
glassware
  chilling, 84–85
  coating rim of, 79–80, 115

sizes, for recipes, 199
substituting, for recipes, 200
types of, 131–33
Glenkinchie Clincher, **262**
Goddaughter, **262**
Godfather, **263**
Godmother, **263**
Godson, **263**
Golden Cadillac, **263**
Goldfish Cocktail, 35, **264**
Gotham Cocktail, **264**
grapefruit juice, 114
Grasshopper, **264**
grater, 126
grenadine, 111
Greyhound, **265**
Grog, origins of, 3

Haigh, Ted, 46, 135, 160
Harvey Wallbanger, **265**
Hawaiian Cocktail, **265**
Hawthorne strainers, 86, 124
Haymaker Special, **266**
"Hell on Wheels" bars, 9
Hemingway Daiquiri, **266**
herbs, fresh, 120
Highballs, 146–48. *See also* Florida Highballs; New England Highballs
Bourbon and Branch, **228**
Bourbon and Coke, **229**
Brandy and Soda, 23, **229**
comparative charts for, 176–78
Cuba Libra, **244**
Dark and Stormy, **245**
Gin and Tonic, 24, **261**
Gin Buck, **261**
history of, 23
Jack and Coke, **272**
Mamie Taylor, **284–85**
Moscow Mule, 42, 43, **307**
Pimm's Cup, **315**
preparing, 85
Presbyterian, **319**
Rye and Ginger, **328**
Scotch and Soda, **333**
Scotch and Water, **333**
serving glass for, 133
Seven and Seven, **334**
Vodka and Tonic, **347**
Hop Toad Cocktail, **266**
horseradish, 109
hot drinks, 148–49
Café Brûlot, **233**
Hot Buttered Rum, 113, **267**
Hot Toddy, 122, **267–68**
International Coffees, **270–71**
Irish Coffee, 111, **269–70**
hot sauces, 109
Hurricane, **268–69**
Hurricane glass, 133

ice buckets, 128
ice crushers, 128
ice scoop and tongs, 128
ice storage, preparation, and service, 128
Income Tax Cocktail, **269**
Infusions, 149–50
Lark Creek Inn Tequila Infusion, **278**
Limecello, **280**
Limoncello, 101, **281**
preparing, 98–102
Raspberry Vodka, **322**
ingredients. *See also specific ingredients*
for coating glass rims, 115
high-quality liquors, 74
pouring method, 81–83
pouring order for, 80–81
testing for freshness, 81
International Coffees, **270–71**
International Sours, 159–60
Apple a Day, An, **206**
Aviation Cocktail, **209**
Bistro Sidecar, **215**
Canteen Martini, **235**
Charlie Chaplin Cocktail, **238–39**
Chatham Cocktail, **239**
Chaya Candy Apple Cosmo, **239**
comparative charts for, 185–88
Delmarva Cocktail, **247**
Delmarva Cocktail No. 2, **247**
Delmarva Cocktail No. 3, **248**
Disaronno Margarita, **248**
El Floridita No. 1, **251**
El Floridita No. 2, **251**
English Rose Cocktail, **252**
Fernandito Cocktail, **254**
Gotham Cocktail, **264**
Hop Toad Cocktail, **266**
Jockey Club Cocktail No. 2, **275**
Kretchma Cocktail, **277**
Leap-Year Cocktail, **278–79**
Millionaire Cocktail No. 4, **300**
Millionaire's Margarita, **300**
Modernista, **304–5**
Paradise Cocktail, **313**
Quick Little Pick-Me-Up, **320**
RBS Special Cocktail, **322**
Stiletto Cocktail, **340**
Twentieth-Century Cocktail, **346**
Irish Coffee, 111, **269–70**
Irish Coffee glass, 133
Irish Peach Cream, **272**
Irish Squirrel, **272**
Jack and Coke, **272**

Jack Rose, **272–73**
Jack Rose Royale (Bottled), **273**
Jamaican Cobbler, **274**
Jamaican Ten-Speed, **274**
James Joyce Cocktail, **274**
Jelly Shots, 150–51
  Banana Daiquiri Jelly Shot, **211**
  history of, 15–16
  ingredients in, 115
  Margarita Jelly Shot, **292**
  Whiskey Sour Jelly Shot, **350–51**
jiggers, 17, 81, 82, 128
Jockey Club Cocktail No. 2, **275**
John Collins, 23, **275**
Johnson, Harry, xi, 16–17, 27, 47, 158
juice, clam, 109
juice, fruit. *See* fruit juices
juice, tomato, 81, 109
Juleps, 152
  Massa Mojito, **297**
  Mint Julep, 2, 120, **301–3**
  Mint Julep No. 2, **304**
  Mojito, 120, **305**
  Southside Cocktail, **339**
  Southside Fizz, **339**
julep strainer, 124

Kamikaze, **275**
Kentucky Longshot, **276**
Kentucky Squirrel, **276**
Kir, **276–77**
Kir Royale, **277**
knives, paring, 125
Kretchma Cocktail, **277**

Lager and Lime, 111, **277**
Lark Creek Inn Tequila Infusion, **278**
layering drinks, 91–92, 201
Leap-Year Cocktail, **278–79**
Lemon Drop, 104–5, **279**
lemon juice, 113–14
lemon twists, 77–78, 118
lemon wedges, 77–78, 117–18
lever-pull juice extractors, 127
Lewis & Martin Cocktail, **279**
Libation Goddess, **280**
Limecello, **280**
lime cordial, 111–12
lime juice, 113–14
lime twists, 77–78, 118
lime wedges, 77–78, 117–18
Limoncello, 101, **281**
liquor
  alcohol by volume, 356–57
  brand-name products, 197–98
  densities of, 92–96
  high-proof, diluting, 99, 101
  infusing, 98–102
  for medicinal purposes, 3
  serving glasses for, 132
Lola Martini, 112, **281**
Long Island Iced Tea, **282**

Madras, **282**
Maiden's Blush Cocktail, **282–83**
Maiden's Prayer Cocktail, **283**
Mai Tai No. 2, **284**
Mai Tai (Original), 41, **283–84**
Mamie Taylor, **284–85**
Mandrintini, **285**
Manhattan, **285–87**
  Bottled, **289**
  Dry, **288**
  early recipes for, 39
  Kentucky's Best, **289**
  Perfect, **288**
  popularity of, 27, 28, 44
  stirring, 87
Manhattan Club (NY), 13
maraschino cherries, 120
Maravel Sling, **290**
Margarita, **290–92**
  Bottled, **292**
  coating glass rim for, 79
  Jelly Shot, **292**
  origins of, 45, 160
Marin-i-Tini, **293**
Martinez, **293**
Martini, **293–96**
  Circa 1900 (Bottled), **296**
  garnishes for, 120–21
  history of, 22, 39, 43, 293–94
  popularity of, 27, 44
  stirring, 87
  variations on, 70–71, 294–96
Martini glass, 133
Martini pitcher, 125
Maryland Squirrel, **296**
Mary Pickford Cocktail, **297**
Massa Mojito, **297**
Maurice Cocktail, **298**
measured pourer, 129
measurements, in recipes, 199
measuring devices, 81–82, 128–29
measuring spoons, 128
Metropolitan, **298**
Metropolitan Hotel (NY), 14
Mexican Squirrel, **298**
Milanese drinks
  Americano, **205**
  Astor Martini, **209**
  Blood Orange, 70, **219**
  characteristics of, 152
  Negroni, **308–9**

Teresa, **342**
Valentino, **346**
Valentino (Vodka), **346**
milk, 81, 113
Millennium Cocktail, **299**
Millennium Manhattan, **299**
Millionaire Cocktail No. 4, **300**
Millionaire's Margarita, **300**
Mimosa, **300–301**
mint, for juleps, 120, 152
Minted Simple Syrup, **303**
Mint Julep, 2, 120, **301–3**
Mint Julep No. 2, **304**
Missing Link, **304**
"mix and chill" instructions, 201
mixed drinks
history of, 1–4
serving, 129–30
serving glasses for, 133
mixing glass, 84, 132
mixology
accommodating individual tastes, 73–74
achieving balance of flavors, 71–73
adding garnishes, 80
blending frozen drinks, 97–98
building drinks, 85–86, 201
chilling glassware, 84–85
coating rim of glass, 79–80, 115
flaming drinks, 97
floating ingredients, 201
infusing spirits, 98–102
layering drinks, 91–92, 201
mixing and chilling ingredients, 201
muddling drinks, 90–91, 201
order of ingredients poured, 80–81
pouring ingredients, 81–83
precision and speed, 76–77
rinsing ingredient, 201
rocking or rolling a drink, 89
serving drinks, 83–84
shake and strain instructions, 201
shaking drinks, 26, 84, 87, 88–89, 201
squeezing garnish into drinks, 77–78
stirring drinks, 26, 84, 87–88
straining drinks, 86–87, 201
theory behind, 69–75
using high-quality ingredients, 74
Modernista, **304–5**
Mojito, 120, **305**
Monkey Gland Cocktail No. 1, **306**
Monkey Gland Cocktail No. 2, **306**
Moon Walk, **306**
Moscow Mule, 42, 43, **307**
Mount Gay Rumrita, **307**
Mouresque Cocktail, **307**
Muddled drinks, 153
Caipirinha, 90, 110–11, **234**
Caipiroska, **234**
preparing, 90–91, 201
Whiskey Old-Fashioned, 23, 39, 90, **348–49**
Whiskey Old-Fashioned (Fruit-Style), **349**
Whiskey Old-Fashioned (Peach), **350**
muddler (wooden pestle), 90, 125
muddling, method for, 90–91, 201
Muddy Waters, **308**
Mudslide, **308**
mulled wines, about, 1–2

napkins, 83–84, 130
Negroni, **308–9**
Negroni (Vodka), **309**
Nelson's Blood, **309**
New England Highballs
Bay Breeze, **211**
Cape Codder, **235**
comparative charts for, 180–81
Madras, **282**
Sea Breeze, **334**
Sex on the Beach, 69–70, **335**
Woo Woo, **352**
New Jersey Squirrel, **309**
New Orleans Sours, 160–62
Beachcomber Cocktail, **212**
Between the Sheets, **214**
Big Pine Key Cocktail, **214–15**
Blue Train Cocktail, **224**
Cacharita, **232–33**
Calvados Cocktail, **234–35**
Caribbean Cosmopolitan, **236**
Cherry Blossom Cocktail, **239**
Classic Cocktail, **240**
comparative chart of, 189–92
Corpse Reviver No. 2, **242–43**
Cosmopolitan, **243**
Crux Cocktail, **244**
Deauville Cocktail, **246**
Footloose Cocktail, **256**
James Joyce Cocktail, **274**
Lola Martini, 112, **281**
Maiden's Blush Cocktail, **282–83**
Maiden's Prayer Cocktail, **283**
Margarita, 45, 79, 160, **290–92**
Marin-i-Tini, **293**
Metropolitan, **298**
Millionaire's Margarita, **300**
Oriental Cocktail, **312**
Pegu Club Cocktail, **313**
Pink Lemonade Cocktail, **316**
Rosebud Cocktail, **326–27**
Sage Margarita, **329**
Sidecar, 39, 43, 79, 160–61, **335–36**

Oatmeal Cookie Cocktail, **310**
Old Cuban Cocktail, **310**
Old-Fashioned. *See* Whiskey Old-Fashioned
old-fashioned or rocks glass, 133
Old San Juan Sour, **311**
olives, 120–21
OP Lemonade Cocktail, **311**
orange bitters, 106–8
Orange Bitters No. 5, Regan's, 107–8
orange-flower water, 115
orange juice, 114
orange twists, 77–78, 118
orgeat syrup, 112
Oriental Cocktail, **312**
Orphans, 154–55
  Baileys Chocolate Martini, **210**
  Banana-Split Martini, 80, **211**
  Betsy Ross, **214**
  Blow My Skull Off, **222**
  Bobbo's Bride Straight Up, **225**
  Boston Cream Martini, **228**
  Dreamy Dorini Smoking Martini, **249**
  Elegant without Number, **251**
  Flame of Love, **255**
  Flirtini Martini, **256**
  Gimlet, 111, **261**
  Glenkinchie Clincher, **262**
  Hawaiian Cocktail, **265**
  Haymaker Special, **266**
  Jamaican Ten-Speed, **274**
  Kentucky Longshot, **276**
  Kir, **276–77**
  Lewis & Martin Cocktail, **279**
  Libation Goddess, **280**
  Mandrintini, **285**
  Mary Pickford Cocktail, **297**
  Millennium Cocktail, **299**
  Monkey Gland Cocktail No. 1, **306**
  Monkey Gland Cocktail No. 2, **306**
  Mouresque Cocktail, **307**
  Oatmeal Cookie Cocktail, **310**
  Royale, **327**
  Russian Walnut Martini, **328**
  Satan's Whiskers, **330**
  Sazerac, 20–21, 41, **330–31**
  Tart Gin Cooler, **341**
  Tiramisu Martini, **343**
  White Wine Spritzer, **352**

Pacific Rim Martini, **312**
Paddy Cocktail, **312**
Paradise Cocktail, **313**
paring knives, 125
peach puree, preparing, 213
Pegu Club Cocktail, **313**
Pernod and Cider, **313**
Peychaud's bitters, 5, 43, 106
Phoebe Snow Cocktail, **314**
Pierce Brosnan, **314–15**
pilsner glass, 132
Pimm's Cup, **315**
Piña Colada, 112, **316**
pineapple garnishes, 119–20
pineapple juice, 114
Pink Lemonade Cocktail, **316**
Pink Squirrel, **316–17**
Pisco Sour, 112, **317**
pitchers, 127
Planter's Cocktail, **317**
Planter's Punch, **318**
Pogash, Jonathan, 47
Pompier Cocktail, **318**
Pousse-Cafés, 155–56
  Angel's Tit, **206**
  AWOL, 91, **209**
  B-52, **214**
  Black-and-White Cocktail, **216**
  Blue-Eyed Blonde, **224**
  Fifth Avenue, **254**
  French-Kiss Shooter, **257**
  preparing, 91–92
  serving glass for, 133
Preakness Cocktail, **319**
Presbyterian, **319**
Pretty in Pink, **319**
Princess Mary's Pride Cocktail, **320**
Prohibition, 28–36
proof, measures of, 356–57
Punches, 156–57
  Artillery Punch, **208**
  Bolo's Pomegranate Sangria, **227**
  Bolo's White Peach Sangria, **228**
  Fish House Punch, 3, **255**
"Punk Cocktails," 45–47
Punt e Mes Fizz, **320**

Quick Little Pick-Me-Up, **320**

Ramos Gin Fizz, **320–21**
  history of, 21, 43, 320–21
  ingredients in, 112, 115
Raspberry Martini, **322**
Raspberry Vodka, **322**
RBS Special Cocktail, **322**
Red Snapper, **323**
red-wine glass, 132
Regan's Orange Bitters No. 5, 107–8
Remember the Maine, **323**
"rinsing" instructions, 201
Ritz of New York, **323**
Riveredge Cocktail, **324–25**
Rob Roy, 43, **325–26**

Rob Roy (Dry), **326**
Rob Roy (Perfect), **326**
"rocking or rolling" ingredients, 89
Roosevelt, Franklin Delano, 36
Rosebud Cocktail, **326–27**
Royale, **327**
Rum Runner, **327**
Russian Squirrel, **327**
Russian Walnut Martini, **328**
Rusty Nail, **328**
Rye and Ginger, **328**

Sage Margarita, **329**
Salty Chihuahua, **329**
Salty Dog, **329**
San Pellegrino San Bitter, 116
Satan's Whiskers, **330**
Saunders, Audrey, xii, 46, 81
Savoy Hotel (London), 30
Sazerac, 20–21, 41, **330–31**
Scofflaw Cocktail, **332**
Scorpion, **332**
Scotch and Soda, **333**
Scotch and Water, **333**
Scottish Squirrel, **333**
Screwdriver, **333**
Sea Breeze, **334**
Seelbach Cocktail, **324**
Seven and Seven, **334**
Sex on the Beach, 69–70, **335**
"shake and strain" instructions, 201
shakers, Boston, 84, 86–89, 124
shakers, cocktail, 84, 86, 125
shakers, short, 125
shaking drinks, 26, 84, 87, 88–89, 201
Shandy, 23, **335**
sherry copita, 132
Shmitt, Stuffy, 45, 47
short shaker, 125
shot glass, 132
shots, per bottle, 356
Sidecar, **335–36**
  coating glass rim for, 79
  Deluxe (Bottled), **336**
  origins of, 39, 43, 160–61
Simple Syrup, **110**
Simple Syrup, Minted, **303**
Singapore Sling, 41
  No. 1, **337**
  No. 2, **338**
sipsticks, 83, 85–86, 129–30
Sloe Comfortable Screw, **338**
Sloe Gin Fizz, 43, **338**
Snappers, 157–58
  Bloody Bull, **219**
  Bloody Caesar, 109, **220**
  Bloody Mary, 30, 42, 43, 44, 89, 109, 120, **220–21**
  Bloody Mary Martini, 109, **222**
  Bullshot, 109, **231**
  Red Snapper, **323**
sodas, 116
Sours, 158–59. *See also* International Sours; New Orleans Sours; Sparkling Sours; Squirrel Sours
  Amaretto Sour, **205**
  Apple Sidecar, **207**
  Apricot Sour, **207**
  Bacardi Cocktail, 26, 30, **210**
  Bennett Cocktail, **213**
  Bolero Cocktail, **227**
  Clover Club Cocktail, **240–41**
  comparative chart of, 182–84
  Daiquiri, 44, **245**
  Delicious Cocktail, **246–47**
  El Presidente, **252**
  Fish House Cocktail, **254**
  Jack Rose, **272–73**
  Lemon Drop, 104–5, **279**
  Old San Juan Sour, **311**
  Pisco Sour, 112, **317**
  Scofflaw Cocktail, **332**
  serving glass for, 133
  Tea Tini, **341**
  Tropical Cocktail, **345**
  Ward Eight, **347–48**
  Whiskey Sour, 90, **350**
Southern Comfort, 44
Southside Cocktail, **339**
Southside Fizz, **339**
Sparkling Sours, 162–63
  Apricot Fizz, **207**
  Carbonated Piston Slinger, **235**
  comparative chart of, 193–94
  John Collins, 23, **275**
  Long Island Iced Tea, **282**
  Maravel Sling, **290**
  Pretty in Pink, **319**
  Ramos Gin Fizz, 21, 43, 112, 115, **320–21**
  Singapore Sling No. 1, 41, **337**
  Singapore Sling No. 2, **338**
  Sloe Gin Fizz, 43, **338**
  Tom Collins, 23, 90, **344**
speakeasies, 28–36
speed pourers, 129
spirits
  alcohol by volume, 356–57
  brand-name products, 197–98
  densities of, 92–96
  high-proof, diluting, 99, 101
  infusing, 98–102
  for medicinal purposes, 3

Squirrel Sours, 163–64
British Squirrel, **230**
Caribbean Squirrel, **236**
comparative chart of, 195
Dutch Squirrel, **250**
French Squirrel, **258**
Irish Squirrel, **272**
Kentucky Squirrel, **276**
Maryland Squirrel, **296**
Mexican Squirrel, **298**
New Jersey Squirrel, **309**
Russian Squirrel, **327**
Scottish Squirrel, **333**
Starry Night Cocktail, **340**
Stiletto Cocktail, **340**
Stinger, 24, 87, **340**
stirrers, 129–30
stirring drinks, 26, 84, 87–88
strainer, Hawthorne, 86, 124
strainer, julep, 124
straining drinks, 86–87, 201
strawberry puree, to make, 343
straws, 130
sugared vanilla beans, preparing, 310
sweetening agents, 110–12
Syrup, Simple, **110**
Syrup, Simple, Minted, **303**

Tabasco sauce, 109
tamarind juice, 114
tangerine juice, 114
Tart Gin Cooler, **341**
Tbilisi Royale, **341**
tea, 115
Tea Tini, **341**
teetotalers, 24
temperance movement, 24–28
tequila, in mid-1900s, 45
Tequila Sunrise, **342**
Teresa, **342**
Third Degree, or Martini with a Spot, **342–43**
Thomas, Jerry, xi, 7, 14–16, 47, 136, 155, 158, 161, 223
Tiepolo, **343**
Tiramisu Martini, **343**
Toasted Almond, **344**
tomato juice, 81, 109
tomato water, 109, 222
Tom Collins, 23, 90, **344**
tonic water, 24, 116
tools and vessels, 123–30
Tremblement de Terre (Earthquake), **344–45**
Trios. *See* Duos and Trios
triple sec, buying, 198
Tropical Cocktail, **345**
Tropical drinks, 164–65
Bahama Mama, **210**
Fog Cutter, **256**
history of, 41
Hurricane, **268–69**
Mai Tai No. 2, **284**
Mai Tai (Original), 41, **283–84**
Piña Colada, 112, **316**
Planter's Punch, **318**
Scorpion, **332**
Zombie No. 1, 97, **352–53**
Zombie No. 2, **353**
Tsar's Champagne Cocktail, **345**
Tulio Oro, **345**
Twentieth-Century Cocktail, **346**

Valentino, **346**
Valentino (Vodka), **346**
Van Gogh O'Magnifique triple sec, 198
vanilla beans, sugared, preparing, 310
vermouth, popularity of, 21–22
Vesper Martini, **347**
vodka, during mid-1900s, 42
Vodka and Tonic, **347**
vodka-based French-Italian drinks. *See* French-Italian drinks
vodka glass, 132

Waldorf-Astoria Hotel (NY), 12–13, 27
Ward Eight, **347–48**
Washington, George, 3, 255
Wassail, origins of, 1
whiskey-based French-Italian drinks. *See* French-Italian drinks
Whiskey Old-Fashioned, **348–49**
Fruit-Style, **349**
history of, 23, 39, 348–49
Peach, **350**
preparing, 90
Whiskey Sour, 90, **350**
Whiskey Sour Jelly Shot, **350–51**
White Russian, **351**
White Spider, **351**
white-wine glass, 132
White Wine Spritzer, **352**
wine, flavored, history of, 1–2
wine service glassware, 132
Woo Woo, **352**
Worcestershire sauce, 109

zester, 80
Zombie
No. 1, **352–53**
No. 2, **353**
origins of, 97
serving glass, 13

Bicycling Magazine's
COMPLETE GUIDE TO
RIDING
AND
RACING
Techniques

POINT LOMA NAZARENE COLLEGE
202832
RYAN LIBRARY

Bicycling® Magazine's

COMPLETE GUIDE TO

RIDING AND RACING *Techniques*

By Fred Matheny

Rodale Press, Emmaus, Pennsylvania

Printed in the United States of America on acid-free paper containing a high percentage of recycled fiber.

Editor: Kim Anderson
Principal photographer: Ed Landrock
Book designer: Darlene Schneck

Library of Congress Cataloging-in-Publication Data

Matheny, Fred. 1945–
Bicycling magazine's complete guide to riding and racing techniques / by Fred Matheny.
p. cm.
Includes index.
ISBN 0-87857-804-8 hardcover ISBN 0-87857-805-6 paperback
1. Bicycling. 2. Bicycle racing. I. Bicycling! II. Title.
GV1041.M37 1989
796.6–dc19 88-31654
CIP

2 4 6 8 10 9 7 5 3 1 hardcover
2 4 6 8 10 9 7 5 3 1 paperback

Contents

Introduction: Bicycling: The Urge to Ride 1
Chapter 1: Mounting Up 7
Chapter 2: Basic Training for Bicyclists 31
Chapter 3: Bicycling Essentials 51
Chapter 4: Basics of Shifting and Braking 65
Chapter 5: Special Techniques 73
Chapter 6: Advanced Riding Techniques 81
Chapter 7: Time Trials 105
Chapter 8: Quick Tracks: Criteriums, Circuit Races, Long and Short Road Races 115
Chapter 9: Fast Recreational and Endurance Cycling 127
Chapter 10: Off-Road Cycling 147
Chapter 11: Special Circumstances 163
Chapter 12: Building Strength and Endurance in the Off-Season 179
Chapter 13: Developing Speed 199
Chapter 14: Diet and Nutrition 211
Chapter 15: Medical Self-Care 223

Photography Credits 235
Index 237

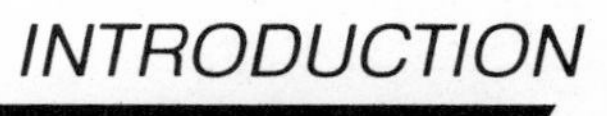

Bicycling: The Urge to Ride

Cycling has been one of the fastest-growing sports during the '80s. The United States Cycling Federation (USCF), the governing body for amateur competition in this country, claimed only about 8,000 license holders in 1980. By the end of 1987, that figure had grown to more than 28,000 and was expected to reach 35,000 by the end of the decade. That's nearly a fourfold increase in ten years–a phenomenal growth rate for a sport that has historically received little attention.

In places as divergent as Boulder, Colorado; New York, New York; San Francisco, California; Athens, Ohio; Austin, Texas; and Phoenix, Arizona, spectators are turning out in unprecedented numbers to see fast, exciting action in short and long road races.

And such numbers aren't limited to the competitive end of the sport. Recreational cycling has grown proportionally all across the country. In 1987, for example, over 12,000 riders participated in a mass-start ride lasting from 10 to 100 miles in Wichita Falls, Texas–the Hotter 'n' Hell Hundred. New cycling clubs are forming all over the country, every town seems to feature an evening race for low-key competition or fun, and mountain bikes–a kind of bicycle that barely existed at the start of the decade–have attracted thousands of new riders to the sport. Why is cycling growing so rapidly?

Birth of the Boom

One reason for cycling's phenomenal growth is publicity. U.S. amateur cyclists enjoyed highly visible success in the 1984 Olympic Games in Los Angeles, taking home nine medals–including a gold collected by Connie Carpenter in the first-ever women's Olympic road race. In 1985, the U.S.-based 7-Eleven professional team made its first foray into European racing. The team held its own–even for a while holding the lead in the most visible and prestigious bicycle race in the world, the Tour de France. And American Greg LeMond–who began racing in Europe in 1981 on his own, without the support of a U.S. team–not only won the coveted rainbow jersey of a professional champion but in 1986 achieved victory in the Tour de France itself.

The Body and Mind of a Bicyclist

But cycling isn't a sport that relies solely on publicity and spectators for popularity. Much of its thrill is intrinsic, an intangible something that happens each time you get on a bicycle and ride. The tangible benefits, however, can be divided into two categories: physical and mental.

The Body

The biggest physical benefit of cycling is improved cardiovascular fitness. Competitive cyclists are among the most aerobically fit athletes in the world. Cyclists routinely record maximal oxygen uptake values (a measure of the body's ability to use oxygen and therefore a measure of fitness) of 80 ml per kg of body weight (divide your weight by 2.2 to get your weight in kilograms). Fit athletes in other sports like basketball score at three-fourths that figure.

A second advantage: Cycling gets you into shape without undue risk of injury. In running, your joints endure thousands of pounding contacts with the pavement. And while some runners can handle training loads of over 100 miles a week without injury, others break down at just 20 or 30 miles.

Cycling, on the other hand, is a smooth, rhythmic, fluid activity that is easy on knees, muscles, and ligaments. The kind of mileage that would put a runner under is almost easy for a cyclist. You can ride a long way in another sense of the word, too—cyclists often continue to compete and tour well into their 70s and 80s. It's a lifetime sport.

Cycling also develops muscular strength. Top riders, both men and women, have legs that are lean, defined, and powerful. Cyclists also work their arms and shoulders, pulling on the handlebars when climbing and leaning on them during steady riding. The net result: Good cyclists have *balanced* muscular development.

Because risk of injury is low, cycling is a lifetime sport.

A final physical benefit of regular cycling is increased stamina—something more complex than simple endurance. Cycling many miles does improve endurance, so much so that even recreational riders can enjoy 100-mile rides if they train moderately and wisely. But cycling develops more than simple endurance. Regular riding strengthens the whole body, training it to withstand exertion, temperature extremes, and all the vagaries of the open road. If you become a cyclist, you'll find that you have more energy for your career, family, leisure time—all the important things in life. The benefits of cycling don't stop when you get off the bicycle.

The Mind

Effective as it is at enhancing your sense of physical well-being, cycling is even better at improving your mental outlook. Easy spinning or hard sprints up killer hills–they both capture the mind. Lost in the pedaling motion, the demands of the route and the fine-fiddling details of gear selection, you momentarily forget the problems of everyday life–and consequently return from your ride better able to solve them.

Cycling cuts stress another way: You're usually out in the fresh air surrounded by back-road scenery. If you live in a town or small city, you can often reach the country in 15 minutes. But even the most urban of bicyclists can escape these concrete canyons by riding in city parks–or loading the bicycle onto the car for a weekend getaway.

Cycling can be a family activity, even for children too young to pedal.

Training for cycling encourages balanced muscular development.

Networking via Bicycle

Cycling is a great way to meet new friends. Socializing, the new-generation psychologists tell us, is good for our health. You can join your local cycling club, go to group rides or low-key time trials, or take off for a week of touring with friends and club-mates.

Finally, riding together is one of the best family activities imaginable. The drafting of cycling lets different people of wide-ranging fitness and strength ride together, stronger ones at the front with the rest riding easy in their draft. Many cycling families begin by riding to museums and parks, and on family picnics. Then they progress to day rides and perhaps longer tours. Even racing can be a family affair. Because of age-graded competition, cycling is one of the few sports in which all generations can compete in the same activity.

Recreational Riding

What are cycling's possibilities if you don't want to compete but you do want to reap all the benefits of the sport? Cycling's activities are incredibly varied.

Fitness Riding

Cycling is an excellent activity for improving aerobic fitness and lower-body muscular strength. Contrary to the usual belief, it isn't limited to fair weather. Cycling can be done in most weather conditions, thanks to modern rain gear, or indoors on training stands when darkness or frigid weather preclude outdoor riding.

Centuries

One-hundred-mile rides—"centuries" for short—are among cycling's most popular challenges. Organized centuries may have thousands of participants, aid stations every 10 miles, and patches as a reward for successful completion. But you can do an unorganized century on your own (or with a couple of friends) whenever you feel like going for a long ride.

Touring

"Touring" is yet another way to enjoy the bicycle. Some cyclists like to tour in style by riding hard all day, then treating themselves to five-star accommodations and gourmet meals. You can take weekend trips carrying just a credit card and a change of clothes if you stay in motels and eat at restaurants.

Or you can camp, carrying lightweight equipment on your bicycle in specially designed bags called panniers. Posh or primitive, these tours can last for several days or several weeks, meandering around a state, or crossing countries or continents.

Racing

If competition is what you crave, cycling action can be fast and furious or low-key—your choice. On the local level, most clubs sponsor evening time trials where you can test your riding ability against the clock. You'll ride an out-and-back course of 5 to 10 miles by yourself, trying for the best time possible. Time trials are great for beginning competitors: Pack riding skills aren't needed because riders start at 1-minute intervals and no drafting is allowed.

Many clubs also stage evening or weekend "criteriums" (relatively short mass-start races of 10 to 20 miles around short courses of a mile or less). They are often graded according to ability with a novice race first and a longer, more-intense event for experienced riders. Club races are ideal for learning how to ride comfortably in a racing pack.

For serious racers of all ages, the USFC sanctions thousands of events all over the country. Both men and women USCF racers age 18 to 34 are ability-grouped from Category Four (novice) to Category One (international caliber). Age-graded racing for children starts at age nine and continues for older riders (at five-year intervals) starting at age 35. USCF races run the gamut from regional criteriums and road races, to district championships on the road and track, to national championships and Olympic selection races.

Mountain Biking

The parallel organization for mountain bikes is the National Off-Road Bicycle Association (NORBA). Races under NORBA's aegis are also ability-grouped, and include hill climbs, downhill events, circuits, point-

Touring means camaraderie, scenery, and a leisurely pace.

to-point races, and trials competitions. The association also sponsors national championships each year.

Other forms of competition are less formal, but just as much fun. Any group ride can become intensely competitive, depending on the people involved. Century rides, for example, often become 100-mile races as packs form and riders try to better their personal records for the distance.

Endurance-oriented riders can pick between 12- and 24-hour record attempts on the road or on the track. Several city-to-city records circulate informally (Seattle to San Diego, for example), but the ultimate endurance ride is the Race Across America. The current record for this roughly 3,000-mile test of physical ability and mental toughness: less than nine days.

But often the most meaningful competition is against yourself. Many riders have personal records for various loop rides or long hills near their homes, and they try to better those marks with all the enthusiasm and planning of Olympic riders mounting assaults on the Gold Medal.

The Aim of This Book

It's hot, it's fun, it's *bicycling*. Want in? Want more? Then read on. This book is designed for both the novice rider and the experienced cyclist who want to perfect their technique and get faster, stronger, and more enduring.

It will show and tell you what equipment and training techniques you'll need to become a safe and competent rider.

It will prepare you for fast recreational cycling, either by yourself or with friends and club-mates.

Finally, this book will equip you with the skills you need to begin racing.

RIDE A
FOR GOOD HEALTH-IT'S FUN
EXIT

Mounting Up

Until fairly recently, basic bicycle design and construction had stayed the same for almost 100 years—a diamond frame built of steel tubing. Cheap bicycles used heavy, seamed steel tubes. Racing and sport bicycles were made of seamless—and in many cases double-butted—tubes whose walls were thicker on the ends where the stress was greatest. Frame dimensions and angles were standardized, and upright track cycles varied by only a few inches and degrees from long-wheelbased touring cycles.

Wheels usually had 36 spokes and alloy rims. Tubular tires and wheels were used for racing and fast sport riding, heavier clinchers (wired-on tires) for touring. Derailleurs (devices that move bicycle chains from gear to gear) were traditionally designed and operated over a 5-speed—or at most 6-speed—freewheel. The best frames and components had Italian names, and serious cyclists would accept nothing less. Those same serious cyclists wore wool shorts and jerseys, leather shoes with *nail-on* cleats, cloth cycling caps, and leather hairnet helmets.

Enter the Space Age

In the last decade, all the old verities have been demolished. Frames are made of steel, aluminum, titanium, or composites of carbon fiber, boron, and other space-age materials. Some frames are still brazed, but others are welded, glued, laminated, or even *moulded.* Frame angles and dimensions have remained much the same, but there's a whole new breed of bicycle—the mountain bike or all-terrain bike (ATB)—that's rewritten the rules concerning what a bicycle can do.

Derailleurs now shift over seven- or even eight-cog freewheels, and the shift levers click neatly from one gear to the next—a design called indexed shifting. Many pedal designs have shed toe clips and straps, and others have eliminated all but the axle.

Wheels have been trimmed down, too—32 spokes (down from 36) is the road racing standard, with 24- or 28-spoke wheels in common usage. Racers still use tubulars for big events, but everyone else is on narrow, high-pressure clinchers that run as fast and true as all but the most expensive

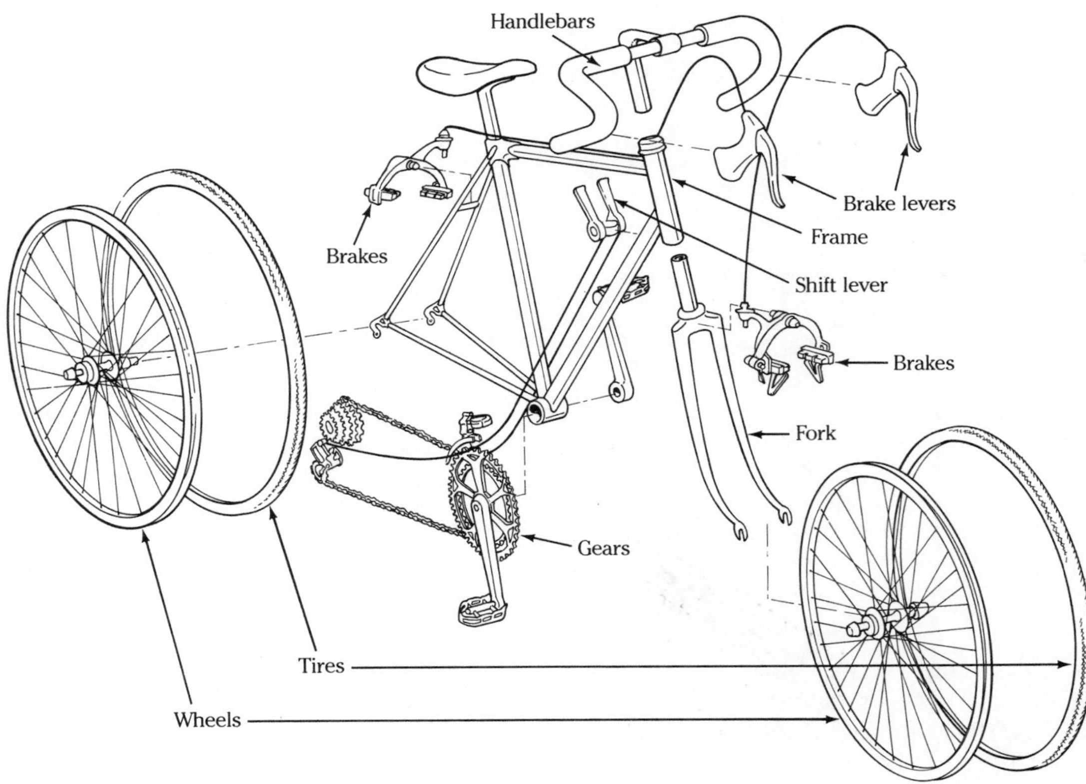

tubulars with a fraction of the expense and maintenance time.

And cyclists have discarded wool jerseys and shorts for skin-tight suits of Lycra, Swisstex, and other synthetics in all the colors of the rainbow–and some that can't be found anywhere in nature.

In short, the bicycle market used to be traditional, conservative, and stable. Now, the summer's newest and hottest component is obsolete and forgotten by the following spring. How can you make wise buying decisions in a market so volatile? By making yourself an informed shopper.

Frames

Steel. The traditional steel bicycle is still alive and well in spite of aluminum and carbon fiber competition. Steel's most obvious advantage is tradition. Bicycles made from steel tubing look and ride like lots of us think bicycles are supposed to. Steel frames can also be painted in any color imaginable and repainted over and over again. Such options are limited on anodized aluminum or unpainted carbon fiber frames. Repairability is another big plus for steel frames. Bent tubes can be tweaked back into true (properly aligned with each other and the rest of the bicycle) by experienced mechanics and crumpled ones replaced entirely. Such repair jobs are either difficult and expensive or impossible with many newer materials. Finally, unlike composites and aluminum, steel cracks *before* it breaks–early warning of a potentially disastrous frame failure.

Aluminum. These frames are sometimes lighter than steel, but they often achieve that weight by compromising stiffness. Many aluminum bicycles solve the problem by using oversized tubes for extra rigidity, but some riders object to this design modification on aesthetic grounds. Aluminum dampens road shock and vibration well, so it's often used by racers competing on rough roads or cobblestones and by tourists who want comfort over the long haul. Although aluminum can be corroded by salt from sweaty bodies or slushy roads, it doesn't rust, making it a good choice in rainy climates.

Composite. Composite frames–made from ultra-high-tech materials like carbon and boron–are so new that a full assessment would be premature. The materials currently used promise lightness, rigidity, and strength undreamed of in traditional steel bikes. But no concensus has been reached on the best way to use the new materials to reap all those advantages. Some composite cycles have standard construction while others, attempting to use the qualities inherent in the material, have experimented with moulded frames.

Only time will tell if the enormous potential of composite construction will be realized in actual bicycles. But in the meantime, there's a whole new world of *components* that make cycling easier and more fun. Derailleurs, pedal/cleat systems, wheels, and tires–all have been improved to work better with fewer problems.

Components

Shifting systems. Indexed shifting (when each move of the gear lever moves the chain a preset distance, and the rider can feel each gear "click" into place) is the most visible recent development in component design. Several manufacturers tried out indexed systems in the past, but none of them caught on with the buying public. But when Shimano introduced its system in 1986 it quickly became the hottest-selling new component on the market. Other makers quickly followed suit, and now there are several different systems to choose from.

Composite frames promise to change the shape of cycling.

Indexed shifting differs from traditional friction shifting in that the shift lever clicks from one gear to the other in *precise* increments. The advantages? No more almost-shifts or backing off on the lever to center the chain after a shift. Indexed systems do shift well under load, a plus for off-road riders or road racers who need fast shifts on hills. For the racer in a flat-out competitive sprint, or the commuter popping into a gap in traffic, operation is so precise that missed shifts are history. And indexed shifting makes learning to ride a derailleur-equipped bicycle much easier, too–a real selling point for new riders.

The major disadvantage is a somewhat higher maintenance level, although an occasional twist of the derailleur's barrel adjuster to take up cable slack is usually all that's needed. Indexed systems also work best on perfectly aligned frames. If your bicycle is out of line or gets that way in a crash, the derailleur won't work well. However, most indexed systems are designed so that they can be converted easily to standard friction mode while riding. That feature also means that you can switch rear wheels among bicycles equipped with different derailleurs–indexed or not indexed–an advantage for people who need fast wheel changes–racers, for example, or riders touring in a group.

Indexed shifting for front derailleurs hit the market for the first time in 1988, courtesy of Shimano. Less precise–but generally more available–friction shifting, however, doesn't present any problems on front derailleurs because they operate on double or triple chainrings or gear wheels rather than six or seven cogs on a freewheel. Nonindexed front derailleurs do have a problem shifting under load, however, so an electronic derailleur system–the Browning Automatic Transmission–is now offered. Two buttons on the handlebars do all the work. One moves the chain from small cogs to big cogs; the other reverses direction (for upshifting or downshifting). Such systems aren't quite as fast as the manual variety, weigh a bit more, and clutter the bicycle with wires and battery.

The Browning Automatic Transmission system.

But a more serious problem is keeping water out of the electronics, a difficulty that has not been satisfactorily solved as of this writing. But if waterproof electronic shifters arrive, and if they can be adapted to rear derailleurs, manual shifting may become obsolete rather quickly.

Pedals. Conventional pedals with toe straps and clips have always had several severe drawbacks. They were hard to get into, for one thing. Novice riders gave themselves away by pawing blindly at the pedals as they tried to begin their ride gracefully. And the conventional retention system–to keep your feet where they belonged–was uncomfortable and unpredictable. If you pulled the straps tight for a sprint or a steep climb, you risked numb toes. What's worse, you were locked in if you crashed or had to put a foot down quickly in an emergency. If you left the straps loose while you were cruising along, you could exit easily; but if you needed security for a sprint or to jump a set of railroad tracks, you then were forced to bend over and pull the straps tight.

To remedy these ills, a dozen manufacturers now market step-in pedal/cleat systems that are modeled on downhill ski binding technology and do away with toe clips and straps entirely. Although each system operates a bit differently, most feature a cleat on the bottom of the shoe that clicks into a spring-loaded platform on the pedal spindle. The shoe is held tightly during normal pedaling but can be released easily with a simple twisting motion. Inadvertent releases are rare.

Pluses for step-in pedals include ease of entry and exit. Your foot is held firmly at all times, so you can sprint all out or spin along normally without adjusting toe straps. There's no strap encircling your foot and exerting uncomfortable pressure. Cleat systems are great for winter riding, too, because you can wear thick shoe covers without worrying if they'll fit in your toe clips. And the best of the new pedals are constructed as well as the traditional models–often with sealed bearings–guaranteeing years of trouble-free pedaling.

But cleat systems aren't without drawbacks. They're impractical for mountain bikes because they don't accommodate shoes suitable for walking or running. Some manufacturers have tried to develop off-road cleats, but they inevitably clog with dirt as soon as they touch the ground. Step-in pedals aren't recommended for loaded touring (riding with full packs) for the same reason. They won't allow you to ride in your walking shoes if your cleats break–a possibility on long rides–or if your cycling shoes get soaked. And you can't make camp, change into walking shoes, and then ride a mile to the store.

Wheels and tires. These key components have also undergone a revolution. The sole choice used to be either heavy clincher wheels with matching tires or lightweight but fragile tubulars. But clincher tire technology has now progressed to the point where clinchers are as light and roll with as little resistance as the best tubulars. They are available with a Kevlar bead so they fold up just like a tubular. For long rides, there's no need to carry more than one spare tube because clincher tubes can be patched again and again. With tubulars, on the other hand, you need a new tire for each puncture, unless you're willing to spend half an hour sitting by the side of the road unstitching and patching a sew-up (wheels with tires that are literally sewn on). Lightweight, high-pressure clinchers are also available in treadless designs for low rolling resistance and excellent dry pavement traction.

Look pedals started the clipless revolution.

If you are a racer, however, don't throw away your old set of tubular wheels. At present, clinchers can't equal the low weight of the tubular tire-rim combination. Although clincher tires and tubes are as light as quality tubulars, clincher rims or wheels are still heavier than tubular rims of similar strength. Because clinchers are attached to the rim with air pressure, they require a hooked lip that adds weight. Tubulars, on the other hand, need less rim wall because they are attached with glue. Lighter rims mean you can accelerate faster and climb with less effort on tubulars.

Tubulars are safer in race conditions, too. If they puncture in a corner, the tire will stay on the rim, so you have a chance to maintain control. Because clinchers are held on only by air pressure, once they puncture you are riding on bare metal. And finally, most racers believe they have better control with tubulars, especially in the rain.

An exception might be time trials, where clinchers may have an edge. Clincher tires are available in a treadless design (sized 700C × 19 mm) with extremely low rolling resistance and the ability to hold 130 to 140 pounds of pressure. The accompanying rims are 20 to 30 grams heavier than tubular wheels suitable for time trialing. But the extra weight isn't much of a disadvantage in an event that doesn't involve climbing or require numerous acclerations to high speed. Clinchers have another advantage: They last longer on the shelf and cost less to replace. You'll use your time-trial wheels relatively infrequently, and fragile tubular tires left on the rims for several years often deteriorate. So does the glue that holds them in place. Conversely, clinchers are inexpensive enough to replace if they show signs of wear.

A word on rim shape. A wheel's shape is a trade-off between weight and strength, convenience and aerodynamics. Standard rims are strong and present a flat braking surface for better control. Streamlined aero-rims cheat the air and, because of their triangular shape, are stronger than their box-shaped cousins. But aero-rims slope away from brake pads. If they get out of true, they make braking a dicey proposition as the sloping surface wobbles into and away from the brakes. Finally, aero-rims cover up more of the valve stem, making it harder to keep the pump attached.

Recommendations? For loaded touring, choose 1¼-inch rims and matching tires. For light touring, go with 1-inch clincher rims mated with 700C × 28 mm high-pressure tires. If you plan on training for fitness or fast recreational rides, use 1-inch rims and narrower tires, perhaps 700C × 25 mm. Only if you plan to race should you go with tubulars—and even then many racers train exclusively on clinchers to hold down expenses.

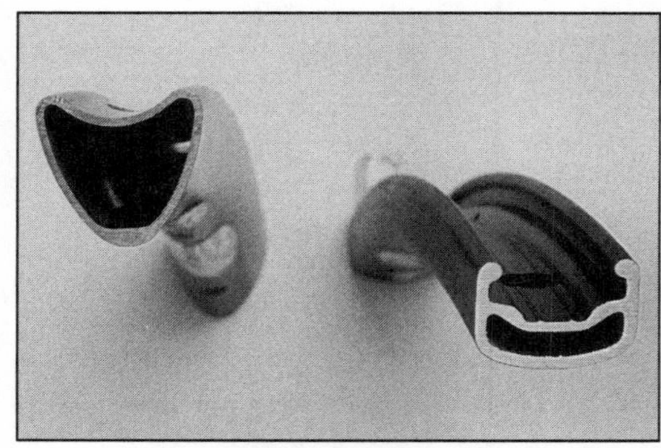

Cross section of tubular, left, and clincher rims.

Mountain bike tires are always clinchers. Choose narrow (26 × 1.5 inches), slick clinchers for easy-rolling road use. If you plan to ride mostly on pavement with an occasional excursion onto the dirt, pick a medium-width tire (26 × 1.75 or 1.95 inches) with knobbies on the shoulders and a quiet "highway band" in the middle of the tread. But for aggressive riding in the dirt, go with wider (26 × 2 inches or more) tires for maximum flotation in soft sand, more protection for the rim, and a cushier ride. As with road tires, folding Kevlar-beaded models are available, useful as spares for extended off-road tours.

The Extras: Accessories

Pumps. Frame pumps are plastic or metal tubes that affix firmly to the bicycle for on-road repairs. They are not designed for day-to-day pumping chores. Make sure that you choose a model with the proper valve design for your tires. *Schraeder valves* are the type normally found on automobile tires and most mountain bikes, and on less-expensive road bikes. Narrower *presta valves* are found on tubulars and high-pressure clinchers, as well as top-end mountain bikes.

On a road bike, the frame pump should be carried between the bottom bracket and top tube, if you have only one water bottle cage. To allow two water bottle cages to be mounted, most newer bicycles have a pump peg behind the head tube, so the pump can be carried below and perpendicular to the top tube.

On mountain bikes, mount the pump behind the seat tube. Some frame pumps designed for off-road use slip down the seat tube itself. Rubber gaskets or tape stop rattling. This trick works only on mountain bikes, because their quick-release seatposts make access to the pump possible without tools. It won't work, however, if the bike has a Hite-Rite (a device that lets the rider use his weight to change seat height).

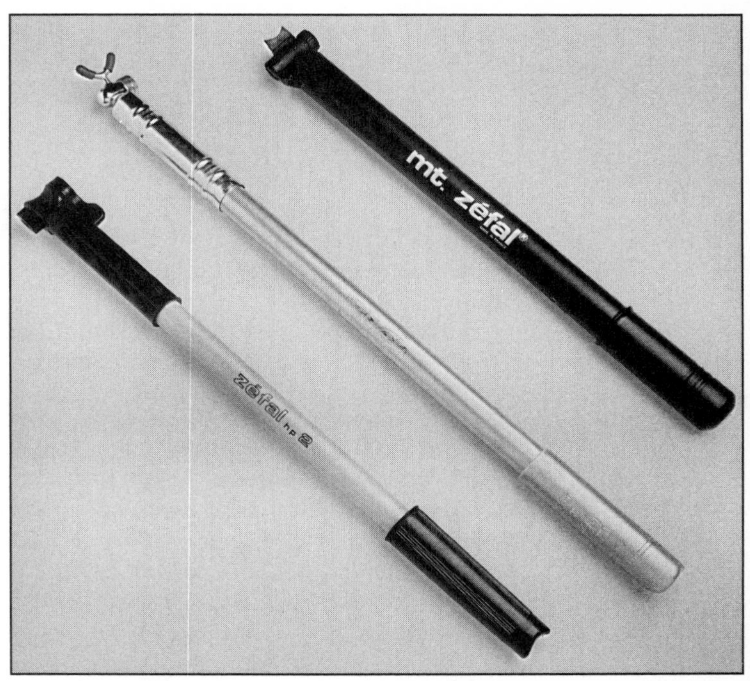

Light, portable frame pumps will keep you going after a flat.

Floor pumps make tire inflation chores a breeze.

Frame pumps lead a hard life because they are exposed to road spray. And they are often used to threaten approaching dogs. It makes sense, then, to check your frame pump monthly as part of normal maintenance. Relubricate the gasket or replace it if necessary. But if the tube is dented or cracked from use as a weapon against man's best friend, replace the whole pump.

Floor pumps make periodic inflation of your tires a snap. If you use clinchers or tubulars with butyl tubes, you'll need to reinflate every week or so. But expensive tubulars or lightweight clinchers with porous latex tubes need a *daily* shot of air because the latex bleeds air much more rapidly than butyl.

Choose a floor pump with the correct kind of chuck, or valve attachment–Schraeder or Presta–for your tires. And remember that many floor pumps have interchangeable chucks. Inflation will be easier if your pump has a large-volume cylinder so you can reach maximum pressure in a few strokes. And you'll want a pump with a built-in pressure gauge. Additionally, look for a stable base, comfortable handles, and a sturdy hose.

Tool kits. If you maintain your bicycle regularly, you won't need to carry a tool kit on normal road rides. A spare tube, patch kit, identification, and some money are all you'll require. But on longer road rides–and any time you ride off-road away from immediate help–tote along several allen-head wrenches or keys, sized to fit your components; a spoke wrench; a small adjustable wrench; and a small screwdriver. Add a chain tool, a freewheel remover, and several spare spokes, and you'll be all set for most repairs.

For your home workshop, the first basic is the stand discussed below–it's hard to work with your bicycle on its side. But you'll also need the additional tools listed below for successful home maintenance. If you don't know how to use them, consult a bicycle repair manual like *Bicycling Magazine's Complete Guide to Bicycle Maintenance and Repair.*

Don't buy them all at once. Make purchases as they are needed, and learn how to use your new tools one at a time. And don't buy expensive things you don't need–frame-preparation tools, for instance. You'll perform these tasks so infrequently that they are best left to your local bicycle shop.

Allen keys in assorted metric sizes.
Open-end wrenches in metric sizes.
Adjustable wrenches, 6, 8, and 12 inches.
Freewheel puller for your freewheel brand.
Cog remover and freewheel vise.
Spoke wrench.
Crank pullers to fit your cranks.
Chain tool.
Headset and bottom bracket tools.
Pedal wrench.

Water bottles. Water bottles don't seem like a technical or glamorous piece of equipment, but they are vital to your performance and safety. Try riding 100 miles without them! Bottles should be made of tasteless and odorless plastic, shaped to fit your bottle cage. Choose the standard size for most conditions and the oversized bottles for hot, humid rides.

The best bottles have a two-position spout: half-open for a cooling spray, all the way out for a drink. Replace your bottles frequently as they get worn or dirty–and don't forget to wash them periodically.

Computers. Bicycle computers range from complex units with multiple functions to relatively simple electronic speedometers. The high-tech models can tell you current speed, average speed for the ride, elapsed time, heart rate, cadence, and serve as a stopwatch if you try for a new record on your local time trial course. Some can even be programmed to beep at set intervals.

You pay a price for these innovations–more initial expense and slightly greater weight. Computers generally also have more wires and magnets to attach to your bicycle. But some units dispense with wires and actually radio the data to the handlebar-mounted monitor. Simpler models have only speed and distance functions but are lightweight and don't clutter your bicycle. Make your choice on the basis of use. Touring cyclists often like all the trip information they can get, while racers are generally interested in just two things: how far they've gone and how fast they did it.

Most computers get their information from a sensor attached to the front fork and a magnet fixed on the spokes of the front wheel. But if you plan to use your bicycle on a training stand, buy a computer designed to mount on the rear wheel, so the computer will be fed information as you pedal. You'll have to put up with more wire, but there's no other choice if you want training information while riding indoors. The one exception: if you ride on rollers, where the front wheel turns as it would on the road.

Here's a trick for attaching wires to your frame. Instead of using the plastic ties that come with most units, use transparent Scotch tape. The wires will be nearly invisible if you route them along the inner sides of the frame tubes and use long strips of tape laid *parallel* to the wire rather than wrapped around the wire and tube. Choose tape a bit wider than normal for more security, and remember: The tape will stick better if you clean the bicycle with rubbing alcohol first.

Another way to reduce clutter: If your computer runs off the front wheel, wrap the wire that travels from the monitor to the fork sensor around the front brake cable and tie it off neatly with a cable tie.

The Whole Bicycle Guide

How do you choose a bicycle and components, given the tremendously wide range of options discussed above? You can make sense out of the confusing bicycle market if you follow several simple rules:

Weigh cost against value. In cycling, as in most other consumer choices, you get what you pay for. Competition among manufacturers is so great that bicycles at similar prices are almost always of similar quality.

Base your selection on intended use. There is no need to spend $1,500 or more for a flat-out racing bicycle if you lean toward 5-mile rides around town on warm summer evenings. Of course, most choices aren't so black and white. For instance, if you want a mountain bike for fitness riding and weekend jaunts to the mountains, you certainly don't need a racing version, but you do need something almost as stiff and durable or you'll probably be disappointed.

Make sure you get the right fit. The most expensive frame will feel uncomfortable and ride like a truck if it doesn't fit you properly.

Learn as much as you can before you buy. Talk to cycling friends. Read books—like *Bicycling Magazine's Complete Guide to Riding and Racing Techniques.* Pore over magazines. Grill bicycle shop personnel. Look at what other people are riding when you go to group rides, centuries, or races. The more you know, the more informed your buying decision will be.

Clothing and Personal Equipment

Nothing can ruin your cycling experience faster than ill-fitting, uncomfortable clothing. Cycling garb looks unusual—even bizarre to the uninitiated—but the sleek shorts and jerseys, the form-fitting shoes, and the protective helmet are all important to a safe, enjoyable bicycling experience. Over nearly 100 years, bicycling clothing has evolved into apparel that looks much different from the uniforms of other sports—but it works *perfectly* for the unique demands of cycling.

Shorts

Most riders will be happiest with form-fitting synthetic shorts, available in traditional black, a variety of colors so jersey and bicycle match, or shorts with contrasting side panels.

Put quality first: Look for six- or eight-panel contruction, so the shorts bend and move with the contours of your body when you are in a cycling position. Check the quality of the seams, because poor sewing will inevitably come apart when the shorts are wrung to dry. You really *shouldn't* wring synthetic shorts after washing–you'll break seam threads. But everyone does it anyway to hasten the drying process, and sturdy seams stand up to this sort of abuse better.

Examine the material, too. Cycling shorts come in everything from traditional wool to the newest synthetics. Thinner synthetic fabrics may be cooler than wool but won't withstand abrasion or protect your skin in a crash. Thin Lycra will fall apart in off-road use–it gets torn by bushes or sandpapered through in the seat by the granite boulders you perch on for lunch. Several manufacturers now make Kevlar-reinforced shorts that are a bit stiff and quite expensive, but *highly* protective in crashes. Since abrasions on the hip are the slowest to heal, such crash-proof shorts may be worth the money if you plan to compete.

Cycling shorts should have a high-quality pad in the crotch to protect this vulnerable area from abrasion and jarring. Formerly, all good shorts sported a leather pad called a "chamois"–even though the leather was really cowhide. The chamois has been replaced by synthetic substitutes on most shorts.

Still, some riders prefer the real thing. Leather quickly gets slippery when treated with ointment and subjected to sweat–an advantage, since your skin will slide on the chamois and reduce the abrasion that causes skin irritation and leads to saddle sores. But leather chamois has to be washed carefully by hand in a mild soap after each use, then dried slowly away from direct sunlight or heat. To keep the leather soft, it has to be "rubbed up" before it has dried completely and then treated with a special chamois ointment. In fact, it is a cycling ritual to hand wash shorts immediately after a ride. But shorts equipped with chamois dry so slowly that you'll need several pairs if you ride frequently or are on a multiday tour.

Synthetic chamois, on the other hand, can be tossed into the washer and dried quickly in the sunlight or in a dryer. This makes it the choice of tourists who often need to throw rain-soaked shorts into a dryer for use the next day. On the negative side, synthetics don't seem to offer the lubricating advantages of leather. You'll have to try both, and see what fits your riding–and laundering–style. Some riders use real leather for long weekend rides and stick with synthetics for shorter evening sorties where abrasion resistance isn't so crucial. Bear in mind, also, that some riders are mildly allergic to the substances used in tanning; changing from leather to synthetic chamois often clears up otherwise mysterious cases of saddle sores or rash.

Regardless of the kind of chamois you choose, you'll need to wash your shorts thoroughly after each wearing. Perspiration and road grime build up quickly in the groin area, and if you ride a second time in dirty shorts, the soiled saddle pad will abrade your skin and increase the chances of infection. If you absolutely can't wash out shorts, at least scrub down the chamois with rubbing alcohol to remove most of the encrusted sweat.

Shorts come in regular or bib models. Regular shorts can be pulled down without taking off your jersey, a real advantage for quick pit stops, especially for woman riders. But they often work their way down gradually as you ride or fall abruptly and embarrassingly when you stand up to climb or sprint, *unless* they have a drawstring at the waist.

Bib shorts move with the rider and stay up in sprints!

Bib shorts stay up better without a tight drawstring, but if you still prefer the regular kind–and if you dread the thought of inadvertently mooning your training partners in a sprint–consider suspenders. They hold your shorts in place just as well.

For people who feel uncomfortable in form-fitting cycling shorts, touring models that resemble hiking or running shorts are available. On tours, these shorts–which also contain a chamois–help you blend in with the crowd if you plan to combine riding and sightseeing. They have pockets that supplement the load-carrying capacities of your jersey. And for riders who can't seem to achieve the slim silhouette of the professional racer no matter how hard they ride, the looser cut is more forgiving of a little excess flesh.

Try on several pairs before buying. Make sure the legs are long enough so they don't ride up and expose the inside of your thighs to irritation from the saddle. The waist should be cut high, especially at the back, to avoid a gap between shorts and jersey when you're bent over in a normal riding position. An elastic or drawstring waistband is more comfortable than belt loops, although suspenders work as well with touring shorts as with Lycra models.

Shoes and Socks

Socks are easy. They should be either a nylon-and-wool blend or nylon and polypropylene. Look for ankle-length socks. They'll be cooler than higher ones and restrict your Achilles tendon less. And if you ride in the rain, shorter socks don't droop as badly from the weight of accumulated water.

White socks are preferred by racers chiefly because the United States Cycling Federation requires them, but others like socks with graphic designs on the side. Suit yourself, but in either case, choose those with a white foot area so dye–which can cause infection–can't get into blisters.

Choose touring shoes without cleats if you are a casual rider or if you plan to go on a tour that features quite a bit of walking. Good ones have stiff soles to protect your foot from pedal pressure and to help you avoid the numb and burning feet long rides can produce. They also should have firm heel counters, much like running shoes, to resist excessive pronation–the inward roll of the anklebone–as you pedal. Look for sturdy toe caps so toe clips don't irritate your toes. Another plus is a leather reinforcing patch where the outside of the toe strap comes over the foot.

Nylon mesh uppers work better in hot or wet climates because they dry rapidly. If you plan to ride in cold weather, opt for the greater protection of predominantly leather uppers. And remember: Leather will give

Touring shoes have stiff sole inserts for painless pedaling but are comfortable for walking, too.

with wear and conform to your foot, while nylon mesh will always be the same size.

Soles of touring shoes should be slightly patterned for easy walking on slippery surfaces. Shoes should slip into the pedals and straps readily, yet grip the rear cages of the pedals almost like cleats. Finally, they should be comfortable for walking.

You'll have to try on several pairs to find what you want. Bring the same thickness socks to the store that you plan to use on the bicycle so you can get a correct fit. You don't want your foot slipping around in the shoe as you pedal.

Cycling shoes with cleats are preferred by all racers and the majority of strong recreational and fitness riders. They are stiffer in the sole for better power transfer, and the cleats align your foot properly on the pedal to eliminate knee problems. Also, cleats encourage a smoother and more efficient pedaling motion, because you can pull the pedal through the bottom of the stroke more powerfully.

But–they're awkward and uncomfortable to walk in. In fact, continued walking will ruin the cleat, so if you plan to see the sights while you tour or if you have to walk a 200-yard gravel driveway each time you ride, you may want to stick with touring shoes.

Soles should be stiff and drilled for both conventional cleats and the three-hole Look pattern that is rapidly becoming an industry standard. The shoes should slip easily into pedals with toe clips, so look for smooth undersections in front of the cleats–ribbed patterns often hang up on the front cages of the pedals. And finally–if the store will allow it–try engaging and disengaging the shoes using your step-in pedal system. Each one seems to have its own idiosyncrasies when mated with different shoe sole designs.

Step-in pedal/cleat combinations are safe and increase cycling efficiency.

Choose either mesh or all-leather uppers on the basis of climate and rainfall conditions. Traditional shoes used laces. But with step-in bindings, the uppers of laced shoes have a tendency to pull away from the soles, because there is no toe strap resisting the upward pull of hard pedaling. As a result, most cycling shoes now use Velcro fasteners with straps that circle the upper and attach firmly to the sole. Velcro has two additional advantages: It can be adjusted while you are riding, and it's makes getting out of the shoes quick and easy—a real plus for triathletes.

With any shoe, the most important criterion is proper fit. Many otherwise fine shoes may not be comfortable on your particular foot, so try on as many pairs as possible before you make your choice. If the shop has a stationary bicycle or a wind trainer, ask if you can pedal for a while—shoes that are perfectly comfortable when you try them on often become unbearable 5 miles down the road.

You don't want to purchase cycling shoes from mail-order catalogs. Sizes vary widely, and a European size 44 from one manufacturer may be a full size different when it comes from another maker. And you can't try on catalog shoes to see how they feel. Unless you are willing to invest time and effort sending shoes that don't fit back to the mail-order company, stick with your local bicycle shop.

Jerseys

Cycling jerseys—shirts to the rest of the world—are available in lightweight fabrics for summer, with ventilating mesh under the arms and down the side. For cooler climes, manufacturers provide long sleeves, heavier materials, and even light fleece linings and a wind-breaking nylon front panel.

You can choose from solid colors, wild combinations, or the jersey of your favorite pro team emblazoned with your favorite manufacturer's name. But regardless of what they look like, a jersey's most important functions are protection from the elements, load-carrying capacity, and visibility.

The amount of protection you get is directly related to the material you choose. Cycling jerseys were traditionally made of wool or wool blends. Although they are increasingly hard to find, they still have advantages. Wool is warm when wet, wicks moisture away from the body, and it's a fabric with body, so a jersey with heavily-loaded pockets retains its shape. Unfortunately, wool is scratchy, prone to shrinkage, and in better grades, expensive. As a result it has been almost totally replaced by synthetic materials—Lycra, lined with polypropylene, for example, or Thermax.

They have all the advantages of wool but don't shrink, irritate the skin, or cost as much. Earlier synthetics tended to absorb and retain body odor so efficiently that a jersey quickly became unwearable in polite company—despite repeated washings. But in modern synthetics, that problem has been virtually eliminated.

Match jersey fabric to the weather. Choose light Lycra and mesh jerseys for hot and humid summer rides close to home. In the spring or fall, go one grade heavier with a polypropylene or Thermax short-sleeved jersey, adding arm warmers for cool mornings or evenings. When the temperature gets down into the 50s, don a short-sleeved jersey over a lightweight, long-sleeved polypropylene top—if you get too warm, pull up the sleeves.

When rain threatens or an approaching front promises much cooler weather before your ride is over, stash a waterproof but breathable (ala Gore-Tex) windbreaker in a pocket. In really cold weather, go for wool or polypropylene cycling jackets with zipper fronts and nylon wind facing. Or go for the ultimate in winter protection—a jersey with a layer of neoprene laminated inside. These are somewhat stiff, but in cold, wet conditions they are unbeatable. They are a major reason modern professionals can race in the bitter cold of a European February that would have forced out half the field in the days of wool jerseys and plastic raincoats.

Two special situations merit discussion here.

Situation one: If you are racing or riding in a group where crashes are a possibility, always wear a thin short-sleeved shirt under your jersey no matter *how* warm it is. If you fall, the jersey will slide on the undershirt and dissipate some of the friction, saving your skin. A short-sleeved polypropylene T-shirt works well as does a much lighter polypropylene "liner shirt" available in some bicycle shops. Traditionalists still choose wool T-shirts although they are nearly impossible to find. Avoid cotton T-shirts. A wet cotton T will chill you no matter how warm the weather.

Situation two: Cycling in the mountains. Large elevation changes produce rapid and unpredictable temperature and weather changes. In a single hour you can be laboring up a mountain pass in intense sunlight, caught in a bone-chilling mountain shower, and descending at 40 or 50 mph in a snow flurry. When riding in the mountains, either on the road or on a mountain bike, wear a polypropylene or wool undershirt, and a warm jersey, and carry a jacket. You can always take off the undershirt for a hot, extended climb, but if you get chilled on the descent, hypothermia–a life-threatening loss of body heat–is a constant danger.

Regardless of fabric, jerseys should fit snugly. You don't want excess fabric flapping in the breeze or the jersey sagging when you put a banana or extra water bottle in the pocket.

As with shorts, check construction, especially zippers and pockets. Poor-quality zippers will shorten the life of the garment, since they are hard to replace if they fail prematurely. Metal zippers are cold against the skin and often irritate it, so look for nylon zippers instead. If the pockets are sewed on insecurely, you may lose car keys or other important cargo in midride.

Look for a jersey with three pockets so heavy objects can be carried in the middle.

The second important function of a cycling jersey is load-carrying capacity. Choose jerseys with three rear pockets. Many models have only two, but that's a design flaw with several disadvantages. You can't get as much payload in two pockets as you can in three, but the balance problem is more critical. If you put something heavy–a water bottle or folded windbreaker for instance–in one of your jersey's two pockets, the weight will be off-center. As you ride, the object will work its way around to your side and make you uncomfortable. When you stand to climb, it will bob and sway, tugging you subtly off-center on each pedal revolution. With a three-pocket jersey, on the other hand, you can put heavy items in the middle pocket, where they'll ride securely–and balanced–in the small of your back.

Old-fashioned jerseys often had buttons to close each pocket, but newer models either have an elastic pucker string sewed in or are cut on a bias, so they are closed while you ride. Pockets that hang open are bad news–they let valuables fall out and they catch air like a drogue parachute.

High visiblity is the criterion for a good jersey. Choose bright colors that show up against the background of highway and horizon. Yellow, orange, white, and bright red are all good choices. Some professional jerseys resemble rainbows. If the aesthetics are questionable, they nonetheless advertise your presence very effectively.

Earth tones and pastels, on the other hand, don't give approaching drivers nearly as much warning—you blend in too well with the background.

Leg Warmers and Tights

Jerseys keep your upper body warm in inclement weather, and that's important. But it's even more important to protect your legs. They work so hard when you ride that they often don't feel cold, but they get the brunt not only of windchill but road spray, too.

Cold muscles are more likely to cramp, and cold tendons are more susceptible to tendinitis. Knees are an especially crucial area. If your hamstrings cramp from the cold, fixing the problem mostly means getting inside to warm up. But if you succumb to patellar tendinitis—an inflammation of the tendons that flex the kneecap—recovery involves time off the bicycle.

Leg warmers can be taken off later in the ride as the day warms up. Always wear them under *shorts.*

The best way to protect your knees? Always wear tights or leg warmers if the temperature is below about 65°F. Some racers are even more cautious: They ride with covered legs until the weather warms well into the 70s. Personal experience is clearly the best guide, because some riders seem to have more resistance to cold than others. And 65° on a calm, sunny day will have a far-different effect on your knees than 65° in the wind with melting snowbanks along the road.

Use leg warmers for variable conditions. Put them on in the morning cold, take them off in the afternoon heat. Good ones reach from your ankles to the tops of your thighs, with stretchy ankle bands so they pull on or off over your shoes but stay out of the chain as you pedal. With a little practice, you can even pull off well-designed leg warmers while riding, but don't try this trick if the ankle band is too snug. One caution: Avoid leg warmers with ankle zippers—an unnecessary refinement that only adds weight.

Cycling leg warmers go on under shorts, not on top, so the legs of the shorts help hold them in place. Pull your leg warmers on first, then your shorts. The best leg warmers are made of synthetic blends, which fit snugly without creeping down during use. They may also have elastic at the top—but watch out for elastic that's too tight. It can constrict circulation, leaving a compressed line in your thigh for hours after a ride. What's worse, even the best elastic bands don't usually do what they're supposed to—keep the leg warmers up. That's more a function of fit and fabric. Whatever your leg warmers are made of, they should cling to your shorts. To reduce slippage, some makers add rubber inserts at the top of their leg warmers. But if you still have trouble, consider using small safety pins front and back to cinch the leg warmers tighter.

For colder conditions, use tights. If temperatures won't go much below 50°F, synthetic tights are best. They are sleek and aerodynamic with enough thickness to hold some insulating air against your body. In colder temperatures, go with thicker fabrics like polypropylene or wool. For extreme cold, add nylon wind panels on the front. And if you're male, be sure these panels extend into the frontal crotch area: Penile frostbite is a real possibility in temperatures below freezing. The neoprene-lined material mentioned in the section on jerseys is also available for tights, although some riders find the stiffness and increased bulk bothersome.

Because tights are thicker and more protective than leg warmers, they don't have as much elasticity at the ankle. That makes zippers a good idea. Look for nylon zippers, securely sewn.

Unlike shorts, tights are usually designed to be worn with suspenders. Bib tights are available that eliminate the bulk and occasional problems with twisting experienced with suspenders, but they have their own disadvantage–they're impossible to remove without taking off your windbreaker or parka.

Rain Gear

The cheapest rain gear is a plastic garbage sack with holes in appropriate places for your arms and neck. Pull it on under your jersey for emergency rain protection. The plastic won't breathe, so you'll soak in your own sweat, but at least you'll stay warm in the typical summer shower.

But cyclists are usually affluent enough to enjoy more sophisticated rain gear–suits made of water-repellent but breathable fabrics like Gore-Tex. These materials–which let sweat vapor escape but keep rain water out–are far better than earlier attempts at rain gear for active people, but they're still a compromise. If completely waterproof, they trap the sweat from hard cycling and soak you from the inside. But if they ventilate well, rain seeps through. In short, the perfect rain gear doesn't yet exist. It is currently impossible to ride for long periods in heavy rain and stay completely dry. With that in mind, think of rain gear as a way to trap enough warm air so that you don't get chilled–you're going to get wet, but you don't have to be cold.

For warm-weather rides when showers threaten, pack along a light rain jacket made of Gore-Tex or similar material. The best models have hoods that either detach and fold into a pocket or roll up into a zippered compartment in the collar. Hoods aren't all that useful when you're actually on the bicycle because they usually aren't cut large enough to fit properly over a cycling helmet. They also limit peripheral vision unless they're cut perfectly so that they rotate when you turn your head. Still, they're a useful accessory because you'll often use them *off* the bicycle–on touring trips, for example, when you're hiking through the woods at your destination, or when you're using the jacket as a windbreaker for jogging, or just walking around the neighborhood.

The most expensive jackets have underarm zippers for maximum ventilation. If it is cold or you're not moving around, keep them zipped up. But when you are tackling a tough climb in the rain, unzip them all the way and open the jacket at the neck. The cross ventilation will help you stay cool without letting in a significant amount of rain.

Rain jackets should also be cut long enough in the back to protect you from spray off the rear wheel. Some models have a spray flap that tucks up underneath and secures with a Velcro flap when not in use. And pockets are always useful–securely fastened, of course, with nylon zippers.

Rain jackets can be purchased with as

many options as the typical car: full-length nylon linings, elastic cords at hood and waist (secured with plastic cord locks), and multiple pockets with zippers or Velcro. Many of these bells and whistles are useful, but they come at a price. Such jackets are not only more expensive, they're often heavier and bulkier, too. Try this test before you buy one: Roll it up and see if it fits neatly into a jersey pocket. If it doesn't, you probably won't tote it along–and a jacket lying in your closet won't keep you warm and dry when the deluge arrives.

Consider buying matching rain pants when you purchase your jacket–it's nice to be dry, top *and* bottom. Get them big enough so they are comfortable when you're crouched over in riding position and long enough to cover your ankles even when your leg is bent at the top of the pedal stroke. It won't matter if they're a bit baggy. If it is pouring so hard you need rain pants, a little extra wind resistance won't matter.

You'll also want elastic (and a drawstring) at the waist, ankle zippers for quick suit-ups when it begins to rain, and a Velcro ankle strap to snug the fabric around your leg so it doesn't foul in your bicycle's chain.

Buy only the brightest colors. A cyclist's naturally low visiblity is worse in flat light

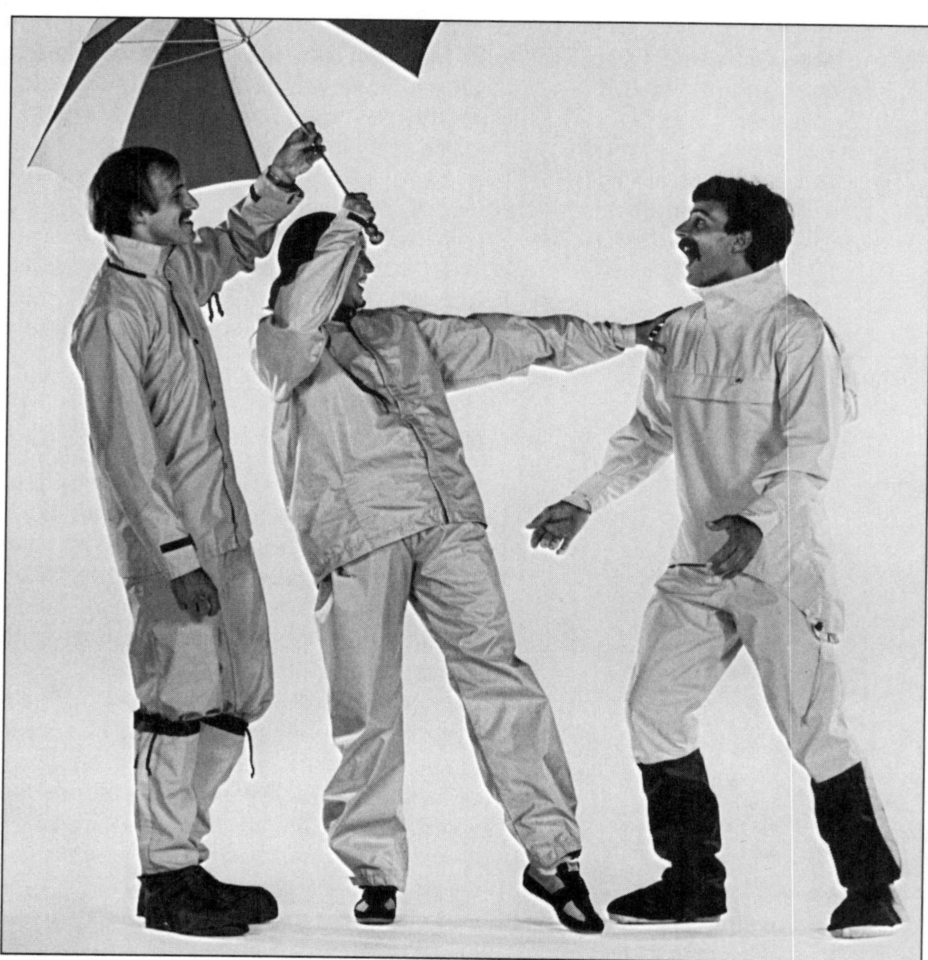

Look for roomy, bright-colored rain gear made from breathable fabric.

and fog–the very conditions in which you're most likely to wear rain gear. Choose colors like yellow, orange, or red that broadcast your presence even in gloomy rain or the swirling spray kicked up by passing trucks.

Shoe Covers

For long rides in rainy weather, you'll need several other pieces of equipment. First in importance are shoe covers, manufactured from a variety of materials.

Models made of plastic-impregnated fabric are waterproof but hold moisture inside. In addition, water often leaks through the needle holes in the seams, so if you want a truly waterproof shoe cover, treat the seams with a brush-on seam sealer (available from backpacking or mountaineering shops).

Shoe covers made from a Gore-Tex fabric are a fairly water-repellent alternative and breathe well in most conditions. But many shoe covers today are made from neoprene, modeled after wet suit socks. They are warm and dry but, again, neoprene retains perspiration.

Neoprene shoe covers will keep your toes toasty on cold, wet rides.

Regardless of material, shoe covers should fit snugly. Look for sturdy soles you can walk in without shredding. If you wear cleated cycling shoes, you'll have to cut holes in the bottoms of the shoe covers to expose the cleats. But if the holes are precut, make sure they are the correct size and in the right positions for your cleats. Regular cleats, for example are both smaller and farther back than Look cleats.

Zippers should be on the back of your leg so they don't soak through as quickly. And no matter how waterproof the fabric or well-designed the zipper system, most shoe covers fail around the top as water hits your legs and runs down into the shoes. A tip: If you're wearing rain pants, don't tuck them into your shoe covers–they'll funnel water directly into your shoes. Overlap them instead with the rain pants edged over the shoe covers like shingles on a roof.

Without rain pants, look for shoe covers that seal tightly against your leg with a Velcro tab. They'll still leak, but they won't scoop up water the way a loose-fitting pair will.

Gloves

Even when your hands don't need protection from the weather, they still need protection from two other hazards: road shock when you ride rough pavement and deep palm abrasions if you crash. Traditional fingerless cycling gloves perform both functions admirably.

Look for leather palms and either a mesh or Lycra back. The mesh is cooler, but Lycra is more aerodynamic and provides a snugger fit. Try on gloves before you buy to be sure they are large enough when you have your hand wrapped around the bars and brake levers.

In warm rain, wear your regular

Gloves protect your hands from road vibrations and crash abrasions and are colorful, too.

(fingerless) cycling gloves. But if it is cold, protect your hands with long-fingered gloves; if your hands get numb, it is impossible to work shift levers properly. What's worse, you may be unable to brake with precision and power. Finding the ideal wet-weather glove isn't easy. Fleece-lined leather gloves work great until they soak through, at which point they are nearly useless.

Gore-Tex gloves keep your fingers dry but cost a lot and aren't very durable—a real liability if you brush debris off the tires with your gloved hand and the whirring tread abrades your investment. Neoprene gloves are durable and keep your hands warm, but they're stiff, they don't breathe well, and unless the fingers and palm are studded with rubber, slip disastrously on wet handlebar tape. As in much other wet-weather gear, compromise is in order.

To complete your foul-weather outfit, wear a billed cycling cap under your helmet to keep flying raindrops out of your eyes. Some cyclists like to wear goggles in the rain, but others find that they fog up and quickly go opaque from road grime.

Skin Suits

Skin suits are specialty items—formfitting jersey and shorts one-piece combinations designed for speed. Although they aren't practical for long rides because they don't have pockets, they are so comfortable that many riders wear them anyway, carrying gear in a fanny pack or under the seat in a wedge pack. They really shine in time trials or short, fast criteriums where load-carrying capacity isn't an issue but air friction is. Because they fit literally like a second skin—without wrinkles or loose material to catch the wind—skin suits are ideal for these high-speed events.

Trim, formfitting skin suits are sleek and fast.

Try on the skin suit you plan to buy. Size means little. Two 6-footers, for example, who technically would wear the same size, can have vastly different leg lengths. What's that mean when buying a skin suit? If you normally wear a "medium" jersey, a skin suit in that size may be too tight in the legs and too short in the body–but it may fit your equally tall buddy perfectly. It is generally better to buy a suit slightly oversized in the upper body so it won't constrict your breathing when you go for speed. Beyond sizing, look for the construction features that distinguish good-quality cycling garments: sound seams, a good zipper, and correct cut.

Helmets

In many ways, a protective helmet is the most important piece of equipment you can buy. Cycling is a reasonably safe sport, but when accidents happen your head is in *immediate* jeopardy. Pavement is hard, rocks and trees line the road, and automobiles are made of a notoriously unyielding substance. It is perilously easy to bump your head when you fall, and the results are almost always serious. Abrasions, cuts, even broken bones generally heal up with no trouble, but head injuries can have a lasting impact on your life–if they don't end it. Even the most minor of head injuries can be deadly.

The heart of a protective helmet is the lining, usually made of a crushable foam material. When you hit your head, the lining deforms to absorb the impact. Most helmets have an additional outer shell of hard plastic, but newer models dispense with the shell to save weight. Helmets without shells would seem to be less protective, but in actual practice they pass the toughest certification tests with ease. Many riders, however, like hard-shell helmets for off-road riding, where the danger of falling on sharp rocks is greater, and save the lighter models for the road.

Some experienced cyclists disdain quality helmets and ride bareheaded. They argue that bicycle handling skill keeps them out of most accidents, and their tumbling and general athletic agility allow them to avoid or minimize the impact of occasional crashes. But head injuries are all too common among the best cyclists in the world–the European professionals–who either don't wear helmets at all or don flimsy leather strap models that provide psychological protection at best.

The fact is, helmets are essential to your safety. Every time you ride, wear one–and make sure it's a helmet that meets the standards of one of the two helmet-testing organizations: The Snell Foundation or ANSI (Amercian National Standards Institute). You can be sure you are getting an approved helmet when the box advertises Snell or ANSI, and the helmet itself carries a matching sticker. Certification by one of these two agencies is the most important thing to look for when buying a helmet.

Fit is second. A helmet that is too tight will generate splitting headaches on the shortest ride–and in short order will be relegated to the closet. An oversized helmet, on the other hand, will flop around when you stand up to climb or slide over your eyes when you ride down a hill.

Most helmets come in three or four shell sizes, with removable foam pads in various thicknesses to customize the fit. Find a shell size that lets you use thin pads, since thicker ones often let the helmet wobble.

The pad that contacts your forehead doubles as a sweatband to keep perspiration from trickling down onto your goggles. If the pad becomes saturated, push the front of your helmet against your forehead, (make sure you're looking down so the sweat doesn't pour into your eyes) to wring it out. You can wear a sweatband instead of sizing pads, but remember: The sweatband completely encircles your head and is therefore warmer than pads spaced intermittently around the inside of the shell.

Ventilation is the third priority. Riding with a properly designed helmet should be as cool as riding bareheaded. Good ones achieve this miracle with air vents in the front of the shell that scoop air as you ride, circulate it inside the helmet, and then expel it out the back. Before you buy a helmet, check for generous vents, especially in the front just above your forehead.

Another crucial construction detail is the buckle. It should be made of high-impact plastic and be easy to engage and disengage even with cold hands. Straps should be nylon, firmly attached to the helmet. A helmet that comes off on impact won't do much to protect you.

Caring for your helmet is a cinch. After each ride, wash out the pads by holding the helmet under the faucet and running cold water over them. Press the pads against the shell with your fingers to wring them out. *Don't* remove the pads from the helmet to clean them–over time that weakens the glue that holds their backing in place.

You'll often see white stains–dried salt–on the straps at the nape of your neck, where perspiration has accumulated and dried. To avoid this, wash the sweat off the straps regularly. Scrub the strap where it goes under your chin because dried sweat can irritate tender skin. And every couple of weeks, sponge off the shell with mild soap and water.

One warning: Don't paint designs on the shell or put on decals. Paint and decal adhesive can corrode the shell material, weakening the helmet and, in many cases, voiding the warranty.

And finally, remember that the best helmet on the market won't save your head unless you wear it. Store your helmet on a hook right next to your bicycle so you put it on as a matter of course each time you ride–a life-saving habit!

Extras

Cycling shops and catalogs are full of tempting goodies. Most aren't vital, but they can make cycling a lot more fun.

Training stands or wind trainers. These allow you to use your own bicycle for indoor training in bad weather. Some models have small fans turned by the rear wheel–the harder you pedal the harder it *is* to pedal. These are thunderously noisy, so if you live in an apartment or want to listen to music while you ride, check out the newer models that use much quieter magnets to provide resistance.

Whatever you buy, the way your bicycle attaches to the trainer stand is of key importance. Standard models clamp the front forks and bottom bracket. Make sure the platform that holds the bottom bracket has channels to accommodate cable guides. Such trainers provide a secure mount for the bicycle, but the rear triangle–the back half of the frame–often moves around as you pedal. To avoid this–and the necessity of removing the front wheel–other models clamp the rear axle.

Rollers. The most traditional indoor training device is a set of rollers. Unlike training stands that clamp the bicycle upright, rollers force you to balance and steer the bicycle as you ride, developing handling skills. The major drawback of rollers is low resistance. Although they are great for developing a smooth spin–an efficient, circular motion–they don't provide the leg workout of wind or magnetic trainers. To surmount that problem, some rollers come equipped with fans, combining road-like resistance with the fun of balancing.

The ergometer/stationary bicycle. Long used in health clubs and exercise physiology labs, ergometers (known to everyone except scientists as stationary bicycles) provide rigorous and easily calibrated workouts. Avoid the inexpensive models with mattress seats and plastic pedals. An ideal ergometer for training purposes has dropped bars, a narrow saddle, and pedals with sporting clips and straps so it can be set up exactly like your regular bicycle. A heavy flywheel–more weight equals less vibration–will smooth out the pedal stroke and provide some momentum. Details to look for include a resistance device that can be easily adjusted while riding, a monitor that displays resistance in watts or calories and an rpm gauge.

The best wind trainers, rollers, and ergometers share certain characteristics. Frames should be sturdy for a lifetime of use. Look for metal parts that are either anodized or protected by heavy enamel to resist the corrosive effect of sweat in large volumes. Bearings on wind trainer fans should be sealed for longer life. Belts on rollers or ergometers should be well-constructed, with replacements easy to find in your area.

Repair stands. Nothing beats a repair stand for cleaning and maintaining your bicycle. It clamps the bicycle gently by the seat tube, allowing you to rotate it 360 degrees for easy access to all components while still working the brakes and derailleurs. Look for a stand with a wide, stable base; a tray for quick access to tools; and a pad on the jaws so your bicycle's finish is protected.

Less-expensive, collapsible models are the ticket if you want a stand for use at home as well as in motels or at races. They aren't sturdy, but they make up for it in easy portability.

Pulse monitors. Pulse rate monitors have become nearly indispensable for modern training. But buying the right one for your needs and budget is a lot more complicated than it appears.

First, be prepared to spend a substantial amount to get a quality unit. As with other cycling purchases, you get what you pay for, and a good monitor is the biggest single expense in cycling next to the bicycle itself. If you spend $200 to $350, you'll get a quality piece of electronics. For $25, you get junk.

Cheap, badly designed models are either grossly inaccurate or give inconsistent readings, because they often gather data through a sensor that attaches to your earlobe or thumb. More-expensive models have chest straps with three electrodes. The chest straps should also have additional straps that go over one shoulder to hold the electrodes in place when you stand up to sprint or when you wear the unit for other sports like running. If the model you buy doesn't have the shoulder strap, fabricate one with a length of shoelace or nylon webbing.

Most units have a monitor that attaches to your wrist like a watch, instead of to a handlebar. They aren't as easy to read when riding, but they go with you automatically when you leave the bicycle–theft is not a problem. And you aren't hooked to the bicycle with a wire in the case of a crash or quick dismount, although that isn't a problem with wireless models. Wrist-mounted units can also be used for other sports like running or cross-country skiing. But don't automatically eliminate handlebar-mounted monitors–they are easier to read, and you can easily jury-rig them to mount on your wrist.

Try out the monitor in bright sunlight, dim shadow, and other conditions you are likely to encounter on the road. Some displays are easy to read in all lighting conditions; others work well only in moderate and indirect light. Look for a display of adequate size, too. Some are so small that it's hard to read them under the best of conditions and almost impossible when the sweat is in your eyes and your head is rolling with fatigue–exactly when you need that electronic feedback the most.

Check to see how easy it is to change batteries. Some units conceal them under a simple plate, while others require a mechanical engineering degree just to find them.

If the unit has a wire from chest strap to monitor, make sure it is long enough to reach from your chest to handlebars or wrist, via your jersey sleeve, with some to spare. If the unit has no wire, but transmits the signal instead, does it still work when your jersey is sweaty? When you are wearing a thick winter cycling jacket? A nylon windbreaker?

Other questions: Are replacement parts easily procurable–spare batteries, electrode pads, and chest straps? Can the chest strap be washed when it gets encrusted with sweat?

And last, don't make a substantial investment in a heart rate monitor until you've talked to other riders. Find out what they are using, which ones they like, and which ones they regret buying. Experienced riders can tell you the advantages and foibles of each brand and steer you away from poorly designed models.

Car-top carriers. If you have a choice, transport your bicycle inside the car, where it will be protected from rain, road grit, and small debris that can fly up from the road and chip the finish. Inside, it is safe from the thin film of smashed bugs that inevitably coats bicycles carried on rooftop racks.

Most car trunks have room for a bicycle if you take off the wheels. Tie up the chain with a used toe strap, put the frame in the trunk with the rear derailleur up, pad it with an old blanket, and put the wheels on top.

Be careful when you close the trunk–the hinges may descend directly on the fragile wheels. And you'll protect other trunk contents from chain grease if you bag the frame in a plastic garbage sack.

If necessary, the bicycle can also fit in the backseat. Remove the front wheel, cover the chain, and stand the bicycle on its front forks and rear wheel directly behind the front seats. If your car is small, you'll have to remove the rear wheel, too.

But if your trunk is full of luggage and the rear seat is full of passengers, you'll have to carry the bicycle outside.

That means buying a carrier. Some carriers mount on the rear of the car, while others are roof-mounted. In general, the bicycle is better protected from rear-end collisions and flying road debris if it's carried on top of the car.

When buying any kind of bicycle-carrying system, the two most important considerations are how securely the rack attaches to the car and how tenaciously the rack grips the bicycle. Bicycles that fall off car roofs at 55 mph are usually totalled.

Racks most often attach to the car's rain gutters with clamps. Be sure the rack fits your car before buying. Many aerodynamic-shaped cars don't have visible rain gutters, so racks hook on with a tower-and-strap arrangement. These are secure enough *if* they are installed correctly. A useful extra is a locking system, so the whole rack can't be stolen, bicycles and all.

Many racks require removal of the front wheel. The front forks clamp to the rack with a quick-release skewer, the rear wheel is secured with a strap or cam device, and the detached front wheel rides in its own inverted fork. Other racks accommodate fully assembled bicycles, using a mounting arm that steadies the upright bicycle.

Before buying any rack, be sure it fits your car, and ask around among other cyclists to get recommendations.

LT
700

CHAPTER

Basic Training for Bicyclists

It doesn't take long for beginning cyclists to get hooked on the sport. One of the fascinations of cycling is in seeing how previously unthinkable distances become commonplace, how complex bicycle handling skills become ingrained. And once the initial skills are mastered, most new cyclists want to know just how good they can get. In the next four chapters, we're going to show you how to do exactly that–get good, starting with what you'll need to find out to improve your fitness and cycling ability, starting with a comprehensive training plan.

Facing Facts

Physical improvement, satisfying as it is, has built-in limits. If you don't recognize and accept those limits, frustration is an inevitable consequence. It's a basic fact of athletic training that performance = heredity + luck + training, and two of the three are factors over which you have *no* control.

One unalterable limit to your aspirations is your genetic ability. Some people are endowed from birth to be great cyclists. Their original equipment includes superior oxygen utilization capacity, the proper blend of fast and slow twitch muscle fibers, perhaps a greater ability to endure pain. As exercise physiologists put it: They chose their parents well. But there's little you can do about the genetic cards you're dealt. If you weren't blessed with a tough grandmother, you can't alter that fact. But worrying about what your personal genetics mean for your performance won't accomplish anything, and can in fact be counterproductive–so much so that it's probably best to forget about it.

You can't do much about luck, either. Good riders frequently seem lucky. They avoid flat tires, because they watch the road ahead for glass or gravel, while lesser cyclists blunder into obstacles. They practice their bicycle handling, so they don't crash on rain-slick corners. They choose the right "breaks" (opportunities to break away from the pack) in a road race and stop at just the right aid stations during a century. But all these examples, while they look like luck to the uninitiated, are actually the result of skill and experience. Accomplished cyclists often *make* their own luck.

But even the best rider can lose a tire to slivers of glass or crash when another rider goes down right in front of him. Perhaps a better definition of bad luck is ignorance. If we knew about the glass or saw the crash coming, we could do something about it. Bad luck, then, is what happens to us when our knowledge isn't up to the situations in which we find ourselves.

But the most important variable in the performance formula–training–is firmly in your control. Organized training centered on a training plan that's based on sound scientific principles helps you maximize your inherited ability *and* your luck.

Training plans aren't just for racers, either. If you ride for fitness, a training plan helps you get the most out of the time you spend on the bicycle. You'll complete club rides and centuries with less strain and more enjoyment. In fact, if you are at all serious about having fun on a bicycle, a few hours spent planning out your program will pay big dividends each time you ride.

The best time to put together your yearly training plan is at the end of the cycling season. In November, when the weather turns bad and the return of standard time darkens your training rides, take some time off the bicycle, stay fit with other activities, and plan your workouts for next year.

Setting Goals

You can't establish a training program unless you know what you want to accomplish. You need a clear set of goals for your cycling season so that when you head out the door, you know exactly what you want to achieve on that day, on that ride.

With goals, your training is directed and effective. Without them, you're just riding around–and if you don't know where you are going, any road will do.

The first step in goal-setting is to determine your strengths and weaknesses. If you've ridden before, objectively assess what you did well and what you did badly. Did you lack power on the hills? Then incorporate weight training, mountain biking, and climbing into your training plan. Were you always beaten in training-ride sprints for city limit signs? In that case, you need an organized program of speed work and–if you're really serious about turning on the afterburners–a comprehensive weight-training program. Learn from experience, and use that learning as you plan your next cycling campaign.

But what if you don't have any cycling experience? If this is your first season of riding, list goals as problem areas emerge. Analyze your performance weekly: Can you ride farther? Is your time up a local hill improving or getting worse? Can you suddenly keep up with training partners who used to leave you in the dust? The point: For effective goal-setting, be a thinking rider who analyzes his performance and learns from it.

Establish your goals on the basis of those events that matter to you. Don't train for centuries if you harbor a secret desire to be a criterium flash. If you hate long rides but love to go out for an hour and sprint against everything that moves, accept that fact–your goals should reflect *your* interests and talents.

Goals shouldn't be set too high, either. You can even state this principle in a formula: Goals = reality squared. When you set goals for the upcoming cycling season, cast a cold eye on your available time, your level of commitment, and your physical talent. Factor in all those potential anchors on your ambitions, then square their limiting effect. It is easy to overestimate your time, your talent, and your capacity for squeezing workouts into a tight time frame.

And while hovering on the brink of your ability to recover might be challenging and fun for a week or so, it can get old in a hurry over the full season to say nothing of a lifetime. It is better to set your immediate goals a little lower and still be riding and improving a year or two down the road than to set them so high that you burn out in months.

Finally, don't be afraid to alter your stated goals as the season progresses. Goals set up a year in advance are going to get compromised by changing circumstances in your life. If you planned to ride 1,000 total miles by June, but you accomplished that goal in May, upgrade your goal to 1,500 miles. If you planned to ride a century in September, but you got a promotion at work and have been putting in 60-hour weeks, the century may have to wait until next year.

Training Diary

The best aid in the struggle to learn from experience is the training diary–your personal daily record of your cycling experiences. Why? You won't get better in a gradual, steady curve. Improvement, when it comes, is usually an abrupt jump up to another step on the long stairway of physical training, followed by a long plateau–the time you stay on that step. The closer you get to your genetic limits, the harder the improvement comes and the longer you stay on each plateau. And doing *more* doesn't necessarily mean climbing faster. If you make the mistake of overtraining, you won't improve at all. Your performance may actually drop. So how do you decide if you are improving–doing enough but not too much? The answer: Your training diary, which lets you look back over a week, a month, or a whole cycling lifetime, plotting your performances against your training.

If you aren't keeping a training diary, start one with your next workout. It doesn't have to be expensive or elaborate. All you need is space on paper to record pertinent data each day. This will allow you to more objectively track satisfying progress or frustrating failure–and more importantly, to do something about it.

You can, for example, look back in your diary to see that two weeks ago, after averaging 150 miles a week all season, you threw in a 250-mile week that included a long ride, three interval sessions, and a race. And you were working full time. The diary also reveals that your resting pulse went from 48 beats a minute at the start of the week to 59 by Thursday, while your previously stable weight dropped 5 pounds. No wonder you feel flatter than a bladed spoke–you were seriously overtraining.

Training diaries let you catch mistakes like that–to see if you're doing just enough work for improvement, degenerating into sloth, or riding yourself into the ground.

Your diary doesn't have to be elaborate. You can, of course, buy a commercially designed model that has separate columns for heart rate, miles, body weight, and other information. Or you can buy a small vest-pocket calendar, and write in the workout each day. Some riders just divide sheets of paper horizontally into the days of the week, vertically into different data columns, and get 100 copies made every couple of years. The point here is that it doesn't matter what your diary looks like, as long as the information is readily accessible and in permanent form–some riders have diaries that date back a dozen years.

Keep the entries simple. Many riders get so enthused about charting their workouts that they fill pages each day with long narrative accounts of where they rode, what gears they used, and how the weather was. What they end up with is more journal than workout diary. One result: They find it difficult to separate the important information from the mass of recorded trivia.

So–stick to basic information. Start with the length of the ride, and use a cyclecomputer (a device for measuring distance) so you have an accurate measure. Many riders prefer to record all workouts by time rather than distance, figuring that time is a more accurate measure of effort–20 miles with a tail wind is a different ride than 20 miles head down into a gale–but the best plan is to record both because the two together provide the most accurate picture of the workout's intensity.

Many cyclecomputers have an average speed readout, invaluable information for smart training. You can use it for each training ride to compare your average speeds over a season, or use it for sections of the same ride. If your computer *doesn't* have the average speed function, you can compute it easily from time and distance figures.

Make a note of your route. Different training routes have different levels of difficulty. Don't describe the rides in detail. Instead, assign names to each of your half-dozen favorite rides. "Seven Hills," for instance, or "the Springville Loop." When you look back in the diary to discover how hard you worked on a particular day, you'll be able to evaluate the influence of terrain on your training, too–the flats of the loop, the long climbs on Seven Hills.

Your diary should also include an objective assessment of how you felt. The fact that you averaged 20 mph on two different rides on the same route isn't very useful information if you breezed through one and were gasping in the other. So include a subjective rating of your perceptions in your diary. A simple system is modeled after school grades. "A" means that you went fast, maybe even set a personal record, and felt great doing it. "B" means that you felt good. Reserve this rating for rides that were solid, businesslike, and productive. "C" means that you felt mediocre. As you rode, statements went through your mind like, "There's no snap in my legs today," or "Man, that hill felt hard." Designate the ride a "D" if major problems develop–you took 30 minutes to do a 10-minute hill. And "F" means that you were so exhausted that you couldn't complete the planned workout–or that you didn't even get out the door (OTD). In fact, an OTD is the ultimate check on your readiness to train. Workouts rated "A" through "C" are definitely worth doing. They improve your fitness and your skills. But a string of "Ds" in your diary indicates a problem–you're getting stale, you're overtraining, or experiencing a health problem. And if you can't get OTD at all, it's time to back *way* off and revaluate your plan.

Also include in your diary a short note about equipment or position changes. Have you changed your saddle height? Are you wearing new shoes or newly adjusted cleats? If you start having mysterious knee trouble, entries like these can help spot the problem. Did you ride on light wheels and tires instead of your normal training wheels? Maybe that sudden improvement in average speed was due to equipment and not to superior fitness.

Make a note of whether you trained alone or with others, since hammering along in a paceline (a group of riders moving at identical speeds one behind the other) will increase your speed several miles per hour.

And you'll want to record two important numbers: pulse and weight. Start with your body weight. Weigh yourself under consistent conditions–always just before breakfast but after visiting the bathroom, for example. There's no need to weigh in every day, but checking weekly helps you spot the insidious gains of winter overeating and the sudden weight loss that can signal overtraining.

For similar reasons, record your resting heart rate. Take it just as you wake up while still lying quietly in bed. Count for 15 seconds, with the first beat as zero, and multiply the result by four to get beats per minute. Then stand up and retake it. Record both figures in your diary like this: 48/56. Over a period of time, you can judge your fitness accurately by your idiosyncratic pulse rate fluctuations. Be forewarned that heart rate is a highly individual thing, so comparing your cardiac behavior to that of other riders is essentially meaningless.

Finally, record your time for key *sections* of the ride. For instance, you may want to time yourself up a certain hill every week or two so you can note your progress over the season.

Making all of these entries sounds time-consuming but actually takes no more than a minute or two. And if you keep your diary with your bicycle, you'll remember to actually record the data after each ride.

A sample entry might read like this:

Thursday, June 14.
HR. *48/58*
Weight. *165*
Training. *1 hour, 30 minutes on Orchard Loop, solo, 30 miles, avg. speed 20.0. B-. Cloudy, warm, light rain. Jammed all hills in 42/19 (2:45 on Coal Creek hill). Three downwind sprints (52/17). New pedals, saddle seemed too low. Legs still tired from Sunday's century.*

Once you've filled in your diary, remember to look back periodically to *use* all that accumulated information. Each January, review the previous year. Look for patterns and compare them. Be especially aware of periods when your performance declined. What changed? The diary can often help you see what you did or didn't do that led to the slump. And if you know what went wrong, you can keep it from happening again.

During the riding season, check your diary each week to find the reasons for problems or successes. A training diary gives you some hard information that can help you set up your goals.

The first step in creating your personal training program? Taming time. You have to determine how much time you have available to train. There's a direct relationship between training time and what you can accomplish as a cyclist. You can't, for example, do justice to the Race Across America if you train only 5 hours a week. Noncycling responsibilities cut deeply into the time most of us have available to train and recover—but that doesn't mean you should try to cram a professional racer's volume of training into *your* day. The usual result is a high level of stress and—quite often—*decreasing* performance. Too much too soon can put you out of the race. But administer the right amount of stress, and you'll get faster, instead.

Consider the following example. A top pro might train 4 to 6 hours a day. But then his masseuse massages him, the team mechanic tones his bicycle, and the sports director does all the rest: sets up his training program, makes travel arrangements, and evaluates his results.

You, on the other hand, train only 1 or 2 hours a day, but you work for 8 or 9, stop at the grocery store on the way home, and then watch your son or daughter play baseball. Your total stress load for the day is probably *higher* than the pro racer's, even though—technically—you trained only one-quarter as much.

There are two secrets to the prodigious performances of the pros. They train long hours, of course. But perhaps more important, they also rest long hours. Cycling is their job, and they are insulated from the extraneous demands of life the rest of us must deal with by a support structure of coaches and team personnel.

So—look at your responsibilities. How much time can you train and still do justice to your job, your studies, or your family—or all three? Don't forget to factor in rest. Time to recover from the training is important, simply because it is during rest that the improvement hard training initiates takes place. Your body repairs itself during sleep,

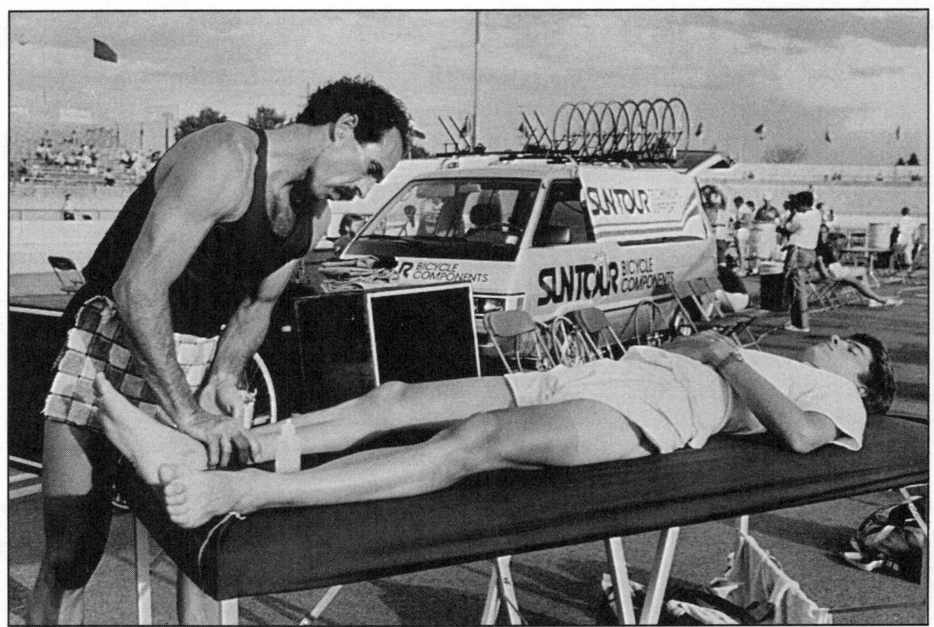

Massage is relaxing and aids recovery.

and when it's done, you're a little bit stronger than you were the day before.

As a rule of thumb, it is difficult for people working full time to ride more than 10 hours a week under the best of circumstances. Add overtime at work, heavy family responsibilties, and bad weather to that equation, and 5 or 6 hours can be a real accomplishment.

Evaluating Your Commitment

You also need to honestly evaluate your commitment. What do you want out of the sport? If it is basic fitness, you need to ride only about three times a week for 45 minutes to an hour each time. There's no need to compromise the rest of your life with long rides and hours of intense interval training. If riding strongly in club outings and local low-key competitions is your goal, move your commitment level up another notch. But if you want to race in United States Cycling Federation events, ride centuries competitively, and in general seriously compete, then you'll have to pay the price–large amounts of time and energy.

Be honest with yourself, too. Don't try to convince yourself that you want to race if you really enjoy casual rides in the country more. Ask yourself if you have fun racing. A surprising number of racers don't really like competition but keep at it because of peer pressure, or because they can't train for fitness without the specter of an upcoming race to goad them. What you want to do determines how much time you'll need.

The next step is taking a realistic look at how many *miles* it will take to achieve your goals.

Pros race between 90 and 180 miles more than 100 times a season. The average pro trains for this load by riding about 450 miles a week. In other words, his weekly training equals about three times his average race distance.

Let's use the same formula to estimate how much mileage you need. Suppose your cycling interest is racing. Junior or Category Three or Four road races seldom exceed 60 miles, and criteriums are in the 20-mile range. To do well in these races, riders need only 150 to 180 miles a week. Some Category Three riders will argue that they need more training to get ready for longer races when they advance to the more difficult Category One and Two competitions. But they have to get out of Category Three first by winning races, and they won't if their training makes them too tired to race well.

Women and riders over age 35 need even less mileage. In the USFC Road Championship, for example, the over-35 race is usually less than 50 miles, and the women go even shorter distances, so a training load of 150 miles a week is plenty.

But what about fast recreational riders who want to prepare for longer rides like centuries? They don't need 300 miles a week in training (three times the longest event) because centuries aren't ridden at road race pace. Fast recreational riders, like most amateur racers, can be successful and have fun on about 150 training miles a week if they're in reasonably good shape. But to prepare for centuries, they need to ride longer less frequently–about 4 hours every 10 days to 2 weeks. Average weekly mileage adds up about the same.

If your goal is fitness, you can get away with riding even fewer miles. You want to be fit enough to ride 25 miles on the weekend? Seventy-five miles a week will do it comfortably–4 or 5 hours on the bicycle, or four 1-hour-long sessions on the stationary bicycle.

Hard and Soft: Building Rhythm into Your Training

When you have a realistic estimate of how much time you need to spend on the bicycle, set up a yearly schedule that divides the year into distinct parts.

Off-season (November, December, and January)
Preseason (February and March)
Early season (April and May)
High season (June through October)

Coaches call this periodization, and it's as important to the recreational rider as it is to the pro. The idea is to use different types of workouts in each period, all designed to help you reach your goals in one way or another–maintaining strength in the off-season, for example, or building speed during the preseason.

The trick is to choose the right fitness and cycling activities, those that will help you be at your best when you want to be. Also, you must be careful to avoid the staleness and fatigue that come from too many hard miles and too much emotional energy poured into training. Workouts appropriately structured for each segment of the year lead to a higher level of cycling fitness just when you want it.

By periodizing your training you can plan your yearly training priorities. For example, it makes little sense to pile on the miles in March and build great endurance early if your century rides don't come until late summer. The time and energy spent on long miles will sap the speed and power you need for summer criteriums, time trials, or weekend 50-milers with the club. Early September, when the hot and busy summer is over, is the time to build the endurance necessary for 7 hours in the saddle. Of course, if you are shooting for the 100-mile USCF District Road Championship in June or your club's annual century ride on Memorial Day, you'll need your endurance earlier. Remember: Your training must be adjusted to fit your objectives.

Here's a sample yearly plan for a strong recreational rider or someone who so aspires.

Off-Season (November, December, and January)

Aerobics. Early darkness and bad weather conspire to limit your time on the bicycle. Don't worry. If you hammer hard all winter, you'll be tired and short of enthusiasm when you want to be sharp and eager to ride. So cut back your riding to perhaps twice a week, and reduce both intensity and distance. Get out for an easy spin on the weekend and again in the middle of the week. Use the wind trainer or ergometer indoors if weather or darkness keeps you off the road. Or ride in the snow and sleet on a mountain bike.

And don't worry too much about losing your wind if weather socks you in for weeks on end. You can retain your aerobic base and still have variety if you use the off-season to get your heart rate up in some noncycling activity. Try running, skiing, swimming, team sports, or brisk hiking.

Strength. Winter is the time to build the strength in your upper body that cycling doesn't. A comprehensive weight program takes little time and minimal equipment, and if it's done right, the risk of injury is low. Yet this modest investment will build the strength you need to stabilize your position on the bicycle, protect against injury if you crash, and improve your speed and endurance.

Preseason (February and March)

Aerobics. At this time of year, you'll want to make your workouts more directly related to cycling. A greater percentage of your time will be spent on the bicycle, either out on the road or on a wind trainer. These workouts should be done religiously and at a steady pace to build the aerobic base you need for the harder training to come.

Early season is also the time to get out on your mountain bike to work on bicycle handling and power while you're improving aerobic fitness wind. Plow through mud or snow, slide around corners, or chase your riding partners around a makeshift dirt criterium course. Get out and get dirty, and you'll be amazed at the power and bicycle handling improvements you'll experience.

Strength. Continue your weight program at this time of year, but ease off to accommodate the greater energy you are putting into riding. Preseason is the time to make the transition from overall body conditioning to training directly related to riding.

Early Season (April and May)

Aerobics and strength. Now, you'll need to emphasize the bicycle in your training. Stop doing the alternate aerobic activities like running, and spend the bulk of your training time actually on the bicycle. The exception: maintenance weight training twice a week to make sure that your hard-won strength doesn't vanish by the middle of the summer. Your cycling schedule at this point becomes fairly structured, including long rides for endurance, interval sessions, and several easy recovery rides each week. Now that the weather is better and you're on the road regularly, you'll also begin to reap the benefits of your year of training either by winning competitions or having more fun on solo and group rides.

High Season (June through October)

Here's the payoff for training wisely and well all winter. You're ready for your new program: training in two- and three-week cycles, aimed at specific races or noncompetitive events that you want to do well in or merely enjoy. Your early training has given you a solid base of aerobic fitness, power, and speed. Now take advantage of those skills.

Finding Time

As you can see, a yearly plan is an invaluable aid to help you become a better cyclist. But many cyclists can't think in terms of years–they have enough difficulty finding time each day to squeeze in their training. Let's look at some strategies to shoehorn enough fitness time into a busy schedule to be able to take advantage of carefully planned yearly schedules.

Unless you are working 14 hours a day, you can find some time to train in even the busiest schedule. The traditional training time is late afternoon following the workday. But darkness, late meetings, bad weather, or any number of other problems can nix your planned ride. The trick is identifying suitable blocks of time and organizing your day so you can take advantage of them. Let's look at some nontraditional workout times and how to use them:

The Early Bird Special

Early morning is a great time to train. It is cool at the height of summer, there's less traffic, and a brisk workout is an excellent way to start your day. If you make a habit of commuting to work, you probably know all about the advantages of early morning riding and have the routine down to a science. If not, you'll need to know both the advantages and drawbacks of early bird training.

The drawbacks start with the struggle to get out of bed. You'll have to discipline yourself to set the alarm early and roll out

Early-morning training is a great way to start the day.

when it rings. Another drawback of early workouts is that they rob you of sleep. Most people can discipline themselves to get up an hour early, but they find it impossible to get to bed early enough to make up for the lost sleep. As a result, they get tired instead of fit. The solution? Don't train early every day. Try it once a week, and assess how you are recovering. If all is going well, increase to two or three days. Trying to train hard five mornings a week without making up for the lost sleep somewhere else in your schedule is a recipe for overtraining.

Early workouts are also difficult because you'll have to do them before breakfast. It is nearly impossible to ride for more than an hour when you haven't eaten since the evening before. You can try a piece of toast while you are getting dressed, but substantial food right before riding sits heavily in your stomach when you try to do a quality workout. For this reason, limit your morning rides to an hour or less, and eat breakfast after the ride–even if you have to munch on a sandwich at your desk. Don't skip breakfast–you'll be famished by lunch.

For a quick getaway, prepare your bicycle and clothing the night before an early ride.

You can save time by putting out all workout clothes the night before, so you don't waste precious riding time fumbling around in the darkness looking for your shorts or shoes. Have your bicycle ready to go, water bottles filled, and tires pumped. Use butyl tubes for training, because they don't bleed air like the latex tubes used in expensive tubulars. Save the hot tires for important events in which you want to do well, not for everyday training when time is of the essence.

If it is still dark when you leave the house, be sure your clothing has reflectorized material sewn on and your bicycle has reflectors and lights. You may want to find a lighted residential loop near your house to ride around until it gets light enough to venture out on the open road.

Midday Motion

If you have an hour for lunch, you can fit in a worthwhile workout. Many people don't train at lunch, because they don't think it is worth the trouble to miss a meal, get dressed and cleaned up, and overcome the logistical problems of bringing the bicycle to work, all for a 45-minute workout. But 45 minutes a day equals 3 hours and 45 minutes a week or nearly 75 miles–plenty of exercise for fitness cyclists and a great start on a week's training if you have larger goals in mind.

The secret to lunchtime training is organization. You have to get on the bicycle as soon as possible, then get cleaned up and back to work in minimum time. With little planning, you should be able to be on the bicycle within 10 minutes. Practice will cut it down to almost 5. Again, have your workout clothes readily accessible, either laid out where you change or stacked in your gym bag in the order you'll put them

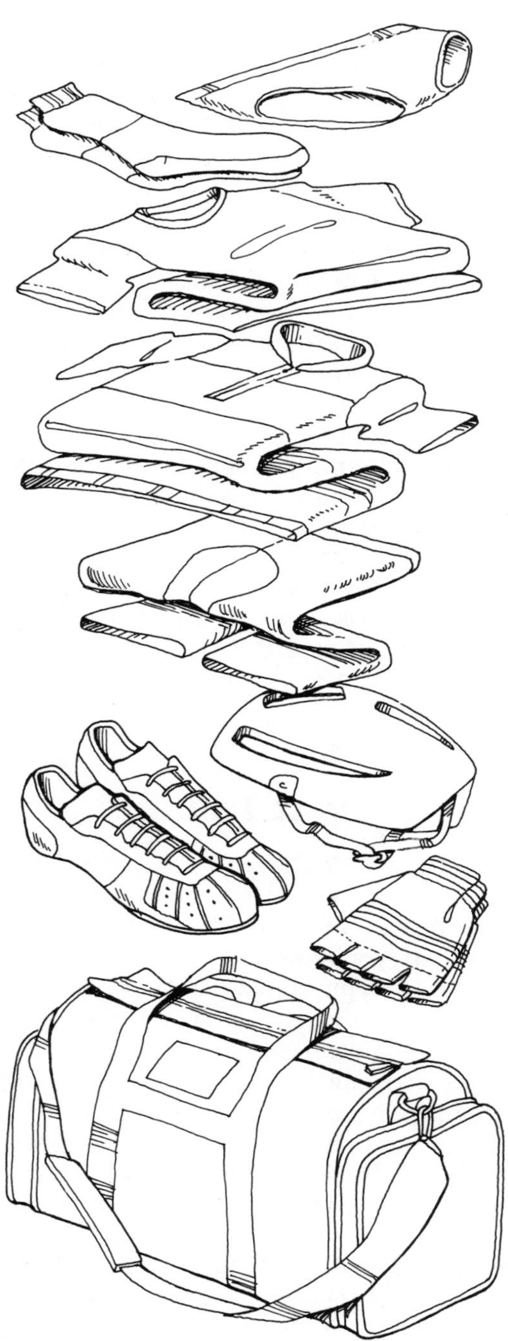

What goes on first goes in your gym bag last.

on: shorts, socks, and polypropylene T-shirt on top; then jersey and tights; finally shoes, helmet, and gloves. Hang up your good clothes in the same organized way to speed getting dressed after the ride.

Back at work, reverse the procedure. Take a quick shower if facilities are available, or towel off using rubbing alcohol. Seven or eight minutes should find you back on the job.

It's not a good idea to skip lunch for the sake of your workout. The best solution is to eat half your lunch at your morning break, the rest in the afternoon. You can also eat a banana or some fruit bars on the ride, but it is hard to eat and ride hard at the same time.

The stress of hurrying through the workout or worrying about getting back to work on time means daily lunchtime training may not be smart. If you have flexible lunch hours or just handle the stress well, you may find that lunch hour workouts are relaxing and make you more productive later in the day. But if you have to hurry frantically to fit them in, you may want to consider working out at a different time.

Night Owl Workouts

Night owl training is a workable option, especially with the advent of improved bicycle lighting systems. But the biggest drawback remains the danger of darkness. Make sure your bicycle glows like a disco, and choose safe, lightly traveled roads for your training. A lighted loop in a park or residential area may be a bit boring but better safe and bored than excited and injured.

Note, however, that some personality types simply can't handle late workouts. They get so emotionally charged by the ride that it takes them hours to fall asleep. The next day they're dragging. So try the midnight training special only if exercise *relaxes* you.

The Splits

Another option: Do part of your workout in the morning before work, and then finish it at lunch, after work, or in the evening. The big advantage of split workouts is versatility. Two-hour rides are possible even when you can't find an uninterrupted two-hour chunk of time. Just do an hour at 6:00 A.M. and another hour at 5:30 after work. Or ride before work, and take advantage of your company's fitness center to lift at noon. The possibilities are endless.

Exercise Efficiency

One secret to efficient workouts is making every second count. Take a tip from the efficiency experts, and examine your routine for ways to use the time you have to more effect. Some pointers:

Pursue quality rather than quantity. An hour at a brisk pace is worth more than 2 hours dawdling along. If you have 1 hour to ride, warm up for 5 minutes instead of 15 or 20. Then do sprints, intervals, long climbs, or time trials. You'll be amazed at how much improvement you can pack into 60 minutes.

Use a heart rate monitor. It keeps your training heart rate at optimum levels. Monitors eliminate wasted training time by providing objective information about how hard you are working.

Eliminate junk miles. A training ride with ten sprints has, as the core of the workout, ten repetitions of about 15 seconds each, separated by 1:45 of rest. But some cyclists do those ten sprints in a 2-hour ride. That constitutes an hour and 45 minutes of low-quality training. As an extreme example, suppose you have only 30 minutes to train at lunch. Warm up for 5 minutes, do your ten sprints in the next 20, and warm down the last 5. The mileage total won't be impressive, but you'll have ridden the miles that count.

Look for time-saving tricks. Use tires with butyl inner tubes rather than porous latex to save time pumping them before each ride. If you need to drive to work at 8:00 A.M., get up at 6:00 A.M., hit the road at 6:15, ride until 7:30, and shower and dress in 15 minutes. You'll still have an additional 15 minutes to eat a quick breakfast. Hint: Try oatmeal. It is easier to eat quickly than crunchy cereals like granola.

Ride by yourself to save time. Group rides may be fun, but driving to the meeting place, waiting for latecomers, and riding slowly while the inevitable puncture victims catch up eats time. Solo rides, involving none of the above, are simply more time-efficient.

Make minutes count with weight training. If you have only 45 minutes to ride before darkness, ride through the dusk, come home and do squats for 15 minutes, then warm down on the wind trainer. Squats provide intense work for your quadriceps, the muscles that propel you down the road, and in conjunction with riding, they will help you improve.

Heart-Smart Training

An important key to effective limited-time training is heart rate monitoring. Your heart rate is an excellent measure of how hard you're working. As you speed up from an easy pace, your heart rate increases proportionally. But at a certain point, called the anaerobic threshold (AT), your heart rate's increase slows, and you start approaching exhaustion. At your AT, your muscles can no longer eliminate lactic acid and the other byproducts of exercise that together produce the sensation of fatigue.

Exercise physiologists speculate that exercising at or just below your AT is the most efficient way to improve your overall aerobic power–the foundation of cycling prowess. And cyclists who train guided by

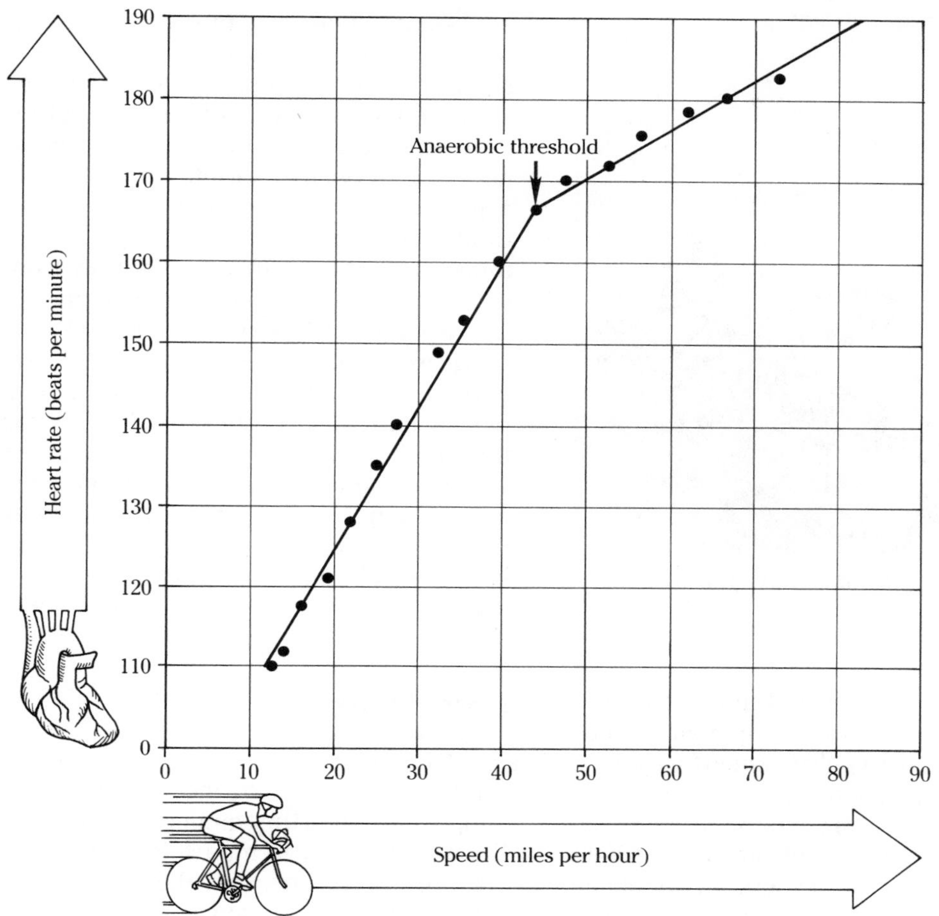

The Conconi graph shows how heart rate is plotted against speed to identify a rider's anaerobic threshold.

their heart rates have made some remarkable improvements.

The question then: How can *you* use heart rate training to become a better cyclist?

Buy a heart rate monitor. The best ones use three electrodes on a chest strap instead of earlobe or finger sensors. Some units connect the electrodes to the monitor with a wire, while others telemeter (radio) the information to the monitor. Monitors are relatively expensive, but like many high tech products, the price is coming down rapidly.

Determine your maximum heart rate. The most accurate figure is obtained from the results of a maximal oxygen uptake (VO_2 max) test that can be administered at a university human performance laboratory. A local sports medicine clinic can often provide the same service. The test measures the amount of oxygen your tissues can process–vital to endurance performance–but also gives an accurate estimate of your maximum safe heart rate. Because the test is done under medically supervised situations, the extreme exertion

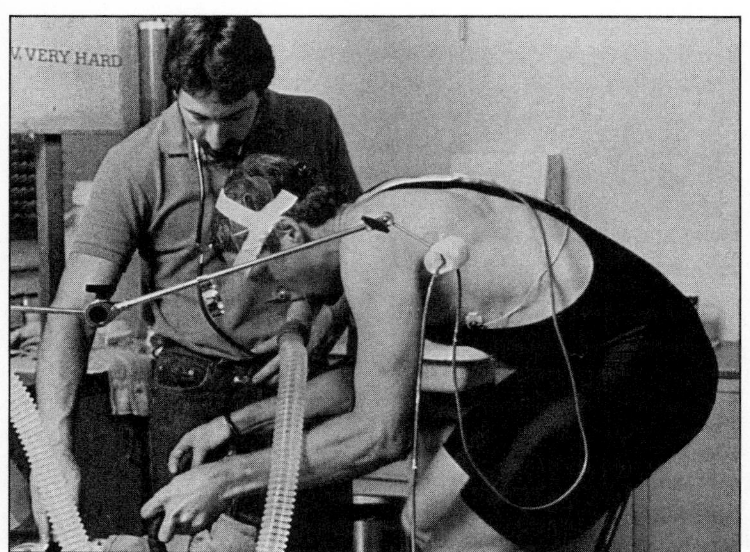

Physiological testing reveals your strengths–and where you need to improve.

levels required are safe. But ask that the test be done on a bicycle ergometer rather than a treadmill. If you've trained for cycling, running may give inaccurate results.

You can, however, determine your maximum heart rate without drawing a single deep breath. Calculate it yourself. Subtracting your age from 220 gives you a good, reasonably reliable estimate, and one that is safe, quick, and painless.

Calculate exercise intensity levels. For endurance training, 65 to 80 percent of your maximum is usually recommended. For instance, if your maximum heart rate is 190–the result if you're 30 years old–you'll train for endurance at a heart rate of 123 to 152. Anaerobic threshold training demands more–most experts recommend training at about 80 to 90 percent of maximum. With a top end of 190, you'd do anaerobic threshold training at 152 to 171. Your estimated anaerobic threshold is 88 percent of your maximum heart rate. Sprints and short intervals call for 90 to 100 percent of maximum.

Wear a heart rate monitor. It ensures that you are exercising at the correct intensity for that day's workout. After a few rides with the monitor, you'll develop a feel for the correct heart rate, and you can do endurance rides as well as sprints without it. It is a good idea, however, to wear it for AT training, because the 85 to 90 percent effort range is the most difficult to identify from subjective feelings of effort and fatigue.

Be careful when riding with a monitor. Look down at the display a second too long, and you may hit something big and hard–like a parked car. Never wear the monitor in mass-start races, because you'll need all your attention on the pack around you. Many top time trialists wear them in races against the clock so they can keep their effort hovering at most efficient levels.

Overtraining

One of the most insidious enemies of superior athletic performance is overtraining. Simply put, when the training load exceeds the body's ability to repair itself, performance levels decline, and the athlete gets frustrated and depressed, and eventually is forced to stop training to recover.

Overtraining is a serious problem for highly motivated athletes. The more dedicated they are, the more common overtraining problems become. Anyone training hard enough to improve significantly is at risk. Personality plays an important, but ironic, role. Athletes who always need to be pushed in training rarely overtrain. But disciplined athletes who are strongly self-motivated regularly do. They will accept nothing less than perfection, and eventually that drive to improve overloads their ability to recover from the training load.

How to avoid it? Understanding some key principles helps. The most basic principle of athletic training, for example, is that if you apply stress to the body by using it, your body will *adapt* to the stress and get faster or stronger or whatever's required to meet the new demand. But if you apply too much stress, your body will be unable to recover. The result: chronic fatigue and lower performance.

Frequency of stress is important, too. Well-trained cyclists can recover from the most exhausting workouts if they have enough time between training sessions to replenish the glycogen in their muscles and allow the cells to repair the damage caused by the workload. But if they try to repeat the hard workout before that recovery is complete, detraining (the opposite of improvement) takes place.

And it is the *total* stress load that determines the breaking point. The stress of your workout has to be added to the other stressors in your daily life: pressure at work, family responsibilities, financial worries. Pro cyclists who do little but eat, sleep, and ride can train the enormous miles their job requires without breaking down, in part because they avoid the debilitating effects of noncycling stress.

The Warning Signs

Fortunately, the symptoms of overtraining are well documented. If you are training heavily, be alert for several subtle but important signals of chronic fatigue and staleness.

Poor performance is the most obvious overtraining tipoff. If your times or placings nosedive, you need to reduce your training load. More gradual declines are harder to spot, so check your training diary periodically to make sure your improvement hasn't stalled. You should, for example, be able to ride longer with less effort as the season progresses. Review mileage figures in your diary as well as the subjective rating ("A" through "F") that you assigned to each ride. Effective training also allows you to recover faster. If you feel tired and still lack the desire to ride several days after a race, your body isn't adapting to the training stress.

Finally, your speed on shorter efforts should increase. Weekly club time trials or short timed intervals provide an objective way to measure your improvement. Always write down your times so you can refer to them later. If your times are stagnant or declining in spite of hard training, suspect chronic fatigue brought on by overtraining.

Increased resting heart rate is another sign you have done too much. Take your morning pulse under standard conditions as described earlier in this chapter. A heart rate eight or ten beats higher than normal usually indicates incomplete recovery and is a sign that you should go easy in your training, or even take rest days, until it drops back to normal. Not all athletes respond to fatigue in the same way, however, so wide fluctuations in resting heart rate don't always indicate high fatigue levels. You'll have to monitor your diary entries over a period of time to see if elevated resting heart rate has predictive value for you—whether or not it corresponds with performance declines.

Be alert for lack of enthusiasm, too. This is the OTD (out the door) test mentioned earlier. If you somehow can't generate your normal enthusiasm and excitement about training, you've probably overdone it. When your body signals your mind that it is tired and needs rest, your mind reacts by reducing the anticipation you'd normally feel at the thought of riding. Many cyclists berate themselves for a lack of will power and motivation when they lose enthusiasm, but trust yourself—if you don't feel like training, you almost certainly shouldn't.

Another common overtraining signal: the washed-out, draggy lethargy of chronic fatigue. If you have little energy for the normal responsibilities of life, it is a warning that your body's ability to recover has been pushed too far. If it takes all your energy to train, your body shuts down during the rest of the day.

Muscle soreness is another strong indicator of overdone training. After an initial conditioning period, the smooth motion of cycling shouldn't cause soreness. If you suffer from persistent soreness in your legs, even after easy rides, suspect overtraining. Chronic aches and pains mean that muscle fibers aren't recovering from training stress, and continued hard riding on sore legs can not only reduce performance levels dramatically but may even *damage* individual muscle fibers.

Can't get rid of that sore throat? Try taking a nap. An athlete who gets chronic infections like one nagging cold after another is probably overtrained. All the body's energy is going into training and recovery, leaving none for the immune system to operate properly. Cyclists often experience chronic infections of another kind, too: saddle sores that hang on stubbornly in spite of cleanliness and proper treatment. Road rash and other nicks that heal slowly or get infected in spite of good medical care are also good indicators of overtraining.

Severe cases of overtraining can cause major dietary disorders. The body is literally too fatigued to process food adequately. Seriously fatigued cyclists suffer from chronic diarrhea or, less freqently, recalcitrant constipation. These digestive problems reduce the amount of food energy available to the cyclist, making the onset of fatigue even more pronounced and the subsequent diarrhea worse. If overtraining has progressed this far, it feeds on itself in an ever-widening vicious circle.

Severe overtraining can also lead to psychological problems. Dr. William Morgan, a sports psychologist who has worked extensively with overtrained athletes, says, "I've never seen a stale athlete who wasn't clinically depressed." Morgan cites studies that show normal athletes exhibiting the so-called iceberg profile: high in vigor at the tip of the iceberg, low in anxiety and fear. Overtrained athletes, on the other hand, reverse this distinctive pattern and score low in vigor, high in anxiety and related traits. So overtraining has both physical and mental ramifications, both leading to poor performance.

Overcoming Overtraining

How do you combat overtraining? The first step is prevention. Plan your schedule so it includes plenty of rest days to allow your body time to recover from your training. Some athletes need more recovery time than others, so refer to your training diary and listen to your body until you discover the right mix of rest and stress for you.

Use periodization (breaking your routine into hard and soft workouts) to build in longer periods of rest during the year. Have a definite off-season when you enjoy *active* rest, keeping fit with activities other than cycling. Hammering away on the bicycle all winter is a recipe for mental and physical depletion by early summer.

If you do fall victim to overtraining, remove the cause. Start by taking a week off so your body can recover. Advanced cases may require as much as a month of rest. It may be difficult to slow down, but rest is the only cure for overtraining. You can ease the psychological distress of forced leisure by finding other things to do during your normal workout time: Go for a walk, go fishing, do chores, reaquaint yourself with your family. Make the rest period a *positive* experience.

When you fire up your training again, do it at a lower level. Cut distance and effort by one-third. Include more rest days or easy days on the bicycle. Monitor your body *carefully* during this recovery period so the pattern doesn't repeat itself. And don't be in a hurry to increase your training load—a

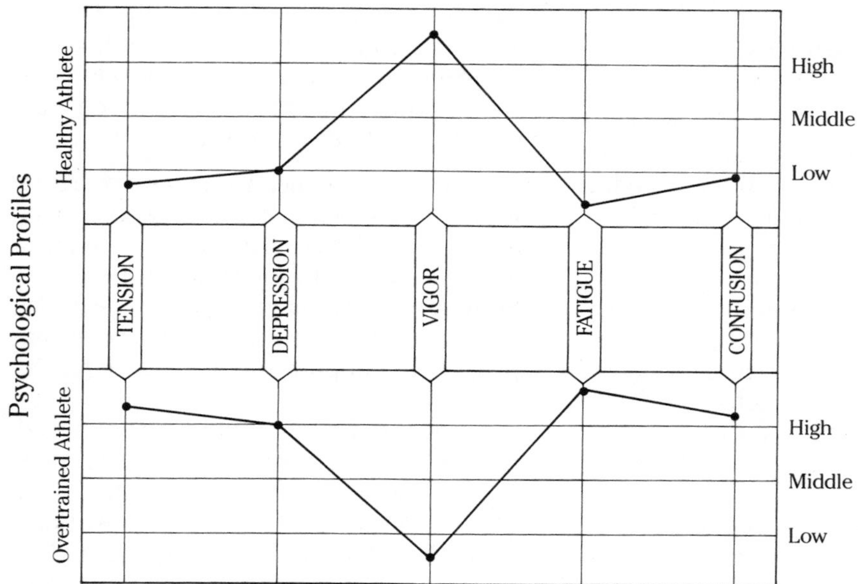

The so-called "iceberg profile" demonstrates the psychological differences between trained and overtrained athletes.

body overtrained once seems to be more susceptible to future overtraining.

Sample Schedules

The following weekly schedules are intended as suggestions for a cyclist with a nine-to-five job and family responsibilities who nonetheless wants to race or ride in fast club tours of 60 miles or so each weekend. *Don't* follow this or any other schedule blindly! Base your own training program on *your* situation, time, and goals.

Off-Season

Monday. Rest and recuperate. Clean and repair your bicycle. Spend time with your family. Run errands and do household chores. Negotiate a deal with your boss to work longer on Mondays and Fridays in return for more training time on other weekdays.

Tuesday. One hour on bicycle or indoor trainer. Steady ride with several sprints.

Wednesday. Run, cross-country ski, aerobics, circuit weight training.

Thursday. Mountain biking.

Friday. Rest.

Saturday. Aerobics or team sports for a warm-up followed by weight training.

Sunday. Ski, run, swim, family activities. Have fun!

Preseason

Monday. Rest and recuperate.

Tuesday. One-hour ride with several sprints and light weight training.

Wednesday. Mountain biking.

Thursday. Road ride at steady pace. If the weather is bad, run or ride on the wind trainer. Light weight training.

Friday. Rest.

Saturday. Easy ride, run, alternate sport, weights, etc.

Sunday. Endurance day. Long hike, run, or cross-country ski. Two hours on the bicycle or wind trainer at an endurance pace, or mountain biking.

Early or High Season

Monday. Rest.

Tuesday. One-hour ride with sprints or short intervals. An hour is usually easy to fit in before or after work. Trade a coffee break for an extra 15 minutes, and train at noon. Too dark, too early? Do the same workout on a wind trainer or ergometer.

Wednesday. Ride 90 minutes at your anaerobic threshold. If a big chunk of time isn't available, try 1 hour before work and 30 minutes at lunch. If you get off work late and darkness threatens, try 1 hour on the road, followed by 30 minutes on the wind trainer.

Thursday. Two-hour endurance ride. In terms of time, this is the tough one. Use a wind trainer for part of the ride or split the workout, doing 1 hour before work, 1 hour after. Or you could ride in darkness the last half hour or so, using appropriate lighting and reflectorized clothing.

Friday. Same as Monday.

Saturday. Ninety minutes at a steady but moderate pace. If you ride early in the morning, you'll have the rest of the day free for house chores and family activities.

Sunday. Sixty miles at a strong pace with a group, a fast solo ride, a race–use your fitness to enjoy your long ride.

These schedules won't get you ready for the Tour de France. But they do provide about 150 miles (or the off-bicycle equivalent) each week of varied training intensities. From April to October, they include a long ride and three medium-length rides that provide the opportunity for high intensity work.

You should, of course, adjust any schedule up or down to suit your cycling goals. Never adopt someone else's training schedule just because it seems to be working. Tailor it to fit your own unique situation and goals. For instance, if fitness is your priority, cut the Wednesday and Thursday rides to an hour or less. If you want to ride centuries, lengthen the Sunday ride to 80 or 90 miles, and cut the Thursday ride back to an hour. You'll still have the same time commitment each week, but the long ride will get you fit for those 100-milers.

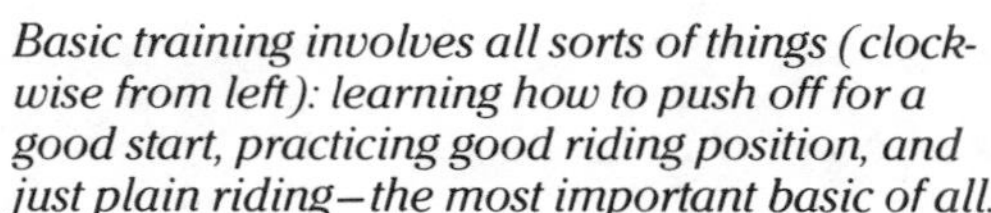

Basic training involves all sorts of things (clockwise from left): learning how to push off for a good start, practicing good riding position, and just plain riding—the most important basic of all.

13
BICYCLE CLASSIC
Levi's
RALEIGH
RALEIGH
SHIMANO

Bicycling Essentials

Like any sport, cycling has basic techniques you need to learn to enjoy the activity. Tennis isn't much fun if your stroke is ragged, and golf is a drag until you develop a smooth swing. If you just want to ride your bicycle around the neighborhood, the riding skills you learned as a child are sufficient. But when you become more serious about having fun on a bicycle–when you want to go for longer rides or use the bicycle for fitness –then you'll need to learn cycling basics to get full enjoyment out of the sport. In this chapter we'll look at techniques that every cyclist should know.

Proper Position

It's easy to recognize accomplished cyclists from a distance. The single most distinguishing characteristic of top riders, male or female, is their position on the bicycle. They have an unmistakable silhouette: comfortable and powerful, aerodynamic and relaxed. Bodies and bicycles meld into one, and above all, they look efficient: no wasted motion, no energy lost to wind, excess movement, or discomfort.

Of course, top riders reach the peak of their profession because of many factors, including inherited ability, time to train, and good coaching. But their position on the bicycle is the result of knowledge and practice–it's something you can emulate. You may not have the inherited cardiovascular ability of a Tour de France winner, but you *can* have an equally efficient position on your bicycle. And *unlike* many cosmetic touches–a fancy jersey or the latest Italian frame–a good position will not only make you look like a real rider, it will improve your riding significantly.

Some years ago, this was the standard advice on position: Buy copies of European cycling magazines, study pictures of the pros, and attempt to imitate them. This advice got quite a few riders in trouble. For one thing, action photos don't always show riders when they are employing perfect form. They may have been dying on a hill in the last stages of a 150-mile race when the photographer snapped the picture. And some pros seem to win in spite of atrocious position on the bicycle. Their natural strength is simply so great that they beat more efficient riders.

But among current professionals, Greg LeMond–first American to win the Tour de France–is widely thought to have exemplary form. LeMond himself singled out world record holder Franceso Moser as having the most nearly perfect form in Europe but criticized him for his tendency to slide forward on the saddle during hard efforts. Sean Kelly, a world-class Irish professional, is castigated for sitting too far forward and too upright. But he keeps winning. In the early days of his career, Belgian Eddy Merckx was a rough pedaler but had a solid position. After a serious crash, however, he was never again comfortable on a bicycle. He made all sorts of adjustments, his position changing subtly from one race to another, but to no avail. The point here is that even the pros aren't always the best models. A further lesson: Position is a highly individual thing. Although all top riders are positioned on the bicycle within a certain range, there is room for variation within that range depending on each rider's body type, flexibility, and personal preference.

Many theories have evolved over the years in the attempt to match the rider perfectly to the bicycle. And thinking has changed recently, so that a position judged perfect 15 years ago is slightly dated today. Some of this change is due to the influence of biomechanical studies on cycling. Several European professional teams have done studies on rider position in an attempt to find the most efficient position for the long, hilly races of Western Europe. Five-time Tour de France winner Bernard Hinault's position was changed in midcareer because of these findings, moving him higher and farther to the rear in relation to the bottom bracket.

In amateur ranks, the Eastern Europeans have led the way in applying the science of biomechanics to rider position. But the United States is close behind. In fact, a 1982 study by exercise physiologist Mark Hodges at the U.S. Olympic Training Center in Colorado was used by national road coach Eddie Borysewicz to help set the position of U.S. Olympic team riders. And Borysewicz notes today that position has changed in the past 15 years because roads are smoother, races shorter and faster, and equipment lighter.

You may not have access to the experience of a Greg LeMond or an Eddie Borysewicz, but almost anyone can find a good local source for coaching on position. Your local bicycle shop is the first choice. A salesperson who is experienced in fitting riders to bicycles often can give useful advice. Local racers or experienced riders are another useful source of advice. When you ride with them, ask if they'll ride beside you and check your position. And don't be shy. Good riders are invariably flattered if you ask for their help, and you'll often get a precise assessment of your position.

If you are fortunate, you may be able to find an actual coach in your area. Ten years ago, there were virtually no qualified coaches in this county. But that situation is changing rapidly as cycling becomes more popular. The Olympic Training Center has been conducting coaching seminars across the nation, and as a result, more people have been introduced to correct position as well as to the techniques necessary to teach it to others.

But you can learn these basics for yourself. Let's start with a look at the components of bicycle fit and rider position and how they are determined:

Bicycle Fit

The first step is to determine what size frame you should be using. Frames that are too large have major disadvantages. They are heavier than smaller frames and usually not as rigid. Because bicycles frames are designed proportionally, a frame that is too long in the seat tube is probably too long in the top tube. Such a frame stretches you out uncomfortably or requires using a stem far too short for the bicycle—a cause of steering problems.

An undersized frame also has liabilities, although they usually aren't as severe. In fact, many experienced riders like a frame on the small side for increased rigidity, lighter weight, and better positioning. The major drawback is that a small frame usually dictates a fairly large differential between the height of the saddle and the height of the handlebars, because most stems have a relatively small range of vertical adjustment. Fixing the problem with a long-shank stem makes the bicycle look funny and handle unpredictably, because it alters the weight distribution that the builder had in mind when he designed the frame. The result: Radically undersized frames compromise comfort and bicycle handling.

The easiest way to determine correct frame size on a road bike is to stand over the bicycle wearing either socks or low-heeled shoes. With your feet close together, there should be about 2 inches of clearance between the top tube and your crotch. This method is a bit rough-and-ready, but it does provide a starting point.

A more sophisticated method is to use one of the commercial frame and bicycle fit systems. An example is Bill Farrell's Fit Kit, featured by many good bicycle shops. Farrell, a longtime racer, was frustrated that so many young riders who came to his New England Cycling Academy showed up on ill-fitting frames. Some of them were on bicycles so large that they hardly had any seatpost showing at all. So Farrell measured the bicycles and bodies of hundreds of top riders, reasoning that good cyclists had positions that were efficient and rode frames that fit. From these measurements, Farrell derived the Fit Kit charts and tables that provide parameters for sizing a rider's frame, stem length, saddle height, and other variables. (Other systems include American framebuilder Ben Serotta's Size-Cycle.)

Experienced salespeople who have fit a lot of customers often have an excellent eye, too, and can tell at a glance what frame size fits. A good bicycle shop is your ally here. Look around for a reputable shop with salespeople who are sympathetic to your needs and willing to take the time to fit you personally.

Finally, frame size can be determined after, rather than before, sizing the rider to the bicycle. Once you know your correct saddle height, choose a frame that allows 8 to 12 cm (3 to 4½ inches) of round seatpost to protrude from the frame.

A quick method to determine frame size: There should be about 2 inches of clearance between the top tube and the rider.

Saddle Height

This is the crucial position measurement, subject of numerous scientific studies as well as cycling folklore from the beginning of the sport. A saddle set at the wrong height reduces efficiency, making the rider work harder for a given speed. In addition, it can cause knee injuries as tendons and ligaments struggle to compensate for less than ideal range of motion. In fact, Bernard Hinault's career was almost ended by knee problems aggravated by a poorly adjusted saddle. Only an operation and careful adjustment of the saddle over a 2-year period allowed him to go on to five Tour de France victories. So it pays to make sure your saddle height is optimum for you.

Approximating correct saddle height: With knee straight, the heel should brush the pedal.

The traditional method of determining saddle height is to have the rider, wearing cycling shoes, sit on the saddle in normal position and pedal backward with the heels on the pedals. If you can just barely keep your heel in contact with the pedal at the bottom of the stroke, the saddle height is adjusted correctly.

A few suggestions to make this technique easier: If your pedals have cages that are thicker on one side than the other, remove the toe clips and straps so your heel can rest on the top side. If your shoe soles are thicker under the cleat than at the heel, you'll have to make allowances when you adjust the saddle height. The same idea in reverse applies to touring shoes with a built-up heel. And if you have one of the strapless pedal systems, like Look, you'll need to adapt this technique to the pedal you are using.

This method usually produces a conservative saddle height that reduces maximum power output but lessens the chance of injury while increasing efficiency over long distances. If you ride casually, take long tours, or have knee problems, the saddle height is the best place to start. Also, this lower position often works best if you use cleatless touring shoes.

Another method of setting saddle height is widely used by fast recreational riders, racers, and serious century riders. First, determine your crotch-to-floor (CTF) measurement. Remove your shoes and stand with your feet about 6 inches apart. Have a friend measure the distance, in centimeters, from your crotch to the floor. You'll need a precise figure, so try this trick: Stand against a wall with your legs together. Insert a record album between your legs. Raise it until it touches your crotch. Then, measure from the top of the album to the floor.

After you have your CTF measurement,

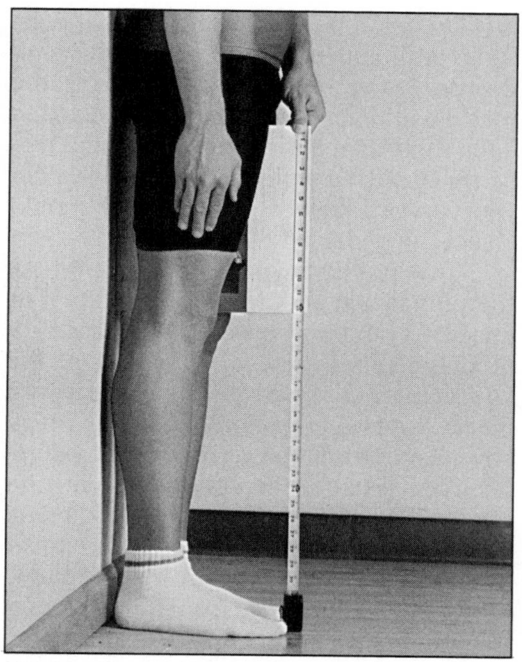

Measuring crotch-to-floor distance.

you can determine the distance from the top of the saddle to the middle of the bottom bracket spindle by using these guidelines: If your CTF is 79 cm or less, subtract 9 cm. If it's 80 to 89 cm, subtract 10 cm. And if it's 90 cm or greater, subtract 11 cm.

Another method, yielding nearly the same result, involves multiplying your CTF by 0.885. For example, if your CTF is 88 cm, the distance from the middle of your saddle to the middle of the bottom bracket axle is 78 cm (88 cm − 10 cm) or 77.88 cm (88 × 0.885).

Remember that two other factors will influence the effective height of your saddle. One is crankarm length—the length of the arm your pedal is attached to. The figures above are based on standard 170 mm crankarms. If yours are different—172.5s for instance—adjust your saddle height accordingly. Longer crankarms mean you need to lower your saddle. You might also want to add the thickness of your shoe sole to your CTF, because thicker soles have the effect of lengthening your leg, thus necessitating a higher saddle.

For example, let's assume your CTF is 88 cm, your crankarms are 172.5s, and your shoe sole under the cleat measures 4 mm. Your saddle height should be set at 78 cm + 0.25 cm (cranks) + 0.4 cm = 78.65 cm. How close does the result have to be? Most coaches say that a 1 cm variation is permissible because your legs will get used to the position when you train over a period of time.

Finally, some riders like their saddles set as much as 1 cm higher than this figure.

The correct way to measure from the top of the saddle along the seat tube to the middle of the bottom bracket spindle.

These riders specialize in short, fast events like sprints or criteriums where maximum power output (from a high saddle) is more important than discomfort over long distances and the increased chance of injury. Riders with long feet or who pedal with their toes down also need a higher saddle, since both those situations have the effect of increasing effective leg length.

Several cautions: Make all saddle height adjustments gradually so your tendons and ligaments have time to get used to the new position. Never raise or lower your saddle more than 2 or 3 mm at a time, and ride at least 100 miles before making another adjustment. Also, most riders don't need extreme positions, either low or high, so moderation is the key. It is tempting to think that you'll generate more power and speed if you have your saddle jacked up to extreme heights, but such extremism usually leads to decreased efficiency, comfort, and sometimes injury.

Fore-and-Aft Positioning

After you have your saddle height adjusted correctly, you'll need to position it properly fore and aft. Saddles slide forward or backward on their rails in the seatpost clamps, so this is an easy adjustment to make. Getting it right is a bit tougher, but important nonetheless, because it determines where you will sit on the bicycle relative to the bottom bracket and the pedals. Too far forward and you'll be unable to get the power of your lower back into the pedal stroke. The bicycle also will have too much weight on the front wheel for efficient steering and bicycle handling. Too far to the rear, and you'll be apt to develop a sore lower back.

To determine correct saddle fore-and-aft position, it's best to put your bicycle on an indoor trainer so you can duplicate road conditions as you make the adjustments. Pedal until you feel that you are sitting on the saddle the way you normally do on the road. Position the crankarms parallel to the floor, then have a friend drop a plumb line (a string with a weight on one end) from your forward knee. The plumb line should bisect the pedal axle.

Two methods of determining where the plumb line should be placed on your knee are commonly used. One method is to hold the plumb line at the front of the kneecap. This results in a more rearward position, designed for long distances, rough pavement, and climbing. It's favored by European professionals, century riders, and others who log long hours in the saddle and need comfort as well as power on the climbs.

But some coaches advise that the plumb line should be dropped from the bony protuberance just below the kneecap instead of the kneecap, itself. This measurement results in a more forward position, favored by sprinters, criterium riders, and some time trialers.

If you are not sure what category you fit into, try a middle-range position, and adjust as you gain experience and discover your preferences and style of riding. Again, make any adjustments gradually, always allowing plenty of time for your body to get used to them.

Regardless of the method you use, it is important to make sure that you are sitting normally on the saddle and that your foot is in the same position it is in when you pedal on the road–not angled up or down more than normal. Try the measurement several times and have a friend watch carefully to see that your pedaling position is the same.

Also, adjusting the fore-and-aft position can change the saddle height, so when you change fore-and-aft position, recheck saddle height–it may take a bit of experimenting to get both right.

Pedal Position

This is another area in which incorrect choices can lead to inefficiency and injury. The key to preventing both is the angle of your shoe on the pedal—not too much toe-in or toe-out. Incorrect angles lead to knee injury because your knee has to compensate for the out-of-line foot.

In the bygone era of nail-on cleats, riders cruised around without cleats until the rear cages of the pedals made marks on the leather soles. Then they nailed on the cleats so the groove was parallel and slightly forward of the mark. Now, with adjustable cleats, more precise methods are available. The best is the Rotational Adjustment Device (RAD) that comes with the aforementioned Fit Kit. Another Farrell invention, the RAD is a special pedal that replaces your own. When you ride on a training stand, the RAD pedal indicates exactly when your foot is properly angled. The cleat is then tightened, and you are ready to ride without danger of knee problems.

Nearly as important is the location of the ball of your foot in relation to the pedal axle. Most riders prefer to have the ball of their foot directly over the axle. Sprinters usually like to be more on their toes with the axle a bit in front of the ball of the foot, while power riders and time trialers prefer to pedal more flat-footed, with the foot a bit forward on the pedal. Make the adjustment by sliding the cleat forward or back on the shoe. But remember that doing so may change your carefully established lateral angle. Proceed slowly and recheck often.

To find the ball of your foot, Farrell recommends drilling a small hole through the sole of the shoe about where you think it is. Then, while wearing the shoes, push a spoke dipped in white paint through the hole, and see where the mark appears on your foot. If the mark is ⅛ inch behind the ball of your foot, then the hole in the shoe is also ⅛ inch behind where the pedal spindle should be.

Farrell's method is quite precise, but since you can come reasonably close by feel, most riders don't go to the trouble of drilling their shoes unless they are having physical problems. The most common ailment caused by improper fore-and-aft cleat placement is an Achilles tendon strain, the result in nearly every case of having the ball of your foot too far behind the axle.

Stem Length and Handlebar Height

Stem length is usually determined by glancing down while you are pedaling normally with your hands on the drops (the lower loops of the handlebars). The tops of the bars should obscure the front hub. This suggestion allows you to make a rough estimate of proper stem length. Obviously it doesn't take into consideration things like riding position or fork rake mechanical exotica. But since stem length isn't as crucial as other position variables like saddle height, a little variation is acceptable.

Remember that you adjust stem length by getting a new stem, not by moving your saddle forward or backward on the rails until the bars obscure the hub. As mentioned earlier, saddle fore-and-aft position is fixed first, then a correctly sized stem is fitted. Good bicycle shops should be willing to change stems when you buy a bicycle, especially if they're doing the fitting. If not, it is easy to buy a new one and change it yourself.

Most riders like the top of the stem to be 4 to 8 cm lower than the top of the saddle. The lower the stem, the more aerodynamic your position, but the less comfortable you're likely to be. As a result, time trialists and sprinters like low stems; tourists and century riders prefer theirs a bit higher.

Remember that stems have a limited amount of vertical adjustment. Never raise your stem so much that the maximum height line shows above the headset lock nut. At least 2½ inches of the stem should be hidden, or the expander bolt may put a bulge in the top of the steering tube when it is tightened. Also, an overextended stem might break off on rough roads or during sprints and emergency maneuvers. If your stem is up as far as it will safely go, and it is still too low in relation to your saddle, your frame is too small.

Bar Width and Brake Lever Placement

Handlebars normally come in widths ranging from 38 to 44 cm, measured from the outside of the ends of the drops. Choose bars approximately as wide as your shoulders. Narrow bars hinder your breathing by constricting the expansion of your chest, and they reduce control of the bicycle because they offer less leverage. Bars that are too wide spread your arms so far that they ride outside the silhouette of your body and create extra wind resistance. For racers, wide bars make it harder to fit through narrow openings in a racing pack. In more pedestrian group rides, they can catch on another rider as you pass to trade places. And they also weigh more than correctly sized bars.

Handelbar selection isn't as easy as just picking the right size, however, because the design of the bar can alter the way it feels. Some bars (like the Cinelli Model 64, for instance) are fairly compact–they have little drop (height) and a short reach (distance from the back of the bars to the curve). Other bars, like the Cinelli Model 66, with greater drop and reach change the effective shape and width of the bar. And of course a bar with more reach requires a proportionally shorter stem to maintain the same distance from your saddle to the brake levers.

Choose a bar that fits your hands and riding style. For instance, some smaller racers refuse to consider conservative bars like the Cinelli Model 64, because they are often used by tourists and casual riders. They opt for the greater reach and drop of the Model 66 when their small hands would actually be better accommodated by a smaller bar. Base your choice on comfort and efficiency, not peer pressure.

Position your brake levers so that their tips are level with the bottom of the drops. On most bars, such placement means that you can get at the brakes as easily from the drops as from the tops of the brake levers. On bars with a large drop, you may feel as though your hands are too far down the curve when you are on the tops. If so, the bar probably has too much drop for the size of your hands.

Once your position on the bicycle has been established, leave it alone. It is tempting to think that you can tailor your position to suit different events. Some riders push their saddles back for long, hilly rides, and then push them forward for short time trials or criteriums. But the concensus is that every rider has an optimum position that falls within a fairly narrow range of adjustment. Meddling with it leads to reduced efficiency, discomfort, and even injury as the muscles of the back and tendons in the knees fight to adjust to frequent changes.

Hand Placement

The dropped bars on your bicycle are among the great inventions in cycling equipment. The unique shape has been refined over the years until the result is a piece of equipment that we hardly think about but that is highly functional.

Handlebars are ergonomic. That is, they are designed to fit the body, yet allow for a wide variety of hand positions. Skilled riders change from one position to another frequently during long rides to vary the weight and pressure on their hands. If you suffer from numb hands on long rides, the solution is probably not padded handlebar covering or thicker gloves but rather relieving the constant pressure on one part of your hand by altering your hand placement.

But changing your hand position does more than keep your hands comfortable and functional. It also distributes the strain on your upper body. For instance, compare the effect of an upright position with your hands on the tops of the bars to your position at speed with your hands on the drops–the lower arms of the handle bars. With your hands on top of the bars you are sitting relatively upright with much of your weight on seat and pedals. Your neck and the small of your back both get a rest, compared to riding with your hands on the drops. Experienced riders change positions frequently, even in races or group rides–hands on the tops when the pack is cruising along, moved more forward to the tops of the brake levers as the pace picks up, back down on the drops when an aerodynamic position is needed in a break.

Let's look at some common hand positions and a few unusual variations, taking it from the top. Remember that good riders will use all of these in the course of a ride:

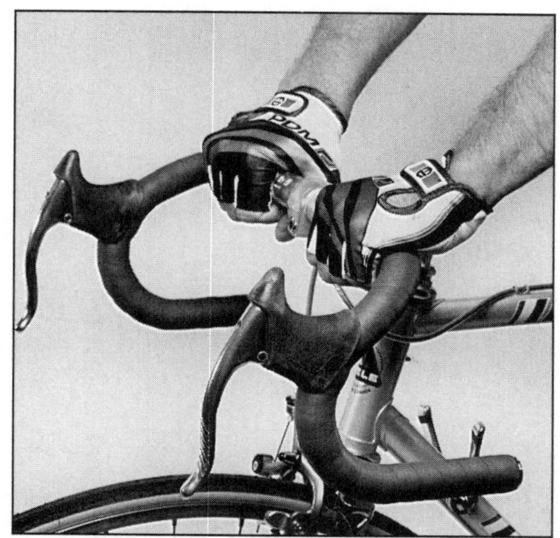

Hands on the tops.

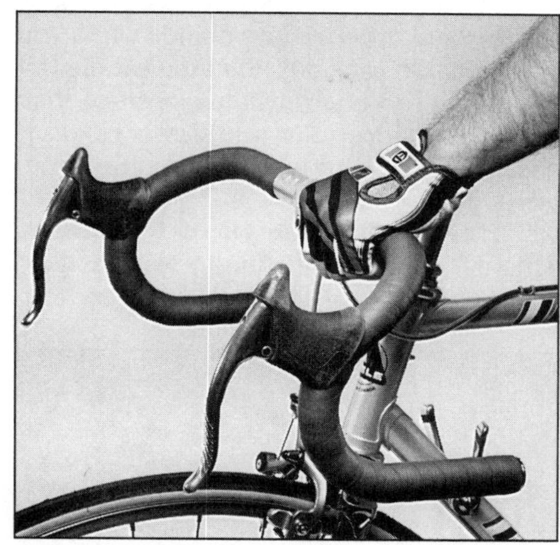

One hand on the top.

Hands on the tops of the handlebars. This position is used for steep, seated climbing because it lets you slide back to the rear of the saddle to get the power of your lower back into the pedal stroke. For the same reason, it's sometimes used on rolling terrain when a small rise requires a short burst of power. And it's used for rolling along with a friend and talking about the scenery.

One hand on the top. Any time you want to ride one-handed (when eating or drinking for example) hold the bar on the top with your hand near the stem. That way, an abrupt movement of your upper body won't affect the steering of the bicycle as much as it would if you were holding the bar farther out, where leverage is greater.

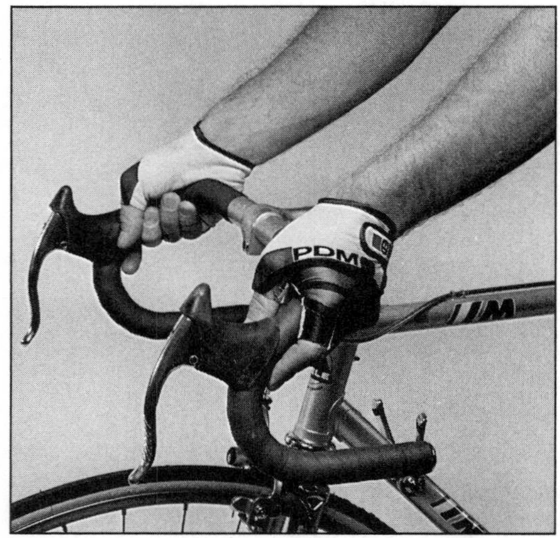

Hands on the upper bends.

Hands on the upper bends. This position is used on moderate climbs when you want to slide back a little in the saddle but maintain a more aerodynamic position than hands-on-the-top allows. In slower riding, it eases the strain on your back resulting from lower positions.

Hands on the tops of the levers. This is the standard riding position, used

Hands on the tops of the levers.

for a variety of situations. Solo, it's reasonably aerodynamic and can be made more so for short periods of time by merely bending your elbows. The brake levers are readily accessible, so it's a safe position, too. In fact, its stability is the reason some coaches recommend it on high-speed descents instead of placing your hands on the drops, explained below. It's great for pack riding, because you are a bit upright and can see what's going on ahead. And it's the standard position for climbing while standing.

The split-finger special.

The split-finger special. No, it's not a baseball pitch–but it *will* keep long rides from throwing you a curveball. Wedge the tops of the brake levers into the forks between your index and middle fingers. The brake levers aren't quickly accessible, so use this position only when you can see ahead.

Hands on the tips of the levers. If you have levers with concealed cables, you have another option. Lean a bit forward, put the middles of your palms on the tips of the levers, and hook your little fingers under the levers, themselves. This stretches you out a bit, providing a more aerodynamic position while still maintaining reasonable comfort over long distances. The major disadvantage: The brakes aren't rapidly accessible.

Hands forward on the drops. This is the standard position for time trialing, fast riding in a break, fast descending, and sprinting. It is also used for explosive acceleration from a standing start, necessary in a time trial or pursuit on the track. The advantages: You can maintain an aerodynamic position and still get at the brakes in a hurry. The disadvantages: It's not very comfortable over long distances and has a tendency to cause numb hands.

Hands forward on the drops.

Hands back on the drops.

Hands back on the drops. In a hard effort, many riders slide their hands back on the drops because they need to slide to the rear of the saddle for greater power.

Your Body on the Bicycle

Let's assume that your frame is the right size, your saddle is adjusted properly, and your stem is an appropriate length. That means that your position is automatically correct, right? Not at all. The flexibility of your body allows for a wide range of variations. That's good, because you can achieve greater comfort. But that's bad, because it's possible to have a bicycle that fits you perfectly and is still uncomfortable, inefficient and awkward. Here are the components of good position.

Head up. You have to be able to see where you are going. Some of the worst accidents in cycling have resulted from riders who pedaled along while staring at their front hub. Sacrifice a bit of the aerodynamics for safety. Speed is pointless if you run into the rear of a parked car.

Upper body relaxed. Inexperienced racers often give themselves away by their white knuckles. They are so frightened by riding in a pack that they squeeze the bars in a death grip, tying up their forearms, shoulders, and neck. And recreational riders are often guilty of the same form flaw. You need a firm but light grip—not a stranglehold—on the bars so a hidden bump won't knock them out of your hands. By the same token, relax your lower back. You'll be surprised how much easier this small trick makes it to get lower and more aerodynamic on your bicycle.

Good position on the bicycle: back flat, arms relaxed, head up.

Elbows bent. Stiff, locked elbows mean that any road shock is transmitted directly to the rest of your body. And if you are in a group, a slight bump on your arm or shoulder will send you to the pavement, because stiff arms transmit the shock directly to the handlebars and steering. Concentrate on keeping a slight bend in the elbows.

Back flat. Some riders look like the Hunchback of Notre Dame. A rounded back means that you are too inflexible, or that your bicycle's top tube-stem combination is too short. A flat back opens up your chest cavity so you can breath freely, and it flattens your whole body so you're more aerodynamic.

Mounting and Dismounting

Getting on and off the bicycle seems to be a skill so obvious that there's no technique at all. But as the crashes at the start of novice races prove, it's not as simple as it looks.

Avoid the technique you might have used as a child, putting your left foot in the left pedal, pushing scooter-fashion with the right, and then swinging your right leg over the saddle once you gain momentum. It may have worked on your faithful balloon-tire Schwinn, but it's outmoded. It is unstable from a standing start, because your cleated sole is apt to slip as you push off. It doesn't work well with cleated shoes, because they don't allow the varying angles of the left foot on the pedal necessary for the pivoting motion of a leg-swinging mount. And reversing the procedure at stoplights is just plain awkward. For normal road riding, there's a better way.

Start by swinging your right leg over the rear wheel and sitting in the saddle with the left foot on the ground. Engage your right foot in the pedal using the technique your pedals require. Rotate the right pedal backward until it is in the ten o'clock position. Then push off gently with your left foot as you simultaneously push down with the right foot.

The Ins and Outs of Pedals

Pushing off was the easy part. Much more difficult is getting the *left* foot into the pedal once you get going. Even veteran riders sometimes have trouble–the start of every group ride or race seems to feature several riders fumbling in vain for their pedal. But it isn't clumsiness. Seemingly insignificant factors like wet shoe soles, gravel in the cleats, or simple haste can change a graceful acceleration into a lurching search for that elusive pedal.

Practice is the key, since every combination of shoes and pedals seems to require a slightly different technique. You may find it helpful to pedal several strokes with your left foot on the bottom of the pedal and the toe clips hanging downward. You may scrape the clips, but the added speed will make it easier to maintain momentum while you flip the pedal up with your toe. This momentum is especially important in an uphill start.

If you are using pedals with toe clips and straps, make sure the pedals have small tabs on the backs of the cages to help you flip them horizontal with your toe. If your pedals don't have this feature, consider bolting or gluing on makeshift substitutes. And because plastic shoe soles often slip on the rear of the pedal cage, you might want to glue a thin strip of old inner tube on the toe for more grip.

If you have the newer step-in pedals, your technique will vary with the type of pedal. With Look pedals you push the tip of the cleat into the front of the pedal, then push down to engage the locking mechanism. The pedal is counterweighted so it hangs in the right position to make this maneuver easy. With the AeroLite system, however, you push the cleat directly down on the pedal spindle.

Regardless of the system you have, you'll need to practice until the motion is second nature. Take every opportunity to practice during the course of your normal training rides. For instance, instead of working on your track stand at traffic lights, stop and put one foot down. When the light turns green, work on getting started smoothly, clicking into your pedal and riding a straight line. Once you have the technique down to a reflex, try not to think about it–you'll mess up for sure if you do.

Shifting Gears

Another area where cyclists get into trouble is in choosing the right gear for starting up. You need to shift *before* you come to a stop so you are in the moderate gear that makes accelerating from a standing start easier. Nothing is more embarrassing than stopping abruptly at a traffic light, then struggling furiously to acclerate in the wrong gear.

Under normal circumstances, it is often easiest and most efficient to merely shift chainrings. For instance, if you are in a fairly large gear (say 52/18) and have to stop for a light, shift the chainrings to the 42 before you stop. Then you'll be in a 42/18 and can accelerate smoothly without dangerous wobbles or waste of energy. But if you have to start on a substantial grade, either shift to a lower gear or stay in a moderate gear and stand up for a dozen pedal strokes to get rolling.

If you want maximum speed away from a dead stop, as in a time trial or to get into traffic flow, choose a larger gear and use the technique described in detail in chapter 4.

Normal Dismounts

Dismounting is normally a simple matter. As you approach the stop, loosen your left toe strap or twist out of your step-in pedal. Slow to a stop, and put the left foot down to steady the bicycle. Remember to lean slightly to the left just as your momentum stops, or you'll fall toward your strapped-in foot. But don't be too embarrassed if it happens anyway. Every beginning cyclist–and some with a great deal more experience–has stopped for a traffic light, put down the left foot, and toppled over the other way.

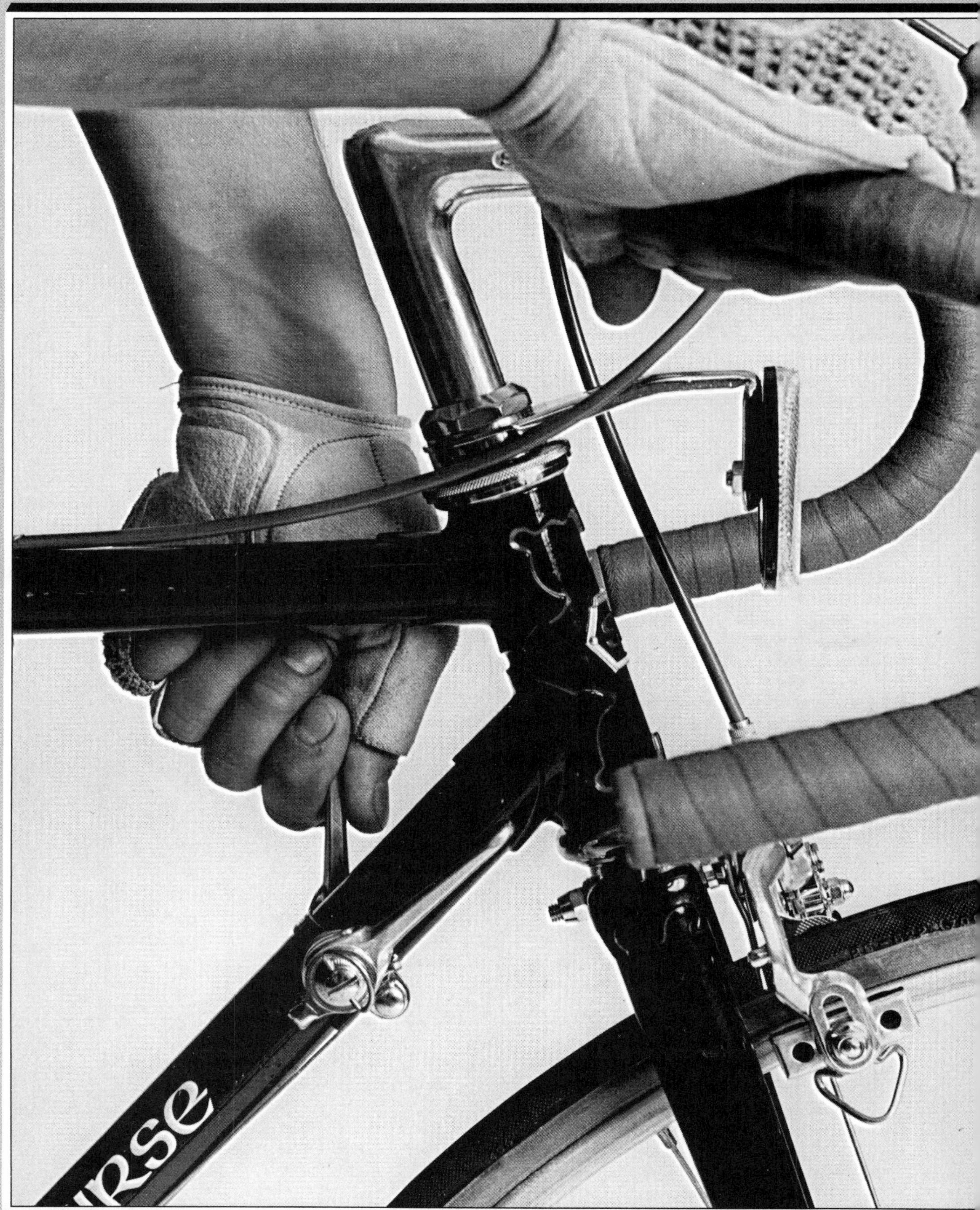

CHAPTER

Basics of Shifting and Braking

Knowing where the parts of your body should be when you're riding is important. But knowing *how* to perform certain necessary chores is just as important. One of the most important is shifting.

Shifting: Putting the Wheels in Motion

Skilled cyclists used to be easily recognizable by their shifting technique—changing gears with a hand that moved like a striking snake. They seemed to barely touch the shift lever before they were back on the bars. No clattering gears, no fooling with the shift lever, no wasted motion. The new click shifters make shifting almost as smooth for the novice, but knowing *when* to shift is still an art.

First, a word on location of shift levers. Skilled road bikers, almost without exception, prefer shift levers mounted on the down tube. They are easy to reach just by dropping the hand from its normal position on the bars. Unlike stem-mounted shifters, they are out of the way of inadvertent bumps when you move your hands to different positions on the bars. And if you crash and go over the front, they don't project upward to cause injury. Some cyclists use bar-end shifters in special circumstances—mountain biking or during criteriums for instance—where it is important to keep both hands on the bars all the time. However for most cyclists in almost all situations, down tube shift levers are the best bet.

Front and Rear Derailleurs

Normally, it is better to use your left hand to shift the front derailleur and your right hand to shift the rear. It's faster to shift both levers with the right hand—reaching through the frame to shift the front derailleur—but it isn't a good technique to cultivate. One reason: It's easy to bump the right lever as you reach across to shift the other one. And shifts on the left lever are rarely as precise when done with the right hand. You'll see many racers shifting with one hand simply because they value speed over precision and long practice has made the technique effective. But if your riding interests tend toward touring and fitness, learn to shift with both hands.

If you have a click system on the rear derailleur, learning to shift gears smoothly is a snap. Just move the lever crisply from one detent to another while easing off slightly on your pedaling pressure. Nothing could be simpler–as long as the system is in adjustment! For easy click shifts, spend the time needed to keep that cable tight.

Friction shifting (on all front derailleurs and nonindexed rear shifters) is a bit more difficult. Here again, practice is the key. When you are first learning, roll along at a moderate speed on the flat, and shift from one rear cog to another and back again. You'll soon get the hang of how far to move the lever and how much you need to ease off on pedal pressure for smooth shifts (on hills, you'll need to soft-pedal more to get a quiet gear change).

With either kind of equipment, anticipate shifts, and make them *before* you are straining to turn a too-large gear or spinning furiously in one that's too small. In the first case, you'll be forced into shifting when the pedals are under load to keep your momentum. The result, at best, will be premature wear on chain and cogs; at worst, a broken chain from the lateral pressure of the derailleur. In the second case, you'll spin out with legs flailing wildly before you shift–not a good way to use limited energy.

But don't shift too soon. For instance, if you are going fast on the flat approaching a hill, an early shift means that your cadence will be inefficiently high at the base of the climb. Better to wait until your cadence begins to slow on the upgrade but before you begin to lose momentum. At that point, shift smoothly into a gear that allows you to keep an efficient and comfortable pedaling rate.

Cadence and Gear Selection

One of the most important cycling skills is also one of the most neglected: the art of keeping an efficient cadence while pedaling smoothly with round strokes.

Style first. Poor cyclists are said to "pedal squares." They fight the circular pattern the pedals make by hammering on the downstroke and resting on the upstroke. Their legs look like pistons pushing an ill-balanced counterweight instead of arms spinning a flywheel smoothly. And awkward cyclists move around on the saddle, a sure tipoff that their position is inefficient. Their upper body bounces, too, wasting some of the energy that should be transferred to the pedals. In contrast, efficient cyclists are smooth as silk regardless of terrain or speed. The French use the word *souplesse* to describe the phenomenon: a supple, liquid, flowing motion that generates great power without appearing forced.

Although an elegant style is partly hereditary–some of the greatest racers have been a bit rough–practice will help you smooth out your pedal stroke and increase your power output. Spend ten minutes of every ride concentrating on a round pedal stroke. Get a friend to videotape you as you ride, and then analyze your style. Ask the opinion of more experienced riding companions or a knowledgeable coach. Buy videotapes of European races, and compare the styles of the great cyclists with your own. And above all, focus on your style when you get tired: at the end of a long ride or when you are going fast. In these conditions, it is easy to get sloppy, which slows you down just when you need speed the most.

The Most Efficient Cadence

Cadence is important, too. If you pedal at too low a rate, your pedaling style will be awkward and labored. The low rate forces you to push too hard, tiring your leg muscles without working your cardiovascular system.

A slow cadence also makes rapid acceleration harder, a problem for your training ride sprints when you need evasive action to outrun the neighborhood canine. It's often argued that slow pedaling in a big gear makes you strong. That may be true, but it also makes you slow—no snap in your legs when you need it for a training ride or a race that heats up.

It's not very elegant, either. If one of the most beautiful sights in sport is a classy pedaler stroking smoothly along, one of the ugliest is an awkward cyclist, overgeared and struggling, pedaling big "squares." And slow pedaling can cause knee injury—your patellar tendon (in the knee) struggles against the heavy load on each pedal revolution.

A cadence that is too rapid is nearly as deadly. It wastes energy, because some of your power output is used just to coordinate the rapid leg movement. An overly fast cadence often leads to form faults—you have a tendency to bounce on the saddle with each revolution and sit more upright to counter it.

Contrary to popular belief, a fast cadence is no protection against injury. A slow cadence tends to irritate the tendons on the front of the knee from pushing too hard, but a rapid cadence may injure the tendons and ligaments on the *back* of the knee. The injury comes from trying to pull the foot through fast enough to keep the pedal stroke round.

So what's the best cadence? Cyclists have been arguing that question for years, and while there's now a concensus, it is by no means unanimous. English time trialists, between the two world wars, turned in times averaging about an hour for 25-mile races on bicycles with single fixed gears of between 75 and 85 inches. They needed to pedal fast, but they also needed control. In those time trials, a cadence of 110 to 120 revolutions per minute (rpm) was not unusual. Conventional wisdom of the time had it that bigger gears and a slower cadence would merely tire out the cyclist and lead to rapid slowing near the end of the event. So for years, the small gear/fast spin theory dominated English time trialing. But once thinking began to swing the other way, it went rapidly and to extremes. Time trialists were soon using 56- or 58-tooth chainrings, gears in excess of 120 inches, and plodding cadences of 60 or 70 rpm.

Not surprisingly, the most efficient cadence for most cyclists is somewhere in between. A number of studies have been done seeking that elusive perfect cadence. Most have found that trained cyclists are most comfortable and efficient somewhere between 80 and 100 rpm on flat or slightly rolling roads. Remember, however, that this is a *range,* and your personal cadence will vary depending on the type of riding you are doing, your experience, and the terrain.

Some examples: Coach Eddie Borysewicz recommends a cadence between 86 and 92 in time trials. The East Germans shoot for 90. Bernard Hinault was accused of pushing big gears slowly but maintained that he stayed above 70, even on long climbs. And fast criterium cyclists have such a finely honed pedal stroke that they can spin along in the shelter of the pack at over 100 rpms for an hour or more.

Most cyclists should aim for a steady 90 or 95 rpm on the flat in training rides. On long climbs, cadence may drop slightly but should never fall below 65 or 70, even when standing. And on fast downhills, spin it out at 110 or 120 (but be careful to retain good form). On long loaded tours, cadence will be a bit lower—but don't get bogged down. Better to shift to a lower gear and keep some snap in your legs if you still have 50 miles to go.

If you have trouble keeping your cadence up, the best time to practice is during the first 15 minutes of a ride as you warm up. Start out in a small gear (say 42/20), and spin smoothly and steadily at a progressively faster rate until you feel yourself begin to bounce on the saddle and lose form. Then cut back a few rpm and hold that cadence for several minutes. Then go to your next bigger gear (maybe 42/19) and repeat the process. Top sprinters can fan a 42/18 or 20 at 120 or 130 rpm for miles on end while sitting rock steady in the saddle.

Choosing Chains and Cogs

Gears are designated by the number of teeth in the chainring, followed by the number in the freewheel cog. For example, common chainrings on road bikes have 52 teeth on the large or outside ring, and 42 teeth on the smaller inside one. A 6-speed freewheel may have sprockets of 13-15-17-20-24 and 28 teeth. So the low gear in this arrangement would be referred to as a 42/28 while the highest gear is a 52/13.

Remember that this gearing designation tells nothing about the actual mechanical advantage—the gear ratio—of the gear in question. You can calculate by dividing the number of teeth on the chainring by the number of teeth on the freewheel cog and multiplying the result by the wheel diameter in inches. That gives you a number, but the best way to get a feel for what it means is to visualize an old-fashioned penny-farthing bicycle with a large front wheel, driven directly by attached pedals. The larger the circumference of the wheel, the faster you could go at a given cadence. The disadvantage was that to change "gears," you had to change wheels. With a derailleur, you achieve the same affect by changing from one sprocket or chainring to another. The formula tells you the diameter of the front wheel that would be on your bicycle when you are in a certain gear. So a 42/17 works out to about 67 inches of gear—in other words it is equivilent to a direct-drive front wheel with a diameter of 67 inches.

As you can see from the foregoing discussion of cadence, gear choice is not an absolute matter but depends on several factors. Training programs that dictate a certain gear—a 42/17 on the flat, for example—ignore the obvious fact that every cyclist has different levels of strength and a different optimum cadence. Choose gears that enable *you* to keep your cadence at appropriate levels on all terrain. If you can handle the hills with a 42/19, fine. If you need a freewheel cog of 28 or 30, use it. Don't let your ego get in the way of mechanical efficiency.

Gear selection tends to bring out the technical side of many cyclists. These "gear freaks" love to plot out exotic combinations of freewheels and chainrings on log paper, searching for the perfect ratios. Unless you enjoy such things, it isn't necessary to get quite so involved. Racers, who worry more about riding than computing, are notorious for using ratios that duplicate gears. For instance, a standard racing setup is a 42/53 chainring combination with a 13-14-15-16-17-19-21 7-speed freewheel. The 53/19 virtually duplicates the 42/15, but that's fine with racers who want to keep it simple. They run the 53-tooth chainring from the 13- to the 17-tooth cogs, then make one double shift to the 42/15 and stay in the 42 chainring all the way to the 21-tooth low gear. Simplicity overrides the fact that the 53/19 is usually wasted.

For most unloaded road riding, a double crankset is adequate. Triples are great for the steep climbs of mountain biking or hauling full panniers over mountain passes. For normal riding, however, they have disadvantages. They are more expensive, trickier to shift, and more trouble to maintain. And unless you live in extremely hilly country, they aren't necessary.

Braking Techniques

Brakes are among the most efficient and trouble-free components on your bicycle. With minimum maintenance, they'll be there when you need them. But mechanical reliability isn't the whole story. Safe braking requires learning certain key techniques and practicing them until they become automatic. After all, when someone unexpectedly opens a car door right in front of you, there's no time to think about which brake lever to clamp on harder!

Front and Rear Brakes: The Right Way to Stop

The first thing to remember is that squeezing your front and rear brakes with the same amount of hand pressure has different effects. If you apply just your rear brake, the bicycle will stop in a reasonable distance. Apply the front brake just as hard, and you'll catapult over the handlebars as your weight abruptly shifts forward and the front brake locks up the wheel. Proper braking, therefore, involves knowing how to balance the different results of front and rear braking.

First, know which lever controls each brake–make sure it is the same on all your bicycles. It is traditional to attach the left lever to the front brake, the right one to the rear. Some cyclists like the reverse because they think the brake cables run more smoothly. Normally, it doesn't matter, as long as you get used to one method and stick to it. But if you plan to race, learn the traditional method: If you have a mechanical failure or crash and have to switch bicycles in midrace, there won't be any surprises.

For a normal stop, begin by squeezing both levers, putting slightly more pressure on the rear brake. Gradually increase pressure on the front lever as deceleration shifts your weight to the front of the bicycle. Push with your arms to avoid being thrown too far forward. Don't squeeze so tightly that you lock up either brake. Locking the front may put you over the bars, and locking the rear scrubs expensive tread off your tire–but doesn't stop you any faster and can lead to skidding and loss of control.

Rain Brakes

Braking in the rain poses some special problems. Rain makes the road slippery, especially when it first begins to fall. The water brings up oil from the asphalt. To make things worse, accumulated dust turns to a nearly invisible layer of slippery mud. The rule for braking in the rain–or for that matter making any other maneuver–is to be steady and not to make any abrupt movements. And remember: Rain-wet rims reduce the gripping power of your brake pads until friction dries them again. So, anticipate stops and allow plenty of time to slow down.

Pack Brakes

When you are riding in a pack–typical during a race–braking requires different techniques and a lighter touch. Pack riding can be a dicey business when someone is grabbing at the brakes, alternately slowing abruptly and spurting ahead. Brakes designed for racing, consequently, don't have the immediate response of touring models–they feel a bit mushy and take more lever travel before they take hold with authority. But this feel is designed into the brake to avoid the problems that overresponsiveness would cause in a racing pack.

In a pack, don't use the brakes unless you have to. Instead, control your relationship to the wheel in front of you by anticipating the minute accelerations and slowdowns that are part of pack riding, and soft-pedaling to maintain your distance from other bicycles. If you must brake, feather the levers lightly! The abrupt movement of a grab at the brakes may cause other cyclists to bump your rear wheel and hit the pavement. The same thing holds when the whole group brakes for corners: Easy does it.

Downhill Brakes

Long, steep descents, especially with a loaded bicycle, require another technique. The idea: to control speed periodically throughout the descent rather than letting it build up to uncomfortable levels and then overreacting. Feather the brakes lightly at regular intervals. Use both front and rear brakes, but compress the rear lever a bit harder than the front.

On tight downhill corners or mountain switchbacks, let the bicycle run on the straights, brake fairly hard just before the corner, and then release the brakes before you lean the bicycle into the turn. The trick is knowing just how fast you can go approaching the corner and how close to the corner you can get before applying the brakes. You'll learn only through practice, since conditions vary so greatly.

Avoid continual braking on steep descents. The brake pads can overheat, causing the brakes to fade just when you need them most. Cyclists with sew-up tires need to be especially careful, because a buildup of heat in the rims can soften the glue that holds on the tires, and they may roll off as you take the next corner. This problem doesn't occur on any but the longest and most severe mountain passes, and it usually isn't a problem with clincher (wired-on) tires, because pressure, not glue, holds them on the rim.

Emergency Stops

Emergency stops require differing braking techniques depending on the situation. If you need to stop quickly but have some room to maneuver, squeeze both brakes, then increase pressure on the front until you are about to skid. Remember that you'll be braking hard enough so that much of your weight will be thrown forward onto your arms and the front wheel. Push back hard with your arms and try to get your rear end back on the saddle.

If you succeed in stopping the bicycle before contact with whatever made you hit the brakes, you can generally get one stabilizing foot down at the last minute. Don't worry about style. Even the best European pros have been known to descend steep passes in the rain with both feet held out to the side, outrigger fashion. Whatever works, works.

If you have toe clips, make a habit of riding with them slightly loose so you can pull out if you have to. Snug them down all the way only for sprints or other maximum efforts. You'll be more comfortable without the strap pushing hard against your feet, and you'll be able to get out with a quick wrench of your foot in an emergency. With step-in pedal systems, your normal reflexes usually suffice to release you from the pedal. The first year that European pro cyclist Bernard Hinault used Look pedals in the Tour de France, he was involved in a big pileup in the sprint at the finish of an important stage. He popped right out of the pedals on impact and saved himself from a potentially serious injury.

In a panic situation–a car pulling out in front of you as you're going through an intersection–don't worry about getting a foot down to avoid a fall. *Stopping* is the important thing. Brake hard, push your weight to the rear, and worry about staying upright *after* you've avoided the car.

In extreme situations, you may have to lay down the bicycle and just accept the resulting scrapes and abrasions to avoid the more serious injuries that would result from a high-speed collision. When you realize you can't stop in time to avoid contact, you need to do several things at once. Lean hard to the left at the same time you twist the handlebars the same direction. Simultaneously, brake as hard as you can with the rear brake. Release the front brake lever completely, put the right pedal down with all your weight on it, and skid broadside into the pavement.

Even though you hope you never have to use this technique, it is worth practicing in case of emergency. And practicing it is actually fun.

Use an *old* road bike or a mountain bike–slick tires work best. Don't forget a helmet, gloves, and sweatpants. If you have them, knee and elbow pads are a good idea. Find a flat field–wet grass works the best. Begin practicing at slow speed. Clamp on the rear brake, and try to skid the bicycle to a stop just like a hockey stop on skates or a full christie on skis. Put your inside foot down like a motocross racer at first, then try to control the skid with both feet in the pedals. It really isn't necessary to take the skid to the ground, but with enough padding and soft grass, it won't hurt if you do–or at least not much. This drill will help you out in emergency situations, and it will improve your general bicycle handling even more.

Special Techniques

You know the basics now—but what do you do when something nonbasic leaps out of the bushes at you? You respond with one of the special techniques listed here.

One-Handed Riding: Shifting, Brushing Off Tires, and Drinking

It's normally best to keep both hands firmly on the bars. One-handed riding can be dangerous, because your weight shifts to one side to compensate for the removal of half your upper body's support system. Any unexpected jarring of the bicycle, like a pothole hiding in a shadow, can cause a crash. And riding no-hands is usually asking for trouble. You not only have little control over the steering of the bicycle, you are also sitting in a more upright position than the bicycle's design was intended to accommodate. And it takes a long time to get to the brake levers when you're sitting there peeling a banana.

Having said all that, it's nonetheless a fact of cycling life that riding with less than a full complement of hands on the bars is often necessary. Skilled cyclists do it all the time and it *is* safe—as long as you know what you are doing.

You necessarily have to ride one-handed when you shift gears. Look ahead to anticipate trouble, and learn to shift without looking down at the levers. With practice, your hand should fall directly to the lever every time. Don't look back between your legs to see what cog the chain is on. European professional Gerrie Knetemann once experienced a serious crash during a race when he ran into the back of a car doing this very thing. Keep track of your gearing as you ride, and soon it will be second nature.

You'll also need one hand free to drink from your bottle. Experienced cyclists drink several ounces every 10 minutes, more frequently in hot weather, so here's a technique you'll need a dozen times on a ride of even moderate length, and much more during a hot century.

While it's not usually necessary when shifting gears, it's a good idea to hold the bars on the tops next to the stem when you are reaching for a bottle. This grip makes the bicycle more stable, since it assures that any movements you make while drinking will have minimum impact on the bicycle's steering. Your upper body will also be more upright, making it easier to swallow.

If you are riding solo, make sure that the road is clear ahead. If possible, choose your terrain. A flat stretch or a slight downhill section is best. Avoid one-handed riding on steep downhills for reasons of control, on uphills because you'll need both hands to pull on the bars. Another reason to drink (or eat) before uphills is the difficulty of choking down a sports drink while you're breathing hard. If you are in a group, take a drink at the back of the paceline, not when you're pulling out in front.

Just as you learned to find the shift lever without looking, the grab for the bottle will soon become automatic, too. More difficult is learning to put it back without looking. But when you drink every ten minutes on a ride, you'll get lots of practice.

Another application of the one-handed riding technique is for wiping road debris off your tires. The rubber compound that makes up tire tread is designed to be a bit sticky so the tire will adhere in corners. Unfortunately, that same stickiness means the tire is apt to pick up tiny pieces of glass, sharp pebbles, thorns, and all the other detritus that litters highways. Any sharp piece of debris that adheres to the tire gets ground into the tread on subsequent revolutions and finally ends up piercing the carcass of the tire and puncturing the tube. But if you can wipe off the junk with your fingers before the tire makes too many more revolutions, you can avoid that roadside repair job.

The lighter your tires, the more often you need to perform this operation. If you ride sew-ups or narrow, high-pressure clinchers, brush off your tires any time you go through the triangles of road grit that accumulate at intersections; again if you ride through a patch of broken glass; and periodically as you ride on clean pavement. Remember: It's the stuff you don't see that gets you. On heavier touring tires you don't need to be as vigilant, but an occasional cleansing will save you grief down the road.

Keeping your tires clean will keep you rolling on your wheels instead of repairing them.

It looks unnerving to stick your fingers on a rapidly whirling tire, but the technique is really simple, safe, and easy to learn. For the front wheel, drop your right hand to the top of the front tire just ahead of the brake. The motion is similar to reaching for the shift lever. Lightly brush your fingers over the top of the moving tire. Don't push too hard or the friction will burn your fingers. And there's no need to bear down; you can flick off most road debris with a light touch. If you feel the bump-bump-bump of a firmly embedded piece, stop and pick it out of the tread so it doesn't work its way into the tube.

Cleaning off the rear tire is a little trickier. With one hand, reach back between your legs, hooking your thumb on the seat tube and letting the backs of your fingers ride lightly on the tire. Touching the seat tube gives you a reference point so you won't reach too far and inadvertently put too much pressure on the tire. Or, as occasionally happens, put your fingers into the whirling spokes.

You also need to be careful to brush the tire fairly high up, not too far forward of the rear brake. If you go lower, where the curve of the tire approaches the seat tube closely, the downward movement of the turning tire can grab your hand and jam it between the tire and the seat tube. The result is one of the most gory crashes in cycling. Even experienced cyclists sometimes get caught. Several years ago in a big amateur stage race in Europe, the race leader suffered this mishap and not only crashed painfully but also had most of the skin flayed from his hand. As with all of these techniques, practice brushing off your tires at a slow speed in a parking lot or other safe area *before* you try them on the road.

There are still other times when you may want to ride with one hand on the bars. You'll need a free hand any time you want something from a jersey pocket: sunglasses, food, sunscreen. And professionals who have to drink enormous amounts during their 5- to 7-hour road races have even learned to make moving pitstops, further proof that the peloton (the main body of the pack in a race) is truly international—at first you're Russian, then European, finally you're a Finnish.

Riding No-Hands: Eating on the Bicycle

Eating on the bicycle is a necessity in long races, a convenience on long tours or day rides. Your muscles store only enough glycogen to last about 2 hours, so you need to eat periodically after the first hour of any long ride. You could stop and have a roadside picnic, but in races or competitive centuries when you are riding with a pack, you'll get dropped if you stop to eat, and it's tough chasing to get back on when you have a full stomach.

On long solo rides, it's often better to stay on the bicycle while you eat so your legs don't stiffen up during the break. Although you can eat on the bicycle while riding with one hand on the bars, it's easier and more efficient to ride no-hands and devote full attention to the chow.

The first step is learning to ride with no hands. Before you begin, be sure that your bicycle's headset is adjusted properly. A tight headset, or one that has pits worn in the races, makes no-hands riding nearly impossible. Your headset has to turn smoothly and freely. Quite a few cyclists having difficulty learning no-hands riding have blamed their own clumsiness or lack of balance when it was really the fault of a poorly adjusted headset.

Practice on a flat stretch of road without traffic (or intersections) or a deserted parking lot. Sit up and grip the bars lightly until you have little weight resting on your hands. Continue to pedal smoothly and let go, leaving your hands within easy reach of the bars. When you feel confident, sit upright, arms at your sides, and ride several yards at a time before you grab on. Soon, you'll be able to avoid road hazards just by using body-lean to steer the bicycle. Skilled cyclists can go for miles on curvy roads without touching the bars, and one continental thrill-seeker has made a career out of descending the most difficult passes in Europe no hands. To make sure he doesn't cheat, his bicycle doesn't have handlebars!

When you reach into your jersey pockets for food, the motion should be smooth. If you are jerky and rough, it's easy to make the front wheel wobble and lose your balance.

Prepare your road rations in advance so they are easy to eat. Quarter apples and peel oranges at home. Carry the sections in a small plastic bag with the top folded over rather than tied shut. The pros like small sandwiches wrapped individually in aluminum foil. And bananas are the cyclist's favorite, because they come prewrapped in convenient yellow packaging.

Eating on the bicycle is no time for table manners. Take big bites, chew fast, and get it down. Then get a hand back on the bars, take a drink, and continue normal riding. When Jonathan Boyer won the Race Across America in 1985, he rode no-hands for miles, eating meals from a specially designed plate that looked like an inverted Frisbee. But you won't be dining in this kind of style on centuries or long day tours, so practice until you can get that banana or fig bar down quickly.

Riding a Straight Line and Following a Wheel

The skill of riding in a straight line is vital to solo as well as group rides. Novices who weave on the road are a danger to themselves and a definite menace if they're in a group. No other habit, short of toting a gun along, will make you less welcome on group rides.

Practice this skill by trying to ride on the white line for 100 yards at first, then a mile or more. Don't stare at the line on the road. Learn to *sense* where it is while looking ahead. If you have problems learning, check your headset for adjustment. Sometimes it is a matter of concentration—if your mind wanders as you ride, your bicycle may too. But the most common reason for erratic cycling is poor riding form. If your pedal stroke is rough or your upper body moves around excessively, your bicycle handling is often compromised. Smooth out your form, and your ability to ride a straight line will improve.

Although pack riding techniques are discussed elsewhere, you'll need one additional basic skill—following a wheel—even if you rarely ride in a group. Any time two cyclists can take turns breaking the wind for each other, they'll be able to go farther and faster with less effort. A long grind into a head wind can be teeth-clenching misery by yourself, but quite bearable if you can rest half the time behind a companion. And part of the thrill of cycling is the speed, shared effort, and camaraderie of taking pace with another cyclist, whether it's in a two-person breakaway in a big race or out on a training ride near your home.

Remember that the drafting effect is greater as you get closer to the cyclist in front. So learn to ride as close as possible while still maintaining a sufficient margin of error. Team pursuiters on the track will ride with their wheels nearly touching, but if the gap is more than 3 feet, the drafting effect will be minimal. So for most recreational riding, keep your front wheel 1 to 2 feet from your partner's rear wheel, varying distance to suit speed, quality of the road, and your skill level.

In normal circumstances, avoid overlapping the wheel in front of you. If the lead cyclist swerves and clips your front wheel, you'll probably crash, since it is the front wheel that controls the steering and the balance of the bicycle. Elite cyclists can sometimes touch wheels and stay up, but they've practiced the maneuver countless times and have reflexes honed over many years. And even they aren't immune. One of the most common crashes in racing packs results from a momentary overlapping of wheels—often all it takes is just a touch to cause a chain reaction crash that brings down half the pack.

Don't grab the brakes if you feel yourself running up on the wheel ahead of you.

Soft-pedal instead until you regain the proper spacing. Or you can drift to one side slightly out of the drafting pocket, so the increased wind resistance will slow you down. Try to be as smooth as possible. If you feel that you are getting too close to the wheel and grab the brakes, you'll slow abruptly and find yourself 10 feet back in the wind. Then you'll have to accelerate to get back on–if you haven't gone down in a pileup. Jerky riding wastes tremendous energy. A few miles of yo-yoing back and forth and your companion will ride off into the sunset, leaving you gasping.

Don't stare at the wheel ahead of you. Look past the lead cyclist so you can see what's coming. It's easy for the leader to drift around potholes or junk in the road, but the cyclist behind invariably rides right over them. For the same reason, always ride a bit to one side rather than directly behind. And if the lead cyclist should slow abruptly, you have a little more room to take evasive action.

If the wind is from the side, a position directly behind the lead cyclist isn't as efficient as when you are bucking a head wind. You'll need to move over to the downwind side to get maximum protection. In windy races the whole pack huddles on the protected side of the road resulting in a staggered riding formation called an echelon.

With only two cyclists, the lead cyclist needs to move toward the wind to give you room to echelon a foot or so to the lee side. If the wind is from the right, for example, the lead cyclist rides on the white line while you ride about a foot to the left. If it's a crosswind from the left, reverse those positions.

But in really strong crosswinds, you'll need to violate the rule that says never to overlap a wheel. In fact, you may want to ride nearly alongside your training partner, tucked in close with your handlebars even with his hip. You'll get more wind protection that way, but the danger of a miscalculation is greater. For safety, make sure both you and your companion feel comfortable in such close proximity before you try it.

Finally, remember that when you are riding with a crosswind, the lead cyclist always pulls off into the wind. You'll be following on the lee side–so if he pulls off that way, he'll hit your overlapped front wheel. Also, when you turn a corner and the wind is coming from another direction, be sure you remind each other. You don't want any surprises in an echelon!

Falling

The last special cycling technique is one you'll hope you never have to use: falling. But knowing how to fall properly when you just can't avoid it is a crucial skill.

Cyclists don't fall very often, but given the natural tendency of two-wheeled vehicles to topple over sooner or later. And probably sooner. Most crashes occur during the first year or so of serious riding, before the reflexes and anticipation skills you need for safety are fully developed.

Naturally, try to avoid crashes if possible. As you become a more experienced cyclist, you'll develop a kind of sixth sense that will set off alarm bells before the situation gets critical. Is the driver of that parked car about to open the door in front of you? Is that dark shadow on the corner ahead leakage from a lawn sprinkler making the road slippery? Good cyclists note these situations automatically and adjust.

And, practice your bicycle handling skills. Specific suggestions can be found in the section on advanced drills, but it's sufficient at first to just get the feel of riding a bicycle on the edge of control. A mountain bike or old road bike is best. Put on a helmet, gloves, and sweats, and ride around in the dirt or on the local kids' BMX practice routes. You'll slip, skid, and slide around

Even experienced riders sometimes fall.

in the ruts, having a great time while you hone the reflexes needed to keep you upright on the road. If you do crash, grass and dirt are a great deal more forgiving than asphalt.

Third, do some tumbling drills to learn to fall without injuring yourself. You don't need a mat or special equipment. Just find some soft grass and practice the forward and shoulder rolls of a high school gym class. Start out slowly, and increase your approach speed until you can dive over a 2- or 3-foot obstacle, absorb the shock with your arms, and roll smoothly to your feet. Ex-U.S. national team coach Eddie Borysewicz sent his cyclists through tumbling drills every winter as part of off-season training camps and attributes their good luck in crashes to improved agility.

Even with all this preparation, crashes on the road will still come as a big surprise. All sorts of theories have been advanced about how to fall and how to protect yourself as you hit the tarmac. But the truth is that most crashes usually happen so fast that you are on the road before you can make any conscious effort to protect yourself—all the more reason to work on your tumbling drills until they become automatic.

Sometimes you have enough time to react. This happens more often in sliding falls—the most common fall—when your wheels go out from under you in a corner. In this case, you'll automatically fall on your side and slide on the road. Although you'll collect some abrasions on your leg and hip—fondly called "road rash" by experienced cyclists—the injuries from sliding falls in corners are usually minor. The most common serious injury is a broken collarbone or wrist, caused by the reflex action of sticking out your arm to absorb the impact of the fall. That's a perfectly normal reaction—

who wants to lose skin–but one that you should try to avoid, because at the speeds you are traveling on a bicycle, the extended arm does *nothing* to protect you. You'll just break a bone. So if you have time to think, do what many professional cyclists recommend. Hold on to the bars all the way to the ground. You'll get scraped up, but you won't have an arm flailing around and getting injured.

The next most common fall usually happens when you run into an object on the road and go over the bars. In races, the obstacle is apt to be another cyclist who falls directly in front of you before you have time to react. By yourself, potholes hidden in shadows or filled with water, dogs charging from the roadside, and flotsam on the road (like discarded pieces of lumber) are the usual offenders.

If you have enough time to react, try to tuck your head and roll on contact to help distribute the impact. After the initial roll, try to slide on one side, like a motorcyle racer, so that the inevitable abrasions are limited to half your body and you can at least sleep on the other.

Although cycling is a relatively safe sport, especially if you learn correct basic techniques, an occasional fall is inevitable. Crashes are the least pleasant aspect of cycling, but with careful riding, bicycle handling drills, and reflexes sharpened by tumbling, you can avoid most trips to the pavement and minimize the impact of the others.

KILLIANS

Advanced Riding Techniques

As you become more at home on your bicycle, you'll probably want to expand your cycling horizons. You'll want to tackle more demanding terrain. And you'll want to become more efficient, covering ground without wasting energy: cornering, climbing, and descending, with precision and grace. The first of these advanced techniques? Cornering–how to survive the bends in the road.

Cornering Basics

Fast, safe cornering is not just a vital skill, it's fun, too. Bends in the road can be the best part of the ride–leaning into turns and sweeping through, balancing the downward tug of gravity against the outward pull of centrifugal force. Part of the thrill of cycling is orbiting through those turns like a planet. But if you don't have the ability to change direction at speed, you'll mince gingerly through corners and miss out on all the fun. Or if your courage outstrips your technique, you'll run the risk of crashing and possibly taking down others riding with you.

Cornering, nonetheless, isn't black magic–although skilled cyclists sometimes make it look that way. They know *exactly* how far they can lean the bicycle over without losing control. They skim through gravel-littered turns that cause cyclists of more modest skills to grab at the brakes in panic. But that cornering competence isn't the result of superior heredity or daring. It's based on simple techniques that you can learn and perfect.

Basic cornering technique stays the same regardless of how sharp the turn or what condition the road. A bicycle at speed is turned by shifting your weight and leaning, not by turning the handlebars. Shifting weight with your hips, instead of steering with the handlebars, makes a turn happen.

Cornering unavoidably puts extra strain on your equipment, which can lead to problems. And a mechanical failure almost always means a crash–you are leaned way over with much less control of the bicycle. Tires are the major source of mechanical trouble in corners. If you ride on sew-ups, be sure they are securely glued to the rims, because if they roll off in a corner, you'll crash when the rim's exposed metal slides

Good cornering technique: outside pedal down, arms relaxed, weight balanced.

on the pavement. Inflate clinchers to appropriate levels, and check them periodically to be sure the bead is seated firmly. Inspect both types often for cuts in the tread or blisters that might blow out in corners. And make sure your headset is adjusted properly. The bicycle needs to be able to swing freely through the corner, and you don't want to be fighting a rough headset all the way.

On the open road, signal your intention to turn about 50 yards in advance of the corner. If you are turning left, point in the direction of the turn with your left arm. And for a right turn, *don't* raise your left arm at a 90-degree angle over your head pointing right. That technique was necessary in a car because the driver couldn't reach over and signal out the right window. On a bicycle, just point to the right with your right arm. Stop signaling about 10 yards from the corner, and get both hands back on the bars before you lean the bicycle over to initiate the turn.

You may have seen cyclists with unusual positions on the bicycle as they cornered–their weight far forward or their inside knees sticking out like a motorcycle road racer's. Don't do it–these unnatural positions are unnecessary and inefficient. Bicycles are designed to track with stability when the cyclist's weight is distributed in normal fashion–about 45 percent of the weight on the front wheel and 55 percent on the rear. That's the way you ride down a straight road, and it is also the way you should corner. If you put excessive weight on one wheel–which riding too far back or forward will do–that wheel is more likely to skid out in the turn.

Basic to good cornering is choosing the correct line. The general rule is to approach a turn from the outside, cut as close to the apex as possible, and exit the turn the way you entered, on the outside. This technique has the effect of decreasing the angle of the turn. It allows greater speed if you are racing and more stability if you aren't.

In competition when the entire road is closed to traffic, take the whole road as you go through corners. On a cleanly swept corner in a closed criterium course, for example, you'll be able to start the turn at one curb and sweep through the corner ending at the other. In this way, sharp angled turns are smoothed out into gentle arcs. But remember to leave enough room for other cyclists to get through underneath you.

On your training rides or tours, you'll have to adjust your line to account for all the exigencies of real life: cars, gravel, pedestrians, oil slicks, and so on. That means approaching the corner more cautiously and using your lane only, leaving extra room to steer clear of gravel and other obstacles. The basic line, however, is still the same.

For a normal right-hand turn, signal, move as far to the left side of the right lane as you can with safety, cut through close to the curb, and complete the turn on the left side of the new lane. Then move to normal road position.

For a left-hand turn, signal, move to the left side of the lane, and arc across the intersection to the middle of the right lane. Then move to your normal riding position at the right side of the road.

Once you have chosen your line and started to lean the bicycle, it is difficult to change line to avoid unforeseen obstacles in the corner. So in competition or fast training on rural roads, develop the ability to read a corner in advance. As you approach, look it over and ask yourself these five questions:

How sharp is the turn? The sharper the turn, the slower you will have to go to negotiate it successfully, and the wider you'll want to go on both the approach and exit. Gentle curves on a meandering road require little adjustment, and 90-degree corners–like those found in criteriums–can usually be handled without braking. But sharper turns require a more precise line and greater control of your speed. Experience will teach you how to judge a corner in 1 or 2 seconds as you approach it.

Is the corner banked or off-camber? The steeper the bank, the faster you can proceed, but an off-camber corner–a left turn where the left side of the road is higher than the right, for example–requires caution, especially if it is wet or gravelled.

Is the road surface clean and dry? Or is it littered with gravel, slick with water and oil? Always corner with discretion, leaving yourself a margin for error. If you blast into a turn at maximum speed and suddenly find a hidden patch of gravel, you won't be able to alter your line in time to avoid it.

Are there any obstacles–like potholes, manhole covers, rocks, or pedestrians–that might force you to take a less-than-ideal line? If so, slow down before the corner, and take a line that will let you avoid them. The most dangerous situation in this regard is a corner that lies in shadow. Your eyes need extra time to adjust from sunlit road to sudden darkness. Rocks or potholes hidden in the shadows leap up unexpectedly, so be cautious when entering the darkness.

What gear will I need after the corner to accelerate quickly back to speed? If you fly into a tight corner in a 52/15 and brake to get around, you'll have to stand up and grind away at 40 rpm to get that big gear moving again. If you'll lose speed because you have to brake for a sharp corner or because the corner is uphill, choose the proper gear before you start the turn. Cornering requires too much concentration to allow for shifting at the same time.

On the basis of your precorner evaluation, adjust speed to corner safely without losing too much momentum. Like a race car driver, you want to brake before the corner and accelerate out of it, instead of grabbing nervously at the brakes after you have entered it.

Position on the Bicycle in Corners

OK–you are set up properly to get around a turn. Next question? What does good cornering technique look like? Approach the corner on the outside of the road with your weight distributed normally. Bend your elbows slightly to absorb the shock of unexpected bumps. Relax your upper body–a death grip on the bars will make you too rigid and awkward, increasing the chances of a mishap. Stay *loose!*

As you begin to lean the bicycle, stop pedaling and put the outside pedal down with most of your weight on it.

Normally, it is best to stop pedaling when the bicycle is leaned over. If you lean too far, the descending inside pedal can strike the road at the bottom of its stroke.

The rear wheel hops and you end up crashing. Racers develop a feel for just how far they can lean over without catching the pedal. In fact, they often buy pedals based on their cornering clearance and choose bicycle frames with high bottom brackets for the same reason. But not all of them. You lose so little time if you stop pedaling for a few strokes that 1986 Tour de France winner Greg LeMond says he *never* pedals through corners.

Cornering in a Pack

Cornering in a pack is more difficult than cornering by yourself. You not only have to contend with the turn itself but with the presence of other cyclists as well. What they're going to do is often unpredictable, so you'll need to leave even more margin for error than when riding alone.

When riding casually with another cyclist, it is usually best to go through corners single file, each cyclist using normal cornering technique. If you're in the rear, stay back far enough to avoid the cyclist in front if he falls, or changes lines abruptly to avoid an obstacle.

If you're confident in your riding partner's ability, try riding through corners side by side. Use the normal technique, but *always* be aware of your companion. Don't, for example, dive into the corner and shave the curb closely if you're the outside cyclist—you'll nail your partner. Leave enough room for the other cyclist to corner properly.

Taking the correct line becomes even more important in a large group. Several cyclists can negotiate a corner abreast if they all take concentric lines and ride predictably. Pro racers in packs of more than 100 routinely handle corner after cor-

If everyone takes the correct line through corners, a large pack can proceed without mishap.

ner at high speeds on bumpy cobblestones without mishap. Each cyclist knows intuitively what the others will do. But if even *one* cyclist is unpredictable or erratic, the whole group is in danger.

As you gain confidence cornering in a group, you'll develop the ability to bump shoulders or elbows and recover without falling. The key is to stay relaxed, with elbows bent to absorb the shock. When you feel contact, don't panic. If you tighten up with fear, the bicycle won't track naturally through the corner, and your upper body won't flex to absorb the contact. Only a relaxed upper body can soak up the shock without transferring it to the handlebars, which can lead to a loss of control.

Pros develop an uncanny ability to bump each other incessantly in corners and take it—practiced cyclists can get a shoulder under a falling cyclist and hold him up, saving the cyclist and themselves from a crash.

You'll feel more comfortable in group situations if you practice cornering with others while riding an old bicycle slowly on the grass. Get several friends together, and lay out a course around cones on a playing field. Then ride abreast, working on taking the right line and recovering from accidental contact.

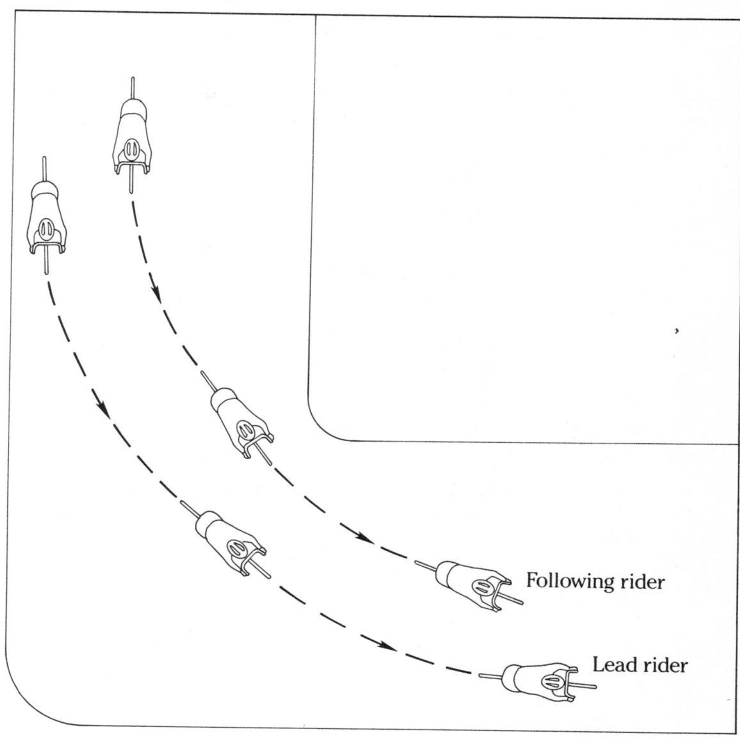

The correct position for two riders cornering together is single file, wheels slightly overlapped as shown.

Cornering in Wet or Hazardous Conditions

Cornering becomes a whole new ball game if the road is wet. The first rule on a wet road is to slow down until you get a feel for how much traction you have. Remember: The road is more slippery in the early stages of a shower than it will be later, when the rain has had time to wash away the film of oil and mud. Even in a race, professional cyclists often slow almost to a stop at sharp corners when the rains first hit.

You can test traction by wiggling the bicycle back and forth as you ride. Do this gingerly at first, steering an imaginary slalom course about a foot wide. Accentuate each turn with your hips. With a little practice, you'll feel the bicycle began to lose traction slightly on each arc—and just how much is a good indicator of road slickness.

Many cyclists reduce pressure for wet roads. When it begins to rain at the starting line of a criterium, you'll often hear the hiss of released air when the racers go from 110 pounds of air pressure to perhaps 95. The theory is that a tire at lower inflation compresses more under load and presents a greater surface patch to the road. A minority of racers recommend the opposite and put in 5 more pounds of pressure, claiming that a harder tire gives them a better feel for the limits of tire adhesion in the wet.

That doesn't mean *you* have to, though. If you are on a casual ride and it starts to rain, leave your tires alone—just take it easy, instead.

The second wet-road rule: Be smooth. Don't make any abrupt movements that might break your tires away from the road. Initiate all turns smoothly, in a wide arc. Don't wait until the last minute and then heel the bicycle over all at once. If the road is really slippery, you can crash making even straight-line maneuvers. Standing to sprint, for instance, often causes crashes when pedal pumping combines with the side-to-side pull on the bars to break the tires loose from the asphalt.

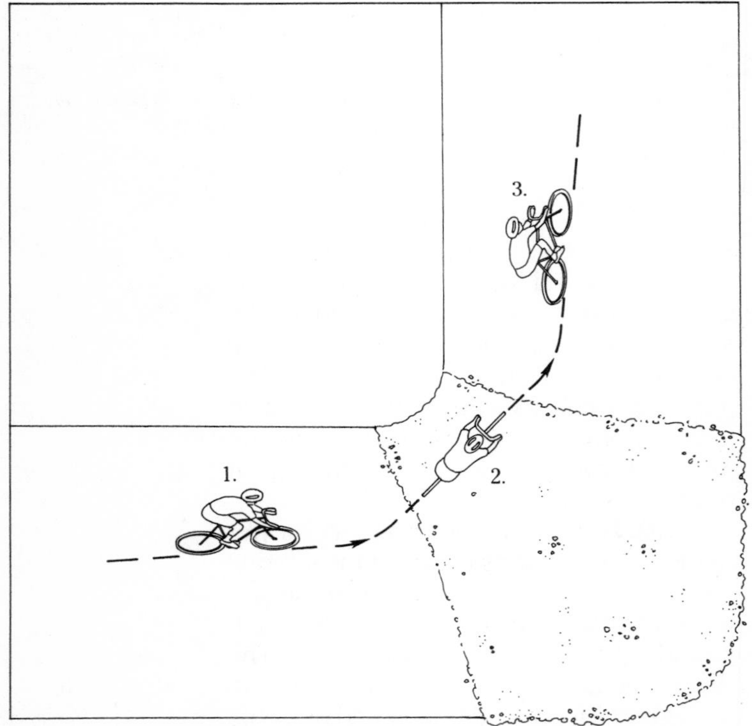

The three parts of the three-part turn: Lean the bike over, straighten up to go through the gravel, then lean it back over to complete the turn.

Wet-road rules also apply if the road is dry but littered with gravel, fallen leaves, or other slippery stuff. You can, however, corner quickly in gravel if you learn to change your line slightly. The technique can be thought of as a three-part turn. One, approach the corner normally and lean the bicycle over on the clear pavement leading into the corner. Inititate the second part—just before you hit the fan of gravel that accumulates at the apex of the turn—by straightening up the bicycle and riding through the slippery spot square and upright. And then lean the bicycle over again, and complete the turn on the other side of the gravel.

This technique works equally well for wet spots, potholes, or any road hazard you encounter in corners. But you need to give yourself extra room on three-part turns simply because they need more room than the smooth arc you'd use otherwise. Don't do it while riding side by side with an unsuspecting companion—you'll send him flying.

What happens if you approach a corner too fast and feel you can't make it through? Generally it is better to increase your angle of lean even though you may lose traction and fall to the inside. Why? It's almost always better to fall and slide rather than to run off the outside of the road and hit obstacles at speed. The exception: if the road shoulder is smooth and carpeted in soft grass, in which case running off the road makes good sense.

But you'll rarely have time to check on the suitability of your landing zone, so remember: Avoid running head-on into trees, rocks, cliffs, and other immovable objects at all costs. Fall instead, because the normal reaction, to stay upright for as long as possible, usually leads to more severe injuries than if you just let yourself go down.

Avoid braking hard when cornering. In a pack, you'll cause a chain-reaction crash when people behind you try to adjust. Braking when you are leaning over also causes the brake pads to grab and chatter, decreasing your control of the bicycle. If you *must* drop speed after you've entered a corner, feather the rear brake lightly—the front brake will affect your steering.

Climbing: The Wise Way Up

The ability to climb is one of the most important skills in cycling. Without it, you'll suffer inordinately whenever the road heads up. Lack of climbing ability can severely limit your riding options—anything with hills is out. It limits you on group rides, too, if you can't keep up on hills and everyone has to wait. And in races, the pace picks up at the *hint* of a hill as strong climbers try to drop weaker cyclists and reduce the pack to a more manageable size. Remember: The most blazing sprint counts for nothing if you never get to the finish line because a hill got in your way.

Good climbing is probably 60 percent physical ability, 20 percent technique, and 20 percent mental. Outstanding climbers have a high power-to-weight ratio. They are lean and short. It is often said that great climbers are born, not made, simply because stocky, muscular cyclists are usually at a disadvantage on hills. But don't cash in your climbing chips just because you don't have the perfect body—you *can* improve your technique, and consequently your performance climbing, considerably.

Cadence and Gearing for Climbing

Start by maintaining a strong cadence on climbs. Good climbers rarely let their rpms fall below 75 seated, 65 standing. A slower cadence means pushing a larger amount of resistance on each pedal stroke, possibly leading to injury of the patellar tendon. It also means that the quadriceps, the muscles on the fronts of your thighs, have to work harder then they would at a higher cadence—they'll fatigue faster and recover more slowly. Racers often say that their legs go dead from using oversized gears on climbs. The result: nothing left for the finish line sprint. And on long rides or day tours, if you labor up early hills at a low cadence, you'll be tired long before the end of the ride.

To help maintain a strong cadence on climbs, consider purchasing a cyclecomputer with a cadence counter. A glance at the readout tells you if you are spinning along or just plodding. It will also remind you to shift to a lower gear if you are getting bogged down.

Choose the right gears for the terrain. Don't choose a gear because it is the one you think you *should* be using on the climb. Remember: *Cadence* determines gears. Cyclists who insist on having it the other way around soon find that when gears determine cadence, every climb becomes an exercise in misery.

The point here: Don't let vanity influence your gear selection. If you need a 42/28 to handle a hill, use it. Struggling up in a 21 because that's what everyone else says they use is asking for injury. And contrary to popular belief, pushing a big gear at a low cadence on a climb won't make you more fit either. It just trains you to pedal slowly, and a common result is that your enthusiasm for cycling oozes away with all that extra sweat pouring off you.

Seated Climbing

At least half your climbing will be done seated. Place your hands on the tops of the bars and sit upright—more than you would on a flat. Your hill-climbing speed doesn't require an aerodynamic position, and you'll appreciate how sitting up straight lets you breathe more freely.

Slide back to the rear of the saddle to put the power of your lower back muscles into the pedal stroke. Sitting on the rear of the saddle has the same effect as raising your saddle, thus increasing your power.

Pedal smoothly and powerfully with a round stroke. Push down evenly, and claw the pedal around on the upstroke. If you have never tried them, you'll be amazed at how toe straps and cleats, or one of the step-in pedal systems, will improve your climbing by letting you apply pressure to the pedals *all* the way through a stroke.

Don't rock the bicycle in time with your pedaling or let your head and shoulders bounce up and down. Stay smooth, work toward round pedal strokes, and stay on top of the gear. Excessive upper body motion is usually a dead giveaway that you had delusions of grandeur when you chose your gearing.

Climbing Out of the Saddle

You won't want to stay in the saddle all the time. Stand up to roll over small hills without losing momentum. As you approach the hill, look it over and decide if you can stay in the same gear or need to downshift. As you roll into the hill and your cadence begins to slow, stand up smoothly with your hands on the tops of the lever hoods. Rock the bicycle slightly from side to side in time with your pedal stroke, but avoid excessive and energy-wasting side motion.

Pull on the bars to counteract the powerful downward push of your leg muscles. Keep your head up and your back flat. When you get to the top, don't give in to the urge to rest and settle back into the saddle–accelerate so you don't lose momentum. Sit back down as you begin the descent, and recover while you pedal smoothly down the hill. When you hit the flat, you'll be able to resume your normal cadence and speed.

On longer climbs, most cyclists like to alternate sitting and standing in a ratio of about two to one. Generally, lighter cyclists stand up more often than heavier ones. This is partly a matter of personal preference. but physiology plays a role. When you stand up, you can push down with your body weight and generate more power. But you pay a price: Your leg muscles have to support you as well as move the bicycle up the hill. Seated, you have only the power of your leg and back muscles for locomotion, but your weight is carried by the saddle. The net result is that heavier cyclists often find it more efficient to sit most of the time. They stand only to keep up their cadence when a grade gets steeper. Light cyclists, on the other hand, often stand and "run" up the hill on the pedals using their superior aerobic ability.

The bottom line: If you stand up for more power, you'll tire faster. Seated, you are more efficient over the long haul but slower. You'll find your own best mix of climbing styles by climbing a lot, but to speed things up, time yourself on a favorite climb using different techniques. Stand all the way one time, stay seated the next, then mix the two in different ratios. Over a period of several weeks, the mix that works best for you should become obvious.

Circumstances may change your usual technique. On a long tour with a loaded bicycle, you'll probably want to sit nearly all the time to save energy. Going up a hill a minute or two faster makes little difference when you are looking at a whole day in the saddle. And a loaded bicycle is hard to ride out of the saddle because the panniers, no matter how carefully designed and packed, tend to wobble and throw you off balance.

You may also alter your accustomed climbing style if you ride in unfamiliar terrain. Midwest cyclists used to short, rolling hills often have to sit a greater percentage of the time when they ride the Rockies with their long, steady grades and high elevations.

You'll usually need gears a tooth or two higher when you go from sitting to standing. For example, if you are climbing in the saddle in a 42/21, you'll probably want to shift to the 19 when you stand up. Your cadence will slow about 5 rpms, but the bigger gear will keep your speed steady.

Climbing in a Group

If you are climbing in a group, it's usually better to go at your own pace. If you try to stay with faster climbers, you'll get so far into oxygen debt (the difference between how much you need and what you actually get) you'll be out of the running long before you reach the top. It is better to pace yourself, losing a little ground steadily, but still reaching the top. The exception is if you begin to fall back near the top. In that case you may want to push beyond your anaerobic threshold to stay with the group, hoping to recover on the descent.

Although drafting has little effect at slow climbing speeds, it's an advantage to ride behind a powerful climber, concentrating on the other cyclist's rear wheel or turning legs. You'll often be able to get into a rhythm that carries you all the way up faster than you would on your own. Additionally, shadowing an accomplished climber is a good way of honing your own uphill techniques. Use the same gears and cadence, stand at the same times, imitate the style, and generally get a feel for what the rhythm of a top climber is like.

But *don't* follow as closely as you would on the flat. When the cyclist in front stands up, the bicycle often jerks backward because of the weight shift–making it easy to get your front wheel clipped. By the same token, if you are the lead cyclist, stand up smoothly so others aren't taken down.

The Inner Climber

Finally, remember that climbing is at least 20 percent mental. All the physical ability and technique in the world won't help if you hate to climb. And many otherwise accomplished cyclists dislike climbing simply because it *always* requires more work than riding on the flat. There's no getting around it: Going uphill fast takes a great deal of old-fashioned hard work. Learning to live with the pain that results is an inescapable part of climbing well.

Although you can't cheat gravity, you *can* kid yourself about it. Focus on the positive elements of the climb–the scenery can help take your mind off how far you still have to go to the summit. If you are riding with a partner, take turns leading and setting the pace. Hum a tune to yourself, and pedal in time to the beat, but choose a fast number so your cadence doesn't slow down. Tell yourself how much the climb is doing for your fitness. Play mental games, imagining yourself in a champion's yellow jersey, blowing away your competition in the Alps. Think about the sense of accomplishment you'll have at the summit, the fun you'll have on the descent, the cool drink from your bottle at the next bend in the road. Think about anything *except* the discomfort.

Another useful mental technique: Divide the climb into several segments, and concentrate on completing them one at a time. A 4-mile climb is easier if you don't think of it as one long grind. Think of it as a steep 1-mile ride to the false flat, then a rolling 2-mile middle section, and finally a fast 1-miler to the summit.

Confidence helps. If you think of yourself as a strong climber, you are more apt to ride like one. If you climb more slowly than your companions, think about how strong and steady you are over the long haul. If you are just beginning to ride, think about how good you're going to be in a few months. In climbing, negative thoughts weigh a lot more than the heaviest of bicycles.

Remember that everyone hurts on climbs, regardless of ability. Many average cyclists think that top climbers don't suffer, that they float to the summit on lightness and lungs. But no one escapes gravity. Top cyclists hurt just as much as you do—they just do it a little faster.

Descending: The Road Back Down

While much of climbing is based on inherited ability, descending is nearly all technique. Although heavier cyclists go faster downhill because of the effects of gravity, that's the sole physical advantage. Safe and fast descending depends on skills that you can learn and practice each time you ride. You don't need a daredevil mentality, either. Some cyclists *love* to scream around switchbacks at the limits of control, but a more controlled and generally saner approach will get you to the bottom almost as quickly.

Position on the Bicycle While Descending

A good descent begins with the right position on the bicycle. You have probably seen pictures of racers flying down the hill in exotic postures: weight forward on the front wheel, rear end raised a foot above the saddle or back over the rear wheel. None of these positions is especially safe.

The best descending position balances your body on the bicycle without placing an excessive amount of weight on either wheel. Bicycles are designed to support the cyclist's weight between front and rear wheels, and there's no reason to alter that balance on downhills. A radical descending style with too much weight to the rear can cause uncontrollable shimmy in the front end. Excessive weight forward makes the bicycle's steering wash out in corners, and even small, unexpected bumps can put you over the bars.

Generally speaking, for good downward-bound position, you'll want to flatten your back in an aerodynamic position, slide to the rear of the saddle, and place your hands on the drops within easy reach of the brake levers. Hold your head up so you can see down the road, but relax your upper body. On straight stretches of road, keep the pedals parallel with about half your weight on them, half on the saddle. If you support *all* your weight on your legs, they'll fatigue on long descents. The exception is bumpy pavement: Put all your weight on the pedals, and lift your buttocks slightly off the saddle to use your legs as shock absorbers.

If the descent is extremely steep and curving, or the pavement is bad, ride with your hands on the tops of the levers. You can brake just as powerfully from the top, and you can also sit up a bit more to see where you're going.

You'll want to use this technique in a big pack—the larger the crowd, the more important it is to see what is happening ahead of you. But it also works well on twisting, tree-lined downhills where visibility is limited. And if it's windy, sitting up often makes the bicycle more stable.

Many cyclists descend with their hands on the tops of the bars near the stem, with

Downhill technique with hands on the drops.

The correct line through a switchbacked mountain turn.

their elbows tucked underneath. This technique is aerodynamic and will save you a little time but makes it much more difficult to reach the brakes quickly in an emergency. And the narrowness of the grip means that you don't have quite as much control of the bicycle. As a result, this position is recommended only when the descent is straight and fast with good visibility at least 50 yards ahead.

Cornering on the Descent

In curves, use standard cornering technique but with extra caution. Going faster than on the flat means the penalties for a mistake are greater. Put the outside pedal down with most of your weight on it to help maintain speed around the turn. Approach it from the outside of your lane, cut across the apex, and finish once again on the outside of the lane.

You can go faster in corners by using both lanes, in effect widening the road and lessening the angle of the turn. But it's a dangerous move if there's any chance of oncoming traffic. Stay in your own lane unless you are *absolutely* sure both lanes are clear. If you need to brake, do it before the corner and not when the bicycle is leaning over.

Judging your speed through downhill corners is the real art in fast and safe descending. It takes balance, depth perception, aggression, and a finely tuned sense of speed to consistently corner near the point of failure. Practicing on curvy descents will improve your skill, but always leave yourself a little room in case you encounter hidden gravel or have a mechanical problem.

Cornering in the rain.

Let the bicycle run on the straights and brake hard at the last minute, then accelerate out of the corner. Give yourself more room on blind corners. You never know how tight the curve will be, and you don't want to trust your life to the highway engineer. Blind corners also often hide approaching cars, dogs in the road, or rocks rolled down from overhanging cliffs. In the rain, remember that the pavement is slick and your brakes won't work as quickly. Allow extra time to slow down.

If you're following other cyclists down the hill, you can use them to gauge your speed through corners. Stay back about 10 yards to allow yourself a margin for error, and follow their line–chances are if they make it through the corner without mishap, so will you.

Tricks of the Pros

Check equipment. It's always a good idea to give your bicycle a quick mechanical inspection before any ride, but if you're going to be roaring down long descents, it's even more important. Squeeze the brake levers hard several times, and make sure the pads are centered. Check tires for glass cuts, sharp objects embedded in the tread, or sidewall bulges that may blow out unexpectedly. Examine your wheels for trueness, flat spots, or bulges that might make braking uneven. If you are carrying a load, be sure that no dangling straps or stray pieces of baggage can foul in the spokes and cause you to crash.

Wear eye protection. At great speeds you have to be able to see curves in the road, but it's also important to spot potholes and debris, because the smallest imperfection in pavement is magnified by velocity. You can be temporarily blinded by a bug in your eye or just the flow of tears from the wind, so wear a good pair of sunglasses designed for cycling. If you sweat all over the lenses on the climb, you might want to stow them in your jersey pocket until you reach the top. It is often more convenient to attach a keeper strap to the glasses and let them dangle on your chest, but you may still drip sweat onto the hanging glasses as you labor upward. Just don't forget to put them on before you begin the descent.

Control the shimmy. Some bicycles have a tendency to vibrate, or shimmy, on fast descents. This is dangerous–it can cause loss of control so severe you are literally thrown from the oscillating bicycle. Even in cases of moderate shimmy, you'll be so concerned about hanging on that you may lose concentration on the road ahead and run into trouble. If your bicycle has the shakes, check the headset adjustment first. A loose headset is often not a problem at normal speeds but causes vibration on fast descents. Bent forks or a front wheel that is out of true are other possibilities, but the most frequent cause is a misaligned frame. If your headset and front wheel both check out, get your frame examined at a competent shop.

Suspect alignment problems if you've recently crashed or entrusted your bicycle to an airline luggage attendant.

If the damage is slight, it's often possible to bend the frame gently back into shape by using a process called cold setting. But if all else fails, follow the advice of the great Belgian cyclist Eddie Merckx: Throw away the bicycle and get a new one. Why? A bicycle that wobbles on high-speed descents isn't safe, and a new frame is cheaper than hospital bills.

If your bicycle unexpectedly gets a bad case of the shakes halfway down the hill, don't panic and grab the brakes. That almost certainly will make the situation worse. Instead, shift your weight forward onto the front wheel. This change often stabilizes the bicycle enough that you can then gently apply the rear brake and slow enough to stop the shimmy.

Another trick: Squeeze the top tube between your knees on all fast descents. This often stops the shakes before they start. Many a bicycle slightly out of alignment has been ridden without mishap because the cyclists made habits of clamping down on their top tubes on every descent.

Staying Safe

The sheer speed of descents frightens many beginners. And it's unnerving to hear the wind whistling in your helmet at 50 mph while the pavement rushes past in a blur. A good rule: Never ride at speeds that make you nervous. If you get uneasy at 30 mph, brake gently to slow down. Given time and experience, you'll be surprised at how soon previously terrifying speeds start to feel safe. But let that happen on its own schedule. There's never a reason to take unnecessary chances on descents.

One of the most frightening events in cycling is a tire blowout during a fast descent. But even though that loud pop seems to spell disaster, it often doesn't. If your rear tire's blown, you can usually keep the bicycle up. Stay calm and steer to the middle of the lane to give yourself room to maneuver, and gently brake to a stop. Don't clutch at the brakes or you'll skid–a blown rear tire means much less control.

If your front tire blows out abruptly, you'll have much less of a chance of staying up. The front wheel controls the steering and balance of the bicycle. Without an inflated tire, you'll lose almost all control. Remaining upright depends almost entirely on your bicycle handling skills–and luck.

Again–don't panic and grab at the brakes. Many front wheel blowout crashes aren't the result of the tire failure but the cyclist's overreaction. The cyclist locks up the front wheel and goes over the bars. One tip if it happens to you: Your front brake can snag on the deflated tire as it flops around. Use your *rear* brake to scrub speed. Even if you can't stop completely, you'll slow down enough to make the crash less severe.

Strong winds on descents can be dangerous. They're especially unpredictable in canyons descending from high mountain passes–they seem to swirl around in every direction.

Your bicycle will be more stable in the wind if you can keep pedaling. Applying power to the rear wheel makes the bicycle more controllable. It is often worth the effort, in fact, to install an oversized gear–maybe a 53/12–if you suspect you'll encounter gusty winds on long descents. The big gear lets you keep power on the wheel when you'd be spinning furiously on something smaller.

Another problem: In a strong crosswind, you'll often feel like your bicycle is moving sideways–and occasionally it is. The best way to combat this eerie feeling is simply to get into the most aerodynamic tuck possible, to present less side surface to the wind. And again–keep pedaling if you can.

Descents are often much colder than climbs because you aren't working as hard. And windchill is greater due to the breeze descending at speed generates. If you know you have to deal with long descents, plan ahead. Take a windbreaker along in your jersey pocket. Tips for the race-minded: Most windbreakers fit loosely, and their incessant flapping creates significant drag. Racers often forego them for a 2-foot-square piece of plastic. At the summit, tuck the plastic up under your jersey to protect the vulnerable chest area. And in colder weather, you may want to add long gloves. Numb hands make it difficult to work the brake levers.

Speed: Putting Sizzle in Your Cycling

Many recreational cyclists never practice sprinting because they see no need for a quick burst of speed in everyday riding. But speed has many uses. Spirited training rides, for example, always seem to feature sprints for the city limits, with the winner owning bragging rights until the next suburb. In city commuting, it helps to change lanes and dart safely and authoritatively into gaps in traffic. Even on long tours, when endurance reigns supreme, the power and fast-twitch muscle fibers that speedwork develops come in handy–for making the most of a tail wind, for example, or outracing a thunderstorm.

A sprinter practicing his craft.

And fast is just plain *fun*. Quality bicycles and fit bodies beg to fly. So don't condemn yours to a pedestrian pace. Fortunately, developing your afterburners is a lot simpler than you'd expect.

Authorities say that speed can be developed in two ways: by increasing your cadence (pedaling faster) or by increasing your power (pedaling harder) so you can use a bigger gear. This is true–as far as it goes. But there is a third key to quickness that is often neglected: technique and especially one in particular that racers call a "jump"–the ability to reach top speed fast. Without efficient form, a cyclist with the speed of a cheetah and the power of a Mack truck will spend most of it on flying elbows and bobbing shoulders. Speed is a combination of cadence, power, and technique, and in this section we'll look at ways to boost all three.

Lightning Legs

The most basic way to build leg speed is to pedal fast and smoothly in low gear, for 10 minutes on each ride–preferably right after the warm-up. If your normal cadence is 90 rpm, for example, start there and gradually increase it to 100, 110, 120–until you're bouncing on the saddle and your legs are flailing. Ease back 5 rpm, hold it there for a minute, and then speed up again. Repeat the sequence four or five times. Not only will you find this to be an effective way to prepare for the rest of the ride, but both your maximum cadence and your comfortable cruising cadence will increase in just weeks–the result of being a more efficent pedaler.

To break the monotony, alternate a second good technique for building leg speed–low-gear intervals. Instead of 45 seconds in 52/16 at 90 rpm, try 42/16 at 120. Your legs won't burn as much as in the higher gears, but you'll burn oxygen like a charging elephant.

Power: Putting Punch in Your Pedaling

Don't do all your speedwork in low gears, however, because the *second* component of speed is power–the ability to exert force at speed. If you can use a bigger gear at the same cadence, you'll go faster. Top sprinters, for example, can turn the power on until their legs blur–*in a 53/12.* Clearly, leg speed alone isn't enough.

If you're really serious about going fast, you'll need to work on building a base of power off the bicycle. How? By lifting heavy objects repeatedly. Weight training is gospel for track sprinters, and what helps them go fast will help you, too.

During road training, hard accelerations in a big gear will help you build power, also. For instance, roll along at 40 rpm in 52/16, stay seated, and accelerate for 10 seconds as hard as you can. Recover fully by shifting to a lower gear, and then repeat. You can accomplish the same thing with short, steep hills. Charge over them, seated, in a big gear.

Sprinting Technique

Steve Bauer of Canada, one of the pro peloton's fastest sprinters, has thought long and hard about good sprinting technique. He has identified three major technique flaws that show up in most cyclists when sprinting out of the saddle.

One, they move their upper bodies too much. Bauer explains that your back is like a fulcrum and shouldn't move. The upper body should be almost perfectly still, serving as a brace for the power of the legs, while your bicycle sways back and forth beneath it.

Two, cyclists tend to put their weight too far forward. Bauer maintains that your shoulders should be only as far forward as the front axle. More, and you'll encounter several speed-sapping problems. You'll have too much weight on your front wheel, which makes the bicycle unstable and hard to handle. Your hips will be too far forward in relation to the bottom bracket axle, which means you won't be able to get as much leverage on the pedals. And your head will be down, so you won't see where you are going–not smart in an all out sprint.

Finally, cyclists tend to use their upper body incorrectly. When sprinting, you should pull on the bars with a rowing motion to balance the power of your legs. If you don't, the bicycle will flop around dangerously, and you'll waste power on waste motion instead of pedaling. It follows that a strong upper body is just as important as strong legs, another reason to look at the weight training suggestions elsewhere in the book.

Bauer suggests doing your sprint workout once or twice a week, year-round, during short, routine rides. Warm up for 10 minutes, do five to eight sprints with full recovery in between, then pedal slowly to cool down. The whole workout takes about an hour. After a few weeks there should be noticeable improvement in your top end speed.

Of course, speed isn't just 10 seconds of bicycle-crunching frenzy. Short bursts of speed are useful for closing a 10-meter gap to a cyclist in front. Jump hard á la Bauer, and that gap closes like a door.

Other situations require both a quick "jump" and the ability to sustain high speed, and it's possible to train for both. But in most recreational riding, all you need is a *minute* at high speed to drop your training partner, bridge the gap between you and your vanishing riding partners, or just for the joy of making that bicycle fly.

Once you've built a bit of leg speed and refined your technique, don't forget to put it all together in longer efforts. A good way to build on your newly acquired power and speed: short, explosive bursts whenever the spirit moves you. Don't do these as structured intervals with incomplete recovery between them. This is a valid technique for serious competitors, but incorporating it into your program too soon can ruin your enthusiasm for cycling in a hurry.

Scatter three or four such efforts through your normal training ride instead—and take advantage of spontaneous situations. For example, a training partner opens a gap while you sit up to adjust your helmet; you jump hard and chase him down. Or you're rolling down a little hill and start losing speed; jump hard and keep it going. Make a *game* out of speed training.

Spirited training rides in small, closely matched groups are good ways to push yourself just a little bit harder. Someone jumps for a road sign, for example, and everyone else chases. The escapee is caught, others sit up to recover, and someone else explodes out of the pack in a fever to be first to the pop machine at the country store. If you can find a group of like-minded friends to train with, you'll have too much fun to notice how much faster you've become.

Riding in a Group: The Fun Crowd

Cycling, more than other endurance sports like running, is a group sport. Crowds are an inevitable consequence of practicing a sport that pits hundreds of cyclists against each other in single events. But cycling is also done with others, because part of the thrill of the sport is the way drafting (riding in the stream of quiet air behind someone else) opens up a whole new world of shared effort in training rides and new strategy in races. If you are feeling confident with your solo riding skills, you are ready to move on to groups of two or more.

To be comfortable in group riding situations, you need to learn to live with *proximity* and *contact*. It is often unnerving for a novice cyclist to be traveling within 6 inches of someone else's rear wheel at 40 mph. But it's possible to learn how to actually enjoy the situation—taking advantage of the opportunity for conversation that such contiguity allows or simply enjoying the drafting effect.

First, a couple of general rules for riding with other people:

Be predictable. Sudden and unexpected maneuvers frequently cause a crash and are certain to arouse the ire of your riding companions. So—ride a straight line. If you must brake, do so smoothly and gradually. And take the correct line through corners. Flamboyance and nonconformity are wonderful characteristics in their place, but they don't belong in a group ride.

Know the other cyclists. If you ride often with the same people, you'll develop your own "book" on everyone's dangerous riding habits. That guy stands up roughly when climbing, so don't follow too closely, while she corners hesitantly, so give her a little more room in corners. After a while, you'll react so automatically to these idiosyncrasies that you'll be able to anticipate them.

If you are racing against people you don't know, you'll have to form some opinions fast. Watch for cyclists who don't go straight, and stay as far away from them as possible. Cyclists who are all over their bicycles—riding as if they're uncomfortable—aren't good bets either. You'll soon learn to recognize smooth, competent cyclists. And they aren't always the strongest people in the group. Some extremely fast cyclists are rough and dangerous without the experience (or patience) to be good cycling citizens.

Look ahead for trouble. Learn to spot dangerous situations before they happen. In a group, ride with your hands on the lever hoods unless you are pulling at the front of a fast paceline. You'll have better visibility that way and quicker access to the brakes if you need them. And braking from the top can be done more subtly if you need to slow down slightly without disrupting the whole group. Learn to spot danger ahead. Approaching a stoplight that is about to turn yellow is an example: Will the cyclists ahead of you shoot through at the last minute or brake suddenly?

Be ready for accidental contact. Bumping shoulders or handlebars is inevitable in group riding but shouldn't cause a problem if you are prepared. Ride relaxed with slightly bent elbows and a light touch on the bars. When you see someone moving into your space, don't tense up. If you are loose and relaxed, you'll absorb the impact without affect on the steering and balance of your bicycle. Good cyclists, in fact, can bump shoulders all day and never go down.

It's best to start practicing group riding with a more experienced cyclist. Find a lightly traveled rural road or long, empty parking lot and ride side by side with your handlebars perhaps a foot apart. Practice reaching over and touching the other cyclist on the back or hip, lightly bumping his bars with your hand. As you become more confident, ride closer together and practice bumping shoulders without tightening up. Practice drafting, too, so you develop a feel for protecting your front wheel.

And remember to be patient with yourself. It is normal to be apprehensive about falling, so give yourself some time to get accustomed to close riding.

When you feel confident with one other person, venture out on a group ride. A group of four or five other people is about right, and it helps if they are experienced cyclists who can offer constructive tips but are willing to go slowly enough to let you concentrate on technique rather than merely keeping up.

Single Pacelines

Begin with a single paceline (a group of cyclists pedaling in single file). The idea is to share the work at the front, each cyclist breaking the wind for 30 seconds or a minute and then back to the rear of the bunch to rest in its draft. In a group this size, skilled cyclists can go 3 or 4 mph faster than they could as individuals, eating up the miles with shared effort.

Start out single file about 6 inches to the left of the white line. "Draft" the cyclist in front of you with your wheels about a foot apart. When you are in the middle of the line, ride smoothly without letting gaps open. Don't overlap the wheel of the cyclist in front of you. If the gap closes too fast, soft-pedal or sit up more to catch enough wind to slow you down slightly.

When you are the lead cyclist you're in charge of setting the pace. Take pulls (turns at the front) of reasonable length. A minute is standard in a small group, but sometimes—in a hard wind, for example—you may want everyone to ride only 20 or so pedal turns before they pull off to the rear.

The lead cyclist is also the eyes of the group, in charge of watching for obstacles in the road. But don't yell, "Glass!" or "Pothole!" when you see them. Point them out with the hand on the side of the hazard, instead. It's also traditional for the lead cyclist to warn the group of approaching cars by saying "Car up!" The last cyclist in the line also checks behind occasionally to warn of overtaking traffic with "Car back!"

When your "pull" is done and you're ready to move to the rear, wave your fingers without taking your hand off the bars on the side opposite the direction in which you plan to pull off. And remember to always pull off into a side or quartering wind. In calm conditions or into a head wind, it is usually safer to pull off to the left toward the traffic lane so that only one cyclist at a time is exposed.

After you've signaled, move to the side about a foot and soft-pedal. The next cyclist is now at the front and should continue pedaling at the same speed, taking over the duties of the leader. Pedal easily, letting the paceline go by on your right. Glance back to locate the end of the line, and when you're within one person of the end, accelerate slightly so you can swing over smoothly into the last person's draft.

Some hints: Don't drink from your bottle unless you are at the *end* of the paceline. If you reach for a drink in the middle, you may ride erratically and cause problems.

When you are second in line and the leader pulls over, keep a steady pace. It is common for cyclists to get so excited about being at the front that they pull through too fast and make everyone else chase, but the whole idea is to work smoothly together so everyone conserves energy.

By the same token, don't pedal at the front 2 or 3 mph faster than the group's been traveling. It is tempting to take monster pulls to show other cyclists how strong you are, but it won't win you any friends. If you are that much stronger, take longer pulls rather than faster ones.

One last tip: If you puncture while riding in a paceline, don't grab the brakes and slow abruptly. Tell your companions what happened, pedal softly, and ease out of line.

Double Pacelines

A larger group can use a double paceline if the road is wide enough to accommodate two cyclists abreast. If yours holds ten people, divide them in half and ride side by side in two lines of five. Every minute or so, the lead cyclist in each column drops back to the outside of his respective line. In effect, you'll have two single pacelines riding side by side and coordinating the length of the pulls.

This type of paceline is ideal for casual rides, because you can talk to the cyclist next to you—and if the two lines have unequal numbers, you'll get a new partner each time through. The disadvantage is that the group is actually four cyclists wide as the former leaders drop back along the double paceline. For this reason, this technique should be used only on almost-deserted roads.

In a large, fast group, try a rotating paceline (two parallel lines, one line moving about a mile per hour faster than the other). When you hit the front, don't stay there and take a pull, but move immediately over into the other, slower-moving line. On your way back down the slower line, check behind by glancing under one arm or over your shoulder to locate the end of the other line. Don't be late moving over into it because if you miss the train, you'll be dangling off, disrupting the whole rotation.

Once you have developed the ability to follow a wheel, ride a single paceline in a small group, and handle double pacelines with more cyclists, you'll be equipped to deal with practically every group riding situation. However, to be a truly finished cyclist, you need to know how to handle two special cases.

Echelons

When the wind is from the side or quartering from the front, cyclists don't look for draft directly behind other cyclists but slightly to the side—away from the wind. The formation that results is called an echelon. For single pairs of cyclists, this staggered formation doesn't present any

A double paceline.

special problems. But when a large number of cyclists become offset to get shelter from the wind, the situation changes.

Cyclists in an echelon take up more room in the traffic lane than they do when riding single or double file. In a strong side wind, as few as four or five cyclists can spread across a whole lane, making this technique dangerous on the open road. Echelons, as a result, usually form only in races when at least one lane of the road is closed to nonbicycle traffic.

Because an echelon can travel much faster than a lone cyclist exposed to the wind, cyclists who can't find a place in the echelon invariably get dropped—a strong incentive to squeeze in, even if it means dangling out in traffic if the wind is from the right or riding in the grass if the wind is from the left.

An echelon with the wind from the rider's *left.*

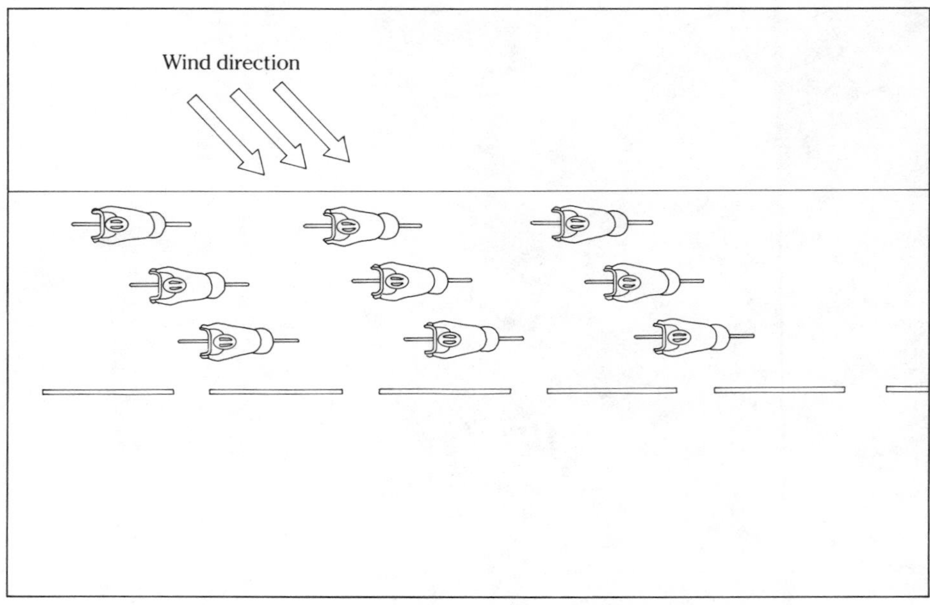

Echelons form when lines of riders move together in this pattern.

When more cyclists try to squeeze into an echelon than will fit into the single lane available, the group can spread out over the whole road—a dangerous situation when dealing with oncoming traffic. In a race with a blustery crosswind, this means that the strongest cyclists will jam to the front, and an echelon will form early in the race.

Echelons are usually self-selecting, because only the strongest cyclists have the power to get to the front where they form and the assertiveness to squeeze into the limited number of spaces available. Everyone else gets left behind—unless they can form their own echelons and tuck in behind the first one.

In group rides where the purpose is to help each other, you can take a tip from the racers and form a series of echelons—but echelons that not only help you in strong winds but also take up a minimum of road space. The trick: Form a series of three-person echelons that nestle close to each other like stacked spoons, with enough room between for cyclists to trade off. Each group of three gets shelter as its members rotate in normal fashion among themselves, but they also get a bit more wind protection, courtesy of the echelon ahead.

Echelons of any type are elegant and fast moving, but they are hard enough to organize that they often don't get used when they're most needed. That's not good, because a well-oiled echelon gives each cyclist feelings of incredible speed and camaraderie that are hard to match.

Riding in a Racing Pack

While a training group will usually cooperate and form predictable pacelines, cyclists are everywhere like a swarm of insects in a race or at the beginning of a competitive century ride. All the cyclists are out for themselves (or for a small number of teammates), and they will cooperate only when it is to their advantage. In addition, everyone is "pumped" psychologically–the resulting tension often leads to miscalculations and accidents. Survival in a racing pack demands a *firm* grasp of all the pack riding skills mentioned so far–plus several more.

First, be wary at the opening of any mass-start race or tour. If 50 cyclists start a race, that means that 50 nervous, pumped-up, fallible humans have to get their feet into their pedals and proceed down the road in something resembling a straight line. Not surprisingly, you can count on several cyclists blowing it.

The safest place to be at the start is the front row. It is often worth it to cut your warm-up short and line up as soon as the chief official gives the word. If you arrive late and can't line up near the front, get into your pedals smoothly at the gun, and look ahead for early warning of mishaps: collisions and pileups.

If you survive the start, your need for caution isn't over. Even experienced cyclists often take several miles to settle down into something resembling a predictable pattern. Early in the event, cyclists will jockey for position, cutting you off if you aren't careful. The first corner in a criterium is especially dangerous because the pack is bunched up, and no one knows the best line through the corner or exactly how fast to take it. The result: A criterium often features a pileup on the first corner. But races get safer the

A racing pack bunched together.

farther you get from the starting line. After they've gone around the course a few times, racers spread out, and most have a better feel for the turns. The same holds for road races or centuries where you see each corner only once on a point-to-point or big loop course.

Skill number two–stay at the front–is the best defense against these problems. Make every effort to stay in the first dozen cyclists, especially approaching corners, so you can choose your own line without worrying about other cyclists crashing in front of you.

Another reason for staying at the front through corners has to do with something called the "accordion effect." The first cyclists through the corner can choose the fastest lines, but cyclists farther back in the pack have to slow and wait a bit for everyone else to funnel through. As a result, those through first can ride smoothly with little loss of speed, saving energy for later in the race or tour. But cyclists held up in the corner have to sprint hard to catch back up to the leaders. Every corner extracts its quota of energy, and soon they are in the rear for good.

Corners aren't the only danger spots in races, so the more you can stay at the front, the safer you'll be. Some of the biggest pileups occur on flat, straight stretches when the pack is bunched up. Someone touches a wheel and falls, taking down those behind in a massive chain reaction.

Skill number three: Be ready for anything. Erratic riding is a case in point. Cyclists who are models of competence and decorum in casual rides with their training partners sometimes become squirrelly and undisciplined in the excitement of a big event. The training ride rule about never overlapping wheels is even more important in competition because of the incessant switching and jumping about that takes place.

Be especially wary of overlapping wheels in corners. Inexperienced competitors are often amazed at the speed they achieve in a racing pack. When they try to carry that speed through corners, they can't make it without changing line in midturn. If you happen to be next to them when they straighten up the bicycle halfway through a corner, you and your bicycle may end up in the cheap seats.

The fourth skill: Realize that sometimes it's smart to cooperate with other cyclists, but at other times you're better off on your own.

Training rides reward cooperation. If you and your training buddies can take turns breaking the wind, you'll go farther and faster getting a better workout. In organized rides like centuries, some cyclists want to set up a paceline, others prefer to go it on their own. But in races, no one wants to cooperate for fear of giving someone else an advantage. There *are* times in races, however–in a break with five or six other strong cyclists, for example–when cooperation is important. If the break members work together, they'll often be able to stay ahead of the pack until the finish, increasing each cyclist's chances for victory, or at least assuring a high placing. That cooperation will often last for miles as the break works together to lengthen their lead over the pack, only to dissolve all at once as the finish line approaches. The trick is knowing when to cooperate, when to free-lance.

That knowledge comes only with experience, so skill number five is: Ride in big packs as often as possible. The more you ride, the more at home you'll become in a swirling sea of bicycles. Strategic decisions become automatic, physical reflexes are honed. And you don't have to travel the country to find big events, either. Evening criteriums put on by local clubs are just as useful for sharpening your skills. Or organize low-key group rides yourself, motivating other cyclists to attend by talking a bicycle shop into donating prizes for a drawing at the finish.

Don't be afraid to try competition, though. The foregoing survival suggestions make even casual group rides seem dangerous and frenzied, but the reality is that most races proceed safely. Competition isn't for everyone, naturally. In fact, some of the strongest cyclists never race, being content to hammer away by themselves on country roads enjoying the thrill of going fast under their own power. But competition is more than just exciting. Learning to handle the challenges of racing makes you a better and safer bicycle handler and all-around cyclist.

RALEIGH

Time Trials

Bicycle racing is exciting, challenging, and an increasingly visible sport in the United States. If you enjoy riding and competing against yourself, you'll probably be tempted to give racing a try. This chapter and the next are designed to describe tactics you'll need to make your first forays into competition rewarding and fun.

Be forewarned: Effective race tactics are complicated. It takes years to learn what to do and how to do it. But this chapter and the next will provide the basics you need to get started in competition. The learning process, however, is never over for even the most experienced professional.

The Cyclist versus the Clock

At first glance, time trials are the simplest form of cycling competition. Cyclists start at intervals, usually 1 minute apart, and ride the course as fast as possible alone. The object is to complete the distance in the least amount of time. You ride as hard as you can from start to finish.

Yet in another sense, time trials are the most complex event in cycling. The aerodynamic requirements of the sport are one reason. At speeds greater than 20 mph, almost all the cyclist's power output is used to overcome wind resistance. Obviously, the cyclist who best slices through that invisible wall of air has an advantage. As a result, time trialing is the most equipment-oriented sector of cycling. Disk wheels, aerodynamic frames, shoe covers, and aero helmets are a few of the ways cyclists in search of high performance try to cheat the wind.

Training for varying distances complicates the sport, too. Local time trials are usually contested on courses from 5 to 10 miles long. The United States Cycling Federation (USCF) district and national championship distance is 40 km, or about 25 miles. Medium-length time trials are unusual in this country. In England, where time trialing is a popular and respected form of the sport, contests covering 100 miles or 24 hours are common. But Americans have embraced the ultimate time trial: the Race Across America, a 3,000-mile cross-country odyssey.

Time trials are also technically demanding. The skills required are so important in other kinds of events that no cyclist with hopes to become a solid competitor can avoid them. For instance, time trials are a vital part of stage racing (races conducted in separate pieces or stages, with victory going to the rider with the best combined times). Cyclists can gain or lose substantial amounts of time since no drafting—slipstream riding, which is more forgiving of bad form on your part—is allowed. It is often said that cyclists who can't race the clock effectively can't win a stage race.

And finally, time trialing is *demanding*. It involves the most severe form of self-discipline. Good time trialists can push themselves to the absolute limit for the duration of the contest. In physiological terms, they hover on the very brink of their anaerobic threshold where the slightest increase in speed would drive them into irrevocable oxygen debt and a lost race. Psychologically, top time trialists must learn to overcome pain and blot out all other distractions in their quest for speed. But the difficulty—and ultimately the fascination—of the sport arises out of this perilous quest for human limits, both mental and physical.

The Race of Truth: Whys and Wherefores

If time trialing is so painful and demanding, why do it? The answer lies in both the nature of the sport and the advantages it offers for competitors and fitness cyclists alike.

A major appeal is the event's absolute purity. The Europeans call it "the race of truth" because you cover the distance alone, with no one else to break the wind, relying on your own strength, talent, and determination to get to the finish. And although it is natural for everyone to compare times after the last cyclist streaks across the line, the real competition is always *you*.

Time trialing also happens to be a good way to sample competitive cycling, regardless of age or sex. For starters, it's convenient. Almost every town with an active bicycle club has a local time trial series or can easily start one. You don't have to drive across the state, spending time and money to race in a crowded and sometimes dangerous event like a criterium.

And you don't have to disrupt your training schedule with daylong drives that keep you off the bicycle. You can train *through* time trials instead of tapering all week for one big effort. The race becomes one of your weekly hard workouts.

Time trialing is fun, too. Like a running race, people gather around after everyone has come in off the course to compare times and talk about the head wind or what gears they used. Time trialing also seems to encourage more camaraderie than road racing, perhaps because so many cyclists see it as a way to improve their own performance rather than as a serious competition with other cyclists.

Time trials offer variety, which may sound like a strange claim for an event whose basic format is so simple. It's nonetheless true. If you are a muscular cyclist who is short on endurance, for example, try a 1,000-meter time trial on the track or a 10-miler on the road. These put a premium on explosiveness and high, steady energy expenditure.

Are you more of an all-rounder with fitness as your goal? Then the 25-mile (40 km) time trial is your ideal. And what if your forte is endurance? Use it—in 50- to 100-mile time trials or even the Race Across America.

For cyclists wanting a special challenge, ultradistance time trials such as Bicycle Across Missouri and the Race Across America offer unique challenges. But there are also recognized records to break from city to city like Seattle to San Diego. And you can always devise your own course and go for a personal record—your driveway, for example, to that town 37 miles away. With investigation and imagination, you can almost always find time trials that suit your particular blend of physical and mental strengths.

One major advantage of time trialing is simply safety. Because each cyclist starts alone, you are on the course by yourself without the crowd that characterizes mass-start races. No drafting is allowed. The emphasis, therefore, is on sheer riding ability and fitness, instead of esoteric skills like following 6 inches behind a speeding wheel or cornering in a tight pack.

While these challenges make road racing a fascinating challenge, they also increase its risk. Time trials are the best way to sample the thrill of speed and competition *without* major hazards. You can, of course, get injured in a time trial if you ride along with your head down and collide with a parked car. But in general, time trialing is the least hazardous form of bicycling competition.

Time trialing is safe for another reason, too. Because the race requires a steady expenditure of effort for the distance, you can eliminate the potentially injurious speedwork that road racers find mandatory. You simply don't *need* that kind of explosiveness.

Training time is another area in which time trials beat out other kinds of races. If you stick to races from 5 to 25 miles, you can tap most of your potential on a total training mileage of perhaps 100 miles per week—a light load. Given one weekly endurance ride of 40 miles or a bit less, this adds up to perhaps 5 or 6 hours a week on the bicycle—well within reach for recreational racers with family and career responsiblities.

If you are considering mass-start racing, time trials are the best way to gauge your fitness. Many would-be racers are hesitant to try the sport simply because they're afraid they can't keep up. Time trials give you the opportunity to compare yourself with more experienced racers to see if you have the power and speed to give mass-start racing a try. If you do, you can start learning the intricasies of road racing that we cover in the next chapter. If not, time trials will tell you that, too, and you can postpone your first mass-start race until you do have the necessary punch.

One final word: Time trialing doesn't have to be expensive. If your goal is to better your own performances, the races can be ridden on the same bicycle you use for everyday training and pleasure riding. Of course, if you're seriously trying to better your personal record or beat someone else's, you can spend large sums on special time trial bicycles and aerodynamic disk wheels. But such expenditures just aren't necessary to meet most people's goals.

Equipment

In 1984, Francesco Moser broke the world hour record—often thought to be the ultimate time trial—by riding 31.7 miles aboard a space-age composite frame with $2,000 disc wheels. His feat revolutionized equipment at the top of the sport, but it hasn't changed the look of small-town bicycle club events. You can get started in time trialing with the bicycle you are currently riding. In fact, if you are primarily interested in personal improvement, it's probably the smart thing to do—changes in your times will reflect your fitness level instead of your equipment.

If you get bitten hard by the competition bug, however, it won't be long before you start wondering how you can make your bicycle just a little faster. Wheels are the place to start.

You'll want the light weight and low rolling resistance offered by narrow tires, coupled with the low wind resistance of fewer spokes. A hot setup for racing the clock begins with a rear wheel with 28 bladed (or elliptical) spokes laced two-cross on the freewheel side and radial on the opposite. Choose V-section aerodynamic wheels shod with narrow, 18 mm tubular tires. Front wheels can be even more radical—smooth cyclists racing on reasonable pavement can get away with 18 spokes and radial lacing.

With the advent of quality clincher tires with low rolling resistance, many time trialists are switching from tubulars. Clincher rims are a bit heavier but are relatively inexpensive, have low rolling resistance, and require less upkeep. If you hate to glue tubulars or want to avoid their expense and fragility, consider 19 mm clinchers with a slick tread design.

One word of caution concerning your wheels. The *quality* of the wheel is considerably more important than the number of spokes. Be sure your wheel-builder knows the craft before you trust your performance—not to mention your safety—to his products. Many wheelbuilders are perfectly competent as long as they limit themselves to durable road racing wheels with conventional lacing patterns, but they lack vital experience in more exotic—and important to racing—techniques like radial lacing. But a crumpling front wheel is as dangerous in a time trial as in any other race, so choose a wheel-builder with impeccable credentials.

Another good time trialing investment is a skin suit (a one-piece Lycra suit, which fits like a second skin). Your body is the main contributor to air resistance. A regular road jersey, with the rear pockets gaping open and catching air like a parachute, acts like an air brake. The skin suit significantly reduces your air resistance. Remember, also, to pin on your number securely so that it doesn't flap and rattle in the wind. A trick: Tape down the edges for a windproof seam.

Other aero tricks: Use brake levers with concealed cables. Take off your bottle bracket before the race. Remove your pump or place it lengthwise under the top tube. Use step-in pedals to eliminate the wind drag of straps and clips. Tape down your shoe laces or Velcro straps. Wear Lycra-backed gloves, because the coarse netting on the backs of conventional gloves catches the wind. Shave your legs—and don't laugh, if you're male. Studies indicate that hairy legs cost you 5 seconds in a 25-mile time trial—perhaps the margin of victory.

And finally, don't forget a hard-shell helmet. Although time trialing is a safe form of racing, accidents can happen when judgment and reflexes are dulled by effort. You'll be faster in a good helmet, too. Almost all ANSI-approved helmets are more aerodynamic than a hairy head, and an aero helmet can save you over half a minute on a 25-mile course.

Training

Training for low-key time trials isn't complicated, and it doesn't differ greatly from the training you are probably doing now for general fitness. Start with a solid base of endurance riding to strengthen your cardiovascular system as well as muscles and ligaments. One ride per week should emphasize endurance at approximately 65 to 75 percent of your maximum heart rate. If you are aiming at time trials up to 25 miles, this long ride can be limited to 2 hours. If you are preparing for longer events, you'll have to increase the distance—but not necessarily proportionally. Quality is much more important than quantity.

Twice a week—no more than that—do some specific time trial training. Intervals and repeats make the best use of your training time, and they can be serious fun instead of major boredom. Here's a sample interval workout that will improve your performance as a time trialist.

Warm up for 15 minutes in a low gear, using a cadence between 90 and 100 rpm. Then hit it hard for about a minute using a bigger gear, one that makes you work hard but not so hard that your form deteriorates. Keep your cadence steady at around 90. Maintain an aerodynamic position like you would in a race: back flat, hands on the drops, elbows bent, head up for safety. After the burst, roll easily in a lower gear for several minutes until your heart rate drops to about 120. Use a heart rate monitor or check your pulse manually. Then shift into the big gear, and go again for another minute. Repeat four or five times, then pedal easily for the rest of the ride. As the season progresses, gradually increase your speed and gearing while decreasing the rest time between efforts.

Another way to build time trial power is with repeats. These are longer than intervals, but you take correspondingly longer rest periods between them. Warm up for 15 minutes, then ride 3 miles hard. Don't go all-out, though—shoot for about an 85 percent effort or about 85 percent of your maximum heart rate. Concentrate on good form. After the distance, roll easily in a small gear until your heart rate drops substantially and your legs feel good again. Then repeat the effort, rest, and go once again. Three times is plenty to start with. Later, you can increase the repeats until you reach five. But don't be in a hurry, or your desire to get faster may outstrip your ability to recover. Remember to emphasize quality. Three strong repeats are better than five ragged ones. The training maxim that says it best: *Train,* don't strain.

Even though time trials are usually flat, time trial power can also be built on hills. If you have long ascents available, ride them at a strong, steady pace once a week. This is anaerobic threshold work that simulates time trialing's cardiovascular demands at the same time that it builds leg strength. If short hills are all you have in

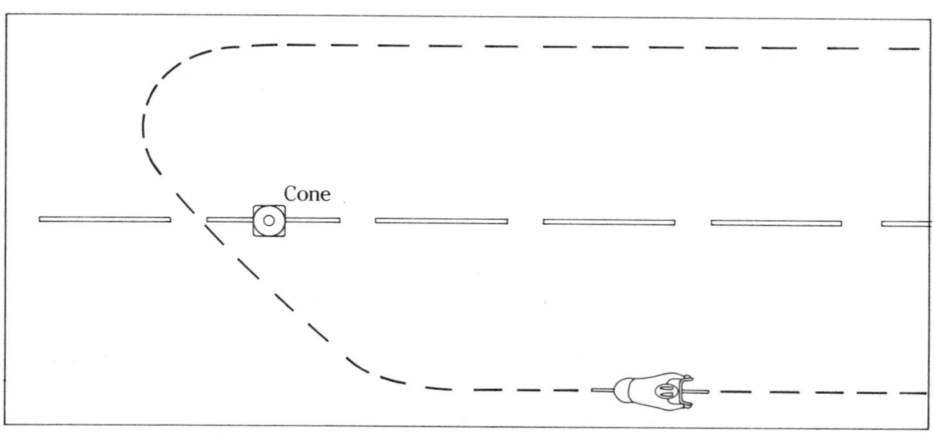

The correct path for a quick racing turn.

your vicinity, do repeats in a gear that enables you to keep a cadence of 85 to 90 rpm and a heart rate at or slightly above 85 percent of maximum.

Training time trials also help prepare you for the real thing. Find a 3-mile stretch of lightly traveled road with no stop signs or traffic lights. Ideally it should be a good warm-up ride away from home. Don't use the same course that you ride in local club competition, because different scenery will ease the boredom of several weeks of training.

Measure a course with your cyclecomputer starting at a conspicuous landmark: a mailbox, sign, or big tree. Use another such object for the turnaround. You won't need a holder–the person who braces you and your bicycle in a real race–for training time trials. Either start from a track stand or a slow roll. Some cyclists like to hold onto a roadside sign to simulate a race's standing start.

Ride the course all-out every two or three weeks, and practice *all* your time trial techniques. That's enough training time, simply because time trialing is such very hard work that if you do this workout too frequently, you'll lose enthusiasm quickly.

Last, practice the specific skills of time trialing. Get someone to hold you upright so you can work on your standing start. Learn the right gear to use and how to come off the line smoothly without wobbling or wasting energy. Put a cone in the road and practice your turnaround until you can circle it at maximum safe speed. A little time spent working on these simple skills can save you time and embarrassment in competition.

Peaking

When you are ready to compete in an important time trial–your club's final event of the summer, for example, or the USCF district championship–you'll want to cut back on rigorous training so both legs and mind are strong for the big race.

The week before, cut your training volume down about one-third. If you normally ride 30 miles on Tuesday, cut it to 20. Reduce the number of repetitions, too. If you've been doing six intervals, do four. However, don't reduce your intensity–do those four intervals at your usual pace.

Don't stay off the bicycle the day before the event. Instead, take a day off two days before. Then you can spin during the afternoon the day before the race to eliminate the stiffness that a day off the bicycle seems to produce. And if you've driven a substantial distance to the race, an easy spin will put life back in your legs.

Spend your day off working on your bicycle. Put on your race wheels and closeratio freewheel if you have them. Change to a chain that you've used with that freewheel–your old chain may skip on the new cogs. Check the bicycle thoroughly before your final training ride: Tighten all nuts and bolts that may have worked loose, and examine the tire tread for small cuts or tiny pieces of embedded glass that may work their way into the tube during the race. Nothing is more frustrating than to be on your way to a personal record only to lose it to a puncture in the last mile. Finally, take the bicycle for a short ride, running through all the gears. Bicycles have a disturbing habit of operating perfectly on the workstand but malfunctioning on the road. If there is a problem, *now* is the time to discover it, not during your prerace warm-up.

Registration and Warm-Up

On the day of the race, get to the course an hour before the start, so you have plenty of time to register, put your bicycle together, and warm up. Add a few minutes for eventualities like getting lost on the drive or changing flat tires during your warm-up.

Warm up *completely.* Time trialing

requires an intense, continuous effort from the start to the finish, so be ready to go hard from the first pedal stroke. Start the warm-up by spinning in a low gear for at least 15 minutes. Work up a sweat, and get your muscles loose until your pedal stroke feels fluid. Then do several short repeats, but don't exert too much. Go just hard enough to start stressing your body, waking it up for the impending effort.

Finish with several short sprints in your starting gear to make sure your chain doesn't skip under load or your rear wheel pull over in dropouts. And time your warm-up so you have 5 more minutes to spin easily before you come to the line. You should be sweating, but not breathing heavily, when your minute man sprints away. If you have a stopwatch, start it when he leaves so you'll be able to determine your elapsed time by merely subtracting a minute.

The Start

The holder will grab your bicycle so you can reach down and get both feet strapped in. Roll the pedals over until they are horizontal, then relax and concentrate on a good start. When the timer counts down to 10 seconds, squeeze the rear brake lever to keep the bicycle from spurting forward, and get out of the saddle, balanced over the pedals.

On "Go!" sprint steadily away from the line until you get the initial gear rolling, then sit down and spin it up to a cadence of about 100. Shift to a bigger gear, build up the cadence again, then settle into the gear you know you will use for the majority of the ride. You'll know that gear from your training—the one that allows you to main-

A rider being held at the start of a time trial.

Out of the saddle, accelerating at the start of a time trial.

tain a cadence of about 90 with your heart rate hovering near your anaerobic threshold. *Don't* let the race's excitement and your ego tempt you into using a larger gear, or your cadence and speed will drop as your muscles fatigue. Speed is the product of a steady cadence and energy output, not pure gear size.

Once you have settled into a rhythm, focus on keeping the same aerodynamic position that you practiced in training. The most ultramodern disk wheels and skin suits won't help at all if your upper body catches the air like a sail. A good image to help you position yourself properly: a shark knifing smoothly through the water.

Hills, Wind, and Traffic

U.S. time trial courses have traditionally been flat, a tradition inherited from England where time trialing is a revered art form. European time trial courses, on the other hand, have been more like road courses–twisting and hilly–and the European model is increasingly influencing American races against the clock.

Handle short hills of less than 100 yards by standing to keep your gear rolling. Don't let your cadence drop too much–it's OK to go mildly into oxygen debt because you can recover on the downhill–but don't overdo it, either. A course with short hills favors more experienced cyclists, because they know exactly how much to save on the flats so they can push hard on the ascents without blowing up. Rookies, on the other hand, tend to go so hard on the easy sections of the course that they are left with nothing when the terrain demands everything.

On longer hills, you'll have to gear down and stay seated. You are better off keeping enough in reserve so that you arrive at the top breathing instead of gasping. The key to time trialing is to portion out your energy throughout the *entire* race instead of blowing it all on one section.

Wind is the time trialist's nemesis. A windy day is always a slow day. And no matter how much faster you go with a tail wind, you'll lose that extra time and more when you turn around and face it. Head winds are the worst, but crosswinds are almost as bad. And while a quartering tail wind helps everyone, a quartering head wind on the return trip hurts weaker cyclists most.

Wind, however, is a fact of life in time trials. And every cyclist is out there under the same conditions. So you need to fight the wind effectively to do well.

Start with a good aerodynamic position. Always important, your position on the bicycle becomes *vital* in windy conditions when the effect of any body part protruding more than necessary into the slipstream is magnified.

Keep low on the bicycle. At the world championships one year, the victorious Italian team rode with thin pieces of wire attached between their waists and their bicycles. The harness gave them something to push against as they pedaled a big gear, forced them to maintain an aero position, and while it wasn't comfortable, it nonetheless kept them low and out of the wind.

Don't overgear into a head wind. If you can handle a 52/16 on calm days, you'll probably need a 52/18 or lower when it's blowing hard. Don't let your ego interfere with your judgment, either. Use whatever gear you need to keep your cadence at optimum levels.

The best way to conquer the wind? Fight it mentally. Windy days discourage some cyclists so much they perform poorly. Often, they're the ones who stay at home on windy training days. Remember: If you train in the wind, you'll race well in it.

Nearly all time trial courses are open to traffic. Safety is the first consideration: Keep your head up and be alert for vehicles, especially at the turnaround. But traffic isn't all bad. Overtaking vehicles can actually improve your race time. As they pass, the draft increases your speed slightly for several seconds. Take advantage of this suction by raising your cadence about 5 rpm when you hear an overtaking car or truck. Then hold the higher cadence as long as possible after the vehicle has passed.

Incidentally, this technique is legal as long as you don't *linger* in the draft of a slow car.

Approaching traffic, of course, slows you down with a wall of wind, but since it's farther away–in the other lane–the effect is less significant than a passing vehicle's. When you see an approaching car, raise your cadence and check your position to be sure it's as aerodynamic as possible. Then power through the turbulence and resume your normal cadence as soon as possible.

The Turnaround to the Finish

As you approach the turnaround, shift to the gear you need for reacceleration. Soft-pedal to catch your breath, but don't brake until the last second. Here's where practice can give you a real edge. Start the turn from the far right side of the road, and shave the marker cone. As soon as the bicycle straightens up, get out of the saddle, and sprint back to race speed. Resume your most efficient gearing/cadence combination as soon as possible.

From a mental standpoint, the quarter of the race that follows the turnaround is the most difficult part. You've pushed yourself to the limit, but you are only halfway home. And the course always seems to be uphill and into a head wind after the turn. Prepare yourself mentally for the letdown that almost always accompanies the third quarter of the race by vowing that you will push through the discouragement and pain. But don't neglect the physical half–smart competitors save a little during the initial leg of the race so they are fresher starting the return leg. They often gain back the time lost with their moderate start and occasionally pile up big time gains as they power by their disheartened rivals.

During the last quarter of the race, push the pace over the distance. Don't wait until the final 300 yards for an all out sprint that will gain you only a few seconds. Instead, try to spread that energy out over the last several miles. Take a chance on going into oxygen debt to gain time, because if you blow up, you don't have far to go. In fact, if you plan your finishing surge correctly, you'll finish with the feeling that you are completely expended.

Don't stop immediately after you cross the line. Cool down instead by shifting to your lowest gear, and spin around for 10 or 15 minutes to help blood circulate in your leg muscles and to catch your breath. Then join the group at the finish line comparing notes on times and experiencing the satisfaction of having gone to the limit.

Assessing Your Performance

Time trialing is about improvement, but it's important to note that there will be events in which you *don't* improve. In fact, you'll often go slower than your previous best. Don't be depressed by these dips in your performance graph. Sometimes wind or rain can slow you down even though you actually felt stronger on that particular day. Equipment makes a difference, too, as well as what you ate for supper. Everyone also has an occasional bad day that just can't be explained. If you consistently experience slower times in spite of hard training, suspect overtraining and chronic fatigue. But never forget: If you train consistently, moderately, and well, you will improve.

79
79

Quick Tracks: Criteriums, Circuit Races, Long and Short Road Races

Most cyclists begin racing in criteriums or short road races–popular, crowd-pleasing events. The tactics, training, and equipment are the same whether the event is an around-the-block criterium, a circuit race on a 1- or 2-mile course, or a short road race of 30 to 50 miles. But at the end of this chapter, we'll provide additional information for longer road races.

Preparation

Assuming that you have a good general training base, what's the best way to prepare for short races? First, if you have been riding long distances, cut back. You don't need to train for a century if you plan to ride 20-mile criteriums. When endurance goes up, speed goes down–and speed is what you need to win shorter races. Cut your weekly endurance ride to about 2 hours, or roughly the length of your longest race. Don't go over 40 miles if you plan on doing mostly criteriums and circuit races. Keep your heart rate at about 80 percent of maximum on these training rides–just a bit harder than you would normally work on endurance days. The shorter distance makes it possible to recover before the next day's training.

Two days each week, work to improve your recovery from short, hard bursts. Criteriums require the ability to go flat out for 20 or 30 seconds, recover briefly and incompletely, then do it again. This is the usual pattern in short-course racing, so it's the best recipe for training.

Warm up thoroughly, sprint hard for 8 to 10 seconds to wind up your gear, then sit down and keep it going for another 15 to 20 seconds. Your pedal rpm should be in the 100 to 120 range. Gear down at that point, and spin briskly until your heart rate drops and the burning in your thighs cools a bit. When your heart rate reaches about 120 beats a minute, go hard again.

Start with relatively few intervals, say five or six, and build up to a dozen or more. Use a cyclecomputer to measure the speed you can maintain during the effort. Note it in your diary, and compare the speeds over the season. Your top sustainable speed, along with the number of intervals you can perform at that speed, should increase with proper training. Train like this no more than twice a week with at least one day of easy spinning in between. Remember: Competition on the weekend or in the evening counts as one of your hard days.

Top racers vary this workout by motorpacing (riding in the draft of a motorcyle or car). The increased speed simulates race pace and develops greater leg speed, but because of the obvious danger isn't recommended for inexperienced cyclists. Train instead with three or four other cyclists of about equal ability, and do the intervals in a paceline, taking fast 30-second pulls just as you would in a race breakaway. You'll get a great workout and improve your ability to follow a wheel.

Bicycle handling is the most obvious challenge in short-course racing, but most beginning cyclists don't try to meet it in a systematic way. They jump blindly into a race with little understanding of the skills required and even less knowledge of how to apply them. That's a recipe for disaster. But bicycle handling isn't some mysterious black art–it's a skill that is learned.

Start with traffic cones. Lay out a six-cornered course in a field that has firm ground and short grass so you can ride reasonably fast. Use an old bicycle and wheels, and then get going–ride the course in every imaginable way. By yourself, ride the course to learn the correct line through each turn. Ride it in both directions, try it in wet weather, and then change the cones to make it even tougher. Ride some of your laps smoothly and steadily, but then hit others with reckless abandon.

Next, get four or five training partners, and stage a "grass criterium." Wear long tights, a long-sleeved jersey, a hard-shell helmet, maybe even elbow and knee pads. The purpose of this drill is to develop bicycle handling, not fitness, so restrict everyone to the same low gear.

Restart the race every five or six laps to give everyone a breather and to practice getting your feet into the clips at the start. Squeeze through the corners riding side by side. Bump elbows. Overlap wheels, and see if you can get into and out of trouble. Stage sprints every other lap, and take a dangerous inside line through the last corner, fighting aggressively for the best position. An hour of this gonzo riding will give you more close calls and probably more crashing experience than three years of riding actual races. You'll escape injury because of the protective clothing, slower speeds and grass surface, but the savvy you'll acquire will help enormously to make competition a safe, pleasant experience.

The last step in this progression: Ride local club criteriums to hone your skills in a low-pressure setting. View these races as practice instead of competitions you need to win. Try various strategies–sit in and wait for the sprint one time, attack early the next. Go with an early break this week, try a solo flyer next time out. Local races are excellent places to learn your strengths and weaknesses while developing your race strategy.

Ready for your first real race? Start out with the same comprehensive warm-up you used for time trials. Short-course races, like tests against the clock, demand a full effort right from the start. If your body isn't ready to function at 100 percent efficiency when the starter's gun goes off, you'll be left in the dust. The rule of thumb: The shorter the race, the more important the warm-up.

Prerace and Warm-up

To get a good warm-up, you'll have to arrive at the race early enough to get all the "administrivia" out of the way. Mass-start racing always involves more prerace hassles than time trials because of the increased danger of group racing. You have to find a place to park, stand in line to register, get your bicycle ready, and have it inspected. You may face a helmet inspection, too. After you have survived the bureaucratic machinery, roll easily for 15 minutes until you are sweating and feeling loose. Then do some sprints and longer accelerations. Finish about 10 minutes before the start.

At some races, you won't be able to warm up because of other events, and sometimes the surrounding roads are too heavily trafficked to allow a safe warm-up. If that's the case, pack along a training stand and use it for your normal warm-up. Choose a model that attaches to the rear wheel and doesn't take up much room. Stationary warm-ups aren't quite as effective as the real thing because you aren't actually riding and honing your balance and bicycle handling, but in center-city criteriums or races where a glass-strewn road is the only option, they are often your best bet.

At most races you'll have a few minutes to ride the course between events. Use this time to get a feel for the corners and look for trouble: potholes, gravel, sewer grates, potentially slippery manhole covers. Course-side obstacles are often barricaded with hay bales, and errant hay can make the road surface extremely slippery. Watch out for places where spectators or wind have scattered the bales. If the course is wet, check traction in the corners. Be on the lookout for painted lane lines; they can be as slippery as ice. And finally, check the wind direction to see which side of the road is sheltered.

Warming up on rollers before a race.

The Start

When you are called to the start, get a place near the front so you won't be caught behind 40 cyclists at the first corner. This position is so important that it is often worth cutting short your warm-up to line up in the first or second row. If you're late, try to squeeze in near the curb. Or have a

Hay bales provide crash insurance in tight criterium corners.

friend save you a place in the front by taking up more room than necessary with his bicycle and body.

At the sound of the gun, pedal a few strokes with your free foot on the bottom of the pedal, then quickly snap in. You'll appreciate all the practice you had grass racing. Sprint away from the line, and go hard from the gun. The first several laps are usually fast, as strong cyclists try to secure places in the lead and burn off less-skilled competitors.

The best-positioned rider in this pack is five or six places from the front.

Pack Position and Cornering

Establish a good position in the pack as soon as possible. The ideal location: five or six cyclists from the front, so you'll get plenty of draft but be able to see and react to moves. It will take hard work and close attention to the ebb and flow of the action to stay there, but it's worth the struggle. At the front, you're less likely to get stuck

In corners, the "accordion effect" strings out riders at the back of the pack, forcing them to sprint out of each corner.

behind a crash, a common problem for cyclists in midpack. You'll avoid less-fit cyclists with reflexes dulled by fatigue. And you'll be in position to go with a break. Mired in the last third of the bunch, you would be unable to do any of that. Remember: The race is at the front!

Another advantage of being a front-runner is that you'll lose less time in corners. In large packs, the first half-dozen cyclists can choose the best line and funnel through at top speed, but the remaining cyclists have to start braking. This initiates the infamous "accordion effect," in which the cyclists near the back are still braking for the corner while the leaders are already accelerating over the horizon. Instead of riding at a smooth, steady, energy-conserving pace, back-of-the-pack cyclists have to sprint hard out of *every* corner to catch up, a situation that will rapidly exhaust even the best prepared cyclist. Consider: A 30-lap criterium with six turns per lap means 180 sprints. How many sprints have *you* been doing in training?

If you haven't yet developed the fitness and skills needed to stay at the front, you can still get a taste of racing—just sit back in the pack and try to hang on as long as possible. Because the risk of crashing increases with distance from the front line, racing in packs of superior cyclists isn't recommended. Stick with racers of similar ability, and don't let your vanity get you in over your head.

Tactical Decisions and Primes

Nonracers love to talk about tactics—how some famous cyclist won through a combination of clever moves or brilliantly planned maneuvers. As a result, many beginning racers believe that the key to winning lies in outthinking the rest of the pack. They believe that superior tactics can overcome deficiencies in power, speed, or the ability to suffer. Not so.

The truth is that a given tactic is only as good as the legs of the cyclist using it. Clever moves are useless unless you have the physical ability to make them happen. The point here? Don't be discouraged if a particular move doesn't work. Perhaps the move was tactically sound, but you haven't yet developed the speed to make it work for you. Experience will teach you what you can and can't do at a particular level of fitness.

Spectators love criteriums and circuit races because midrace action is encouraged by primes (pronounced "preems," sprints for prizes, points, or in a stage race, time bonuses). It is a good idea to chase some primes to see how your legs feel in an all out sprint. This experience will help you plan your strategy for the finish as well as evaluate your competition. But beware: The best sprinter may be saving himself or herself for the sprint that counts the most—the run for the finish.

Be aware that in a race with several primes, race-winning breaks often develop after a sprint. Someone wins the prime, looks back and sees that he has a sizable gap, and decides to go for a solo win. A few other cyclists who were strong enough to stay at the front during the windup for the prime sprint bridge up to the escapee. The result is a small but high-powered break that gains 30 or 40 seconds almost immediately over the dispirited pack.

Even if you don't plan to contest primes, stay close to the action.

Hills

The important thing to remember about hills in a criterium or circuit race is that you'll be climbing the same ones over and over again–once per lap. Obviously you can't go all-out each time up or you'll wear out long before the finish. Instead you have to ration your energy for the whole race.

On the other hand, you need to be mentally prepared for the speed that a racing pack maintains on hills. If you have never raced before, you'll be amazed at how fast the pack climbs–and how fast *you'll* have to go to avoid being dropped. Racing can lose its appeal quickly in the suffering necessary on the climbs.

Yet there are excellent tactical reasons for the cruel climbing pace. Pack speed on short hills is high because of the drafting effect. Although drafting is a minor factor on a long climb at 12 or 14 mph, it's important in a 20 or 25 mph jam over a half-kilometer hill on a criterium course. The result: Racing packs power over hills at speeds you would never attempt on a training ride.

The pace also picks up on hills, simply because strong cyclists recognize them as the best places to pare down the pack to a reasonable size. Hills nearly always cause a selection process to take place–if not the first time up, then certainly by the 10th or 15th ascent. For this reason alone, you should be ready for attacks each time around or at least until a small lead group forms.

Once that happens, the break is more likely to keep the pace steady on the hill so it can keep total lap speed high and remain away from the rest of the pack until the finish. Of course, in the last few laps, the climbers will attack again–to try for a solo win and to avoid a pack sprint that they probably couldn't win.

If you have good basic fitness and climbing talent, the key to surviving lap after lap of hill jams is good position in the pack. Again–leading is better than following. Locate yourself near the front where you can get a good draft but won't have to work too hard to maintain the pace. Starting the climb up front means you can drift back a little when you start to get tired. But if you *start* the climb at the back, there's just no room for taking it easy.

Another problem with climbing at the rear of the group is that slower cyclists block your progress. On narrow climbs, the bunch often splits and leaves behind cyclists otherwise strong enough to stay at the front. But they get caught behind cyclists who are slowing down, have to slow down themselves, and then can't recapture the leaders.

A tactic that can help you avoid that bottleneck is to follow a strong cyclist. Get on his wheel, and just follow it up the hill. But look for a steady climber, not one who ascends in a series of bursts. You'll get dropped during his surges and catch up just in time to get squirted off the wheel again at his next sprint.

The Free Lap Rule

If you crash or have a mechanical problem during most criteriums, the free lap rule applies to you. The free-lap rule simply states that you can take the time the pack needs to complete one lap for repairs to yourself and the bicycle, without penalty. Then the mechanic will push you back into the race so you end up in the same relative position you occupied when the mishap occurred.

Know where the pit area is on the course, and get there as quickly as possible. If you crashed and your bicycle is unridable, you may have to pick it up and run to the pits. And once there, don't panic–relax and let the mechanic change the wheel or straighten the bent derailleur hanger. Catch your breath, so when you reenter the race, you can flow back into the action.

If you crashed, evaluate your own physical damage while the mechanic repairs your bicycle's. You'll probably know immediately if you can resume racing; but if you suspect a broken bone or other major

Mechanics pushing a rider back into action after a wheel change.

problem, err on the side of safety, and hang it up for the day. There's no reason to continue and risk permanent harm.

But if everything seems intact, don't be too quick to give up either. Many racers who crash and sustain minor injuries come back and *win* the race, riding an adrenaline charge that carries them to victory.

Assessing Breaks

The most crucial tactical decision in mass-start races comes when you must either let a break go or try to catch it. Base your decision on your reading of the race and knowledge of your opponents' strengths and weaknesses. Generally, a solo break in the first half of a race is doomed unless the cyclist competely outclasses the competition or has a strong team blocking in the pack and thwarting attempts to chase.

The larger the break, the more strong cyclists it contains; and the closer it is to the end of the race, the greater its chances of succeeding. That's why cyclists who don't sprint well may try it anyway with one or two laps left to ride. They hope that no one will decide to chase them down, because whoever does make that effort with other cyclists drafting behind will probably ruin his own chances of winning.

The Final Sprint

In spite of all the tactical jockeying, many criteriums come down to a mad gallop for the finish line. The action starts several laps early as teams lead their designated sprinter into position, strong cyclists without a good sprint try to get away early, and the general excitement caused by the impending finish raises the speed several miles per hour.

Be ready for the crunch–a surprising number of races are won not after the final corner, but two or three corners back, when the strongest cyclists fight for the best position. Pure speed aside–the more experience and race savvy you have, the better your chances.

If you're a team member, decide before the race who is the designated sprinter. And decide which team members will be assigned to lead that sprinter out at the finish. Several laps before the sprint, the sprinter must find his teammates in the pack and get on their wheels to rest for the final sprint. The lead-out cyclists' job is to tow their champion to the front and install him in a good position, then gradually increase speed to a peak about 200 meters from the line. At that point the sprinter can come out of the last lead-out cyclist's draft and charge the line. A well-drilled team works together with precision and harmony to catapult their designated sprinter to the line, but it is a skill that takes practice, talent, and plenty of race experience.

Evaluating Your Performance

After the race, cool down by riding easily for several extra laps. Then take a few minutes to evaluate your performance while the experience is still fresh. Modify your training schedule accordingly. If you have a personal coach, ask him to critique your race and offer advice. For beginners, a great advantage of short-course racing is that much of the action can be seen from the curb, so a coach can help you more than in any other type of bicycle racing. And finally–if you can–have a friend videotape the event. Review your successes and failures on film when you have the time and energy to do it most effectively.

Longer Road Races

The tactics above work equally well for road races on longer, hilly circuits or point-to-point courses. But you'll need to make a few additions and modifications to criterium tactics when races stretch out over 50 miles or more.

You'll need to be more patient, for one thing. Early breaks rarely succeed in long races, simply because the distance is so great. One exception is when many strong cyclists are in the break. The pack in that case may simply lack the horsepower to reel in the break.

Another case is when nearly all the strong teams place one or two cyclists in the break with several other teammates remaining in the pack to block. The pack goes slowly because no one wants to chase down a teammate who may have a chance to win.

In most cases, however, early breaks in long road races are doomed. So–sit back and relax, and save your energy for important moves later.

Longer races change the way you look for opportunity and danger, also. The most difficult aspect in this regard is that you can never let up mentally, something the sheer length of the race makes difficult. Halfway through, the pack takes off without you, or you're involved in a crash you might have avoided had you been more alert. Eternal vigilance is the price of success–and even survival–in the racing pack.

Another difference between a criterium and a long road race is that in a criterium, corners are the most dangerous part of the course. But in a long road race with few corners, the straight open road becomes the enemy. Attention wanders. In a large pack cruising at a steady speed, it is easy to waver just a bit from a straight line while talking to teammates or reaching for a bottle. And all it takes is *one* cyclist overlapping a wheel to produce a crash that takes down half the pack.

One danger sign: rapidly varying speed. Racing packs have personalities, just like the individuals they're made of. Sometimes the pack proceeds sedately; at other times it is undisciplined, nervous, and excitable. If cyclists are popping off the front frequently, the speed will rise abruptly as the pack chases them. When the gap's closed, things slow down just as quickly. Cyclists not in tune with this yo-yoing can overreact to the bursts of speed and run up on the rear wheels of cyclists in front, creating gruesome crashes.

Unlike criteriums or circuit races, road races sometimes feature long climbs that require a different approach than short "sprinters hills." Position in the pack is still crucial, and you'll still have to fight for it before the hill. But because you can lose so much time on a long ascent, it's vital to understand the best ways to control your losses.

The pace of the climb is important. Instead of an all out charge, long hills have to be ridden at a steady pace designed to get you to the top without blowing up. If you go deeply into oxygen debt in a flat road race, you can often soft-pedal to recover, since a level road just doesn't eat speed as much as a hill does. On a steep hill, though, if your power output lessens a little, you'll slow down markedly as gravity tries to pull your bicycle and body back down the slope. Cyclists who go into oxygen debt in the middle of a 5-mile climb can lose 5 to 10 minutes on others in the group, a gap that's almost impossible to close.

The solution: Climb at your own pace. If you try to keep up with faster cyclists, you'll blow up for sure and lose great chunks of time. But if you ride steadily, you'll probably be close enough at the summit to get back on.

Good climbers often punctuate their steady climbing with hard jumps and accelerations of 50 or 100 yards in an attempt to lure less-gifted ascenders into irrevocable oxygen debt. When those human antigravity machines start playing their games, don't try to follow, but keep steadily plugging along. Unless they're much more fit, they'll slow down before they get too far ahead and–if you have the discipline to stay with a steady pace–you'll reel them in. And if not, you won't be too far behind at the summit. You'll at least have a chance to catch up, a chance you'd lose if you exhausted yourself in vain efforts to keep up.

In the high mountains, be wary of the effects of altitude. Even if you are acclimatized, you'll probably be unable to make the kind of repeated jumps that you could get away with on a sea level climb. Recovery from hard effort is slower at altitude, and indiscriminate spurts of effort are much more difficult to recover from.

Descending techniques are covered in detail elsewhere, but the following general tips should be emphasized.

In a large group, give yourself plenty of room to maneuver. Crashing when wheels touch in a pack descending at 50 mph usually has serious consequences.

Higher speeds also mean that the drafting effect extends several feet behind the lead cyclist. Use this larger wind shadow to give you more room for evasive action. Don't be concerned about staying on top of the competition during the steep and dangerous parts of the descent. The pack naturally regroups at the bottom of the hill.

If it is cold, carry a piece of plastic about 2 feet square. Slip it under the front of your jersey at the summit to break the wind on the descent. Long-fingered gloves are a good idea, too. Unprotected hands quickly get so numb that operating the brake levers becomes nearly impossible.

Long races force you to carry enough food and drink to get you to the finish line–or at least the cyclist refueling area. Experience will teach you how much and what to carry. Cyclists used to carry solid food like small sandwiches, but those rations were hard to eat while breathing heavily and difficult to unwrap while riding in a pack. The nourishment of choice among racers today is a high-carbohydrate liquid, carried in water bottles for easy access. Try several different products until you find something that you can stomach without distress at racing speeds. A drink that works fine in training may make you sick in the stress of competition.

For races in cold weather, some cyclists still prefer solid food, feeling it gives them more energy. And in stage races, where the food you consume in the race today is the energy that keeps you going tomorrow, most cyclists *demand* solid food. But interestingly, participants in the Race Across America have been successfully using liquid diets during their eight- or nine-day trek across the country, so solid food may not be necessary after all, even for the extreme demands of multiday racing. Experiment to see what works best for you.

Races over 70 or 80 miles have feed zones so that cyclists don't have to weigh themselves down with three or four water bottles and a bunch of bananas at the start. For safety reasons, feed zones are usually located on a hill where cyclists are going more slowly. The feed zone is still dangerous,

U.S. pro rider Andy Hampsten picking up his musette in the feed zone.

though, as a result of cyclists jockeying for position on the right side of the road, trying to get their handups (prepacked sacks of food and fluid), and sprinting back into the pack.

Know in advance where the feed zone is located so you can get good pack position early. Make sure that the support person handing you the food or bottles is dressed in clothing you can spot from a distance.

Large amounts of food–several bottles, fruit, and some fig bars–are usually handed up all at once in a musette bag. The handler runs along the roadside with the bag dangling from his outstretched hand. The cyclist picks it up by grabbing the shoulder strap or sticking his hand through the strap and letting the bag dangle until he is clear of other cyclists, then unpacking the bag and stowing the contents in jersey pockets and water bottle cages.

Handups of single items–a water bottle for example–are done without the musette by using the same technique. But the cyclist has to be going slower–a water bottle is harder to grab on the fly than a musette.

The last important difference between circuit races and road races is the finish. The final straight is almost always much longer. The length allows you more time to choose the wheel you want to follow and get positioned in the pack. But it also means that you won't be able to rely on your cornering skill to gain an advantage at the last minute.

Road race sprints are also more like long windups, covering several hundred meters, instead of the lightning-fast sprints won with a superior jump that are characteristic of the shorter races. So think ahead, and use your strengths to advantage. If you have a good jump, try to slow down the sprint until the last possible minute so you can use your short-term speed to advantage. If you are more of a chaser who can sustain a high rate of speed over a long distance, it is often worth the gamble to lead the sprint out early in hopes that you can wear out the real speed burners during a long final stretch.

One final caution if you do: Remember the wind. If you try to lead out a long sprint into a head wind, you'll rarely succeed. Other cyclists will get so much shelter from you that, no matter how strong you are, they'll be able to come around. But with a *tail wind* on the finishing stretch, an early jump often works.

Deciding to race involves the rider in all sorts of new experiences (clockwise from bottom): the jostling of a mass start, the pressure of shoulder-to-shoulder sprints for the finish line, and the pure exhilaration of breaking away from the pack.

Fast Recreational and Endurance Cycling

Competition is fun and exciting, but many cyclists find that noncompetitive activities are just as challenging. Recreational cycling, one-day endurance rides, and multiday tours provide opportunities for a cyclist to push to the limit or to relax, depending on the mood of the day. And many dedicated racers enjoy these less-competitive rides, too, either during the off-season or after their racing career is over.

Club Rides

Cycling can be a solo sport. Long rides through the spring countryside, mountain bike rides in the hills, weekend tours to scenic areas–all can be enjoyed with only your own thoughts for company. In fact, many cyclists prefer to go alone, because they can choose their own route, set their own timetable, and generally be free to ride hard or just stop and smell the flowers as their fancy dictates.

But cycling is also the perfect group sport. Part of the thrill of riding a road bike is the drafting effect of other cyclists in close proximity. A group lets you meet more people, expanding your social horizons. Racing is inevitably a group activity, so if you plan to compete, it is almost mandatory to train with other racers at least part of the time.

And finally, small group rides are faster and safer. They are faster, because you can share the work at the front and cover more ground during your training time. And they are safer, because a large group is more visible to motorists than a single cyclist. And if you have trouble of any sort, help is readily available. For all these reasons, it's a good idea to join a cycling club even if you plan to ride alone most of the time. But which one you pick depends on what you want to do and how you want to do it.

Racing Clubs

Some clubs are strictly racing organizations. They exist to help talented cyclists achieve competitive goals. If racing is your

Former U.S. national cycling coach Eddie Borysewicz instructing coaches at a clinic.

top priority, look first for a club that provides qualified coaching. The coach at such a club will often have volunteered time at the Olympic Training Center in Colorado Springs to learn leading-edge techniques from the U.S. national team coaching staff. But best of all is a club coach certified by the United States Cycling Federation.

Good coaches, however, are often identifiable more by intangibles than by certificates. They have time to devote to working with young or inexperienced cyclists. They have the patience to bring beginning cyclists along slowly, letting them develop at their own rate without undue pressure. And finally, good coaches aren't slaves to one coaching system. They don't blindly follow some cycling guru but instead devise training and racing strategies empirically for individual cyclists. They are interested in what *works*.

Good racing clubs have a comprehensive year-round program. In the winter, club

Riding with a group means that you'll have help if you puncture.

members meet for weight training and stationary bicycle work. They train together in the early season, then travel to races in team vans. They engage in team tactics and practice these techniques together on team training rides.

Outstanding race clubs also promote races—usually a local time trial series and a weekly evening criterium in which members hone their skills for the weekend's competitions. These races should be open to everyone, not just club members, both to increase the level of competition and to recruit additional cyclists. And the races are a good measure of the club—look for events that start on time, are well-organized, and take place on safe-but-challenging courses.

Cycling is an expensive sport, so good clubs also work hard to secure sponsorships from noncycling companies as well as from bicycle shops. Sponsors often have fairly large advertising budgets that help the clubs buy equipment and meet travel expenses for members, but affiliation with a bicycle shop is important so cyclists can get mechanical work done. Shops may also offer discounts on parts and service to club members.

In spite of the emphasis on competition, exemplary racing clubs offer friendly, supportive environments. Team members encourage each other with advice and consolation. Their training rides are designed to help everyone improve, and race strategy is based on *teamwork* rather than on showcasing star athletes. One sure sign of a poor club: Team members yell at each other on training rides, dispensing criticism instead of support.

Touring Clubs

These clubs are designed to promote touring and recreational cycling. Good ones offer full schedules of rides on weekends plus longer tours. These rides are often graded in terms of distance and ability so that new recruits don't accidentally bite off more than they can chew. One sure tip-off to a poor club: You choose a ride rated "easy" that turns into a race as the leader shows off his fitness and power.

Top touring clubs have family rides that encourage participation by the whole family. They often sponsor low-key time trials and encourage everyone, regardless of fitness or skill, to participate. And they regularly have social gatherings like potlucks or "restaurant rides" that bring people together for the sole purpose of getting to know one another.

They are active in local politics, too, working to make cycling safer and more enjoyable for everyone. Cycling clubs are often the political force behind bicycle path construction, traffic ordinances favoring cyclists, and campaigns urging residents to reduce air pollution by commuting to work by bicycle.

In the winter, cycling clubs often sponsor cross-country skiing trips or week-long charters to warmer climates for leisurely cycling. They often arrange for discounts at local health clubs for winter workouts. And some clubs have a modest gym of their own. Finally, good touring clubs sponsor an annual major ride, often either a century or a double century. These rides are well organized, safe, and promoted among the regional cycling community.

Obviously, good clubs are extremely hard to find. You may live where you have little choice—there may be only one cycling club in your area. In that case, try to make it the best possible so it conforms to the ideal.

If you have a choice, though, shop around. Get to know the cyclists in several clubs. Go to club races and time trials, watching the organization and the atmosphere. Participate in club rides, and be alert for the tenor of the group—whether it is supportive or critical of other cyclists. If you can, go to several meetings to discover the club's backing and policies. Remember: If you enjoy cycling, you are going to be on the road frequently with your fellow club members, so it pays to make your decision carefully.

Holding Your Own during Fast Club Rides

The major activity of any cycling club–racing or touring–is the group ride. Whether you get together with a couple of friends for a fast 20 miles after work or ride a weekend century in a pack of 15, the most important cycling club activity takes place on the road. As a result, it's important to know how to not only hang in on these club rides but make yourself welcome again. And success is often due to more than merely fitness.

First, know the traditions of the group. Some clubs like to start all rides–no matter how fast they'll eventually become–with a 20- or 30-minute easy warm-up. If you are impatient early, you can cause hard feelings or crashes by chafing at the bit to go faster. But if you know the pattern, it's easier to be patient.

Next, find out what kind of ride is scheduled. A fast training ride? A leisurely spin? Paceline practice? It is dangerous to have most of the group thinking one thing while one or two cyclists are on a different agenda. If an easy recovery ride is scheduled, but two cyclists think they are out for hard training, people are going to get angry. So–if you don't know the group goal before the ride, ask.

When the pace heats up, do your best to stay with the group. If you are having trouble taking your pulls at the front, move through the front and rotate back as quickly as possible to get maximum draft. It is far better to let others do the work than to slow down the whole pack.

If you often get dropped on hills, use a racing trick. As the climb begins, nestle in the front third of the bunch, getting as much draft as possible. If you can't hold the pace, you can slide back through the group but still be in contact at the top. Stronger cyclists will sometimes give you a helpful push on the shoulder as they ride by or even grab the rear of your saddle and push you along for part of the climb. Don't be embarrassed by their help–they probably got towed up quite a few climbs when they were starting, too. And a short push often allows you to regain breath and climbing rhythm so you can continue on your own.

If you are really having difficulty keeping the pace, it sometimes works to follow just one strong, accomplished cyclist. Get on his wheel and mirror his technique. Use the same gear, stand up when he does, take a drink as soon as he reaches for the bottle. This teaches you good cycling habits, but emulating his movements also takes your mind off your own effort and helps you over the hard spots.

Don't be afraid to tell fellow cyclists that the pace is too hard. It's a good bet that other cyclists probably feel the same way but have been reticent to speak up–or couldn't, because they were breathing too hard to talk. Perhaps even the cyclists who have been setting the pace are having difficulty but continue to go hard out of vanity or because they think everyone else expects a hard pace. A little communication goes a long way in making a group ride a pleasant and productive experience.

If you consistently have trouble holding the pace, look for another group, one closer to your ability level. There's no shame in rationally assessing your strength and choosing cyclists who share it. You'll actually improve *faster* if you ride with a group you can stay with to practice paceline cycling, proper climbing techniques, and following a wheel.

Conversely, cycling over your head week

after week can hurt your progress. You'll always be tired, for one thing, so you won't be improving as rapidly as you might with more rest. A pace too fast for you will hurt you mentally, too–you'll begin to associate cycling with pain and misery. And other cyclists don't like to be held up by the same person they always have to wait for on hills, either. So don't let your ego overpower your better judgment. An appropriate dose of humility now will pay dividends later.

Century Rides

The highlight of many cyclists' season is the 100-mile ride called a "century." Centuries are often held in late summer when legs are fit from a whole summer of cycling. And while 100 miles seems daunting to many novice cyclists, the distance is actually well within the grasp of any reasonably fit beginner. In fact, if you follow five simple rules, you can ride a century successfully and have fun doing it.

Prepare properly. It doesn't take a massive volume of training miles to ride a century. You don't have to complete exhaustive training sessions in the weeks before the event. And you don't need high-intensity speedwork. Of course, if you are already training long and hard, a century won't be much of a challenge. But we are concerned here with recreational cyclists who put in 50 or 75 miles a week, whose longest ride is perhaps 30 miles. If you meet this description, can you become fit enough in two months to ride a century in 8 or 10 hours? Sure–and the secret is how you spread your training miles out over the next eight weeks.

Let's assume that you ride about 30 miles once a week on Sunday, and you do a Wednesday evening ride of perhaps 20. Several other days of the week you spin around for 10 or 12 miles–all for a total of from 50 to 80 miles each week. Begin preparation by gradually increasing the length of your long weekend ride. If you have been doing 30 miles on Sunday, boost it 5 miles the first weekend, 8 miles the next, and 10 miles on succeeding Sundays until you reach 75 miles on Sunday of the sixth week. On the seventh week, go about the same distance–perhaps 75 miles. The following weekend is the century–25 miles longer but now well within your reach.

On top of that, increase the length of your midweek evening ride by 5 miles per week, from the 20 you began with up to a maximum of 35 or 40. You'll hit those figures the fourth or fifth week. Then stabilize at about 30 or 35 until the week of the century. At that time, cut back to 20. Your two longer rides per week will look like this:

Week	Sunday	Wednesday
One	30 miles	20 miles
Two	35 miles	25 miles
Three	43 miles	30 miles
Four	53 miles	35 miles
Five	63 miles	30 miles
Six	73 miles	30 miles
Seven	75 miles	30 miles
Eight	100 miles	20 miles

The remaining two or three rides each week should be no longer than 15 miles.

Several cautions. First, don't pick up the pace of your rides. An occasional burst is fine, but if you try to increase mileage at the same time you are increasing intensity, you'll end up slower and with *less* endurance. This is a program to let you complete the century, not race it.

Second, if you experience the symptoms of overtraining, reduce your mileage and intensity. It is better to be undertrained for a century than to go into it exhausted.

Know yourself. The training described prepares you for 6 to 8 hours in the saddle. But there's another reason for two months of regular cycling before a 100-mile effort:

You'll learn the art of pacing–finding out how fast you can go, how often you have to stop at aid stations, and how intensely you can ride and still finish in good order.

One way to learn your body's limits on long rides is to wear a heart rate monitor in training. Check it occasionally to find the rate your body settles into naturally during steady effort over long distances. You may find that you are comfortable at 110 or 120 beats a minute. Or you may be able to cruise along at 140.

Keep tabs on harder efforts too: hills, quick bursts to get on a faster moving paceline, short head wind sections. In short order, you'll develop a feel for how many harder stints you can put in and still settle back into your cruising pace.

You can also check your effort by feel rather than with a monitor. It isn't as accurate, but it's a lot less expensive and much less trouble. You'll also find that it works just as well after you become accustomed to listening to your body. A final advantage: Some heart rate monitors are notoriously unreliable. You'll be on your own if it blinks out in midride. But if you've learned to feel how hard you're working, you won't have to rely on the electronic crutch.

The best specific advice for completing your first century: start out slowly. Ride the first half well within yourself. Don't be tempted to go fast, pulled along by the excitement and high velocity pacelines. You can always pick up the pace later if you feel fresh. But if you go out too fast, you'll pay the price in the last 30 miles in fatigue, cramps, and general discomfort.

Choose your century ride with an eye on terrain. Look for a *flat* course with light winds and at least several hundred cyclists. Hills make 100 miles seem like 150. The rest you gain on the way down doesn't begin to make up for the effort of climbing.

Hard wind is another surefire way to get discouraged. There aren't any guarantees, but autumn rides are usually calmer than spring spins. Check the prevailing weather pattern before any long ride. More experienced club members are another good source of information, as are the ride's promoters.

And remember: The more cyclists, the more pacelines available. If you get into cohesive groups, you can draft and save energy that may make the difference between struggling to finish and having a great time.

Eat and drink as you ride. A century burns about 4,000 calories and takes anywhere from 4 to 10 hours to complete, depending on fitness, weather conditions, and the course. Yet your leg muscles can store only enough glycogen for about 2 hours of hard effort. The point: Even in the best of circumstances, you can carry along only enough internally stored fuel to go about half the distance. But don't panic–there's a solution. The secret to overcoming this fuel shortage is to eat and drink as you ride or at rest stops along the way. If you replenish food supplies and stay well-hydrated, you'll finish comfortably. But if you get caught up in the excitement of the ride and forget to eat and drink, you'll run out of gas long before the end of the ride. The result will be the infamous "bonk," cyclists' shorthand for running out of fuel. You'll feel weak, listless, hungry, and your motivation will vanish mysteriously.

Fluids first. As a general rule, drink a quart of either plain water or sports drink in the first quarter of the century. You'll need at least one more by the halfway point. But here's where experience is important. If you drank two 1-quart bottles in 50 miles, simple arithmetic says you should need four to complete the full distance. But your initial rate of consumption won't hold up until the end because you can't replenish liquids by drinking as fast as you use them up by sweating. You'll need more than two bottles in the last 50 miles, because you'll be repaying the dehydration debt incurred in the initial half of the ride.

Plan on at least three bottles during the last half of the ride, maybe four, and err on the side of prudence. Remember that high temperatures increase the body's demand for fluid, so it's common to need 8 or more quarts to cover a hot 100 miles.

Food consumption works the same way but at a slower rate. If you ate a good preride meal, you probably won't be hungry until you reach 60 or 70 miles. But if you wait to eat until then, you'll *bonk* before the finish. Why? Because food, unlike water, needs time to get into your bloodstream where it helps you out.

Start eating at 25 miles and keep putting it down until the finish. Munch a fig bar every 5 or 10 miles, take a swig of sports drink, eat a banana. And after you have finished, eat a good postride meal–it will cut your recovery time, and you'll feel much better the day after the century, You'll also be able to resume normal training and home activities much sooner.

Take advantage of faster cyclists. One of the charms of century rides is the variety of people they attract. All skill levels are represented, and it's common for some cyclists to blast across the finish in 4 hours while others, having just as much fun, take three times that long. Faster cyclists invariably achieve their times by working together in pacelines, and if you want to finish with less effort, look for pacelines to join along the ride.

The best way to do this is to start early. Most centuries don't feature a mass start but allow cyclists to begin whenever they want. If you get a head start, you'll soon find faster cyclists passing you in pacelines of three or more cyclists. Glance behind you to see these pacelines approaching. Choose one that is going slightly faster than you are, and as it draws near, increase your speed. Then latch onto the back as it goes by.

Find out immediately what kind of paceline is operating. Is it a single paceline? A double paceline? Accidents happen when newcomers fail to blend harmoniously into the pattern.

One caution: In some parts of the country, cycling etiquette requires that you ask permission to join the group. For example, a club cycling a century to work on the members' paceline technique won't welcome intruders. But, in most cases you'll be more than welcome to join in and share the work. The more cyclists in the paceline, the faster everyone goes.

If the paceline is too fast for you, drop off the back instead of working hard to stay with the group. You'll just waste energy trying to keep up with a group with superior fitness. Instead, slide off the back, continue at a moderate pace, and wait until a slower group comes along. In a big century ride, there will be no lack of opportunities.

If the group is too slow for you, join faster groups as they motor past. Remember to be predictable as you move into the other group. Don't dart out unexpectedly from the middle of your present paceline into the passing group. Such behavior won't endear you to your erstwhile companions and certainly isn't a recommendation to members of your new paceline.

Another way to make a century faster and more fun is to ride the whole thing with one or two others of similar abilities and goals. But try to find a more experienced cyclist to guide you through your first attempt at the distance. Of course, there's nothing wrong with going it alone. You may want to see how fast you can time trial the century without drafting, or you may just want to enjoy the effort and the scenery without talking to others.

After you finish, secure your bicycle and get something to eat and drink as you sit around and share the experience with other cyclists–a gold mine of information. When you drive home, reflect on your preparation and the actual ride. What worked? How could you have had more fun? Each time you do a century, you learn more techniques for increasing your efficiency and pleasure.

Tours

A bicycle is a sophisticated instrument for fast cycling fitness, but one of the pleasures of cycling is just taking off for a day or a month and going wherever your interests and fancy lead you. A bicycle's gearing system allows you to ride at an aerobic, conversational pace regardless of terrain and still cover plenty of territory in a day. And because cycling doesn't extract a toll on your joints, you can do it for days on end.

Touring is such a pleasure in large part because it combines speed with intimacy. You go faster than you would walking or running, so you can travel to different places significantly far away. But go slowly enough that you can see the country you're passing through.

Most casual touring rides don't develop fitness to any significant degree, partly because of the slower pace but primarily due to frequent stops. No matter–that's not the purpose of bicycle touring. If you hammer through the ride nose to stem with the countryside going by in a blur, you'll be missing the whole point. Look at touring rides instead as another way to enjoy the fitness you've already built from shorter, faster training.

Day Tours

Short rides of several hours to a whole day are merely extensions of your normal training rides–slower and more leisurely to be sure, but requiring few modifications in equipment or technique.

You can usually carry all you need in your jersey pockets. Include a banana and some fig bars, a windbreaker or leg warmers depending on the anticipated weather, maybe a map if you are venturing into unknown territory. If you add two full bottles, a frame pump, and a patch kit and spare tube (with clinchers) or an extra tire (with tubulars) tucked under your saddle, you'll need only two more vital items.

For a ride of any length, *always* carry along money and identification, wrapped in a plastic bag and secured with a rubber band. There's no need to tote along your wallet on day trips. It takes up too much room, and no matter how well protected, it can get wet from perspiration or rain, ruining money or other important contents.

Instead, write pertinent information with an indelible marker on a 3-by-5-inch piece of high-quality paper. Include your name, address, and phone number, along with the name and number of someone to contact if you should be injured. Add any allergies you may have–to penicillin, for instance. Note any medical conditions like diabetes that could alter treatment you might receive in case of an accident. Finally, make a note of any medicine you are currently taking.

Fold the card in half, sandwiching it between the halves of about ten one-dollar bills with two dimes and a quarter inside. Roll it up in two plastic sandwich bags, and secure with a rubber band. Store this emergency packet next to your helmet and gloves so you always remember to carry it along on rides. Hospitals and police will be able to notify your family or friends much faster in the event of an emergency. With the money, you can buy food or drink along the way. If you have an insurmountable mechanical problem–your frame breaks, for instance–call home from a pay phone or even pay a reluctant motorist to taxi you to your door.

Remember to change the information as conditions warrant. For example, if you go on vacation and begin your rides from the motel, list the motel's name, room number, family or friends you are staying with, and possibly the motel manager.

Another useful piece of equipment for

A lightweight cable lock deters theft during short stops.

day tours is a light cable and lock. You may want to leave the bicycle while you go into restaurants or walk a short distance to some scenic attraction along the way. Even if you lean your bicycle against a wall in plain sight, it can vanish when your back is turned. The cable doesn't have to be heavy enough to withstand professional bicycle thieves' metal cutters, but its presence alone will act as a deterrent and keep honest people honest.

For longer day trips, especially in uncertain or changeable weather, you'll need to carry along more items than will comfortably fit in your jersey pockets. If it is cold when you leave but warms up during the day, you'll want a place to stow leg warmers, a windbreaker, maybe even shoe covers and long-fingered gloves. One way to handle the problem is a fanny pack, especially popular with off-road cyclists because the weight is carried close to the body rather than hanging on the bicycle where it can wobble or shake loose over rough terrain. It has the added advantage of going with you when you leave the bicycle.

Choose models that ride securely in the small of your back, without bobbing up and down when you stand to climb. Look for outside straps that cinch down to accommodate smaller loads. Other useful features include external strap-attachment patches so you can tie on jackets or other items too big to fit inside. Try on the pack before you buy to see if the waist strap constricts your breathing in cycling position. Some packs have buckles so large they press into your abdomen when you are crouched over on the bicycle.

Fanny packs are great for carrying assorted paraphernalia, but on long road rides their weight is added to your own and can make saddle pressure increasingly uncomfortable–it feels like you've gained 10 or 15 pounds. If you spend most of your ride sitting down, you might be better off with a wedge-shaped bag that attaches under your saddle. Choose one that fastens securely to the saddle and seatpost without wobbling. The best models retain their shape with a plastic insert even when empty, something that makes getting items in and out easier.

One real disadvantage of both fanny packs and wedge packs is their relative inaccessability while cycling. It is easy to slide your hand into a jersey pocket for sunglasses or food, but much harder to reach back and unzip a pocket on the fanny pack. And with a wedge pack, it's virtually impossible–you have to stop if you want something. On the other hand, with the wedge pack you can still stow oft-needed items in your jersey pockets–an impossibility with a fanny pack because it covers them up.

Outfitted with a small pack and some money, you can tour comfortably all day. Stop at roadside stores to replenish food, get water from pumps in picturesque town parks, lock your bicycle and wander through small-town stores. Explore all the back roads you never had time to visit on training rides. Leave early and ride 100 miles across the state, meeting your family at the beach for a swim.

On a mountain bike, you can ride gravel or dirt roads to trailheads, lock the bicycle to a convenient tree, and take short hikes to scenic overlooks. Explore canal banks, fire roads, and old trails through the woods. The possibilities for simple day tours are as rich as the countryside, itself–anything within 50 or 75 miles of home is yours to explore.

Sag Tours

Once you gain some experience with one-day rides, you'll probably want to try trips that span a weekend or longer. Touring with a small group, it's convenient to use an accompanying car–a sag wagon in bicyclist's slang. The idea is for the vehicle to haul all your equipment for camping or staying at motels. All *you* need to carry is the one-day equipment described above. You tour lightly loaded but still have all the comforts of a well-equipped camp or motel at the end of the day.

A sag wagon ready to roll.

The single drawback is finding someone to drive. Occasionally a noncycling spouse will volunteer, but failing that, members of the group can take turns driving and cycling, switching off every 50 miles or so at prearranged spots along the route. Another option is to have the driver leave in the morning when the cyclists do, drive to the day's destination, then ride the route backward until he meets the others. The inconvenience is more than balanced by the pleasure of riding an unencumbered bicycle.

A third alternative is to go on an organized tour. Commercial touring organizations usually supply sag wagons, maps, advice on the day's route, and someone to pitch camp and cook dinner at day's end. Large group tours, like the Denver Post's "Ride the Rockies," rent semis to haul camping gear for over 2,000 cyclists.

Credit Card Tours

Another way to tour for several days without carrying heavy loads on your bicycle is to add one lightweight but important piece of equipment to your usual day touring load–a credit card. With it, you can get a motel and meals each night. In essence, a nearly weightless piece of plastic substitutes for tent, sleeping bag, and cooking gear.

If you opt for "plastic fantastic" touring, plan out your route carefully–and make motel reservations in advance for each night's stop. Carrying camping equipment, you can improvise if you can't find a campsite. But it's impossible to improvise a motel. So you'll have to sacrifice the spontaneous nature of a camping tour for the added comfort and security of motel lodging.

Here's a suggested list of equipment for a long weekend tour of this type. Remember: The whole purpose is to go light, ride hard all day, then get a good night's sleep, You won't need elaborate clothes for evening activities.

1. Credit cards, money, identification, emergency phone numbers.
2. Water bottles, food for the day, lightweight cable and lock.
3. Leg and arm warmers, light rain jacket, spare cycling shorts, socks, and jersey.
4. T-shirt and shorts to wear off the bicycle, light running shoes if you wear cleated shoes while cycling.
5. Patch kit and spare tube, small screw driver, 6-inch adjustable wrench, assorted allen keys, chain tool, two spare spokes, and a small aerosol can of chain lube.
6. Lip salve, sunscreen, chamois ointment, toothbrush and paste, other toiletry items.

With careful packing, all these items can be carried in both your jersey pockets and in a large wedge seat bag, although your jersey can hang uncomfortably from the load. To overcome this problem, some cyclists combine a fanny pack with the wedge bag. Add a handlebar bag if you need more room, but use it only for light items—handlebar bags can affect the bicycle's handling. If the above equipment list still seems a bit spartan, use small front panniers for additional "luxury" items like camera and extra clothes.

All of the lightly loaded tours described here can be done on the same bicycle you use for training and recreational rides, but two modifications will make your tour more fun:

Mount heavier tires for additional puncture protection. The tires should be new. Never start a multiday tour with worn, uncertain tires. Replacements, especially in 700C size, are often hard to get outside of larger cities.

If the route is hilly, install a wider-range freewheel. If you normally ride a low gear of 42/24, change to a 26 or even a 28. You'll be carrying a little more weight than on training rides, and you'll be cycling for longer periods of time. A low backup gear can get you over that last hill when worn-out legs are cramping and a strong head wind's trying to push you back down.

Loaded Tours

For a real get-away-from-it-all cycling experience, consider carrying camping equipment on your bicycle and traveling self-contained. The advantage is freedom to ride as far as you want each day without worrying about whether the next town will have a motel. You'll be free to wander at your own pace, cycling fast between scenic destinations or just cruising along with an eye toward the unusual or picturesque. And for many people, camping out each evening is as much fun as the cycling.

Choosing Touring Companions

One of the first decisions you'll have to make if you decide to give touring—regardless of the kind of touring you pick—a try is whether to go alone or with a companion. Two people can share the camping and route-finding tasks. They can trade places at the front in strong head winds. And if one person becomes injured or ill while on tour, another cyclist offers security and safety.

But traveling companions are liabilities, too. The most common disagreement involves pacing. One cyclist is comfortable at 15 mph on the flat, while the other likes to go faster. Rest stops are also potential problems if one person likes to get off the bicycle and stretch every hour, while the other eats, drinks, and sleeps in the saddle.

And even a relatively smooth tour can strain a friendship. Part of the challenge of touring is overcoming the little hardships that continually crop up: punctures, getting lost, cold rainstorms for three days in a row. Don't even think about touring with another person unless you talk out the possible problems in advance and keep the communication lines open along the way. This advice goes double if your potential touring partner is your spouse. The best way to discover the strength of a relationship is to share cold food in a soggy tent during the third day of continuous rain.

Touring Style

Another decision involves your touring *style.* If you choose campsites in advance from a map or a campsite directory, you'll have the security of knowing where you'll stop each night. But you'll lose the spontaneity that makes touring fun, and you'll be locked into a specific amount of mileage each day. Too, campsites are often located at inconvenient distances from one another. Even if you spot two campgrounds on the map that are the perfect distance apart for a day's ride, you may not discover until too late that the evening's destination is at the top of a 10-mile climb. So it's often better to use a map or campground directory as a general reference rather than a device for planning a specific itinerary. Have a basic idea of where campsites are located on your planned route, but be flexible to suit the circumstances.

If you are touring in heavily populated areas or popular tourist destinations, you may have to camp in commercial campgrounds. If you have a choice, *don't* stay at the first one you happen upon. Be selective. Look for places that have shade, water, and grass under your tent. Hold out for a view if possible. Avoid low, soggy meadows that are breeding grounds for mosquitos. Equally noxious are noisy four-wheelers, dirt bikes, and other mechanical distractions. If the campground seems to attract such noisemakers, look elsewhere.

You'll probably be happier if you avoid the large campgrounds that cater to the recreational vehicle set. But when you have no choice, find one that has a separate area for small tents. If you are assigned a crowded site between two metal behemoths, you may be able to discreetly move your tent later in the evening to a quieter, outlying area. But be aware that changing sites without telling the owners can mean trouble—like getting run over by a vehicle because your tent's not where it was supposed to be.

In some more rural areas, especially in the West, look for Forest Service or Bureau of Land Management campsites. They usually have minimum facilities—a water faucet and pit toilets—but they are inexpensive and often located in scenic areas. You can camp anywhere in national forests where overnight stays aren't expressly prohibited, so keep your eyes open as you ride along near the end of the day. Your dream campsite may be just around the next bend.

If you can't find a formal campground, ask permission to stay on farmland or pastures. If you can't find the owner, it is usually OK to camp overnight if the land isn't posted. But that's not a hard-and-fast rule, so be as unobtrusive as possible. Get out of sight of the road, shield your tent in trees or bushes, and generally maintain a low profile. When you are ready to leave in the morning, clean up so completely that no one could tell you were there.

The major problem with camping in undeveloped areas is finding drinking water. If you know you'll be staying in a field 20 miles up the road, plan to arrive with full bottles. Carry along inexpensive water purification tablets, and treat *any* water you use from an uncertain source. The most sparkling stream or inviting spring can harbor bacteria that will bring your trip to a dismal conclusion.

If your route includes small towns, the local authorities will sometimes allow you to camp in the town park or on school playgrounds. And often, people who see cyclists ride into town have a pleasant habit of inviting them to stay in the spare bedroom or camp in the backyard. People seem *drawn* to the independence and freedom the touring cyclist represents. The price for such hospitality? Usually an evening of conversation and a wonderful chance to meet new people.

Loaded Bicycle Handling

The drawback of loaded touring is, of course, the load. A lively and responsive bicycle turns into a recalcitrant pack mule when festooned with panniers and laboring under 30 pounds of gear. So–to avoid surprises–get used to the difference ahead of time. Attach the panniers you plan to use, fill them with a light load of clothes or a sleeping bag, and try out the bicycle on your favorite training route. You'll be amazed at the difference in handling. In the days leading up to your departure, increase the weight until you duplicate your traveling load.

No matter how you choose to carry your equipment, though, or how much you practice, your formerly predictable bicycle will acquire a mind of its own. Front panniers make the bicycle unstable at low speeds. In a crosswind, they catch much more air than an unloaded bicycle. Equipment mounted on top of the rear rack makes the bicycle top-heavy and hard to handle in corners. A handlebar bag can create a dangerous instability problem on descents. And no matter how securely the load is attached, it still seems to swing and sway, making out-of-the-saddle climbing nearly impossible. Translation: Be *sure* to try out your equipment before you leave on a long trip, making necessary modifications in the safety of your home instead of the open road.

Cycling and Camping Equipment

If you've never camped before, rent or borrow equipment and try out the whole concept with a one-night trial trip. You may find that no matter how romantic camping sounds, you *despise* the reality. Many cyclists would agree with you–they like to go hard all day, then shower, have a good meal, and relax in a soft bed instead of a rumpled sleeping bag. The trial run lets you find out which side–camping or moteling–of the touring community you belong to.

If you are an inexperienced camper or if you have just purchased a new tent, set it up and take it down in the backyard several times. You don't want to be learning the foibles of your particular model in a bone-cold thunderstorm at the end of a 100-mile day.

Try out your stove, too, if you plan to carry one. Stoves are nearly indispensable for modern camping where open fires are either illegal or impractical for lack of wood. Choose a small one-burner designed for backpacking. The best ones burn readily available white gas, but many campers prefer the convenience of butane gas cartridges.

If you plan loaded tours, you'll want a bicycle designed for the job. Good touring bicycles have relatively long wheelbases to absorb shock and provide a smoother ride with heavy loads. The length makes the bicycle more stable in straight-line cycling, so you don't have to use energy fighting twitchy steering on long, straight roads. The other advantage of a long wheelbase is heel clearance. If the chainstays tape around 17 inches, your heels will clear loaded rear panniers at the back of the pedal stroke.

Of course, a long wheelbase and stable steering also means that a touring bicycle is slow on corners and usually flexible at the bottom bracket. But while that's a liability for racing or fast day touring, it's just the ticket for loaded touring. You won't be flying around corners with 40 pounds of camping gear along for the ride, anyway.

Good touring bicycles also feature extra sturdy wheels and tires–the major problem areas on long tours. The best bet for loads over 20 pounds includes 36 spokes,

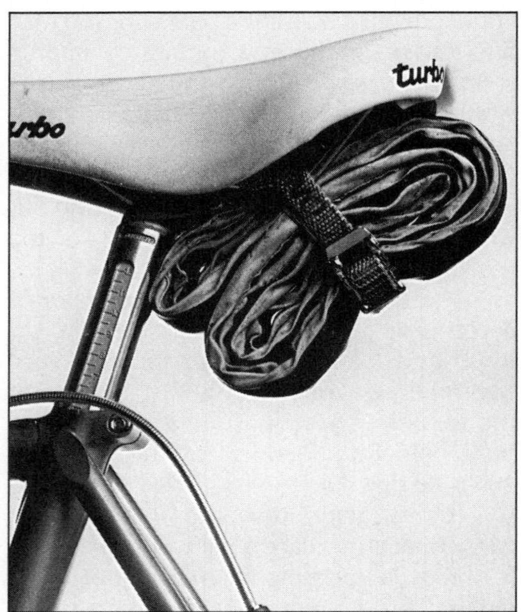

Here's how to fold a clincher and stow it beneath the saddle.

sturdy alloy clincher rims in size 27 × 1¼ inches, and matching tires designed for loaded touring. Some experienced tourists like 40-spoke wheels for added security, but replacement rims are hard to find in any but the best bicycle shops. If you foresee small towns and rough pavement–or no pavement at all for substantial stretches–opt for readily available 36-spoke wheels.

The 27 × 1¼-inch rims have traditionally been chosen for the same reason–they are easier to find than 700Cs. That situation is changing, however, and most bicycle shops carry a stock of both sizes. *Don't* try loaded touring on 1-inch wheels. The rims are probably strong enough, but the tires' significantly more narrow profile and low air volume don't provide enough protection for either tire or wheel. When you hit a pothole's jagged edge, for example, 1-inch tires can compress, pinching the tube and creating the classic "snakebite" puncture. When that happens, the wheel is usually bent or knocked out of true from the impact. Fatter tires provide substantially more protection and, therefore, less grief on the road.

When choosing tires, look for an easy-rolling tread pattern, strong sidewalls, and a cut-resistant rubber compound. The rear tire will wear faster for two reasons: It supports more weight, and it is subject to the forces of accleration. So on long tours, rotate the front and rear tires at regular intervals for more uniform wear.

Most tourists don't carry spare clinchers because they are bulky and hard to pack. The rely instead on a roll of duct tape to repair cuts caused by glass. But if you still want the added security of a real spare, choose a folding clincher with a Kevlar bead. They are lighter and more fragile than standard wire-bead touring tires but they will get you to the next bicycle shop in an emergency.

It is a good idea to learn how to true your wheels before you go on tour, since you'll need to maintain them at least once a week, depending on the quality of the wheelbuilding job, the road surface, and your own cycling habits.

Your touring bicycle should have plenty of clearance between the tires and the frame so you can install fenders. You may resist using them for reasons of style, but in rainy conditions they work remarkably well in keeping your feet dry from all the water kicked up by the tires. Look for sturdy eyelets on the front and rear fork for mounting both fenders and pannier racks. Sealed bearings on hubs, bottom backet, and headset also help keep grit and road slop out during long rainy stretches.

Touring bicycles have low gears for hauling big loads over mountain passes and up steep eastern hills. Choose your gearing for the terrain. In the mountains, go for a triple crankset with a low gear of at least 28/30. For flatter roads, a double

A fully loaded touring bicycle.

crankset with a low of 38/28 will usually suffice. But remember that gearing is an indivdual decision based on fitness and cycling style–don't let ego enter into it. Those hills can get mighty steep when gravity is in league with a heavy load. Pedaling in the wrong gear just because it's the one a cycling champion uses makes no sense at all.

Touring frames are often chosen an inch or so larger than racing or sport bicycles. A larger frame allows a higher handlebar position–a real advantage over hundreds of miles. You may want to install padded handlebar covering for comfort, but most cyclists find that well-padded gloves work just as well. Generally, you should keep the same saddle height you use on your sport bicycle, but if you tour in different shoes, the change in sole thickness may make an adjustment necessary.

Many cyclists are now touring on mountain bikes, modified for more comfort on the road. Mountain bikes may seem heavy and slow, but they have a number of important advantages for loaded touring. They are stable under load, for one thing, and their low gearing makes them a natural for touring in the mountains. They also have the long wheelbase, fender clearance, and predictable steering of the best road touring machines. But their biggest advantage is adaptability. If your route contains gravel or dirt roads, a mountain bike will be right at home. In fact, they make possible great loop tours (trips that include both paved and gravel roads, jeep trails, and whatever lies beyond).

The most important modification a mountain bike needs for touring is the installation of dropped bars so you can change hand position during the course of a long day. Consider switching tires, too, to slicks designed for the road or modified knobbies with easier-rolling tread patterns. And finally, install toe clips and straps.

Panniers and Packing

Once you've chosen a bicycle and settled on the gear you'll tote along, you'll need something to carry it in. The best bet is a sturdy set of panniers, chosen to handle the load you plan to carry. There's no reason to invest in large panniers suitable for a cross-country ride if you're only going out for weekends. Conversely, if you have too much gear for your panniers' capacity you'll have to tie the excess on the outside, creating a dangerous and unstable load.

A good combination for light touring is a set of low-rider front panniers and a large wedge pack under the seat. With this combination, you can carry a compact sleeping bag, a small plastic tarp or bivouac sack, clothes, and other necessities for up to a week of camping and restaurant meals.

If you want to cook, you'll need more room for a small stove, pots, and other kitchen supplies. In that case, use larger rear panniers with room on top of the rear rack for light but bulky objects like sleeping bag or foam pad. If you are carrying a big load, you'll probably need both front and rear panniers to balance the weight for better bicycle handling. But always remember: The more weight you load onto your bicycle, the less pleasure you'll get from the cycling. The old rule of thumb for backpacking applies: If you don't *know* you'll need it, you probably don't.

When packing for the trip, cut weight wherever possible. If water is available along your route, use your bicycle bottles rather than carrying a plastic canteen in the panniers. You won't need a fork–a spoon works fine for everything. Ditto for a plate–carry a plastic bowl instead.

Cut half the handle off your toothbrush, and buy a small tube of toothpaste instead of the larger pump container. Pack Lycra and polypropylene leg warmers instead of more bulky wool ones. Nylon running shorts are suitable off-bicycle wear in temperate climates, and they compress into virtually nothing. Your rain jacket doubles as protection against evening chill.

Think carefully about each item you pack because you'll have to haul it up every climb on the tour. To help decide, ask yourself: Can I leave it at home? Duplicate its function with something else? Or find a lighter model?

Check for adequate heel clearance when you buy rear panniers.

After you gain experience, you can cut your load even more. Use another old backpacker's trick: When you return from a trip, put everything you toted along in one of three piles. In the first pile, include items you used every day. In the second, stack those things you used occasionally. Relegate equipment you never used to the third heap. If you really want to go light on your next trip, take only the contents of the first pile and at the most, a few selected items from the second stack.

Whatever kind of panniers you purchase, look first for a stable and secure mounting system. The material should be waterproof and abrasion-resistant. If you plan on encountering wet weather, consider additional rain covers, available from most manufacturers, since even the best waterproof material lets water in through needle holes when it's subjected to both pelting rain and road spray.

It's a good idea to choose brightly colored panniers for safety on the road. They should be easy to take off the bicycle for security–when you want to shop for food or walk around some scenic attraction, you can remove the panniers and carry them like luggage with shoulder straps.

Finally, panniers should provide easy access to their contents, with a combination of zippers and Velcro. Pockets, both sewn to the outside and inside the main compartment, make organization of your gear easier.

A tip: You can make things easier to find and pack in the panniers by using plastic bags of various sizes. They help you quickly locate lunch, spare socks, or the toilet paper, and they add another layer of waterproofing to key supplies.

Pack your gear with an eye toward bicycle handling. The general rule is to put heavy items like food and stove fuel as low and close to the frame as possible. Put light but bulky objects on top of the rear rack.

But like any other rule, this one has to be broken occasionally. For instance, bicycle tools are heavy but should be packed in an outside pocket where they are readily available. Keep your stove and fuel bottle in an outside pocket, too–so if they leak, they won't befoul everything else. For the same reason, put them on the opposite side of the bicycle from food supplies. Better to have your spare jersey, rather than your supper, smell like white gas. And stash your rain jacket just under the top flap of the main compartment along with your walking shoes, camera, and map–all of which can use the extra protection.

Vital belongings, however–your wallet, money, and identification–belong on your person in a jersey pocket, again well protected from rain and sweat with plastic bags.

Rain

Rainy weather is the bicycle tourist's nemesis. It's cold, it makes the road slippery, it plasters your bicycle with grit, and the swirling clouds obscure the beautiful country you set off on the tour to see. But unless you are singularly blessed, you *will* encounter rainy spells–and they may last the whole trip. But with the right gear and know-how, a rainy tour can be a real high point in your cycling adventures.

First, keep a good mental attitude. Remind yourself that rain is an inconvenience, not a disaster. The resulting discomfort is a little thing that can be borne. If you grimace at every dark cloud or head for a motel when you hear a threatening weather forecast, you'll miss the best part of your tour.

Next, prepare for rain with the right gear. Pack neoprene shoe covers and long-fingered gloves, plus a waterproof but breathable rain suit of Gore-Tex or similar material. Unfortunately, even breathable fabrics retain a considerable amount of body heat–you'll still get wet from sweat. But the shell garments will keep you warm.

Carry several changes of shorts, jerseys, and socks so you have dry clothes each morning. Nothing dampens enthusiasm faster than climbing into a pair of soggy shorts for the third day in a row. And add a cycling cap with a bill to keep rain out of your eyes. (Some cyclists like cycling goggles with clear lenses for the same purpose, but others think they get too smeared and fogged up to be of use. Try it both ways.)

In warm summer rain, you can probably get by with just a rain jacket to hold in body heat. Your feet and legs will get soaked, but that's OK if it isn't too cold. The big problem regardless of season is getting dry at the end of a rainy day. If you are staying in motels, strip off the wet clothing as soon as you check in. After dinner, simply wash out the road grime and stick the clothes in the dryer at the motel. Synthetic fabric and artificial chamois work better in the rain than wool for this reason. Stuff your shoes with newspaper to absorb the day's moisture, and you'll be able to start off in the morning with dry clothes and only mildly wet shoes. Incidentally, shoes with synthetic uppers are easier and faster to dry than all leather models.

If you're camping, the problem is more severe. The solution: Take several sets of cycling clothes. After you pitch your tent and spread out your foam pad, take off the wet clothes and isolate them in a plastic bag so they don't soak other gear. Put on dry clothing so you don't get chilled during the evening in the tent. Stuff your shoes with the newspaper you bought in the last town for that purpose. (It's OK to read it first.) The next morning, put on your second set of cycling shorts, jersey, and socks. If it is still raining, don rain gear. And as you ride, watch for laundries–when you spot one, take a break from cycling and dry yesterday's clothes for use tomorrow.

If the day dawns sunny, hang the wet clothes on your panniers to dry as you ride. With a little luck in finding laundries or occasional sunny days, you should be able to tour for a rainy week with only two sets of cycling clothes plus something warm to wear in the tent each night.

The other rainy weather problem is keeping your bicycle running smoothly. If you are staying in motels, clean and lube your bicycle each evening. Don't, however, work on it in your room where dirt and grease may stain the carpet. Ask the management if it has a maintenance room or a protected area with access to a hose. It may also have old rags you can use.

Hose road grime off the bicycle gently so the force of the spray doesn't drive grit into the bearings. Then relube the chain and other moving parts. If you have to ride in the rain for several days, the chain and freewheel will get pretty gritty. But it shouldn't affect the performance markedly. When you return home, clean all components thoroughly, replacing any parts that show signs of excess wear.

If you are tent camping, finding a dry place to clean the bicycle is more of a chore. In commercial campgrounds, ask about a storage room. The public rest room facilities often have overhanging roofs and hoses. In primitive campgrounds, you'll have to save the cleaning chores for another day or spray the bicycle as best you can with water from a bicycle bottle, then relube. It isn't pretty, but it works.

Sometimes inclement weather is too bad to ride through. You'll have to hole up and wait it out. Examples are severe lightning storms, seasonal hurricanes in southern states, tornado warnings, and cold rain in the valleys that turns to snow on mountain passes. But most of the time, unpleasant weather can be viewed as a challenge.

Sample Equipment List for a Week's Camping Tour

The following list is not exhaustive. In fact, experienced tourers will undoubtedly find that it leaves out items they can't live without and includes several things they wouldn't dream of carrying along. You'll have to modify it to suit your own situation and experience. But it is a good starting point for a beginner's touring adventures.

Camping gear. Sleeping bag, foam pad, small tent or bivouac sack.

Cycling gear. Bicycle with appropriate gearing for the trip, racks and panniers, patch kit and spare tubes/tires, tool kit, frame pump, water bottles, lock and cable.

Food. Stove and fuel, matches, pot, plastic bowl, cup, spoon, pocket knife with can opener, water purification tablets, biodegradable dishwashing soap, and plastic pad.

Clothes. Helmet, cycling cap with bill, cycling glasses, gloves, cycling shoes, walking shoes if you ride in cleats, shoe covers, leg warmers, rain suit, two pairs of cycling shorts, two jerseys, two pairs of socks, sweatpants and polypropylene sweater for off-bicycle wear.

Miscellaneous. Sunscreen, lip salve, first aid kit with any personal medication required, repair kit, toilet paper, camera, maps, insect repellent.

Off-Road Cycling

Your cycling doesn't have to end when the pavement does. More and more cyclists are discovering the thrill of adventuring off the blacktop on gravel roads, canal banks, fire paths, and—where it's legal—trails. Most were introduced to the dirt with the arrival of mountain bikes on the cycling scene. Mountain bikes were developed in the late 1970s by fun-seeking cyclists in California who wanted to descend fire roads on old clunkers, then pedal back up again. The heavy 1-speeds that made screaming descents so much fun were definitely not the ticket for the climb back up. Gears and derailleurs hit the scene quickly with lightweight frames and alloy rims not far behind. In the space of a few years, California gave birth to a whole new segment of the bicycle industry—and one that is now growing faster than any other. Along with that growing popularity, a growing desire to compete on mountain bikes also has developed. And even if you aren't interested in actually racing, competition techniques like those discussed later in this chapter can make you a better all-around cyclist.

Choosing Your Mountain Bike

Mountain biking has increased rapidly in popularity in large part because of the bicycle itself. With their wide tires, upright position, and flat handlebars, mountain bikes are stable and forgiving machines. They encourage you to try slippery downhills and boulder-strewn slopes that would mangle the standard touring bicycle.

When you pick a mountain bike, forget the road bike frame size recommendations elsewhere in this book. Your off-road frame should be 2 to 3 inches smaller than your road frame, so you have plenty of top tube clearance in case you have to bail out over the front of the saddle. A smaller frame is stiffer, too, and its naturally shorter top tube places you in a more upright—and therefore more stable—cycling position.

Choose the model you want based on what you intend to do. Mountain bikes cover the spectrum, from inexpensive models designed for urban commuting to top-of-the-line racing bicycles for gonzo descents

A mountain bike designed for performance riders.

on treacherous terrain. But at price points between these extremes, plenty of solid and reliable bicycles are available. And just as in choosing a road bike, a reputable shop is your best ally in the search for the perfect mountain bike.

If you want a practical bicycle for urban errands or commuting, check out a "city bicycle." These differ from full-bore mountain bikes in several ways, the most obvious being narrower tires with tread patterns designed for pavement rather than for dirt. Some bicycles destined for use only on pavement have easy-rolling slicks, while bicycles that may see double duty–commuting during the week, an occasional weekend romp in the backcountry–have dual-purpose tires with moderate knobbies on the shoulder and a smooth band in the middle for lower rolling resistance on pavement.

Some city bicycles come complete with fenders, too, so you don't get your Brooks Brothers suit wet commuting in the slop. Style-conscious cyclists generally dislike fenders, preferring the aesthetics of the stripped-down racing bicycle. But in countries where commuting by bicycle has a long and honorable history–Great Britain or the Netherlands, for instance–fenders are *de rigueur*. In fact, European road racers use detachable models for training in spring conditions. If your bicycle doesn't come with fenders, at least make sure it has fittings so you can add them later.

A city bicycle generally has more upright handlebars, putting the cyclist in a more vertical position for better visibility, and the wider saddle provides comfort on short rides. Their components, however–while adequate for commuting–aren't designed to withstand the abuse of serious off-road use.

Frame angles are also more relaxed, and wheelbases are longer for easier cycling, more predictable steering, and plenty of fender clearance. Choose a city bicycle if you plan to run errands around town, commute short distances, ride around the neighborhood with the kids, and sample real dirt and gravel roads only occasionally.

One step up from the city bicycle is the mountain bike, usually medium-priced, designed for general off-road cycling. They sport real mountain bike tires with gravel-grabbing knobbies that usually work well in loose surfaces but on pavement tend to be noisy and slow. Components are upgraded to offer greater resistance to crashes and the abrasive effect of clinging mud. Head angles are more upright than on city bicycles for greater rock-dodging agility and quicker handling in corners. Seat angles are distinctly more upright, also, positioning the cyclist over the bottom bracket for greater power on climbs. Yet the frame angles are still a compromise, relaxed enough for touring or pleasure cycling.

Choose a bicycle like this if you want to get off the road and explore the trails and dirt roads, maybe plan to sample some off-road racing, or just like to bash around with friends. Medium-priced bicycles cover a lot of territory, some designed for off-road touring, others for beginning racing and fast sport cycling. To find the one for you, describe your needs to the people at your favorite shop before you lay down your money.

At the top of the mountain bike line are hard-core racing bicycles, machines built with no-quarter competition in mind. They have aggressive tires for maximum traction in muddy conditions, mounted on rims that strike a precarious balance between strength and weight. Frame angles are upright, often duplicating the angles on a quick-steering road bike. The tubing is light enough to sometimes sacrifice crash-worthiness for performance, since factory-sponsored pros view frames as expendable components.

If you plan to race off-road seriously, you'll want to consider one of these machines. But don't pass them by if your interests don't include racing. The racing mountain bike works well for high-performance touring, sport cycling, or fitness. There's something about the ride, quick handling, and lightness of a racing bicycle that makes a winding dirt road irresistible.

Clothing

Many off-road cyclists use the same clothes they'd use while cycling on a road bike. A good helmet is, of course, indispensable. Regular cycling shorts, even thin Lycra models, eliminate chafing from the saddle while still providing some protection against brambles and sharp tree limbs. A standard cycling jersey is cool enough for sweaty ascents, and the pockets are handy for stashing a snack or a windbreaker if it gets too breezy at the summit.

Gloves are even more essential off-road than on. They'll soak up the increased vibration and shock from bumpy terrain, and in minor falls they'll protect your palms from scratches. For shoes, choose among the many models offered by manufacturers eager to provide top quality to the burgeoning army of off-road cyclists.

Some manufacturers offer specialized mountain bike clothing: shorts and jerseys made from more durable fabric to withstand the abuse of the wilderness. You can also buy knicker-length pants to protect your knees from trailside thorns and brush. Some jerseys even come equipped with elbow and shoulder pads. If you habitually ride in rough terrain that might mangle you, especially at high altitudes where it's colder, the heftier clothing might be worth the extra weight and increased warmth while climbing.

Cycling in the mountains also means that you'll need to pack along a wind shell made of Gore-Tex or similar fabric to protect you from sudden showers or snow squalls. No matter how warm the weather at the start, no matter how blue the sky, stick that jacket in your pocket or bag. Conditions can change quickly in mountain country, especially with a few thousand feet of elevation gain, and the shell can protect you from hypothermia, the potentially lethal loss of body heat.

Customizing a mountain bike with dropped bars, bar end shifters, and an upright stem.

Customizing the Bicycle

Because mountain bike design is continually evolving, most cyclists can't help trying out different ideas on their own bikes. Two favorite modifications of stock bicycles: dropped bars and toe clips.

A traditional mountain bike has straight bars, a design based on motorcyle handlebars. In fact, early mountain bikes used motorcyle brake levers. Nearly all stock mountain bikes come with some version of straight bars, and many cyclists prefer them. But although the mountain bike's basic design has been steadily improved since its invention, the perfect off-road handlebars have yet to be invented. Straight bars have drawbacks that we'll discuss in a moment, so many cyclists customize their mountain bike and install the characteristic dropped bars of road biking. Should you? Consider the advantages and drawbacks of each, and then decide.

The advantages of straight bars begin with greater control on downhills. Their extra width lets the cyclist exert the leverage he needs to yank the bicycle around obstacles and wrench the front wheel through mud or weeds. They allow an upright position for better visiblity and promote a more stable center of gravity. And finally, they allow the use of thumb shifters (changing gears can be done without taking a hand off the bars on the sort of bumpy terrain where such a move invites a crash).

But straight bars aren't perfect. For one thing, they offend the aesthetic sense of some cyclists, reminding them of noisy motorcycles powered by smelly engines instead of silent human muscles. They feel and handle differently from dropped bars, disconcerting if you switch back and forth frequently from road bike to mountain bike. Their biggest disadvantage is the inability to vary hand positions. You can't get down on the drops for an aerodynamic shape on smooth downhills or move your hands around on the bars during long climbs. And if you ride for more than an hour, the constant, unchanging hand and upper body position is guaranteed to leave you sore and stiff.

Conversely, dropped bars offer the usual half-dozen hand positions familar from road biking so there's greater comfort on long rides and more efficiency on climbs. Although thumb shifters don't work well on the dropped bar design, they *can* be fitted with bar-end shifters so you don't have to let go to shift.

In fact, the only disadvantage that most cyclists cite is a lack of control on steep and bumpy downhills. But this is only a relative disadvantage, because cyclists who have gotten used to dropped bars report that they actually prefer them, even on the sort of downhills that leave the toughest competitors bathed in cold sweat.

Which type to choose? Try dropped bars if you ride moderate distances, either racing or training, and have had wrist or lower back problems from a static position. If you use your mountain bike for long distance loaded touring, dropped bars are a necessity. And if you ride on mild terrain free of terrifying downhills, you won't have to worry about their single disadvantage—less control on high-speed descents. Finally, go for the drops even if you simply like them for aesthetic reasons.

Conversion to dropped bars is relatively easy. A good bicycle shop should be able to suggest what stems and bars to purchase. In general, look for a stem that has a short reach and a long shank. You want to approximate the upright position of straight bars, and a stem with a long reach will put you too far forward, while a short shank will put you too low.

Stems should have a hole or pulley arrangement for the front brake cable so you don't have to resort to a headset cable hanger. And stems designed for mountain bike use should be sturdy. A little extra weight is a small price to pay for peace of mind when you are bouncing down a rocky trail.

For the same reason, dropped bars suitable for mountain bikes are a bit stronger than road bars. They are wider, too, for more leverage. Some manufacturers flare the ends slightly for this reason. They should have a short drop-and-reach so you aren't spread out too far. If your hands get numb from the pounding, try lightly padded handlebar tape.

If you are going to use your mountain bike for anything but short city errands, add toe clips and straps. Bare pedals have an advantage only in stop-and-go city traffic where you have to put your foot down incessantly, and only if you don't want to devote the small amount of time to learning how to get into clips quickly and efficiently. In every other application, toe clips are the way to go. They'll keep your feet from bouncing off the pedals on rough terrain. Toe clips also let you pull up on the pedal, making you a more efficient climber, while smoothing out your pedal stroke on the flat for more efficient cycling.

The step-in pedal revolution hasn't hit the off-road scene yet. The problem is that the required cleat would get ground down quickly by all the running and walking on rocky terrain. And shoes suitable for step-in pedals wouldn't be comfortable for walking.

Equipment

A piece of equipment crucial to off-road cycling is a good repair kit. If you have a mechanical breakdown on asphalt, you are usually within walking distance of a phone booth or a farmhouse. But 20 miles up a lonely fire road, you'll wait a long time for help if your bicycle breaks down. Current off-road racing rules forbid outside mechanical assistance—competitors have to make all repairs themselves with tools they carry on the bicycle. Here's a list of basic necessities for your off-road tool kit.

1. Spare tube.
2. Patch kit.
3. Tire levers.
4. Frame pump, or one-shot inflating cartridge (for races).
5. Small screwdriver.
6. Chain tool.
7. 6-inch adjustable wrench.
8. Spoke wrench.

These tools weigh little and pack neatly under the saddle in a nylon bag. Wrap them in cloth so they don't rattle, and you won't even notice they're aboard, waiting to help you fix most common off-road problems and get home to tell the tale.

Mountain Biking Techniques

You'd rightfully expect a mountain bike to be used in mountainous terrain, so it follows that two basic cycling techniques involve climbing and descending steep hills. Although power is still an indispensable component, handling off-road hills requires different techniques than cycling their paved cousins.

Climbing

In climbing, use low gears so you don't get bogged down. Muscling up a climb while overgeared wastes energy and courts knee injury. It is true, however, that experienced off-road cyclists usually use a lower climbing cadence than their road riding brethren because the ascents are so much rougher. To increase leverage, most mountain bikes sport longer crankarms than similarly sized road bikes.

As you approach a steep hill, shift into a lower gear before you need it; shifting is much harder under the kind of loads characteristic of off-road terrain. Trying to force a late uphill shift may ruin your derailleur or break the chain, and it certainly doesn't do anything for your smoothness, efficiency, or sweet-tempered disposition.

Most off-road climbing is best done seated, because your weight is over the rear wheel for maximum traction. On moderate grades, shift your weight to the rear of the saddle, and grind it out. When the angle steepens so much that the front wheel begins to flop from side to side or threatens to come off the ground, lean forward at the waist so you have the weight of your upper body on the front wheel to keep it down while still keeping the weight of your hips on the rear wheel for traction.

From the side, you'll look more spread out than when climbing on the road, with a greater bend at the waist. Biking steep hills often becomes as much a balancing act as a display of power. Experience will tell you just how much weight you need at either end of the bike for maximum efficiency, and soon you'll adjust to subtle changes in gradient without thinking about it.

Another hint for seated steep climbing: Keep your elbows low and tucked in. If you pull on the bars with flaring elbows, you'll disturb the bicycle's steering and cause even more front wheel flop than you'd get naturally from the terrain.

Stand up on short, moderate climbs to maintain your momentum—just as you would on a road bike. It is possible to climb steep grades standing if your bike has short chainstays so your weight is over the rear wheel. Help your frame's geometry along by modifying your position—shift the weight of your hips back while bending forward at the waist to keep the front wheel down. Slow your cadence and avoid abrupt accelerations, or you'll tear the rear wheel loose and lose traction.

When the hill gets too steep to ride, get off the bike with a racer's dismount. Anticipate the *need* to dismount, too, or you'll hop off awkwardly, lose momentum and grind to a halt. It's easier to make the transition from cycling to running (or walking) with the bicycle if you retain some forward speed during the switch. Again, practice will teach you when the grade flattens out enough, and long enough, to warrant remounting.

Get back on again using a technique borrowed from mountain bike racing. Swing your bicycle-side leg just high enough to clear the saddle, then slide over into cycling position. Getting in the clips is the next key step, so pedal a few strokes with your feet on the bottom of the pedals before you try to flip them over and get in. Most mountain bike pedals are designed for easy entry under trying conditions. If you are having trouble after repeated practice, consider replacing your pedals or shoes if the ribbed sole hangs up on the rear of the pedal cage.

Seated climbing with weight to the rear of the saddle for maximum power and traction.

Descending

Off-road downhills often separate the bike handlers from the power cyclists. Ride smooth, moderate downhills like you would on a road bike: head up, aerodynamic position, brake levers in easy reach. As the grade steepens, you'll need to shift your weight farther back over the rear wheel to keep from going over the bars–either from sheer steepness or hitting bumps that slow the bicycle so abruptly that you catapult forward. On near-vertical pitches, your hips will be hanging *over* the rear wheel.

It is easier to get your weight back if

Climbing steep grades, standing with weight forward to keep the front wheel down.

A rider "dabbing" on an intricate trials course.

the saddle is lower than normal on long descents, so use the quick-release seatpost—standard on most bicycles—to lower your saddle several inches. Mark your seatpost with a small file, so you can reposition it accurately at the bottom of the hill. Racers often use a device called a Hite-Rite that allows saddle height adjustments en route (a spring automatically pops the saddle back to the correct height).

On bumpy terrain, raise your rear off the seat several inches, and support your weight on the horizontal pedals. Using the strength in your arms, shoulders, and legs as shock absorbers, let the bicycle bounce beneath you while still maintaining control. One secret of safe descending is to go fast over ruts and bumps—the increased speed seems to flatten them out, and you bounce around less than when you pick your way gingerly through.

Look ahead as you descend, and pick your line through the rocks and stumps like a downhill skier picks a line though the moguls. If you focus your eyes and attention on the obstacle just ahead, you'll be through it and into other difficulties before you can adjust. Good descenders have learned the knack of figuring out in advance how to get over or around a rock, then letting their body do it while their mind is already working on the next obstacle.

In downhill corners, brake before the turn so you can go around without skidding. A clean cornering technique is much faster and less destructive to the environment than a dirt-spraying skid. If you misjudge the turn and have to brake in the middle, use the rear brake so the front wheel doesn't lock up and wash out. Skids involving the rear wheel are much easier to control than those in front.

Modern mountain biking tires have amazing traction on loose surfaces, and bicycles can be leaned over frighteningly far on the most rubble-strewn corners. But off-road surfaces are considerably less predictable than pavement, so corner conservatively—the tire-gripping hardpack in the first third of the corner often deteriorates to loose gravel in the middle.

When you are cycling on the flat in loose and unstable surfaces—mud, sand, or deep gravel—sit back on the saddle for traction and *power* your way through. If the bicycle starts to fishtail, don't panic and grab the brakes. Instead, keep pedaling—you need power from the rear wheel to accelerate out of the situation.

Races

The infinite variety of courses and conditions in mountain bike racing makes specific suggestions impractical. Instead, let's look at some general rules that apply equally to any off-road race.

Off-Road Racing Techniques

Start by getting to the front. Most mountain bike races are conducted on narrow trails or dirt roads where passing is difficult. This means that if you get caught at the back early, you'll be slowed by cyclists ahead and have trouble maintaining your pace. Nothing is more frustrating for a skilled, conditioned cyclist than to be stuck behind slower cyclists, crashes, and cyclists with poor technique who can't get their feet back into the clips after steep run-ups.

Avoid the problem by going as hard as possible from the line. Most races start on a wide stretch of road or in a field, the course narrowing in a half mile or less to a dirt road or single track. The idea is to get good position early in the race when you still have room to pass, then hold on during the narrower sections. Leisurely starts don't cut it in mountain bike racing.

Warm up sufficiently before the race so your body is ready for maximum effort from the time the gun goes off. Preride at least the first mile of the course to learn just where it gets narrow and to scout out the obstacles. If you didn't get to the starting line early enough to line up near the front, slink up the side if you have to. Practice your starting technique before the race, so when the gun goes off you can smoothly push off, get into the clips, and accelerate to high speed. Remember where the course narrows—make sure you are in good position relative to those around you to funnel into the single track.

Next, pace yourself. Drafting is not a factor in most off-road races because speeds are slower and packs don't form due to the obstacles. So the exertion called for is more like the steady pacing of a road time trial than the fast/slow pattern of a road race or criterium. Once you achieve good position, settle into a speed and a rhythm that you can maintain for the whole race.

Cyclists get into trouble when they jam hills so hard that they get into oxygen debt and have to slow way down to recover. You'll cover the course faster if you keep tabs on your breathing and exertion levels, holding a *steady* pace all the way.

Don't forget to maintain technique, however. No matter how strong you are, you can lose tremendous amounts of time by clumsy execution of the technical parts of the course. Fumbling with toe clips costs 5 or 10 seconds. Missing a shift and being forced to walk up part of a steep hill is worth another 10 or 15. And taking the wrong line through a corner and dumping it in the weeds may add half an hour while you rebuild your bicycle.

Practicing the technical aspects of the sport before the race helps, but so does careful pacing during competition. Many cyclists go so deeply into oxygen debt on climbs that when they have to do something other than just blindly pedal–pick their way around boulders for instance–they are so fatigued they can't control the bicycle. *Always* keep a little energy in reserve. It's better to go a little slower and be able to negotiate the course's hard parts than to lose big chunks of time to accidents or clumsiness.

Spare your equipment. Off-road cycling is hard on bicycles. Mud clogs moving parts, trailside bushes claw at derailleurs, rocks and ruts lie in wait to flatten wheels and crumple frames. Since all mechanical work has to be done by the cyclist with no outside help, it pays to take it easy on the rough sections. You may lose seconds here and there, but you won't lose minutes bending your forks back into line. And if you are racing recreationally, you'll want your bicycle to have as much fun as you are. Factory team cyclists can get a new frame issued to them after a mishap, but you probably will have to go to the shop on Monday and *buy* a replacement.

As in any competition, drink during the race. Hydration is crucial to performance. A loss of only a few percent of your body weight severely compromises your work output, so experienced road racers drink every 10 or 15 minutes. It is much more difficult to drink regularly during off-road races, because the terrain is so bumpy and irregular that it's often impossible to take one hand off the bars to get at the bottle. And when you have it up to your mouth, chances are you'll hit a bump and jam the nozzle into your gum or split your lip with the edge.

Avoid do-it-yourself "plastic surgery" by checking out the course in advance. If the race is a circuit, note the smoothest place each lap and drink there each time around. On loops or point-to-point races, take advantage of every break in the undulations to grab a quick drink.

Observed Trials

A relatively new event in off-road racing, observed trials are rapidly increasing in popularity. The basic format is simple. Cyclists try to navigate short obstacle-strewn sections without falling or putting down a foot for balance. Elapsed time doesn't matter, but each time the cyclist touches the ground with a foot (called a "dab"), points are added to the score. Falls are penalized more heavily. As in golf, the cyclist with the lowest score wins. The sport places a premium on bicycle handling, agility, and concentration. Fitness and power are important, but less so than in other events since the event is so much shorter.

When observed trials are part of off-road stage races, cyclists usually have to use the bicycles they use for the other stages of the race. Sometimes they are allowed to remove the outer chainring for more clear-

A skilled rider on a trials bicycle can climb about anything!

1. Saddle up!
2. Mosey on down those front steps.
3. Watch out for that critter on the right.
4. Use the cinder block to get over the wall.
5. Don't get hog-tied by those tree roots.
6. Hop along the curb.
7. Giddap and over that ledge.
8. Don't let a little brick buffalo you.
9. Dig in your spurs and clear that high-jump bar.
10. Steer clear of that oil spot (cow chip?) in the garage.
11. Now's the time for some real hossin' around.
12. Giddap and over that ledge one more time.
13. Ride herd into the backyard for some more adventure.

ance over rocks and logs. As a specialized event, cyclists use trials bicycles with tiny seats, wide tires, a low fixed gear, and perhaps a skid plate so the chainring doesn't catch on obstacles. Skilled trials cyclists can ride over picnic tables, up stairs, or sidestep up steep hills by hopping the bicycle.

The key to trials riding is practice. You need to be completely at home on the bicycle, able to balance for long periods of time on the pedals, hop the bicycle sideways up steep grades, and pivot around obstacles on the rear wheel. Good cyclists routinely balance on the front wheel.

The key to such wizardry is a practice course at home. The front yard works fine. Route the course over the curb, around planter boxes and shrubs, and perhaps up the front steps. Insert additional obstacles like rocks, pieces of firewood, or children's

Going down takes as much skill as going up.

toys, and then *use it*—practice negotiating your homemade obstacles as smoothly as possible.

Another key to trials riding is to imitate the technique of accomplished cyclists. Go to trials competitions and see how they handle obstacles. Seek out the best cyclists near your home and work out with them, making it a point to be always open to advice and tips. Good trials technique is reinforced by example.

Off-Road Riding for Road Riders

The preceding discussion has emphasized the competitive aspects of off-road riding. But cycling in the dirt is fun even if you never turn a pedal in competitive fever. And it can pay big dividends if your major interest is road biking, either noncompetitive events like group rides and centuries or striving for the top on the racing circuit. Think of it this way:

Most recreational cyclists and novice racers lack two major skills: climbing and cornering. They get burned off on the hills, terrified in corners. But it's relatively easy to improve in both these areas by doing what top U.S. amateurs have done for years as part of their winter training program: Get out and do mountain bike workouts as part of your normal off-season routine. Recreational cyclists who can only envy the acrobatic bicycle handling and overwhelming power of the top racers can use off-road riding to develop these skills.

A fat-tired mountain bike or a modified klunker are just fine to practice on. Either type bicycle will work—the trick is to get out and get dirty. The benefits? Improved bicycle handling leads the way. Navigating through icy ruts, powering up muddy hills, and slithering down steep embankments puts a premium on body control, balance, and a feel for the limitations of a two-wheeled vehicle in the presence of gravity. No matter how skilled you are at keeping the rubber on the pavement, there will always be challenges: lousy drivers, snarling dogs, or slippery corners. Riding a mountain bike on dirt, snow, mud, or grass is the best and safest way to improve balance and control. You'll learn to handle far more difficult terrain than you'll ever meet on the pavement this side of Paris-Roubaix.

Some off-road cyclists develop a wizard's bicycle-handling touch. On a mountain bike you often lose traction in corners, so you get used to the feeling of sliding around and soon learn the knack of staying loose when the rear tire is traveling sideways. Then when the same thing happens on the road, you don't panic and dump it. The art can be honed to a high degree. A few combination off-road/road racers are comfortable skidding their skinny tires through wet downhill corners on high-speed descents.

You can develop bicycle handling skills faster off-road because the penalities for a crash are less severe. Soft dirt is a lot more forgiving than blacktop. You learn how far you can lean the bicycle over in a corner only by pushing closer and closer to the edge until you eventually crash. That sort of experimentation just isn't done on the road—at least not willingly. So you don't learn where the limits are. But if you choose a grassy field or soft dirt paths, you can be more daring without fear of serious injury. The result: A faster learning curve *without* undue risk of injury.

Power is another plus. Wide off-road tires produce extra rolling resistance. Add a little mud, sand, or loose snow to an uphill grade, and your local killer hill will seem much less formidable. You don't need big dirt hills, either. Even a gentle grade can be demanding when gravity is in league with quagmire. Riding regularly through the glop can start you on the way to power that cracks crankarms and strips freewheels.

Riding off-road also strengthens your upper body, as you pull on the handlebars to conquer hills and lurch over obstacles. One of the disadvantages of cycling as an all-around builder of fitness is that it emphasizes the legs and shortchanges the upper body. That isn't as true of off-road rides. Many newcomers to mountain bikes comment that their arms and shoulders get as tired as their legs on their first few excursions. That power above the waist increases your overall fitness, makes you a stronger, more effective cyclist, and helps prevent injury to your shoulder girdle if you fall.

Don't forget variety. Most cyclists train on the same roads all season. On a mountain bike the number of possible training routes is almost infinite. Dirt and gravel roads, canal banks, jogging trails—they're all open for exploration. And when you get jaded with pavement and civilization, go take a roll in the dirt.

And there's a final advantage. In spite of rocks, overhanging tree limbs—and the serious danger of being buzzed by flying squirrels—off-road biking is actually less dangerous than pedaling along a city street. Unpaved roads are less traveled by motor vehicles, making them much safer since getting beaned by a squirrel is a lot less traumatic than a close encounter with a truck. And if you crash, the landing is *much* softer.

All these advantages don't require a major investment. You can train off-road on your regular road bike equipped with sturdy wheels and knobby tires. Use clincher rims and Specialized 700C × 35 Tri-cross tires. It's not a good idea to bang around on your best road frame, though. The inevitable minor crashes, as well as the shock of bouncing around on rocky terrain, can throw your good frame out of alignment. An old frame and cheap components make a better beater.

If you own a mountain bike, you already have the ideal setup. But to get the power and bike handling benefits while avoiding injury, it is important to maintain proper riding position. Your pedaling efficiency will increase and your risk of knee problems will decrease if you approximate the same saddle position on your mountain bike that you use on your road bike. Small variations are permissible, however. Some off-road racers like their mountain bike saddles farther back, so they can push down and pull up on the pedals with maximum force even though they aren't wearing foot-securing cleats. Other dirt track demons like their saddles a bit forward to ease the strain on their backs during climbs.

Equip the pedals with toe clips and straps to keep your feet secure on bumpy terrain and to give you more power on climbs. Some cyclists install dropped handlebars and bar end shifters so that their position is even closer to that on their road bike, but former U.S. national team coach Eddie Borysewicz says that this isn't necessary. He's more concerned about duplicating saddle height than upper body position.

You'll have to experiment to find your ideal saddle position, but it's a cardinal rule not to overgear. Plodding up hills at 40 rpm will prevent you from developing valuable power, and it will probably destroy your knees. Choose gears for your mountain bike that are low enough to allow you to spin over the tough spots. Even strong cyclists in the mountain bike mecca of Crested Butte, Colorado, often pack a granny chainring of 26 or 24 teeth.

A mountain bike set up this way also makes a good bicycle for road training in early season rain or slush. The sealed bearings and components resist moisture and mud, and the earth-mover tires rarely puncture. In fact, if you need one *more* good excuse to buy a mountain bike, think of all the wear and tear you'll save on your road bike in abysmal spring conditions.

Be sure to mix your mountain bike and road biking wisely, however, if your main interest lies with road events. It is easy to lose the snap and spin that good roadies have, with too much power-intensive trail riding, becoming a plodder instead. If you balance the two types of riding, though, you can enjoy the extra power development and still retain leg speed, too.

No matter where you live, you can find good terrain for off-road training, but it may take some looking. In a city, your best bet is a park with jogging or horse trails. Vacant lots often have ready-made trails, courtesy of kids on BMX bicycles.

In rural areas, look for fire trails, backcountry dirt or gravel roads, irrigation ditch roads, jeep roads, towpaths, or the farmers' tractor roads around corn fields. (Ask permission first!)

No matter where you find the dirt, you can reap all the benefits of off-road riding without formal practice. You'll learn most necessary bicycle handling skills by just haphazardly meandering on trails and through the brush. If the terrain in your area isn't too severe, you can increase the difficulty just by increasing the speed.

Or you can set up a more formal practice area, copying a typical course. In fact, it may be worth your time to attend a local mountain bike circuit race just to get an idea of what sort of obstacles these cyclists contend with. The ideal: a challenging 1- to 3-mile circuit that begins about 5 miles from your house. You can warm up on the way, ride the circuit for 30 to 60 minutes, throwing in all the variations that the terrain and topography will allow, and then cool down on the way home. If you get cold or have a mechanical problem, you won't be stranded on some mountain ridge 20 miles from home.

An ideal course includes at least one longer, steady climb; several short, abrupt hills; tight corners; and some flat sections. The idea is to challenge all your abilities each time around.

Don't ride the circuit the same way every time–always pushing the hills and cruising the flats, for instance. Instead, use the terrain the way a good downhill skier works the moguls. Bang up a hill in a big gear one time, finesse it the next. Take a corner at high speed on the most efficient line, then take a more difficult line, and see if you can get yourself into and out of trouble. Ride the course in each direction to create different challenges.

You don't have to be content with natural features, either. Dig a small ditch, position a log or rock, and learn to jump the bicycle over the obstacle–a skill that will come in very handy the next time you're forced into the curb or over a pothole in a race.

And don't keep your circuit a secret. Because bicycle handling skills change in a pack, ride the loop with three or four friends. Stay close together and jostle each other on the flats. Try to sneak through corners on an inside line. Purposely touch wheels to learn the correct reaction. Some crashes are inevitable in this sort of training, so wear a hardshell helmet and thick clothing, and choose a circuit with soft landing places instead of trees and rocks. A few bruises are a small price to pay for the vastly increased confidence and pack riding skills you'll gain. Greg LeMond certainly benefitted back in 1979 when he won the Junior World Road Championship. Another cyclist forced him off the course twice, making him ride over a row of automobile tires. He didn't fall and later gave the credit to the type of off-road training just described.

Do a mountain bike workout twice a week in the early spring, and you'll see a big improvement in your skills when you start reemphasizing road biking. And don't quit when summer hits–even when the season is in full swing, it's smart to head for the dirt periodically to sharpen reflexes and get a break in your training routine.

ARDY
BOOK SALE

Special Circumstances

Cycling is a unique sport in that its arena is the open road–full of traffic, potholes, snarling dogs, and absent-minded pedestrians. Basketball players can count on a court free of potholes and strolling passersby, and no one jaywalks on a tennis court. But cyclists have to share the public roads, and since they do, it is important to learn how to deal with road hazards and traffic–skills that open up a whole new world of cycling.

Road Hazards

First, a few general rules that apply to any kind of cycling. Always ride with your head up. Cruising along on a lonely stretch of rural road, it is tempting to stare at the whirling pattern of the front spokes, mesmerized by their patterned spinning. And in a hard effort like a time trial, some riders try to ignore the pain by looking down at their pumping legs. But resist these impulses, and keep an eye on where you are going. Although cycling is generally safe, the roads are full of potential dangers that can easily be avoided if you see them in time. But it is all too easy to let a momentary downward glance last just a second too long.

Don't let your mind wander any more than your eyes. The smooth and rhythmic motion of cycling can have a hypnotic effect, lulling the daydreaming rider into a languorous and somnambulant state of lethargy and inattentiveness (a bit like this sentence). Daydreaming riders have crashed into the back of parked cars or run blithely off the road, separated from the outside world by the vivid canvases created by their imagination. But the reality of the road consists of semis, 2-ton cars, and gravel in the turns, so it's best to stay firmly in touch with it.

The last general rule for dealing with road hazards: Be sure your bicycle is in excellent mechanical condition. Worn tires with cracked tread and bulging sidewalls won't hold up when you encounter the inevitable patched and broken pavement of an American road. And it is impossible to avoid collisions with all the flotsam and jetsam littering the tarmac if your brake pads are worn to the metal or adjusted badly. Your first line of defense against the challenges of the real world is a bicycle with everything in good working order.

Glass and Gravel

Anything that punctures your tires is a road hazard, and both glass and gravel can do it. Experienced riders avoid frequent punctures by choosing their line with care to avoid road rubble and potholes. They brush off their tires frequently and inspect the tread after every ride for clinging debris. And they replace worn tires before they fail. These measures work–it isn't uncommon for careful cyclists to go 3,000 miles or more without a flat, even on tubulars. But no matter how lucky and careful you are, the gremlins in charge of punctures will get you eventually, and probably when it's least convenient.

Prepare for the inevitable flats by always carrying a frame pump. If the gods are with you, it won't get used very often, so check periodically to see if it still works. Nothing beats the frustration of flatting, mounting a new tire, and then finding that your pump doesn't work.

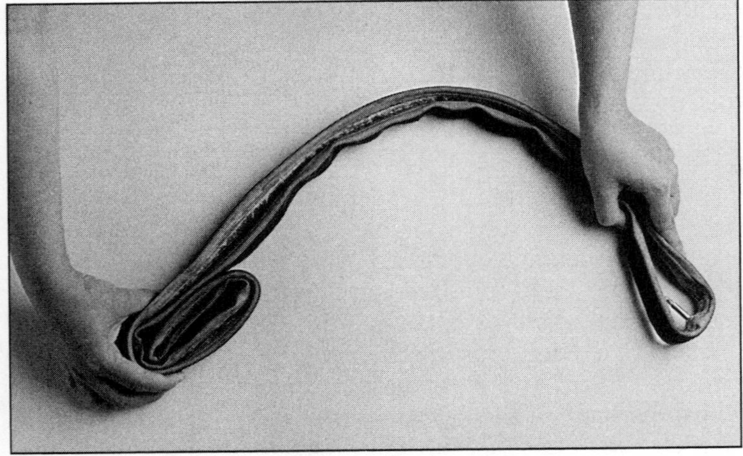

Folding a tubular tire, glue portions to the inside.

If you ride tubulars, carry at least one spare tire. On a long solo ride, you may want to carry two, since a prickly patch of road that gets one tire can get the other at the same time. If other riders in your group are on tubulars, one spare each is plenty since you can share if the need arises.

Pack your spare in a small bag designed for the purpose or an old sock, to protect it from road debris kicked up from the rear wheel and also from the deteriorating effects of the sun. Secure it beneath your saddle with a toe strap.

If you need to carry two spares, put one in your jersey pocket. You can strap them both beneath the saddle, but the added bulk sometimes makes them protrude enough to rub the back of your thigh on each pedal stroke. If that happens, you'll wear a hole through your skin in 10 miles.

Be sure that any spare tubular has been prestretched on a wheel so you can get it on easily when you need it. By the same token, give the base tape of the tire a coat of glue and let it dry before you pack it along as a spare. The glue will help the spare stick to the wheel, but a newly mounted tubular is never as secure as one carefully glued at home–be careful in corners.

Make sure all the air is out of the tire, and then fold it lengthwise with the glued sections facing each other so you won't get glue on the tread. Fold up the resulting strip, snugging the last two folds over onto the previous ones. Secure with a rubber band, and put it in your tire sack.

If you are riding on clinchers, carry a spare tube and a patch kit. Tubulars are easier to change on the road–just peel off the old one and stick on the spare–but clinchers have the advantage of multiple repairability. If you puncture three times, just keep patching–but don't forget to look for the offending material before you replace the tube. You'll just puncture again if the sliver of glass or thorn that caused the first flat is left embedded in the tire casing. Use the spare tube for the first flat only to save time, or if the original tube is damaged too extensively to repair.

Although supernatural forces often seem to blame, nearly invisible shards of glass are the usual culprit. Prevention is the best cure. If you don't have the good fortune to live in a state with a bottle law, be on the lookout for the telltale glitter of shattered glass when you ride. Weekend mornings are especially risky–most of the glass on our roads comes from late-night partiers tossing empty bottles out car windows. If you spot the patch of glass in time, swing wide to avoid it. But if you are riding by yourself, check behind for traffic before switching lanes–better to get a puncture than be rear-ended by a car. If you are riding with others, don't swerve abruptly to avoid glass–you'll run the risk of taking down another rider. And even if you think you successfully avoided the glass, immediately brush off your tires with your fingertips to remove any of the small splinters that were inevitably scattered across the road.

When you don't see the glass in time, or if traffic or your riding companions make evasive action impossible, you'll have to ride through the shards. But a puncture is *not* inevitable. Try to avoid the biggest pieces by slight alterations of line. An inch or two either way can help you escape the large chunks of glass that are most likely to cut through the tread, sometimes severing the whole tire right down to the rim like a deli clerk slicing a submarine sandwich. If that happens when you are riding clinchers and carrying a spare tube, you are out of luck–the tire is ruined beyond repair. To handle the situation, riders tote along a folding spare tire with a Kevlar bead on long solo rides. A lighter solution: duct tape and a 3-inch-square piece of sturdy cloth, all you need to fabricate an emergency boot for the slashed tire. Major tread cuts ruin tubulars past all repair, also, so in either case try to avoid the biggest pieces of glass waiting to hack at your tires.

If you ride through a patch of small, broken-up pieces, they may not have an immediate effect, but they'll stick to the tread and eventually burrow into the tube. Wipe off your tires immediately, and if you feel anything still sticking to the tread, stop and pry it out before it penetrates.

If you can't swerve away from the glass before you get to it, you are usually better off riding straight through. Abrupt turns while you are riding on glass tend to puncture the more fragile sidewalls of your tires as you lean them over to swerve. The general rule is to keep as much tread as possible between you and the glass, and hope for the best.

Sharp pieces of gravel can wreak as much havoc on your tires as glass. Be on the lookout at intersections, where gravel tends to get swept up by passing cars and deposited in a river-delta shape, fanning out from the corners. Broken glass accumulates in these alluvial deposits, too, another reason to avoid them. Move to the middle of the lane when you approach intersections to dodge these gravel bars and to increase your visibility to motorists.

The worst kind of gravel occurs when roads are resurfaced with what is called chip-and-seal. In this operation, road crews first apply a layer of sticky tar, then top it off with small, jagged pieces of rock. The tar makes your tires sticky, and the gravel clings to the tread, digging closer to the tube with each turn of the wheel. And it is almost impossible to brush off the gooey stuff with your hand.

The danger of encountering miles of new chip-and-seal is a good reason to ride heavy tires if you are on a long tour. When you leave from home for normal training, scout out local roads that are being repaired, and take alternate routes until the gravel is ground into the tar and the road crew has returned to sweep the streets. On rural roads, however, sweeping is a haphazard process done by passing cars. The result is that lightly traveled roads, the sort that make cycling a pleasure, generally take longer to become ridable than less pleasant, high-traffic routes.

Cactus spines and thorns of various kinds are the other major causes of punctures in certain sections of the country—the Southwest, for example. When you are riding in thorn country, stay a foot or so to the left of the white line—a part of the road where passing traffic has had a chance to sweep the road clean. And if you wheel your bicycle off the road to take a break, brush off your tires before you resume riding in case you accidentally pick up some prickly hitchhikers.

Consider mounting tire savers. Available in most bicycle shops, they are flexible wire devices that ride just above your tires, skimming off debris at every rotation before it can get ground in through the casing and into the tube. Although they are most useful in thorn country, where the danger of punctures is always present, many riders in other parts of the country regularly use them. A big advantage: If they're cleaning your tire, you don't have to, although you should supplement the tire saver's vigilance with your own.

In country where thorns seem to grow out of the pavement, you may still get a high frequency of punctures in spite of these measures. The solution: sturdier tires and tubes. Consider tires with protective Kevlar strips under the tread, and use so-called "thornproof" tubes—extra thick on the road side. Plastic tire liners are also available.

The desert is tough on tires.

Dogs

Dogs are road hazards that cause many cyclists great concern. To deal with roving canines, they carry noxious chemicals in spray cans or detour miles out of their way to avoid the beasts. Granted, there is something unnerving about a snapping mutt yapping at your heels. But most strong reactions are unwarranted.

The majority of dogs who chase bicycles are merely defending their territory. When you pedal off the section of road that they consider to be their turf, you no longer pose a threat to their ancestral instincts, and they lose interest. Dogs who home in on you like an Exocet missile and chase for miles are fortunately in the minority.

Although danger from dogs is usually overrated, it does exist—they can cause crashes if you are paying more attention to Fido than to the road. And it's undeniable that some dogs will bite you or run in front of your wheel, taking you down. But where there's a problem, there's usually a solution, and evasive action is one of them.

You can often outrun charging dogs,

especially if they aren't too serious about attacking but have just come out to look you over. If the road is flat or downhill, stand up and sprint, keeping one eye on the dog. Experienced riders quickly develop the knack of assessing a dog's fitness and speed, and adjust their escape tactics accordingly. Is it fat and out of shape? Sprint on by with a smile. But if it's lean and mean, agile, mobile, and hostile, better try another approach—like hitting the rocket assist.

The dog is gaining in spite of your best efforts. Or the road is uphill and you can't sprint fast enough to escape. Resort to Plan B. Look authoritatively down at the dog, and cover two bases at once by raising your hand threateningly as if it contains a rock, then yelling "No!" or "Stay!" in as loud and commanding a voice as you can muster. If the dog is reasonably well-trained, it will hesitate in response to the command. And outlaw mutts usually have had plenty of experience with what comes flying at them after a human raises an arm in a throwing gesture. Either way, you will probably have enough time to get down the road.

If you can't outrun or outbluff the dog, get off your bicycle and hold it between you and the threatening canine. Then use the bicycle or your pump to fend off the charge until help arrives. If it comes to this, report the attack to the county sheriff or other authority as soon as you get home. Include the location, a description of the dog, an account of what happened, and the owner's name and address if you know them. Then follow up with a call to the authorities to find out what action was taken.

Some riders swear by small aerosol cans of ammonia that they clip to their handlebars and spray in the dog's face when one attacks. The ammonia stings its eyes but doesn't cause any lasting damage. But most dogs can be repelled simply by spraying them in the face with water from a bottle. A few cyclists go so far as to carry rocks in their jersey pockets to hurl at every approaching hound. But such militant behavior is usually unwise for several reasons.

One, it is dangerous to throw something or spray a charging dog from a moving bicycle. It's easy to crash when your attention is on the dog. They also usually attack from the rear so you'll have to look back to deal with the attack—you may as a result run into parked cars or go off the road. And most cyclists really don't want to hurt someone's pet, understanding that it isn't the dog's fault that it isn't versed in the niceties of civilized behavior. Most dog problems, in fact, are really problems with people—people who allow their animals to run free or who don't train them to stay in the yard. Don't, in other words, take it out on the dog. If you consistently have problems with the same dog, get the address of the owners, and write a polite letter asking them to restrain their dog. Send a copy to the local law enforcement agency, too, so you'll have proof of previous problems if the dog bites you or causes a crash, and the affair goes to court. Cyclists have the right to use the roads without fear of animal violence, so don't be afraid to assert your rights.

Potholes and Railroad Tracks

Another common road hazard is the pothole in all its forms: deep, round craters, shallow gouges with jagged edges, and miniswamps filled with water and hidden from view. Hitting normal potholes can bend your rims beyond repair, and if they're deep enough, they'll send you hurtling over the bars when the bicycle suddenly stops.

Note where potholes lurk on your normal training routes, and remember to avoid them. But don't expect the road to be in the same condition every day. Keep your eyes open, because potholes have a habit of sprouting up overnight, especially in the spring after winter's alternate freeze-and-thaw opens yawning chasms in the pavement.

Treat potholes like glass and ride around them, first checking behind for traffic and always mindful of training partners when you change your line. Newly minted potholes present a double hazard—the chasm, itself, and the fragments of shattered pavement around it. If the pothole doesn't bend your wheel, the sharp bits of rubble will puncture your tire. So give these highway craters a wide berth.

Skilled riders can jump their bicycles over potholes when they're unable to avoid them because of traffic or adjacent riders. Learn this move on a grassy field first. Jump over a line on the ground, then graduate to higher but soft objects like a small cardboard box. As you approach the obstacle, stop pedaling with the crankarms horizontal. Crouch with your weight lifted slightly off the saddle. Clear the obstacle by springing upward, taking your feet with you and simultaneously pulling on the handlebars so the bicycle comes up smoothly with both wheels the same distance off the ground. Limit the impact of landing by using your legs like shock absorbers, or your wheels may develop flat spots from the impact.

Jumping over obstacles. Note bent knees for a soft landing.

Jumping is easier if you tighten your straps first so your feet don't come out of the pedals. Step-in pedal systems are an advantage here because you are always locked in. If an obstacle looms unexpectedly, you can hop over without scrambling to tighten the straps. BMX riders can jump their bicycles without toe clips by rolling their wrists forward and putting rearward pressure on the pedals, but it's a technique that is much easier on a BMX bicycle than a road bike.

Railroad tracks are a very common road hazard. And they are harder to avoid because, unlike all but the most cavernous potholes, they extend all the way across the road. You can't ride around them, so you have to develop ways to get over them without mangling your wheels. In normal riding, where speed isn't crucial, slow down for the tracks, rise slightly off your saddle to absorb the shock, and cruise gently over the rails.

If the tracks cross the road on a diagonal, you'll have to turn across the road and approach the tracks square. If you hit them on an angle, the rails can twist your front wheel off-line and produce a crash. Be especially wary if it is raining. Bare-metal railroad tracks are incredibly slippery when wet, and the slightest abrupt move can take you down.

If you need to cross tracks at maximum speed, you'll have to jump them. Use the same technique that worked for potholes (see above), but remember that you have two rails to jump so you'll need more speed and lift. If you misjudge and come down too early, your rear wheel will hit the second rail with great force, almost guaranteeing a ruined wheel or a puncture.

If the railroad crossing has more than one set of tracks, it's impossible to jump them all at once unless you wear a cape and change clothes in a phone booth. Either slow down and cross gingerly, or do it in two jumps: first one set, then land and jump the next.

White Lines, Oil Slicks, and Fallen Leaves

Potholes and railroad tracks are obvious road hazards, but the streets are full of other less-visible dangers. Painted white lines, especially the wide pedestrian crossing markings at intersections, are especially dangerous. The thickly applied paint fills in the tiny spaces between the bits of crushed rock in the asphalt, producing an extremely slippery surface that is uncertain when dry but *deadly* when wet.

Always use caution on these surfaces. The danger increases when the paint is new because, as it wears down with use, traction increases.

Oil slicks are another nearly invisible danger. Look for darker streaks on the gray pavement, especially in corners. You aren't safe if you ride through oil on the straights, because it can cling to your tires, producing greased tread that can dump you in the next corner. Oil becomes especially slick in the rain. In heavy rain, an oil slick that was originally limited to a small patch can grow until it covers the whole lane, so be on the lookout for the telltale rainbow-colored water. There's no pot of gold at the end of this rainbow–only an unscheduled meeting with the pavement.

In the autumn, watch out for thin carpets of fallen leaves on the road. Secluded, tree-arched lanes are great to ride on, but they often collect a thick coating of leaves since they aren't swept often by passing cars. Fallen leaves are more dangerous when wet, but even when dry, they form an unstable surface on top of the pavement.

Metal Grates

Some city streets have metal sewer grates with the bars spaced just wide enough to trap a bicycle wheel. Many of these wheel manglers have been replaced with bicycle-friendly models, but be careful in case your community hasn't gotten the message yet.

A close cousin of the sewer grate is the metal expansion strip sometimes installed where roads join bridges. Designed to accommodate the expansion and contraction of the bridge in varying temperatures, they are more difficult to avoid because they extend completely across the road. Although newer designs have solid strips spaced at intervals along their length so bicycles can pass safely, older ones seem to be constructed for the sole purpose of swallowing bicycle wheels. Jump them, or walk across.

In many parts of the western United States, you'll have to watch out for cattle guards (large grates extending completely across secondary roads). With bars that run across your direction of travel, they often have the rails placed close enough together so you can ride uncomfortably but safely across at reduced speed. You can also jump them, but even the best riders are often cowed by a 4-foot expanse of hard metal. You'll need considerable velocity to jump the gap, and the penalties for a mistake are *all* painful.

Be particularly cautious when you ride on any metal surface when it is raining. Wet metal is literally as slippery as ice. It is nearly impossible to stay up if you change your line the slightest bit. These surfaces are particularly dangerous after a clear, frosty night–the melting frost makes the surface wet and treacherous without the rainfall that would normally put you on guard. But if you inadvertently ride onto a metal bridge before you realize it's wet, *don't* grab at the brakes or make any other sudden moves; just continue pedaling smoothly, and try to ride it out.

Riding at Night

The most dangerous of all road hazards is darkness. You can't see the road clearly, so it is easy to run into potholes or other nocturnal obstacles like roaming skunks or raccoons. And drivers are even less likely to see you, so the normal danger from vehicular traffic is vastly increased.

Step one in cutting your risk is to mount a good headlight. Battery-powered lights are preferable to generator-driven models, because they maintain a steady brightness even when stopped–at traffic signals, for example. And they can be dismounted and used as flashlights if you need to change a tire or make mechanical repairs in the dark.

On the debit side, batteries have the annoying habit of running low just when you need them most. If you ride in the dark regularly, consider paying more for rechargeable batteries that can be plugged into a recharger each day. Another option is a generator light for the open road, with a battery-operated handlebar light that takes over at intersections when you stop.

You'll also need a good taillight so overtaking motorists can see you. The brighter the better–most car-bicycle accidents after dark are rear-end collisions caused by the motorist's inability to see the cyclist. One superior choice is a flashing beacon that attaches to your bicycle or your waist. You may look like a moving highway barricade when you're wearing it, but it's guaranteed to get the attention of overtaking drivers.

Reflectors are usually the first things that get discarded on a new bicycle, simply because they're often so cheaply made they rattle madly at every bump. That's too bad–reflectors *do* light up your bicycle effectively in the glare of headlights. Pedal reflectors are especially noticeable, because their unusual circular motion is like nothing else on the road. They wake up the most inattentive driver. But they have the disadvantage of making the rear of the pedal cage thicker, so cleats don't engage as well, and the step-in pedal systems don't accomodate them.

One alternative to the usual bulky metal-and-plastic reflector is reflective *tape*. Available in any hardware store, this adhesive-backed tape can be cut into appropriate lengths and stuck to frame tubes, crankarms, and pedal cages–even you. It is highly reflective and lightweight. So decorated, your bicycle lights up like a Christmas tree in car headlights.

If you don't plan to ride in the dark but might get caught in it–on a long tour, for instance, or training after work–consider carrying a battery-powered leg light. These ingenious devices are inexpensive, lightweight, and take up little room in jersey pocket or touring bag. Combined with reflectorized tape, they make you much more visible in the dangerous twilight period.

The leg light/tape combination works well alone for serious training in darkness, too, but only in reasonably well-lit residential areas. Find a quiet residential loop brightly lit with streetlights. You can dispense with bicycle-mounted lighting systems, and you'll be able to go fast enough for a training effect because you'll be able to see the road. Going around the same loop gets boring, but it beats facing the much greater dangers of darkened roads.

Riding in Traffic

Because cyclists must share the road with cars, farm vehicles, logging trucks, and stretch limos, traffic is an inescapable fact of cycling life.

One way to minimize problems with heavy vehicular traffic is to choose lightly traveled roads for training and commuting.

It pays to search them out and plan how to get to them from your house with the minimum of riding on busier streets.

If you are new to an area, stop in a bookstore and get a county map showing all the local roads. Study it in the evenings, and try new routes whenever you ride. Carry the map in your jersey pocket, folded in a plastic bag to protect it from sweat and rain, until you are sure you know the way back as well as the way out. Most maps make even mountainous terrain look one-dimensional, but once you get familiar with the country, the map that really matters—the one you carry along in your head—will show every mesa and hollow, valley and dell.

Another good source of information on local roads is an area bicycle shop. They often have wall-sized maps of the area with good cycling routes highlighted in colored pen. Some shops also carry specially designed cyclist's maps of the city and surrounding countryside.

Ask salespeople at the shop about their favorite routes, too, and whether they sponsor group training rides. Going along on a couple of these excursions may tip you off to enjoyable new territory you'd otherwise miss. And local racers and recreational riders know all the shortcuts, lanes, and ridable dirt paths that connect the lightly traveled roads so you don't have to make otherwise necessary detours on major highways next to the 18-wheelers.

Asserting Your Vehicular Rights

You can't, of course, always avoid traffic. Getting to most places requires riding on major arterials at least part of the time. And if you want to take long rides to scenic attractions, you'll have to share the road with drivers who have the same idea. And while riding in heavy traffic is never pleasant, if you practice certain simple technques, it *can* be safe and fast.

First, remember that a bicycle is a vehicle, and as a cyclist, you have the same rights and responsibilities as any motorized road user. You have to stop for traffic signals, obey speed limits, and signal for turns. But you also have a right to a safe share of the road, and motorists are legally required to allow you that space.

The law in most states requires cyclists to ride as far to the right of the roadway as is "practicable." Practicable means the same thing as practical, but perhaps a better translation of this legalese is "safe." You are required to ride as far to the right as you safely can, not as far to the right as possible.

On a road with a wide shoulder, ride about a foot to the right of the white line.

In addition, you are allowed to move left to avoid road hazards and obstructions.

On rural roads with a safe, wide shoulder you should ride about a foot to the right of the white line. If the shoulder is strewn with glass, move to the left to avoid it. Look ahead to see if the shoulder narrows unexpectedly for bridge abutments or is blocked by parked cars. When that happens, look behind, signal your intentions, and move smoothly left into the traffic lane. Stay there until you can *safely* return to the shoulder.

On rural roads with no shoulder, you have little choice but to take space in the traffic lane. If that's the case, ride about a foot to the left of the white line. It is tempting to ride right on the line to give passing motorists as much room as possible but—contrary to appearances—tightroping down the white line is much more dangerous than riding a foot to the left.

Why? If you ride on the line, drivers think that they have enough room to go around you at full speed even if another car is approaching in the opposite lane. Cars buzz by your left shoulder at maximum speed with little room to spare. And riding on the line puts you so close to the edge of the road that you have almost zero space to maneuver if a car comes too close and you have to swerve to the right. You are likely, in fact, to be run off the pavement.

But if you assert your rights to the road by riding a foot or so to the left of the white line, drivers slow down and pass you as they would any other slower-moving vehicle—when it is safe to move out into the other lane and go by.

On the open highway, be aware of the effect of passing trucks and buses on your bicycle's handling. A fast-moving semi rocketing past your elbow creates a partial vacuum in its wake, pulling you along and increasing your speed momentarily. Experienced time trialists competing on busy roads take advantage of this legal draft by increasing their rpm as they feel the swirling tug of the displaced air.

The disadvantage of high-speed traffic is the tendency for the induced vacuum to pull you slightly to the left and into the traffic lane. A fast-moving rig passing within a foot of your shoulder can physically pull you into its wake and cause loss of control—all the more reason to leave yourself some space to maneuver between your line of travel and the pavement's edge.

Take your legal share of the lane on city streets, too—if anything, ride a little *farther* to the left. It is dangerous to hug a line of parked cars, because the occupants often open their street-side doors without looking, and connecting with an open car door at 20 mph is no fun at all. Getting "doored," as it is called, is reason enough to ride far enough to the left for safety. But there's more: Pedestrians can also step out from between parked cars, but if you ride several feet out in the lane, you'll have time to avoid them. And finally, wheel-eating sewer

On a road with an unsafe shoulder or none at all, ride about a foot to the left of the white line.

Take your legal share of the lane in city cycling.

grates, potholes, and piles of broken glass are more common near the curb.

The biggest reason to assert your right to lane space is to diminish the danger caused by overtaking drivers turning right directly in front of you. If you are hugging the curb, you lose the only advantage you have in this situation: visibility. For some reason, many drivers will treat you as if you weren't there, pass you closely, and then turn right so abruptly you either brake quickly or get forced into the curb. If the car isn't quite past you when it begins to turn, you have little choice but to turn with it—always a dicey maneuver, but especially so if the driver cuts too close to the curb to let you through. Riding out in the traffic lane forces overtaking motorists to slow and wait until you are through the intersection before they turn right—exactly what they'd have to do if you were driving a car.

In fact, many experienced urban riders always take the whole lane as they approach and cross intersections. Drivers behind may have to slow, but they won't be able to hook you as they turn right. And you are much more visible to oncoming motorists who may be turning left in front of you and to others who may be sneaking across the intersection against the light.

In the city, ride well out in the lane, so drivers turning right won't cut you off.

Another trick at intersections is to make eye contact with drivers who are stopped and waiting to pull out. If they focus on you, they may actually see you instead of darting out as you pass by. But it's not a sure thing. For some reason, many drivers look right at you and then blithely pull out in front of you. Make eye contact anyway, but watch the front wheels–the car can't move before the front wheels do, so they are often your earliest warning of movement in an unexpected direction.

Be ready for drivers who pull out just far enough ahead of you that you have to brake abruptly. In most cases, these motorists acknowledge your presence with eye contact–and then pull out anyway. But usually, they aren't trying to get you–they're simply used to children's bicycles traveling at slow speeds, and they forget that fit adult cyclists roll down city streets at 20 to 25 mph. They are halfway out on the street, you are almost upon them, and their surprise is palpable. This sort of incident is fortunately decreasing as motorists become more used to faster cyclists and learn to equate bicycle speed with that of cars and motorcycles.

Making Right and Left Turns

When you want to turn right or left in traffic, follow the same laws that govern motor vehicles. Position yourself in the correct lane well in advance of the turn, signal your intentions, and take a smooth line through the corner. Don't try to take any corner in traffic at high speed. Leave plenty of margin for pedestrians who step off the curb unexpectedly, slippery lane markings, and parked cars that pull away from the curb without looking. Remember: A fall in traffic is much more dangerous than a fall on a rural road. In traffic, not only do you pick up the usual array of road rash, but you may hit a car as you crash or get run over by a vehicle that can't stop in time.

Coexisting with Vehicles and Their Drivers

Whenever you share the road with motorized traffic, you'll be safer if you go about your business in a professional way. Very few cyclists can be professional racers, but we can all look and behave professionally on our bicycles. And motorists are much more likely to treat you with respect if you demand it with your actions and demeanor. How do you do that? Wear bright colors that give motorists advance notice of your presence. Look sharp in your position on the bicycle. Wear a good helmet that indicates your seriousness about safety. And in dusk or darkness, use reflectors and lights.

Be predictable. Don't weave around on the road or wobble as you ride. Instead, ride a straight line so overtaking motorists feel secure about passing you. Survival in traffic boils down to riding in such a way that you confidently and competently assert your control of the road.

What do you do if you are threatened or hassled by motorists? Fortunately, this doesn't happen very often, but every cyclist of more than a month's experience can tell one or two horror stories of flying beer cans, unexpectedly opening car doors, and verbal abuse. The best reaction is to ignore the affront and ride calmly on. In most cases, the driver will have gotten rid of his frustrations by the initial action and will drive off, leaving you in peace. But if you react with shouts or gestures, he may return and continue the assault. The point here is that ignoring them takes all the fun out of the assault, which usually puts an end to it.

If the harrassment is repeated or more serious, try to get pertinent information for a police report. Check for a license number, a description of the car and occupants, an account of the incident, and the names of any witnesses. If you can, write all this down at the scene, borrowing paper and pencil from a bystander or storekeeper. And if you can't find conventional writing materials, *chalk* the pertinent data on the sidewalk with a rock.

Be sure to report the incident to police. They usually refuse to take action unless they have seen the incident, but if you supply them with a license number and description of the people involved, at least the information will be on record. If you or other cyclists are then confronted by the same party, the police can act–the driver is now a repeat offender. Your only other option is to file a complaint with the district attorney. Unless you have witnesses and complete information, however, you stand little chance of making a charge stick.

Harrassment of cyclists is often the work of a very small percentage of the driving population, so chances are the police have run across this particular license number and description before. If all cyclists would report incidents and pursue them to a satisfactory conclusion, the roads would be safer for everyone.

If you have the misfortune to be knocked off your bicycle by a car, don't scream obscenities or insults at the offending driver. Lie still until you are *sure* that your injuries are only superficial. Only then, get the name, license number, and insurance company of the driver as well as a description of the car. Also get names and addresses of witnesses, asking one of them to write everything down if you can't. One caution: Even with minor injuries, you're going to be shaken and angry. Make it a point to control your emotions at least until you get the information you need.

Above all, don't let the driver talk you into replacing your bicycle or a similar deal in exchange for not reporting the accident. Call for the police so they can write up an accident report. Ask for medical help if you are injured, no matter how minor, and get all injuries and their treatment documented. If the driver leaves, it then becomes a case of "leaving the scene of an accident." And if the driver stays, you have all the information and legal framework you need to pursue the case in court.

Commuting by Bicycle

Commuting is one of the most satisfying uses of a bicycle. On lightly traveled roads, you avoid the traffic jams and irate motorists of rush hour and get a dose of fresh air instead of freeway fumes. Commuting rides can also double as training, keeping you fit with very little extra time expenditure.

It's fast, too–in a number of studies, door-to-door travel by bicycle has been shown to be at least as fast as auto travel for trips of 5 miles or less in urban areas. In a car, you have to fight traffic and search for a parking place. But on a bicycle, you can choose less-traveled side streets and ride directly to a bicycle rack–or even wheel your mount right into a building.

Bicycle commuting is considerably less expensive than making the same trip by car, too. For the price of a bicycle and accessories–that you probably already own–you save the price of gas, oil, parking, and wear and tear on your car. Figured on the basis of a 20-mile round-trip 200 days per year, savings can easily exceed $2,000. And the exercise is free!

Equipment for Commuting

You'll need some accessories to make your commute safer and more enjoyable. Start with a protective helmet containing a sticker asserting that it is certified by either ANSI or the Snell Foundation. A good helmet should be worn anytime you are on the bicycle, but it is *the* basic piece of safety equipment for commuting.

You'll want to wear your regular cycling garb for commutes of more than a mile or two, simply because the time needed to change at work is more than compensated for by greater comfort and efficiency.

Wear the same cycling shoes, shorts, and jersey you normally do on recreational rides. In winter, add shoe covers, long tights, gloves, a windbreaker, and perhaps a helmet cover. And if it is raining, a suit made of Gore-Tex or similar material will help keep you dry while still letting perspiration escape. Even if it isn't raining when you leave, it's a good idea to stick a jacket in your pack or handlebar bag in case it clouds up during the day. It doesn't matter too much if you get wet in a warm rain on the return trip because you can jump in the shower and relax at home. But even short rides in cold rain or sleet can mean real trouble from hypothermia, so it is always best to be on the safe side.

It is possible to commute occasionally on the same bicycle that you use for recreational and fitness riding. But if you plan on pedaling to and from work day after day in all weather, you'll want a bicycle that is specially modified to make your trip more enjoyable. A commuting bicycle doesn't have to be lightweight, expensive, or fancy–only reliable. In fact, more expensive bicycles are often a liability in suburban and city commuting, because their light tires and rims don't hold up to the daily pounding. And while the aerodynamic position with dropped bars of a racing bicycle is great for slicing through the wind on a training ride or the winning break in a race, you can't see traffic patterns and potential problems nearly as easily. Your best bet: a medium-priced bicycle with relaxed touring geometry, plenty of fender clearance, and gravel-crushing tires.

Some commuters like to shop around for well-thrashed used bicycles for their daily encounters with mean streets. If the bicycle already has peeling paint and frayed handlebar tape, they don't feel bad about riding it through the snow and slop. And a bicycle that is obviously destined for the junk heap is unlikely to get stolen.

But if you go this route, be sure you know enough about bicycle mechanics to pick a safe klunker. Many used models have been badly cared for and have unsafe tires, wheels out of true, brakes that need adjustment, and derailleurs that won't shift properly. A used bicycle picked up for a song at a yard sale can look a bit tattered and still work well, but it sometimes takes an expert's eye to find it.

Some riders go so far as to artificially age a new bicycle to make it less attractive to thieves. If keeping your mount is more important to you than cosmetics, take off all the decals–including the ones that reveal the tubing manufacturer, because expensive tubing is a tip-off to a top-line bicycle. Scratch up the existing paint or repaint sloppily from a spray can. File the logos off quality components or substitute cheap derailleurs and brakes–the first places that bicycle thieves in a hurry look to assess the worth of a potential target. Finally, put on a cheap saddle. An expensive model is easily spotted in a whole rack of parked bicycles and invariably signals a bicycle worth stealing.

Another commuting option is a lightweight mountain bike with upright bars and road tires. A number of manufacturers offer these as city bicycles, less rugged versions of true mountain bikes, designed specifically for urban use. They work well for short commutes of 10 miles or less. They go perhaps 2 mph slower than road bikes for the same amount of effort, but for short distances the actual added time is insignificant. And it is more than made up for by the upright rider position, which gives greater stability and better vision in traffic. The tires are virtually impenetrable, also, while their rugged mountain heritage fits them well to handle potholes, rough pavement, construction zones, and other obstacles of the urban wilderness.

Regardless of the type of commuting bicycle you choose, be sure it has sturdy tires, tubes, and rims, so you can bash through the worst roads or glass-strewn intersections without worrying about flats. Fragile tubulars or high pressure clinchers have their place, but it *isn't* on Main Street during the morning rush hour.

Carry a spare tube, patch kit, tire levers, and a pump—even if you ride bombproof tires. Don't forget to tote the pump with you when you leave the bicycle, or it may be missing on your return. If your bicycle has a quick-release seatpost, you'll have to take the saddle and seatpost, too. One tip: Replace the quick-release lever with a binder bolt.

You'll also want a good cable and padlock or one of the ultrasecure U-shaped locks that provide virtually 100 percent protection against theft. These locks are expensive, bulky, and hard to carry, but if you have to park your bicycle in a high-risk area, they are certainly worth the price and the inconvenience. Get a lock even if you can park your bicycle in a secure area in your workplace—you may want to stop on the way home for an errand and leave the bicycle outside a store. And some "secure" areas turn out to be a lot less secure than supposed.

Unless it never rains or snows in your neck of the woods, install fenders, too. Invaluable for keeping road slop off your shoes and clothes, they also help keep the brakes and other working parts of your bicycle clean. If you buy a bicycle without fenders, be sure it has enough clearance between the tires and the brakes to mount them properly if you decide later that fenders are the way to go. Plastic models attach neatly to fork eyelets and don't rattle nearly as much as metal fenders.

You'll also need some way to carry necessities. Try a rack and a small set of panniers if you haul big loads: papers, perhaps, and a change of clothes. The traditional rear rack works fine for light commuting loads and is readily available in a variety of prices and designs. You can even purchase a lockable plastic box that bolts securely to the rack—a sort of trunk for your bicycle. But remember: Racks and panniers that attach to the *front* fork—so-called low-riders—offer greater stability in tight traffic maneuvers.

If you don't like to clutter your bicycle with a rack, another option is a handlebar bag that can be detached quickly and carried with you when you leave the bicycle. Some riders like small backpacks, although they are unstable when you stand up and the weight often presses you down uncomfortably on your saddle. Fanny packs ride more securely but usually have less capacity. Specially designed models that accommodate the cyclist's crouched position are available, but for the ultimate in commuting cool, try a bag modeled after the sacks carried by New York City bicycle messengers.

Any pannier or pack that you choose should be sturdily made of coated waterproof fabric so you don't arrive at work with a bag of waterlogged clothes or papers. If the bag attaches to a rack, it should be easy to remove, but remain securely attached on bumpy pavement and in sprints for stoplights. Make your choice on the basis of capacity, too. You don't want to lug around panniers designed for transcontinental tours if you only need room for lunch and a change of clothes.

If you don't want to carry clothes on your bicycle, you can alternate driving and riding on different days, taking several day's clothes to work on days you drive. For instance, drive on Monday, leaving clothes for the next three days. Ride Tuesday through Thursday, and take the week's outfits home in the car on Friday. This schedule is particularly good if you race or ride hard on the weekends, since you'll probably want to take Mondays and Fridays off the bicycle anyway.

Building Strength and Endurance in the Off-Season

Cycling is an endurance sport: It requires cardiovascular and muscular staying power sufficient to meet the demands of races and tours that last anywhere from a single hour to several days. Cycling is also a power sport: Riders need it to climb fast, accelerate explosively, and sprint at high speeds. And finally, cycling is a strength sport: Riders need strength to withstand the rigors of pulling on the handlebars in sprints and to hold good pedaling form during centuries.

How do you acquire all three: endurance, power and strength? Not overnight. These abilities can't be developed in the few short weeks just before the start of the summer cycling season–they require *months* of preparation. But it can be done. And a good way to start is to work on aerobic fitness: your "wind."

General Aerobic Fitness

It's a mistake to ride hard *all* year around. Your mind, of course, needs a break from cycling, but so does your body–you need alternate activities that develop the muscles cycling doesn't touch. So–when bad weather and shorter daylight hours force you to cut back on your riding, don't begrudge the time off the bicycle. Instead, look at it as an opportunity to mix other activities with a moderate schedule of easy riding (a good idea even if you live in a temperate climate where you can ride 12 months of the year).

Running

Running is an excellent winter activity. It is convenient, possible even on slippery snow-covered roads, and reasonably safe even in darkness if you wear reflective clothing and choose lighted suburban loops or parks. Because it is steady exercise, you can get in a great workout in a limited time. Running is mentally refreshing, too, simply because you do it in places–forest trails and park jogging paths–you didn't see all summer riding.

Before you begin a running program, go shopping for sturdy shoes with good support–you'll only get injured if you run

Seek out earth trails to avoid running injuries.

with inadequate shoes. And if you run in cold rain, snow or slush, good shoes will protect your feet and provide traction on uncertain surfaces.

After a summer on the bicycle, start your running program gradually, to let your joints and tendons get used to the pounding. Cycling builds up your cardiovascular system strongly enough that you could probably run quite a few miles the first time out. But leg muscles used to pedaling instead of running would be unbearably sore the next day.

Begin by walking briskly for 3 or 4 miles. After several walks, alternate short jogs of about a half mile with walking breaks. Gradually increase the running and cut back the walking until you reach 30 minutes of continuous running. Then you are ready to increase speed and vary the terrain. To further minimize the road shock, avoid hard surfaces—run on dirt roads, gravel running trails, or equestrian paths in parks. And if you have to pound the pavement, remember: Asphalt is considerably softer than concrete.

Running on level ground is fine, but hill running works your cycling muscles more specifically and boosts your heart rate quickly, too. Be careful running downhill—gravity intensifies the shock. One option is to run up but *walk* down. If you are blessed with long ascents, you may want to arrange a car shuttle for the return trip.

Skiing

If you live in a snowy climate, don't curse the white stuff that keeps you off the bicycle. Dive right in with cross-country skiing. It is an exercise that conditions most of the important cycling muscles. In addition, the poling motion required exercises the upper body, too—often neglected on the bicycle itself. One tip: The diagonal stride may be an old standby, but the newer technique called skating is even more specific to cycling.

Dry land ski training has as many aerobic advantages as the real thing plus one: It can be done even when nature doesn't cooperate. Ski the roads on roller skis or RollerBlades, which are basically just skis with wheels. Ski-bounding (running up hills while using ski poles) is another good training technique that works your upper body and increases your heart rate.

Though somewhat out of fashion as a cycling conditioner, downhill skiing nonetheless can build iron quadriceps and improve bicycle handling skills. Choose a steep mogulled (for nonskiers, that means one littered with bumps) run and ski it as

Cross-country skiing works legs and arms.

"Skating" on skis builds strong legs.

aggressively as you can. Bomb down, get on the lift, and hit it again. Aggressive skiing stresses the same things–reflexes and body control–needed to stay upright on a bicycle.

Snowshoeing is an excellent winter cycling conditioner, and many parts of the country have regular competition.

Snowshoeing

Another excellent off-season aerobic workout for snowy climates is snowshoeing. The pace is slower than skiing, but moving snow-clogged snowshoes up mountain trails in a foot of new powder is a guaranteed workout for your cycling muscles, especially the hip flexors that pull the pedal through the dead spot at the top of the stroke.

Swimming

If you have access to an indoor pool, swimming is an overall body workout with a significant aerobic advantage–there's no pounding, which makes it ideal for staying in shape if you are injured. A tip: Use pull buoys (floats attached to your legs) to support your legs, swimming only with your upper body for a great arm and shoulder workout.

Aerobics

One of the best ways to get a total body workout in a short time and have fun while you're at it is to take regular aerobics classes at a local health club. The stretching movements help your flexibility, a fitness component often neglected by cyclists. Strength develops without boredom, since much of an aerobics workout consists of calisthenics set to music—a sort of symphonic circuit training. Fit cyclists who complain that the workload just isn't strenuous enough to raise their heart rates to the level of aerobic benefit simply need to try an advanced class.

If you don't have a health club nearby, you can do a beneficial aerobics workout in your own home even if you don't have much room. First, set up your bicycle on a training stand, and turn on some motivational music. Then do a series of calisthenics, following each exercise with a minute of fast pedaling in a moderate gear. For instance:

1. 20 push-ups, indoor trainer.
2. 30 sit-ups, indoor trainer.
3. 20 jumping jacks, indoor trainer.
4. 5 pull-ups, indoor trainer.
5. 30 seconds running in place, indoor trainer.
6. 20 step-ups, indoor trainer.

Repeat this sequence three times, and you won't doubt the benefits of aerobic workouts. For variety, change the exercises: Use light barbells, and do basic movements like curls, presses, and rows. If you have a partner, the workout can be even more effective, the product of both competition and camaraderie. One of you can do push-ups or jumping jacks while the other hammers on the bicycle, and then switch places. And with several trainers, a whole cycling club can put winter evenings to good use.

Team Sports

Finally, don't ignore team sports like basketball, soccer, or lacrosse. You'll get plenty of running, some body control work, and have fun with other people, too.

Often neglected in cycling is the idea of teamwork. If you plan to compete on a cycling team, playing a team sport in the winter with your fellow cyclists will foster the camaraderie and cohesiveness so important to success. And if you're a recreational rider, team sports can make you a more polished athlete—the name of the game in the search for fitness.

Indoor Cycling

Although alternate aerobic workouts are fun and add variety to a dreary winter, ride the bicycle several times each week to retain the cycling-specific fitness you'll want come spring. Cyclists used to take the whole winter off, starting road training in March and riding in April and May races to get in shape for the midsummer events that really counted.

No more. Racers who hope to be competitive have to *start* the season with their endurance and strength at high levels. The same is true for recreational riders. Because we have become more fitness-conscious, average performance levels have risen drastically. Now even early-season Sunday group rides are quite fast, and April races go from the gun at midseason pace. Century rides used to be scheduled in late summer when riders had plenty of miles on their legs, but April 100-milers are now popular in many parts of the country. It is no longer enough to use winter for alternate sports—the serious rider has to stay in cycling shape all year.

Training-Stand Workouts

Fortunately, year-round fitness isn't a hardship for enthusiastic athletes. Riders used to train indoors on rollers, but while these devices improved balance and the ability to spin the pedals rapidly, their inability to provide serious resistance was a drawback. Now, however, the invention of the training stand has made getting in your winter miles easy, with resistance supplied by fans or a magnetic field. Don't give up on rollers, though, if you like them–some manufacturers now offer models with fans that add pedaling resistance rivaling that of wind trainers.

Training stands have important advantages. Averaging about one-fifth the cost of a good road bike, they let you train in the warmth and comfort of your own home. Even in blizzard conditions and sub-zero temperatures, you can get in a hard ride–it just happens to be in your living room. And in winter's early darkness, simply do your after-work training indoors.

Training stands simulate real riding. On the road, your speed is strongly influenced by air resistance. At speeds over 20 mph, much more of your energy is used to overcome air resistance than rolling friction. A wind trainer's cleverly designed fans produce the same type of resistance you'll experience on the road–resistance that increases geometrically compared to speed. The harder you pedal in a given gear, the more resistance you'll encounter. On a wind trainer, turning a big gear at 100 rpms is a tough workout for the most superbly conditioned rider. Magnetic trainers produce similar training effects with less noise.

You can use your road bike on the trainer (or fan-equipped rollers), so you don't have to worry about saddle height or stem length. Your miles of indoor cycling convert directly when the weather improves –no painful adjustment period required.

Indoor training is convenient. Most

Indoor training stands provide either wind resistance with fans, above, or magnetic resistance, below.

training stands require only removal of the front wheel. Then your bicycle is clamped by the bottom bracket, and you are ready to go. The whole operation takes less than a minute. Some models don't even require front wheel removal but attach by the rear axle.

Finally, riding indoors is time-efficient. You are *always* pedaling, so every minute counts. If you have a mechanical problem, you can fix it right away, because your tool kit is an arm length away. You also save on cleanup time: Riding on winter's sloppy roads requires substantial bicycle maintenance, but *your* bicycle stays clean during indoor riding.

Indoor training does have some disadvantages, but they can be overcome if you know a few tricks. The first problem is simple boredom. On the open road, cycling is the least boring sport imaginable. You are continually aware of the wind in your face, the speed, the sounds of cars, birds, and pedestrians. Your mind is working overtime to monitor your speed, keep track of your effort, and calculate how far to lean over in corners. There's never a dull moment.

Inside, on the other hand, most of the sensory richness of the open road is lost. The wind trainer is clamped into a stand so you can't crash. No charging dogs or competitive training partners keep you on your toes. It's just you listening to your own labored breathing and the rhythm of dripping sweat.

The best way to avoid these problems? Create an indoor environment designed for efficient training. Start with proper clothing. Excess heat buildup is a significant problem—you'll sweat much more noticeably training indoors than outdoors (where cooling breezes allow perspiration to evaporate quickly). So dress for comfort in cycling shorts and an old T-shirt. There's no need to wear a good jersey—the sweat will ruin it, and you don't need the jersey's pockets to carry food since you aren't going anywhere. A training stand is one place where you can ride safely without a helmet, but a sweat-band will help keep stinging perspiration out of your eyes.

Set up your trainer in a cool room, well ventilated with fans. If possible, put your trainer in front of a window—fresh air and a view make training more enjoyable. Set up the fan so it blows on you as you ride. Some experienced indoor cyclists use two large floor fans placed directly in front of the trainer. If you can create an artificial head wind of 15 mph, you'll avoid overheating and get a more efficient workout.

If the heat generated by spirited indoor cycling still bothers you, ride outside wearing leg warmers on an apartment balcony, covered deck, or a patio. You won't be moving, so you'll be warm even in frigid temperatures—no windchill.

The major problem associated with heavy sweating isn't physical, it's mechanical—the salt in perspiration can wreak havoc with your bicycle's finish. Protect it from sweat's corrosive effects by covering the top tube and stem with a folded towel or a commercial bicycle protector. Spray frame tubes lightly with WD-40 (silicone spray) for more protection. Grease your stem and the expander bolt frequently so sweat doesn't seep into the steering tube and freeze the parts with corrosion. After each ride, wipe down the bicycle and trainer with a lightly oiled rag. Once a week, put a light coat of wax on the frame, concentrating on vulnerable areas like the top tube and down tube.

Have a water bottle handy as you ride, also, to replace the fluids you lose in perspiration. If you will be training for more than an hour, use your favorite sports drink to keep your energy level high. If you place the bottle on a table next to your trainer so you can reach it easily, you'll avoid getting sticky sports drink all over your bicycle. A folding plastic tray table that can be wiped dry and stowed out of the way between sessions is a good choice.

Other items you'll want on the table: a towel for wiping sweat off your face, spare sweatbands to replace the saturated original, and an extra, dry T-shirt for long training sessions.

Attack the boredom problem in a variety of ways. Start with a cyclecomputer to keep track of how far and how fast you are riding. If the computer has an average speed readout, you can do 5- or 10-minute time trials and compare your progress from week to week. The speed function helps you do a series of repeated intervals at the same level of effort. Check your rpms periodically so you don't lapse into a slow cadence and spend all winter practicing bad habits (like being slow). Monitoring your speed and cadence will keep your mind occupied and alert. Be sure, though, to choose a cyclecomputer with a sensor that mounts on the rear wheel–the front wheel is either removed from your bicycle or is stationary when you ride on a wind trainer.

You'll usually want to listen to music while riding indoors. Use headphones if you have a wind trainer–the fans are noisy enough at a slow pace, but at high speeds, music turned up loud enough to hear while riding will disturb everyone around you. A magnetic trainer or an ergometer, on the other hand, is usually quiet enough to ride sans headphones. Regardless of which route you go, remember to choose fast music with a strong beat, and pedal to the rhythm.

You can also watch television while training indoors at a moderate pace, but most riders can't concentrate both on the tube and on their effort effectively enough to do hard workouts while boosting the Nielsen ratings. The one exception might be watching videotapes of European races–seeing the stars in action can be a powerful motivational force.

Several manufacturers offer computer programs designed especially to beat boredom. The best programs offer visuals of famous race courses, simulate riding in a pack, and graphically portray changing terrain and strategy. You can program in the amount of effort you want to expend, struggle furiously to keep up with the pack, or make an attack. Their one drawback? High cost.

If you have a vivid imagination, however, you don't need computer simulation. After a warm-up, visualize yourself in varying race or touring situations. Jam a hill, attack on the flat, beat the world champion in a time trial. These visualization techniques are effective, they improve your ability to concentrate on the bicycle, and–best of all–they don't cost a cent.

Another way to fight boredom is to keep indoor workouts short, but high in quality. An hour on a wind trainer is about the limit for even the most dedicated cyclists, so the trick is to make training short but intense. Do intervals, time trials, jams–all the speed-building techniques talked about in the chapter on speed. Hard effort makes the time go faster, too.

Alternatives to Wind Trainers

A useful alternative to a wind trainer is a bicycle ergometer. Standard equipment at most health clubs, ergometers provide a wide range of pedaling resistance, from no resistance at all to simulated mountain climbing. Good ergometers cost about four times as much as wind trainers, but are sturdily built for years of use. With anodized or enameled frames, they are virtually sweatproof. You can't attach a cyclecomputer, but most models come equipped with a cadence counter and a gauge that measures resistance in watts. Quality ergometers have one other major advantage: Because they don't rely on whirring fans for resistance, they are much quieter than wind trainers and therefore preferable for use in apartments or college dorms where noise might disturb your neighbors.

One drawback to a bicyle ergometer as a serious training device is the difficulty of achieving the same position as on your road bike. Most ergometers have wide saddles, upright bars, and flimsy pedals without clips or straps. The solution is to buy a model with a racing saddle, dropped bars, and quality pedals. Then you can adjust it the same way that you adjusted your road bike. Another option is to buy a standard ergometer and replace the saddle, handlebars, and pedals.

Weight Training

Weight training can make you a better cyclist. Although many cycling coaches derided weights for years, most of the critics have since changed their tune. The East Germans pioneered progressive resistance training with their cyclists, but American amateur road riders today use weights at the Olympic Training Camp, and track riders routinely spend nearly as much time in the weight room as on the bicycle.

Weight training isn't just for racers. A good weight training program offers many advantages to the recreational cyclist. Cycling, for example, develops leg muscles but leaves most of the upper body untouched. The result is muscle imbalance and the potential for injury. A strong upper body, on the other hand—the kind that weight training builds—stabilizes your position on the bicycle for more efficient pedaling. Strong arms, shoulders, and trunk also act as a foundation for your pedaling motion. And finally, a stable position helps you resist the fatigue of long rides. If you've ever completed a century with aching shoulders and a stiff neck, weight training is for you.

The strength developed in the weight room helps you resist injury if you fall, too. A strong shoulder girdle protects against broken collar bones, the most common serious cycling injury. With the acceptance of hard-shell helmets, head injuries are decreasing, but a weak neck is still vulnerable. A neck-strengthening routine can bolster this crucial area very effectively.

Weight training is an ideal activity in the winter months when you can't ride as frequently, chiefly because you can design a program that increases aerobic power as well as strength. A good "circuit program" of the type outlined later in this chapter will increase your endurance even if you can't get on the bicycle.

Contrary to popular opinion, weight training *won't* add unwanted bulk unless that's what your particular regimen is intended to do. Weight training programs can be designed for about any athletic goal. Some people do experience extreme muscular hypertrophy (enlargement), but this is due in large part to heredity, sex—men consistently experience much more hypertrophy than women—and training programs specifically designed to increase bulk. In addition, it is a long-term process. Cyclists who want to gain strength and endurance without size need only choose the right training regimen and monitor their progress, backing off a bit in the unlikely event that they grow too fast.

Finally, exercises like squats and lunges develop power that converts readily to the bicycle. If you want to climb more efficiently and improve your time trialing ability, the combination of weights and the right exercise helps you improve your power-to-weight ratio—the *key* to cycling performance.

Many different methods of progressive resistance exercise exist, and most of them will help you improve. The key is not what kind of apparatus you use but the fact that you are lifting. Machines like the Nautilus are available at most health clubs, where staff will teach you how to use them. But the remainder of this chapter will suggest some routines for free weights.

Free weights have many advantages: They are relatively inexpensive, so you can purchase a set for your home and save the time necessary to commute to the club as well as the cost of membership. A good set of weights will last several lifetimes. Free weights are also adaptable, enabling you to custom-design exercises for cycling. Finally, exercises using free weights demand balance and technique, both qualities important to cycling and which have more carryover value to riding than strength developed on a machine that does it all for you.

Equipment

You can set up a weight room in your own home or apartment. A small space of about 6 by 8 feet is adequate, and the weights can be stored when not in use. You'll need a:

110-pound barbell set. Look for quality cast-iron plates, a 5- or 6-foot bar with a knurled grip, and collars that are easy to tighten securely. You won't need more weight for your initial training. As you get stronger, you can purchase additional plates. Sophisticated and expensive "Olympic" sets are impractical for most home training, but they are fun to use for advanced lifting at a club.

Sturdy bench. The best is one with a rack to hold the weights, adjustable for flat bench presses or incline presses.

Squat rack. Squats are an integral part of a cycling weight program, and a rack is vital for safe execution of this lift.

Lifting belt. These wide leather belts provide support for your back. They aren't mandatory, but many lifters use them. They aren't recommended unless you are lifting extremely heavy weights.

Preliminaries

Get qualified instruction if you are beginning a lifting program. Start with the illustrations and directions in this book, but remember that nothing replaces personal instruction.

Check at your local gym, university, or health club for weight-training classes. Ask around among cyclists for names of qualified instructors. Experienced lifters can be good bets, but make sure anyone who is helping you is aware of your goals—and knows what they're talking about. You want a program to improve your cycling, not one that makes you into a power lifter. Finally, even though weight training has been criticized as being dangerous, it actually has a very low incidence of injury if you take the time to learn safe form.

Some weight training jargon: A "repetition" or "rep" is one complete movement of an exercise. A "set" is a series of reps. A workout is often recorded in shorthand. Four sets of 10 repetitions each with 100 pounds would be written $4 \times 10/100$.

Weight training is intense work, so give your muscles plenty of time to recover before the next session. Never lift two days in a row—that's for body builders, not bicyclists. For building strength in the off-season, three times per week or every other day is sufficient. In the cycling season, one or two maintenance sessions per week will retain the gains you made in the winter.

Always do a progressive warm-up before lifting. Start with several minutes of stretching exercises and some calisthenics like jumping jacks, side bends, and toe touches. Move the activity level up a notch with running in place or easy spinning on the wind trainer. Then do the first set of each exercise with low weights. For instance, if you usually do three sets of 10 to 20 bench presses with 100 pounds, warm up using 75 pounds, then start your normal three sets. This is a minimal warm-up to avoid injury. For a more comprehensive warm-up, see below.

You'll make more progress if you use relatively low weights coupled with high repetitions. Low weights reduce the possibility of injury from wrestling with training poundages too heavy for your stage of development. Your form tends to be better, too, because you won't be tempted to "cheat" to complete a rep, and good form is usually safer form. And another advantage of low weights is that you don't need a "spotter" to help if you need assistance. It is safer and more fun to work out with a partner—who will "spot" or lift the weight when you can't—but if you must lift alone, low weights and high reps are safer. As a general rule, do 10 to 25 reps per set for your upper body, 15 to 50 for your legs.

Weight training should be progressive. Weight training works because it uses the principle of progressive resistance: Start with a light weight and increase it as your body grows stronger. For example, start bench pressing at three sets of 10 to 15 reps. When you can do 15 reps for the three sets, add weight and cut the reps back to 10. Build up to 15 and add weight once again. In this way, you'll get stronger while minimizing your risk of injury.

Beginning Program

Here's a good program for cyclists who are weight training beginners. Start with one set of each exercise, choosing a weight that lets you perform 10 to 25 reps on upper body exercises, 15 to 50 for your legs and midsection. Don't strain to complete the desired number of repetitions. As you get stronger, increase the number of sets to two and then three, reducing the reps if necessary.

Warm-up. Weight training is intense work. Injury is much more likely if you don't prepare your body in advance. The warm-up activities described above are the recommended minimum. If you have the time, go through a full warm-up sequence that includes stretching, calisthenics, and some tumbling drills to build reflexes that will protect you in a crash. Conclude with 10 minutes on the wind trainer, and then begin your warm-up sets of each exercise. The complete routine should take about 15 or 20 minutes, unless you opt for the alternative: a 45-minute aerobics class before you lift.

The Exercises

Power cleans work the entire body: legs, back, chest and arms.

Begin with the barbell on the floor, hands not quite shoulder-width apart, head up, knees bent, and back straight.

Start the lift by pulling hard with the legs. Your arms should not be bent in the initial stages of the lift but should act like cables attached to the bar.

Starting position for the power clean.

Ending position for the power clean.

When the bar reaches your waist, dip the knees, pull with the arms, pull the bar to your shoulders, rolling your elbows down underneath. Finish with the bar supported across your hands and shoulders.

Power cleans can cause injury if done incorrectly, so be sure to get qualified coaching. Have a knowledgeable observer watch you periodically to spot dangerous form flaws you might be developing unconsciously. And again—use light weights and build up slowly.

Bench presses build the muscles that support your upper body on the handlebars, thus lessening fatigue on long rides. They also develop the front of your shoulder girdle, helping to protect your collarbone in falls.

Lie on your back on the bench with feet flat on the floor. Don't arch your back to complete the lift. Grip the bar with your hands about shoulder-width apart. Lower the bar slowly and steadily to your chest, pause a second without actually resting the bar on your body, then return to starting position. Remember: Don't arch your back off the bench.

Upright rows develop the muscles in shoulders and upper back that pull on the bars in hard climbing or sprints, and

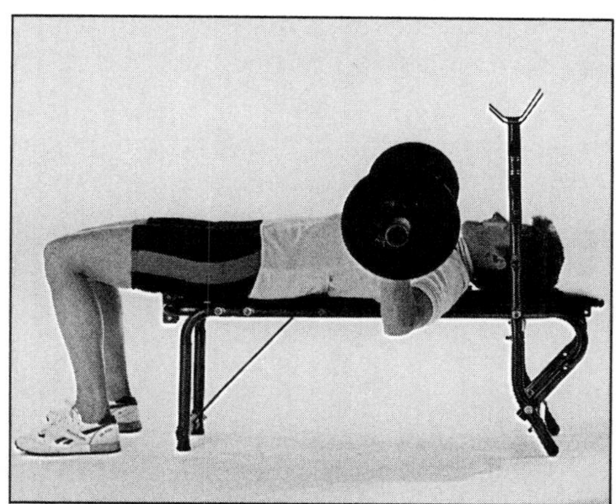

Beginning position for the bench press.

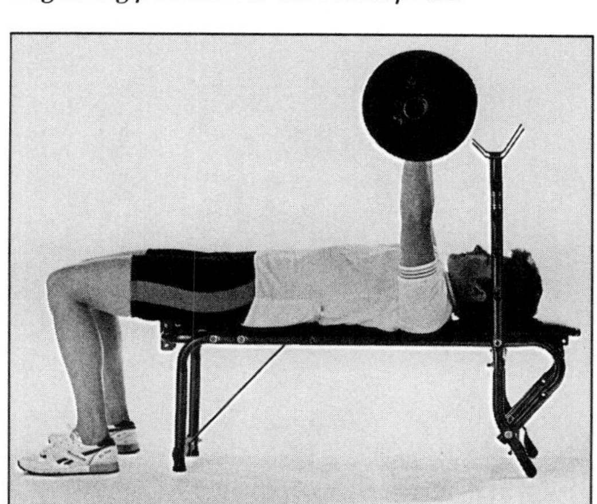

Second position for the bench press. Keep the back flat on the bench.

Beginning position for the upright row.

Finishing the upright row.

strengthen your hand grip for less fatigue holding the brake levers. They build the muscles that help protect your shoulder girdle and neck in falls.

Stand upright with a light barbell hanging from straight arms. Your hands should be 4 to 8 inches apart. Raise the bar slowly and steadily to your chin, pause, then lower smoothly to the starting position. Don't rock your upper body or cheat by rising up on your toes, and keep your elbows up and out.

Starting position for the military press.

Completing the military press. Don't arch the back!

Military presses behind the neck strengthen your triceps, the muscles on the backs of your upper arms that support your weight on the handlebars. It also builds up the deltoids that cover the points of your shoulders.

Start with a barbell resting on your shoulders behind the neck. Press the weight upward slowly until your arms lock. Lower the weight in a controlled fashion, or you'll hit yourself on the head or bruise your neck. Repeat.

Bent rows, like upright rows, develop the pulling muscles, but a different set: those in your back instead of your shoulders. The bent-over position can cause injury, so wear a belt and use light weights.

Start bent over 90 degrees at the waist, feet apart for stability, head up, and arms

Bent rows. Keep the back flat and still.

Pull the bar to your chest, pause, then let it back down.

straight, holding the barbell with hands at least a foot apart. Raise the barbell steadily to your lower abdomen, just above the navel. Keep your head up, your back flat, and your knees slightly bent. Lower to original position.

Crunchers develop the key abdominal region. Cycling doesn't build abdominal strength, but having it is vital for stability on the bicycle.

Lie on your back with your legs bent. Fold your arms over your chest. Raise your shoulders 4 to 5 inches off the floor, and hold for 3 seconds before lowering.

Squats are the single most important exercise for cycling power, simply because they work the big muscle group on the front of your thigh–the quadriceps–that does most of the work. They are also the exercise with the most potential for injury if done incorrectly or with too much weight. Use a belt, spotters, a solid rack, sturdy shoes with good heel and arch support, and *caution*.

Full squats, with the tops of the thighs going just below parallel to the floor, are undoubtedly the most efficient form of the exercise. They are also dangerous, hard to learn to do properly, and require a long apprenticeship period. So cyclists without a lifting background are better advised to squat only far enough to duplicate the amount of bend the knee usually has at the top of the pedal stroke.

Begin with the barbell across the shoulders. Keep your head up, back straight,

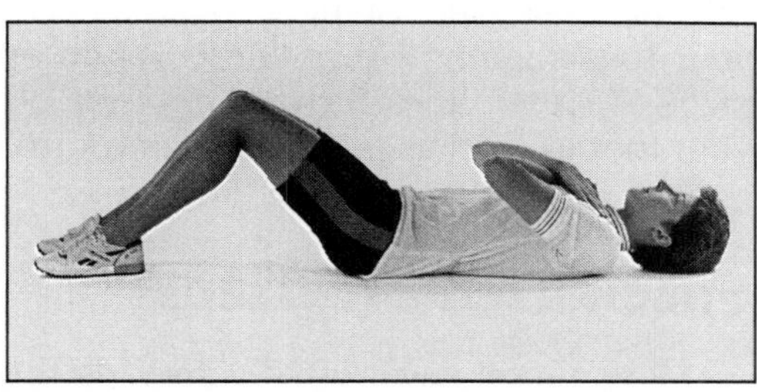

Starting position for abdominal cruncher.

Completing the abdominal cruncher. Hold the position for about 3 seconds.

Starting position for squats.

Low position for squats. Keep the back flat, head up, and tops of the thighs parallel to the floor.

Starting position for curls.

Top position for curls. Keep the upper body motionless.

and feet about shoulder width apart. Squat down until your knee duplicates the bend at the top of the pedal stroke. You may want to squat down to an appropriately sized chair or box until you learn how deep to go, but don't bounce off the chair. Instead, let it touch the backs of your upper thighs lightly as a signal to return to the starting position.

Curls work the biceps that flex the arm when you pull on the bars. For cycling purposes, they get enough stimulation when you do rows and cleans. But because the tricep is worked so hard with bench presses, adding curls to your program keeps the arm in balance.

Stand upright, holding the bar with hands shoulder-width apart, palms outward. Raise the bar to a position just below the chin. Keep your elbows pinned against your sides. Don't cheat by rocking your upper body or rising up on your toes.

Wrestler's bridges are important, because a strong neck is important to your safety if you fall. In addition, it supports your head and helmet in comfort on long rides.

Although health clubs have sophisticated machines specifically designed for neck development, the simplest and least expensive neck exercise is the *wrestler's bridge.* Lie on your back with your arms folded on your chest. Use a mat or choose a thickly carpeted floor to protect your head, or wear an old cycling helmet. Arch your back and support your weight on your head and feet. Roll back until your forehead nearly touches the floor, then back the other way so your shoulders just brush the floor. After 10 to 30 reps, roll over on your stomach and repeat.

Calf raises work the muscles on the backs of your calves that are important in sprinting and climbing. Because they're used so much in daily life, they are among the hardest muscles in the body to develop. For that reason, use higher numbers of repetitions in this exercise.

Position the barbell over your shoulders as if you were doing a squat. Elevate your toes slightly with a barbell plate or piece of wood. Rock forward and rise on your toes as high as possible, then return.

Specialized Programs

If you have never lifted before, do the general program just outlined for about six weeks in November and early December. You should experience good gains in strength. Even if you are a weight-training veteran but didn't lift during the cycling season, start with this general program to reaccustom the muscles to exercise. Once you have established a foundation of strength, you can move on to other forms of weight training, depending on your goals and preferences. In any event, changing your program every six weeks or two months is advisable to avoid boredom and stalled progress. Additional weight training programs useful for cyclists include:

Circuit Training

Circuit training consists of a series of exercises done for 15 or 20 seconds each with the same amount of rest between. A circuit commonly contains 8 to 12 exercises that work different muscle groups, alternating between upper and lower body movements.

Circuit training is one of the most advantageous weight programs. Because weights are low and speed of movement is emphasized, circuit training provides some aerobic benefit in addition to strength. As a result, it is an excellent program to use in the winter when you can't ride as frequently.

The chance of injury is low, also due to the light weights used. Several cyclists can work out together by alternating exercises. There's little chance of boredom, too, simply because different combinations of exercises can be used every workout. Circuit training is widely used by Eastern European cyclists and American riders at the Olympic Training Camp.

A sample circuit workout requires only a barbell, a bench, and a wind trainer. Do as many reps of each exercise as possible in 20 seconds while still retaining good form. During the 20 seconds between exercises, change the weight on the barbell for the next movement. Use light weights. The object isn't to lift impressive poundages but rather to exercise all the muscles rapidly. Be sure to warm up properly before you begin.

1. 1 minute on the wind trainer at a brisk pace. If you don't have a wind trainer, substitute running in place.
2. Press behind the neck.
3. Squat.
4. Crunchers.
5. Bent rows.
6. 1 minute on the wind trainer.
7. Bench press.
8. Calf raises.
9. Crunchers.
10. Upright rows.

In the calf raise starting position, elevate your toes with a board for maximum stretch.

Ending position for a calf raise.

Go through each exercise once the first time you try the circuit. Then add a second set with 2 or 3 minutes rest between. Add a third set when you can handle the added work. You may have to reduce weight as you add sets, but that won't compromise the quality of the workout. The additional repetitions will more than compensate for lowered resistance.

Vary your circuit routine in a number of ways:

Use different exercises for each section of the body. For instance, substitute push-ups for bench presses or step-ups for squats.

Alternate each exercise with a minute on the wind trainer. It will elevate your heart rate more than the exercises alone and have the additional advantage of being specific to cycling.

Alternate each exercise with running in place. Or try a 100-yard jog down the sidewalk, or some other aerobic activity like a rowing ergometer. Use your imagination: If you have a gym handy, run around the perimeter, jumping up to touch the net on each basket.

In-Season Maintenance

A good off-season weight program will do wonders for your strength, power, and enjoyment on the bicycle. But if you abruptly stop lifting in March when you increase your cycling mileage, all the strength you developed over the winter will be gone by midsummer. You can't, however, both lift and ride intensely all spring. The solution? A maintenance program that will let you keep your hard-won strength with a minimum investment of time and energy. The following tips will help you make it happen:

Use light weights and high repetitions. This combination builds endurance instead of big muscles.

Don't go to exhaustion. The muscles should feel tired during the last few reps but not exhausted.

Spare your legs. Most riders find that their legs get plenty of work on the bicycle without including legwork in their maintenance program. But if time constraints limit your riding time, include squats to make up for the decreased road time.

Simple exercises that work a large number of muscles are best. A good routine includes pull-ups, push-ups, light cleans, crunchers, and wrestler's bridges. You can also do an abbreviated version of the general weight-training program outlined above, including exercises for the main upper body muscles. And don't neglect your abdomen and neck in the cycling season! These muscles get little work on the bicycle but must be kept strong for your safety and cycling efficiency.

Power Program

If you are a serious competitor in short-distance events like sprinting, you'll want to increase your commitment to weight training. Criterium racers and road riders whose usual events are less than 50 or 60 miles can benefit, too, because these races require power and speed rather than great endurance–and in actual practice, this description applies to nearly all U.S. racers with the exception of talented Category One and Two riders. The following program is designed to increase your speed and power for sprinting, time trialing, short hills, and hard chases in modern American racing.

Several cautions first: These workouts are intense, so they should be used only by highly motivated competitors. Recreational riders can build sufficient power with the normal winter weight training and indoor cycling described above.

Use them only after you have a good fitness base on the bicycle as well as in the weight room. Heavy squats will make your legs extremely sore if you aren't accustomed to them and can injure your knee tendons. By the same token, don't try heavy squats without a spotter to take the weight if you can't complete a repetition.

Use this program in the off-season and early season to build a power base. Switch to the maintenance program outlined above about a month before your important events.

Squats

The squats you did in circuit training or general weight training were light, and you concentrated on high repetitions. Now you'll use heavier weights, multiple sets, and varying numbers of repetitions. The idea is to do a progressive workout of perhaps six sets, starting with light weight and high reps for a warm-up, then decreasing the reps each set as the weight increases. The last set returns to light weights and high reps to build endurance. Remember that the weights listed are only examples. Use what you can handle for the required number of reps.

1. Standard warm-up: stretching, calisthenics, light aerobic exercises.
2. 1 × 30/95 (1 set of 30 reps at 95 pounds) to warm-up.
3. 1 × 25/135.
4. 1 × 20/165.
5. 1 × 15/185.
6. 1 × 12/205.
7. 1 × 50/95 (endurance set).

Wind Trainer or Ergometer

Indoor cycling is good aerobic exercise as previously mentioned, but if you have access to an ergometer, the greater resistance can be used for power development. Wind trainers work, too, but you'll need larger gears. If you are too strong for a standard wind trainer even in monster gears, buy a model that comes with two fans to increase resistance.

Here are two sample power-building workouts on an ergometer or wind trainer:

Workout One

1. Warm up with 15 minutes of spinning at low resistance.
2. Select a resistance that enables you to pedal 3 minutes at 90 rpm. At the end, your heart rate should be about 85 percent of maximum.
3. Pedal easily for 3 minutes.
4. Repeat number 2. This time, your heart rate will be slightly higher at the end of the 3 minutes, and your cadence may drop, but don't let it go below 85 rpm. If it does, your resistance is too high.
5. Repeat number 3.
6. Repeat number 2. Your heart rate should be about 90 percent of maximum during the last minute.
7. Cool down with 15 or 20 minutes of easy spinning.

Variations: Do three times 3 minutes as above, but increase the resistance each time. For instance, you might do the first set of 3 minutes in a 52/19, the second in 52/18, and finish in 52/17. You'll have to experiment to find what gears produce a heart rate of between 85 and 90 percent of maximum during the last minute of the last set. Do a ladder: 1 minute the first set, 2 minutes the second, and 3 minutes on the third. Then come back down.

Workout Two

1. Warm up with 15 minutes of easy spinning.
2. Ride steadily for 5 minutes at a cadence of 90 finishing with a heart rate of about 85 percent of maximum.
3. Spin easily for 3 minutes.
4. Hit it hard five times 1 minute on and 1 minute off. Select a resistance that you can turn between 80 and 90 rpm for a minute. Your heart rate should be about 90 percent of maximum at the end of each minute. Pedal easily for 2 minutes between each hard effort.
5. Spin easily for 5 minutes.
6. Hit it hard five times 30 seconds on, 2 minutes off. Select a high resistance that you can turn between 70 and 80 rpm for 30 seconds. Your heart rate should approach your maximum at the end of

the 30 seconds. Spin easily for 2 minutes between each hard effort.

7. Cool down with 15 minutes of easy spinning.

Combination Workouts

You can combine squats and ergometer riding for an extremely hard workout that builds great power. For example:

1. Warm up with light stretching and calisthenics.
2. Continue the warm-up with 15 minutes of easy spinning on the ergometer.
3. Complete the warm-up with squats: 1 × 25/light weight.
4. The core of the workout consists of squats alternated with a minute hard on the ergometer. For instance: Squats: 1 × 25/100. Ergometer: 1 minute at 90 rpm, heart rate 90 percent of maximum. Rest for 2 minutes between each set by spinning easily on the ergometer.
5. Cool down.

This workout stresses the quadriceps intensely and has the advantage of being specific to cycling. You work the quads hard with the squats then again with the pedaling motion.

Remember: Any of these workouts can be varied infinitely by simply changing the weight, number of sets, or the ergometer workout.

Early Season Training on the Bicycle

For racers, indoor power development in the weight room and on the ergometer is not enough. A really solid aerobic base requires miles of road riding also. The same is true for recreational riders who want to ride centuries or fast club rides. Like competitive riders, they need actual road miles as soon as the weather permits outdoor cycling.

These early miles should be done both on the flat, for basic aerobic fitness, and in the hills, to continue your power development. If you race on the weekend or do weekend club rides, schedule your long ride for Tuesday or Wednesday. When the weather improves and you can get on the road regularly, increase the length of your endurance ride each week. But remember to keep it gradual, both to avoid overuse injuries and the staleness that comes from doing too much too soon. A rule of thumb: Limit weekly mileage increases to 10 percent or less of current mileage.

You should aim for a weekly endurance ride about the length of your longest race, club ride, or hard solo effort—say 50 or 60 miles or about 3 hours of cycling. Combined with the rest of your weekly schedule, this is adequate endurance training. But if you want to ride centuries, take one longer ride about 5 hours long every 10 days or two weeks during the two months before the event.

Increasing Early Season Mileage

Here's a sample 10-week program of increasing mileage for a recreational rider aiming at 3-hour club rides. Monday and Friday are not listed, because they are always rest days.

Week 1: Tuesday–10 easy. Wednesday–20 steady. Thursday–10 fast. Saturday–10 easy. Sunday–25 steady. Total–75

Week 2: Tuesday–10 easy. Wednesday–20 steady. Thursday–10 fast. Saturday–10 easy. Sunday–30 steady. Total–80

Week 3: Tuesday–10 easy. Wednesday–20 steady. Thursday–15 fast. Saturday–10 easy. Sunday–35 steady. Total–90

Week 4: Tuesday–10 easy. Wednesday–20 steady. Thursday–15 fast. Saturday–10 easy. Sunday–40 steady. Total–95

Week 5: Tuesday–10 easy. Wednesday–25 steady. Thursday–15 fast. Saturday–10 easy. Sunday–45 steady. Total–105

Week 6: Tuesday–10 easy. Wednesday–25 steady. Thursday–15 fast. Saturday–10 easy. Sunday–50 steady. Total–110

Week 7: Tuesday–10 easy. Wednesday–30 steady. Thursday–20 fast. Saturday–10 easy. Sunday–50 group ride. Total–120

Week 8: Tuesday–10 easy. Wednesday–30 steady. Thursday–20 fast. Saturday–10 easy. Sunday–55 group ride. Total–125

Week 9: Tuesday–10 easy. Wednesday–30 steady. Thursday–25 fast. Saturday–10 easy. Sunday–60 group ride. Total–135

Week 10: Tuesday–10 easy. Wednesday–30 steady. Thursday–25 fast. Saturday–10 easy. Sunday–65 group. Total–140.

During all steady conditioning rides, keep a smooth, fast cadence in moderate gears and concentrate on supple pedaling. Work on your riding position: flat back, elbows slightly bent, head up and tipped slightly to one side, and arms and hands relaxed.

Your heart rate during these rides should be about 10 percent below your anaerobic threshold. This is a level of exertion that is not painful but makes you feel like you are working hard, pedaling briskly. You should end the ride feeling tired from the miles, not the speed. And while group rides are fine, they should be done steadily–riders who turn training into racing may have fun, but that's not good training.

In the early season, don't neglect the hilly courses so useful in power development. Just ride them at a steady pace. Shift down and spin uphill seated, or stand and climb rhythmically. Avoid oxygen debt on days when your purpose is building endurance.

And finally, while long climbs are fine in the early season, in the raw weather of early spring, you'll get sweaty going up and cold on the long descent, so rolling terrain with a series of short climbs is preferable.

WOLBER

Developing Speed

In the last chapter, we talked about building a good foundation for a successful cycling season. November through February should be devoted to developing aerobic fitness and overall strength. When that foundation is firmly established, your attention should turn to speed and power.

The Benefits of Fast Training

Speed is where it's at. Whether your cycling interest is racing, touring, or fitness, it pays to devote some time to improving your ability at getting down the road in a hurry. Here, speed means the ability to go fast over longer distances: from 100 yards up to 2 or 3 miles.

Why is this sort of speed important? For fitness riders, the ability to go faster means you're in better shape. Fitness is nothing more than ability to do work, so if you can ride a 10-mile time trial in 30 minutes in March but improve to 27 minutes by July, your fitness has improved along with your performance levels. Your heart and lungs have become more efficient, and your leg muscles can deliver more power to the pedals. Your engine works better.

Long rides are more enjoyable if you have developed speed. On tours, the power and fast-twitch muscle fibers that speedwork builds come in handy on rolling hills for making the most of a tail wind or outracing a thunderstorm. With power, you can haul a loaded touring bicycle up the meanest hill with aplomb. Increased speed also means that you'll be more efficient over the long haul. Improve your pedal stroke, and you improve your speed. The intervals and other techniques we'll discuss in this chapter hone your sheer physical ability to ride, but they also make you a more efficient user of that power.

Speed isn't wasted, even if you ride primarily in the city or commute. In this context, speed means security—you can change lanes and dart safely and authoritatively into gaps in traffic.

For recreational riding, speed means enjoyment and competence. Spirited training rides always seem to feature sprints for city limit signs, with the winner owning bragging rights until the next suburb. A quick burst will put you out of reach of a dog defending its territorial imperative. In a fast-moving paceline, speed enables you to take your pulls, rocket back to the group after a pit stop, or just hang on when the ride starts to sizzle.

For racers, of course, speed is the essence of success. The most basic element separating top riders from pack fodder is the sheer ability to make that bicycle go fast. This talent to kick in the turbo when it counts is more important than tactical savvy, reading a race, or hanging on to a wheel like grim death. You can have all these technical skills and still be off the back in a hurry if you don't have the horsepower on steep climbs, flat windy sections, and those long uphill grades that grind off weaker riders no matter how doggedly they stare at the wheel in front. If you can't bridge gaps, counter attacks, or launch aggressive moves yourself, you'll always be a defensive rider, stuck in the pack, unable to control the action or react to it.

Finally, fast is fun. The term speedwork has painful connotations among many cyclists, because they associate building speed with timed interval training, painful lactic acid accumulation, or seemingly endless sprints up the same hill. It doesn't have to be that way. As we'll see in this chapter, developing your afterburners is simpler, and considerably more fun, than you'd expect. Quality bicycles and fit bodies beg to fly. Don't condemn yours to a pedestrian's pace.

Structured Intervals

Speed development boils down to one thing: You have to go fast in training if you want to go fast in a race. The principle of physiological specificity states that your body will do most efficiently only what it is trained to do. If you want to jump high, you have to practice jumping high, not jumping long. If you want to shoot 80 percent from the free throw line, you'll have to shoot 100 free throws a day. And if you want to go fast on the bicycle, your training has to include some fast riding. Only in this way will your cardiovascular system, as well as your leg muscles, receive the stress that adapts them to the demands of fast cycling. If you always ride slowly in training, you can't expect your body to go fast on command. There aren't any miracles.

The best method of developing speed has traditionally been interval training, a technique originated by runners and later adopted by cyclists. Although interval training can become extremely complex, the basic idea is simple: Go hard for 1 to 5 minutes so your heart rate reaches about 90 percent of maximum, then take it easy. Spin easily for several minutes or until your heart rate returns to perhaps 60 percent of maximum. Then repeat the cycle as many times as possible.

Interval Training Tips

Before you begin any sort of speed training—especially structured intervals—consider a few suggestions. Several important variables can be manipulated to increase the stress and therefore the effectiveness of interval training. You can increase the speed of the hard effort as your cardiovascular system adapts. When you begin, your heart rate might reach 90 percent at a speed of only 20 mph for a minute. But in short order, it takes 21 or 22 mph, as well as larger gears, to produce the same heart rate. This means that your body is becoming a more efficient energy pump. To keep progressing, pedal faster.

You can also increase the length of each hard effort as you improve. Starting out with 30 seconds at 20 mph may drive your heart rate to 90 percent of max. Within a few weeks, you can handle 1 or even 2 minutes at the same speed and heart rate.

The recommendation for continued progress, again, is to ride longer.

The final variable is to decrease the rest period between efforts. Exercise physiologists maintain that the rest period helps you improve by giving your body a chance to adapt to the stress. The hard effort is important only because it provides that stress, acting as a kind of catalyst that begins the adaptive process. Decreasing the amount of rest is an excellent way to artificially increase the stress your body experiences—the exhausted muscle has to struggle to meet the demands of the next interval, and the more struggle, the more adaptation.

Any kind of speedwork is more efficient if you monitor your heart rate. As we have seen, the effectiveness of interval training depends on the effort expended and the length of the rest period, both of which can be tracked precisely with a heart rate monitor.

If you don't own a monitor, you can check heart rate manually. After an interval, feel your pulse in the carotid artery of your neck next to your windpipe. Ride with one hand on the bars, and check your pulse with the other. The pulse is sometimes difficult to find when you are at rest but will be evident when your heart is beating rapidly. You'll need bare fingers to feel the heartbeat, so in the winter, when you are wearing long-fingered gloves, slip one off before you check your pulse. Glance down at your watch, count the beats for 6 seconds, then simply add a zero to get beats per minute. This method is an approximation but is close enough for most hard training. For a more accurate reading, count beats for 15 seconds and multiply by four.

Generally speaking, your heart rate should rise to between 80 and 90 percent of maximum during the final third of the work interval. For example, if you are going for 1 minute, your heart should reach its target rate during the last 15 or 20 seconds. During the rest interval, heart rate should drop to about 60 percent of maximum or around 120 beats per minute.

Search out a suitable road for interval training. Ideally, it will be a good warm-up ride, 5 to 8 miles, away from your home. You'll be going at maximum effort, so the less traffic the better. For the same reason, find a stretch of road without stoplights or intersections. A 1-mile-long course is sufficient, but 2 or 3 miles is even better. Don't worry about rolling hills on the course. Just adjust your gearing so you maintain the desired heart rate both up and down the inclines. However, long steep hills should be avoided unless you are training specifically for mountainous races with hill intervals.

Because interval training is so stressful, don't do it too often. When you begin, once per week is plenty for any kind of formal speedwork. Later, as you adapt and grow stronger, you may want to add another weekly session. Remember that hard group rides, races, or any fast ride in the hills has the same effect on your recovery as a hard interval session. Be sure to count them when you total up your weekly effort. Generally speaking, there's no reason to schedule more than two hard workouts of any type each week. If you do more, you are courting overtraining, chronic fatigue, decreased performance, and lessened enjoyment.

For the same reason, don't do intervals for more than a month at a time. Prolonged hard training means that you'll burn out—increasing lack of enthusiasm is a warning that each workout has become less effective at the same time that it has become more and more like drudgery. For best results, do intervals once or twice a week for a month, then take a week of easy spinning on scheduled interval days. When you begin speedwork again, it will be at a higher level of intensity and enthusiasm.

Never do speedwork without a substantial mileage base. Most cyclists know that rushing into interval training early in the season can lead to knee problems, but there's a more important reason. You need a sound aerobic foundation to build your speedwork upon. Without that base, you'll reach your peak performance sooner, but performance levels won't be as high as if you had exercised more patience. The adage that "haste makes waste" is nowhere more true than in cycling–you'll get wasted if you try to do too much too soon!

As you can see, traditional interval training has some serious disadvantages. It is hard work, requiring great motivation and intense concentration to do it well. As a result, many cyclists hate intervals and won't subject themselves to the regimen unless they are forced by a coach or by peer pressure.

Hard intervals over several months can also lead to psychological problems: burnout and loss of interest in training. Don't even consider serious interval training unless you have a burning desire to improve and are willing to pay the price in sweat, discomfort, and fatigue. If your cycling aspirations are more modest, you are better off with the recreational intervals, jams, and group training discussed later in the chapter.

Ladder Intervals

Still want to try some hard-core intervals? The following workouts will get you started. To keep fresh, manipulate the length or intensity of the work interval, as well as the length of the rest period.

Workout One

1. Warm up with 15 or 20 minutes of spinning. Increase the pace and the gearing during the last 5 minutes.
2. Shift to a fairly large gear that you can turn at between 90 and 100 rpm for the duration of each work period. As an example, use a 52/17. Get out of the saddle and sprint hard for several seconds to get the gear moving. Then go hard and steadily for 1 minute and 30 seconds. During the last 20 or 30 seconds, your heart rate should be about 90 percent of maximum.
3. At the end of the work period, shift to the small chainring (42/17 in our example), and spin easily until your heart rate returns to about 60 percent. You can also calculate the rest period by time. Usually about 2 minutes will lower your heart rate to 120, but because the actual time will vary with your fitness, a heart rate monitor is more efficient.
4. After your heart rate comes down to 60 percent, shift to the 52/17 again and repeat step two. However, go only for 1 minute and 15 seconds. The shorter work period will allow you to maintain full effort in spite of the fatigue built up from the first work phase.
5. Repeat step three.
6. Continue to alternate fast riding and easy spinning, but decrease the work interval by 15 seconds each time, until you reach 30 seconds, like this: (1) 1:30 (2) 1:15 (3) 1:00 (4) :45 (5) :30.
7. Warm down with 15 or 20 minutes of easy spinning on the way home.

Workout Two

1. Warm up as above with 15 to 20 minutes of easy spinning.
2. Go for 1 minute in a big gear–say 52/16 –that allows you to maintain an rpm of about 90. During the last 15 seconds of the effort, your heart rate should reach about 90 percent.
3. Spin easily in 42/16 until your heart rate falls to about 60 percent.

4. Go hard for 1 more minute, but this time use a lower gear–say a 42/15–that allows you to maintain a higher cadence of about 120 rpm.
5. Continue to alternate large and small gears for about five repeats of the cycle.
6. Warm down with easy spinning.

Recreational Intervals

Frankly, most riders, even serious racers, hate the type of structured interval program described above. Hard-core intervals are effective but extremely difficult. Fortunately, speed training doesn't have to mean pain and agony for everyone. If you're not a serious competitor, there's an easier way to get most of the benefits of intervals without the drawbacks. Instead of rigid and structured intervals, use recreational interval training to get faster–effective speedwork without the pain.

Nonstructured Intervals

The simplest form of recreational interval training involves the fast-slow pattern of hard-core intervals without the strict time and heart rate monitoring. After a warm-up, simply jam hard for 1 minute or so whenever the spirit moves you. For instance, after a good warm-up, jump hard out of the saddle as if you were doing a sprint. When you get the gear rolling, sit down, pedal it up to about 120 rpm, and stay with it for a minute. After the effort, continue with your ride, rolling at a moderate and comfortable pace. When you are thoroughly recovered and mentally ready to go again, repeat the jump.

Don't treat this sort of training as you would structured intervals with an incomplete recovery between efforts. That can ruin your enthusiasm for cycling in a hurry. Instead, scatter three or four such efforts through your training ride with no regard for rapid repetition to maximize the training effect.

Take advantage of different terrain to add variety. For instance, do the first interval on the flat with a tail wind. Do the second jam after your normal training route has turned back into the wind, using a lower gear to compensate for the head wind. Wait until you come to a small hill for the third effort, and work hard going up. The idea behind these unstructured jams is to keep them fun and spontaneous.

When training by yourself, look for possibilities: You've rolled down a little hill and started to lose momentum. Jump hard and keep it going on the flat. Or you hear a car coming up from behind, so you jump hard and race the car for several hundred yards. A dog charges menacingly out from a farmhouse. Sprint away from the snarling canine. Unstructured intervals turn the acquisition of speed into a game.

But do they work as well? It would seem that if they are easier than structured intervals, they should be less effective. There's no free lunch, right? Actually, nonstructured intervals accomplish almost everything their more rigid counterparts do except for two things. First, it is harder to accurately gauge your improvement over time, because you aren't doing a set workload each session. Secondly, your recovery from the work phase won't improve as much, because the rest interval between hard efforts is at best inconsistent, at worst considerably longer.

Hills

Speed and power can also be developed on the hills. If you are fortunate enough to have varied terrain, do your climbing on long hills one day each week. On your other weekly hard workout, hit shorter, more

Jamming up a short hill out of the saddle.

intense hills. If you train hard only one day each week because of weekend races or fast group rides, alternate every other week between long and short hills.

The best training technique on long hills of 2 miles or more mimics racing: steady and hard. You must learn to apportion your energy so you go up fast but don't blow up before the top. Keep a little in reserve, because strong climbers will attack at intervals during the ascent or just below the crest when everyone else is easing from the effort.

In training, climb at a pace just below your anaerobic threshold. Here's a simple trick that will tell you when you're working hard, but not too hard: On a steady grade, gauge your level of exertion so that if you increase your cadence about 5 rpm, you'll be forced to slow down in less than 1 minute. For example, if your cadence counter registers 80 rpm and you are working hard, increase cadence to 85. If you can maintain the effort, try 87. Keep pushing until you get into oxygen debt and slow down. Then back off about 5 rpm and hold it to the top. You'll soon develop an accurate feel for what, if anything, you have left at any point in the climb.

Learn how to alternate sitting and standing on long climbs while keeping your heart rate steady. Many riders are most efficient if they sit for two-thirds of the climb and stand for the remainder, alternating sitting and standing every 200 or 300 yards. Cadence drops off when you stand up, so to maintain forward speed, you must shift to a cog about two teeth smaller–from a 21 while sitting to a 19 while standing, for example.

For variety on long climbs, do a series of harder accelerations. Go as hard as you can for 200 yards in a fairly big gear, say

42/18, keeping the cadance above 80. Then shift to your lowest gear. Pedal as easily as the hill's steepness allows until you have recovered. Then do it again. These repeated bursts will do wonders for your power and are great practice for the surges that good climbers keep dishing out on long ascents. After 4 to 6 weeks on a program of long climbs, you'll be happy to discover that your power and speed on the flats has improved along with your climbing ability. But a steady diet of extended climbing can rob you of acceleration, so don't neglect short hills that build snap and anaerobic power. Road races in most parts of the United States are on rolling terrain, not mountainous grades. Even on the Coors Classic's fabled Morgul-Bismarck course, the longest hill is only half a mile. And most riders live in an area of short, rolling hills rather than 10-mile mountain grades.

While long hills should be ridden aerobically, keeping something in reserve, throw caution to the wind and attack on short rises. Hit the bottom spinning hard in a moderate gear, and halfway up go one tooth smaller (from 42/17 to 42/16 for instance), get out of the saddle, and explode over the top. The last 100 yards or so should be anaerobic but not so hard that your form deteriorates.

If you are in a group, there will probably be a miniature race each time one of these short climbs looms—it is cycling tradition to jam hills. These impromptu competitions will give you a feel for how hard you can go, what gears to use, and how you compare to other local riders. And as a bonus, your power will improve without the drudgery of solo intervals.

Head Winds

If there are no hills in your area, you can still build power. But you'll have to use head winds instead of hills to provide resistance. Fortunately there is no lack of wind in most sections of the country, especially in the spring when power training is most important.

Repeats can be done into the wind to build power.

To use head winds, warm up well first, riding both with and against the wind so your muscles and mind get accustomed to the effort. Warming up into the wind also gives you a feel for the gear you'll need for the ride itself.

When you are ready to go, find a flat, unprotected stretch of road that goes directly into the teeth of the gale. Choose a gear that enables you to keep your cadence between 80 and 90 rpm with a heart rate that tops out around 90 percent of maximum at the end of the effort. Do repeat grinds into the wind of from 1 minute to as long as 5 minutes in duration. Recover between efforts by rolling easily downwind.

In many flat, windy parts of the country, you'll find roads laid out in 4-mile squares, and they work great for head wind training. Go hard on the head wind mile, easy the next leg with a quartering tail wind, hard and fast with the tail wind for leg speed, and easy on the fourth side of the square going back into the quartering head wind. Repeat as often as desired.

If you have easy grades instead of real hills, use the head wind to make them steeper. Or ride a mountain bike with fat tires for more rolling resistance. With careful choice of wind conditions, terrain, and gearing, nearly any geographic location can be coupled with weather patterns to provide power training.

Group Training

Although solo training is time-efficient and practical, the best way to acquire speed and power is on spirited training rides in a small, closely matched group. Riding with others simply seems to inspire most of us to greater effort.

Choose a group to train with based on mutual goals. If your interest is in low-key fitness riding, you'll be unhappy training with a group of racers who will undoubtedly be more concerned with developing a jump, aggressiveness, and superior climbing ability. If you like long recreational rides and centuries, look for fellow riders who pile on the miles, rather than people whose schedule allows only 45 minutes on the bicycle.

Look for a group that meets at a convenient time. If you have to alter your schedule significantly or make major changes in your lifestyle just to ride twice a week, you'll be unlikely to stick with the program very long. Finally, it is worth the effort to find riders you like and get along with in a social way as well as in a cycling environment. Many long-lasting friendships spring from training rides, but the bottom line is simple: You're more likely to train if you like your training partners.

Look for group rides advertised by local cycling clubs. Bicycle shops are another good source of information. Top shops often sponsor rides at various times of the day, graded as to ability level and goals.

Once you have found a group, be aware of some unwritten but important riding traditions that have grown up through cycling's history. First, be on time for the ride. No one wants to waste precious cycling time waiting around for latecomers. Most organized rides take off at the appointed time, and if you are late, you'll be off the back before you start. On smaller rides with a couple of friends, it is often tempting to wait another 5 minutes for laggards, but such well-meaning gestures only encourage the tardy rider to repeat the mistake. Do your best to be on time.

Another tradition is that each rider carries food, water, tools, and a spare tire sufficient to get through the ride. Also, each rider should have the basic mechanical skills needed to adjust a derailleur or change a flat. Relying on friends is inescapable sometimes, but generally speaking, prepare for a group ride as if you were going alone —as you will be if you get dropped, lost, or abandoned.

The better groups make it a rule to never yell at erring riders or criticize them for mistakes in judgment or balance. Helpful advice is welcomed by most cyclists, but rude and inconsiderate remarks have no place in what should be recreation rather than serious business.

Finally, respect the wishes of the group. If you feel like going 50 miles today but everyone else planned on 30, compromise by riding with the group then continuing if you want more miles. Don't try to embarrass others into a longer ride.

Performance Tips for Competitive Riders

If your group is primarily interested in increasing performance, here are some useful techniques.

Form a paceline and go hard for 10 miles, alternating the lead every minute. Essentially you'll be doing a team time trial, although the pulls at the front will be a bit longer than they would be in competition. This technique works well in groups of mixed ability, because stronger riders can take longer pulls, while weaker riders either take short turns at the front or merely pull over and rotate to the back.

Simulate a road race by giving one rider a 50-yard lead. He tries to stay away, while the group attempts to get organized and chase down the lone break. Decide in advance how long the escapee has to stay away to "win." Vary this game with breaks of two or more people depending on the size of the group.

Race up hills and cruise on the flat to recover. The finish line should be about 100 yards past the top of the hill. In competition, if you apportion your effort so you are exhausted just as you hit the top, other riders will attack shortly before the crest and drop you on the flat after the climb. Use these uphill group dashes to become accustomed to riding over the hill rather than merely to the top.

Sprint for imaginary finish lines. Riders are allowed to use regular race tactics as the sprint approaches, including making temporary allegiances for lead-outs. Don't take unnecessary chances. Emphasize safety so you don't have a painful crash in a race that doesn't count.

Take advantage of unfolding situations as you ride. Someone jumps for a road sign and everyone else chases. The escapee is caught, everyone sits up to recover, and someone else attacks treacherously to be the first to the county line. Let's say a training partner opens a gap while you sit up to unzip your jacket or adjust your helmet. Jump hard and chase him down.

Training Time Trials

Training time trials are extremely useful for building speed and power even if you don't compete in real time trials. They improve your position on the bicycle as you strive to keep an aerodynamic position. You'll develop mental toughness as you work at your anaerobic threshold for several minutes at a time. You'll be able to judge your improvement accurately as you compare times on the same course over a month or a season.

Training time trials can be random affairs that you do whenever the spirit moves you. In the middle of a ride, go as hard as possible for 3 miles, figuring the distance on your cyclecomputer and timing yourself. If your computer has an average speed readout, you have one more piece of data to file away in your training diary. Don't forget to record wind conditions, and take them into account when comparing times.

Most riders like more formal training time trials. Choose a course on a lightly traveled road with no traffic signals and few intersections. Measure off a 1-mile-long course and do 2-mile repeats going out and back. Many riders like longer efforts of 5 or even 10 miles, but repetitions of the 2-miler will enable you to practice your start and turnaround techniques more frequently. You'll be able to ride at a higher heart rate because of the shorter distance. And you can increase distance in smaller increments for better training. Increasing from one 5-mile time trial to two of them in a single workout is a huge increase in effort, but adding a 2-miler to the 3 you are already doing is easier for the body to handle.

Start training time trials from a track stand or a momentary hesitation. There's no need for a holder to steady your bicycle. Push the button on your watch a second before the start, then put your hand back on the bars so you can stand up and accelerate powerfully away from the start. Your time won't be totally accurate, but if you follow the same procedure each day, your results will be comparable. As you cross the finish line, hit the stop button, but roll around a bit before you check the results. It is dangerous to stare down at the watch when you are cross-eyed with fatigue from the time trial. Also, if you went slower than you had hoped, it is bad for your attitude to discover the bad news when you are still hurting from a tough effort. Better to wait until you have recovered and are in a better frame of mind to receive the results, good or bad.

Don't be afraid to do training time trials in windy or rainy conditions. Your times may suffer, but you'll still be putting out the effort and getting the physical benefit. You'll learn how to handle those adverse conditions, too. Make a note in your training diary of wind and weather conditions so you can accurately compare your times to those in more favorable conditions.

Don't do training time trials too frequently. All out efforts for 3 to 10 or more minutes are so tough that you are liable to get physically and mentally exhausted. One session per week is the maximum, and most riders who train with varied techniques should limit themselves to once every two weeks or less.

Motorpacing

One technique that racers often use to increase their speed is motorpacing (riding in the draft of a motorcyle or small car). Road riders often warm up behind the team van while track racers string out behind special motorcyles—called "dernies" in Western Europe—that pull them around the track at breakneck speeds. Professional track riders even have a world championship motorpaced event.

Although it seems like an exotic and dangerous training technique, motorpacing has many advantages. The greater training speeds possible more closely imitate racing speeds and accustom your leg muscles to the effort. Although it would seem that training at lower speeds but equal effort without the motor would be as beneficial, it doesn't work out that way in practice. In the smooth pocket of air behind the motor, you can hover on your anaerobic threshold longer than you can fighting inconsistent gusts of wind by yourself.

A small motorcycle can accelerate smoothly at increments of less than 1 mph, so you can increase speed slowly but inevitably until you just can't keep up anymore. You can simulate sprints by accelerating behind the motorcycle to high speed, then sprinting around it. Another advantage of motorpacing is greater visibility on the highway—the motorcycle and bicycle are more noticeable than the bicycle alone.

But for all its allure, motorpacing has a number of pronounced drawbacks that cause most recreational riders and many racers to reject it as a training aid. For one thing, it is technically illegal on public highways because you would be "following too closely." And your driver might be cited for "careless driving" too.

Expense is another problem. This training requires a special motorcyle to motorpace correctly and safely. Such motorcyles have relatively low power, so they don't accelerate too fast for the bicycle and rider. And they have a roller attached to the rear forks, at the height of the bicycle's front axle, in case the rider comes too close and bumps the motorcycle with his front wheel. Without the roller, the result is almost inevitably a dangerous, high-speed crash. With the roller, the bicycle's front wheel spins the roller harmlessly.

The motorcycle driver needs experience to know when to change speeds and how to do it safely. In fact, most motorpace drivers are bicycle racers themselves and have an uncanny feel for exactly how much effort the following rider is expending as wind and terrain change during the ride.

The speed alone makes motorpacing more dangerous than normal riding. The consequences of a crash are more severe. You are riding within a foot of a hard, unyielding fender or frame that promises injury

Motorpaced training is safest in the controlled conditions of a velodrome.

if you hit it as you fall. The pacing vehicle hides potholes and other road obstacles from view until your front wheel is virtually in contact, making evasive action nearly impossible.

Finally, motorpacing is dangerous because it disrupts the normal expectations of other highway users. Drivers expect motorcyles to travel about as fast as cars and bicycles at about a third that speed. Motorpacing destroys drivers' preconceptions because the motorcycle is going too slowly and the bicycle is going too fast. Robbed of their normal speed perceptions, even good drivers often make mistakes in depth perception or judging distance.

Motorpacing Alternatives

Fortunately there are some excellent motorpacing alternatives that feature most of the advantages of the real thing while eliminating the danger and illegality.

A fast paceline simulates motorpacing because it provides both the draft and the high speed. In fact, before motorcycles were in common use, cyclists used teams of other riders to pace them to long-distance records. Find a fast training group, and you'll get great motorpaced training without the motor. A fast group in a big century ride or long road race works well, too.

By yourself, look for fast downhill stretches where you can turn a big gear at high speeds. Ideal is a long canyon that slopes gently downhill. Work on your climbing on the way up, and get a gravity-assisted motorpace coming home.

In many ways, a tail wind is the ultimate motorpacing substitute. You can ride on the flat so you aren't assisted by gravity, but the tail wind enables you to keep your speed high. The drawback of this type of training is the head-down grind back home into the howling wind. Overcome the problem by arranging for someone to drive and pick you up at the end of the downwind run. Failing that, you'll just have to tough it out. However, you can build great power coming back into that wind.

Diet and Nutrition

Proper nutrition is the area of athletic performance most replete with misinformation, myths, and old wives' tales. Even the history of how to determine position on a bicycle is lucid and concise compared to theories of optimal athletic nutrition.

Cyclists have been urged to become vegetarians, eat bee pollen, take megadoses of vitamins, and generally worry to distraction about what should be a natural and pleasurable act. To make it even more difficult, solid, scientifically researched findings about carbohydrate ingestion, fluid replacement, and cholesterol levels are sprinkled in among the quackery. The trick? Separating the valid suggestions from those with little or no validity.

Advantages of Low Body Fat

Top bicycle racers are distinguishable from sedentary citizens, casual riders, and even strong recreational cyclists by an incredible leanness. The best cyclists, male or female, carry so little body fat that the skin on their legs seems nearly transparent.

A male professional rider may have only 5 percent body fat–dangerously close to the 3 percent that physiologists deem the minimum essential for health. Although equally fit women generally have 5 percent more body fat because of childbearing demands, they still score a svelte 8 to 10 percent. What are the advantages of these extremely low levels of stored fat for the cyclist?

Better performance in the heat is a major advantage of lower body fat. Fat is excellent insulation–useful if you are cast adrift in the North sea, but the last thing you want when you are riding a century on a hot day. Poor heat tolerance means that your blood supply will be diverted to the skin for cooling when you'd really rather have all that oxygen-carrying red stuff feeding the muscles with nutrients and hauling away waste products.

Less body fat also means improved cardiovascular performance. Your maximal oxygen uptake, the measure of how efficiently your body processes oxygen, automatically increases as you lose weight. This value is expressed in "liters of oxygen per kilogram of body weight," so if you lose 5 pounds, simple math automatically increases your performance potential. Some studies have shown that a 1 percent loss in body fat automatically produces a 1 percent rise in aerobic performance.

Finally, trim down, and you'll enjoy a better power-to-weight ratio that translates into improved climbing ability. You don't want to carry more dead weight than you need, and fat is essentially nonfunctional tissue in cycling. If your body is lighter, your heart and lungs won't have to work as hard during a climb. You'll be able to go faster if you are racing or proceed more comfortably if you are touring or riding a century.

Suppose, for example, that you weigh 150 pounds and can generate 300 watts of power going 10 mph on a climb. Lose 15 pounds of unnecessary fat, and your 300 watts of power will have to lift 10 percent less weight up the hill. Your speed will increase enormously with no increase in power output! No wonder competitive cyclists place such a premium on the lowest possible body fat levels.

Strong male cyclists usually carry from 8 to 12 percent of their body weight as fat. Subtract another 2 or 3 percent if they are racers. Women at the same level of fitness will usually test about 5 percent higher. Those are fairly low figures, since the average American male is usually over 15 percent, the average woman over 20.

Remember that scale weight means little because it tells you nothing about what percentage of your weight is fat. Lean body mass, composed of muscle and bone, helps you go faster and resist the effects of crashes. But the scale can't distinguish between muscle and useless fat. It only records weight. A 5-foot-11-inch male who weighs 165 pounds may have a low 10 percent of body fat. Another male cyclist of the same height and weight may carry over 25 percent. The scale tells the same tale in both instances, but their performance on the bicycle is likely to be vastly different.

Dieting: Why You Shouldn't

Don't rush blindly into a restrictive diet in hopes of improving your performance on the bicycle. Although weight loss seems to be pure plus, losing too much weight–or losing the wrong kind of weight–can have negative effects on your cycling and your health. Many riders diet obsessively, figuring that if they improved by losing 10 pounds, they'll be world beaters if they lose 20. Not so. In fact, they might actually be better off eating more and riding more.

Why? Simply because there's a difference between the kind of weight lost during exercise and the kind lost during dieting.

Many dieters like to weigh themselves periodically. If their scale weight declines, they believe that they are less fat, and therefore more fit, than they were previously. Not necessarily. The weight lost exercising is mostly fat. The weight lost dieting is mostly *muscle*–the very tissue you want to preserve because it burns calories like no other part of the body.

If your diet leaves you with less muscle–and dieting without exercise will–you'll be less able to burn off excess calories in the future and you'll regain the weight you lost. This is the reason that many dieters who lose weight through diet alone gain it back–and more–when they return to normal eating.

It is possible then to impede your performance, even to compromise your health, if you allow your body fat to drop too low. Male riders often experience a higher incidence of colds and other minor infections like saddle sores if their body fat percentage falls much below 6 to 9 percent

(10 to 15 percent for women). Low body fat may also contribute to insidious tissue breakdown that causes injuries like tendinitis or unexplained muscle strains.

Determining Body Fat Percentage

Fortunately, it is easy to discover if your body fat percentage is too low or too high. Three methods are commonly used to determine percentage of body fat. However, each is an approximation since they rely on indirect measurements.

The traditional method involves being weighed underwater. While submerged in a tank, subjects are weighed and the results compared, in a complex formula, to normal scale weight. Because fat is more buoyant than muscle and bone, total percentage of body fat can be calculated using Archimedes's principle. Eureka!

This process has several drawbacks, though. First, it costs $20 to $40, usually at a sports medicine or similar specialized clinic. Second, accuracy depends on the experience and skill of the technician. Third, you may find the process extremely uncomfortable, because you must exhale as much air as possible underwater, then remain submerged while the readings are taken. Blowing all the air out of your lungs while you are underwater is hardly a natural act, but if residual air volume remains, it will make you more buoyant and the results less accurate.

If underwater weighing isn't your thrill, skin-fold measurements, available at most gyms and health clubs, are the way to go. In this process, a trained technician pinches your skin at three or more locations and measures the thickness of the resulting skinfold with accurate, specially designed calipers. These readings are then plugged into preprogrammed calculators. Quick, easy,

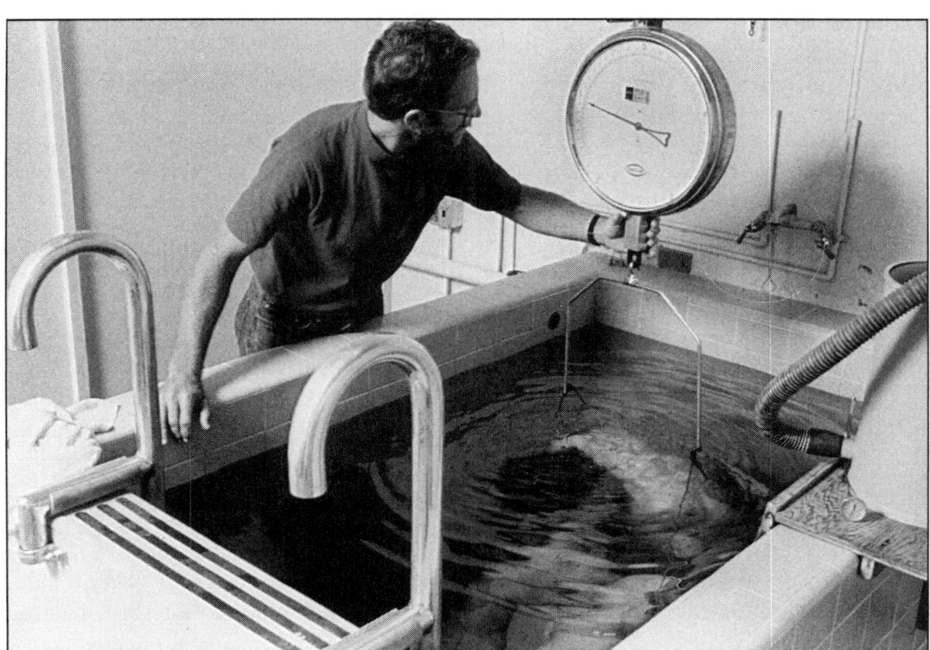

Underwater weighing to determine body fat percentage.

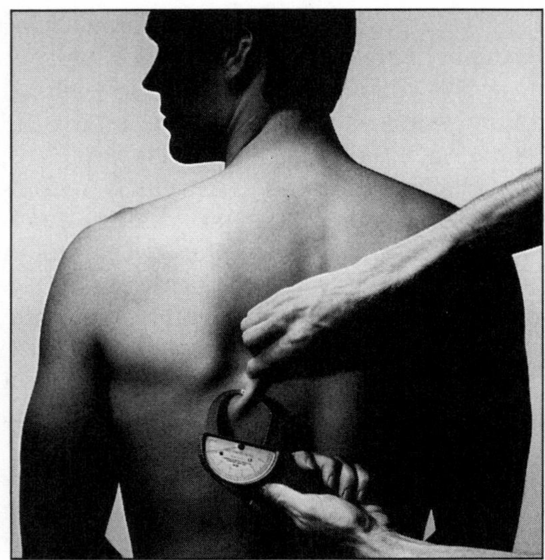

Determining body fat percentage with skin-fold calipers.

and relatively inexpensive ($10 to $25) skin-fold measurement is a good way to keep tabs on your flab.

There are some drawbacks, though. The formulas assume, for example, that fat under the skin is proportional to internal fat stored around bodily organs. In other words, if you hoard most of your fat supply under your skin, the results will be misleading. Also, skin-fold measurements are only as reliable as the person taking them. Different technicians may take samples in slightly different locations. Fat thickness at one location on the frontal thigh may be half as great as it is just an inch away. Or they may leave the calipers on the skin-fold for different amounts of time. Since fat is compressible, the longer the caliper remains on the sample, the thinner the skin-fold becomes.

So if you plan to have skin-folds done every couple of months to assess progress during your weight-loss program, have them performed by the same technician to assure consistency. You can also buy your own skin calipers for about $250. However, it is impossible to take the readings yourself unless you are a contortionist. And without the necessary expertise, results will be, at best, an approximation of an approximation.

A third technique, with limited availability, involves a recent development known as electrical impedence. In this process, electrodes are attached to your foot and hand, then a mild electric current is passed between them. Percentage of fat is calculated indirectly (again) based on the amount of electrical resistance, a number that distinguishes muscle from fat. This method is the quickest and the least expensive (about $20) of the trio. And despite the use of an electrical current, it's painless.

Unfortunately, it is often inaccurate. Results can vary widely depending on your state of hydration and such seemingly unimportant factors as whether your thighs are touching–changing the distance the current travels and therefore the resistance measured.

There is a fourth method of gauging body fat, however, that doesn't cost a thing. Stand naked in front of a mirror and honestly assess what you see. Do you look lean or are there areas of pudge? Do you have the visible ribs of fitness? Or is there a distinct ring of fat at the belt line?

Visual self-appraisal may be the best way to determine if you are at your most effective cycling weight or if you need to lose a few pounds. Take snapshots periodically during your weight-loss process, from the same distance and in the same lighting each time, to provide a visual comparison of changes in body composition.

Achieving Low Body Fat

Suppose all the evidence indicates that you need to lose a few pounds? Surprisingly, concensus does exist on how to accomplish that feat.

As mentioned earlier, don't begin with a diet—at least not in the traditional sense of the word. We have seen the havoc that can wreak with your lean body mass. Instead, change the type of food you eat. Nutritional experts agree that your daily food intake should be about 70 percent carbohydrate, 15 percent protein, and about 15 percent fat. If you are training heavily, increase the carbohydrate intake to as much as 80 percent of the total with proportional reductions in fat and protein.

In fact, adoption of a diet high in carbohydrates and low in fat is probably the most important single thing that you can do, with the exception of a good training program, to improve your performance on the bicycle and your general health.

Why? A high carbohydrate intake fuels your body for endurance exercise. Carbohydrates are converted readily into the glycogen that is the primary muscle fuel in endurance exercise. Your body can metabolize fat, but it does so grudgingly and inefficiently. Eat plenty of carbohydrate and your muscles will be well-stocked with glycogen's energy-producing potential.

Next, carbohydrates provide fiber for better digestion and a greater feeling of satiety. High-fiber diets speed the movement of waste products through the digestive tract and reduce the risk of colon cancer.

A diet of high carbohydrate foods like whole wheat bread, potatoes, fruit, and vegetables is more likely to contain the vitamins and minerals you need for balanced nutrition.

Finally, a high carbohydrate diet contains fewer calories than a diet high in fat. Carbohydrates contain only 4 calories per gram, while the same amount of fat contains a whopping 9 calories. If you eat primarily carbohydrates, you'll feel full on less than half the calories. Put another way, you can eat more, avoid the hunger and discomfort associated with traditional dieting, and still either lose fat or maintain your ideal percentage. Many riders find that they can eat as much as they want, ride hard, and still lose fat until they settle at their most effective weight and body fat percentage.

None of these good things happen, of course, without exercise. If you diet without accompanying exercise, you'll lose at least as much muscle tissue as fat. But with a program combining moderate exercise and a reasonable diet, you'll lose fat and gain muscle.

An exercise program that combines aerobic exercise like cycling with some muscle development work like weight training—the sort of program advocated in this book—produces the best all-around results. You'll burn fat on the long aerobic-paced rides while you build muscle tissue with faster anaerobic intervals and weight training. The result will be a leaner, faster body that metabolizes food more efficiently.

Don't attempt to calculate calories consumed against calories expended in exercise, either. For example, since a pound of fat contains about 3,500 calories you may think that by reducing your calories by 500 per day and increasing your mileage so that you use another 500 (about 45 minutes of riding at 15 mph) you'll be able to lose about 2 pounds of fat a week. Although this is theoretically true, it almost never works out in practice. One problem is the difficulty of calculating precise caloric intake. Unless you know the exact ingredients in all foods you consume and unless you weigh everything you put in your mouth, you'll have at best an inaccurate estimate.

More perplexing is the wide variation in the way different individuals seem to use calories. A study of elite runners showed that some were running over 100 miles a week on less than 2,000 calories a day. That's a mathematical impossibility according to all the calorie-versus-exercise equations, yet they maintained a high level of performance and personal vigor. Obviously there is wide variation in the way individuals store and use the energy from food.

Finally, realize that body fat reduction is a long-term process. Changing your body composition isn't something that can be done overnight or even in a few months. And some people will have a much harder time than others because different individuals have a widely varying hereditary bias when it comes to their ultimate body composition.

In fact, advocates of what is called "setpoint theory" argue that each person tends to gravitate to a unique percentage of body fat. In the theoretical model, one person who rides 100 miles a week and eats a high-carbohydrate diet will settle at 10 percent fat, while another rider putting in the same number of miles and eating an identical diet will stabilize at 15 percent. Because such a theory is nearly impossible to test scientifically, setpoint is still controversial. Yet those who work professionally with nutrition and athletes believe that it exists.

What does setpoint mean for you? Essentially it means to be realistic in your weight-reduction goals. Most cyclists will never approach the one-digit body fat percentages of elite riders because they don't have the hereditary predilection toward leanness, and they don't have time to put in the calorie-devouring weekly mileage that top riders view as a matter of course. A 30-year-old recreational cyclist shouldn't strive for the body fat levels of the pros, because it would involve putting in as many miles as the cashmen–impractical for most people since they don't get paid for it. Realistically, body fat percentages of below 10 percent for men and 15 percent for women are nearly impossible to attain on recreational cyclists' mileage unless they are genetically blessed with a tendency toward low body fat.

The Ideal Training Diet

Let's look at some dietary specifics for the hard-working endurance athlete. How can he decide what to eat each day when the supermarkets and fast-food emporiums are laden with temptations, some enhancing cycling performance, others quite detrimental?

Food Guidelines

First, daily food intake should provide enough calories to meet the energy demands of hard training. Many cyclists make the mistake of thinking that if they eat small amounts, they'll lose weight and get faster. And that process works–up to a point. But as we have seen, when body fat falls below optimum levels, performance declines rapidly. So does the rider's enthusiasm, another element absolutely necessary for effective training.

Additionally, many inexperienced cyclists underestimate the amount of food needed to fuel training rides, tours, or a hard racing schedule. They want to ride to lose fat and are horrified when they find themselves eating more than they did when they were sedentary. How can I lose weight, they ask, when I'm eating everything in sight? Conversely, cyclists who have been at it successfully for a year or so invariably recognize the necessity of eating large amounts so they have the energy to enjoy cycling as well as other activities. But because they choose their food wisely from high-carbohydrate selections, they have the energy to ride well without unwanted weight gain.

Next, a good cyclist's diet should meet nutritional needs. Fortunately, if you eat a varied diet, in the quantities needed for even moderate training, you'll probably get all the vitamins and minerals your body requires for health and food metabolism. Some riders take a multivitamin supplement for dietary insurance. Large doses of vitamins are expensive, unnecessary, and in some cases may actually be harmful.

Third, your diet should provide for adequate hydration–in other words, good fluid intake. Active cyclists perspire heavily but often don't notice it because the body's movement through the air evaporates most of it before they realize how much they are sweating. As a result, many riders don't drink enough. Dehydration severely compromises your ability to do work and upsets your body's electrolyte balance.

Assure adequate fluid intake by drinking several ounces from your bottle every 10 or 15 minutes while riding. Carry two bottles on all but the shortest rides, and replenish your supply at aid stations on organized rides or at wayside stores or parks while training. Don't skimp on the fluids during cold-weather rides. You'll still sweat in the winter, although it may be less noticeable than in hot weather. At home, drink several glasses of water each day, and avoid caffeinated beverages like coffee that increase dehydration, since they act as diuretics.

Fourth, remember to avoid fat. Fat often masquerades in foods that we take for granted. Eliminate them and you eliminate a large percentage of the fat in your diet. Get in the habit of substituting more nutritional items for the fat. Low-fat eating doesn't have to be tasteless.

For instance, butter or margarine is fat, pure and simple. Simply stop using it on toast, bread, cooked vegetables or anywhere it shows up in your daily diet. To make food more palatable, substitute unsweetened applesauce as a topping for your morning toast. Steam vegetables or stir-fry them in water. Put low-fat cottage cheese on your baked potato, or moisten it with a little low-fat milk.

Many riders like salads prepared with various types of greens and vegetables. But they smother the finished salad in high-fat dressing. A 100-calorie salad can easily swell to over 500 calories simply with the addition of a ladle of blue cheese dressing. And most of the additional calories are fat. Substitute lemon juice for the dressing, or eat the salad plain.

Another example: meats like roast beef, pork, or hamburger. The trick is to eat less of the meat dish, and substitute more bread, rice, and potatoes. For instance, at the restaurant, order the 6- rather than the 12-ounce steak–and take half of it home for a sandwich next day.

Low-fat eating can be a problem at home if someone you love is preparing the food but doesn't understand your dietary preferences. Compromise is in order. Suppose dinner is chili with meat. Prepare a large container of brown rice in advance and keep it in the refrigerator. Fill a bowl about three quarters with the rice, warm it in the microwave, and ladle some chili on top. You'll eat about a quarter of the chili you normally would, get the benefit of all the carbohydrates from the rice, and avoid domestic turmoil at the same time. The same trick works with soup and stew.

Snacks are another area often high in fat. There's nothing wrong with snacks. In fact, five or six small meals each day are probably better than three big ones, because they won't overload your stomach and will supply a continuous flow of energy all day without the sleepy feeling that too often follows a big meal. Unfortunately, most common snacks are laden with fat, sugar, and food additives. So choose your snacks with an eye toward nutrition as well as convenience. Fresh fruits and vegetables, whole-grain bread, and dried fruit are all useful snack foods. Stay away from nutritional zeros like potato chips and candy.

Finally, be adaptable. Any diet that requires spartan self-discipline is doomed to fail–if not immediately, certainly over a period of a year or more. If you visit friends and are served a big piece of prime rib, you don't have to jeopardize the friendship by refusing to eat it. One dietary indiscretion won't ruin your health. Similarly, if you are traveling, you often have little choice about what is on the menu. Make the best choice possible and carry on.

A hint for travelers: Eat breakfast in your motel room, and avoid the typically high-fat breakfast of eggs, sausage, bacon, and pancakes that is standard fare in most restaurants. Simply pack a bowl, a spoon, a cold whole-grain cereal, and some powdered nonfat milk. Add raisins or a banana for sweetening, and you can begin the day quickly and inexpensively.

For lunch, stop at a supermarket and buy whole-grain bread, fruit, low-fat yogurt, and raw vegetables, and construct your own roadside picnic. Such improvisations are far healthier than the menu at the standard fast-food franchise, and fun to plan and purchase along the way.

Preparation of road food is easier if you take along a small ice chest for storing fruit, juice, and skim milk if you don't like the taste of nonfat milk. The ice chest is also useful for keeping postride food fresh in a hot car while you are off on a century or group ride.

Low-fat eating is primarily a matter of changing eating habits that have been ingrained. Think before you order at a restaurant or while you prepare food at home. You'll barely miss the fatty portion of your diet, and you'll be rewarded for your watchfulness with better health and performance.

Look for these alternatives when you do your grocery shopping for the week. Soon, it will become automatic to choose more healthful recipes.

Breakfast

Try cold cereal like shredded wheat or Grape Nuts. It comes in many varieties with little added sugar or salt, vitamin and iron enrichment, and no harmful food additives.

Hot cereal, especially oatmeal, is good if you don't cheat and use instant. Try this preparation trick: Put a cup of oatmeal in a bowl, add a little apple juice and some raisins. Then add enough water to thoroughly wet all the contents and float the oatmeal. Microwave the oatmeal for 3 minutes on "reheat" or until the liquid starts to bubble. Drain off excess liquid and add fresh fruit. Oatmeal can also be soaked overnight in the refrigerator instead of cooked in the microwave. Try diced fruit instead of raisins.

Whole-grain bread makes excellent toast. Use unsweetened applesauce instead of butter. If you like jam, look for the low-sugar varieties in the supermarket. Whole-grain bagels or rolls provide variety.

Pancakes or waffles made with whole-grain mix are delicious. Top them with applesauce, fresh peaches, or strawberries instead of syrup.

Nontraditional breakfast items can start your day off right. Try leftover pizza, vegetable sandwiches, or even a nourishing soup.

Lunch

Think of a sandwich as a salad surrounded by bread. Use whole-grain bread stuffed with vegetables and various kinds of lettuce.

Dice fruit with cold, cooked brown rice. The combination mixes well with several spoonfuls of plain low-fat yogurt.

Warm up leftovers from last night's dinner. Spaghetti, casseroles, stir-fried vegetables, and pizza all make great lunches.

Dinner

Modify your favorite recipes. For instance, make meatless lasagna with low-fat cottage cheese. Create vegetarian spaghetti, substituting vegetables like zucchini for meat. When a recipe calls for margarine, cut the recommendations in half.

Center your meal on carbohydrates. Top a baked potato with vegetables. Mix soups or stews with brown rice. Fill up on whole-grain bread instead of another helping of a meat dish. Use beans and legumes, rather than meat, as your primary protein source.

Avoid gravy, cream sauce, and cheese. Skin chicken before cooking. Stir-fry in water rather than oil. Broil meat instead of frying, and carefully trim off all visible fat before cooking.

Snack Suggestions

Cereal.

Air-popped popcorn (without salt or butter).

Fruit.

Raw vegetables.

Whole-grain bread or rolls.

Eating before, during, and after Rides

Food is important to the cyclist at any time. But because it supplies the fuel for endurance exercise, what you eat before and during your ride determines how much you'll enjoy the time on the bicycle if you are riding recreationally and how well you'll perform if you are competing. And what you eat after a hard ride dictates how you will feel the next day—both on the bicycle and in everyday activities.

Preride Meals

The last meal before a ride should be high in carbohydrates (of course) and easy to digest. In addition, eat what you are used to eating so your stomach and digestive tract don't react to the dietary surprise with a surprise of their own.

Timing your meal is important so you have enough energy for the ride without a full stomach that will, for the digestive processes, divert blood from your working muscles. Generally speaking, eat at least 2 hours before a recreational jaunt, a moderately paced training ride, or a long road race. If the ride will be a higher intensity effort like a circuit race, criterium, or a fast training ride with a group, eat your preride meal about 3 hours before the start. For intense efforts like time trials that go flat out from the beginning, most riders prefer to allow at least 4 hours, so their stomachs are empty when the event begins.

A good preride meal for morning training or races consists of a light breakfast of cereal and skim milk topped with a banana. Add a piece of whole-grain toast with applesauce or low-sugar jam if experience has shown that you need it. If you train late in the afternoon, eat your normal lunch, then have a snack of fruit or whole-grain bread about 2 hours before you ride. Otherwise, the 5- or 6-hour gap between lunch and training will be too great—you'll lack energy for hard efforts.

If you plan a long ride at a moderate pace—maybe a century ride—eat a bit more than normal, and don't be afraid to finish the meal fairly soon before the start. You'll avoid stomach upset because of the slower pace, and you'll welcome the energy from the larger meal 75 or 80 miles down the road.

Much has been written about the technique of carbo-loading for endurance events. The theory behind carbo-loading is simple. Go for a long, hard ride three days before the event you are aiming for, depleting your muscles of their glycogen stores. During the subsequent three days, eat a diet as high in carbohydrate as possible. Your muscles will supercompensate and absorb more glycogen than they would under normal circumstances.

In actual practice, endurance athletes are carbo-loading all the time. They train long and hard, then eat high-carbo diets as a matter of course. So you probably won't have to make any special adjustments before a big event. Just be sure that you are getting 70 to 80 percent of your daily calories in the form of carbohydrates.

What to Eat during Rides

Cycling is distinguished from other sports like running, because the cyclist actually can eat while riding, thus prolonging the amount of time it's possible to continue. The body can store only enough glycogen for about 2 hours of intense effort, but by properly replenishing those supplies in midride, cyclists can extend the period of peak performance for hours or days. For example, Race Across America competitors ride nearly continually for almost two weeks, eating in the saddle and maintaining a steady energy output.

Food to eat during a ride should be easy to carry. Avoid gooey sandwiches that squash and smear all over your pockets. By the same token, unwrapped bread or soft fruit often becomes inedible from sweat or rain. Nothing is more disheartening than to reach into a pocket for your ration of goodies 75 miles into a century and come up with a handful of wet crumbs.

Consider the packaging, too. If your midride food isn't easy to get out of your pocket, unwrap, and eat, you won't eat it, and the result will be an attack of the "bonk" 20 miles from home. Like "the wall" in marathon running, the bonk is to be avoided at all costs. Some riders like to line their jersey pocket with a plastic sandwich bag, pinning the mouth of the bag to the opening of the pocket. Then they can reach in with one hand and pull out slices of fruit or fig bars while still riding safely.

Experiment with various food and drink to see what you can stomach in different conditions. Food that slides down easily on a casual ride in the spring may be absolutely unpalatable on hard rides in the heat of midsummer. A sports drink that tastes great in training may make you nauseated in the stresses of competition. Every rider has different food preferences and has to discover them individually.

The best solid food for most rides is undoubtedly fruit. Bananas are a favorite because they are easy to carry and convenient to eat while pedaling. Apples are good, too, especially if you cut them into quarters before the ride and carry them in a small plastic bag. Ditto for orange slices. Pull out the pieces, and eat them one at a time when it's convenient. Avoid soft fruit like ripe peaches, because it will get mangled by the pressure of your jersey. You'll end up with a pocket full of fruit juice.

Some riders like dried fruit like figs or dates, but they tend to be sticky, so be sure they are bagged securely. Fig bars are good, too, because they provide some bread with the fruit. Look for whole wheat fig bars at health food stores or your local supermarket.

Consider riding without solid food, instead substituting one of the glucose polymer drinks available from several manufacturers. These palatable drinks can be carried premixed in your water bottle. They contain carbohydrate in the form of easily absorbed glucose polymer, mixed in the optimum solution. Another advantage is ease of use. Just drink it from your bottle instead of fumbling with solid food. Use the extra space in your jersey pocket to carry along an extra bottle. A hint: Put full bottles (or any heavy objects) in your middle pocket so they don't pull off uncomfortably to one side.

If you use sugary sports drinks, wash your bottles carefully after the ride. Bacte-

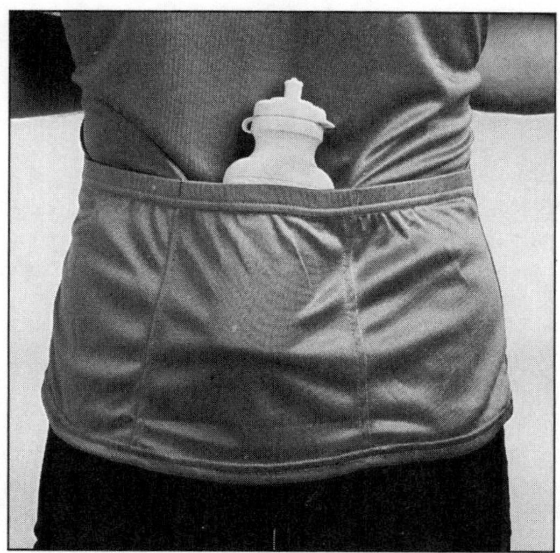

Carry a full bottle in your middle jersey pocket so it doesn't pull off to one side.

ria consider the sugar residue in the bottom of unwashed bottles a perfect environment, and the next time you use it, you may get a shock. Also, the flavor of sports drinks may linger in the plastic if the bottle isn't washed soon after use. Use hot, soapy water and a bottle brush to thoroughly scrub all the recesses inside and out, or put the bottle in a dishwasher.

Postride Nutrition

After a ride, be sure you are fully hydrated. Weigh yourself before and after long rides, and compare the two figures. Short-term weight loss is almost certainly fluid from perspiration, so drink plenty of liquids until your body weight has returned to normal.

You'll also want to replenish the burned calories as soon as possible. In fact, studies have shown that your exercised and glycogen-depleted muscles are most receptive to repacking with glycogen from high-carbohydrate meals within about 2 hours after exercise. So take a shower, clean your bicycle, and eat as soon as you feel hungry. Don't spare the carbos!

One way to increase the total amount of glycogen stored in your muscles during this period of maximum absorption is to consume one of the specially formulated high-carbohydrate drinks. Available in several flavors, the carbohydrate is absorbed more quickly than that in solid food. During periods of heavy training or on long tours, consider supplementing your meals with these products.

26
Candy
del tongo
COLNAGO

CHAPTER

Medical Self-Care

You hurtle down a concrete road at speeds up to 50 mph on fragile tires no wider than your thumbnail. The road is littered with gravel and broken glass. Savage dogs, hostile pedestrians, and careless drivers may strike beyond the next blind curve. And if you are preparing to race, you also face the risks posed by overtraining, overuse injuries, and unskilled competitors. Cycling certainly looks like a dangerous sport.

But appearances are deceptive. Statistically, cycling turns out to be relatively safe. Cycling skill, a protective helmet, and alert riding usually suffice to keep you upright and out of harm's way. But every cyclist's luck turns eventually. The trick is to avoid preventable injuries and learn how to treat the unavoidable–but usually minor–problems that occasionally arise.

A word on treatment. In most cases, it is easier (and certainly less expensive) to treat your own injuries–provided they are minor. But for a serious injury or a minor injury that worsens, see a physician qualified to treat athletic injuries.

Take Preventive Action

Prevention, however, is the key to staying healthy on the bicycle, and it begins with proper clothing.

Outfit Your Body

Wear cycling shorts with chamois, either artificial or the real thing, to cut down on irritation from the saddle. Invest in good cycling gloves, both to pad your hands from the bars and to eliminate painful palm abrasions if you crash. Stiff-soled cycling shoes allow you to pedal hard in comfort without having the serrated pedal cage push painfully into your foot. Cleated shoes also let you align your foot properly on the pedal to eliminate knee strains. In cold weather, protect your knees with tights, either wool or synthetic. Cycling clothing is protective, practical and increasingly stylish, so there's no reason to miss out on its advantages.

Head Injuries

The most severe cycling injury is a blow to the unprotected head causing deep lacerations, concussion, or in extreme cases, a skull fracture. Here's a case where prevention isn't just the best cure, it's the only cure. Because head injuries are life-threatening, wear a hard-shell helmet, approved by either ANSI or the Snell Foundation. And because head injuries can happen at any speed, riding alone or in a pack, on the open highway or just cruising around a parking lot, wear one every time you ride. Consult a doctor for any head injury, especially if the skin is broken, and if you develop persistent headaches, changes in behavior and personality, or bleeding from the ear or nose.

Don't Take Falls

Properly attired, you can prevent a lot of injuries. But clothing doesn't prevent falling. To keep yourself in the saddle, make a practice of riding safely and predictably. Always obey traffic laws, and keep a wary eye on motorists and other cyclists.

Maintain your bicycle, because some crashes are caused by tires that blow out unexpectedly or brake cables that snap during routine stops. Practice your bicycle handling, so you remain vertical in tight spots. For instance, wearing a good helmet and protective clothing, ride an old bicycle on dirt paths to learn how to save it when your wheels start to skid.

If you fall, know how to land properly. During the off-season, incorporate some tumbling routines into your fitness workouts. Practice shoulder rolls, forward and backward rolls, and other agility drills, so you can hit the ground and come up fighting—or at least come up. You don't need a mat for these drills; soft grass in the backyard works fine. But you will need to practice until the correct motion becomes automatic. You won't have time to think as you are crashing, so the reflexes have to be built in to save your skin.

Try Sports Massage

Sports massage is another way to prevent injuries and hasten recovery from hard riding. Long a staple of the professional racer's training arsenal, massage has been adopted by recreational cyclists for its regenerative power. Self-massage is easy to learn, convenient, and costs nothing but time and a little energy.

If you decide to employ massage, the first decision you'll have to make is whether to shave your legs. Top racing cyclists, male or female, shave down as a matter of course.

Why should you consider shaving? First, when you are riding, your legs hang down by the road where they pick up all sorts of grime. Shaved legs are easier to keep clean, minimizing the risk of infection. Second, if you fall and collect abrasions on your legs, skin without hair is easier to clean and bandage. You'll be able to scrub road grit out of the injury with less pain, scabs won't form as readily, and adhesive bandages won't pull uncomfortably. Finally, clean-shaven legs are easier to massage. You can massage hairy legs, but the rubbing often irritates the hair follicles and produces a rash or an infection. For all these reasons, consider shaving down if you plan to do more than casual riding.

Women in our culture don't need advice on shaving their legs. Neither do football players who usually shave their ankles for weekly tape jobs before games. If you fit neither of the above categories, here are some tips. The actual shaving process is easier the first time if you use electric clippers to trim off most of the hair. If you try to shave a normal growth of leg hair with a blade, the razor will clog with every stroke. Then shave normally with a blade and shaving cream. Some riders use an electric razor. In either case, once a week will probably do it.

Next, select a light oil to lubricate the skin—making massage easier. Several commercial brands are available. Almond oil, available in health food stores, works well. Or you can make your own by combining rubbing alcohol, witch hazel, olive oil, and wintergreen. Buy the ingredients at the drugstore, and experiment with the proportions. In cold weather, you'll want more wintergreen for a warming effect.

The technique of self-massage is easy to learn. When you come in from a ride, stretch and cool down. If you have a hot tub or sauna, get in for 10 minutes to aid relaxation. Once you are properly relaxed, sit on the floor with your knees up and your feet flat on the floor. Apply some oil to your legs. Begin the massage with the feet, move up to the calves, spend some time kneading the tendons around the knee, and finish with the large quadriceps muscles of the thighs. Spend about 5 minutes or so on each leg. Always stroke toward the heart. Don't rub so hard that you feel pain in the muscle. Massage should be a healing experience, not a painful one. Experiment with various kneading motions. With experience, you should be able to feel your tired and taut cycling muscles become loose and pliable by massage's end.

Be sure to clean your skin thoroughly after massage so the oil doesn't clog your pores. Scrub off the oil with a washcloth and rubbing alcohol, or take a shower immediately after massage.

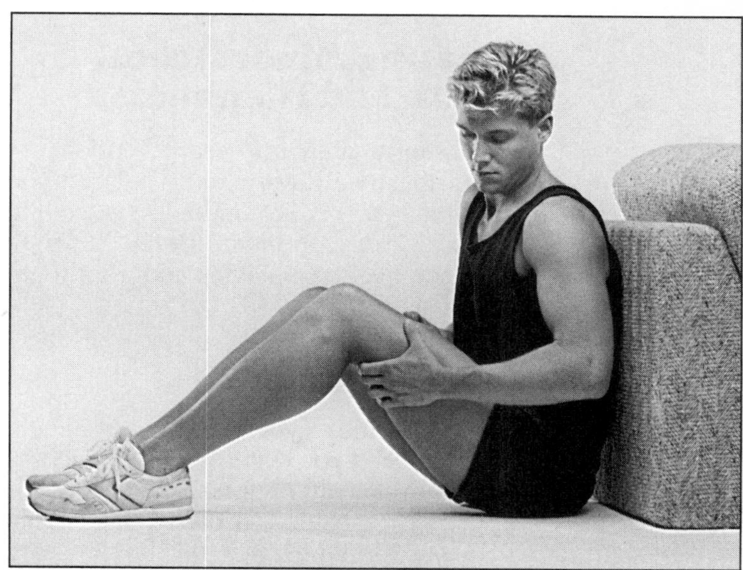

Correct position for self-massage.

Avoid Overtraining

Overtraining produces chronic fatigue, which can lead to injury and illness. If you are tired, you won't be an alert or confident bicycle handler. Fatigue leads to crashes that could have been avoided. European professional racers often say that the first sign of overtraining is a clumsy and embarrassing crash. In fact, minor crashes are often a blessing in disguise, because they force the rider off the bicycle for a week and allow recovery.

Overtraining also leads to injury and illness, because chronic fatigue lowers your immunity. A bone-weary body is less able to fight off infections.

Finally, chronic fatigue leads to overuse injuries. When you are tired, you'll probably go slower in training and be more likely to sit up to relieve tired back muscles or aching legs. Your pedal stroke may change subtly as you become increasingly fatigued day after day. As a result of your changed position and pedal stroke, you may fall prey to overuse injuries even though you are doing less mileage and training less intensively.

The moral is to train wisely and sensibly, always monitoring your body's reactions to your workouts. In that way you'll prevent many of the injuries and illnesses that can keep you off the bicycle for long periods of time.

Treating Minor Aches, Pains, and Numbness

Unfortunately, the best prevention program doesn't always work. What can you do when you do get injured or succumb to an overuse problem? Here's a list of common cycling maladies and what to do about them.

Neck Pain

Sometimes, cycling can be a real pain in the neck. If you suffer from sore, aching neck muscles after a long ride, first check your riding position. If the distance from your saddle to the handlebars is too short, you'll have to really stretch your neck to see the road ahead. Riding for several miles in that unnatural position will quickly fatigue your neck muscles, and you'll probably experience neck pain. Generally speaking, the correct combination top tube/stem length enables you to look down when you are in normal riding position and have the handlebars obscure the stem. The inexpensive way to get that combination is to use a longer stem to push the handlebars out where they belong. A more costly solution is to get a new frame with a longer top tube. Either way, your new position will be more elongated, so you'll be able to see down the road without craning your neck.

Don't overdo a good thing, however. If you are too spread out because of either an oversize stem or a frame that is too large, your neck may still protest. In that case, find a stem a centimeter or two shorter, and see if it helps.

Regardless of position, your neck will still give you fits if the muscles are too weak to support the weight of your helmet and head. Work on those muscles with the exercises suggested elsewhere in the book: basic flexibility movements like neck rolls and strength exercises like neck bridges. A strong and flexible neck won't fatigue easily on long rides and will protect your spinal cord should you take a bad fall.

Stretching lower back while on the bicycle.

Low Back Pain

Low back pain also can result from poor position, so check your saddle height and its fore-and-aft placement. If you are sitting on the bicycle properly and your lower back still hurts, your pain probably stems from weak back muscles. Most people have trouble with back pain early in the season, when they first begin to climb or push bigger gears on the flats, both actions that use the powerful muscles of the lower back. The way to prevent this pain is to keep those muscles in shape with an off-season weight program. It also helps to pace yourself by having a more gradual buildup to long climbs and big gears in your training program.

Finally, vary your riding position. If you ride primarily on the flat, stand up out of every corner and again on long straight stretches, shifting to a larger gear to accommodate standing's slower cadence. In hilly terrain, get out of the saddle for every little roller, and alternate sitting and standing on long climbs to move around the strain on your back muscles.

On-bicycle stretches, above and below, for shoulder and upper back pain.

Hand/Foot/Groin Numbness

Changing your riding position helps prevent numbness, too. Foot numbness is often the result of mile after mile of grinding away while seated, so stand up to vary the pressure on your feet. If standing fails, check your shoes. If they are too tight, either loosen the laces or Velcro fasteners slightly or choose thinner socks. Leather shoes can often be stretched at the places that put pressure on your foot. Try wetting the leather thoroughly at home, then riding until the shoes dry. In stubborn cases, carry a bottle filled with a mixture of 50 percent water and 50 percent rubbing alcohol to spray on your shoes as you ride. Often, the shoe will mold to your foot, eliminating the pressure point.

But sometimes the shoe's basic design may be at fault. If so, you'll have to shop for a new pair until you find a model that works for you. Some riders who have suffered for years from painful feet experienced immediate and seemingly miraculous relief when they switched to shoes built on wider lasts.

Hand numbness usually can be relieved (if not eliminated outright) simply by changing your hand position on the bars at every opportunity. Ride on the tops of the levers for several minutes, switch to the tops of the bars on a climb, go for the drops on the downhill. Move your hands around continually. Dropped bars, because they permit multiple hand positions, are much better than the straight bars commonly found on mountain bikes, so if you have trouble when you ride a mountain bike, consider making the conversion to drops. Numb hands usually respond quickly to this strategy, but if yours don't, try wearing gloves with extra padding, or use padded brake hoods, or thick foam-backed handlebar tape.

While numb hands or feet are usually just inconveniences, numbness of the groin can be a real problem. Extreme cases, for example, can lead to impotency. Most cyclists experience this numbness occasionally. If you've felt numb for more than a few minutes, you'd better take action. Stand up on the bicycle, or stop and walk around. Don't let the numb and tingling sensation persist, because it signals potential damage to the pudendal nerve.

Check your saddle adjustment, too. The top of the saddle should be dead level. If the nose tilts up, it can press on the perineum and cause numbness. Hold a yardstick on the top of the saddle to see if it is parallel to the top tube. If not, adjust it until it is level. In extreme cases, you might have to use a saddle pad.

Knee Strains

Cycling is much easier on the knee joint than impact sports like running or contact sports like football. Nevertheless, cycling can injure your knees if you don't take precautions.

Most knee problems are the result of overuse, which causes the nagging pain of tendinitis. To prevent tendon problems, be sure you have a proper riding style. Use low gears that you can spin at 90 to 100 rpm rather than the higher gears you have to muscle around. Pushing too large a gear can strain the patellar tendon surrounding the kneecap, an injury that has a nasty habit of becoming chronic. Be sure your saddle is high enough. A low saddle forces the knee to bend too much at the top of the pedal stroke, leading to patellar tendon problems. Extremely high saddles, conversely, can put unnatural strain on the Achilles tendon as you toe down to maintain contact with the pedal at the bottom of the stroke. A high saddle can also damage the tendon just behind the knee. Work on a smooth pedaling style, too, since a rough, jerky pedal stroke pulls inexorably against your knee tendons.

Next, keep your knees warm. It is tempting on that first warm day in March or April to strip off the tights and greet the spring. Don't do it. Knees are complicated and vulnerable creations. Their maze of tendons needs warmth to remain supple and well-lubricated with the joint's synovial fluid. When training, wear tights if the temperature is below the 68° to 70°F range, especially if there's a cold wind or if the road is lined with snow. When the temperature is in the 60s, you are probably safe with Lycra tights, but in colder weather, opt for thicker polypropylene models. When it is really cold, down around freezing or below, wear wool tights with nylon wind-breaking panels sewn over the knees.

Racers, who often compete bare-legged in frigid temperatures, take precautions. They rub their legs with an analgesic ointment that feels hot. They also stick adhesive plasters over vulnerable areas. However, these experienced racers know exactly how much tolerance they have for the cold and exactly how much hot ointment to smear on before the race. And they are willing to take a chance with knee problems to gain more freedom of movement in competition. Recreational riders should err on the side of prudence and cover their legs until the temperature is well out of the danger zone.

Knee problems also are caused by improper placement of the foot on the pedal. Each rider has a unique foot position while walking. Some people toe out slightly while others walk with their feet straight ahead or pigeon-toed. That foot position must be duplicated on the pedal. If your cleats are adjusted incorrectly, your knee joint will have to absorb the twisting that results from the improperly aligned foot, leading to pain either on the outside or inside of the knee joint. The solution is to align your cleats with the RAD device in the Fit Kit.

Sometimes your cleats may be aligned perfectly, but the crankarm or pedal spindle is bent, producing unnatural torque on the knee. Suspect this problem if your knee pain mysteriously develops soon after a crash that didn't hurt your knee but damaged the bicycle. Take your frame to a competent shop for an alignment check.

If you develop knee pain, stop riding at once. Call for a ride or hitch home if you have to. Grimly continuing when your knees hurt will only make the injury more severe and the healing time longer. Use ice to reduce inflammation and take an anti-inflammatory medication like aspirin or Advil. Use the forced vacation from your bicycle to find the cause of the problem. When the pain subsides, resume riding carefully, using low gears. Don't push. It is often wise to take the initial rides on a training stand, so you can control the resistance more precisely and stop immediately when you feel pain rather than having to ride home.

Treating Respiratory Problems

We'd all like to think that our fitness lifestyles protect us from minor health problems like respiratory infections. However, cyclists in general run about the same risk as the general population of coming down with the sneezes, sniffles, and aches of the common cold. And as we have seen, if you are overtrained, you are actually more susceptible. Furthermore, a cold can escalate into a more serious condition if you try to train through it without giving your body's defense mechanisms a chance to kill those evil bugs.

Vasomotor Rhinitis

The most common respiratory problem isn't even a disease—but it can be embarrassing and bothersome. It's vasomotor rhinitis, or "skier's nose," that persistently runny nose that most cyclists experience in cold weather. Road riders used to wipe their noses on the backs of their gloves, but now there are several prescription sprays available to keep noses dry for several hours at a time. Check with your physician.

Frequent Colds

Next in order of respiratory severity is the common cold. You usually can train through a cold if no fever is present. Physicians often advise using antihistamines and decongestants to minimize the symptoms, but many riders feel better more rapidly and have fewer unpleasant side effects if they avoid medication. You'll improve faster if you drink hot liquids to keep the membranes of your throat moist, increase the humidity in your house with a humidifier, and use a vaporizer at night. Be sure to get plenty of rest. Reduce the intensity of your training, take it easy during normal daily activities, and get more sleep so your body has the reserves to fight the infection.

If you have more than two or three colds a year or always contract an early-season cold that you can't quite shake, examine your training schedule and your general health habits. Frequent colds are often caused by overtraining because chronic fatigue makes you more susceptible to viral infections. Poor health habits like eating incorrectly or not getting enough sleep will also lower your resistance. Take a week or so off the bicycle, and when you resume training, do so at a reduced level until your body's reserves have been replenished.

Bronchitis

Common colds can escalate into more severe illnesses accompanied by fever, muscle aches, and uncomfortable nasal congestion. If that happens, stop training, rest, and take care of yourself. If you try to train through a fever, your simple cold can rapidly change into various forms of bronchitis or pneumonia. In that case, consult a physician. Viral bronchitis can't be treated with antibiotics and often drags on for weeks. It can turn into bacterial bronchitis, against which antibiotics are often effective. In either case, you'll have trouble training for long periods of time. To avoid the resulting loss of fitness, it pays to take a little time off when your malady is still a cold rather than a more serious illness.

Exercise-induced asthma. Exercise-induced asthma is often triggered by breathing cold air. It's treated with various inhalants that can be prescribed by your physician. Be aware that some drugs present in over-the-counter medications are on the International Cycling Union's banned list, and taking them would make you test positive in a postcompetition drug test. If you are a recreational or fitness rider, you'll have no problem. If however, you'll be competing in national or international competition, be sure your doctor prescribes something that doesn't contain these substances.

Aside from exercise-induced asthma, training in cold weather doesn't cause any real trouble. The nose and mouth are so effective that they warm frigid air before it gets to your lungs. It is possible if you breathe *very* hard in *extremely* cold conditions—doing sprints or intervals for instance—that you could damage your lungs or bronchial tubes. But it is highly unlikely. If you are susceptible, wear a mask or balaclava over your mouth to help in the warming process.

Treating Skin Problems

Many people don't realize that the skin is an organ, just like the heart or liver. In fact, it's your body's largest organ, responsible for such vital tasks as temperature control and protecting your internal organs from bacterial infection. When you are cycling, most of your skin is directly exposed to an often-harsh environment. As a result, it pays to know how to protect your skin.

Saddle Sores

Saddle sores are small boils that form where your tender skin is irritated by the saddle and your shorts. The bacteria that are always present on your skin penetrate through minor breaks caused by an ill-fitting saddle or abrasive shorts. Saddle sores can make riding extremely unpleasant or utterly impossible depending on their severity and your pain tolerance.

Prevention is the best way to handle saddle sores, and cleanliness is the secret. Purchase enough riding shorts so you can wash them *every* time you ride. If they have artificial chamois, just throw them in the washing machine after a ride, and either dry them in a clothes drier or outside, depending on care instructions. Wash real leather chamois by hand with a mild detergent and cold water. Hang them out to dry, but avoid direct sunlight because it dries out the chamois, making it hard and brittle. When the chamois is still slightly damp, soften it by rubbing it briskly against itself, then treat it with Vaseline or one of the commercial chamois creams.

Keep your skin clean, too, by washing your crotch area before each ride with an antibacterial soap. After the ride, shower and again scrub thoroughly. After a race or ride, don't stand around talking to other cyclists, but change into clean clothes. If no shower is handy, clean up with rubbing alcohol and a washcloth. Scrupulous attention to cleanliness prevents most saddle sores from forming.

If you are unlucky enough to sprout one, see a physician who will prescribe oral antibiotics. Stay off the bicycle for several days, and take hot soaks in mildly soapy water. If you have to keep riding, on a tour or in a stage race for instance, consider an injection of an interlesional steroid that often dries up the sore quickly. Severe boils have to be lanced and drained, an extremely painful procedure.

Sunburn

Sunburn has always been considered one of those minor annoyances that cyclists shrugged off and ignored. No more. Now we realize that excessive exposure to the sun leads to premature aging of the skin as well as more serious problems like skin cancer. What's more, skin cancer seems to be associated with burns rather than tans. In fact, the incidence of one of the most deadly forms of cancer–malignant melanoma–has risen nearly 100 percent in the last 10 years, apparently due to our more fitness-conscious lifestyle. And cyclists, who spend more time in the sun than many other endurance athletes, are at proportionally greater risk.

Prevent sunburn by using a good sunscreen with an SPF (Sun Prevention Factor) of at least 15. Products in the 25 to 30 range are a better choice if you ride long miles in the sun or live in areas like Colorado, where the high altitude allows more of the sun's damaging ultraviolet (UV) rays to scorch your skin. Shop around for a sunscreen that stays on when you perspire heavily but still lets your skin breath. In this respect, some of the sunscreens used by surfers don't work well for cyclists. They cling through any amount of moisture, but because they don't let perspiration escape, they may lead to overheating.

Sun damage is more prevalent in the spring when you first shed tights and long sleeves. So remember to apply sunscreen to all exposed skin, especially areas that get the brunt of the sun's rays: your forearms, the backs of your hands, and the backs of your calves. Give your face a good coating too. Your helmet and glasses afford some protection, as does the cyclist's crouched position, but reflected rays can still cause a severe burn. Continue to use a good sunscreen all year if you're serious about protecting your skin. And especially if you're fair or have already had sun-related skin problems.

Lacerations and Contusions

The most common cycling injuries are the bright red results of a fall when your skin slides across the road's hard surface. Called by racers, none too fondly, "road rash," these abrasions are usually painful but minor problems. Avoid them with bicycle handling drills and careful riding. A bit of luck helps, too.

If your luck runs out, the most important treatment is to carefully clean the damaged skin. Begin by thoroughly scrubbing the wound with soap and a washcloth or rough sponge. Icing the damaged area, then washing it with cold water, sometimes helps ease the pain. If the abrasions cover a large area or if the skin is lacerated deeply by rough pavement, you may have to be scrubbed clean by a doctor or nurse with the aid of a local anaesthetic. In most cases, though, gritting your teeth will suffice. But it's important to do a complete job in spite of the pain. It not only prevents infection, it also keeps the bits of gravel and road dirt from becoming embedded in your skin, tattooing it when it heals.

Next, keep the wound clean by scrubbing it frequently during the healing process. Gently scrub at least twice a day with antibacterial soap. Another reason for twice-daily scrubs is to inhibit scab formation. Although scabs are nature's way of protecting the skin while healing takes place, they aren't particularly effective bandages. If a scab forms, you'll end up with a more prominent scar, and the wound will be more painful during the healing process as the stiff scab cracks when you move the body part beneath it. So get in the shower, and gently scrub off developing scabs as they form. Then cover the wound with an ointment like Vaseline to keep it moist and to reduce the pain. Cover with a nonstick pad.

If the wound becomes infected in spite of all these precautions, see a physician for an oral antibiotic to fight the infection. Get a complete examination at the same time, because infections in properly treated abrasions often indicate that your body is too tired from overtraining to fight off the infection. It may also indicate a more serious medical problem. Ice is the best treatment, applied for periods of 5 or 10 minutes out of every half hour as soon after the injury as possible.

Eye Irritations

Prevent eye problems by wearing good glasses or goggles designed for cycling.

Good cycling glasses also protect you from bugs, small pebbles, weed seeds, and other flying objects that seem to have an affinity for cyclists' eyes. If you do get a bug or other foreign object in your eye, most of the time it will wash out by itself on the tears the eye generates when injured. If not, pull the top eyelid over the bottom lid to try to dislodge the irritant. If the pain persists more than 24 hours, see a doctor.

Among cyclists, the most common eye problem is a pterygium (an irritation caused by repeated exposure to wind rushing over the eye). Glasses help, and goggles—especially models with a foam strip on the upper edge—virtually eliminate the problem.

Fractures and Separations

The most common fractures among cyclists are breaks of the collarbone or the small bones in the wrist caused when the rider puts out one hand to break a fall. Although fractures are painful and will keep you off the bicycle for several weeks, they usually heal without trouble.

Shoulder Separations

One of the most common orthopedic problems in cycling is a separation of the acromioclavicular (AC) joint. This is the spot where the collarbone butts up against the shoulder blade. The separation is usually caused by direct trauma, like landing on the shoulder in an over-the-bars crash. AC separations are best treated with rest until the pain diminishes, anti-inflammatory drugs like Motrin, and immobilization with a sling. When the pain and swelling are under control, start rehabilitation until full range of motion is restored.

AC separations can have long-term consequences. One is cosmetic, because separations produce the distinctive "dropped shoulder" look that some riders find merely annoying, others intolerable. Also, during the healing process the cartilage in the joint sometimes calcifies, making shoulder movement painful. It isn't uncommon for degenerative arthritis to attack the joint over a period of 10 to 20 years following the initial injury until range of motion becomes extremely limited.

Fortunately, treatment is a straightforward surgical procedure called a clavicle resection. About an inch of the collarbone's outer end is removed, effectively widening the joint and eliminating irritation from the calcified cartilage. Unlike many operations involving joints, the prognosis is excellent. The surgery is often done on an outpatient basis, and rehabilitation takes only a few weeks.

Collarbone Fractures

Broken collarbones are another common cycling problem. Often, you can start riding on a wind trainer within a week of the crash, since indoors you won't have to contend with road vibration. Riding with one hand on the bars and the other in a sling is feasible, too, although such a position often produces back trouble because you are off-center on the bicycle.

With minor breaks, you'll be back on the road within two weeks, but more serious clavicle fractures may require more healing time. In either case, take it easy and don't try to make up all the lost training time during the first ride. To reduce painful road vibrations, pad the handlebars and use large-section tires with somewhat lower inflation pressures. Choose smooth roads. Mountain bikes work well, because they have fat tires and the upright position takes some of the strain off your shoulder area. However, straight bars may be uncomfortable, so consider installing drops on your mountain bike during the rehabilitation period. Don't race or ride in an unpredictable group until you are competely healed. Another crash on top of an incompletely healed clavicle can be extremely serious—it's possible for the end of the bone to puncture a lung.

Arm or Wrist Fractures

These fractures take longer to heal than collarbone breaks but, paradoxically, they usually necessitate less time off the bicycle, because the cast can be formed to fit the handlebars and brake levers. European pros often race with casts protecting their broken wrists, but again, such a practice isn't recommended for recreational riders because of the danger of reinjury.

Heat Injuries

Heat stroke can kill endurance athletes who compete or train too hard in high temperatures without adequate fluid intake. In fact, the American College of Sports Medicine recommends that running races be cancelled if the temperature and humidity are extreme. Fortunately, cyclists are spared most of this danger. Their increased velocity produces more rapid evaporation of sweat and results in greater cooling. Also, cyclists can carry several bottles of fluid and drink it more comfortably and effectively while riding than runners can while running.

Still, it is wise to be aware of the symptoms that signal overheating. You'll probably notice cramps in your quadriceps and calves first. In fact, another reason cyclists usually avoid heat stroke is because they cramp so badly in the early stages of dehydration that they can't continue riding and so are spared more serious heat-related problems. Cramps appear when you have lost about 3 percent of your body weight from dehydration, so the best remedy is to start the ride well-hydrated and drink at least 3 or 4 ounces of fluid every 10 or 15 minutes on hot rides. Water is the best fluid to drink; little evidence exists that cramps are caused by electrolyte deficiencies in the muscles due to sweating. Water is what you are sweating out and water is what you need to replace. Many sports drinks also contain some carbohydrate so you can replace lost muscle fuel as you ride. But strictly for avoiding heat problems on the bicycle, water is better.

Spraying on a hot day can alleviate burning feet.

Photography Credits

Cover photographs by—

John P. Hamel: front

Ed Landrock: back

Book photographs by—

Angelo M. Caggiano: pp. 92; 118, bottom.

Carl Doney: p. 210.

David Epperson: p. 121.

Bob Gerheart: pp. 36; 80; 82; 94; 209.

Tom Gettings: p. 114.

Seth Goltzer: pp. 99, top; 117, bottom; 222.

John P. Hamel: pp. vi; 3, top; 9; 10; 150; 166; 181, bottom.

Donna Hornberger: pp. 11; 12; 13, top; 17; 18; 20; 24; 40; 59; 60; 61; 117, top; 140; 142; 148; 164; 183, top; 214; 221; 225; 226; 227.

J. Michael Kanouff: p. 126.

Rick Kocks: p. 128, bottom.

Ed Landrock: pp. 2; 5; 49; 53; 54; 55; 62; 72; 74; 84; 90; 99, bottom; 101; 104; 111; 118, top; 125; 136; 146; 168; 171; 172; 173; 178; 180; 188; 189; 190; 191; 192; 193; 198; 204; 233.

Warren Morgan: pp. 30; 39; 205.

Lew Plummer: p. 158.

Anthony Rodale: pp. 78; 124; 153.

Rodale Press Photography Department: pp. 6; 13, bottom; 25; 64; 128, top; 135; 141; 162; 183, bottom.

Team Russell: p. 181, top left.

Beth Schneider: p. 181, top right.

Fred Staub: p. 154.

Christie C. Tito: pp. 21; 23; 44; 213.

Mitch Toll: p. 3, bottom.

Cor Voss: p. 50.

Gordon Wiltsie: p. 156.

Fred Zahradnik: p. 91.

Index

A

Aerobic exercises
- classes for, 182
- early-season, 38
- off-season, 38, 179–82
- preseason, 38
- running, 179–80
- skiing, 180–81
- snowshoeing, 181
- swimming, 181–82
- team sports, 182

Aluminum bicycle frames, 8-9
Anaerobic threshold (AT), 42–43, 44
Arm fractures, 233
Asthma, 230

B

Back, riding position for, 62
Bib shorts, 17
Bicycle(s)
- accessories, 12–15
- brake lever placement on, 58
- city, 148–49
- commuting by, 175, 176–77
- components, 9–12
- cost versus value of, 15
- customizing of, 150-51
- design and construction of, 7
- early-season training on, 196-97
- extras on, 27-29
- fit of, 15, 52-56
- handlebar height on, 57-58
- handlebar width on, 58
- mountain, 141–42
- pedals on, 57
- racks for, 29
- seats. *See* Saddles
- selection of, 15
- stationary, 28
- touring, 139–42
- value versus cost of, 15

Bicycling. *See* Cycling
Bicyclists. *See* Cyclist(s)
Blowouts, tire, 93
Body
- condition of, 2-3
- riding position for, 49, 51-52, 61-62

Body fat
- determining percentage of, 213–14
- low
  - achievement of, 214–16
  - advantages of, 211–12
- setpoint theory of, 216

Brake levers, placement of, 58

Braking
- basics of, 68-71
- downhill, 70
- emergency, 70-71
- normal, 69
- in pack riding, 69-70
- in rain, 69

Bronchitis, treatment for, 229-30
Browning Automatic Transmission, 10

C

Cadence
- efficient, 66-68
- gear selection and, 66
- rapid, 67
- slow, 66-67

Campgrounds, selection of, 138
Camping equipment, 139. *See also specific equipment*
Car-top carriers, 29
Century rides, 4, 131-34
- eating and drinking during, 132-33
- flat course for, 132
- pacelines in, 133-34
- pacing yourself for, 131-32
- preparation for, 131

Chains, 68
Chamois crotch, care of, 16
Circuit races. *See* Criteriums
City bicycle, 148-49
Cleat systems, 11
Cleats, placement of, 57
Climbing
- basic technique of, 87-90
- cadence for, 87
- gearing for, 87
- in a group, 89
- mental techniques for, 89-90
- in off-road cycling, 152-53
- while seated, 87-88
- while standing up, 88-89

Clinchers, folding and stowing of, 140
Clincher tire, 12
Clincher wheel, 11-12
Clothing, 15-27
- gloves, 24-25
- helmets, 26-27
- jerseys, 19-21
- leg warmers, 21-22
- for off-road cycling, 149-50
- to prevent injuries, 223
- rain gear, 22-24
- shoe covers, 24
- shoes, 17-19
- shorts, 16-17
- skin suits, 25-26
- socks, 17-19
- tights, 21-22

Club rides, 127
- holding the pace during, 130-31

Cogs, selection of, 68
Colds, frequent, 229
Collarbone fractures, 232-33
Commuting, 175
- bicycle for, 176-77
- clothing for, 175-76
- equipment for, 175-77

Competition. *See specific competitions*
Components, 9-12
Composite bicycle frames, 9
Computers, 14-15
- for indoor cycling, 185

Contusions, 231-32
Cornering
- approach to turns, 82
- banked, 83
- braking in, 86-87
- in competition, 82
- in criteriums, 119
- descending and, 91-92
- encountering obstacles while, 83
- falling while, 86
- gearing for, 83
- in gravel, 86
- in hazardous conditions, 85-87
- left-hand turn, 83
- off-camber, 83
- in a pack, 84-85
- position on bicycle for, 82, 83-84
- precorner evaluation, 83
- right-hand turn, 82-83
- road surface condition and, 83
- sharpness of turn, 83
- signaling for, 82
- smooth movements in, 86
- speed in, 86
- technique for, 81-87
- on tours, 82

traction in, 85-86
on training rides, 82
in wet conditions, 85-87
Crankarms, length of, 55
Credit card tours, 136-37
Criteriums
breaks in, 121
climbing hills in, 119-20
cornering for, 119
evaluation of performance in, 122
final sprint in, 121
free lap rule in, 120-21
pack position for, 118-19
preparation for, 115-16
prerace for, 116-17
primes in, 119
start of, 117-18
tactical decisions in, 119
warm-up for, 116-17
Crosswind(s)
on descents, 93
riding with, 77
Crotch numbness, 227-28
Crotch-to-floor (CTF) measurement, 54-55
Cyclecomputers. *See* Computers
Cycling
advanced techniques for, 81-103
climbing, 87-90
cornering, 81-87
descending, 90-94
in a group, 96-103
speed, 94-96
basic techniques for
dismounting, 62, 63
hand placement, 58-61
mounting, 62
no-hands, 75-76
one-handed, 73-75
pedaling, 57, 62-63
pushing off, 49
shifting gears, 63
body position for, 61-62
on city streets, 172-73
commitment to, 36-37
in crosswinds, 77
double pacelines, 98
early-season training for, 196-97
echelons, 98-100
falling while, 77-79
as family activity, 3-4
for fitness, 4
following a wheel, 76-77
hazards, dealing with, 163-64
increased stamina and, 2-3
indoor, 182-86
at intersections, 173-74
mental outlook and, 3
mountain, 4-5
muscular development and, 2
at night, 170
off-road
bike selection for, 147-49
climbing, 152-53
clothing for, 149-50
customizing bicycle for, 150-51
descending, 153-55
equipment for, 151-52
for road riders, 158-61
on open highways, 172
physical benefits of, 2-3
popularity of, 1
proper position for, 49, 51-52
racing, 4
in a racing pack, 100-103
on road shoulder
safe, 171, 172
unsafe, 172
on rural roads, 172
saddle fore-and-aft positioning for, 56
saddle height for, 54-56
shoes for, 18-19
single pacelines, 97-98
socializing and, 3
speed for, 199-200
stem length for, 57-58
straight line riding, 76
stress and, 3
time scheduling for, 35-36
touring, 4
in traffic, 170-71
in winds, 77
Cyclist(s)
body of, 2-3
facts about, 31-32
goal-setting for, 32-33
harassment of, 174-75
mind of, 3
off-road riding for, 158-61
time scheduling for, 35-36
training diary for, 33-36

Cyclist(s) *(continued)*
- training for, 32
- vehicular rights of, 171-74

D

Darkness, techniques for dealing with, 170
Day tours, 134-36
Derailleur systems, 7
- electronic, 10
- shifting and, 65-66

Descending
- basic technique for, 90-94
- cornering and, 91-92
- crosswinds in, 93
- equipment check before, 92
- eye protection for, 92
- in long road races, 123
- in off-road cycling, 153-55
- position on bicycle for, 90-91
- safety rules for, 93-94
- shimmy control in, 92-93
- strong winds in, 93
- tire blowout in, 93
- vibration control in, 92-93
- windchill in, 93-94

Diet, training, 216-19
Dieting, 212-13
Dismounting, 62, 63
Dogs, dealing with, 166-67
Double pacelines, 98, 99
Downhill brakes, 70
Drinking, one-handed riding technique for, 73-74

E

Early-morning training, 39-40
Early season
- road riding, 196-97
- training, 38
- weekly schedule for, 48

Eating
- after rides, 221
- before rides, 219-20
- during rides, 220-21
    - no-hands technique for, 75-76

Echelon(s)
- technique for, 98-100
- in windy races, 77

Elbows, riding position for, 62
Electronic derailleur system, 10
Emergency stops, 70-71
Equipment
- camping, 139
- check, before descents, 92
- for commuting, 175-77
- for off-road cycling, 151-52
- personal, 15-27
    - for touring, 142-43
- for time trials, 107-8
- for touring bicycles, 139-42
- for a week, 145
- for weight training, 187

Ergometers, 28
Exercises, 42. *See also* Aerobic exercises
Eye(s)
- irritations, 232
- protection, 92

F

Falling
- prevention of, 224
- technique for, 77-79

Family activities, 3-4
Fanny packs, 135
Fatigue
- injuries and, 225
- overtraining and, 45-46

Fenders
- on city bicycles, 148
- for commuter bikes, 177
- for touring bicycles, 140

Fitness riding, 4
Floor pumps, 14
Following a wheel, 76-77
Food guidelines, 216-19
Foot numbness, 227
Fractures, 232-33
Frame(s)
- aluminum, 8-9
- composite, 9
- correct size of, 53
- design and construction of, 7
- fit of, 52-53
- oversized, 52-53
- steel, 8
- for touring bikes, 141
- undersized, 53

Frame pumps, 12-14
Friction shifting, 66
 system for, 10

G

Gears, 68
Glass, dealing with, 164-65
Gloves, 24-25
Gravel, dealing with, 165-66
Group riding. *See also* Cycling
 accidental contact in, 97
 double pacelines in, 98
 echelons in, 98-100
 racing pack, 100-103
 rules for, 96-97
 single pacelines in, 97-98
 spotting dangerous situations in, 97
 sudden maneuvers in, 96
 technique for, 96-103

H

Hand(s)
 numbness of, 227
 placement on handlebars, 58-61
  back on drops, 61
  forward on drops, 61
  one on top, 59
  split-finger special, 60
  on tips of levers, 60-61
  on tops, 59
  on tops of levers, 60
  on upper bends, 60
Handlebar(s)
 dropped, 151
 height, 57-58
 straight, 150-51
 width, 58
Harassment, dealing with, 174-75
Hazards. *See* Road hazards
Head, riding position for, 61
Head injuries
 helmets and, 26
 prevention of, 224
Head winds, speed development in, 205-6
Heart rate
 maximum, 43-44
 monitoring, 42-44, 201
 overtraining and, 45
Heat stroke, 233
Helmets, 26-27
High season
 training, 38
 weekly schedule for, 48
Hills, speed development on, 203-5

I

Indexed shifting system, 9-10
Indoor cycling
 disadvantages of, 184
 ergometers for, 185-86
 for off-season workout, 182-86
 sample workouts for, 195-96
 wind trainer workouts for, 183-85
Infections, overtraining and, 46
Injuries, prevention of, 225
Intersections, dealing with, 173-74
Interval training, 200-203
 cautions for, 201-2
 monitoring heart rate during, 201
 workouts for, 202-3

J

Jerseys, 19-21
 colors of, 21
 construction of, 20
 fabric of, 19-20
 fit of, 20
 load-carrying capacity of, 20
 pockets in, 20

K

Knee strains, 228-29

L

Lacerations, 231-32
Leaves, fallen, techniques for dealing with, 169
Leg speed. *See* Speed, leg, building
Leg warmers, 21-22
Loaded bicycle handling, 139
Loaded tours, 137
 bicycle handling in, 139
 campground selection for, 138

Loaded tours *(continued)*
camping overnight during, 138-39
packing for, 142-43
panniers for, 142-43
traveling companions for, 137-38
Locks, for commuter bikes, 177
Look pedals, 11
Low back pain, 226-27
Lunchtime training, 40-41

M

Mental outlook, 3
Metal grates, techniques for dealing with, 169
Motorpacing, 208-9
Mountain bike(s)
for city use, 148
customizing of, 150-51
dropped bars on, 151
pedals for, 151
selection of, 147-49
straight bars on, 150-51
for touring, 141-42
Mountain biking, 4-5
techniques for, 152-55
climbing, 152-53
descending, 153-55
Mounting, 62
Muscles, sore, overtraining and, 46

N

Neck pain, 226
Night owl training, 41
Numbness, 227-28
Nutrition
breakfast, 218
dinner, 218-19
fats, 217
fluid intake, 217
high carbohydrate intake, 215
ideal training diet, 216-19
lunch, 218
meats, 217
postride, 221
preride, 219-20
during rides, 220-21
salads, 217
snacks, 217, 219

O

Off-road cycling
bike selection for, 147-49
climbing, 152-53
clothing for, 149-50
customizing bicycle for, 150-51
descending, 153-55
equipment for, 151-52
for road riders, 158-61
Off-season
aerobic workouts, 179-82
indoor cycling, 182-86
training, 38
weekly schedule for, 47
weight training, 186-95
Oil slicks, techniques for dealing with, 169
One-handed riding, 73-75
One-hundred-mile rides, 4. *See also* Century rides
Overtraining, 44-47
avoidance of, 44-45
chronic fatigue and, 45-46
chronic infections and, 46
decrease in speed and, 45
increased resting heart rate and, 45
injuries and, 225
lack of enthusiasm and, 45
muscle soreness and, 46
overcoming, 46-47
poor performance and, 45
psychological problems and, 46
psychological profile of, 47
rest periods for, 46
severe cases of, 46
stress of, 45
warning signs of, 45-46

P

Pacelines
double, 98
single, 97-98
Pack riding, braking in, 69-70
Panniers, 142-43
Pedal(s)
conventional, 10-11
ins and outs of, 62-63
for mountain bikes, 151
position, 57
step-in, 11

Periodization, 37-38
Potholes, dealing with, 167-68
Power, speed and, 95
Practice course, 157
Preseason training, 38
  weekly schedule for, 47
Psychological problems
  internal training and, 201
  overtraining and, 46
Pulse monitors, 28-29
Pump(s)
  floor, 14
  frame, 12-14
Pushing off, 62

R

Racing, 4. *See also specific races*
  clubs, 127-29
  off-road, 155-56
    observed trials, 156-58
  skills for, 100-103
  starting off, 101
Railroad tracks, dealing with, 168-69
Rain, 143-44
  braking in, 69
  gloves, 24-25
  jackets, 22-23
  pants, 23-24
  plastic garbage sack, as protection from, 22
  shoe covers, 24
Recreational riding, 4, 127-45
  club rides, 127
  intervals as, 203
Repair stands, 28
Respiratory problems, 229-30
Rest periods, for overtraining, 46
Riding. *See* Cycling
Road hazards, 163-64
  cactus spines, 166
  darkness, 170
  dogs, 166-67
  fallen leaves, 169
  glass, 164-65
  gravel, 165-66
  harassment, 174-75
  metal grates, 169-70
  night riding, 170
  oil slicks, 169
  potholes, 167-68
  railroad tracks, 168-69
  thorns, 166
  traffic, 170-71
  white lines, 169
Road races
  breaks in, 122
  climbing hills in, 122-23
  descending techniques for, 123
  eating and drinking during, 123-24
  finish of, 124
  handups during, 124
  long, 122-25
  varying speed in, 122
  winds in, 124
Road shoulders, riding on, 171-72
Rollers, 27
Rooftop racks, 29
Running, for off-season workout, 179-80

S

Saddle(s)
  fore-and-aft positioning of, 56
  height of, 54-56
    cautions for, 56
    crankarm length and, 55
    determination of, 54
    measurement for, 54-55
Saddle sores, 230
Sag tours, 136
Seats. *See* Saddle(s)
Self-massage, 224-25
Setpoint theory, of body fat, 216
Shifting, 63
  basics of, 65-68
  cadence and gear selection, 66
  friction, 66
  front derailleurs, 65-66
  levers, 65
  one-handed riding technique for, 73
  rear derailleurs, 65-66
  systems, 9-10
  too soon, 66
Shimmy, in descending, 92-93
Shoe(s)
  covers, 24
  cycling, 18-19
  touring, 17-18
Shorts, 16-17

Shoulder separations, 232
Single pacelines, 97-98
"Skier's nose." *See* Vasomotor rhinitis
Skiing, for off-season workout, 180-81
Skin problems, 230-32
Skin suits, 25-26
Snowshoeing, for off-season workout, 181
Socializing, 3
Socks, 17
Speed
 basic technique for, 94-96
 benefits of, 199-200
 development of
  group training for, 206-7
  in head winds, 205-6
  on hills, 203-5
  interval training for, 200-203
  motorpacing for, 208-9
  training time trials for, 207-8
 leg, building, 94-95
 power and, 95
 sprinting technique, 95-96
Split workouts, 42
Sports massage, 224-25
Sprinting, 95-96
Stationary bicycles, 28
Steel bicycle frames, 8
Stem length, 57-58
Step-in pedal/cleat system, 11
Stoves, 139
Straight line riding, 76
Strength, building, 38
Stress, 3
Sunburn, 231
Swimming, for off-season workout, 181-82

T

Tent, 139
Thorns, dealing with, 166
Tights, 22
Time trials, 105-13
 aerodynamic requirements of, 105
 appeal of, 106
 assessment of, 113
 demands of, 106
 enjoyment of, 106
 equipment for, 107-8
 hills in, 112
 length of, 105
 preparation for, 110
 registration for, 110
 safety of, 107
 speed development for, 207-8
 start of, 111-12
 traffic in, 112-13
 training for, 108-10
 turnaround, 109, 113
  practice for, 110
 variety of, 106
 warm-up for, 110-11
 winds in, 112
Tire(s)
 blowout, during descent, 93
 brushing off
  front wheel, 74
  one-handed riding technique for, 74-75
  rear wheel, 75
 clincher, 12
 pumps, 12-14
 recommendations for, 12
 for touring bicycles, 140
 tubular, 7
 wired-on, 7
Tool kits, 14
Touring, 4
 clubs, 129-30
 equipment list for, 145
 mountain bikes for, 141-42
 packing for, 142-43
 panniers for, 142-43
 personal equipment for, 142-43
 in rainy weather, 143-44
 shoes for, 17-18
 style, 138-39
 traveling companions for, 137-38
Touring bicycles, 139-42
Tours, 134
 credit card, 136-37
 day, 134-36
 fanny pack for, 135
 identification to carry for, 134
 loaded, 137
 money to carry for, 134
 sag, 136
Traffic
 coexisting with, 174-75
 cyclist's rights in, 171-74
 high-speed, 172
 at intersections, 173-74
 left turns in, 174

riding in, 170-71
right turns in, 174
Training. *See also* Overtraining
diet for, 216-19
early-morning, 39-40
early-season, 38
weekly schedule for, 48
efficient workouts, 42
heart rate monitoring in, 42-44
high-season, 38
weekly schedule for, 48
interval, 200-203
workouts for, 202-3
lunchtime, 40-41
midday, 40-41
night owl, 41
off-season, 38
weekly schedule for, 47
periodization of, 37-38
preseason, 38
weekly schedule for, 47
psychological profile of, 47
split, 42
time scheduling for, 39-42
weekly schedule for, 47-48
yearly plans for, 37-38
Training diary, 33-35
Training stands, 27
Traveling companions, 137-38
Tubular wheel, 11-12
Turning, in traffic, 83, 174

V

Vasomotor rhinitis, 229
Vehicular rights, 171-74
Vibration, 92-93

W

Water
bottles, 14
purification, 138
Weather, rainy, 143-44
Weight training
advantages of, 186-87
beginning program for, 188
bench presses, 189
bent rows, 190-91
calf raises, 192
circuit, 193-94
crunchers, 191
curls, 192
equipment for, 187
in-season, 194
military presses, 190
for off-season workout, 186-95
power cleans, 188-89
power program, 194-95
preliminaries for, 187-88
specialized programs for, 192
squats, 191-92, 194-95
upright rows, 189-90
warm-up for, 188
wrestler's bridges, 192
Wheel(s)
clincher, 11
design and construction of, 7-8
following, 76-77
recommendations for, 12
shape of, 12
for time trials, 108
for touring bicycles, 139-40
tubular, 7, 11-12
use of, 7
White lines, painted, 169
Wind(s)
on descents, 93
riding with, 77
speed development in, 205-6
Windchill, on descents, 93-94
Wind trainers, 27
Wrist fractures, 233